Cape Town
& the Garden Route

Around Cape Town
p187

Cape Town
p49

Garden Route
p227

PLAN YOUR TRIP

Welcome to Cape Town & the Garden Route **4**
Cape Town & the Garden Route Map **6**
Cape Town & the Garden Route's Top 15 .... **8**
Need to Know **16**
What's New **18**
If You Like... .... **19**
Month by Month **22**
Itineraries **25**
Getting Around **30**
Eat Like a Local **32**
Wine & Wineries **36**
Activities **42**
Regions at a Glance **45**

ON THE ROAD

CAPE TOWN **49**
Neighbourhoods at a Glance 50
Table Mountain National Park 54
Sights 68
Activities 115
Tours 123
Festivals & Events 125
Sleeping 127
Eating 138
Drinking & Nightlife 156
Entertainment 168
Shopping 172

AROUND CAPE TOWN **187**
Road Trip > Driving Route 62 190
Winelands **194**
Stellenbosch 194
Franschhoek 202
Paarl 207

KIRSTENBOSCH NATIONAL BOTANICAL GARDEN P95

DECORATIVE MASKS, GREENMARKET SQ P69

Contents

Tulbagh 211
Robertson 213
The Overberg 214
The Elgin Valley 215
Hermanus 216
Gansbaai 220
Stanford............... 221
West Coast 223
Darling 223
Langebaan.............224
Paternoster 225

GARDEN ROUTE... 227
Surfing Along the Garden Route 230
Mossel Bay 232
George 235
Wilderness.............237
Buffalo Bay 238
Knysna 239
Plettenberg Bay 246
Nature's Valley 250

UNDERSTAND

Cape Town Today 254
History.............. 256
People & Culture 266
Architecture 271
The Arts............. 273
The Natural Environment 277

SURVIVAL GUIDE

Directory A–Z 280
Transport............ 285
Language 289
Index................ 295

HERMANUS P216

SPECIAL FEATURES

Getting Around........ 30
Table Mountain National Park 54
Driving Route 62 190
Surfing Along the Garden Route 230
People & Culture 266

Welcome to Cape Town & the Garden Route

There's nowhere quite like Cape Town and the Garden Route – a coming-together of the diverse cultures, cuisines and spectacular landscapes of Southern Africa.

Natural Wonders

Table Mountain National Park defines the city. The flat-topped mountain is the headline act, but there are many other equally gorgeous natural landscapes within the park's extensive boundaries. Cultivated areas, such as the historic Company's Garden, Kirstenbosch National Botanical Garden and Green Point Urban Park, also make exploring the city a pleasure. Follow the lead of locals by taking full advantage of the abundant outdoor space: learn to surf; go hiking or mountain biking; tandem-paraglide off Lion's Head; abseil off the top of Table Mountain – just a few of the many activities on offer.

Art & Design

Human creativity is also self-evident here. From the brightly painted facades of the Bo-Kaap, to the Afro-chic decor of its restaurants and bars and the striking street art and design boutiques of the East City and Woodstock, this is one great-looking metropolis. The informal settlements of the Cape Flats are a sobering counterpoint, but these townships also have enterprising projects that put food from organic market gardens on tables, or stock gift shops with attractive souvenirs.

People & Culture

Christian, Muslim, Jewish, Hindu and traditional African beliefs coexist peacefully in this proudly multicultural city. Given South Africa's troubled history, such harmony has been hard-won and remains fragile: nearly everyone has a fascinating, sometimes heartbreaking story to tell. It's a city of determined pioneers – from the Afrikaner descendants of the original Dutch colonists and the majority coloured community to the descendants of European Jewish immigrants and more recent Xhosa (isiXhosa) migrants from the Eastern Cape. They all bring unique flavours to Cape Town's rich melting pot.

Beyond the City

Wrenching yourself away from the magnetic mountain and all the delights of the Cape Peninsula is a challenge, but within an hour you can exchange urban landscapes for the charming towns, villages and bucolic estates of Winelands destinations, such as Stellenbosch and Franschhoek. Hermanus is a prime whale-watching location, and also a base from which to organise shark-cave diving. Further afield, the delights of the Garden Route unfold, with more inspiring scenery to be viewed on thrilling drives down the coast and over mountain passes.

Why I Love Cape Town & the Garden Route

By Simon Richmond, Writer

Mother Nature surpassed herself when crafting the Mother City. Whether jogging along Sea Point promenade, climbing up Lion's Head in the dawn light, clambering over giant boulders at Sandy Bay or driving the amazing coastal roads down to Cape Point, I never fail to feel my spirits soar as I take in the breathtakingly beautiful vistas. You don't need to break a sweat: sipping wine on a historic farm in Constantia or enjoying a picnic at an outdoor concert in Kirstenbosch National Botanical Garden are equally memorable ways to commune with Cape Town's great outdoors.

For more about our writers, see p304

Above: Camps Bay Beach (p93)

Cape Town & the Garden Route

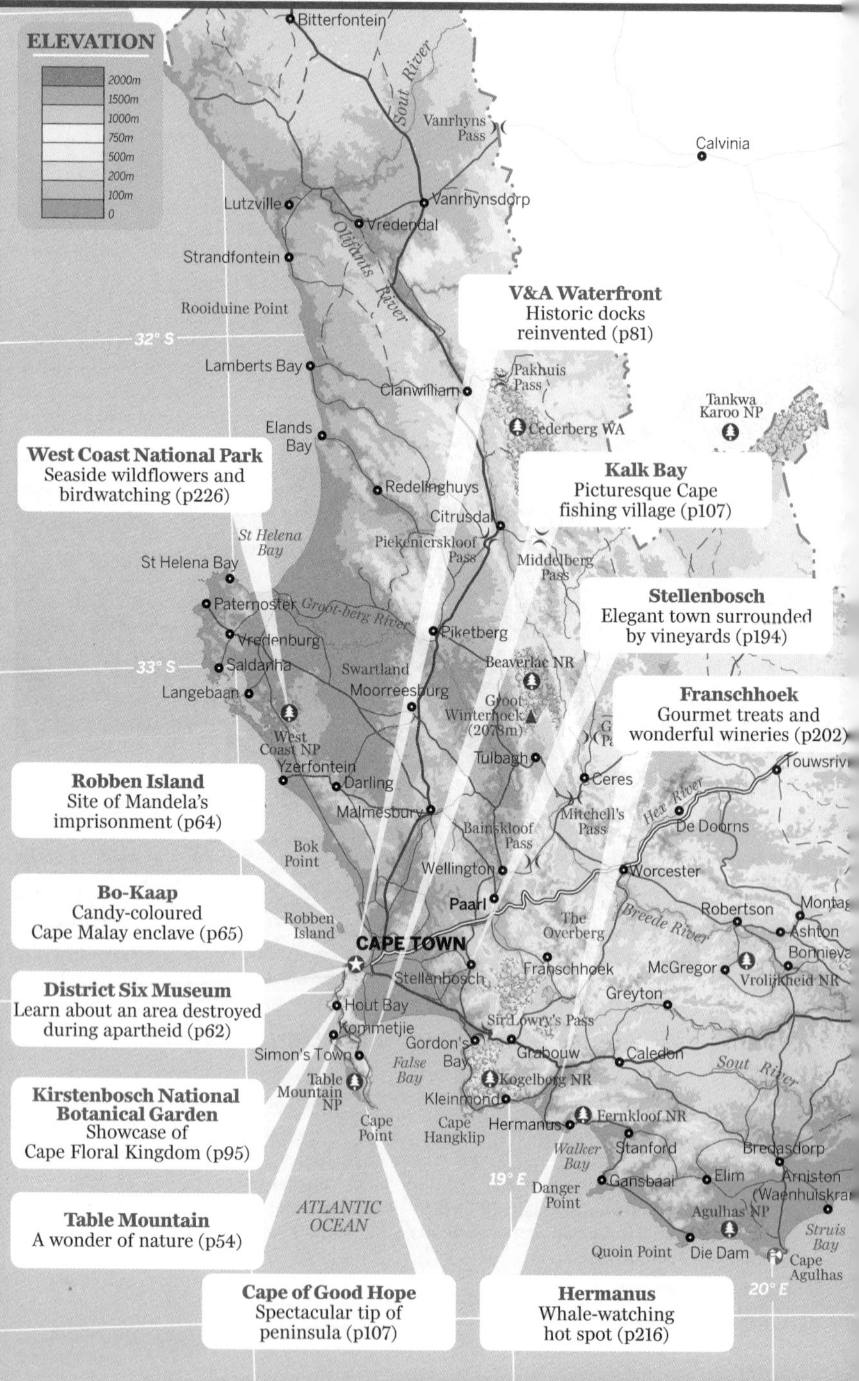

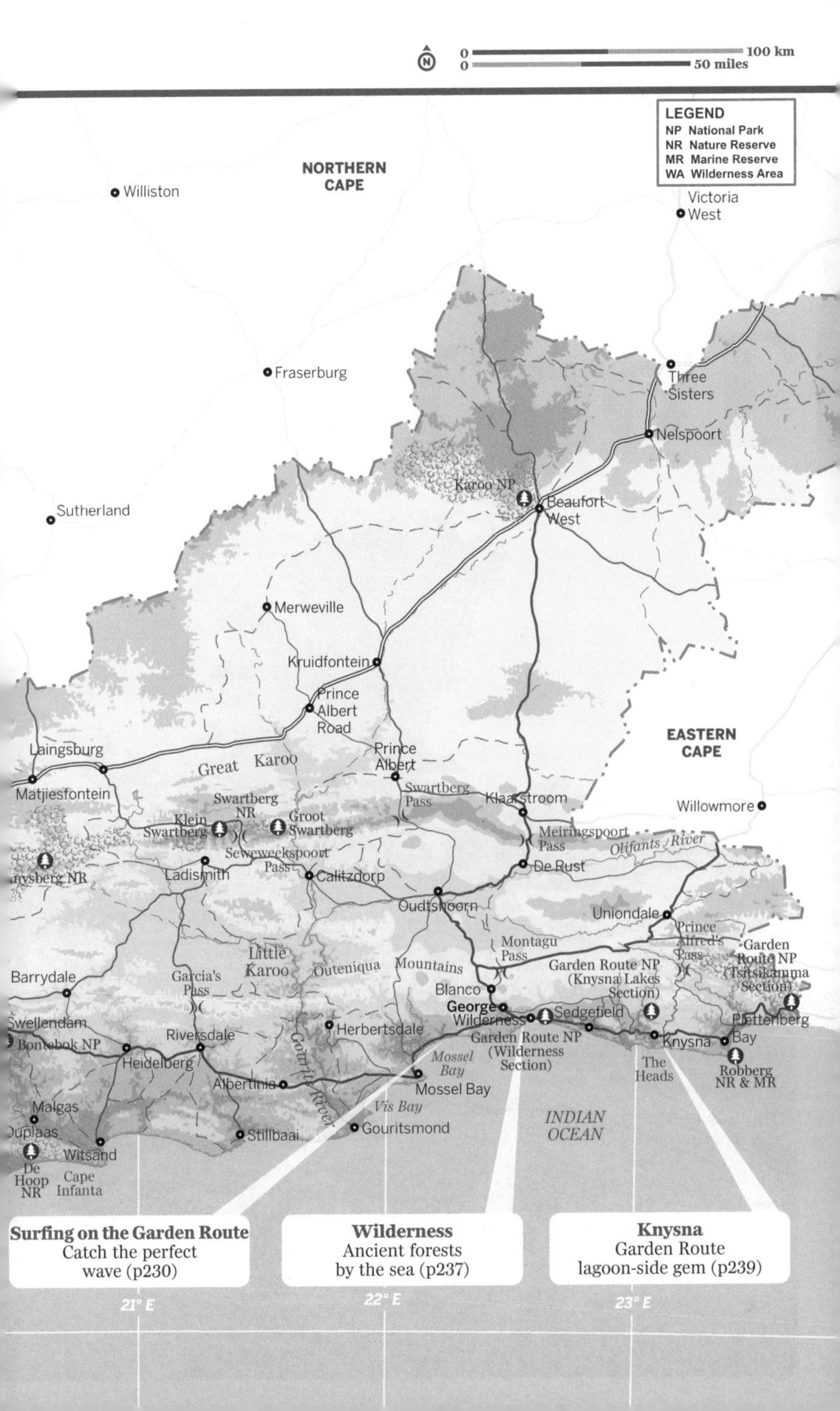

0
100 km
0
50 miles
LEGEND
NP National Park
NR Nature Reserve
MR Marine Reserve
WA Wilderness Area
NORTHERN CAPE
Williston
Victoria West
Fraserburg
Three Sisters
Nelspoort
Karoo NP
Beaufort West
Sutherland
Merweville
Kruidfontein
Prince Albert Road
Laingsburg
Matjiesfontein
Great Karoo
Prince Albert
Swartberg Pass
Klaarstroom
EASTERN CAPE
Willowmore
Swartberg NR
Klein Swartberg
Groot Swartberg
Seweweekspoort Pass
Meiringspoort Pass
Olifants River
De Rust
Ladismith
Calitzdorp
Oudtshoorn
Uniondale
Prince Alfred's Pass
Montagu Pass
Little Karoo
Outeniqua Mountains
Garden Route NP (Knysna Lakes Section)
Garden Route NP (Tsitsikamma Section)
Barrydale
Garcia's Pass
Blanco
George
Wilderness
Sedgefield
Swellendam
Bontebok NP
Heidelberg
Riversdale
Herbertsdale
Gourits River
Garden Route NP (Wilderness Section)
Knysna
Plettenberg Bay
Mossel Bay
Mossel Bay
The Heads
Robberg NR & MR
Albertinia
Vis Bay
INDIAN OCEAN
Malgas
Duplaas
Stillbaai
Gouritsmond
Witsand
De Hoop NR
Cape Infanta
Surfing on the Garden Route
Catch the perfect wave (p230)
Wilderness
Ancient forests by the sea (p237)
Knysna
Garden Route lagoon-side gem (p239)
21° E
22° E
23° E

Cape Town & the Garden Route's Top 15

1

Table Mountain

1 Whether you ride the revolving cableway or put in the leg work and climb, attaining the summit of Table Mountain (p54) is a Capetonian rite of passage. Weather permitting, your rewards are a panoramic view across the peninsula and a chance to experience some of the park's incredible biodiversity. Schedule time for a hike: the park's 245 sq km include routes to suit all levels of fitness and ambition, from gentle ambles to spot *fynbos* (proteas, heaths and ericas) to the two-day, 33.8km Cape of Good Hope Trail.

V&A Waterfront

2 Cape Town's top sight in terms of visitor numbers, the V&A Waterfront (p81) is big, busy and in a spectacular location, with Table Mountain as a backdrop. There's a pirate's booty of consumer opportunities, from chic boutiques to major department stores, plus plenty of cultural and educational experiences, including walking tours of its well-preserved heritage buildings and public sculptures, the excellent Two Oceans Aquarium, and the spectacular new Zeitz MOCAA museum of contemporary art. Be sure to take a harbour cruise, too – preferably at sunset.

BENJAMIN B /GETTY IMAGES ©

2

BRIAN EDEN/GETTY IMAGES ©

3

4

Robben Island

3 A Unesco World Heritage Site, the former prison on Robben Island (p64) is a key location in South Africa's long walk to freedom. Nelson Mandela and other Freedom struggle heroes were incarcerated here, following in the tragic footsteps of earlier fighters against the various colonial governments that ruled over the Cape. The boat journey here and the tour with former inmates provides an insight into the country's troubled history – and a glimpse of how far it has progressed on the path to reconciliation and forgiveness.

Bo-Kaap

4 Painted in vivid colours straight out of a packet of liquorice allsorts, the jumble of crumbling and restored heritage houses and mosques along the cobblestoned streets of the Bo-Kaap (p65) are both visually captivating and a storybook of inner-city gentrification. A stop at the Bo-Kaap Museum is recommended to gain an understanding of the history of this former slave quarter. Also, try Cape Malay dishes at one of the area's several restaurants, or stay in one of the homes turned into guesthouses and hotels.

Cape of Good Hope

5 Make the spectacular journey out to this historic headland (p107), and onward to Cape Point, the dramatic tip of the peninsula protected within Table Mountain National Park: rugged cliffs shoot down into the frothing waters of the Atlantic Ocean; giant waves crash over the enormous boulders at Africa's most south-westerly point; and the Flying Dutchman Funicular runs up to the old lighthouse for fantastic views. Afterwards you can relax on lovely beaches such as the one at Buffels Bay, which is lapped by the slightly warmer waters of False Bay.

District Six Museum

6 More than 40 years on from when most of the homes in the inner-city suburb of District Six (p62) were demolished, and their multiethnic owners and tenants relocated to the blighted communities in the Cape Flats, the area remains largely barren. A visit to this illuminating, moving museum provides an understanding of District Six's tragic history and the impact it has had on the lives of all Capetonians. You can also arrange a walking tour of the area, led by a former resident.

Franschhoek

7 Franschhoek (p202) is the smallest – but for many the prettiest – Cape Winelands town. Nestled in a spectacular valley, Franschhoek is also the country's undisputed gastronomic capital. You may have a tough time deciding where to eat – the main road is lined with top-notch restaurants, some of them among the best in the country. The surrounding wineries likewise offer excellent food and no shortage of superb wine. Add a clutch of art galleries and some stylish guesthouses and it really is one of the loveliest towns in the Cape. Top: Boschendal winery (p202)

Kalk Bay

8 This delightful False Bay fishing village (p103) – named after the kilns that produced lime from seashells, used for painting buildings in the 17th century – offers an abundance of antique, arts and craft shops and great cafes and restaurants, as well as a daily fish market at its harbour. A drink or meal at institutions such as the Brass Bell pub or Live Bait restaurant – nearly as close to the splashing waters of False Bay as you can get without swimming – are fine ways to pass the time. Bottom: Harbour House (p148)

SUBMAN/GETTY IMAGES ©

LENISECALLEJA.PHOTOGRAPHY/SHUTTERSTOCK ©

Kirstenbosch National Botanical Garden

9 There's been European horticulture on the picturesque eastern slopes of Table Mountain since Jan van Riebeeck's time in the 17th century, but it was British imperialist Cecil Rhodes, owner of Kirstenbosch Farm and surrounding properties, who really put the gardens (p95) on the map when he bequeathed the land to all Capetonians. Today it's a spectacular showcase for the Cape Floral Kingdom, which was declared a Unesco World Heritage Site for its incredible biodiversity. Take in the view from the treetop walkway known as the Boomslang.

Surfing along the Garden Route

10 The Garden Route is known for its outdoor pursuits on both land and sea. The coast between Mossel Bay and Plettenberg Bay boasts some of the Western Cape's best surf (p230), great whether you're a pro or just starting out. Herold's Bay and Victoria Bay, near George, are particularly pretty spots to catch a wave, and offer excellent beaches for nonsurfing travel companions. In Victoria Bay you can try a beginner lesson or rent a board and join the experts on a more challenging day trip.

Knysna

11 Although a wildfire in 2017 laid waste to the forests around Knysna (p239) and damaged many homes, the Garden Route's top tourist town has been quick to bounce back. The conflagration cannot detract from Knysna's serene location on a beautiful lagoon (which is best explored on a sightseeing cruise. Hang around to appreciate the town's arty, LGBT-friendly atmosphere as well as its great range of activities, including tours into the local township and the Rastafarian community and a chance to go elephant tracking. Bottom right: Knysna Lagoon (p239)

Stellenbosch

12 At the heart of hundreds of vineyards, Stellenbosch (p194) is an elegant town with Cape Dutch, Georgian and Victorian architecture and good museums. A must-see is the Village Museum, which is spread across a group of buildings charting different periods in the town's three centuries of history. Travellers in search of fine-dining experiences will find they are spoilt for choice by the restaurants in town and on the surrounding wine estates, many of which should be booked ahead.

Wilderness

13 A quieter alternative to Knysna and Plettenberg, Wilderness (p237) lives up to its name. Here you'll find dense old-growth forests on steep hills running down to kilometres of white sand and sheltered lagoons. The village is on the doorstep of a lovely section of the Garden Route National Park that includes lakes, wetlands and estuaries. Hike the park's 5km Kingfisher Trail, which includes a boardwalk across the intertidal zone of the Touws River. There's superlative birdwatching and a host of outdoor activities including kayaking and kloofing (canyoning).

12

DARCY BROWN/500PX ©

PETER CHADWICK/GETTY IMAGES ©

Hermanus

14 Clinging to the clifftops, Hermanus (p216) has pretty beaches, fynbos-covered hills and some of the best land-based whale watching in the world. Between June and November scores of whales converge on Walker Bay to calve. The giant ocean-living mammals often come very close to the shore and there are some excellent vantage points from the cliff paths that run from one end of Hermanus to the other. There's also a whale crier who walks around town blowing on a kelp horn and carrying a blackboard listing where whales have been sighted. Top right: Southern right whale (p216)

West Coast National Park

15 This park (p226), which is easily accessed from Cape Town, encompasses the clear, blue waters of the Langebaan Lagoon and is home to an enormous number of birds. It covers around 310 sq km and protects wetlands of international significance and important seabird breeding colonies. Wading birds flock here by the thousands in summer. The offshore islands are home to colonies of African penguins. The only time it approaches getting crowded is during its famous wildflower display, usually between August and September. Bottom right: Cape gannet

Need to Know

For more information, see Survival Guide (p279)

Currency
South African rand (R)

Language
English, Afrikaans, Xhosa

Visas
Australian, UK, US and most Western European citizens can get a 90-day entry permit on arrival.

Money
ATMs are widely available. Credit cards are accepted at most businesses, but some smaller food places, including weekly markets, are cash-only.

Mobile Phones
South Africa uses the GSM digital standard; check compatibility with your phone provider. Local SIM cards are easy to buy.

Time
South Africa Standard Time (GMT/UTC plus two hours)

When to Go

Warm to hot summers, mild winters
Dry climate
Desert, dry climate

Langebaan
GO Dec–Mar

Cape Town
GO Dec–Mar

Franschhoek
GO Feb, Mar & Nov

Knysna
GO Feb, Mar & Nov

Hermanus
GO Feb, Mar & Nov

Summer (Dec to Feb)

➡ Warm, dry weather and lively festivals.

➡ Peak times are early December to mid-January and around Easter.

➡ Coastal and national-park accommodation books up months in advance. Prices can rise by 50% or more.

Spring & Autumn (Apr–May & Sep–Nov)

➡ Often sunny weather.

➡ Optimum wildlife-watching conditions from autumn onwards.

➡ Wildflower and whale watching season late August to early September.

Winter (Jun–Aug)

➡ Rainy season in Cape Town and the Western Cape.

➡ Accommodation prices are generally low and its a good time to visit arid areas such as the Karoo.

Useful Websites

Cape Town Magazine (www.capetownmagazine.com) Online magazine with its finger on Cape Town's pulse.

Cape Town Tourism (www.capetown.travel) The city's official tourism site is stacked with info.

Lonely Planet (lonelyplanet.com/cape-town) Destination information, hotel bookings, travellers forum and more.

Important Numbers

Country code	☎27
International access code	☎00
Emergency (landline/ mobile)	☎107/112
Table Mountain National Park	☎086 110 6417
Sea Rescue	☎021-449 3500

Exchange Rates

Australia	A$1	R9.62
Canada	C$1	R9.63
Europe	€1	R14.74
Japan	¥100	R10.93
Lesotho	M1	R1
New Zealand	NZ$1	R8.73
Swaziland	E1	R1
UK	£1	R16.78
USA	US$1	R11.86

For current exchange rates see www.xe.com.

Daily Costs

Budget: Less than R1000

- Dorm bed: R250
- Gourmet burger: R70
- Local beer: R30
- Hiking in Table Mountain National Park: Free
- MyCiTi bus from City Bowl to Camps Bay: R11.70

Midrange: R1000–5000

- Hotel room: R1000–3000
- Township/cultural tour: R600
- Kirstenbosch Summer Sunset Concert ticket: R180
- Meal with wine at Waterfront restaurant: R500

Top end: More than R5000

- Hotel room: R3000–6000
- Meal at top-end restaurant: R800–1200
- Full-day gourmet wine tour: R2000
- Thirty-minute helicopter flight: R1650
- Three-hour cruise on luxury yacht: R6800

Opening Hours

The following are general hours. Individual reviews list more specific variations.

Banks 9am to 3.30pm Monday to Friday, 9am to 11am Saturday

Post offices 8.30am to 4.30pm Monday to Friday, 8am to noon Saturday

Shops 8.30am to 5pm Monday to Friday, 8.30am to 1pm Saturday. Major shopping centres are open 9am to 9pm daily.

Cafes 7.30am to 5pm Monday to Saturday. Cafes in the City Bowl are open 8am to 3pm on Saturday and closed on Sunday.

Restaurants Noon to 3pm and 6pm to 10pm Monday to Saturday.

Arriving in Cape Town

Cape Town International Airport MyCiTi bus to Cape Town Train Station is R100; the Backpacker Bus shared minivan taxi is R220 to city centre hotels and hostels; a taxi is around R250.

Cape Town Train Station Long-distance trains and buses arrive at this centrally located terminal; a taxi to most central locations will be under R50.

V&A Waterfront Jetty 2 or Duncan Dock Where international cruise ships dock.

What to Wear

Capetonian dress codes are supremely casual – even at quiet formal events you'll find some people dressed in jeans and T-shirts. It's important to remember that the vast majority of the city's population own maybe just one or two changes of clothing so running around blinged up to the nines is likely to make you stand out for all the wrong reasons. That said, there is certainly a Miami-meets-Monaco beachy fashion vibe in the tonier areas of town, such as Camps Bay and Constantia, and if you are heading to the posher restaurants a smart outfit will help you blend in.

For information on **getting around**, see p30

What's New

Silo District

The Heatherwick Studio–designed Zeitz MOCAA Museum is the star attraction of this revamped Waterfront area, but also worth searching out are The Yard restaurant (p148) and shop and the design gallery Guild (p179).

Mojo Market

Sea Point holds a daily market that's as good a place to shop for fashion and souvenirs as it is for an inexpensive meal or just to enjoy a drink with live music. (p180)

Cape Town Fynbos Experience

Learn all about the flavour profiles and medicinal benefits of various species of fynbos (the local flora) at this tasting experience in the Company's Garden. (p61)

A4 Arts Foundation

Discover new and established artistic talent at this arts centre staging free exhibitions, film screenings, live performances and discussions. (p76)

Arch for Arch

Admire the interlaced wooden arch next to St George's Cathedral, dedicated to Nobel Prize winner Archibishop Desmond Tutu. (p69)

Township Dining & Drinking

Quality refreshments have come to Khayelitsha and Langa in the form of the gourmet restaurant 4Roomed, braii (barbecue) joint Mzansi (p156), and cafes Siki's Kofee Kafe (p167) and Kaffa Hoist (p168).

18 Gangster Museum

This tiny, but imaginatively designed 'museum' in a shipping container teaches about the perils of gang life in the townships. It also runs walking tours. (p124)

New Parks

As well as the Two Rivers Urban Park (p76) near Observatory, on the cards is the development of Maiden's Cove (p93) into a new municipal park linking Clifton and Camps Bay.)

Obz Revival

Observatory has several new and revamped places to eat, drink and shop including AHEM! Art Collective (p78), the force behind the monthly Art Thursday event (p172).

Church Square

There are new places to eat and drink around this attractive and historic City Bowl square that is set to become a venue for a free light and sound show. (p68)

Brewing & Distilling

Craft brewing across the Cape is still going gangbusters with plenty of new microbreweries popping up. They've also been joined by spirits distilleries such as Woodstock Gin Company (p161) and New Harbour Distillery (p82).

Café Roux

Doing it proud for the live music scene is this establishment with bases at Noordhoek (p172) and the City Bowl (p168), both with a packed schedule of concerts by local talents.

For more recommendations and reviews, see lonelyplanet.com/south-africa/cape-town

If You Like...

Beaches

Muizenberg Colourful Victorian chalets, warm(ish) water and fun surfing. (p105)

Clifton 3rd Beach Where the gay community leads, Capetonians follow. (p93)

Buffels Bay Tranquil, with sweeping views across False Bay and a sea pool for safe swimming. (p111)

Sandy Bay The nudist beach also has amazing giant rock formations to explore. (p94)

Noordhoek Magnificently broad, overlooked by Chapman's Peak and with a shipwreck in the sand. (p109)

Viewpoints

Table Mountain Sweeping vistas across the city and peninsula. (p54)

Bloubergstrand Picture-perfect view of Table Mountain north of the city. (p113)

Cape of Good Hope Walk to just above the Cape's original lighthouse. (p107)

Chapman's Peak Drive Take in the elegant sweep of horseshoe-shaped Hout Bay. (p119)

Signal Hill Hear the cannon fire and look out over the Waterfront. (p78)

Free Stuff

V&A Waterfront Buskers, outdoor events, seals, historic buildings, public artworks and the comings and goings of the harbour. (p81)

Table Mountain National Park No charge for hiking the myriad trails on the main mountain, up Lion's Head or along Signal Hill. (p55)

St George's Cathedral One of the few places of worship that was open to people of all races during apartheid. (p68)

A4 Arts Foundation Free gallery featuring contemporary South African art. (p76)

Long Street Stroll from the junction with Buitensingel St north to Strand St. (p69)

Street Art District Six and Woodstock are dotted with impressive large-scale works. (p77)

Nelson Mandela Gateway Learn about the Freedom struggle and life in the prison before heading to Robben Island. (p64)

Parks & Gardens

Company's Garden Relax or stroll through these historic gardens, marvelling at ancient trees and pretty flower beds. (p60)

Green Point Urban Park Enjoy the lovely eco-legacy of World Cup 2010 at this new park showcasing biodiversity. (p82)

Oranjezicht City Farm A beautifully laid-out urban farm on the slopes of Table Mountain. (p83)

Two Rivers Urban Park A new park around the confluence of the Liesbeek and Black Rivers. (p76)

Arderne Gardens The oldest collection of trees in the Southern Hemisphere is a lovely place to escape the crowds. (p103)

Babylonstoren Explore the blissful garden of edible and medicinal plants at this elegantly reimagined wine and fruit estate. (p210)

Art Collections

Zeitz MOCAA Museum Contemporary art from across Africa and beyond displayed in a converted grain silo complex. (p66)

South African National Gallery Prime examples of the nation's art are exhibited in this elegant building. (p78)

Stevenson Major commercial gallery for contemporary artists, with interesting thematic exhibitions. (p78)

Irma Stern Museum Former home of the pioneering expressionist artists, with a lovely garden. (p96)

Casa Labia Cultural Centre Beautifully restored interiors at this Muizenberg villa, converted to an arts and cultural space. (p107)

Historical Insights

District Six Museum Shines a light on the destroyed multicultural inner-city area. (p62)

Robben Island Book ahead for visits to the former prison of Mandela and other freedom fighters. (p64)

Bo-Kaap Museum Learn about the people of the Cape Malay community in this colourful district. (p65)

Iziko Slave Lodge Exhibits on the history of slaves and their descendants. (p68)

South African Museum Lots of natural history and fine examples of San rock art. (p79)

South African Jewish Museum Traces the routes of Jewish migration and settlement in the country; has a section on the Holocaust. (p77)

Hidden Gems

Rust en Vreugd Elegant 18th-century mansion and garden in the midst of the city. (p80)

Tintswalo Atlantic Not staying at this luxe lodge? Call to see if you can visit for lunch or dinner. (p134)

Enmasse Thai massage the modern way, in a historic building tucked away in Gardens. (p116)

Wynberg Village Explore the many Cape Georgian buildings here to find the studios and shops of artists, designers and interior decorators. (p95)

Intaka Island Spot 120 feathered species and 200-plus plant species at this 1600-sq-metre wetland reserve nestled in the Century City development. (p113)

Top: Neighbourgoods Market (p177), Cape Town

Bottom: Babylonstoren (p210)

The Luxe Life

Status Luxury Vehicles Cruise Cape Town's roads in a top-marque convertible, or have a chauffeur drive it for you. (p186)

Prins & Prins Go shopping for diamonds and other precious jewels at this emporium based in a historic City Bowl house. (p175)

Klûk & CGDT Haute couture from a former apprentice to John Galliano. (p174)

Belmond Mount Nelson Hotel Not a guest? Come for afternoon tea or visit the Planet bar and restaurant. (p132)

Sports Helicopters Hire a chopper and take some photos of the peninsula that will really impress your friends. (p119)

Activities & Sports

Hiking in Table Mountain National Park Hire a guide so you don't get lost, and learn more about the Cape floral kingdom. (p54)

Abseil Africa Dangle from a rope off the edge of Table Mountain and take in the view. (p116)

Downhill Adventures Offering a range of adrenaline-fuelled activities, from mountain biking to surf safaris. (p185)

Animal Ocean Flip around with Cape fur seals off Duiker Island (aka Seal Island), either snorkelling or diving. (p119)

Kaskazi Kayaks Close encounters with dolphins, seals and penguins while paddling on the Atlantic. (p116)

Newlands Cricket Ground Judge for yourself whether this is the world's best-looking cricket ground. (p169)

Newlands Rugby Stadium Local team the Stormers play at this home of South African rugby. (p169)

Cape Town Stadium Catch a national Premier Soccer League match here. (p83)

Entertainment

Baxter Theatre Centre Premier theatre and performing arts complex in a striking 1970s building. (p171)

Fugard Theatre Vibrant addition to city's theatre and cinema scene set in a converted church. (p170)

Alexander Bar & Café Upstairs studio space hosts some of Cape Town's most innovative theatre and cabaret. (p168)

Evita se Perron Theatre legend Pieter-Dirk Uys' Darling home for his satirical cast of characters. (p223)

Cape Town Comedy Club Laugh along with South Africa's leading comics at the Waterfront. (p171)

Labia Retro-cool cinema in Gardens specialising in art-house titles. (p170)

Live Music

Studio 7 Sessions Great acoustic sets, up close and personal, at this Sea Point lounge. (p171)

Café Roux Its venues in the City Bowl and Noordhoek can be relied on for up-and-coming and edgy bands and singers. (p172)

Cape Town City Hall Home base for the Cape Philharmonic Orchestra. (p72)

Kirstenbosch Summer Sunset Concerts Picnic while top South African musicians play the beautiful outdoors. (p96)

Crypt Jazz Restaurant Book ahead for shows in the stone crypt of St George's Cathedral. (p169)

Shopping & Markets

Watershed Outstanding selection of local crafts, design and fashion at the Waterfront. (p179)

Old Biscuit Mill Fabulous retail and Saturday's Neighbourgoods Market. (p176)

Kalk Bay Modern Fine art, jewellery and fabrics beside the sea. (p182)

Guild Top-of-the-line South African design from postcards to statement pieces of art. (p179)

OZCF Market Day Fresh locally grown produce, edible treats and crafts. (p177)

Blue Bird Garage Food & Goods Market Fun Friday night bash in Muizenberg, with tonnes of food, some fashion and crafts. (p177)

Bay Harbour Market Seaside market that's great for souvenirs, food and relaxing at the weekend. (p177)

Montebello Design Centre Artists' studios scattered around a central craft shop, stocking a great range of gifts. (p181)

Month by Month

TOP EVENTS

Cape Town Minstrel Carnival, January

Infecting the City, March

Design Indaba, February

Open Book Festival, September

Adderley St Christmas Lights, December

January

Expect packed hotels and restaurants, crowds at the beaches and traffic on main coastal roads. Some restaurants, cafes and shops close for the first week or so of the month.

Cape Town Minstrel Carnival

Tweede Nuwe Jaar (2 January) sees satin- and sequin-clad minstrel troupes march through the city for the Cape Town Minstrel Carnival. There are smaller marches on Christmas Eve and New Year's Eve. Into early February there are competitions between troupes at Athlone Stadium. (p274)

Sun Met

Fancy a flutter? Don your biggest hat for South Africa's richest horse race – with a R2.5 million jackpot. Usually held on the last Saturday in January at Kenilworth Racecourse. (p125)

February

Check for classical concerts at the Cape Town International Summer Music Festival. The city goes into lockdown for the opening of Parliament in the first week of February – avoid anything but essential travel on that day.

Cape Town Pride

Held from the last week of Feburary to early March with events focused in De Waterkant. (p157)

Design Indaba

Bringing together creatives from the varied worlds of fashion, architecture, visual arts, crafts and media, this creative convention is held from late February to early March, usually at the Cape Town International Convention Centre. (p125)

March

The cultural calendar cranks up with a series of arts and music festivals. Cyclists take over the streets (and many of the city's hotels) for the Cape Town Cycle Tour, so forget driving around town on the day of the event.

Cape Town Carnival

This city-sponsored parade and street party celebrates the many facets of South African identity. Held in the middle of the month on the Walk of Remembrance in Green Point. (p126)

Cape Town Cycle Tour

The world's largest timed cycling event, held on a Saturday in the middle of March, attracts more than 30,000 contestants. The route circles Table Mountain, heads down the Atlantic Coast and along Chapman's Peak Dr. (p126)

Cape Town International Jazz Festival

Bringing together big names from both South Africa and overseas, Cape Town's biggest jazz event is usually held at the Cape Town International Convention Centre at the end of March. It includes a free concert in Greenmarket Sq. (p126)

Infecting the City

This innovative performing arts festival is held across Cape Town's squares, fountains, museums and theatres. It's held every two years, and features artists from across the continent. (p126)

Mercedes-Benz Fashion Week

Fashionistas line the catwalks to spot the hottest work from local designers and pick up the latest trends. (p126)

Old Mutual Two Oceans Marathon

This 56km marathon kicks off in Newlands and follows a similar route to the Cape Town Cycle Tour around Table Mountain. It is held in mid-March, and attracts around 9000 competitors. (p126)

April

The weather starts to chill from now through early October, so bring warmer clothes and be prepared for rainy, blustery days.

Freedom Swim

Only thick-skinned and strong swimmers should apply for the solo and team relay events of this swim from Murray's Bay, on Robben Island, to Bloubergstrand. It's held around Freedom Day (27 April). (www.freedomswimseries.co.za)

Pink Loerie Festival

Knysna celebrates its gay-friendliness with a flamboyant Mardi Gras at the end of April and beginning of May. (p243)

May

Head to Kirstenbosch, Constantia and the Winelands to enjoy the blaze of autumnal colours laid on by Mother Nature.

Franschhoek Literary Festival

As if you needed more reason to visit this delightful Winelands town, this literary festival attracts the cream of locally based and expatriate South African writers. (www.flf.co.za)

Good Food & Wine Show

Three days of gourmet goodness can be enjoyed at this event, held at the Cape Town International Convention Centre. (p126)

July

Winter in Cape Town can be very blustery and wet, but it's also one of the best times to spot whales off the peninsula's coast.

Cape Town Nu World Festival

Taking place over Mandela Day weekend (around 18 July), this celebration of global beats and rhythms takes over City Hall and parts of the Grand Parade. (p126)

September

The first official month of spring and it's still prime whale-watching season around the Peninsula and down to Hermanus. The city also hosts a couple of top arts events.

Cape Town Fringe

Organised in conjunction with the respected Grahamstown Festival, this jamboree of the performing arts entertains the Mother City for 11 days in late September and early October. (p126)

Open Book Festival

Cape Town's main literature festival offers a packed schedule of talks, readings and discussions with local and international writers. It's organised by the the Fugard Theatre with events held there, the District Six Homecoming Centre and the Book Lounge. (p126)

October

Well into spring now; enjoy warmer weather and freshly blooming flowers in Kirstenbosch and other parks and country areas.

Cape Town International Kite Festival

This colourful gathering of kite enthusiasts at Zandvlei (near Muizenberg) supports the Cape Mental Health Society. Held at the end of October. (p126)

Mama City Improv Festival

This stand-up comedy and improvisation festival in Observatory includes five laughter-packed days of shows, workshops and performances by local and international talents. (p126)

OUTsurance Kfm 94.5 Gun Run

The only time that the Noon Gun on Signal Hill gets fired on a Sunday is at this popular half-marathon (21km) – competitors try to finish the race before the gun goes off. There are also 10km and 5km races. (p126)

Season of Sauvignon

Sauvignon blanc, Durbanville's signature grape, is the focus of this festival in late October, with most of the area's dozen wineries hosting events from vertical tastings to live music. (p126)

November

Cape Town can be lovely in the spring, although the wind may drive you a little crazy. Various regular outdoor events start their summer seasons in this month.

Galileo Outdoor Cinema

This outdoor cinema operation (http://thegalileo.co.za) starts screenings in Kirstenbosch, the Waterfront and the Winelands.

Kirstenbosch Summer Sunset Concerts

These Sunday afternoon concerts run through until April; expect everything from arias performed by local divas to a funky jazz combo. There's always a special concert for New Year's Eve. (p96)

Miss Gay Western Cape

Glitz and glam are the order of the day at this long-running transgender beauty pageant, usually held in early November. (p126)

Streetopia

The lively street festival is usually held on the last Saturday in November at various locations around central Observatory including the Trill Rd, Station Rd and Lower Main Rd. (p126)

Wavescape Surf & Ocean Festival

This surfing-themed fest includes art shows, movie screenings and masterclasses – which are held at various places around the Cape, including Muizenburg and the Waterfront. (p127)

December

This is the top holiday season, so book well ahead for tickets for popular attractions and to get reservations at top restaurants. New Year's Eve is busy, with fireworks at the Waterfront – one of many special events across the city.

Adderley St Christmas Lights

The Christmas season kicks off on the first Sunday in December, as huge crowds turn out for a concert in front of Cape Town Railway Station, followed by a parade along illuminated Adderley St. A night market is also held in the Company Gardens starting mid-December. (p127)

Cape Town Festival of Beer

The continent's largest beer festival sees more than 200 beers available for tasting over three days in early December. (p127)

MCQP

Standing for Mother City Queer Project, this theme fancy dress dance party is held a different major Cape Town venue each December. Although it's a LGBT event, everyone regardless of sexual orientation, joins in the fun. (p157)

Itineraries

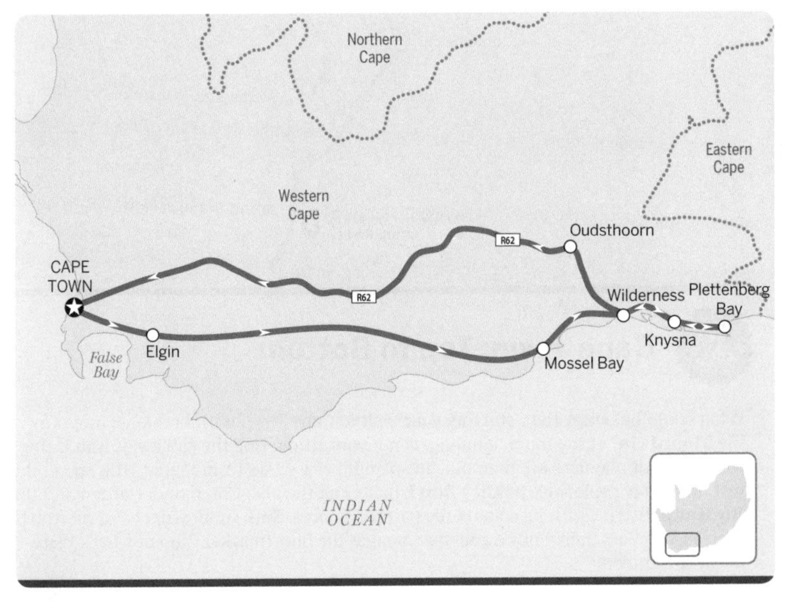

Garden Route Road Trip

The verdant Garden Route endures as one of South Africa's top draws for visitors. Ideally you would spend a week travelling to and exploring the region, but you still get a taste of its pleasures in five days, allowing a couple of days in **Cape Town** at either end.

From Cape Town, head east along the N2, stopping for *padkos* (road snacks) at an **Elgin** farm stall. Spend a night in **Mossel Bay** where you can surf, skydive, hike, dive with sharks or just explore the museum. Resist the temptation to drive right by **Wilderness**: its national park deserves at least one afternoon and accommodation options around town are excellent.

Stop in **Knysna** to hike the forests, take a boat cruise on the lagoon and join a tour of the hilltop township. If you're seeking some beach time, continue to pretty **Plettenberg Bay,** with its seafront accommodation and smattering of wineries specialising in bubbly.

On the return to Cape Town consider driving through **Oudtshoorn** and taking **Route 62** – the arid, winding drive makes for a delightful alternative to the N2.

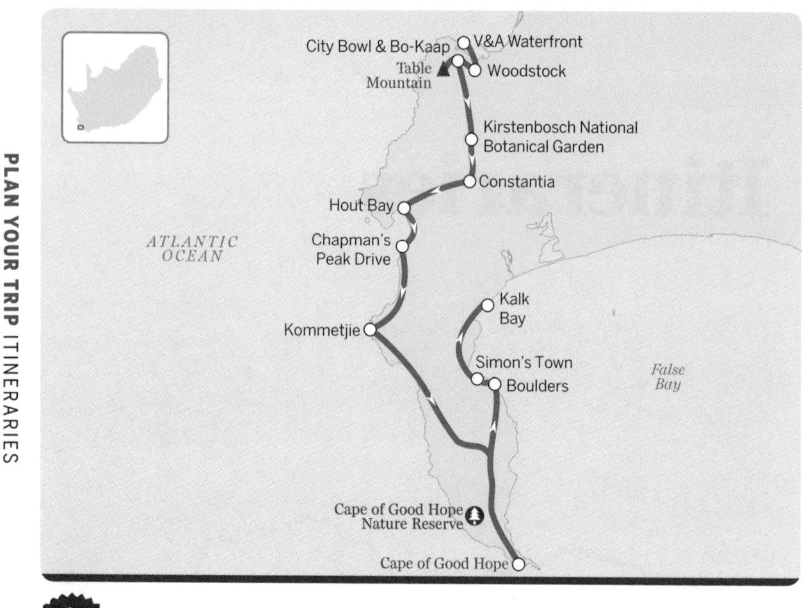

4 DAYS Cape Town: Top to Bottom

What could be better than starting your visit to Cape Town with breakfast atop **Table Mountain**? If the tough climb up is not your thing, ride the cableway. And if the weather's not playing ball, then take in splendid city views from Signal Hill. Spend the rest of the day exploring the **City Bowl**, including the lush Company's Garden and the **Bo-Kaap** district with its colourfully painted houses. Sink sundowners at a rooftop bar, such as The Vue, then enjoy a gourmet meal at the Shortmarket Club or Chef's Warehouse & Canteen.

On day two learn about the city's troubled past at the District Six Museum. Watch the noon key ceremony at the 350-year-old Castle of Good Hope. Head to Woodstock for lunch at Kitchen followed by contemporary art browsing at galleries such as Stevenson and Goodman Gallery Cape. There's also abundant street art around the **Woodstock Exchange**. Art lovers should have the new Zeitz MOCAA Museum at the **V&A Waterfront** high on their list of priorities; hang out in this lively area for a sunset cruise followed by dinner at Harbour House.

Begin day three exploring the beautiful **Kirstenbosch National Botanical Garden**. Book well ahead for lunch at Foxcroft or La Colombe then spend a blissful afternoon sampling your way through **Constantia's** wineries. Motor over Constantia Nek to **Hout Bay**. Enjoy the sea views, beer in hand, from the beachside pub Dunes.

The peninsula's deep south beckons on day four – reach it by driving along spectacular **Chapman's Peak Drive** and the surfing hot spot of **Kommetjie**. Stand at the southwestern tip of Africa within the **Cape of Good Hope Nature Reserve** section of Table Mountain National Park. Enjoy a picnic lunch here then head to **Boulders**, home to a thriving colony of African penguins. The historic naval base of **Simon's Town** is just up the road while further around False Bay is the charming fishing village of **Kalk Bay**, where you can enjoy fresh seafood at many excellent restaurants such as Olympia Café.

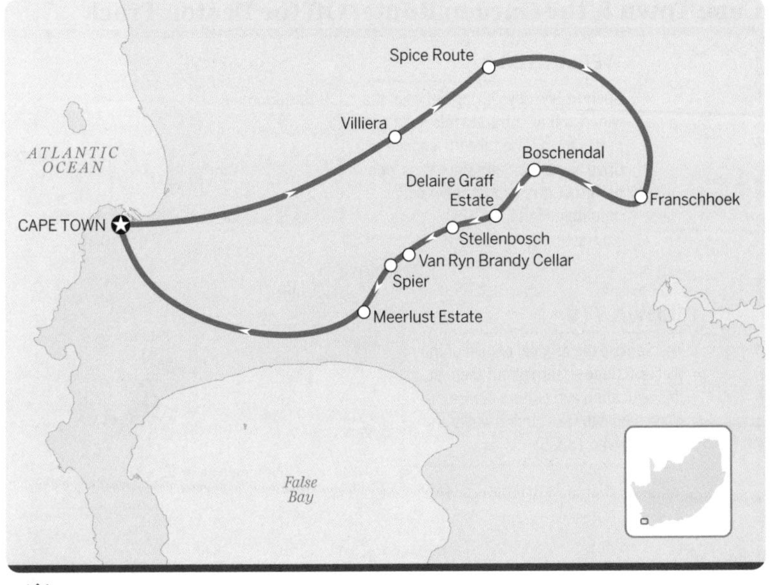

The Essential Winelands

The Winelands make it onto the bucket list of almost every visitor to South Africa. Even nondrinkers are soon entranced by the elegant Cape Dutch mansions, fine food and bluish-grey mountain backdrop. This itinerary could easily be split into day trips. Stick to a maximum of four wineries per day.

Leaving **Cape Town** via the N1, kick off your day with a glass of bubbly at **Villiera** and consider sticking around for a two-hour wildlife drive to see giraffes and zebras. From here it's a 20-minute drive to **Spice Route**, where you can easily spend half a day indulging in all the foodie pursuits. Enjoy lunch with a view then take Rte 45 towards **Franschhoek**, stopping to visit the museums – and tasting room – at Solms-Delta. Overnight in a Franschhoek guesthouse and be sure to book ahead for dinner in one of the town's renowned restaurants.

Wake up and take a stroll around town, stopping to graze in cafes and patisseries as you go. Mix things up with lunch at a local brewery before heading to one of the region's most beloved estates, **Boschendal**, with its stately buildings, huge tree, vineyard tours and mountain biking trails. Route 310 towards Stellenbosch is a winding, scenic road and there's no better spot to enjoy the views than at **Delaire Graff Estate**. Spend the night in one of **Stellenbosch's** historic hotels or long-standing hostels.

On day three, spend the morning exploring the town centre – don't miss the excellent Village Museum and the pretty botanical garden, a nice spot for midmorning coffee and cake. Head out of town on Rte 310 and try a brandy tasting at **Van Ryn Brandy Cellar**, whose brandies are among the most awarded in the world. Mere moments along the same road you will reach **Spier**. It is unashamedly commercial, but few leave disappointed by the restaurants, wine tasting, family-friendly activities and vast grounds.

Continue south, but before you join the N2 back to Cape Town, make time for one final stop at **Meerlust Estate** where there is no restaurant, no kids' corner, pairing experience or on-site cheesemaker. Here it's all about the wine, particularly its signature red blend.

Cape Town & the Garden Route: Off the Beaten Track

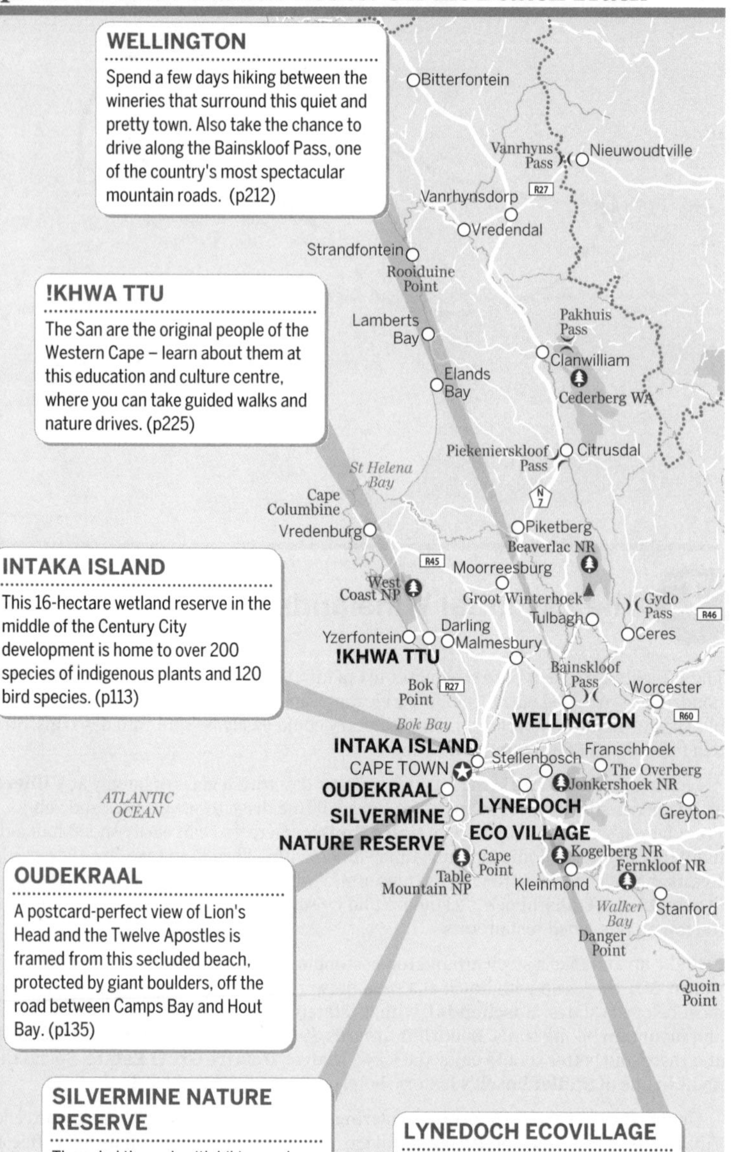

WELLINGTON

Spend a few days hiking between the wineries that surround this quiet and pretty town. Also take the chance to drive along the Bainskloof Pass, one of the country's most spectacular mountain roads. (p212)

!KHWA TTU

The San are the original people of the Western Cape – learn about them at this education and culture centre, where you can take guided walks and nature drives. (p225)

INTAKA ISLAND

This 16-hectare wetland reserve in the middle of the Century City development is home to over 200 species of indigenous plants and 120 bird species. (p113)

OUDEKRAAL

A postcard-perfect view of Lion's Head and the Twelve Apostles is framed from this secluded beach, protected by giant boulders, off the road between Camps Bay and Hout Bay. (p135)

SILVERMINE NATURE RESERVE

Threaded through with hiking and mountain biking trails, this southern section of Table Mountain National Park harbours a reservoir with tannin-stained waters, around which is a wheelchair-accessible boardwalk. (p103)

LYNEDOCH ECOVILLAGE

Near Stellenbosch, drop by this tiny village that challenges the notion that sustainable development and ecological building is too expensive. There's a cafe and simple accommodation here too. (p194)

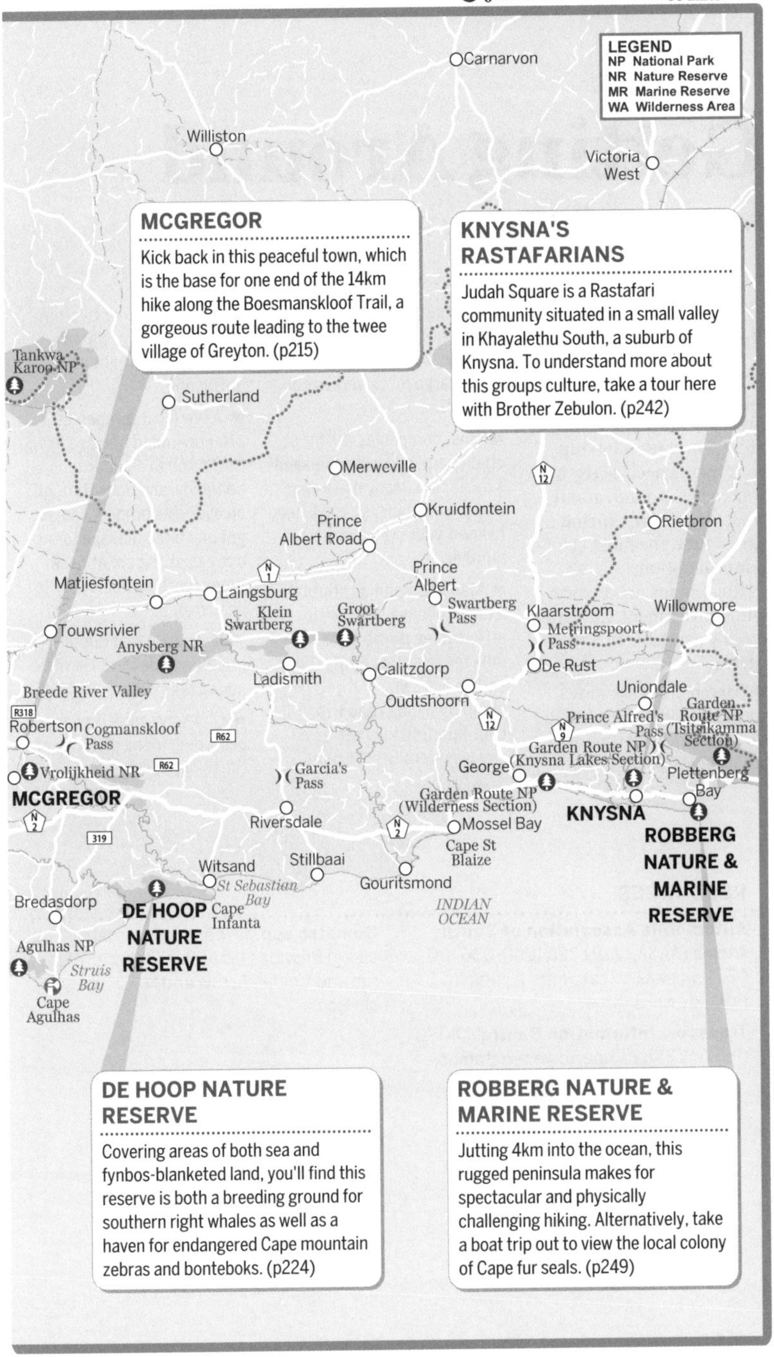

0 — 100 km
0 — 50 miles

LEGEND
NP National Park
NR Nature Reserve
MR Marine Reserve
WA Wilderness Area

MCGREGOR

Kick back in this peaceful town, which is the base for one end of the 14km hike along the Boesmanskloof Trail, a gorgeous route leading to the twee village of Greyton. (p215)

KNYSNA'S RASTAFARIANS

Judah Square is a Rastafari community situated in a small valley in Khayalethu South, a suburb of Knysna. To understand more about this groups culture, take a tour here with Brother Zebulon. (p242)

Carnarvon
Williston
Victoria West
Tankwa Karoo NP
Sutherland
Merweville
Kruidfontein
N12
Rietbron
Prince Albert Road
N1
Prince Albert
Matjiesfontein
Laingsburg
Klein Swartberg
Groot Swartberg
Swartberg Pass
Klaarstroom
Willowmore
Touwsrivier
Meiringspoort Pass
Anysberg NR
De Rust
Ladismith
Calitzdorp
Breede River Valley
Oudtshoorn
Uniondale
R318
Robertson
Cogmanskloof Pass
R62
N12
Prince Alfred's Pass
Garden Route NP (Tsitsikamma Section)
N9
Garden Route NP (Knysna Lakes Section)
Vrolijkheid NR
R62
Garcia's Pass
George
Plettenberg Bay
MCGREGOR
Garden Route NP (Wilderness Section)
KNYSNA
N2
Riversdale
N2
Mossel Bay
ROBBERG NATURE & MARINE RESERVE
319
Cape St Blaize
Witsand
Stillbaai
St Sebastian Bay
Gouritsmond
Bredasdorp
DE HOOP NATURE RESERVE
Cape Infanta
INDIAN OCEAN
Agulhas NP
Struis Bay
Cape Agulhas

DE HOOP NATURE RESERVE

Covering areas of both sea and fynbos-blanketed land, you'll find this reserve is both a breeding ground for southern right whales as well as a haven for endangered Cape mountain zebras and bonteboks. (p224)

ROBBERG NATURE & MARINE RESERVE

Jutting 4km into the ocean, this rugged peninsula makes for spectacular and physically challenging hiking. Alternatively, take a boat trip out to view the local colony of Cape fur seals. (p249)

Getting Around

For more information, see Transport (p285)

Travelling By Car

South Africa is a spectacular country for a road trip. Away from the main bus and train routes, having your own wheels is the best way to get around, and if you're in a group, hiring a car is often the most economical option.

Road maps are a worthwhile investment, and are readily available in South Africa.

- Car rental is inexpensive compared with Europe and North America, starting at around R200 per day for longer rentals. For the lowest rates, book online months in advance. Many companies levy a surcharge for drivers aged under 21.
- Most companies ask for a credit card, and will not accept a debit card. Many use a chip-and-pin machine, so you'll need to know your credit card's pin number.
- Many companies stipulate a daily mileage limit, with an extra fee payable for any mileage over this limit. This can be a drawback if you're planning a long road trip. Four hundred kilometres a day is generally sufficient. If you plan one- or two-day stopovers along the way, 200km a day might be sufficient.
- A few local companies offer unlimited mileage. If you rent through an international company, and book through an overseas branch, you may get unlimited mileage for no extra cost, except at peak times (such as December to January).
- Make sure that quoted prices include the 14% value-added tax (VAT).
- One-way rental is charged according to the distance of the relocation.

RESOURCES

Automobile Association of South Africa (AASA; ☎011-799 1000, 086 100 0234; www.aa.co.za) offers a vehicle breakdown service.

Transport Information Centre (☎080 065 6463) for Cape Town timetables.

Gometro app (https://app.gometro.co.za) Provides timetables for Metrorail and Golden Arrow and MyCiTi bus services.

No Car?

Air

The only local flight you might consider making in this region is between Cape Town and George (at least three daily, 50 minutes).

Bus

Lines including Greyhound, Intercape and Translux are cover the region in comfortable vehicles at reasonable rates. The backpacker shuttle bus services Baz Bus and Mzansi Experience are convenient and social options for covering the Garden Route between Cape Town and the Eastern Cape.

Bicycle

As long as you're fit enough to handle the hills, the Western Cape offers some rewarding cycling. There's scenic and diverse terrain, abundant campsites and numerous quiet secondary roads. The major drawback is sharing the tarmac with South Africa's often erratic and aggressive drivers.

Shared Taxi

These are OK for short journeys but less practical over long distances, as there are various safety and security issues. However, away from train and bus routes, shared taxis may be the only choice of public transport.

- Driving standards and vehicle conditions are poor.
- There are frequent accidents.
- There are occasional gangster-style clashes between rival companies.
- Shared-taxi stations and their immediate surroundings are often unsafe.
- Muggings, pickpocketing, sexual harassment and other incidents are common.
- If you want to try riding in a shared taxi, don't travel at night, read the newspapers and seek local advice on lines and areas to avoid.
- In a few areas, shared taxis are relatively safe during daylight hours. This is notably the case in central Cape Town, where locals from all walks of life use shared taxis.
- Do not travel with luggage, partly because most shared taxis don't carry bags on the roof, and stowing backpacks can be a hassle.

Private Taxi

Cape Town and its surrounding areas has plenty of private taxi services; there are taxi stands in popular areas. Phoning for a cab is often safer; you will have to wait for the taxi to arrive, but the vehicle will likely be better quality than those at the stands. Rates in Cape Town average R10 per kilometre, often with a minimum charge of R30 or more. Uber is popular.

Train

Metro trains connect Cape Town with Stellenbosch and Paarl in the Winelands. Take care to travel on trains during the busy part of the day, for safety reasons.

DRIVING FAST FACTS

- Driving is on the left-hand side of the road.
- Seatbelts are mandatory.
- Speed limits are 60km/h in built-up areas, 100km/h on open roads, 120km/h on most major highways.
- Your home country driving licence is OK, provided it is in English (or you have a certified translation).

ROAD DISTANCES (KM)

	Langebaan	Cape Town	George	Hermanus
Cape Town	125			
George	550	435		
Hermanus	240	120	380	
Knysna	600	490	60	440

Plan Your Trip
Eat Like a Local

Take some black magic, a dash of Dutch heartiness, a pinch of Indian spice and a smidgen of Malay mystery and what you get is an amazing array of cultures, all simmering away in the rich pot of influences that is South African cuisine. The country's culinary diversity reflects its multicultural society, ranging from African staples in the townships to seafood and steaks in globally acclaimed restaurants, and eating is an excellent way to the heart of the rainbow nation.

Opening Hours

Many restaurants and cafes are closed Sunday.

Cafes 7.30am-5pm Mon-Fri, 8am-3pm Sat

Restaurants 11.30am-3pm and 6-10pm Mon-Sat

Reservations

Reservations for popular and trendy places are recommended. A handful of venues need reserving several months in advance; some will also require advance payment.

Guides & Blogs

Rossouw's Restaurants (www.rossouwsrestaurants.com) Sprightly criticism of Cape Town's restaurants online; also publishes an annual print guide.

Eat Out (www.eatout.co.za) Online reviews and annual magazine guide with Cape Town and Western Cape reviews.

Once Bitten (http://oncebitten.co.za) Reviews and features by former *Mail & Guardian* restaurant reviewer Brent Meersman.

Where to Eat

If you're after fine dining in magnificent surroundings, head to the Winelands. Along the Western Cape coast, open-air beachside eateries serve multicourse fish braais (barbecues), with everything cooked before your eyes. A highlight of visiting a township is experiencing some family-style cooking in a B&B or home. In addition to speciality restaurants, every larger town has several places offering homogenised Western fare at homogenised prices (from about R75). Many restaurants are licensed, but there's still a BYO wine option pretty much everywhere – corkage charges almost always apply.

All towns have cafes where you can enjoy a cappuccino and a sandwich or other light fare. In rural areas, 'cafe' *(kaffie)* usually refers to a small corner shop selling soft drinks, chips, basic groceries and braai wood. Most cafes are open from about 7:30am to 5pm.

Larger towns have a good selection of pubs and more upmarket cocktail lounges. Franchised bars proliferate in urban areas, and most smaller towns have at least one hotel with a bar. In townships, things centre on shebeens (informal drinking establishments that were once illegal but are now merely unlicensed).

Throughout South Africa you can buy all alcoholic drinks at bottle stores and wine at supermarkets, though there are few options for take-out booze on Sunday.

Dining Trends

Foraging and use of local flora in cooking is on trend in Cape Town, with restaurants such as Foliage (p206) and Fyndraai (p205) in Franschhoek blazing the trail, along with pop-up feasts prepared by Veld and Sea (p121) at Good Hope Gardens Nursery.

Many places now offer vegetarian and vegan dishes that are both healthy and delicious. In tune with the Mediterranean climate, more restaurants offer small-plate or tapas-style menus for lighter meals, or mix-and-match dining, too. The low-carb, high-fat diet locally known as 'Banting' remains popular. You'll see Banting menu options, such as pizza with a base made from cauliflower, at several places.

The other trend of note is the rise of supper clubs such Reverie Social Table (p145) and **Secret Eats** (www.secreteats.co.za); sign up to their newsletters to find out about their events. If you'd like to dine in a Capetonian's home, **Pozay** (www.pozay.com) can arrange it.

Seafood Galore

Explore local types of fish, including kingklip or even snoek – a very meaty, mackerel-on-steroids type of fish that is delicious barbecued (or 'braaied' as they say in these parts). Watch out for the many small bones, though.

If you see 'line fish' advertised, it means the catch of the day. Deliciously fresh crayfish can also be had – for a price. Before ordering, make sure what you're eating isn't on the endangered list: details can be found at the **Southern African Sustainable Seafood Initiative** (SASSI; http://wwfsassi.co.za).

PRICE RANGES

The following price ranges refer to a standard main course.

$ less than R75

$$ R75–R150

$$$ more than R150

In Cape Town and the Winelands, prices are higher:

$ less than R100

$$ R100–R200

$$$ more than R200

Cape Malay Cuisine

This intriguing mix of Malay and Dutch styles, which originated in the earliest days of European settlement, marries pungent spices with local produce. It can be stodgy, with some dishes on the sweet side, but is still well worth trying.

The Cape Malay dish you'll commonly see is *bobotie,* usually made with lightly curried minced beef or lamb topped with savoury egg custard, and served on a bed of turmeric-flavoured rice with a dab of chutney on the side. Some sophisticated versions of *bobotie* use other meats and even seafood.

There's a great variety of *bredies* – pot stews of meat or fish, and vegetables. *Dhaltjies* (chilli bites) are very moreish, deep-fried balls of chickpea-flour batter mixed with potato, coriander and spinach. Mild curries are popular and are often served with *rootis,* similar to Indian roti bread but doughier. Also from Indian cooking are samosas, triangular pockets of crisp fried pastry enclosing a spicy vegetable filling. Meat lovers should try *sosaties,* which is a Cape Malay–style kebab.

Desserts include *Malva* pudding, a delicious sponge traditionally made with apricot jam and vinegar, and brandy pudding (true Cape Malay cuisine – strongly associated with the Muslim community – contains no alcohol). Also try *koeksusters,* a doughnut dipped in syrup.

RODGER BOSCH/AFP/GETTY IMAGES ©

Top: Two Oceans Restaurant (p154), Cape Town

Bottom: Biltong

LEARNING ABOUT FOOD & DRINK

Cape Town's food and drink scene is spectacular and if you like what you find here it's possible to learn more from local experts. Cape Malay cooking classes in the Bo-Kaap are offered by Gamidah Jacobs of **Lekka Kombuis** (079 957 0226; www.lekkakombuis.co.za; 81 Wale St, Bo-Kaap; cooking class & tour R650; Dorp, Leeuwen) and Zainie Misbach of **Bo-Kaap Cooking Tour** (074 130 8124; www.bokaapcookingtour.co.za; 46 Rose St; per person R825; Church|Longmarket).

Those with a sweet tooth will not want to miss out on the various chocolate making and baking courses at the **Lindt Chocolate Studio** (Map p86; 021-831 0360; www.chocolatestudio.co.za; Shop 2, Silo 2, V&A Waterfront; tastings & classes from R245; 9am-6pm), including ones for kids. You can also book tastings and a bon bon making class with local confectioners Honest Chocolate (p158).

Veld and Sea (p121) runs fynbos and coastal foraging courses. Experienced guides will teach you sustainable techniques to harvest Mother Nature's edibles, including seaweed and mussels (you need to get a mollusc permit for this, available from post offices) from nearby rock pools in Scarborough and the Cape of Good Hope nature reserve. Lunch is made from whatever you find.

Beer brewing courses are offered by **Beerguevara** (021-447 0646; www.beerguevara.com; 20 Brickfield Rd, Salt River; 9.30am-5pm Mon-Fri, 9.30am-noon Sat; Upper Salt River) while you can learn about gin distilling from **New Harbour Distillery** (021-447 3396; http://newharbourdistillery.co.za; cnr Victoria & Woodlands Rds, Woodstock; classes/tastings per person R850/75; by appointment; District Six). There are also home barista classes held at Origin (p160).

African & Afrikaner Cuisine

The staple for most blacks in the townships is rice or mealie *pap* (maize porridge), often served with a fatty stew. It isn't especially appetising, but it's cheap. The same goes for the *smilies* (sheep's heads) that you'll see boiled up and served on the streets. Other dishes include *samp* (a mixture of maize and beans), *imifino* (maize meal and vegetables) and *chakalaka* (a tasty fry-up of onions, tomatoes, peppers, garlic, ginger, sweet chilli sauce and curry powder).

Grilled meats, seasoned and sauced on the braai (barbecue), is a dish that cuts across the colour bar as well as being the keystone of traditional Afrikaner cuisine. The Voortrekker heritage comes out in foods such as biltong (deliciously moreish dried beef and venison) and rusks, perfect for those long journeys into the hinterland. Boerewors (spicy farmer's sausage) is the traditional sausage, and plenty of recipes make use of game; some include venison, which will be some type of buck.

Vegetarians & Vegans

South Africa is a meat-loving society, but most restaurants have at least one vegetarian option on the menu. In larger towns you might find a vegetarian restaurant. Cafes are good bets, as many will make vegetarian food to order. Indian and Italian restaurants are also useful, although many pasta sauces contain animal fat. Larger towns have health-food stores selling tofu, soy milk and other staples, and can point you towards vegetarian-friendly venues.

Eating vegan is more difficult: most nonmeat dishes contain cheese, and eggs and milk are common ingredients. Health-food shops are your best bet, though most are closed in the evening and on Sunday. Larger supermarkets also stock soy products, and nuts and fruit are widely available. Look out for farm stalls selling seasonal fruit and vegetables along the roadside throughout the country.

Plan Your Trip

Wine & Wineries

With over 200 wineries within a day's drive, Cape Town is the natural hub for touring the Western Cape's Winelands. This is where South Africa's wine industry began in the 17th century; today, the annual grape harvest is close to 1.5 million tonnes, most of which is used to make wine and other alcoholic beverages.

Growing Industry

Scores of new wine producers join the industry each year. While many are content to remain as micro-wineries, honing their wines to perfection, others are seeking to capitalise on the industry's popularity by adding museums, restaurants, accommodation, walking trails and other attractions. We review the more notable of these, along with vineyards that are renowned for their fine wines.

Best All-Round Wineries

Babylonstoren (p210) New wines and artisan food on a magnificently reimagined estate with a gorgeous culinary garden.

Solms-Delta (p204) Excellent museum, inventive wines, local music, indigenous garden and a beautiful riverside picnic area.

Groot Constantia (p96) Museum, restaurants and beautiful grounds at this historic estate, where wine making in South Africa began.

Vergelegen (p195) Handsome heritage building, rose gardens and a top-class restaurant.

Fairview (p208) Great-value wine and cheese tasting – plus yoga and tower-climbing goats!

Spice Route (p208) Combines complex reds, chocolate, craft beer and glass-blowing.

Reading Up

Platter's South African Wine Guide (www.wineonaplatter.com) The definitive guide with annually updated tasting notes and star ratings for thousands of bottles.

South Africa's Winelands of the Cape (Gerald & Marc Hoberman; 2014) Over 50 estates are covered in this glossy coffee-table book.

Love Your Wine (Cathy Marston; 2015) Will help you get to grips with wine tasting.

Wine of the New South Africa (Tim James; 2013) Profiles of 150 of South Africa's leading wineries. Also see James' blog **Grape** (http://grape.co.za).

Courses

Cape Wine Academy (☎021-889 8844; www.capewineacademy.co.za; course R1395) Runs wine appreciation courses in Stellenbosch, Cape Town and other locations around the Western Cape.

Fynbos Estate (☎022-487 1153; www.fynbosestate.co.za; 1-day/overnight course per person R750/1500) Hands-on wine-making courses in the Paardeberg mountains, 15km outside Malmesbury (an hour's drive from Cape Town).

For Sparkling Wine

Graham Beck (p213) Sample the award-winning bubbles of this Robertson winery.

Villiera (p196) Produces several excellent Méthode Cap Classique wines.

Haute Cabrière (p203) Marvel at *sabrage:* the method of slicing open a bottle of bubbly with a sword.

For Food

Waterkloof (p195) French chef Gregory Czarnecki has won awards for his creative cuisine at the restaurant here.

Buitenverwachting (p98) Blissful picnics in this old Constantia estate, as well as a coffee roastery, cafe and fine-dining restaurant.

La Motte (p202) Wine-pairing lunches and dinners are served at the Pierneef à la Motte restaurant.

For Families

Blaauwklippen (p198) On weekends there are horse-and-carriage rides around the estate.

Spier (p195) Birds-of-prey displays, Segway tours through the vines, two restaurants, and picnics to enjoy in the grounds.

Villiera (p196) View antelope, zebras and various bird species on a wildlife drive around the farm.

For Accommodation

Grande Provence (p202) Sleep in gorgeously decorated cottages on this estate, which also showcases contemporary South African art.

Delaire Graff Estate (p197) Sleep in pampered luxury at this ultra-modern 'vineyard in the sky'.

Babylonstoren (p210) Super-chic guest rooms, crafted from old workers' cottages.

For Art

Glen Carlou (p209) Among the 65 international artists in this winery's collection are works by Gilbert and George, Frank Stella and James Turrell.

La Motte (p202) Host to a prime collection of works by South African artist Jacob Hendrik Pierneef.

Tokara (p197) Offers a fine art collection, plus a fantastic deli/sculpture gallery.

Planning Your Wine Tour

Just starting out? Heed the following and you'll never be caught confusing your *vin rouge* with your vanity.

Starting Off

Call ahead to any estates you want to visit to make sure they're open and not too crowded (some get very busy from December to February). Allow around an hour for tasting at each estate. It's worth joining at least one cellar tour – these can be fascinating. Appoint a designated driver; for those without their own wheels, there are plenty of guided tours (p38) of the Winelands.

Tasting

Many (but not all) cellars will charge you for tasting – usually a little, sometimes a lot, and often refundable with a minimum purchase. You might get to take home the logo-branded glass you tasted from – it saves them the washing up, and gives you a souvenir. Usually the server (who might even be the wine-maker at a small family winery) will guide you through the range, starting with whites (dry, then less dry), moving through reds, then on to sweet and fortified wines. To get the most out of it all, give the wine a deep sniff and swirl a little around in your mouth – then spit that out in the spittoon provided (save swallowing for the ones you really like).

Ageing

Producers will usually sell their wine soon after it's bottled, and most of it is then ready to drink. Even many serious red wines these days are designed to give youthful pleasure – though an estate may recommend waiting a year or longer to get the benefit of mature flavours. Good restaurants will often sell particular reds and whites after some bottle-ageing.

Buying

Intercontinental delivery is expensive, so check the cost before buying a crate. Wine prices vary hugely, of course: there's a big bulge between R50 and R150 for good reds and whites, and an increasing number of grand wines going for much higher than that.

Winery Tours

African Story (☎073 755 0444; www.africanstorytours.com; R850) Full-day tours include wine, cheese and chocolate tastings at four estates in the Stellenbosch, Franschhoek and Paarl regions.

Bikes 'n Wines (p199) Highly recommended cycling tours with routes that range from 9km to 21km, and take in three or four Stellenbosch wineries. There are also Cape Town city tours and trips to lesser-visited wine regions such as Elgin, Wellington and Hermanus.

Easy Rider Wine Tours (p199) Reliable Stellenbosch-based operation. The day kicks off with a cellar tour and includes visits (usually) to Boschendal and Fairview, as well as a few other estates. It's good value for a full-day trip at R650 including lunch and all tastings.

Gourmet Wine Tours (☎021-705 4317, 083 229 3581; www.gourmetwinetours.co.za; half/full-day tours from R1800/2650) Stephen Flesch, a former chairman of the Wine Tasters Guild of South Africa, has over 35 years of wine-tasting experience and runs tours to the wineries of your choice.

Vine Hopper (p199) A hop-on, hop-off bus with three routes, each covering six estates, the Hopper departs hourly from Stellenbosch Tourism (where you can buy tickets). It also offers a full-day tour that includes brandy and sparkling wine cellars.

Wine Flies (☎021-462 8011; www.wineflies.co.za; per person R820) Fun trips taking in four to five estates, including cellar and vineyard walking tours, cheese, olives and chocolate tastings.

Wine History

Although Jan van Riebeeck, the founder of the Cape Colony, planted vines and made wine himself, it was not until the arrival of Governor Simon van der Stel in 1679 that wine-making in South Africa began in earnest. Van der Stel created the estate Constantia (later subdivided into the several estates in the area today), and passed on his wine-making skills to the burghers who settled around Stellenbosch.

Between 1688 and 1690, some 200 Huguenots arrived in the country. They were granted land, particularly in the region around Franschhoek (which translates as 'French Corner'). Although only a few had any wine-making experience, they gave the infant industry fresh impetus.

For a long time, Cape wines (except those produced at Constantia) were not in great demand, and most grapes ended up in brandy. The industry received a boost in the early 19th century, as war between Britain and France – and preferential trade tariffs between the UK and South Africa – led to more South African wine being imported to the UK.

Apartheid-era sanctions and the power of the Kooperatieve Wijnbouwers Vereeniging (KWV; the cooperative formed in 1918 to control minimum prices, production areas and quota limits) didn't exactly encourage innovation, and instead hampered the industry. Since 1992 the KWV, now a private company, has lost much of its former influence.

THE HUMAN COST

The black and coloured workforce in the wine industry currently numbers over 160,000, most of whom are toiling in vineyards owned by around 4500 whites. Workers often receive as little as R100 a day for 12-hour shifts, with migrant workers from places such as Zimbabwe sometimes receiving even less.

Ripe with Abuse, a 2011 report by Human Rights Watch (www.hrw.org), damned the industry, citing low wages, appalling housing conditions, lack of access to toilets or drinking water while working, no protection against pesticides and barriers to union representation.

There is labour legislation on the books, but it's not always complied with, and unfortunately many workers are unaware of their rights. Wines of South Africa (www.wosa.co.za) runs various programs to improve the industry's human rights and sustainability record. The industry has also increased cooperation with the Wine Industry and Ethical Trade Association (WIETA; www.wieta.org.za), which lobbies for a better deal for those working in the wine industry.

Top: Buitenverwachting winery (p98)
Bottom: Vergelegen winery(p195)

WOLFGANG KAEHLER/CONTRIBUTOR/GETTY IMAGES ©

BRANDY

The Western Cape Brandy Route links up distilleries at 13 wineries; for more information contact the **South African Brandy Foundation** (☎021-882 8954; www.sabrandy.co.za). The Van Ryn Brandy Cellar (p197) in Stellenbosch makes world-class brandy and runs superb tours.

Many new and progressive wine makers are leading South Africa's reemergence onto the world market. New production regions are being established in the cooler coastal areas east of Cape Town, around Mossel Bay, Walker Bay and Elgin, and to the north around Durbanville and Darling. The older vines of the Swartland, northwest of Paarl (and in particular the Paardeberg area), are also producing some very high-quality wines.

Wine Varieties

Reds

Pinotage, a cross between pinot noir and cinsaut, which produces a very bold wine, is the Cape's signature grape. Together with other robust red varieties such as shiraz (syrah) and cabernet sauvignon, it's being challenged by lighter blends of cabernet sauvignon, merlot, shiraz and cabernet franc, which are closer in style to a Bordeaux wine.

Whites

The most common variety of white wine is chenin blanc. In the last decade or so, more fashionable varieties such as chardonnay and sauvignon blanc have been planted on a wide scale. Other widely planted whites include colombard, semillon and sweet muscats. Table whites, especially chardonnay, once tended to be heavily oaked and high in alcohol, but lighter, more fruity whites are now in the ascendancy. For good sauvignon blancs, look to wineries in the cooler regions of Constantia, Elgin and Hermanus.

Rosés

Rosé wines – lightly fruity, crisp and dry – are gaining popularity. Look out for 'pinotage' on the label – not everyone admires this local variety in red wines, but all agree it's great for pink ones.

Sparkling

Méthode Cap Classique (MCC) is the name that South Africa's wine industry has come up with for its champenoise-style wines: many are as good as, or even better than, the real thing.

Fortified

The Worcester, Calitzdorp and Karoo regions are the country's leading producer of fortified wines, including port, brandy and South Africa's own *hanepoot*. This dessert wine is made from the Mediterranean grape variety known as muscat of Alexandria to produce a sweet, high-alcohol tipple for the domestic market.

Workers' Wines

It's worth noting that South Africa has more fair-trade-accredited wines than any other country. Various wineries are leading the way in setting improved labour and fair-trade standards. Both Solms-Delta (www.solms-delta.co.za) and Van Loveren (www.vanloveren.co.za) in Robertson have made their employees shareholders in joint-venture wine farms, while part of the Nelson Wine Estate (www.nelsonscreek.co.za) has been donated to the workers to produce wines under the label New Beginnings. La Motte is also strong on treating its workers fairly; it developed Dennegeur, a model village where workers can own their homes and have access to high-quality social services including health, education and child care.

Other worker or black-owned and -empowerment brands include:

Thandi (www.thandiwines.com) Meaning 'love' or 'cherish' in Xhosa (isiXhosa), and located in the Elgin area, this was the first winery in the world to be fair-trade certified. It's half owned by the 250 farm worker families and produces good single varietals and blends.

M'hudi (https://mhudiwineboutique.com) Owned by the Rangaka family, its range includes a cabernet sauvignon, pinotage and shiraz.

Lathithá Made by wine makers at Blaauwklippen on behalf of Sheila Hlanjwa, it's part of a project to popularise wine drinking in township communities.

Fairvalley Wines (www.fairvalley.co.za) The fairtrade-accredited wines from this venture, located next door to Fairview, are owned by 42 families.

Wine Trends

South African wine makers blend grape varieties for many of their top wines. Red blends, mostly based on cabernet sauvignon, have been around for decades, but recent years have seen something of an explosion in white blends in two distinct, but equally exciting, main styles. First is those mixing sauvignon blanc and semillon, à la white Bordeaux. Vergelegen has been the leader here, with its well-oaked and rather grand semillon-based wine. But now there are many fine versions – like Oak Valley's OV blend, Tokara White and Steenberg's Magna Carta.

The other strand in the white blend story is more indigenous. These wines are often from warmer inland districts, like the Swartland. Most follow the lead of the 'inventor' of this style, Eben Sadie, with his wine Palladius, and use plenty of chenin blanc, along with varieties like chardonnay, roussanne and viognier.

Wine makers are also moving to the coast or climbing mountains in search of cooler areas to make different styles of wine; these wines are more delicate and often have lower alcohol levels and greater freshness. Elgin, a high inland plateau, is gaining increasing recognition for its fine chardonnay, sauvignon blanc and pinot noir.

Pinotage also features in the growing number of 'chocolate coffee' styles of red wine. While generally sniffed at by the critics, these wines have been a hit with the public.

Glossary of Wine Terms

aroma The smell of a wine; 'bouquet' is usually used for the less fruity, more developed scents of older wine.

balance The all-important harmony of the components in a wine: alcohol, fruitiness, acidity and tannin (and oak, when used).

blend A mix of two or more varieties in one wine, eg colombard-chardonnay. You'll see 'Cape Blend' appearing on some reds' labels; it implies at least 20% pinotage.

corked Not literally cork fragments in the wine, but when the cork has tainted the wine, making it (in the extreme) mouldy-tasting and flat.

estate wine This term is permitted only for wine grown, made and bottled on a single property.

finish The impression a wine leaves in the mouth: the longer the flavour persists (and the sadder you are when it goes), the better.

garage wine Wine made in minuscule quantities, sometimes by passionate amateurs – and occasionally actually in a garage.

oaked or **wooded** Most serious red wines, and a lot of smart whites, are matured for a year or two in expensive wooden barrels; it affects the texture of the wine and the flavour. A cheap way of getting oak flavour is to use wood chips or staves in a metal tank.

organic It's the grapes, rather than the winemaking, that can be organic (naturally grown without pesticides, chemical fertilisers etc).

tannin Mostly in red wine and derived from grape skins and pips, or oak barrels; the mouth-puckering dryness on gums and cheeks, which softens as the wine matures.

vintage The year the grapes were harvested; also used to describe a port-style wine made in a particularly good year (the best are often called 'vintage reserve').

Plan Your Trip
Activities

With wind-whipped waves and rugged mountains on hand, surfing, hiking and rock climbing are hugely popular and can easily be organised. For adventures such as shark-cage diving or paragliding, you'll need to travel out of Cape Town as well as wait for the ideal weather conditions. It's not all about thrill-seeking: the Mother City and Western Cape are also fabulous locations for golf, a bike ride or a canter along the beach on horseback.

Resources

Bass Fishing South Africa (www.bassfishing.co.za) Forum and details of fishing sites.

Bike Hub (www.bikehub.co.za) General cycling site, with articles, classifieds and popular forums.

Cape Piscatorial Society (www.piscator.co.za) Licences for sites around Cape Town and the Winelands.

Climb ZA (www.climbing.co.za) News, articles, directory and forum.

Mountain Club of South Africa (www.mcsa.org.za) Information and links to regional clubs.

MTB Routes (www.mtbroutes.co.za) Maps the locations of over 400 bike trails nationwide.

Pedal Power Association (www.pedalpower.org.za)

Table Mountain Bikers (www.tablemountainbikers.co.za)

TASKS: The African Sea Kayak Society (www.seakayak.co.za/tasks)

Wavescape Surfing South Africa (www.wavescape.co.za)

Zig Zag (www.zigzag.co.za) South Africa's main surf magazine.

Birding

There are birdwatching clubs nationwide, and most parks and reserves can provide birding lists, with information available from SANParks (p246). Many parks, reserves and accommodation places also have field guides, but it's still worth bringing your own.

Birding Africa (www.birdingafrica.com) Day trips from Cape Town and tours further afield, covering birds and flowers.

BirdLife South Africa (www.birdlife.org.za) Useful information and links. Promotes avitourism (birding ecotourism) routes.

Bird-Watch Cape (www.birdwatch.co.za) Small, Cape Town–based outfit for twitchers, with tours including a nationwide 17-day package.

Cape Birding Route (www.capebirdingroute.org) Information relating to western South Africa, from Cape Point to the Kalahari.

Canoeing, Kayaking & Rafting

The are various outfits, including Kaskazi Kayaks (www.kayak.co.za), offering sea kayaking in Cape Town. The Western Cape's rivers flow year-round and offer rewarding rafting and canoeing. Rafting is highly rain

African penguins, Boulders Penguin Colony (p108)

dependent, with the best months in most areas from December/January to April.

Diving

Take the plunge off the southern end of Africa into the Indian and Atlantic Oceans. Strong currents and often windy conditions mean advanced divers can find challenges all along the coast.

Along the Atlantic seaboard, the water is cold year-round, but is at its most diveable, with many days of high visibility, between November and January/February. Expect to pay from R5000 for a four-day PADI open-water certification course, and from R350 for a dive.

Fishing

Sea fishing is popular, with a wide range of species in the warm and cold currents that flow past the west coast. River fishing, especially for introduced trout, is popular in parks and reserves. Licences are available for a few rand at park offices, and some shops and accommodation rent out equipment.

Hiking, Kloofing & Rock Climbing

The Western Cape is a wonderful destination for hiking, with an excellent system of well-marked trails varied enough to suit every ability.

Hiking is possible year-round, although you'll need to be prepared in summer for extremes of heat and wet. The best time for Cape Town and the Western Cape is spring (September to November) and autumn (March to May).

Kloofing (called canyoning elsewhere) is a mix of climbing, hiking, swimming and some serious jumping. It can be enjoy in various locations across the Western Cape. There's an element of risk in the sport, so when hunting for operators, check their credentials carefully before signing up.

Top spots for rock climbing include Table Mountain (p54) and Montagu.

Rock climbing, Cape Town (p116)

Paragliding & Microlighting

Favourable weather conditions year-round and an abundance of high points to launch yourself from make South Africa a fine destination for aerial pursuits. Taking to the South African skies is fairly inexpensive; a helpful contact for getting started is the **Aero Club of South Africa** (☎011-082 1100; www.aeroclub.org.za).

South Africa is one of the world's top paragliding destinations – especially Lion's Head in Cape Town, with further opportunities throughout the Western Cape. **South African Hang Gliding & Paragliding Association** (SAHPA; ☎074 152 2505; www.sahpa.co.za) can provide information on flying sites, schools and clubs.

A useful resource with forums and a list of airfields for ultralight aviation can be found at http://microlighters.co.za.

Surfing

The best time of year for surfing is autumn and early winter (from about April to July). Boards and gear can be bought in Cape Town and the larger coastal towns of the Western Cape. New boards start around R4500 – check out www.gumtree.co.za.

A good spot for beginners – with lessons and gear hire aplenty – is Muizenberg in Cape Town.

Mountain Biking

There are trails almost everywhere and Cape Town is an unofficial national hub for the activity.

Regions at a Glance

Cape Town and the Western Cape are refined, developed spots, where you can sip wine and enjoy activities on beaches and mountains. It's also a region packed with sights and activities, so if you have limited time it pays to put some thought into where you might base yourself and what you plan to do. With good roads, not to mention some of the world's most scenic drives, you will not regret hiring a car to get around. Alternatively, it's easy to use public transport to connect up the main locations.

Cape Town

Outdoor Activities
Eating
Shopping

Accessible Adventures

Its mountainous national park, beaches and ocean make Cape Town a scenic hiking and surfing location. Even just strolling along Sea Point promenade is a sheer pleasure. Kitesurfing, rock climbing and paragliding are also offered.

Diverse Cuisine

Cape Town's multiethnic peoples have bequeathed it a range of cuisines. Enjoy mouth-watering meats and fish from the braai (barbecue), world-class restaurants, Cape Malay curries in the Bo-Kaap neighbourhood, and Xhosa dishes in township restaurants.

Contemporary Craftwork

The 2014 World Design Capital is bursting with creativity: intricately beaded dolls, contemporary light fixtures made from recycled plastic, stylish buckskin and leather pillows – Cape Town's emporiums and artisan craft markets have it all.

p49

Around Cape Town

Food & Drink
Landscapes
Nature

Wine Tasting

The Winelands around Stellenbosch, Franschhoek and Paarl are justifiably famous for their beautiful wine estates. Intrepid tasters should also explore areas such as Wellington, Stanford, Tulbagh and Robertson. Pairing wines with chocolate or cheese adds an extra dimension to tastings.

Spectacular Drives

The varied landscapes of this region are stunning. From mountain crossings such as the spectacular Bainskloof Pass and Sir Lowry's Pass, to the coastal Route 44 that brings you to or from Hermanus, this is a wonderful place for a road trip.

Wildlife Spotting

Shark-cage diving is popular but controversial. Hermanus is a wonderful spot for whale watching while the West Coast National Park is renowned for its wide range of birdlife. There's even wildlife to be seen at some of the region's wineries.

p187

Garden Route

Water Sports
Hiking
Food & Drink

Hit the Surf

Among the many water sports and activities taking advantage of the Garden Route's beaches and lagoons are surfing, canoeing and diving. Mossel Bay, Victoria Bay and Plettenberg Bay are all top places to dip your board in the ocean.

Multiday Hikes

The Garden Route National Park and surrounding coastline is threaded through with spectacular hikes such as the five-day, four-night Otter Trail or the week-long Outeniqua Trail. There are plenty of shorter, easier routes to follow, too.

Gourmet Grazing

From farmers markets selling organic produce to fine-dining restaurants and top-class resorts, the Garden Route delivers on the food front. Enjoy freshly shucked oysters in Mossel Bay and game meats in Plettenberg Bay.

p227

On the Road

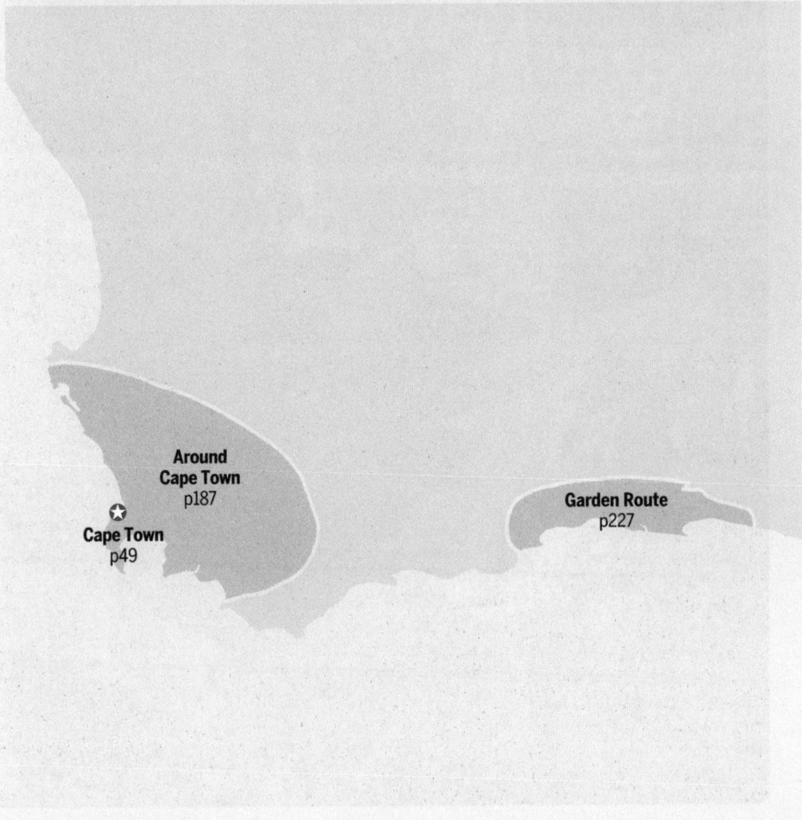

Around Cape Town p187
Cape Town p49
Garden Route p227

Table Mountain Aerial Cableway (p116)

Cape Town

021 / POP 3.74 MILLION

Includes ➡

Neighbourhoods at a Glance 50
Table Mountain National Park 54
Top Sights 58
Sights 68
Activities 115
Tours 123
Festivals & Events 125
Sleeping 127
Eating 138
Drinking & Nightlife 156
Entertainment 168
Shopping 172

Best Places to Eat

- ➡ Chef's Warehouse & Canteen (p140)
- ➡ Reverie Social Table (p145)
- ➡ Foxcroft (p153)
- ➡ La Mouette (p150)

Best Places to Stay

- ➡ Tintswalo Atlantic (p134)
- ➡ Mannabay (p132)
- ➡ Backpack (p130)
- ➡ La Grenadine (p131)

Why Go?

Known as the 'Mother City' for its historical role in modern South Africa, Cape Town is dominated by Table Mountain. This magnificent rock is often draped with cascading clouds, while at its base are sun-kissed beaches. Few cities can boast such a wonderful natural attraction at their heart or provide the wide range of adventurous activities that take full advantage of it.

The city does have desperately poor areas, but the vast majority of visitors will find the country's wealth manifest in the built infrastructure and the fabulous range of places to stay, eat, party and shop. Lessons learned during Cape Town's stint as World Design Capital during 2014 have been used to improve citizens' quality of life across the board. This is also a multicultural metropolis where everyone has a fascinating, sometimes heartbreaking story to tell. When the time comes to leave, you may find your heart breaking, too.

When to Go

Cape Town

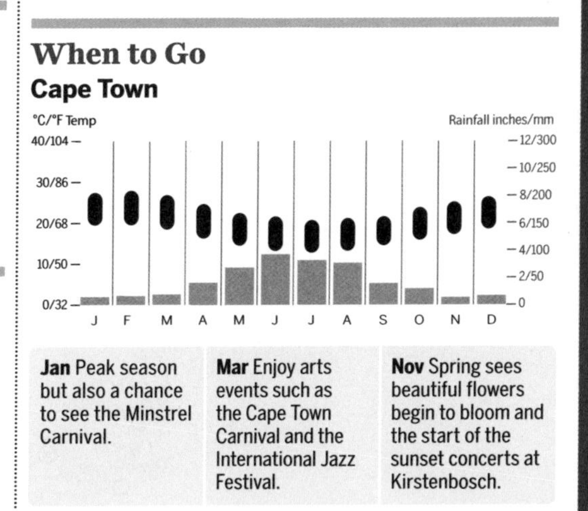

Jan Peak season but also a chance to see the Minstrel Carnival.

Mar Enjoy arts events such as the Cape Town Carnival and the International Jazz Festival.

Nov Spring sees beautiful flowers begin to bloom and the start of the sunset concerts at Kirstenbosch.

Neighbourhoods at a Glance

1 City Bowl, Foreshore, Bo-Kaap & De Waterkant (p68)

The City Bowl, where the Dutch first set up shop, includes many historic sights and businesses. Landfill created the Foreshore district in the 1940s and 1950s, now dominated by Duncan Dock and the convention centre. Tumbling down Signal Hill are the colourfully painted houses of the Bo-Kaap and, to the northeast, Cape Town's pink precinct De Waterkant, a retail and party hub.

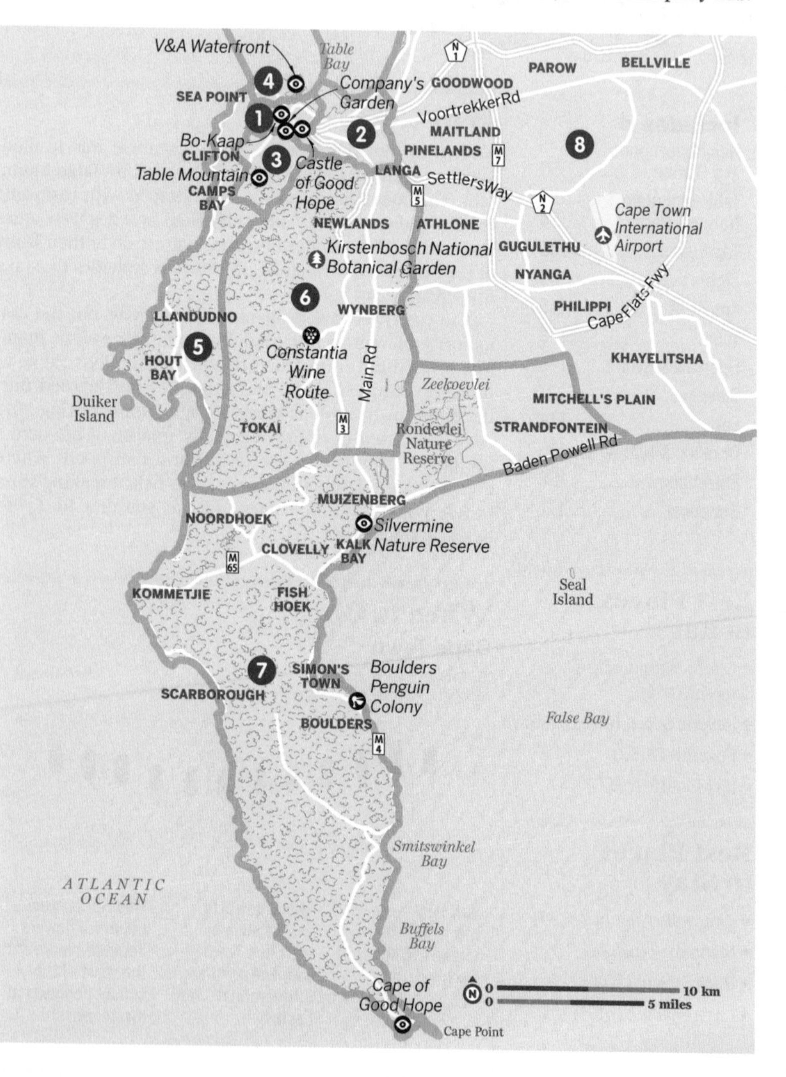

❷ East City, District Six, Woodstock & Observatory (p76)

Immediately east of the City Bowl is what was once the mixed residential area of District Six – it's long been a series of empty plots awaiting development, but in recent years creative types and nightlife operators have started to move to the area. Woodstock and Salt River continue to attract the attention of developers and the art set, but are yet to fully gentrify. Bohemia rules at Observatory near Cape Town University.

❸ Gardens & Surrounds (p77)

Ranging from the cluster of museums at the south end of the Company's Garden, up the slopes of Table Mountain, is the wider area known as Gardens. Neighbourhoods here include Tamboerskloof, Oranjezicht, Higgovale and Vredehoek – all desirable residential suburbs with views of Table Bay and immediate access to Table Mountain. Kloof St and Kloof Nek Rd are the main retail strips.

❹ Green Point & Waterfront (p81)

Green Point's common includes an imaginatively landscaped park and the Cape Town Stadium, built for the 2010 World Cup. There are several pleasant guesthouses and backpacker lodges to stay here too, but if it's luxe digs you're after then head to the V&A Waterfront. Known simply as the Waterfront, this shopping, entertainment and residential development is the city's most popular tourist destination and home to top sights such as the ferries to Robben Island and the new Zeitz MOCAA Museum, which opened in 2017.

❺ Sea Point to Hout Bay (p89)

Sea Point blends into ritzier Bantry Bay and Fresnaye before culminating in the prime real estate of Clifton and Camps Bay, where white modernist villas climb the slopes above golden beaches and models imbibing raw shakes in cafes. South of here, the stunning coast road passes beneath the Twelve Apostles range, and urban development is largely curtailed by Table Mountain National Park until you reach delightful Hout Bay. This harbour town has good access to both the city and, via Constantia Nek pass, the vineyards of Constantia.

❻ Southern Suburbs (p94)

The lush eastern slopes of Table Mountain are covered by the affluent areas known collectively as the Southern Suburbs. Here you'll find Kirstenbosch National Botanical Garden, the rugby and cricket grounds of Newlands, the centuries-old vineyards of Constantia and the shady forests of Tokai. Overlooked by Africa's top university, the University of Cape Town (UCT), this was once the stomping ground of British imperialist Cecil Rhodes and the area retains a strong English flavour in its leafy avenues and prestigious schools.

❼ Simon's Town & Southern Peninsula (p103)

A string of charming and historic coastal communities, including Muizenberg, Kalk Bay and Simon's Town (plus the penguins living at Boulders Beach), line the False Bay side of the peninsula. More wildlife and incredible landscapes are protected within the nature reserve at Cape Point and the Cape of Good Hope. On the Atlantic coast side, Kommetjie is beloved by experienced surfers, and the broad beach at Noordhoek by horse riders.

❽ Cape Flats & Northern Suburbs (p113)

The vast townships and coloured suburbs sprawling alongside the N2 highway east of the city centre are known collectively as the Cape Flats. It's well worth visiting a township – either independently or on one of the excellent guided tours on offer – and even staying overnight, to get a sense of how the majority of Capetonians live.

In contrast, the Northern Suburbs' appeal lies in their beaches and wine estates. North along Table Bay lie Milnerton and Bloubergstrand, while inland is the wine-growing district of Durbanville.

Cape Town Highlights

1 Table Mountain (p116) Riding the cableway to the top of this magnificent rock and looking down on the city.

2 Robben Island (p64) Sailing out to the infamous prison and pondering the country's past and present.

3 Company's Garden (p60) Sauntering through this historic patch of greenery in the city centre and admiring the surrounding architecture.

4 Cape of Good Hope (p107) Encountering the wide open spaces, wildlife, empty beaches and dramatic scenery at the peninsula's rugged tip.

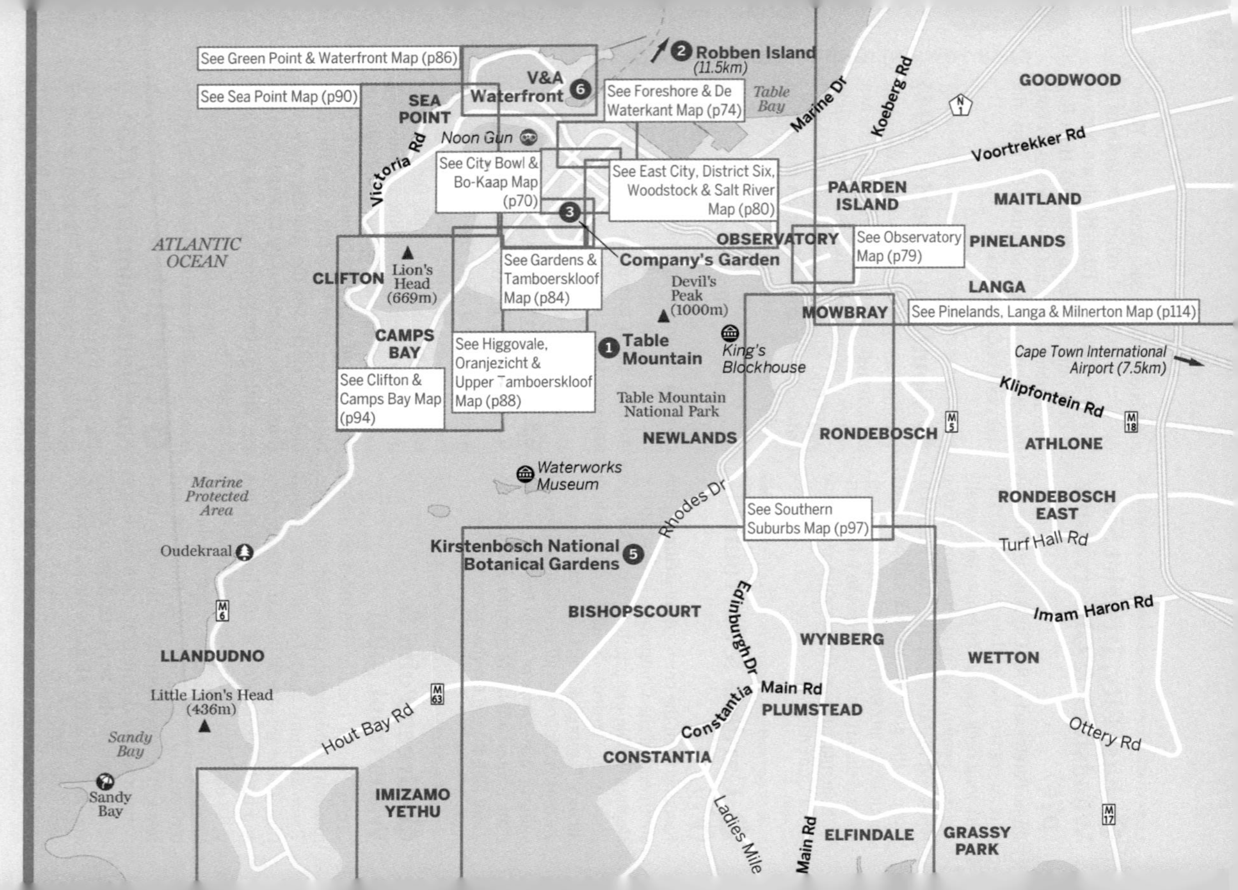

5 Kirstenbosch National Botanical Garden (p95) Wandering through these beautiful gardens and learning about the magnificent Cape Floral Kingdom.

6 V&A Waterfront (p81) Enjoying the attractions, shopping, harbour cruises and buzzing atmosphere of this reinvented historic dock.

7 Boulders (p108) Snapping photos of the superstar African penguins paddling along the beach.

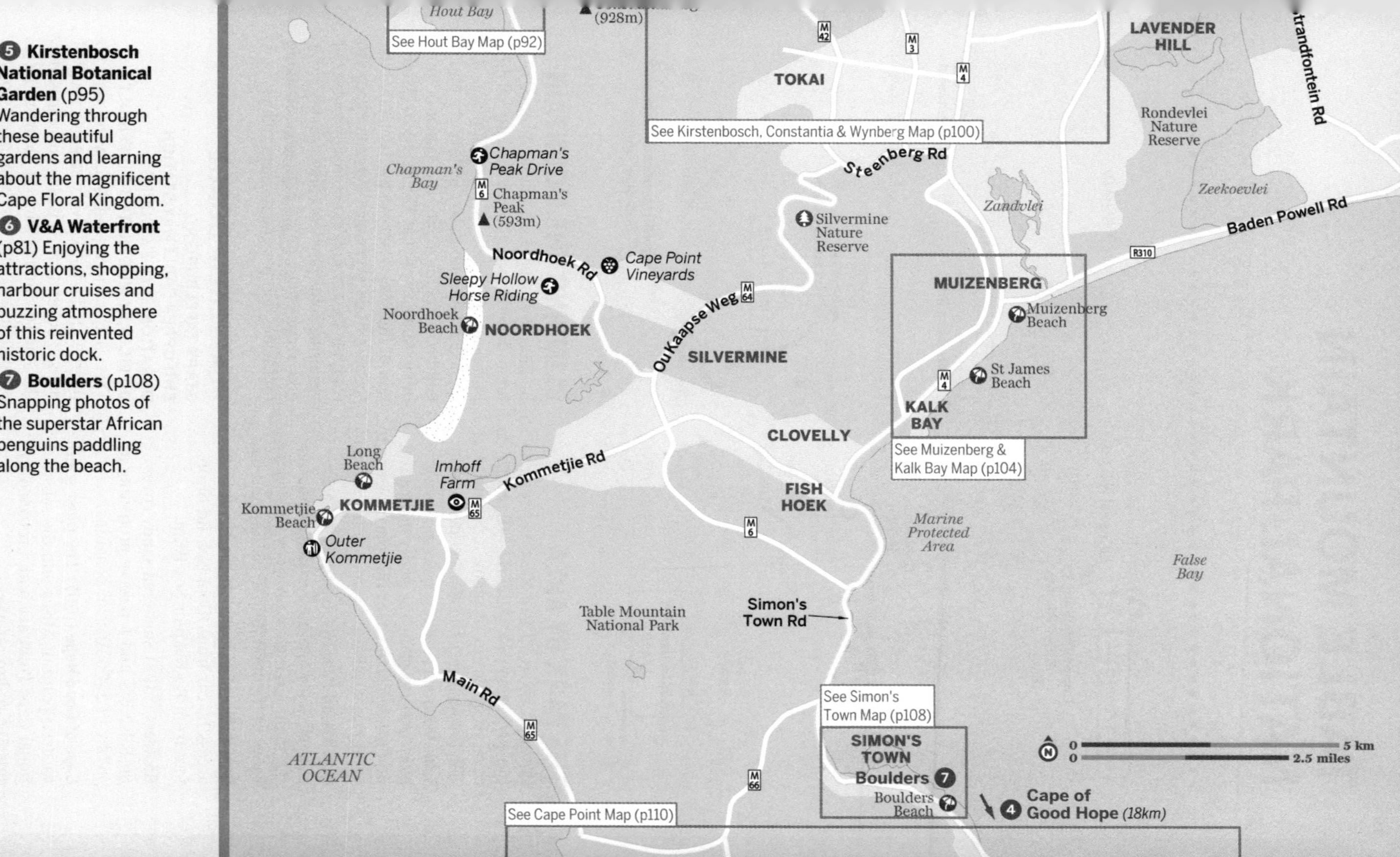

TABLE MOUNTAIN NATIONAL PARK

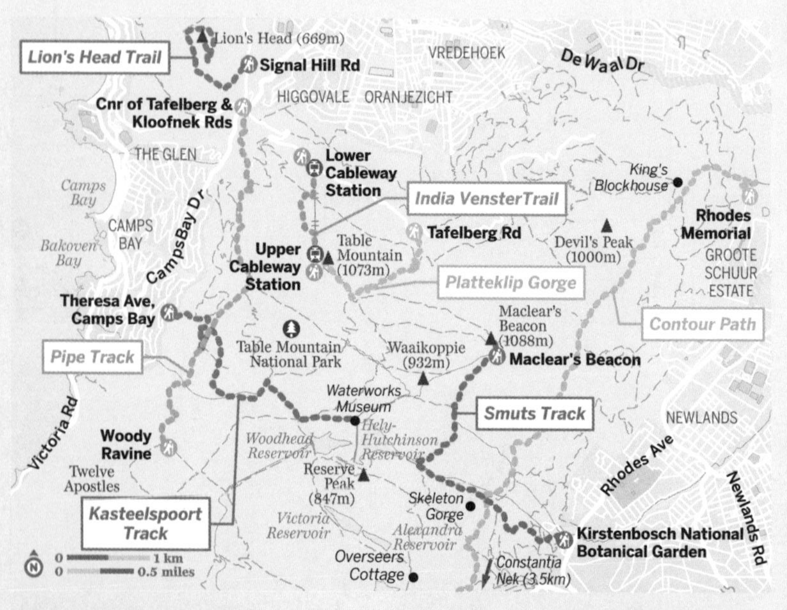

THE PARK BY AREA

Covering about 73% of the Cape Peninsula, the **park** (Map p94; ☎021-712 7471; www.tmnp.co.za) is made up of many different areas. The following are the key sections to visit:

Table Mountain (Map p88; www.sanparks.org/parks/table_mountain) The park's main attraction is here; climb it, or ride the cableway to within easy walking distance of the summit.

Lion's Head (Map p94; Signal Hill Rd, Tamboerskloof; Kloof Nek) An easier climb than the main mountain; provides 360-degree views of the mountain, coastline and city.

Signal Hill (p78) Home of the Noon Gun; access by car from Kloof Nek Rd or on foot from Bo-Kaap or Sea Point.

Boulders (p108) Sheltered sandy coves on False Bay and a reserve protecting a colony of 3000 African penguins.

Cape of Good Hope (p107) The most south-western point of Africa and the sensational Cape Point are both protected by this 77.5-sq-km reserve.

CLIMBING THE MOUNTAIN

In 1503 Portuguese navigator Admiral Antonio de Saldanha bagged the title of 'first European to climb Table Mountain'. He named it Taboa do Cabo (Table of the Cape), although the Khoe-San, the Cape's original inhabitants, knew it as Hoerikwaggo (Mountain of the Sea). Visitors have been climbing the mountain ever since. You can choose to conquer the summit via scores of routes (all requiring some physical effort), or stay lower down traversing around buttresses, climbing up ravines and passing through valleys.

PLATTEKLIP GORGE

START TAFELBURG RD
END UPPER CABLEWAY STATION
DURATION 3KM; 2½ HOURS
DIFFICULTY MODERATE TO DIFFICULT

This is the most straightforward way up the mountain, but it's very steep so you will need to be pretty fit. It is also fully exposed to the sun, so climb as early in the morning as possible in summer and bring plenty of wa-

Stretching from Signal Hill to Cape Point, this 220-sq-km park is a natural wonder. It includes several mountains, boulder-strewn beaches and shady forests, making it ideal for adventure activities.

ter and sunblock. Also make sure you have wet-weather gear packed as the climate can be very different at the top of the mountain.

The well-trodden path is clear, sturdily constructed and buttressed by gabions (wire containers filled with rocks), but it is unrelentingly steep. You can also bake in the wind-sheltered gorge, so make sure you bring more water to drink than you'll think you'll need – you won't regret it. Drinking water from the streams in the gorge is not recommended.

Having followed the zig-zag path up to the aptly named Desperation Corner, you'll encounter the sheer rock walls at the head of the gorge. You'll be knackered, but this is the trickiest part of the climb, with some often slippery boulders to negotiate, so take it slowly. Once at the top, you can relax and take a breath and enjoy the views. Turn right and it's around a 15-minute walk to the upper cableway station.

LION'S HEAD TRAIL

START SIGNAL HILL RD
END SIGNAL HILL RD
DURATION 4.4KM; TWO TO THREE HOURS
DIFFICULTY EASY TO MODERATE

It was the Dutch who coined the term Lion's Head (Leeuwen Kop) for the 669m, nipple-like outcrop that overlooks Sea Point and Camps Bay. This is likely the most climbed peak in South Africa, with over 200,000 people a year attaining the summit. Many Capetonians do the hike as an early-morning constitutional, and it's a local ritual to hike up and watch the sun go down on a full-moon night. The moonlight helps the walk back down, although you should always bring a torch and go with company.

The hike starts near the foot of Signal Hill Rd where there are parking guards and a security hut. Initially you follow a broad gravel track around the mountain to the launch area for paragliding facing towards Camps Bay. The route narrows and becomes more rocky, but is always clear as you twist around to the Signal Hill side of the mountain. Eventually you'll reach a fork where you can either continue on the track ahead or use the metal rungs and chains to climb up a steep cliff face. The two routes meet at the base of a stand of gnarled pine trees, from where it's around another 20-minute climb to the summit.

The walk up is not especially challenging, so it's good for kids, but there are areas that are steep and require rock scrambling. The stunning 360 degree views at the top make the effort well worthwhile.

If you're looking for people to hike with, then check out the calendar on the site of the conservation group **Friends of Lions Head and Signal Hill** (http://friendsoflionshead.org).

SMUTS TRACK

START KIRSTENBOSCH NATIONAL BOTANICAL GARDEN
END MACLEAR'S BEACON
DURATION 5KM; FOUR TO FIVE HOURS
DIFFICULTY MODERATE TO DIFFICULT

This track is named after Jan Smuts, the general and South African prime minister, who was an enthusiastic hiker and a prime mover for securing formal protection for Table Mountain as a national park – he walked this track well into his 70s. It is steep, with ladders in places, and some scrambling over rocks is required – note it can be treacherous after rain, when it is best avoided.

There's shade in the Afromontane forest at the start as you follow Skeleton Gorge up the back of Table Mountain from Kirstenbosch's Fragrance Garden. The climb is steady and requires some effort. About two-thirds of the way up, wooden ladders will help you negotiate the steep and sometimes slippery rocks.

Once on top, turn right at Breakfast Rock and continue for around two more hours to Maclear's Beacon, the summit of Table Mountain (1085.9m). This part of the climb is more gentle but still rises in elevation by about 300m.

From the summit it's around an hour's walk to the upper cable car station for the easy way down. Alternatively you can retrace your steps back to Kirstenbosch. If you wish to avoid the entrance fee for Kirstenbosch, you can also access the route from Constantia Nek by following Contour Path.

HIKING TIPS

- Hike with long trousers. Much of the fynbos is tough and scratchy. There's also the seriously nasty blister bush (its leaves look like those of continental parsley).
- If your skin does brush against the blister bush, cover the spot immediately – sunlight activates the plant's toxins, which can leave blisters on your skin that may not heal for years.
- Tell someone the route you're planning to climb, and take a map (or go with a guide).
- Stick to well-used paths. Don't be tempted to take shortcuts.
- Take plenty of water, some food, weather-proof clothing and a fully charged mobile phone.
- Wear proper hiking boots or shoes and a sun hat.
- Don't climb alone – park authorities recommend going in groups of four.
- Don't leave litter on the mountain or make a fire – they're banned.

INDIA VENSTER TRAIL

START LOWER CABLEWAY STATION, TAFELBERG RD
END UPPER CABLEWAY STATION
DURATION 2.5KM; TWO TO THREE HOURS
DIFFICULTY DIFFICULT

This route up Table Mountain starts from directly behind the lower cableway station and heads straight up; it's recommended for experienced climbers only. The trail is pretty clear and there's one rock scramble where there are chains and metal rungs to assist in climbing. You'll need a head for heights and it should certainly be avoided if wet, as slippery rocks can make it dangerous.

PIPE TRACK

START CNR OF TAFELBERG AND KLOOF NEK RDS
END WOODY RAVINE
DURATION 6KM, TWO TO THREE HRS
DIFFICULTY EASY

The Pipe Track was carved out in 1887 to service a pipeline running below the series of buttresses known as the Twelve Apostles; it carried water from Disa Gorge in Table Mountain's Back Table, via the Woodhead Tunnel, to the Molteno Reservoir in Oranjezicht. Easily accessible (and thus a popular hike), it is rocky in places. If you get tired or want a shorter walk, it's possible to exit onto Teresa Rd above Camps Bay, at the junction with the Kasteelspoort route to the mountain top. Overall the track is reasonably level for most of the way and offers magnificent coastal views, but this also means that it is very exposed to the hot afternoon sun. Hike here early in the day in summer, or follow the track in winter when you'll be able to spot many species of protea in bloom.

CAPE OF GOOD HOPE TRAIL

START CAPE OF GOOD HOPE ENTRANCE
END CAPE OF GOOD HOPE ENTRANCE
DURATION 38.8KM; TWO DAYS
DIFFICULTY MODERATE

You'll need to book to walk the two-day, one-night Cape of Good Hope Trail, which traces a spectacular 33.8km circular route through the reserve, winding its way up and down the peaks on either side of the peninsula and taking you to some beautiful beaches.

Accommodation (R300) is included at the basic Erica, Protea and Restio huts, which offer six-bed dorms, kitchens and hot showers at the southern end of the reserve. You'll need to bring your own food and a sleeping bag, and as long as the bag is under 6kg you can arrange with the park to have it dropped off/collected from the hut for an extra R205. Start the hike before 9am to be sure to get to the huts before sunset. Contact the reserve's Buffelsfontein Visitor Centre (p57) for further information.

CONTOUR PATH: CONSTANTIA NEK TO RHODES MEMORIAL

START CONSTANTIA NEK
END RHODES MEMORIAL
DURATION 11KM; FIVE TO SIX HOURS
DIFFICULTY EASY TO MODERATE

If you're short of time, you could just hike the section of this walk between Kirstenbosch National Botanical Garden and the Rhodes Memorial, but otherwise this a great way to spend a day hiking along the back of Table Mountain. It's a fairly flat route with plenty of shade, so a good one if you're hiking with a mixed-ability group or with children. At the start of the walk, you'll pass through plantation forests and have some wonderful views across the vineyards of Constantia towards Muizenberg Peak. About half way along, you'll skirt the top of the Botanical Garden, where you could pause for a picnic or lunch at one of the cafes. Before dropping down to Rhodes Memorial, make sure you check out the King's Blockhouse, a fortification built by the British between 1795 and 1803.

KASTEELSPOORT

START THERESA AVE, CAMPS BAY
END THERESA AVE, CAMPS BAY
DURATION 8KM; 3½ TO 4½ HOURS
DIFFICULTY MODERATE

This circular routes takes you up from the Twelve Apostles to two of the reservoirs that are atop Table Mountain. You can also join the track by following the Pipe Track for about 35 minutes from its start at the top of Kloof Nek Rd. The path is a steady climb with little shade, but the pay-off is great views. Despite the heat, it's worth doing this walk later in the afternoon to catch the Apostles glowing in the evening light as you descend. If you call in advance you may be able to arrange a visit to the **Waterworks Museum** (☎086 010 3089; Back Table; ⌚9am-4pm Mon-Fri) beside the Hely-Hutchinson Reservoir. It's possible for groups to book a stay in the **Overseers Cottage** (up to six people from R2955) near the Woodhead Dam; contact South African National Parks for details.

GUIDED WALKS

As well as the companies listed below, Abseil Africa (p116), Awol Tours (p125) and Downhill Adventures (p185) all offer guided hikes in the park. Hiking clubs that arrange day and weekend hikes include **Cape Union Mart Hiking Club** (www.cumhike.co.za), **Trails Club of South Africa** (www.trailsclub.co.za) and **Mountain Club of South Africa** (Map p84; ☎021-465 3412; www.mcsacapetown.co.za; 97 Hatfield St; joining fee R175, annual membership from R460; ⌚climbing wall 10am-2pm Mon-Fri plus 6.30-9pm Tue & 7.30-9.30pm Fri; Government Ave) FREE.

Venture Forth (☎084 700 2867, 021-555 3864; www.ventureforth.co.za; per person from R825, minimum three people) Excellent guided hikes and rock climbs with enthusiastic, savvy guides.

Walk in Africa (☎021-785 2264; www.walkinafrica.com) Steve Bolnick, an experienced and passionate safari and mountain guide, runs this company. He offers various half- and full-day hiking trips within Table Mountain National Park as well as further afield.

South African Slackpacking (☎082 882 4388; www.slackpackersa.co.za; under/over 4hrs from R1100/1400) Registered nature guide Frank Dwyer runs this operation, which offers one-day and multiday hikes.

Table Mountain Walks (☎021-715 6136; www.tablemountainwalks.co.za; per person from R550) Offers a range of guided day hikes in different parts of the park, from ascents of Table Mountain to rambles through Silvermine.

Christopher Smith (☎073 727 0386; http://tablemountain.my-hiking.com; from R600 per day) This personable and knowledgeable freelance guide is National Park–trained and has plenty of experience guiding across Table Mountain's terrain.

Karbonkelberg Hikers (Map p92; www.facebook.com/Karbonkelberg-hikers-791126257689574/) Brent Thomas, Donita Puckpas and Colin Delcarme (all Rastafarians) are a team of Hangberg residents, who know the area intimately and can guide ou through this part of the park (do not walk here unguided, the area is a mugging hotspot).

SAFETY FIRST

Accidents on the mountain are common, often due to a climbing expedition gone wrong; more people have died on Table Mountain than on Mt Everest. Mountain fires have also claimed their victims, and muggings on the slopes of Table Mountain and Lion's Head are unfortunately not rare events.

There are staff patrolling the park, but it covers such a large area that they cannot be everywhere, so be well prepared before setting off. Even if taking the cableway to the summit, be aware that the weather up top can change very rapidly. The main emergency numbers are ☎086 110 6417 to report fires, poaching, accidents and crime, and ☎021-948 9900 for Wilderness Search and Rescue.

INFORMATION & MAPS

Signage is improving, but it's far from comprehensive, and even with a map it's easy to get lost.

Table Mountain National Park Head Office (Map p100; ☎021-712 7471; www.sanparks.org/parks/table_mountain/; Tokai Manor House, Tokai Rd, Tokai; ⌚8am-3.45pm Mon-Fri)

Boulders Visitor Centre (Map p108; ☎021-786 2329; Kleintuin Rd, Seaforth, Simon's Town; ⌚7am-7.30pm Dec & Jan, 8am-6.30pm Feb, Mar, Oct & Nov, 8am-5pm Apr-Sep)

Buffelsfontein Visitor Centre (Map p110; ☎021-780 9204; Cape of Good Hope; ⌚8am-5pm Mon-Fri)

Slingsby Maps (https://slingsby-maps.myshopify.com)

TOP SIGHT
CASTLE OF GOOD HOPE

Less than a century ago, the sea lapped up to the bluestone-walls of the Castle of Good Hope. South Africa's oldest surviving colonial building is the headquarters for the Western Cape military command, as well as the location of a couple of interesting museums and a spectacular backdrop for events including festivals, plays and concerts.

The History

Designed to protect the logistical and financial interest of the VOC (Vereenigde Oost-Indische Compagnie; Dutch East India Company) the fortress was constructed between 1666 and 1679, and replaced the original 1652 clay and timber structure commissioned by VOC Commander Jan van Riebeeck just two days after setting foot on the shores of Table Bay.

Governor Simon van der Stel moved into the castle in 1680; it was under his instructions that the main gate was moved from the sea-side of the fortress to between Leerdam and Buuren bastions, where it remains today. In 1795, when the Dutch lost the Battle of Muizenburg to the British, the castle was taken over without a single shot being fired there. The flag of the Batavian Republic fluttered from the ramparts between 1803 and 1806 when the British once more returned to power.

Never lovers of the Dutch fortress, Cape Town's British rulers tried several times to have the castle demolished, to no avail. In 1922 the old South African flag was raised over the castle, to be replaced in 1994 by flag of the new South African democracy. There are military units still stationed here.

DON'T MISS

- Walking the fortifications
- Castle Military Museum
- William Fehr Collection
- Key ceremony

PRACTICALITIES

- Map p70
- ☎ 021-787 1249
- www.castleofgoodhope.co.za
- cnr Castle & Darling Sts, City Bowl, entrance on Buitenkant St; P
- adult/child R50/25
- 9am-4pm
- Castle

The Layout

Shaped as a pentagon, the castle has defensive bastions jutting out from its five corners, each of which is named after the official titles of the Prince of Orange (from left to right from the entrance: Buuren, Catzenellenbogen, Nassau, Oranje and Leerdam). Climb up to and around these to take in the fort's layout, and for the panoramic view across the Grand Parade and towards Table Mountain.

Across the fort's centre and around its walls are various buildings, some of which continue to be used by the military. You can peep into the torture chamber, the 18th-century bakery (Het Bakhuys), a replica of the forge, and the Dolphin Pool, so called because of the ornate dolphin fountain at its centre.

The Museums

The interesting **Castle Military Museum** occupies the castle's original bayside entrance. Inside you can see examples and vivid paintings of different military uniforms down the centuries, as well as a very good exhibition on the Anglo-Boer War, and a shop selling military memorabilia.

A large chunk of the **William Fehr Collection** (www.iziko.org.za) of oil paintings, furniture, ceramics, metal and glassware is displayed in the former Governor's Quarters. Temporary exhibitions with more contemporary themes are also held here. The businessman William Fehr started his collection in the 1920s with South African–related paintings, later adding furniture and other art objects; much of it has been on display at the castle since the 1950s, with works on paper mainly being shown in Rust en Vreugd (p80).

Fronting the former Governor's Quarters is a beautifully restored 18th-century balcony with a pediment bas-relief created by the German sculptor, Anton Anreith.

Next door is the **Secunde's House**, formerly the home of the Cape's vice governor. There's no original furniture here, but the rooms are designed to reflect what they would have looked like during the 17th, 18th and 19th centuries. Restoration has revealed some the house's original wall paintings.

KEY CEREMONY

Catch the key ceremony at 10am and noon, Monday to Friday. At 10am, a key is used to open a wicket gate within the main castle gate, after which a bell is rung and sentries take up positions. A small cannon is fired on the outer bailey and the key is then returned to the Governor's quarters. The noon ceremony repeats the process in reverse.

On public holidays, volunteer guides from the Canon Association of South Africa hold public demonstrations of how to fire a canon.

TOURS

Guided tours (included in the admission fee) run at 11am, noon and 2pm.

TOP SIGHT
COMPANY'S GARDEN

What was once the vegetable patch for the Dutch East India Company (VOC) is now a city-centre oasis, where locals can be found relaxing on the lawns in the shade of centuries-old trees. The primary focus is the Public Garden, but many other interesting buildings and landmarks are found around the garden's main pedestrian thoroughfare, Government Ave.

The Garden's History

The Company's Garden began to be cultivated in April 1652 as soon as the VOC's first officials arrived at the Cape. *Grachten* (irrigation channels) were dug to lead water from the streams that flowed down Table Mountain, and these eventually determined the shape not only of the garden but also of the city's original streets and boundaries. By the end of the 17th century, pathways, fountains and even a menagerie had been established in the area.

It was during the 19th century that the gardens began to take on the shape that they have today. Chunks of the grounds were carved off for buildings including St George's Cathedra (p68)l and the Houses of Parliament (p69). In 1848 the lower part of the area became a public Botanical Garden.

The construction of the **Delville Wood Memorial** in the 1920s radically changed the upper part of the garden close to the South African Museum (p79). The memorial honours the 2000-plus South African soldiers who fell during a five-day WWI battle.

The Public Garden

Planted with a fine collection of botanical specimens, including frangipanis, African flame trees, aloes and roses, the **Public Garden** (Groote Kerk) is the area's highlight. The oldest recorded specimen is a saffron pear tree, in the region of 300 years old and still bearing fruit.

DON'T MISS

- Public Garden
- De Tuynhuis
- Delville Wood Memorial
- National Library of South Africa
- Centre for the Book

PRACTICALITIES

- Map p70
- City Bowl
- 7am-7pm
- Dorp, Leeuwen

The squirrels that scamper around were imported from North America by the politician and mining magnate Cecil Rhodes. A bronze **statue of Rhodes** (Map p70; Groote Kerk) was erected in 1908 on a plinth carved with the phrase 'Your hinterland is there' as the imperialist points towards the heart of the continent.

Also to be found here is a small aviary; a fake 'slave bell' erected in 1911; a rose garden designed in 1929; and the **VOC Vegetable Garden** (Map p70; Company's Garden, Queen Victoria St, City Bowl; 7am-7pm; Upper Loop, Upper Long), installed in 2014 but inspired by the original market garden – some of the food grown here is used in the garden's restaurant.

Along Government Avenue

The original Company's Garden was bisected by the oak-lined Government Ave, which has entrances off Wale St between St George's Cathedral and the Houses of Parliament, and off Orange St. Along here, peer through ornate gates at the **De Tuynhuis** (Garden House; Map p70; Government Ave, City Bowl; Groote Kerk), a handsome building originally constructed in 1700 as a visitor's lodge. From the front gate you'll just about be able to make out the VOC's monogram on the pediment – as close as you'll get, since De Tuynhuis is now an official office of South Africa's president, and off-limits to tourists. The design of the parterre garden dates from 1788 and was recreated in the 1960s.

Further south along Government Ave you'll pass the South African National Gallery (p78; pictured), outside of which is a striking, abstract statue of **Jan Smuts** (Map p84; Paddock Ave, Gardens), the former general and prime minister (1870–1950). It was designed by Sydney Harpley; when the statue was unveiled in 1964, a storm of protest resulted in the second, more traditional statue of **Smuts** (Map p70; cnr Adderley & Wale Sts, City Bowl; Groote Kerk) by Ivan Mitford-Barberton, beside the Slave Lodge.

Libraries

Facing the garden's north end, the **National Library of South Africa** (Map p70; 021-424 6320; www.nlsa.ac.za; 5 Queen Victoria St, City Bowl; 9am-5pm Mon-Fri; Dorp) is a neoclassical building based on the Fitzwilliam Museum in Cambridge, UK. Exhibitions are held here; enter to admire the central rotunda. Housed in a grand domed building to the east of the park, the **Centre for the Book** (Map p70; 021-423 2662; www.nlsa.ac.za; 62 Queen Victoria St, City Bowl; 8am-4pm Mon-Fri; Upper Long, Upper Loop), constructed in 1913, has a beautiful central reading room and is sometimes used for concerts.

INFORMATION

The **Visitor Information Centre** (www.heritage.org.za; information centre 8.30am-3.30pm Mon-Fri, shop 9am-2pm Tue-Sat; Upper Long, Upper Loop) has an exhibition on the garden's development. You can also pick up a good booklet with a self-guided trail of the area's major landmarks, and arrange guided tours here.

The oldest recorded specimen in the Company's Garden is a saffron pear tree, in the region of 350 years old and still bearing fruit. The original trunk collapsed years ago, so what you can see now – behind a protective fence and held up by metal crutches – are the sprouts from the tree's roots.

LEARN ABOUT FYNBOS

In the Visitor Information Centre, **Cape Town Fynbos Experience** (Map p84; 021-426 2157; www.gettothepoint.co.za; fynbos tasting/apothecary workshop R450/1254) run hour-long fynbos tasting courses where you can sample the native aromatic plants in the form of infusions, tinctures and oils.

TOP SIGHT
DISTRICT SIX MUSEUM

It's impossible not to be emotionally touched by this museum, which celebrates the once lively multiracial area that was destroyed during apartheid, its 60,000 inhabitants forcibly removed. Inside the former Methodist Mission Church, home interiors have been recreated, alongside photographs, recordings and testimonials, all of which build an evocative picture of a shattered but not entirely broken community.

The Area's History

Named District Six by the city in 1867, this was for many decades a vibrant, ethnically mixed community of former slaves, merchants, artisans, labourers and immigrants. However, as early as 1901 black South African residents were moved out by the authorities to Langa. Even so, many Cape Malay, white Portuguese, Chinese and Hindu families all continued living side by side here.

In 1966 an order declared District Six a 'whites only' area under the Group Areas Act. For several years little happened, but in 1970 the demolition of buildings started and gradually the residents were moved out to other areas of the city, mostly in the Cape Flats.

The museum's displays include a floor map of what District Six originally looked like, on which former residents have labelled where their demolished homes and features of their neighbourhood once stood. There are also reconstructions of home interiors, and faded photographs and recordings.

DON'T MISS

- Floor map of District Six
- Walking tour of area
- Homecoming Centre

PRACTICALITIES

- Map p80
- 021-466 7200
- www.districtsix.co.za
- 25a Buitenkant St, East City
- adult/child R40/15, guided tour of museum R55, walking tours R80-100
- 9am-4pm Mon-Sat
- Lower Buitenkant

PETER UNGER/GETTY IMAGES ©

Residents' Stories & Tours

The best way to understand the events of District Six's history is to speak with the staff, all of whom have heartbreaking stories to tell. A good example is Noor Ebrahim whose grandfather came to Cape Town in 1890 from Surat in India. Noor grew up in the heart of District Six and his family hung on there until 1976, when they were given two weeks to vacate the house that his grandfather had bought some 70 years previously. By that time, they'd seen families, neighbours and friends being split up and sent to separate townships determined by their race. They'd prepared for this by buying a new home in the coloured township of Athlone.

Noor will never forget the day he left District Six. He got in his car with his wife and two children and drove off, but only got as far as the corner before stopping. He started to cry as he saw the bulldozers move in immediately.

Homecoming Centre

A block north of the main museum is its annex, the **Homecoming Centre** (15 Buitenkant St, East City; 9am-4pm Mon-Fri) FREE, occupying part of the Sacks Futeran Building. Currently there's a wonderful exhibition of the art works created for the *District Huis Kombuis Food & Memory Cookbook,* which includes beautifully embroidered panels detailing family recipes, painted plates and striking portrait photography. You can buy a copy of the book at the museum.

For many generations the Futeran family traded soft goods and textiles from these premises and, before that, part of the building was the Buitenkant Congregational Church.

The Future of District Six

Since democracy, there have been promises to rebuild the 4200-sq-m site but, as the largely empty lots prove, it has been very slow going. It is impossible for everyone to return to where they once lived, because buildings such as the Cape Peninsula University of Technology now occupy large chunks of the area. Many claimants are getting very old and some prefer to take financial compensation rather than land restoration from the government, who keep failing in their pledges to build homes.

On a positive note, in early 2018 the R104-million District Six Community Health Centre opened on the site of the old Peninsula Maternity Hospital. A memory project has seen former residents collaborate on murals decorating the centre's walls.

TOURS & ENCOUNTERS

The museum runs sunset walks on the last Thursday of each month (R100), starting at the museum and finishing at the home of a returned family.

If you'd like to dig deeper into the history, the museum also runs a series of more formal encounters with former residents. Tickets are between R75 and R150, and can be booked online.

BOOKS

Good books to read include *Recalling Community in Cape Town* (eds Ciraj Rassool and Sundra Posalendis), an illustrated account of District Six and how its memory was kept alive by those who once lived there, and the eloquent tales of *'Buckingham Palace', District Six* by Richard Rive.

TOP SIGHT
ROBBEN ISLAND

A Unesco World Heritage site, Robben Island's best-known prisoner was Nelson Mandela, which makes it one of the most popular pilgrimage spots in all of Cape Town. Set some 12km out in Table Bay, the flat island served as a jail from the early days of VOC (Vereenigde Oost-Indische Compagnie; Dutch East India Company) control right up until 1996.

The small island, just 2km by 4km, can only be visited on a tour that starts with a ferry journey (30 to 45 minutes, depending on the vessel) from **Nelson Mandela Gateway** (Map p86; Clock Tower Precinct, V&A Waterfront; ⌚9am-8.30pm; Nobel Sq) FREE. On the ferry a video is screened giving a concise history of the island and its use down the centuries as a prison and a leper colony.

On arrival you'll first take a 45-minute bus ride around the island with commentary on the various places of note, such as the lime quarry in which Mandela and many others did hard labour; the little house where Robert Sobukwe, leader of the Pan-Africanist Congress was held in solitary confinement for six years; the village where the museum's staff and their families still live; and the *kramat* (Muslim shrine) built in memory of the Indonesian prince of Madura, Pangerau Chakra Deningrat, who died in 1754 while exiled on the island by the Dutch.

Back at the old prison a former inmate will be your guide and explain from a highly personal viewpoint what life was like for the prisoners. There's the obligatory photo stop at Mandela's tiny cell and, if you're lucky, you'll have a few moments to linger before heading back to the boat. The tour plus boat transfers take around four hours.

At peak times, tickets can sell out days, if not weeks, in advance, so book well ahead via the website. Also be prepared for changes of schedule, as ferry sailings are weather-dependent.

DON'T MISS

- Nelson Mandela's Cell
- Nelson Mandela Gateway
- Jetty 1
- Photo of Table Mountain from the island

PRACTICALITIES

- 021-413 4200
- www.robben-island.org.za
- adult/child R340/190
- ⌚ferries depart at 9am, 11am, 1pm & 3pm, weather permitting
- Nobel Sq

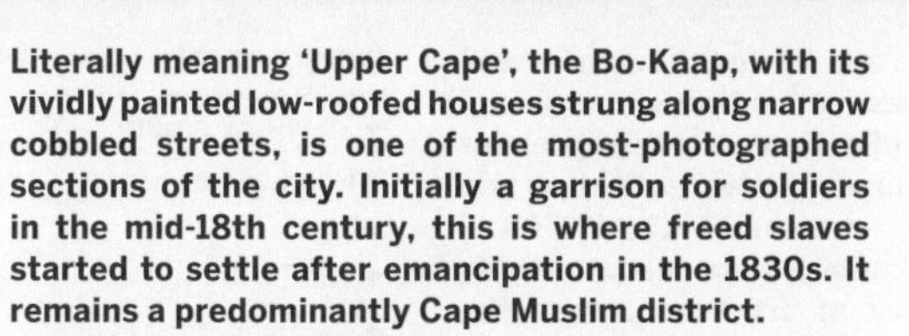

TOP SIGHT
BO-KAAP

Literally meaning 'Upper Cape', the Bo-Kaap, with its vividly painted low-roofed houses strung along narrow cobbled streets, is one of the most-photographed sections of the city. Initially a garrison for soldiers in the mid-18th century, this is where freed slaves started to settle after emancipation in the 1830s. It remains a predominantly Cape Muslim district.

The liquorice allsorts colours of the houses are a relatively new development, appearing after the end of apartheid during which this was classed a coloured-only area. The most photogenic streets are Chiappini, Rose and Wale. However, parts of area remain evidently poor, so it's a good idea to stick to the main streets when walking here after dark.

The small but interesting **Bo-Kaap Museum** (Map p70; ☎021-481 3938; www.iziko.org.za/museums/bo-kaap-museum; 71 Wale St, Bo-Kaap; adult/child R20/10; ⊙10am-5pm Mon-Sat) provides some insight into the lifestyle of a 19th-century Cape Muslim family. The most interesting exhibit is the selection of black-and-white photos of local life displayed in the upstairs room. The house itself, which was built between 1763 and 1768, is the oldest in the area.

The **Auwal Mosque** (Auwal Masjid; Map p70; ☎082 551 7324; http://auwalmasjid.co.za; 34 Dorp St, Bo-Kaap) is the oldest place of Islamic worship in South Africa, established by Iman Abdullah Qadi Abdus Salaam (also known as Tuan Guru) in 1789. This Indonesian prince served time on Robben Island, where he wrote three copies of the Koran from memory, one of which is on display inside the mosque.

The pungent smell of over 100 different herbs, spices and incenses perfumes the air at **Atlas Trading Company** (Map p70; ☎021-423 4361; www.atlastradingcompany.co.za; 104 Wale St, Bo-Kaap; ⊙8.15am-5.15pm Mon-Thu, 8.15am-noon & 2-5.15pm Fri, 8.30am-1pm Sat), a cornerstone of the Bo-Kaap, where generations of cooks have come for essential ingredients (pictured above).

DON'T MISS

- Chiappini St
- Rose St
- Bo-Kaap Museum
- Auwal Mosque

PRACTICALITIES

- Map p70
- 🚌 Dorp, Leeuwen

TOP SIGHT
ZEITZ MOCAA MUSEUM

The Waterfront's old grain silo has been transformed into this state-of-the-art museum for the contemporary Southern African art collection of entrepreneur Jochen Zeitz, as well the museum's own collection and loaned works. Opened in September 2017, MOCAA is still finding its feet as an exhibition space, but already provides a dazzling survey of art from across the continent and beyond.

Transforming the Grain Silo

Easily the most striking thing about the museum is the building in which it is housed. When it opened in 1921, the grain silo was South Africa's tallest building. Disused since 1990, the structure has been spruced up outside and utterly transformed inside in an imaginative design by the studio of British architect Thomas Heatherwick. An atrium has been carved out of the 42 elevator tubes in the building's heart, exposing sections of their circular structure that rise up eight storeys from the basement to a rooftop sculpture garden. Look carefully and you'll see the atrium's shape is that of a corn kernel – one of the crops that used to be stored here.

On the roof, the sculpture garden's glass floor is etched with an invented alphabet – an art piece by Togo artist El Loko. In the basement and around the entrance many of the silo's original industrial fittings have been left intact – providing a visual history of the building. Also used as a gallery for film projections and other installations is the **Dusthouse**, which once operated as an air-filtration plant for the silo.

DON'T MISS

- The BMW Atrium
- Rooftop sculpture garden
- The Dusthouse
- Centre for the Moving Image

PRACTICALITIES

- Map p86
- 087-350 4777
- www.zeitzmocaa.museum
- Silo District, South Arm Rd, V&A Waterfront; P
- adult/child R180/free
- 10am-6pm Wed-Mon, first Fri of month to 9pm
- Waterfront Silo

Museum Departments

There's some 9500 sq m of space for art in MOCAA spread out over 80-plus galleries. It can be a confusing place to navigate with those galleries scattered over several levels around the atrium. However, this does allow for a sense of discovery – and there's plenty of interest to see here.

Few works from the collection of 21st-century art from Africa and its diaspora of artists will be on permanent display. The one piece you will likely see is British artist Isaac Julian's *Ten Thousand Waves*, a nine-screen video installation lasting 55 minutes that is set to remain here for five years. Otherwise, the not-for-profit museum will certainly have works on display by local establishment figures, such as William Kentridge and the US-born, South Africa-based photographer Roger Ballen, who has sponsored the museum's Foundation Centre for Photography (www.rogerballen.org), as well as new stars such as South African photographer Zanele Muhole and Zimbabwe artist Kudzanai Chiurai.

There will also be regularly changing exhibitions in other major sections of the museum, including its **Costume Institute**; the **Centre for Performative Practice**, hosting performance art, talks and other events; the **Centre for the Moving Image** for video and digital art; the **Curatorial Lab**, whose first project has been to investigate the representation of the LGBTQI+ community in South Africa; and the **BMW Atrium**, which will host a major new installation each year.

TICKET DISCOUNTS

It's half-price admission from 4pm to 8.30pm on the first Friday of the month. African citizens get in for free every Wednesday between 10am and 1pm. There's free entry for everyone on **Museum Night** (www.museum-night.co.za; V&A Waterfront) between 5pm and 10pm.

Visit Zeitz MOCAA Food on the museum's fifth floor to have a drink and enjoy the views.

TOURS & EVENTS

Entry includes a free hour-long guided tour of exhibition highlights – good for getting your bearings and understanding the background to some of the works. Check the museum's website for regular events held here such as performances, panel discussions, special film screenings and talks.

Sights

City Bowl, Foreshore, Bo-Kaap & De Waterkant

These areas are where Cape Town was born as a city and thus are crammed with historical sights and places of interest, spanning from the Castle of Good Hope (p58) in the east to the brightly painted houses of the Bo-Kaap (p65) to the northwest. In the middle are the dense grid of streets making up the City Bowl, punctuated by the green lung of the Company's Garden (p60). It's easy to walk between the sights and most can be seen over the course of a full day or a leisurely two days.

Iziko Slave Lodge MUSEUM
(Map p70; 021-467 7229; www.iziko.org.za; 49 Adderley St, City Bowl; adult/child R30/R15; 10am-5pm Mon-Sat; Groote Kerk) Dating back to 1660, the Slave Lodge is one of the oldest buildings in South Africa. Once home to as many as 1000 slaves, the lodge has a fascinating history; it has also been used as a brothel, a jail, a mental asylum, a post office, a library and the Cape Supreme Court in its time. Today, it's a museum mainly devoted to the history and experience of slaves and their descendants in the Cape.

Until 1811 the building housed slaves in damp, insanitary, crowded conditions; up to 20% died each year. The slaves were bought and sold just around the corner on Spin St.

The walls of the original Slave Lodge flank the interior courtyard, where you can find the tombstones of Cape Town's founder, Jan van Riebeeck, and his wife, Maria de la Queillerie. The tombstones were moved here from Jakarta where Van Riebeeck is buried.

The museum also has artefacts from ancient Egypt, Greece, Rome and the Far East on the 1st floor.

St George's Cathedral CATHEDRAL
(Map p70; 021-424 7360; www.sgcathedral.co.za; 1 Wale St, City Bowl; Groote Kerk) Known as the People's Cathedral, this was one of the few places of worship that was open to people of all races during apartheid. Classical concerts are sometimes held here; see the website for details as well as times of daily services. The interior is a cool retreat, but also search out the **Siyahamba Labyrinth** in the cloisters, a paved circular walking path to aid mediation and spiritual relief.

Designed by Sir Herbert Baker at the turn of the 19th century, the church's official name is the Cathedral Church of St George the Martyr in Cape Town. Archbishop Desmond Tutu presided here and made the cathedral a focus of opposition to the Afrikaner regime.

Look around the exhibition in the Memory & Witness Centre in the crypt, where you'll also find the Crypt Jazz Restaurant (p169). The cathedral remains a beacon of hope through its HIV/AIDS outreach programme – note the Cape Town AIDS quilt hanging above the north door.

CHURCH SQUARE

One of the city's most attractive public plazas, Church Sq is surrounded by handsome old buildings including the Herbert Baker – designed National Mutual Building, parts of which date to 1905; it now houses the **Iziko Social History Centre**. The property developer Urban Lime has been buying up and restoring some of the commercial spaces in buildings around the square including **Speaker's Corner** (Map p70; www.speakers-corner.co.za; Church Sq, City Bowl), set to house a restaurant, bar, events spaces and offices.

There are plans to launch a free sound-and-light show in the square by the end of 2018, with the projections screened at night onto the National Mutual Building. Information on the square's history will also be transmitted to visitors via a hi-tech interactive app.

The square's name comes from **Groote Kerk** (p72), the mother church of the Dutch Reformed Church, which borders the square; adjacent is Spin St, where a small circular plaque in the traffic island marks the location of the **Slave Tree** (Map p70; Spin St, City Bowl; Groote Kerk), under which it is believed slaves were sold until emancipation in 1834. In the square itself is the **Slavery Memorial** (Map p70; Church Sq, City Bowl; Groote Kerk), 11 low black-granite blocks engraved with the names of slaves or words relating to slavery, resistance and rebellion. There is also a statue of **Jan Hendrik** (Map p70; Church Sq, City Bowl; Groote Kerk), one-time editor of the *Zuid Afrikaan* newspaper and a key figure behind the drafting of the 1909 South African constitution.

ROCK GIRL BENCHES

As you wander around the City Bowl, as well as up on Signal Hill, at Lion's Head and the V&A Waterfront, keep your eyes peeled for the colourful mosaic-decorated benches created by **Rock Girl** (www.rockgirlsa.org). This inspiring project was started by human-rights lawyer Michelle India Baird in 2010 when she was volunteering at the Red River School in the crime-ridden Cape Flats suburb of Manenberg. There was an urgent need to create safe places there for young girls and boys to sit and not be harassed by gangsters.

Several prominent Capetonian artists and designers, including Lovell Friedman, Laurie van Heerden, Atang Tshikare, Paul du Toit and Lyall Sprong, have since become involved in creating the benches. Most of the ones in Central Cape Town are twinned with a sister bench in the townships, such as in Gugulethu, where there's one at the **Amy Biehl Memorial** (p115), and in Khayelitsha at the **Grassroot Soccer Football for Hope Centre**.

In **Prestwich Memorial Garden** (p121) there are three benches: *Time Out* by artist Paul du Toit, in the shape of a symbolic Rock Girl; an oversized wooden bench by Mark Thomas (who also designed the Boomslang at Kirstenbosch National Botanical Garden); and a metal and wooden bench by Laurie van Heerden inside Truth Coffee. You'll find others at the southern end of Long St, outside the **Backpack** (p130), and in the lobby of the **Cape Town International Convention Centre** (p169). If you go for a surf in Llandudno or Muizenberg, look out for benches there as well.

Arch for Arch PUBLIC ART

(Map p70; cnr Wale & Adderley Sts, City Bowl) Unveiled in 2017 for Archibishop Desmond Tutu's 86th birthday, this wooden arch stands next to the cathedral where the Nobel Prize winner presided as a symbol of hope and opposition during apartheid. The monument, commissioned by Design Indaba and designed by Norwegian architectural firm Snøhetta, features 14 interlaced strands inscribed with excerpts from South Africa's constitution.

Houses of Parliament NOTABLE BUILDING

(Map p70; 021-403 2266; www.parliament.gov.za; Parliament St, City Bowl; tours 9am-4pm Mon-Fri; Roeland) FREE A tour around parliament is fascinating, especially if you're interested in the country's modern history. Opened in 1885, the hallowed halls have seen some pretty momentous events; this is where British Prime Minister Harold Macmillan made his 'Wind of Change' speech in 1960, and where President Hendrik Verwoerd, known as the architect of apartheid, was stabbed to death in 1966. Call ahead and present your passport to gain entry.

Long Street ARCHITECTURE

(Map p70; City Bowl; Dorp, Leeuwen) A stroll along Long St is an essential element of a Cape Town visit. This busy commercial and nightlife thoroughfare, partly lined with Victorian-era buildings featuring lovely wrought-iron balconies, once formed the border of the Muslim Bo-Kaap. By the 1960s, Long St had fallen into disrepute and it remained that way until the late 1990s, when savvy developers realised its potential. The most attractive section runs from the junction with Buitensingel St north to around Strand St.

Youngblood Africa GALLERY

(Map p70; 021-424 0074; www.youngbloodafrica.com; 70-74 Bree St, City Bowl; 9am-5pm Mon-Fri, 10am-2pm 1st & 3rd Sat; Church, Mid-Long) FREE The artworks of young South Africans are displayed in this impressive multilevel gallery space and creative studio, where you'll also find the **Food Lab** cafe. Check their website for frequent evening events, including concerts and performances that could be anything from a swinging electronic gypsy jazz band to classical music in the dark.

Greenmarket Square SQUARE

(Map p70; City Bowl; Church,Longmarket) This cobbled square is Cape Town's second-oldest public space after the Grand Parade. It hosts a lively and colourful crafts and souvenir market daily. Apart from the Old Town House, the square is also surrounded by some choice examples of art deco architecture, including **Market House**, an elaborately decorated building with balconies and stone-carved eagles and flowers on its facade.

City Bowl & Bo-Kaap

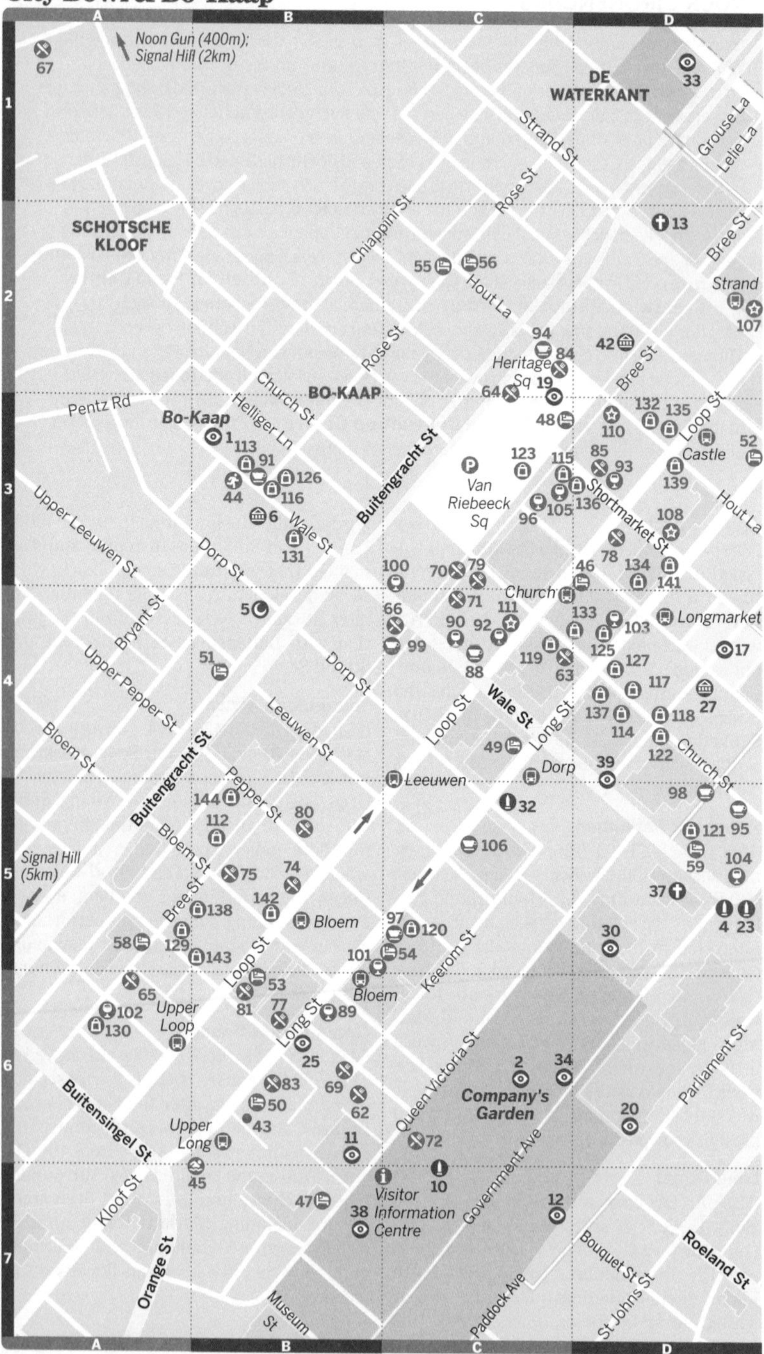

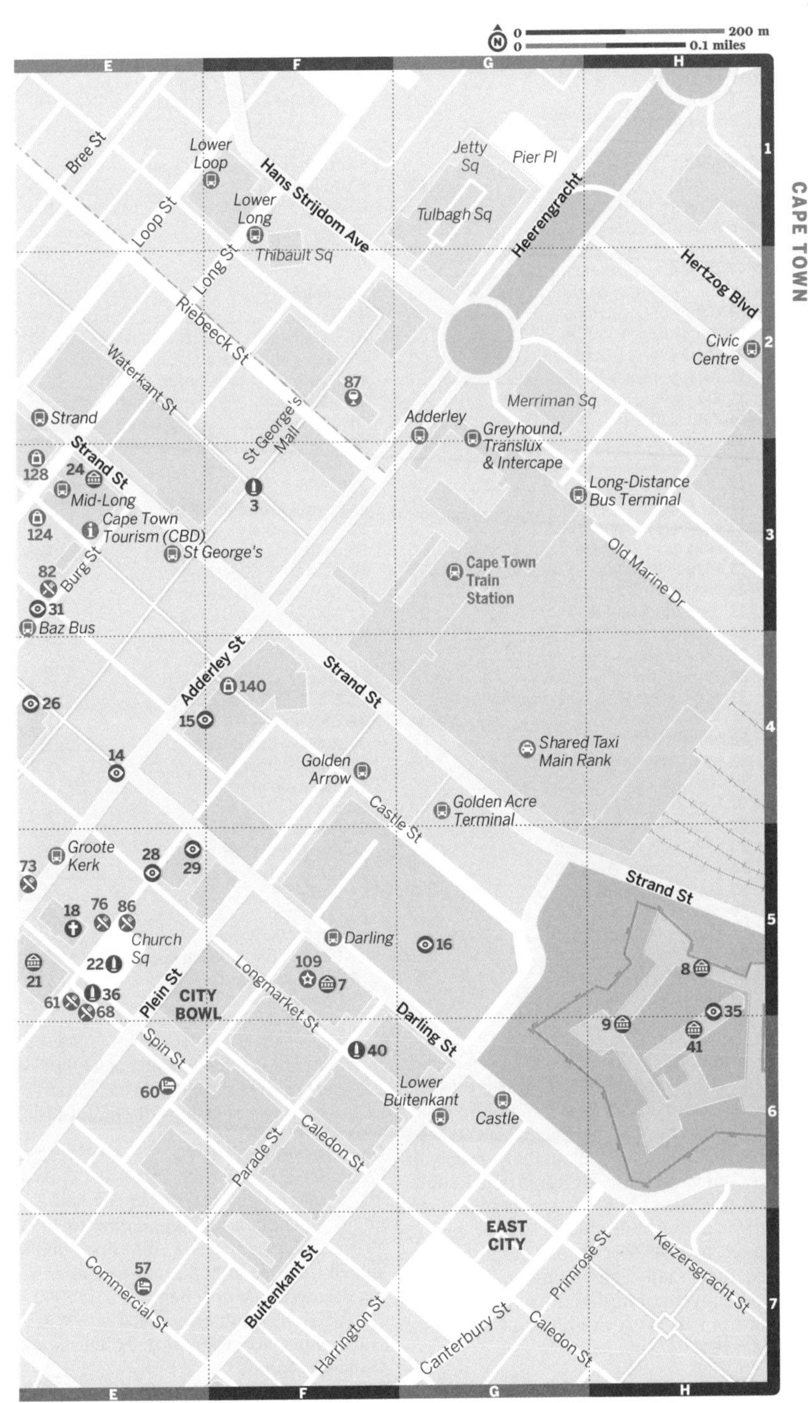
0 200 m
0 0.1 miles
E
F
G
H
1
2
3
4
5
6
7
Bree St
Lower Loop
Loop St
Hans Strijdom Ave
Lower Long
Long St
Thibault Sq
Jetty Sq
Pier Pl
Tulbagh Sq
Heerengracht
Hertzog Blvd
Civic Centre
Riebeeck St
Waterkant St
St George's Mall
87
Merriman Sq
Adderley
Greyhound, Translux & Intercape
Strand
Strand St
128
24
Mid-Long
3
Long-Distance Bus Terminal
124
Cape Town Tourism (CBD)
St George's
Burg St
82
31
Baz Bus
Cape Town Train Station
Old Marine Dr
Adderley St
140
Strand St
26
15
14
Shared Taxi Main Rank
Golden Arrow
Castle St
Golden Acre Terminal
Groote Kerk
28
29
73
Strand St
18
76
86
Church Sq
Darling
16
21
22
109
7
8
61
36
68
Plein St
CITY BOWL
Longmarket St
Darling St
9
35
41
Spin St
40
60
Lower Buitenkant
Castle
Parade St
Caledon St
EAST CITY
57
Commercial St
Buitenkant St
Harrington St
Canterbury St
Primrose St
Caledon St
Keizersgracht St
CAPE TOWN

City Bowl & Bo-Kaap

Top Sights
1 Bo-Kaap ... B3
2 Company's Garden ... C6

Sights
3 Africa ... F3
4 Arch for Arch ... D5
5 Auwal Mosque ... B4
6 Bo-Kaap Museum ... B3
7 Cape Town City Hall ... F5
8 Castle Military Museum ... H5
9 Castle of Good Hope ... H6
10 Cecil Rhodes Statue ... C7
11 Centre for the Book ... B6
12 De Tuynhuis ... C7
13 Evangelical Lutheran Church ... D2
14 First National Bank ... E4
15 Former Standard Bank ... E4
16 Grand Parade ... G5
17 Greenmarket Square ... D4
18 Groote Kerk ... E5
19 Heritage Square ... C2
20 Houses of Parliament ... D6
21 Iziko Slave Lodge ... E5
22 Jan Hendrik Statue ... E5
23 Jan Smuts Statue ... D5
24 Koopmans-de Wet House ... E3
25 Long Street ... B6
26 Market House ... E4
27 Michaelis Collection at the Old Town House ... D4
28 Mullers Opticians ... E5
29 Mutual Heights ... E5
30 National Library of South Africa ... D5
31 New Zealand House ... E3
32 Open House ... C5
33 Prestwich Memorial ... D1
34 Public Garden ... C6
35 Secunde's House ... H5
36 Slave Tree ... E5
Slavery Memorial ... (see 22)
37 St George's Cathedral ... D5
38 VOC Vegetable Garden ... B7
39 Waalburg Building ... D4
40 We Are Still Here ... F6
41 William Fehr Collection ... H6
42 Youngblood Africa ... D2

Activities, Courses & Tours
43 Abseil Africa ... B6
Cape Town on Foot ... (see 135)
44 Lekka Kombuis ... B3
45 Long St Baths ... B7

Sleeping
46 91 Loop ... D3
47 Cape Breaks ... B7
48 Cape Heritage Hotel ... C3
49 Daddy Long Legs Hotel ... C4
50 Daddy Long Legs Hotel Apartments ... B6
51 Dutch Manor ... B4
52 Grand Daddy Hotel ... D3
53 Happy Rhino Hotel ... B6
La Rose B&B ... (see 55)
54 Long Street Backpackers ... C5
55 Rose Lodge ... C2
56 Rouge on Rose ... C2
57 Scalabrini Guest House ... E7
58 St Paul's B&B Guesthouse ... A5
59 Taj Cape Town ... D5
60 Townhouse ... E6

Eating
61 6 Spin St Restaurant ... E5
62 95 Keerom ... B6
63 Addis in Cape ... C4
64 Africa Café ... C2
65 Bacon on Bree ... A6
66 Bocca ... C4
67 Bo-Kaap Kombuis ... A1
Bombay Brasserie ... (see 59)
68 Bread, Milk & Honey ... E5
69 Carne SA ... B6
70 Charango ... C3
Chef's Warehouse & Canteen ... (see 48)
71 Clarke's Bar & Dining Room ... C4
72 Company's Garden Restaurant ... C6
Fork ... (see 134)

Groote Kerk CHURCH

(Map p70; ☎021-422 0569; www.grootekerk.org.za; Church Sq, City Bowl; ⏰10am-2pm Mon-Fri, services 10am & 7pm Sun; 🚌Groote Kerk) The highlights of the mother church of the Dutch Reformed Church (Nederduitse Gereformeerde Kerk) are its mammoth organ and ornate Burmese-teak pulpit, carved by master sculptors Anton Anreith and Jan Graaff. The building is otherwise an architectural mishmash, with parts dating from the 1704 original and other bits from 1841.

While here, ponder the fact that for the first 100 years or so of the church's life, slaves are said to have been sold immediately outside.

Cape Town City Hall HISTORIC BUILDING

(Map p70; ☎021-455 2029; Darling St, City Bowl; P; 🚌Darling) Cape Town's old city hall is a grand Edwardian building dating to 1905. Nelson Mandela made his first public speech from the front balcony here after being released from prison in February 1990.

City Hall's auditorium is one of several venues for the Cape Philharmonic Orchestra (p168).

Hail Pizza..(see 71)
73 Hokey Poke..E5
74 Homage 1862..B5
75 Jason Bakery..B5
76 Kleinsky's Delicatessen..E5
77 Lola's..B6
78 Marrow..D3
79 Mink & Trout..C3
80 Mulberry & Prince..B5
Olami..(see 130)
81 Plant..B6
82 Raw and Roxy..E3
83 Royale Eatery..B6
84 Savoy Cabbage..C2
85 Shortmarket Club..D3
86 Speaker's Corner..E5

Drinking & Nightlife

87 31..F2
88 Bean There..C4
89 Beerhouse..B6
90 Gin Bar..C4
91 Harvest..B3
Honest Chocolate Cafe..(see 90)
92 House of H..C4
93 House of Machines..D3
94 I Love My Laundry..C2
95 Ka Pa Tée..D5
96 La Parada..C3
97 Lady Bonin's Tea Bar..C5
98 Localli..D5
99 Nitro Brew..C4
100 Openwine..C3
101 Orchard on Long..B5
102 Orphanage..A6
Outrage of Modesty..(see 85)
103 Tjing Tjing..D4
104 Twankey Bar..D5
105 Upstairs on Bree..C3
Waiting Room..(see 83)
106 Yours Truly..C5

Entertainment

107 Alexander Bar & Café..D2
108 Café Roux..D3
109 Cape Philharmonic Orchestra..F5
Crypt Jazz Restaurant..(see 37)
110 Gate69 Cape Town..D3
111 OnPointe Dance Studios..C4

Shopping

112 Alexandra Höjer Atelier..B5
113 Atlas Trading Company..B3
114 AVA Gallery..D4
115 Avoova..C3
116 Bo-op..B3
117 Cape Gallery..D4
118 Carole Nevin..D4
119 Chandler House..C4
120 Clarke's Bookshop..C5
121 EarthFair Food Market..D5
122 Eclectica Contemporary..D4
123 Espadril..C3
124 Lucky Fish..E3
Ma Se Kinners..(see 73)
125 Mali South Clothing..D4
126 Mami Wata..B3
127 Mememe..D4
128 Merchants on Long..E3
129 Merry Pop Ins..A5
130 Missibaba & Kirsten Goss..A6
131 Monkeybiz..B3
132 Mungo..D3
133 Olive Green Cat..D4
134 Pan African Market..D3
135 Prins & Prins..D3
136 Real + Simple..D3
137 Rialheim..D4
138 Skinny La Minx..B5
139 Stable..D3
140 Trafalgar Place..F4
141 Tribal Trends..D3
142 Unknown Union..B5
143 What If The World..B5
144 Wild Olive..B5

Grand Parade SQUARE

(Map p70; Darling St, City Bowl; Darling) A prime location for Cape Town's history, the Grand Parade is where the Dutch built their first fort in 1652; slaves were sold and punished; and also where crowds gathered to watch Nelson Mandela's address in 1990. A market is held on part of the square, which is also used for parking.

Mutual Heights ARCHITECTURE

(Map p70; www.mutualheights.info; cnr Parliament & Darling Sts, City Bowl; Darling) Clad in rose- and gold-veined black marble, Mutual Heights is the most impressive of the City Bowl's collection of art deco structures. The facade is decorated with one of the longest continuous stone friezes in the world, designed by Ivan Mitford-Barberton and chiselled by master stonemasons the Lorenzi brothers. Much of the building's original detail and decoration have been preserved, including the impressive central banking space (sadly not open for general viewing).

Commissioned by the Old Mutual financial company, this was once not only the tallest structure in Africa bar the Pyramids, but also the most expensive. Unfortunately, the building's opening in 1939 was eclipsed

Foreshore & De Waterkant

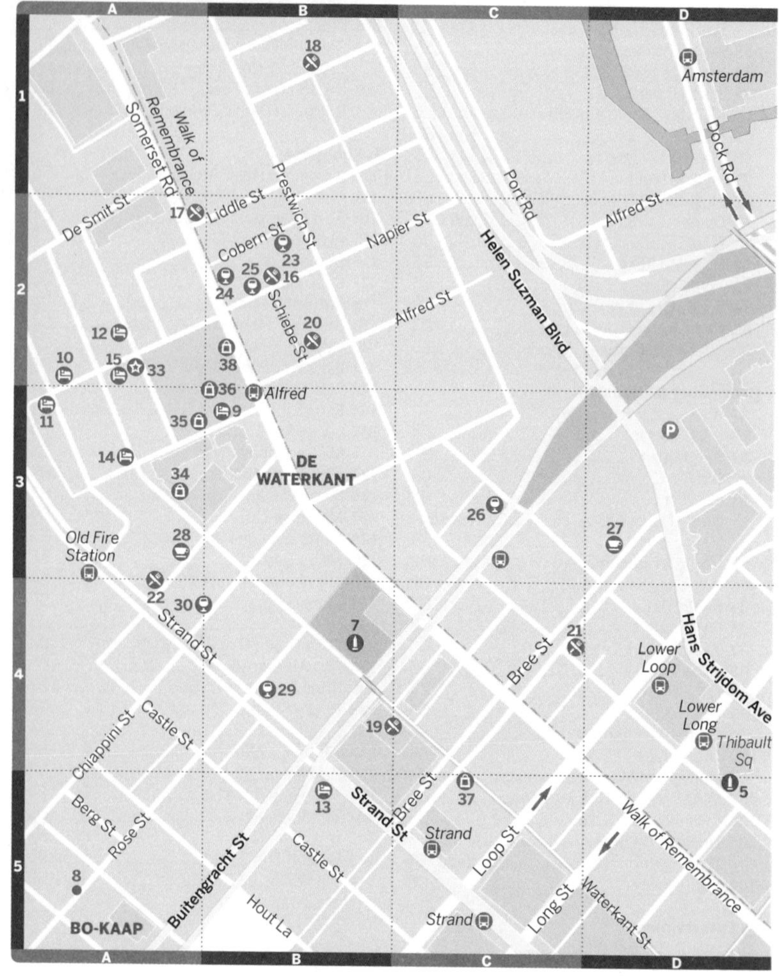

by the start of WWII. Additionally, its prime position on the Foreshore was immediately made redundant when the city decided to extend the land 2km further into the bay. Old Mutual started moving its business out of the building to Pinelands in the 1950s. Made into apartments and renamed Mutual Heights in 2002, it kicked off a frenzy among developers to convert similarly long-neglected and empty city-centre office blocks.

Prestwich Memorial MEMORIAL

(Map p70; cnr Somerset Rd & Buitengracht St, De Waterkant; 8am-6pm Mon-Fri, to 2pm Sat & Sun; Strand) FREE Construction in 2003 along nearby Prestwich St unearthed many skeletons. These were the unmarked graves of slaves and others executed by the Dutch in the 17th and 18th centuries on what was then known as Gallows Hill. The bones were exhumed and this memorial building, with an attractive facade of Robben Island slate, was created. It includes an ossuary and excellent interpretive displays, including a replica of the remarkable 360-degree panorama of Table Bay painted by Robert Gordon in 1778.

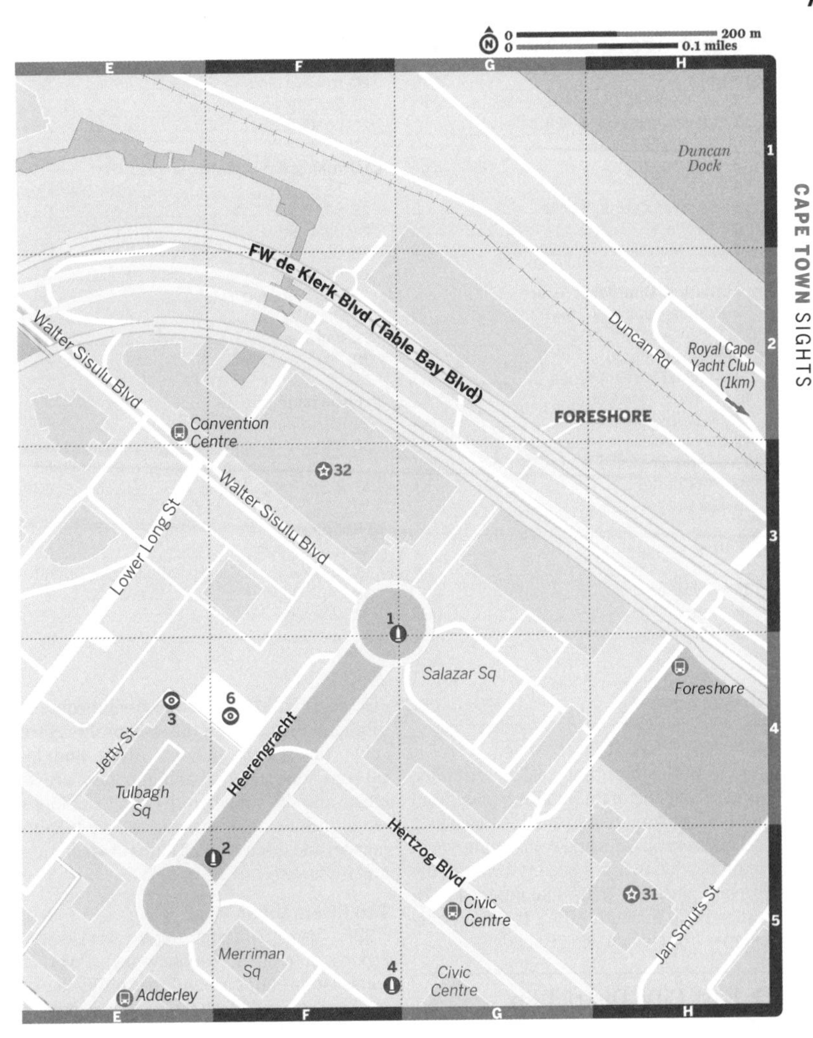

Evangelical Lutheran Church CHURCH

(Map p70; ☎021-421 5854; www.lutheranchurch.org.za; 98 Strand St, City Bowl; ⏲10am-2pm Mon-Fri; 🚌Strand) Converted from a barn in 1780, the first Lutheran church in the Cape has a carved wood pulpit that's a masterwork by the German sculptor Anton Anreith. A pair of muscular figures of Hercules (symbolising the power of faith) hold up the front two corners of the pulpit, above which four cherubs fly and a rococo canopy hangs.

Anreith's work can also be seen in Groote Kerk and at Groot Constantia.

Koopmans-de Wet House MUSEUM

(Map p70; ☎021-481 3935; www.iziko.org.za; 35 Strand St, City Bowl; adult/child R20/10; ⏲10am-5pm Mon-Fri; 🚌Strand) Step back two centuries from 21st-century Cape Town when you enter this classic example of a Cape Dutch town house, furnished with 18th- and early-19th-century antiques. It's an atmospheric place, with ancient vines growing in the courtyard and floorboards that squeak just as they probably did during the time of Marie Koopmans-de Wet, the socialite owner after whom the house is named.

Foreshore & De Waterkant

Sights
1 Bartholomeu Dias Statue ... F3
2 Jan van Riebeeck & Maria de la Queillerie Statues ... F5
3 Jetty Square ... E4
4 Knot ... F5
5 Mythological Landscape ... D5
6 Pier Place ... F4
7 Prestwich Memorial Garden ... B4

Activities, Courses & Tours
8 Bo-Kaap Cooking Tour ... A5

Sleeping
9 African Elite Properties ... B3
10 De Waterkant Cottages ... A2
11 De Waterkant House ... A3
12 Purple House ... A2
13 SunSquare Cape Town City Bowl ... B5
14 The Charles ... A3
15 The Grey ... A2

Eating
16 Anatoli ... B2
17 Beefcakes ... A2
18 Gold ... B1
19 Hemelhuijs ... B4
20 Izakaya Matsuri ... B2
21 La Tête ... C4
22 Loading Bay ... A4

Drinking & Nightlife
14 Stories ... (see 13)
23 Bar Code ... B2
24 Beaulah ... B2
25 Crew Bar ... B2
26 Fireman's Arms ... C3
27 Hard Pressed Cafe ... D3
28 Origin ... A3
29 Pink Panther 2 ... B4
30 The Vue ... A4

Entertainment
31 Artscape ... H5
32 Cape Town International Convention Centre ... F3
33 Piano Bar ... A2

Shopping
34 Africa Nova ... A3
35 Baraka ... A3
36 Cape Quarter ... B3
37 Klûk & CGDT ... C5
38 Spar ... B2

Heritage Square ARCHITECTURE
(Map p70; www.heritage.org.za/heritage_square_project.htm; 90 Bree St, City Bowl; P; Church, Longmarket) This beautiful collection of Cape Georgian and Victorian buildings was saved from the wrecking ball in 1996. As well as a hotel and several cafes and restaurants, you'll also find a vine that has been growing in the courtyard since the 1770s, making it the oldest such plant in South Africa. It still produces grapes from which wine is made.

East City, District Six, Woodstock & Observatory

The top sight of the East City is the District Six Museum (p62) and its satellite Homecoming Centre (p63), but do also check out the exciting art exhibitions at A4 Arts Foundation. Over in Woodstock, Salt River and Obs, there are plenty of commercial galleries that are often worth a look even if you have no intention of buying the art displayed. For some fresh air, birdwatching and great views towards the back of Table Mountain, go for a walk in Two Rivers Urban Park.

A4 Arts Foundation ARTS CENTRE
(Map p80; www.a4arts.org; 23 Buitenkant St, District Six; 10am-5.30pm Tue-Fri, 10am-2pm; Lower Buitenkant) FREE Fascinating multimedia exhibitions are staged at this non-profit centre supporting the arts in South Africa. Both local and international contemporary artists create and show their work here. Exhibitions often include film screenings, live performances and discussions. There's also a library and resource centre.

Two Rivers Urban Park PARK
(TRUP; Map p114; http://trup.org.za; Liesbeek Parkway, Observatory; Observatory) Covering some 240 hectares around the confluence of the Liesbeek and Black Rivers, this new park is one of the city's largest, with the potential to provide a common space for the long-divided communities that surround it. Paths beside the Liesbeek River are pleasant for a stroll, jog or cycle, and the wetlands provide excellent opportunities for bird-watching.

Cape Town Science Centre MUSEUM
(Map p79; 021-300 3200; www.ctsc.org.za; 370B Main Rd, Observatory; R55; 9am-4.30pm Mon-Sat, from 10am Sun; P; Observatory) Occupying a rare example of the work of modernist architect Max Policansky, this is a great place to bring kids for attractions such as the giant gyroscope (R5) and tons of Lego. There's also a replica of the Soyuz

DON'T MISS

DISTRICT SIX & WOODSTOCK STREET ART

Vivid works of street art, big and small, decorate the sides of many buildings in District Six and Woodstock. Street artists who can show you around these areas include **Juma** (p124), a friendly Zimbabwean who also leads tours of Khayelitsha, and **Grant Jurius** (079 066 7055; www.facebook.com/thestreetisthegallery; tours per person R270), who also offers tours around Mitchells Plain. Khayelitsha and Mitchells Plain are both areas where you'll find more eye-catching works.

I Art Woodstock (Map p80; btwn Gympie & Hercules Sts, Woodstock; Woodstock) FREE The sketchy grid of streets off Albert Rd is a canvas for some amazing street art, much of it created during a collaborative project between a collective of street artists and Adidas Originals in 2011. More pieces have been added since, such as *Raised By Wolves* by Nardstar, and the *Freedom Day Mural* by Freddy Sam.

Land & Liberty (Map p80; Keizersgracht; Hanover St) Prolific street artist Faith47 (www.faith47.com) created this eight-storey-tall mother with a baby strapped to her back pointing up towards Lion's Head.

Harvest (Map p80; Picket Post 59-63 block, cnr of Cauvin Rd & Christiaan St; District Six) Faith47 designed this proud African woman and her crop of reeds, which integrates an electronic lighting system. It's designed to illuminate every time a donation is made to the #ANOTHERLIGHTUP (www.anotherlightup.com) project, which funds lighting for public spaces in Khayelitsha.

Freedom Struggle Heroes (Map p80; Darling St; Hanover St) Portraits of Nelson Mandela, Steve Biko, Cissie Gool and Imam Haron are painted on the side of a building as if their faces were carved into the side of Table Mountain.

capsule that returned South African tech billionaire Mark Shuttleworth to earth after his trip to the International Space Station.

Heart of Cape Town Museum MUSEUM
(Map p79; 021-404 1967; www.heartofcapetown.co.za; Old Main Bldg, Groote Schuur Hospital, Main Rd, Observatory; R350; guided tours 9am, 11am, 1pm & 3pm; P; Observatory) Booking a two-hour guided tour is the only way you can see the very theatre in Groote Schuur Hospital where history was made in 1967 when Dr Christiaan Barnard and his team carried out the world's first successful heart-transplant operation (sadly, the recipient died a few days later). The displays have a fascinating Dr Kildare–quality to them.

Gardens & Surrounds

Lording it above the area and indeed all of Cape Town is the main attraction: Table Mountain (p54). Climb it or take the cableway up for the amazing views. An easier climb is up neighbouring Lion's Head (p54). Down at ground level, make time to view the excellent South African Jewish Museum and South African National Gallery, the pick of the cultural institutions clustered to the southeast of the Company's Garden.

South African Jewish Museum MUSEUM
(Map p84; 021-465 1546; www.sajewishmuseum.co.za; 88 Hatfield St, Gardens; adult/child R60/free; 10am-5pm Sun-Thu, to 2pm Fri; P; Annandale) You need a photo ID to enter the secure compound that's home to this imaginatively designed museum, which partly occupies the beautifully restored **Old Synagogue** (1863). The permanent exhibition *Hidden Treasures of Japanese Art* showcases a collection of exquisite *netsuke* (carved pieces of ivory and wood). There are also temporary exhibitions that are usually worth seeing.

Your ticket also covers the fascinating 25-minute documentary, *Nelson Mandela: A Righteous Man*, screened in the building across the courtyard from the museum's exit. Upstairs, the **Cape Town Holocaust Centre** (Map p84; 021-462 5553; www.holocaust.org.za) packs a lot in with a considerable emotional punch; the history of anti-Semitism is set in a South African context with parallels drawn to the local struggle for freedom. Also take time to view the functioning and beautifully decorated **Great Synagogue** (Map p84; 021-465 1405; www.gardensshul.org; tours 10am-4pm Sun-Thu), a 1905 building in neo-Egyptian style.

WOODSTOCK & OBSERVATORY GALLERIES

A good reason for heading to Woodstock and Observatory are to check out the many commercial galleries here. All put on interesting shows and there's no pressure to buy.

Greatmore Studios (Map p80; ☎021-447 9699; www.greatmoreart.org; 47-49 Greatmore St, Woodstock; ⏰9am-5pm Mon-Fri; Lawley) This pioneer of the Woodstock art scene provides studio space for local artists and visiting overseas artists, with the idea of providing skills transfer and cross-cultural stimulation of ideas and creativity. Visitors are welcome to stroll around and there are occasionally group exhibitions held.

Goodman Gallery Cape (Map p80; ☎021-462 7573; www.goodman-gallery.com; 3rd fl, Fairweather House, 176 Sir Lowry Rd, Woodstock; ⏰9.30am-5.30pm Tue-Fri, to 4pm Sat; District Six) A big gun of the Jo'burg art world, the Goodman Gallery was one of the few to encourage artists of all races during apartheid. They represent luminaries like William Kentridge and David Goldblatt, as well as up-and-coming artists.

The entrance to the main gallery is around the back of the building, while at the front is a new space showcasing video art.

Stevenson (Map p80; ☎021-462 1500; www.stevenson.info; 160 Sir Lowry Rd, Woodstock; ⏰9am-5pm Mon-Fri, 10am-1pm Sat; District Six) Exhibitions at this well-respected gallery have included the humorous, subversive work of Anton Kannemeyer, also known as Joe Dog, creator of the darkly satiric comic Bitterkomix with Conrad Botes; and the wonderful photographer Zanele Muholi. You can also browse pieces of the distinctive ceramic art of Hylton Nel.

AHEM! Art Collective (Map p114; ☎071 585 3423; www.ahemartcollective.com; 77 Lower Main Rd, Observatory; ⏰9am-5pm; Observatory) Shining a light on the graphic art and illustration talents of local artists, as well as importing some great pieces from France and elsewhere, this gallery/cafe/co-working space is at the vanguard of Obs' arty revival. Works are affordable and exhibitions change regularly.

There are plans to provide basic overnight accommodation in the gallery for R300 per person: contact them for further details.

South African Print Gallery (Map p80; ☎021-462 6851; http://printgallery.co.za; 109 Sir Lowry Rd, Woodstock; ⏰9.30am-4pm Tue-Fri, 10am-1pm Sat; District Six) Specialising in prints by local artists – both established and up-and-coming – and likely to have something that is both affordable and small enough to fit comfortably in your suitcase for transport home.

Also within the compound is the kosher **Café Riteve** (Map p84; ☎021-465 1594; http://caferiteve.co.za; 88 Hatfield St, Gardens; mains R60-90; ⏰8.30am-5pm Sun-Thu, to 3pm Fri; ; Annandale) and a gift shop.

Signal Hill VIEWPOINT

(Map p90; Kloof Nek) The early settlement's lookout point is so named because it was from here that flags were hoisted when a ship was spotted, giving the people below time to prepare goods for sale and dust off their tankards. Walk, cycle or drive to the summit, which is part of Table Mountain National Park, by taking the first turn-off to the right off Kloof Nek Rd onto Military Rd.

South African National Gallery GALLERY

(Map p84; ☎021-481 3970; www.iziko.org.za/museums/south-african-national-gallery; Government Ave, Gardens; adult/child R30/15; ⏰10am-5pm; Annandale) The impressive permanent collection of the nation's premier art space harks back to Dutch times and includes some extraordinary pieces. But it's often contemporary works, such as the *Butcher Boys* sculpture by Jane Alexander – looking rather like a trio of Tolkienesque orcs who have stumbled into the gallery – that stand out the most.

Also note the remarkable teak door in the courtyard, carved by Herbert Vladimir Meyerowitz, with scenes representing the global wanderings of the Jews; his carvings also adorn the tops of the door frames throughout the gallery.

Observatory

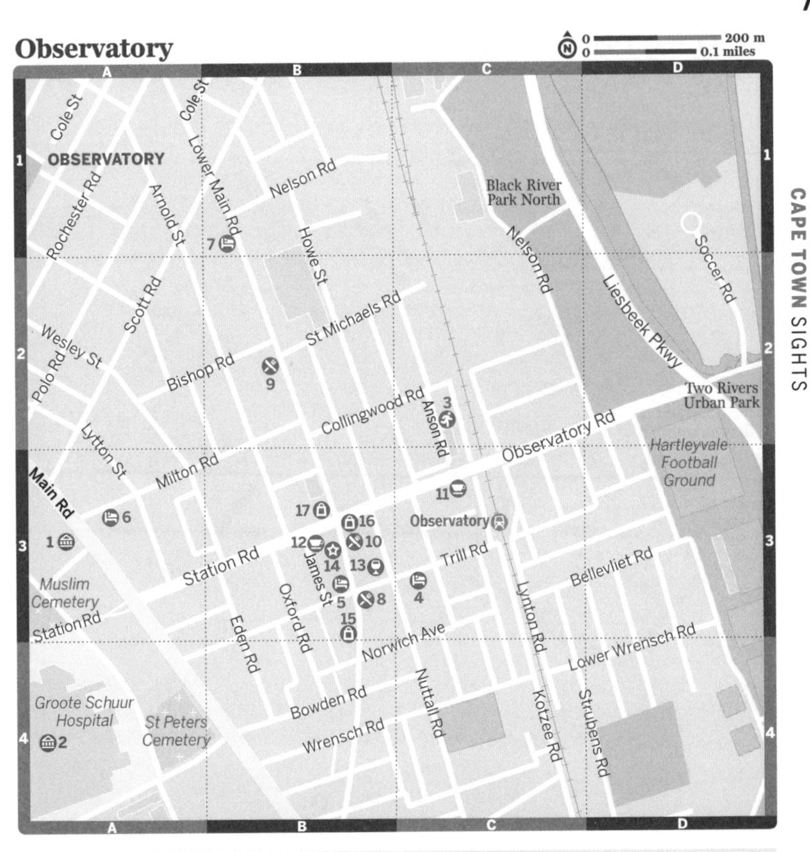

Observatory

Sights
1 Cape Town Science Centre A3
2 Heart of Cape Town Museum A4

Activities, Courses & Tours
3 City Rock C2

Sleeping
4 33 South Backpackers C3
5 Bohemian Lofts Backpackers B3
6 Green Elephant A3
7 Observatory Backpackers B1

Eating
8 Café Ganesh B3
9 Ferdinando's B2
10 Hello Sailor B3

Drinking & Nightlife
11 Drawing Room Cafe C3
12 Saint James B3
13 Touch of Madness B3

Entertainment
14 Obviouzly Armchair B3

Shopping
15 AHEM! Art Collective B3
16 Black Chillie Style B3
17 Mnandi Textiles & Design B3

South African Museum MUSEUM
(Map p84; 021-481 3800; www.iziko.org.za/museums/south-african-museum; 25 Queen Victoria St, Gardens; adult/child R30/15; 10am-5pm; Michaelis) South Africa's oldest museum was undergoing renovations at the time of research, so some galleries were closed. The museum contains a wide and often intriguing series of exhibitions, many on the country's natural history. Look out for an amazing example of San rock art – there's an extraordinary delicacy to the

East City, District Six, Woodstock & Salt River

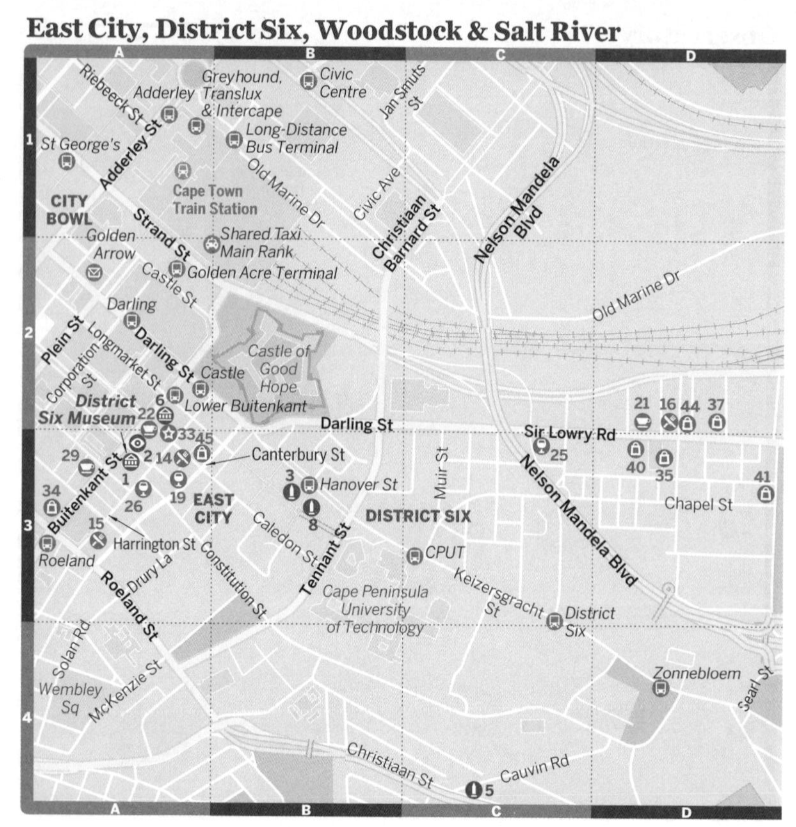

paintings, particularly the ones of graceful elands. Another highlight is a 2m-wide nest – a veritable avian apartment block – of the sociable weaver bird, in the Wonders of Nature Gallery.

The atmospheric Whale Well is hung with giant whale skeletons and models, and resounds with taped recordings of their calls. The terracotta Lydenburg Heads, the earliest-known examples of African sculpture (AD 500–700) are currently removed from the African Cultures Gallery, which is undergoing a major revamp.

Rust en Vreugd GALLERY, GARDEN

(Map p84; ☎021-467 7205; www.iziko.org.za; 78 Buitenkant St, Gardens; adult/child R20/10; ⊙10am-5pm Mon-Fri; Roeland) This delightful mansion, dating from 1777–78 and fronted by a period-style garden (recreated in 1986 from the original layout), was once the home of the state prosecutor. It now houses part of the Iziko William Fehr collection of paintings and furniture (the major part is in the Castle of Good Hope); you may see detailed lithographs of Zulus by George Angus and a delicately painted watercolour panorama of Table Mountain (from 1850) by Lady Eyre.

TABLE MOUNTAIN FRAMES

A legacy of Cape Town's World Design Capital program are the **Table Mountain Frames**. Giant, bright-yellow metal frames are sited at various locations, including Signal Hill, the V&A Waterfront, Eden on the Bay in Bloubergstrand, on Harrington St beside **Charly's Bakery** (p144) cafe in District Six, and Lookout Hill in Khayelitsha. Sponsored by Table Mountain Cableway, they have proved to be popular, with visitors uploading photos to an online gallery (www.tablemountain.net/galleries).

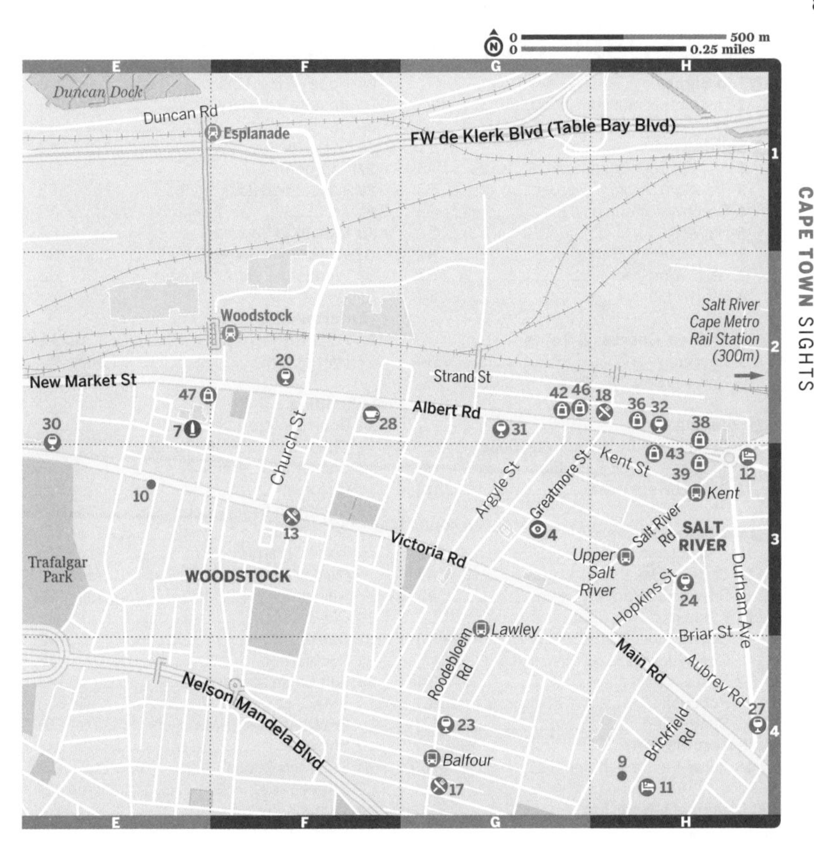

South African Planetarium PLANETARIUM
(Map p84; ☎021-481 3800; www.iziko.org.za/museums/planetarium; 25 Queen Victoria St, Gardens; adult/child R60/30; ⏲2pm Mon-Fri; 🚌Michaelis) The displays and star shows here unravel the mysteries of the southern hemisphere's night sky using images caught by the Southern African Large Telescope (in the Karoo region), which is one of the largest telescopes in the world. Call ahead or check the website for additional show times.

The Planetarium is attached to the South African Museum.

Green Point & Waterfront

Set aside a couple of days to explore the many facets of the V&A Waterfront. Quite apart from shopping and places to eat, drink and stay, this still-functioning harbour has some top sights and attractions including Nelson Mandela Gateway (p64), from where boats to Robben Island (p64) depart, and the dazzling Zeitz MOCAA Museum (p66) in the former grain silo.

The outcrop of largely open land west of the Waterfront is Green Point, where you'll find Cape Town Stadium and the excellent Green Point Urban Park. The area also includes rocky Mouille Point – right on the Atlantic coast and an atmospheric place for a seaside stroll or sunset cocktails and a meal.

★V&A Waterfront AREA
(Map p86; ☎021-408 7500; www.waterfront.co.za; P; 🚌Nobel Sq) This historic working harbour has a spectacular setting and many tourist-oriented attractions, including masses of shops, restaurants, bars, cinemas and cruises. The Alfred and Victoria Basins date from 1860 and are named after Queen Victoria and her son Alfred. Too small for modern container vessels and tankers, the Victoria

East City, District Six, Woodstock & Salt River

Top Sights
1 District Six Museum A3

Sights
2 A4 Arts Foundation A3
3 Freedom Struggle Heroes B3
4 Greatmore Studios G3
5 Harvest C4
6 Homecoming Centre A2
7 I Art Woodstock E2
8 Land & Liberty B3

Activities, Courses & Tours
9 Beerguevara H4
10 New Harbour Distillery E3

Sleeping
11 DoubleTree by Hilton Hotel Cape Town – Upper Eastside H4
12 Wish U Were Here H3

Eating
13 Andalousse F3
14 Charly's Bakery A3
15 Downtown Ramen A3
16 Kitchen D2
Lefty's .... (see 15)
Ocean Jewels .... (see 47)
17 Pesce Azzurro G4
Pot Luck Club .... (see 36)
Superette .... (see 47)
Test Kitchen .... (see 36)
18 Three Feathers Diner H2

Drinking & Nightlife
19 Babylon A3
20 Brewers Co-op F2
Espressolab Microroasters .... (see 36)
Field Office .... (see 47)
21 Flat Mountain D2
22 Haas A2
23 Hidden Leaf G4
24 Hope on Hopkins H3
Rosetta Roastery .... (see 47)
25 Stardust C3
26 SurfaRosa A3
27 Taproom H4
28 Tribe Woodstock F2
29 Truth A3
30 Ukhamba Beerworx E2
31 Woodstock Brewery G2
32 Woodstock Gin Company H2

Entertainment
33 Fugard Theatre A3
Harringtons .... (see 26)

Shopping
34 Book Lounge A3
Chapel .... (see 47)
Clementina Ceramics .... (see 36)
Cocofair .... (see 36)
35 Goodman Gallery Cape D3
Grandt Mason Originals .... (see 47)
Imiso Ceramics .... (see 36)
Mü & Me .... (see 36)
Neighbourgoods Market .... (see 36)
36 Old Biscuit Mill H2
37 One of a Kind D2
38 Recreate H2
39 Salt Circle Arcade H3
SMAC .... (see 30)
South African Print Gallery .... (see 16)
40 Stevenson D3
41 Stockton Goods D3
Streetwires .... (see 43)
42 Threads Project G2
43 Vamp H3
44 Welkin Supply Store D2
45 Woodhead's A3
46 Woodstock Co-op G2
Woodstock Cycleworks .... (see 41)
47 Woodstock Exchange E2

Basin is still used by tugs, fishing boats and various other vessels. In the Alfred Basin you'll see ships under repair.

Two Oceans Aquarium AQUARIUM

(Map p86; ☎021-418 3823; www.aquarium.co.za; Dock Rd, V&A Waterfront; adult/student/child R165/120/80; ⏰9.30am-6pm; 👪; 🚌Aquarium) This excellent aquarium features denizens of the deep from the cold and the warm oceans that border the Cape Peninsula. It's a chance to see penguins, turtles, an astounding kelp forest open to the sky, and pools in which kids can touch sea creatures. Qualified divers can get into the water for a closer look (R870 including dive gear).

Get your hand stamped on entry and you can return any time during the same day for free.

Green Point Urban Park PARK

(Map p86; www.gprra.co.za/green-point-urban-park.html; Bay Rd, Green Point; tour adult/child R35/11; ⏰7am-7pm; 🅿; 🚌Stadium) One of the best things to come out of the redevelopment of Green Point Common for the 2010 World Cup is this park and biodiversity garden. Streams fed by Table Mountain's springs and rivers water the park, which has three imaginatively designed areas – People & Plants, Wetlands and Discovering Biodiversity – that, along with educational information boards, act as the best kind of outdoor museum. Guided tours of the park can be arranged through Cape Town Stadium.

As well as the many types of fynbos (literally 'fine bush' – primarily proteas, heaths and ericas) and other indigenous plants, you can see an example of the kind of structure that the Khoe-San used to live in, and spot beautifully made beaded animals, insects and birds among the flower beds. There's plenty of space for picnics with brilliant views of the stadium, Signal Hill and Lion's Head, and two kids' play parks (one for toddlers and one for older kids).

Cape Town Stadium STADIUM

(Map p86; 021-417 0120; www.capetown.gov.za/capetownstadium/home; Granger Bay Blvd, Green Point; tours adult/child R45/17; tours 10am, noon & 2pm Tue-Sat; P; Stadium) Shaped like a giant traditional African hat and wrapped with a Teflon-mesh membrane designed to catch and reflect natural light, this R4.5-billion stadium, built for the 2010 World Cup, is Cape Town's most striking piece of contemporary architecture. The hour-long tours will take you behind the scenes into the VIP and press boxes and the teams' dressing rooms.

The 55,000-capacity stadium is home ground for the soccer team Ajax Cape Town, and has been used for big pop concerts by the likes of Coldplay and U2, as well as a memorial service for Nelson Mandela.

Across from the new stadium, a section of the old Green Point Stadium forms the viewing platform for a running and cycling track.

Chavonnes Battery Museum MUSEUM

(Map p86; 021-416 6230; www.chavonnesbattery.co.za; Clock Tower Precinct, V&A Waterfront; R70; 9am-4pm; Nobel Square) This museum houses the remains of an early-18th-century cannon battery, one of several fortifications the Dutch built around Table Bay. Although it had been partly demolished and covered over during the construction of the docks in 1860, an excavation of the site in 1999 revealed the remains. You can walk around the entire site and get a good feel for what it would have originally been like.

The Springbok Experience MUSEUM

(Map p86; 021-418 4741; www.sarugby.co.za; Portswood House, V&A Waterfront; adult/child R75/50; 9am-5pm Tue-Sun; ; Nobel Sq) You don't have to be rugby crazy to enjoy this attraction, which celebrates the history of rugby in South Africa and, in particular, the trials and triumphs of the national team, the Springboks. There are several interactive displays (one purports to show whether you'd make the grade as a Springbok player), and the historical aspects – including the international boycotts of the team during apartheid – are covered in detail.

Adults get a voucher with their entrance ticket for a free pint of lager in a nearby restaurant.

Cape Wheel FERRIS WHEEL

(Map p86; 021-418 2502; www.capewheel.co.za; Market Sq, V&A Waterfront; adult/child R130/60; 10am-10.30pm; Nobel Square) What was supposed to be a temporary attraction at the Waterfront has proved so popular that it's been made a permanent fixture. Your ticket

WORTH A TRIP

ORANJEZICHT CITY FARM

In 1709, 'Oranje Zigt' – the original farm on the upper slopes of Table Mountain – was established. By the early 20th century, the once large farm had disappeared, swallowed up by urban development, leaving the small **Homestead Park** (Map p88; Upper Orange St, Oranjezicht; Upper Orange) FREE with its historic farmhouse and a section of old stone wall. There was also an unused bowling green that was inhabited by vagrants. In 2013 local residents and other volunteers began to transform the bowling green into the **Oranjezicht City Farm** (OZCF; Map p88; 083 508 1066; www.ozcf.co.za; Upper Orange St, Oranjezicht; 8am-4pm Mon-Fri, to 1pm Sat; Upper Orange) FREE. You are free to wander around this beautifully designed but functional space and rest on the benches, which provide sweeping views of Table Bay. Guided tours can also be arranged: see the website for details.

The farm's produce and that of other small Western Cape farms is sold at the **OZCF Market Day** (p177), a highlight of the Capetonian week. The organisers are embarking on creating another urban farm in nearby Vredehoek, which will be double the size of the OZCF and include a new high school where there will be lessons on farming and food security.

Gardens & Tamboerskloof

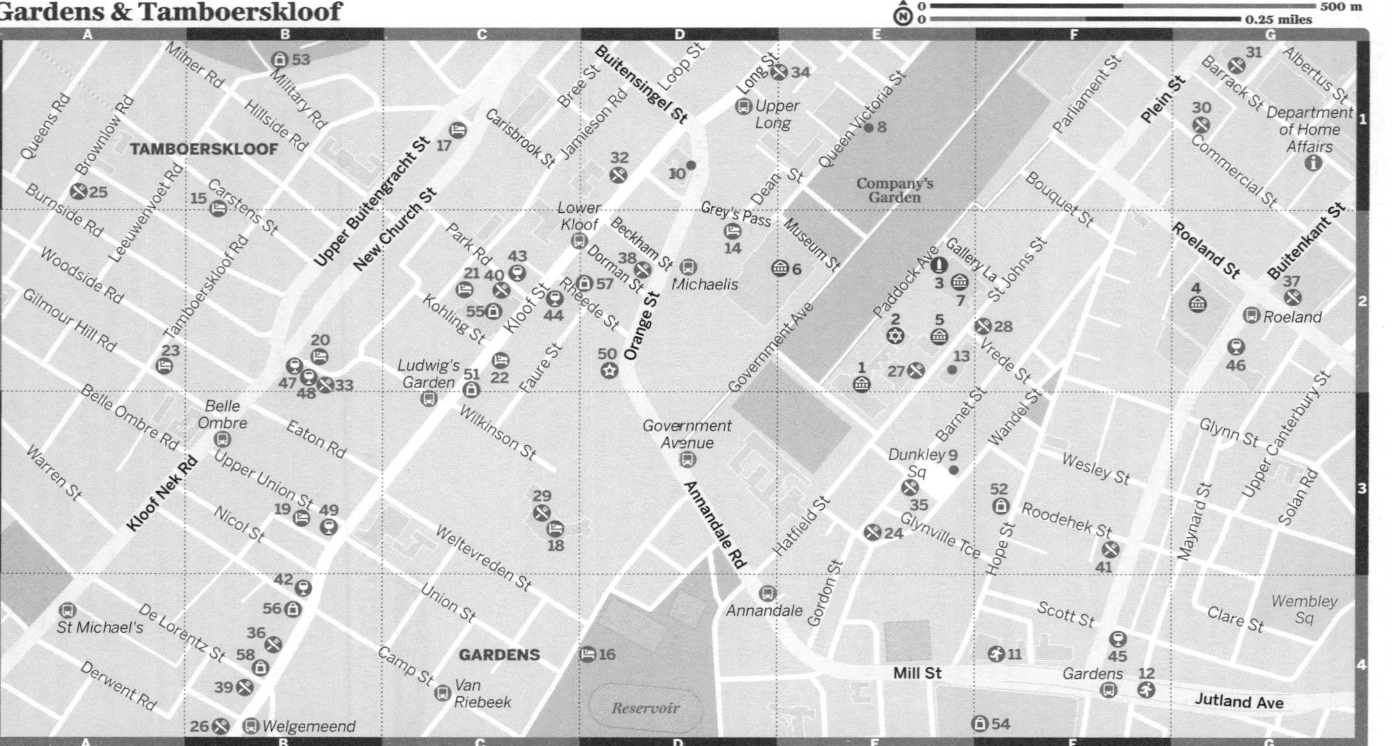

Gardens & Tamboerskloof

Sights
1 Cape Town Holocaust Centre E2
2 Great Synagogue E2
3 Jan Smuts Statue E2
4 Rust en Vreugd G2
5 South African Jewish Museum E2
6 South African Museum E2
7 South African National Gallery E2
South African Planetarium .... (see 6)

Activities, Courses & Tours
8 Cape Town Fynbos Experience E1
9 Coffeebeans Routes E3
10 Downhill Adventures D1
11 Enmasse F4
12 Mill St Bridge Skate Park F4
13 Mountain Club of South Africa E2

Sleeping
14 15 on Orange D2
15 An African Villa B1
16 Ashanti Gardens D4
17 Backpack C1
18 Belmond Mount Nelson Hotel C3
19 Cape Cadogan B3
20 Cloud 9 .... B2
21 La Grenadine C2
22 Once in Cape Town C2
23 Trevoyan A2

Eating
24 Aubergine E3
25 Blue Cafe A1
26 Cafe Paradiso B4
27 Café Riteve E2
28 Chefs F2
29 Chef's Table C3
30 City Bowl Health Kitchen G1
31 Cousins G1
32 Kloof St House D1
33 Kyoto Garden Sushi B2
34 Lucy Ethiopian Restaurant E1
35 Maria's E3
36 Melissa's B4
37 Raptor Room G2
38 Societi Bistro D2
39 Tamboers Winkel B4
40 Thali C2
41 Yard F3

Drinking & Nightlife
42 Asoka B4
43 Cause Effect C2
44 Chalk & Cork C2
45 Deluxe Coffeeworks F4
46 Perseverance Tavern G2
47 Power & the Glory/Black Ram B2
48 Publik B2
The Sorrows .... (see 20)
The Vic .... (see 56)
Tiger's Milk .... (see 44)
49 Van Hunks B3
Yours Truly Cafe & Bar .... (see 22)

Entertainment
50 Labia D2

Shopping
AKJP Collective .... (see 22)
51 Ashanti C2
Bluecollarwhitecollar .... (see 55)
52 City Bowl Market F3
53 Erf 81 Market B1
54 Gardens Centre F4
55 Lifestyles on Kloof C2
56 LIM B4
57 Mabu Vinyl D2
58 Mr & Mrs B4
Wine Concepts .... (see 55)

gives you four spins (lasting around 15 minutes in total) on this 40m-tall Ferris wheel, with a bird's-eye view of the surroundings.

For R240 per person you can also take an extended ride of 30 minutes, that includes a picnic of your choice.

Nobel Square SQUARE
(Map p86; www.nobelsquare.com; V&A Waterfront; Nobel Square) Here's your chance to have your photo taken with Desmond Tutu and Nelson Mandela. Larger-than-life statues of both men, designed by the artist Claudette Schreuders, stand beside those of two other South African Nobel Prize winners – Nkosi Albert Luthuli and FW de Klerk.

Also here is the *Peace and Democracy* sculpture by Noria Mahasa, which symbolises the contribution of women and children to the struggle. It's etched with pertinent quotes by each of the great men, translated into all the major languages of the country.

Robinson Dry Dock NOTABLE BUILDING
(Map p86; V&A Waterfront; Nobel Square) One of the Waterfront's most fascinating sights is this large dry dock, opened in 1882 and still used to repair ships today. Named after Governor Sir Hercules Robinson, it was used to repair over 300 ships during WWII. The Pump House next to it – now housing a comedy club (p171) and food market (p147) – was used to pump out the water.

Diamond Museum MUSEUM
(Map p86; 021-421 2488; www.capetowndiamondmuseum.org; 1st fl, Clock Tower Shopping Centre, V&A Waterfront; admission R50, free with

Green Point & Waterfront

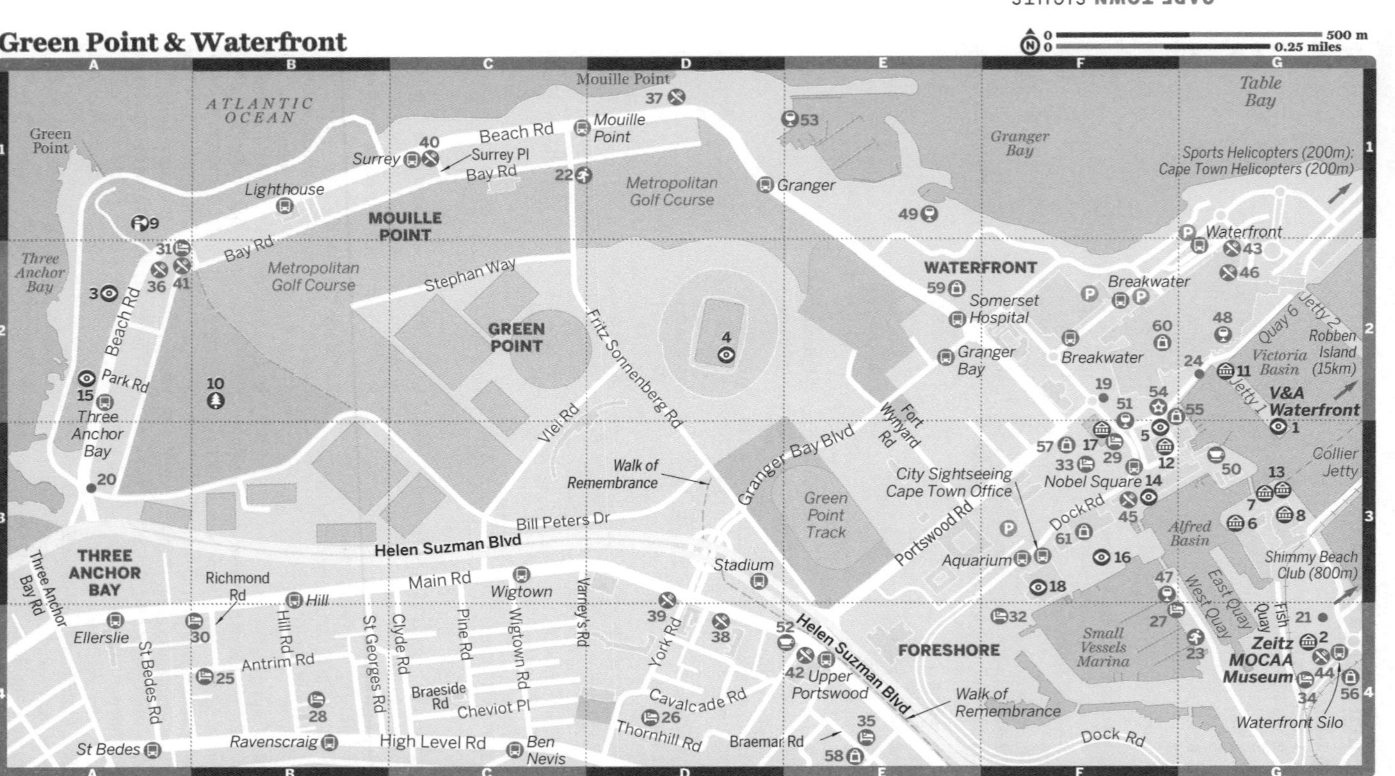

Green Point & Waterfront

Top Sights
1 V&A Waterfront ... G3
2 Zeitz MOCAA Museum ... G4

Sights
3 Blue Train Park ... A2
4 Cape Town Stadium ... D2
5 Cape Wheel ... F3
6 Chavonnes Battery Museum ... G3
7 Clock Tower ... G3
8 Diamond Museum ... G3
9 Green Point Lighthouse ... A1
10 Green Point Urban Park ... B2
11 Jetty 1 ... G2
12 Maritime Centre ... F3
13 Nelson Mandela Gateway ... G3
14 Nobel Square ... F3
15 Putt-Putt Golf ... A2
16 Robinson Dry Dock ... F3
17 The Springbok Experience ... F3
18 Two Oceans Aquarium ... F3

Activities, Courses & Tours
Adrenalised Cape Town ... (see 24)
19 Awol Tours ... F2
20 Kaskazi Kayaks ... A3
21 Lindt Chocolate Studio ... G4
22 Metropolitan Golf Club ... C1
23 Ocean Sailing Academy ... G4
Two Oceans Aquarium ... (see 18)
24 Waterfront Charters ... G2
Yacoob Tourism ... (see 24)

Sleeping
25 Ashanti Green Point ... B4
26 B.I.G. Backpackers ... D4
27 Cape Grace ... F4
28 Cape Standard ... B4
29 Dock House ... F3
30 Head South Lodge ... B4
31 La Splendida ... A2
32 One&Only Cape Town ... F4
33 Queen Victoria Hotel ... F3
34 Radisson Red ... G4
Silo Hotel ... (see 2)
35 Villa Zest ... E4

Eating
36 Café Neo ... A2
37 Cape Town Hotel School ... D1
38 El Burro ... D4
39 Giovanni's Deli World ... D3
Harbour House ... (see 55)
40 Lily's ... C1
41 Newport Market & Deli ... A2
Nobu ... (see 32)
42 Nü ... E4
43 Tashas ... G2
44 The Yard ... G4
45 V&A Food Market ... F3
46 Willoughby & Co ... G2

Drinking & Nightlife
47 Bascule ... F3
48 Belthazar ... G2
Cabrito ... (see 38)
49 Grand Africa Café & Beach ... E1
50 Life Grand Cafe ... G3
51 Mitchell's Scottish Ale House ... F3
52 Shift ... E4
Sotano ... (see 31)
53 Tobago's Bar & Terrace ... E1
Vista Bar & Lounge ... (see 32)

Entertainment
Cape Town Comedy Club ... (see 45)
Galileo Open Air Cinema ... (see 29)
54 Market Square Amphitheatre ... F2

Shopping
55 Cape Union Mart Adventure Centre ... F2
56 Donald Greig Gallery & Foundry ... G4
57 Everard Read ... F3
Guild ... (see 34)
58 Out of this World ... E4
59 OZCF Market Day ... E2
Shimansky ... (see 8)
60 Victoria Wharf ... F2
61 Watershed ... F3

Information
V&A Waterfront Visitor Information Centre ... (see 51)

voucher from website; 9am-9pm; Waterfront Silo) Really an extended sales pitch for the bling on sale in the attached Shimansky Jewellers (p180), the displays at this museum have nonetheless been put together with some style and imagination. There's no obligation to buy, and you can learn a lot about diamonds and how their discovery contributed to the wealth of South Africa.

The guided tours (last one at 7.30pm) are led by one of the sales staff, who will point out replicas of famous rocks such as the Hope and the Taylor-Burton diamonds.

Green Point Lighthouse LIGHTHOUSE

(Map p86; 100 Beach Rd, Mouille Point; P; Three Anchor Bay) Often mistakenly called Mouille Point Lighthouse (the remains of which are in the grounds of the nearby Cape Town Hotel School), this red-and-white candy-striped beacon dates back to 1824 and makes a striking landmark.

Outside on the grassy common beside the Mouille Point Promenade are a variety of attractions that will appeal to families, including a playground, **Putt-Putt Golf** (admission R25; 9am-9pm) and the

Higgovale, Oranjezicht & Upper Tamboerskloof

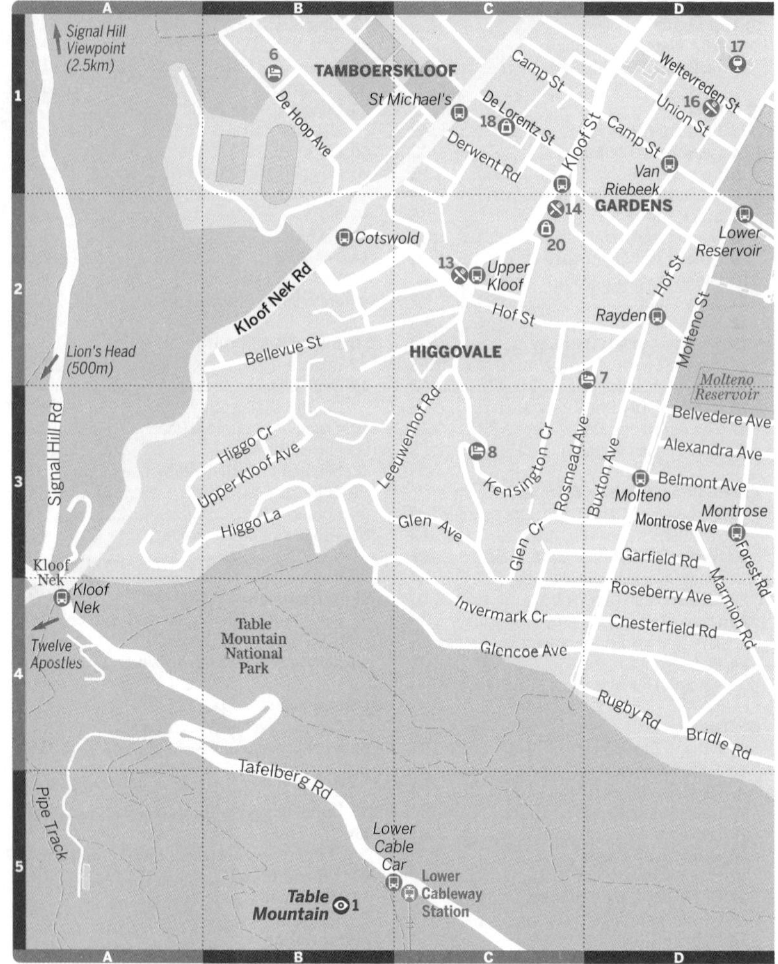

child-sized locomotive of the **Blue Train** (Map p86; ☎084-314 9200; www.thebluetrainpark.com; Erf 1141/1061; admission R25; ⏲9.30am-6pm Tue-Sun) amusement park.

Clock Tower HISTORIC BUILDING

(Map p86; Clock Tower Precinct, V&A Waterfront; Nobel Square) This red-and-grey Victorian Gothic–style building, dating from 1882, is from where the harbour master used to control the comings and goings in the docks.

Maritime Centre MUSEUM

(Map p86; ☎021-405 2880; www.iziko.org.za/museums/maritime-centre; 1st fl, Union-Castle House, Dock Rd, V&A Watefront; adult/child R20/10; ⏲10am-5pm; Nobel Square) This small museum, stocked with model ships, houses the **John H Marsh Maritime Research Centre** (www.rapidttp.co.za/museum), a resource for those interested in South Africa's maritime history. The main exhibit is about the ill-fated voyage of the *Mendi*, which sank in the English Channel in 1917, taking 607 black troops to a watery grave.

Higgovale, Oranjezicht & Upper Tamboerskloof

Top Sights
1 Table Mountain B5

Sights
2 Homestead Park E3
3 Oranjezicht City Farm E3

Activities, Courses & Tours
4 Run Cape Town F3

Sleeping
5 Abbey Manor E3
6 Blencathra B1
7 Four Rosmead D2
8 Kensington Place C3
9 Mannabay E5
10 Platteklip Wash House F5

Eating
11 Deer Park Café F4
12 Lazari F2
13 Liquorice & Lime C2
14 Manna Epicure C2
15 Spirit Cafe E1
16 The Stack D1

Drinking & Nightlife
17 Mount Nelson Lounge D1

Shopping
18 Handmade by Me C1
19 Roastin' Records E1
20 Stefania Morland C2

Jetty 1 MUSEUM

(Map p86; V&A Waterfront; 7am-9pm; Nobel Sq) FREE Preserved as a small museum is the Waterfront's Jetty 1, from where boats sailed to Robben Island when it was a prison. You can view the tiny holding cells here (similar to the cells on the island), with hard beds and empty benches in the waiting room. On the walls are copies of applications for visitors' permits.

Sea Point to Hout Bay

Long popular with Cape Town's Jewish, gay and Chinese communities, Sea Point sports numerous art deco apartment blocks, lending it an almost Miami Beach–like elegance. Main and Regent Rds form its commercial spine, lined with many good restaurants, cafes and shops. Don't miss a wander along Sea Point Promenade (p96), a local ritual especially at sunset and weekends.

Moving south, you'll find prime beach territory: the exclusive and wealthy residential neighbourhoods of Bantry Bay, Clifton and Camps Bay follow hard and fast on each other in a tumble of mansions with to-die-for sea views. These are areas to hit the beach or beautiful-people-watch on a cafe terrace.

Sea Point

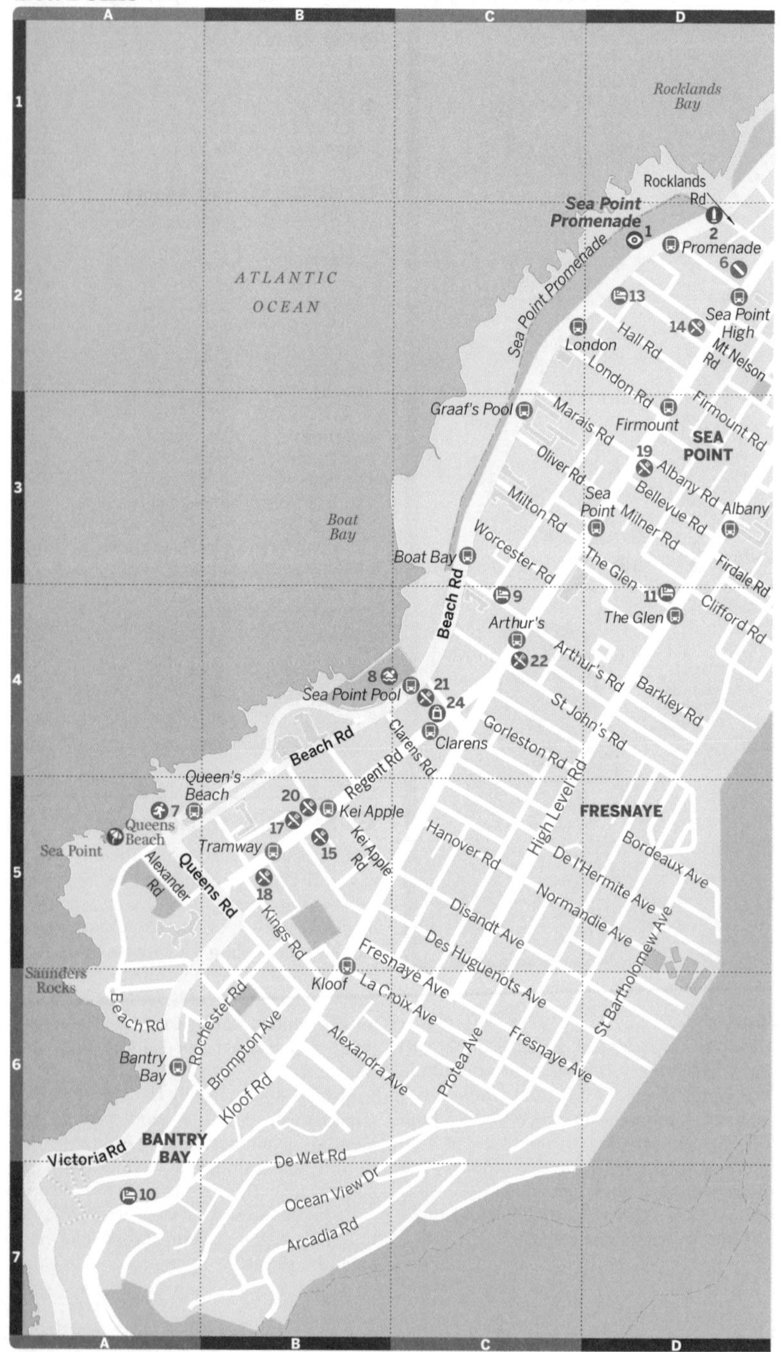
ATLANTIC OCEAN
Rocklands Bay
Rocklands Rd
Sea Point Promenade
Promenade
Sea Point High
London
Hall Rd
London Rd
Mt Nelson Rd
Firmount Rd
Graaf's Pool
Marais Rd
Firmount
SEA POINT
Oliver Rd
Albany Rd
Sea Point
Bellevue Rd
Albany
Milton Rd
Milner Rd
Boat Bay
Worcester Rd
The Glen
Firdale Rd
Beach Rd
Clifford Rd
Arthur's
Arthur's Rd
Barkley Rd
Sea Point Pool
St John's Rd
Gorleston Rd
Clarens Rd
Clarens
Regent Rd
High Level Rd
Queen's Beach
Kei Apple
FRESNAYE
Queens Beach
Tramway
Kei Apple Rd
Hanover Rd
Bordeaux Ave
Sea Point
Alexander Rd
Queens Rd
De l'Hermite Ave
Normandie Ave
Disandt Ave
Kings Rd
Des Huguenots Ave
St Bartholomew Ave
Saunders Rocks
Fresnaye Ave
Kloof
La Croix Ave
Beach Rd
Rochester Rd
Brompton Ave
Alexandra Ave
Protea Ave
Bantry Bay
Kloof Rd
BANTRY BAY
Victoria Rd
De Wet Rd
Ocean View Dr
Arcadia Rd

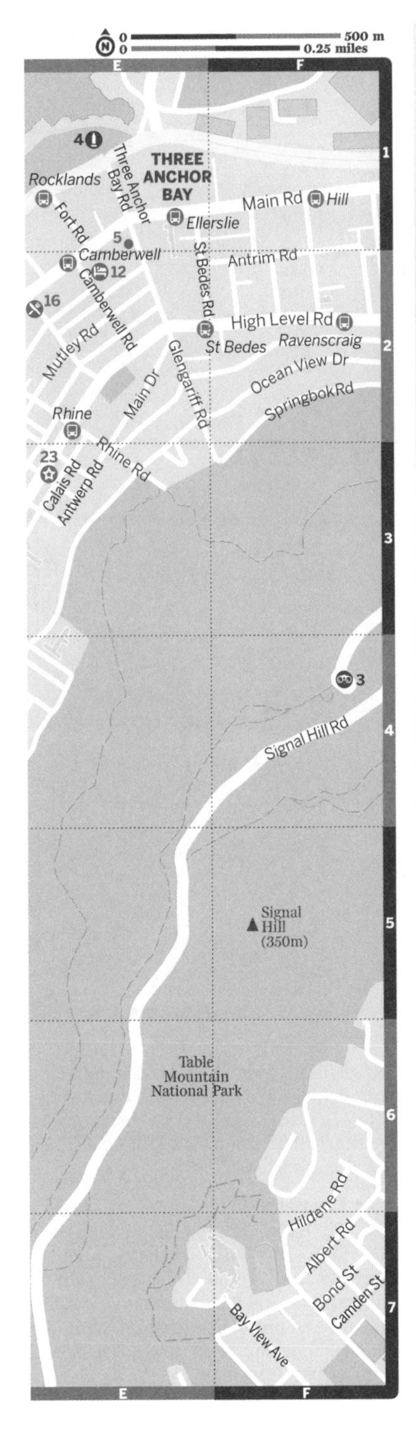

Sea Point

Top Sights

1 Sea Point Promenade D2

Sights

2 Promenade Pets D2
3 Signal Hill F4
4 White Horses E1

Activities, Courses & Tours

5 Cape Sidecar Adventures E1
6 Into the Blue D2
7 Promenade Mondays A5
8 Sea Point Pavilion B4

Sleeping

9 Cascades on the Promenade C4
10 Ellerman House A7
11 Glen Boutique Hotel D4
12 Ritz Hotel E2
13 Winchester Mansions Hotel D2

Eating

14 Duchess of Wisbeach D2
15 Fuego B5
Harvey's .... (see 13)
16 Hesheng E2
17 Jarryds Espresso Bar & Eatery B5
18 Kleinsky's Delicatessen B5
19 La Boheme Wine Bar & Bistro D3
20 La Mouette B5
21 La Perla C4
22 Nü C4

Entertainment

23 Studio 7 Sessions E3

Shopping

24 Mojo Market C4

Follow coastal Victoria Rd over the pass beside Little Lion's Head (436m) to drop down into the fishing community of Hout Bay. Its forests are long gone but Hout Bay's stunning geography remains eternal. The natural harbour and horseshoe sweep of white sand nestle between the almost vertical Sentinel and the steep slopes of Chapman's Peak. Take it all in from the viewpoints on Chapman's Peak Dr (p119).

With its township of Imizamo Yethu (also known as Mandela Park) inland, and its coloured district of Hangberg overlooking the harbour, Hout Bay is like a microcosm of South Africa, and is facing common post-apartheid integration challenges. Its village atmosphere and handy location midway along the Cape Peninsula make it a good base for visitors.

Hout Bay

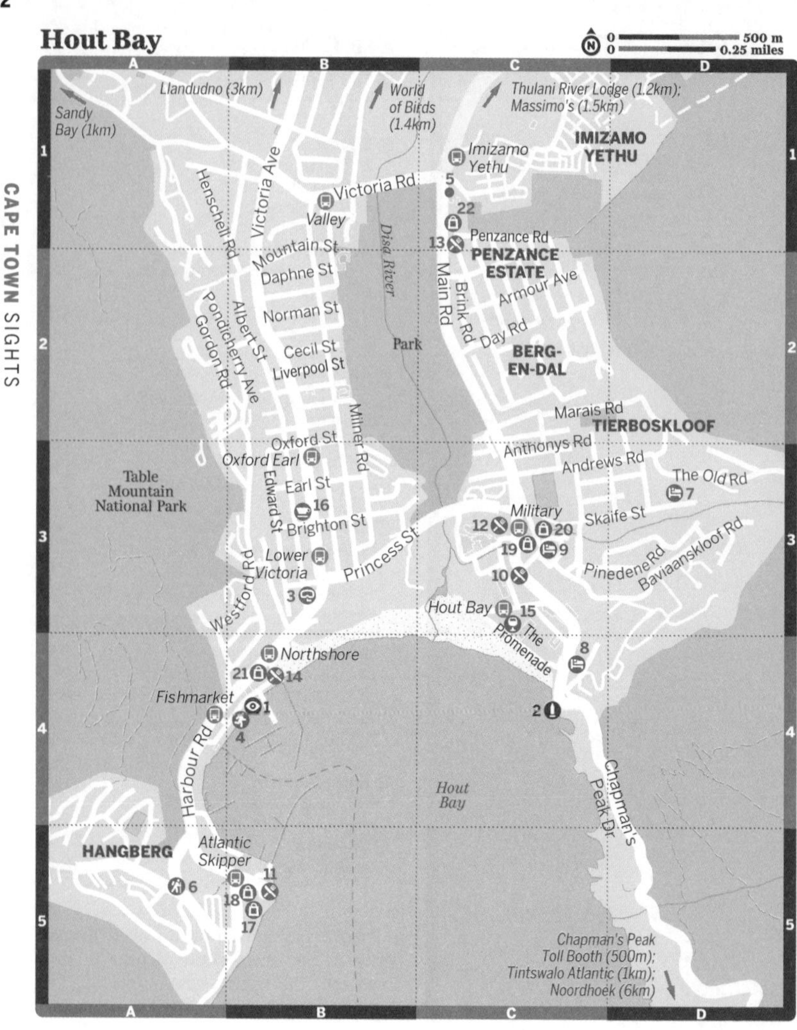

Hout means 'wood' in Afrikaans: Hout Bay is where Cape Town founder Jan van Riebeeck discovered plentiful supplies of timber in the forests that once blanketed the Disa River valley, helping the Dutch East India Company (Vereenigde Oost-Indische Compagnie; VOC) build ships and fortifications including the Castle of Good Hope.

Twelve Apostles MOUNTAIN
(Map p94; Kloof Nek or Dal) The name of the Twelve Apostles is said to have been coined by British governor Sir Rufane Donkin in 1820. There are actually well over 12 buttresses on the sea-facing side of Table Mountain, and none is individually named after an apostle. Called De Gevelbergen (Gable Mountains) by the Dutch, they're best viewed around sunset from Camps Bay Drive.

Hout Bay Harbour HARBOUR
(Map p92; Harbour Rd, Hout Bay) Partly given over to tourism with complexes such as Mariner's Wharf (p150), Hout Bay's harbour still functions and the southern side is a fishing port and processing centre. Cruises and snorkelling/diving trips to Duiker Island (p121) depart from here.

Hout Bay

Sights
1 Hout Bay Harbour B4
2 Leopard Statue C4

Activities, Courses & Tours
3 Animal Ocean B3
Circe Launches (see 4)
Drumbeat Charters (see 4)
4 Duiker Island Cruises B4
5 Imizamo Yethu Tour C1
6 Karbonkelberg Hikers A5
Nautical Charters (see 4)

Sleeping
7 Amblewood Guesthouse D3
8 Chapman's Peak Hotel C4
9 Hout Bay Manor C3

Eating
10 Cheyne's C3
11 Fish on the Rocks B5
12 Hout Bay Coffee C3
13 Kitima C1
14 Mariner's Wharf B4

Drinking & Nightlife
15 Dunes C3
16 Ta Da! B3

Shopping
17 Bay Harbour Market B5
18 Ethno Bongo B5
19 Hout Bay Lions Craft Market C3
20 Iziko Lo Lwazi C3
21 Shipwreck Shop B4
22 T-Bag Designs C1

World of Birds BIRD SANCTUARY
(021-790 2730; www.worldofbirds.org.za; Valley Rd, Hout Bay; adult/child R95/45; 9am-5pm; P; Valley) Barbets, weavers and flamingos are among the 3000 birds and small mammals – covering some 400 different species – at Africa's largest bird park. A real effort has been expended to make the extensive aviaries as natural-looking as possible, with the use of lots of tropical landscaping. In the **monkey jungle** (open 11.30am to 1pm and 2pm to 3.30pm) you can interact with cheeky squirrel monkeys.

The penguins are fed at 11.30am and 3.30pm, the pelicans at 12.30pm, the cormorants at 1.30pm and the birds of prey at 4.15pm. A winner for families, with a cafe (great chips) and sandpit to follow the birdwatching.

Maiden's Cove PARK
(Map p94; off Victoria Rd, Clifton; Maiden's Cove) This coastal parkland on the border of Clifton and Camps Bay is set to receive a billion-rand facelift, which will introduce new boardwalks, braai (barbecue) facilities, an outdoor gym, housing, a hotel, shops and restaurants.

Beaches

Between Sea Point and Hout Bay are a string of beaches each with their own distinctive personality. Before hopping in the sea, remember that the water comes straight from the Antarctic, so swimming here is exhilarating (ie freezing).

Going from north to south, the first beaches you'll encounter are the four at Clifton reached by steps down from Victoria Rd. Vendors hawk drinks and ice creams along the beaches, and sun loungers and shades are available.

Clifton 3rd Beach (Map p94; Victoria Rd, Clifton; Clifton 3rd) is the prettiest of quartet and popular with the Capetonian gay crowd, though plenty of straight folk frequent it, too.

Clifton 4th Beach (Map p94; Victoria Rd, Clifton; Clifton 4th) is the only Blue Flag beach among the four sheltered stretches of sand thus is popular with families. On calm summer evenings, especially the night of Valentine's Day, couples and groups of young people have candlelit picnics on 4th from sunset onwards.

Glen Beach BEACH
(Map p94; off Victoria Rd, Camps Bay; Glen Beach) Escape the crowds on this sheltered stretch of sand, split off from Camps Bay's northern end by boulders. Swimming isn't advised, but if the surf's up this is a popular spot with locals for riding the waves. There's stair access from the main road.

Camps Bay Beach BEACH
(Map p94; Victoria Rd, Camps Bay; Camps Bay) With soft white sand and a backdrop of the spectacular Twelve Apostles range (part of Table Mountain), this Blue Flag beach is one of the city's most popular. However, it has drawbacks: it's one of the windiest beaches here; it gets crowded, particularly on weekends; and the surf is strong. Take care if you do decide to swim.

There's a strip of busy bars and restaurants here, ideal for drinks at sunset or general all-day lounging.

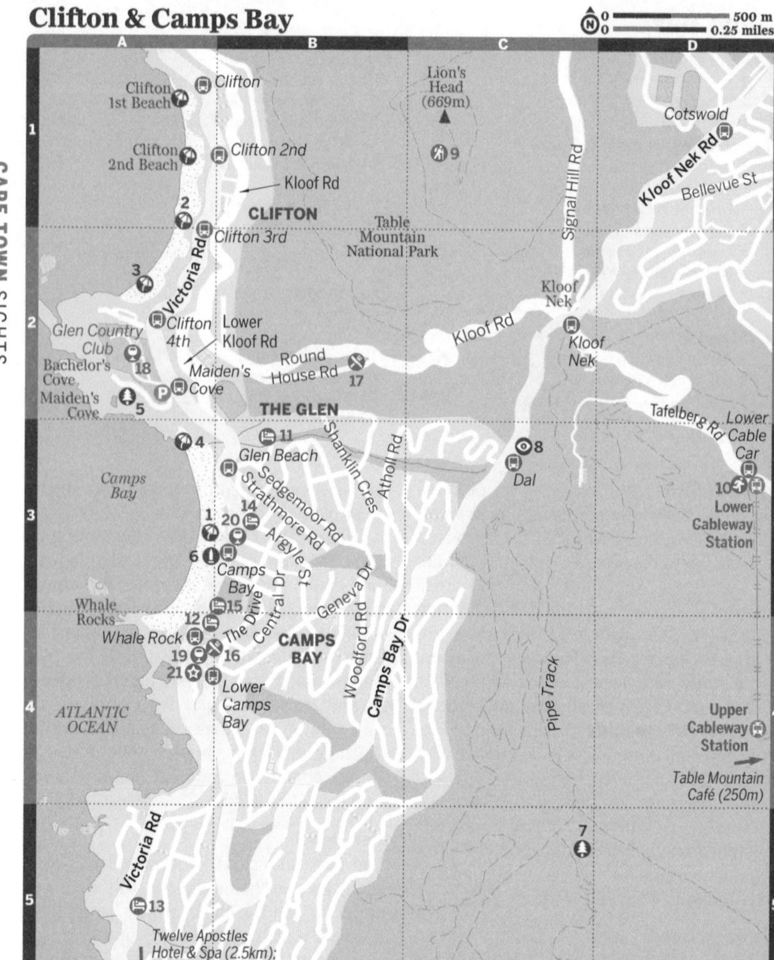

Llandudno Beach BEACH
(Llandudno Rd, Llandudno; P; Llandudno) The exclusive enclave of Llandudno has a giant-boulder-flanked beach that's a beauty. It's a popular spot with families. There's surfing here on the beach breaks (mostly rights), best at high tide with a small swell and a south-easterly wind. Bring a picnic: there are no shops here.

Sandy Bay BEACH
(Llandudno; Llandudno) This particularly beautiful stretch of sandy beach is roughly a 15-minute walk to the south from the Sunset Rocks parking area at Llandudno. As Cape Town's unofficial nudist beach – though there's no pressure to take your clothes off – and is popular with the gay community as a cruising spot. The beach is also of interest to nature lovers, with incredible rock formations and trails through shrubby fynbos (literally 'fine bush'; primarily proteas, heaths and ericas) to explore. Access from Sunset Ave.

Southern Suburbs

If you want to see how the other half of Cape Town lives – the rich half, that is – visit the Southern Suburbs, the residential areas

Clifton & Camps Bay

Sights
1 Camps Bay Beach A3
2 Clifton 3rd Beach A1
3 Clifton 4th Beach A2
4 Glen Beach A3
5 Maiden's Cove A2
6 Royal View A3
7 Table Mountain National Park C5
8 Twelve Apostles C3

Activities, Courses & Tours
9 Lion's Head C1
10 Table Mountain Aerial Cableway D3

Sleeping
11 Camps Bay Retreat B3
12 Marly A4
13 Ocean View House A5
14 POD B3
15 Village & Life B3

Eating
16 Codfather B4
17 Roundhouse B2

Drinking & Nightlife
18 Bungalow A2
19 Dizzy's Restaurant & Pub A4
La Belle .... (see 12)
20 Mynt Cafe B3

Entertainment
21 Theatre on the Bay A4

clinging to the eastern slopes of Table Mountain. Heading south out of the City Bowl on the M3 highway, around Devil's Peak you'll first hit Mowbray and Rondebosch; this is the territory of the University of Cape Town (p103) (UCT), as well as one of Cape Town's premier arts spaces, the Baxter Theatre Centre (p171), and the exotic interiors of the Irma Stern Museum.

Leafy, affluent Newlands and Bishopscourt are where you'll find the area's highlight, Kirstenbosch National Botanical Garden, as well as the city's major cricketing and rugby venues. The area around Claremont Station is a fascinating study in contrasts, with black and coloured traders crowding the streets around the ritzy Cavendish Square mall. It's a similar story in Wynberg, another suburb where the haves rub shoulders with the have-nots. The thatched-roof Cape Georgian homes of **Wynberg Village** (Map p100; around Durban Rd; Wynberg) are worth a look.

Immediately to the west is Constantia, home to South Africa's oldest wineries and where the super-wealthy live in huge mansions behind high walls. It's a verdant area that culminates in Tokai, with its shady forest reserve.

You can cover the Southern Suburbs in a day, with a trip to Kirstenbosch and another sight in the morning, followed by a couple of afternoon wine tastings. With more time available, further explorations might lead up the mountain to the Rhodes Memorial (p103) or along the hiking trails to the historic reservoirs on the Back Table of Table Mountain.

★ Kirstenbosch National Botanical Garden GARDENS

(Map p100; 021-799 8783; www.sanbi.org/gardens/kirstenbosch; Rhodes Dr, Newlands; adult/child R65/15; 8am-7pm Sep-Mar, to 6pm Apr-Aug; P; Kirstenbosch) Location and unique flora combine to make these 52,800-sq-km botanical gardens among the most beautiful in the world. Gate 1, the main entrance at the Newlands end of the gardens, is where you'll find the information centre, an excellent souvenir shop and the **conservatory** (Map p100; 9am-5pm).

Added for the garden's centenary in 2013, the popular **Tree Canopy Walkway** (informally known as the 'Boomslang', meaning tree snake) is a curvaceous steel and timber bridge that rises through the trees and provides amazing views.

The gardens run free guided walks, or you can hire the MyGuide electronic gizmo (R40) to receive recorded information about the various plants you'll pass on the signposted circular walks.

More than 7000 of Southern Africa's 22,000 plant species are grown here, including the Cape Floral Kingdom's famous fynbos (literally, 'fine bush'; primarily proteas, heaths and ericas). You'll find a fragrance garden that has been elevated so you can more easily sample the scents of the plants; a Braille trail; a kopje (hill) planted with pelargoniums; a sculpture garden; a section devoted to 'useful' medicinal plants; two hiking trails up Table Mountain, Skeleton Gorge and Nursery Ravine; and the significant remains of Van Riebeeck's Hedge, the wild almond

DON'T MISS

ART BY THE SEASIDE

Public art is never going to please everyone, but there was a strident outcry in November 2014 when Michael Ellion's **Perceiving Freedom** – a giant metal-and-plastic pair of Ray-Bans – was unveiled on **Sea Point Promenade** (Map p90; Beach Rd, Sea Point; ; Promenade), looking out to Robben Island. Ellion's stated intention was to reference Nelson Mandela, who was once photographed wearing a pair of the iconic sunglasses. Dismissed by the local press as 'corporate vandalism' rather than art, the sculpture was itself vandalised within the month by the guerrilla graffiti group **Tokolos Stencil Collective** (www.facebook.com/tokolosstencils).

Perceiving Freedom was one of several installations by **Art54**, a World Design Capital 2014–endorsed project that was piloted along the Atlantic Seaboard, from Mouille Point to Camps Bay, to increase the city's stock of public art. Some of the works have become permanent fixtures: for example, the **Promenade Pets** (Map p90; Rocklands Beach, Beach Rd, Sea Point; Promenade) benches by Rocklands Beach, which have seats held up by pairs of blue seagulls, black sea lions and pink poodles. At Camps Bay, you can pose like the king and queen of the beach on Greg Benetar's **Royal View** (Map p94; Victoria Rd, Camps Bay; Camps Bay) thrones.

At the Three Anchor Bay end of Sea Point Promenade is Kevin Brand's **White Horses** (Map p90; Beach Rd, Sea Point; Rocklands), which was inspired by the SS *South African Seafarer*'s calamitous visit to Table Bay in 1966. When the ship ran aground, some of its cargo, including some plastic white horses, washed up on the shore nearby. Each of the slightly askew horses sculptures here has a vuvuzela horn in its mouth; speak into one horse and the sound comes out the mouth of another.

hedge planted by Jan van Riebeeck in 1660 to form the boundary of the Dutch outpost.

The outdoor **Summer Sunset Concerts** (Map p100; adult/child from R180/135), held here on Sundays between November and April, are a Cape Town institution. The gardens are a stop on the City Sightseeing (p125) bus. The quiet Gate 3 (aka Rycroft Gate) is the first you'll come to if you approach the gardens up Rhodes Dr from the south. There are three cafes, including the excellent Kirstenbosch Tea Room (p152).

★Groot Constantia MUSEUM, WINERY

(Map p100; 021-794 5128; www.grootconstantia.co.za; Groot Constantia Rd, Constantia; tastings R80, museum adult/child R30/free; tastings 9am-6pm, museum 10am-5pm; P) Simon van der Stel's manor house, a superb example of Cape Dutch architecture, is maintained as a museum at Groot Constantia. Set in beautiful grounds, the estate can become busy with tour groups, but is big enough for you to escape the crowds. The large tasting room is first on your right as you enter the estate. Further on is the free **orientation centre**, which provides an overview of Groot Constantia's history, and the beautifully restored homestead.

The **Cloete Cellar**, with a beautiful moulded pediment, was the estate's original wine cellar. It now houses old carriages and a display of storage vessels. Tours of the modern cellar are also available for R100 including tasting.

You can download two audio-guide apps from Groot Constantia's website and purchase a Visitors Route Experience ticket (R95), which includes a tasting and entrance to the estate's attractions. A wine and chocolate pairing for R125 is another option for visitors.

★Irma Stern Museum MUSEUM

(Map p97; 021-685 5686; www.irmastern.co.za; Cecil Rd, Rosebank; adult/child R10/5; 10am-5pm Tue-Fri, to 2pm Sat; Rosebank) The pioneering 20th-century artist Irma Stern (1894–1966), whose works are some of the most sought-after among modern South African painters, occupied this 19th-century house for almost 40 years. Her studio has been left virtually intact, as if she'd just stepped out into the verdant garden for a breath of fresh air. The flamboyant painter's ethnographic art-and-craft collection from around the world is as fascinating as her own art, which was influenced by German expressionism and incorporates traditional African elements.

Southern Suburbs

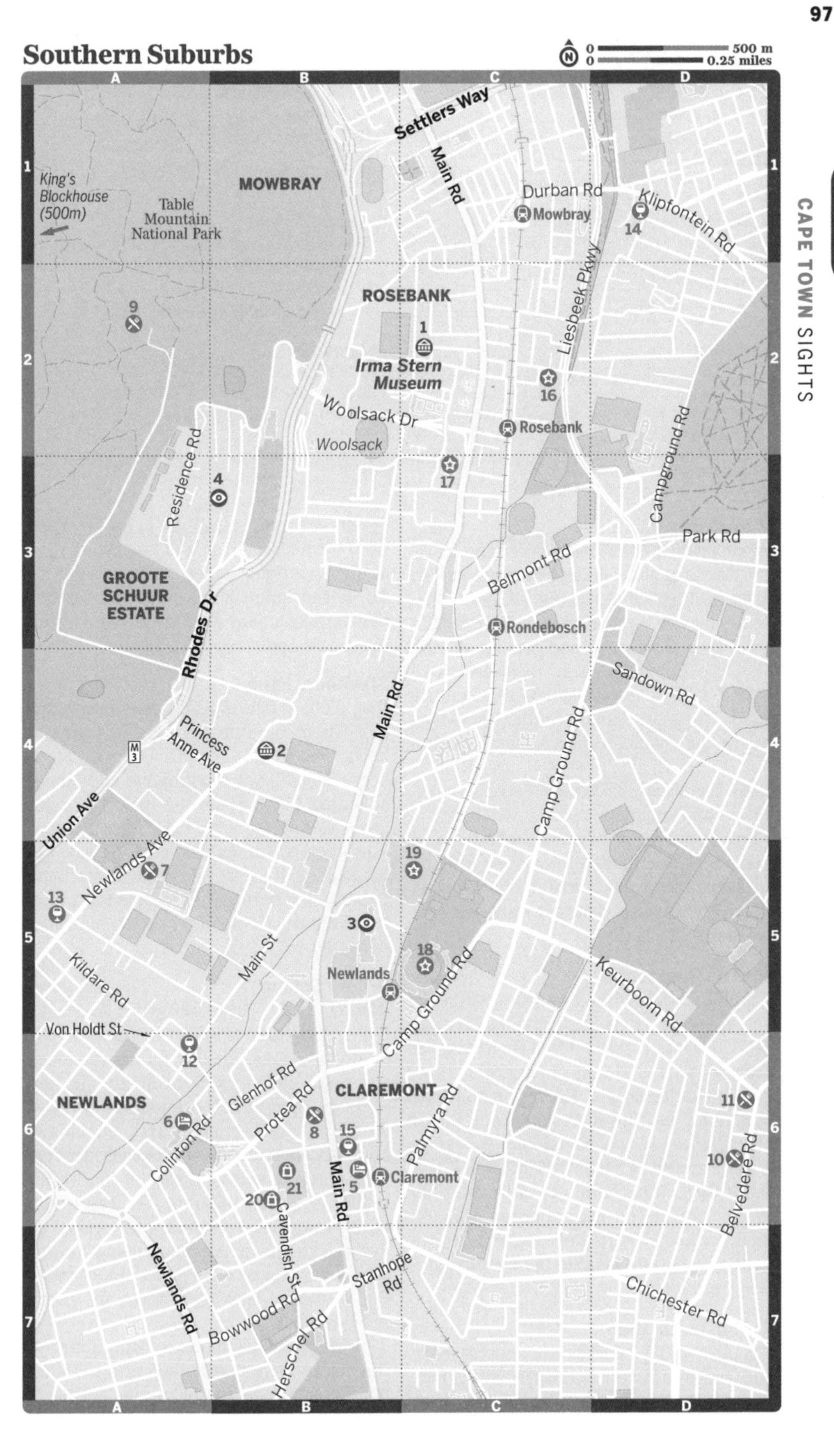

Southern Suburbs

Top Sights
1 Irma Stern Museum C2

Sights
2 Groote Schuur B4
3 Newlands Brewery B5
4 University of Cape Town B3

Sleeping
5 Off the Wall B6
6 Vineyard Hotel & Spa A6

Eating
7 Gardener's Cottage A5
8 O'ways Teacafe B6
9 Rhodes Memorial Restaurant A2
10 Starlings Cafe D6
11 The Eatery D6

Drinking & Nightlife
12 Barristers A6
13 Forester's Arms A5
14 Salt Yard D1
15 Zhivago B6

Entertainment
16 Alma Cafe C2
17 Baxter Theatre Centre C3
18 Newlands Cricket Ground C5
19 Newlands Rugby Stadium C5

Shopping
20 Balu Legacy Boutique B6
21 Cavendish Square B6
Montebello Design Centre .... (see 7)
YDE .... (see 21)

★ **Buitenverwachting** WINERY
(Map p100; ☎021-794 5190; www.buitenverwachting.com; Klein Constantia Rd, Constantia; tastings R50; ⊙tastings 10am-5pm Mon-Sat; P) Buitenverwachting means 'beyond expectation', which is certainly the feeling one gets on visiting this Cape Dutch estate. It's a lovely estate to visit with an unusual late-18th-century manor house overlooking verdant lawns, as well as the Quaffee coffee roastery, **Coffee Bloc** (Map p100; ☎021-794 4468; mains R75-135; ⊙8am-5pm Mon-Fri, 8.30am-3pm Sat) cafe, a restaurant and gift shop.

Beg, borrow or steal to snag a bottle of its delicious – but limited-release – Christine bordeaux blend. The creamy chardonnay and richly textured cabernet sauvignon are also standout wines.

★ **Klein Constantia** WINERY
(Map p100; ☎021-794 5188; www.kleinconstantia.com; Klein Constantia Rd, Constantia; tastings R50; ⊙tastings 10am-5pm Mon-Fri, to 4pm Sat & Sun; P) Part of Simon van der Stel's original Constantia estate, Klein Constantia is famous for its Vin de Constance, a sweet muscat wine. It was Napoleon's solace on St Helena; and in Jane Austen's *Sense and Sensibility*, Mrs Jennings advocates 'its healing powers on a disappointed heart'. There's a small bistro and excellent tasting room – be sure to sample the champagne-style sparkler.

★ **Constantia Glen** WINERY
(Map p100; ☎021-795 5639; www.constantiaglen.com; Constantia Main Rd, Constantia; tastings R45-75; ⊙tastings 10am-5pm Sun-Thu, to 8pm Fri & Sat; P) There's a sweeping view of the vineyards from the terrace in front of the tasting room at this boutique winery, which is known for its sauvignon blanc and bordeaux-style blends. Accompany your tasting with a yummy cheese-and-charcuterie platter.

Steenberg Farm WINERY
(Map p100; ☎021-713 2222; www.steenbergfarm.com; Steenberg Estate, Steenberg Rd, Constantia; tastings R60-80; ⊙tastings 10am-6pm; P) Steenberg's contemporary tasting bar and lounge, adjoining Bistro Sixteen82 (p152), is a gorgeous setting for sampling its great merlot, sauvignon blanc, sémillon and Méthode Cap Classique (MCC) sparkler. The estate is the Cape's oldest farm, dating back to 1682, when it was known as Swaaneweide (Feeding Place of the Swans).

Groote Schuur HISTORIC BUILDING
(Map p97; ☎021-686 9100; Klipper Rd, Rondebosch; R50; ⊙tours 10am Mon-Fri; Rondebosch) The grandest of Cecil Rhodes' former residences was also home to a succession of prime ministers and presidents, culminating with FW de Klerk. The beautifully restored interior, all teak panels and heavy colonial furniture, with antiques and tapestries of the highest calibre, is suitably imposing. The best feature is the colonnaded veranda overlooking the formal gardens, which slope uphill towards an avenue of pine trees and views of Devil's Peak. Advance booking is necessary for the two-hour tour.

Bring your passport to gain entry to this high-security area; the entrance is unmarked but easily spotted on the left as you take the Princess Anne Ave exit off the M3.

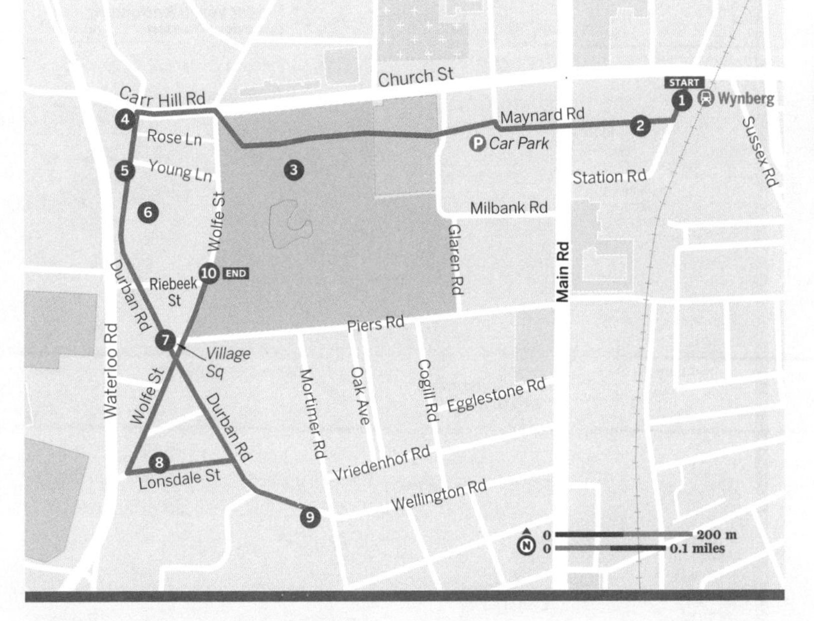

Neighbourhood Walk **Southern Suburbs**

START WYNBERG STATION
END WOLFE ST
LENGTH 2.5KM; ONE HOUR

This conservation area is packed with Cape Georgian and Victorian buildings, some thatched, and many with lovely flower gardens. However, the area around 1 **Wynberg Station**, jammed with taxis and traders, contrasts starkly with the genteel village less than 10 minutes' walk west. The station is a popular transit point for residents of the Cape Flats heading to the Southern Suburbs or the city centre. Opposite it is the restored 2 **Town Hall**, designed at the turn of the 19th century by William Black in Flemish Revival style.

Cross Main Rd and continue west on Maynard Rd. Across from the car park (an alternative start/finish point if you're driving) is 3 **Maynardville Park**. Walk through the park, emerging at the junction of Wolfe St and Carr Hill Rd. The neo-Gothic 4 **Dutch Reformed Church**, up the hill at the corner of Durban Rd, dates back to 1831; inside are four granite supporting pillars donated by Cecil Rhodes.

Turn left (south) at the church and walk down Durban Rd. Many pretty thatched-roof cottages line this street, including 5 **Winthrop House**, which was once the British Army officers' mess, and 6 **Falcon House**, said to be the village's first courthouse.

Where Durban Rd meets Wolfe St is a small square shaded by a pair of oak trees. Around here are interior-design shops; some surround the hidden 7 **Chelsea Courtyard**, a delightful garden. Return to Wolfe St and continue south to the corner of Lonsdale St to admire the 8 **old bakery** (c 1890), with its fish-scale slate turret flanked by gryphons.

Turn left (east) into Lonsdale St and continue to Durban Rd. Detour right to peek through the wire fence at the late-18th-century mansion 9 **Tenterden**. The Cape Dutch Revival veranda was added in the 20th century. The Duke of Wellington once slept at the (no longer existant) coach house that was located on the property.

Head north up Durban Rd until you reach the village square; 10 **Wolfe St** has a parade of shops and places to eat and drink.

Kirstenbosch, Constantia & Wynberg

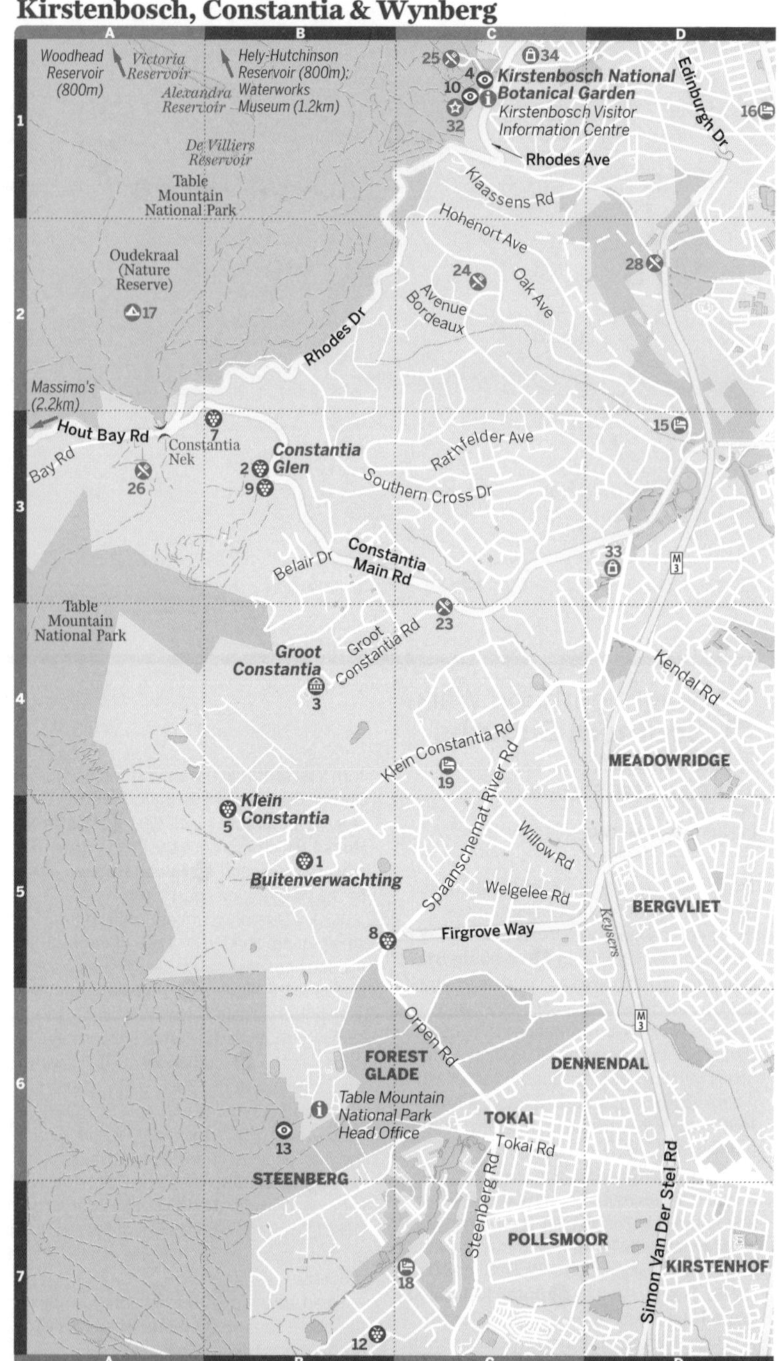

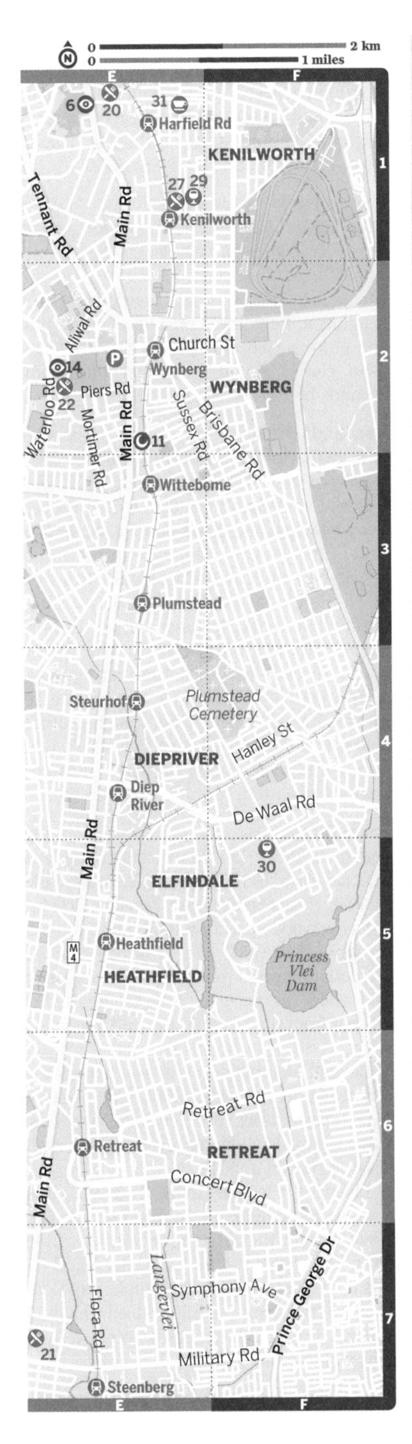

Kirstenbosch, Constantia & Wynberg

Top Sights
1 Buitenverwachting B5
2 Constantia Glen B3
3 Groot Constantia B4
4 Kirstenbosch National Botanical Garden C1
5 Klein Constantia B5

Sights
6 Arderne Gardens E1
7 Beau Constantia B3
8 Constantia Uitsig B5
9 Eagle's Nest B3
10 Kirstenbosch National Botanical Garden Conservatory C1
Maynardville Park .... (see 14)
11 Open Mosque E2
12 Steenberg Farm B7
13 Tokai Arboretum B6
Tokai Forest .... (see 13)
14 Wynberg Village E2

Sleeping
15 Alphen D3
16 Andros Boutique Hotel D1
17 Orange Kloof Tented Camp A2
18 Steenberg Hotel C7
19 Summit Place C4

Eating
20 A Tavola E1
Bistro Sixteen82 .... (see 12)
Coffee Bloc .... (see 1)
21 Earth Fair Food Market E7
22 Four & Twenty Cafe & Pantry E2
23 Foxcroft C4
24 Greenhouse C2
Jonkershuis .... (see 3)
25 Kirstenbosch Tea Room C1
La Belle .... (see 15)
26 La Colombe A3
27 Rare Grill E1
Tashas .... (see 33)
28 The View D2

Drinking & Nightlife
29 Banana Jam E1
Caffé Verdi .... (see 22)
30 Jack Black's Brewery F5
Martini Bar .... (see 24)
31 Twigs with Beans E1

Entertainment
32 Kirstenbosch Summer Sunset Concerts C1
Maynardville Open-Air Theatre .... (see 14)

Shopping
33 Constantia Village D3
34 Kirstenbosch Craft Market C1

Beau Constantia WINERY

(Map p100; ☎021-794 8632; www.beauconstantia.com; Constantia Nek, Constantia; tastings R55; ⏲tastings 11am-6pm Tue-Sun; Ⓟ) Perched high above the vineyards, Beau Constantia's strikingly contemporary tasting room has panoramic views. The viognier is worth tasting and there's a branch of the excellent Chef's Warehouse (p140) restaurant here.

Take care when driving, in as the car park is a little tricky to locate.

Constantia Uitsig WINERY

(Map p100; ☎021-794 6500; www.uitsig.co.za; Spaanschemat River Rd, Constantia; tastings 3/6 wines R50/90; ⏲tastings 10am-6pm; Ⓟ) Call in here to sample a crisp sémillon, luscious chardonnay-based MCC brut or limited-release Red Muscat d'Alexandrie in the tasting room, located at the estate gate. There's also a restaurant and a bike park.

Eagle's Nest WINERY

(Map p100; ☎021-794 4095; www.eaglesnestwines.com; Constantia Main Rd, Constantia; tastings R60; ⏲tastings 10am-4.30pm; Ⓟ) Try the viognier or shiraz at this boutique winery nestling among the Constantia vineyards, and enjoy a deli cuts platter (R145) or artisan cheese board (R165) in the shady grounds beside a stream.

Newlands Brewery BREWERY

(Map p97; ☎021-658 7440; www.newlandsbrewery.co.za; 3 Main Rd, Newlands; tours R80; ⏲tours 11am & 3pm Mon, 10am & noon Tue-Sat, plus 2pm & 6pm Wed, 2pm & 4pm Fri; Ⓟ; Ⓡ Newlands) In the early 19th century, Jacob Letterstedt built the Mariendahl Brewery in Newlands, a handsome building since granted National Heritage status. It's now part of Newlands Brewery and owned by South African Breweries. Fascinating tours of the complex, including the chance to sample Castle, Black Label and the other beers made here, will give you an insight into large-scale beer making. Advance booking essential.

Tokai Forest FOREST

(Map p100; ☎021-712 7471; www.tmnp.co.za; Tokai Rd, Tokai; adult/child R25/15, car R27, mountain biking R80; ⏲8am-5pm Apr-Sep, 7am-6pm Oct-Mar; Ⓟ) This wooded section of Table Mountain National Park (p55) is a favourite spot for picnics, mountain biking (weekends only) and walks. To reach the forest, take the Tokai exit from the M3 highway and follow the signs.

Beyond the picnic area, you'll find the **Tokai Arboretum** (Map p100), a planting of 1555 different trees representing 274 species. Having closed following severe bushfires, it is set to reopen in 2018.

Likewise closed temporarily is the challenging 6km hike up to **Elephant's Eye Cave**, within the Silvermine section of the park. The zigzag path is fairly steep and offers little shade as you climb higher up Constantiaberg (928m), so hikers need a hat and water. The cave is more easily accessed from Silvermine.

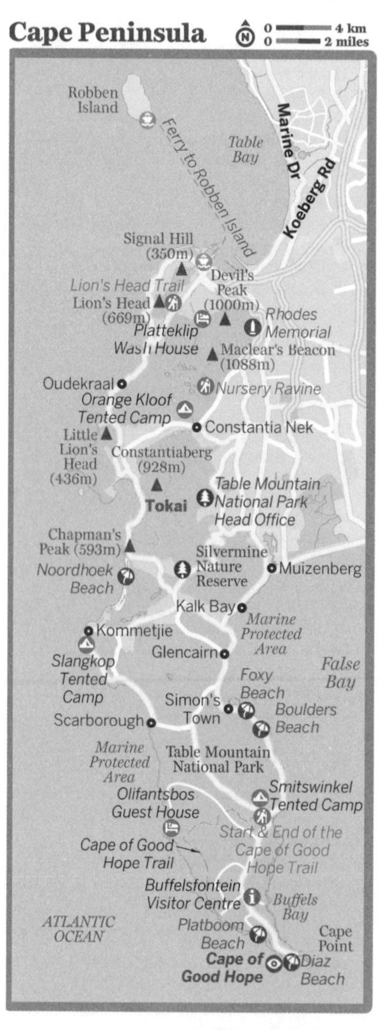

Arderne Gardens GARDENS

(Map p100; www.arderneGardens.org.za; 222 Main Rd, Claremont; by donation; 8am-6pm; Claremont) These shady gardens planted by botanist Ralph Arderne in 1845 represent the oldest collection of trees in the southern hemisphere and include bamboo, fir, gum and enormous Moreton Bay fig trees. It's a lovely place to wander around for an afternoon, and is especially colourful on weekends, when many Capetonian wedding parties come to have their photos taken.

Rhodes Memorial MONUMENT

(Map p102; www.rhodesmemorial.co.za; off M3, Groote Schuur Estate; 9am-5pm; P) Partly modelled on the arch at London's Hyde Park Corner, this monumental granite memorial stands on the eastern slopes of Table Mountain, at a spot where the mining magnate and former prime minister Cecil Rhodes used to admire the view. The 49 steps, one for each year of Rhodes' life, are flanked by pairs of proud lions; the top provides sweeping vistas of the Cape Flats and the mountain ranges beyond.

Rhodes bought all the surrounding land in 1895 for £9000 as part of a plan to preserve a relatively untouched section of the mountain for future generations. His ambition and determination is memorialised by a dynamic statue of a man on a rearing horse (in contrast to the bust of Rhodes himself, which has him looking rather grumpy).

Behind the memorial is a pleasant restaurant (p151) and a steep path leading up to the **King's Blockhouse** (Tafelberg Rd, Table Mountain National Park), a defensive position built by the British between 1795 and 1803. From here it's possible to follow the contour path above Newlands Forest to Skeleton Gorge and down into Kirstenbosch gardens (p95). Don't hike alone, as muggings have occurred in this part of the mountain.

The exit for the memorial is at the Princess Anne Interchange on the M3.

University of Cape Town UNIVERSITY

(UCT; Map p97; www.uct.ac.za; off Rhodes Dr, Rondebosch; P; Rondebosch) For the non-academic there's no pressing reason to visit UCT, but it's nonetheless an impressive place to walk around. Unfortunately, it has experienced violent student protests in recent years. The Upper Campus (west of the M3) presents a fairly cohesive architectural front, with ivy-covered neoclassical facades and a fine set of stone steps leading to the temple-like Jameson Hall. If you call ahead, it's possible to arrange a tour of the library.

If you approach UCT from Woolsack Dr, you'll pass the **Woolsack**, a cottage designed in 1900 by Sir Herbert Baker for Cecil Rhodes. Now a student residence, it's said that Rhodes' friend Rudyard Kipling wrote the poem 'If' during his sojourns here between 1900 and 1907.

OFF THE BEATEN TRACK

SILVERMINE NATURE RESERVE

This less-visited **reserve** (Map p50; 021-712 7471; www.tmnp.co.za; Ou Kaapse Weg; adult/child R50/25; 7am-6pm Sep-Apr, 8am-5pm May-Aug; P) includes the Silvermine Reservoir, a beautiful spot for a picnic or a leisurely walk on the wheelchair-accessible boardwalk. The placid reservoir waters are tannin-stained and, despite the signs forbidding swimming, you'll often find locals taking a dip here. Some excellent half-day hiking trails lead into the mountains from this area, named after the fruitless attempts by the Dutch to prospect for silver here in the late 17th century.

Simon's Town & Southern Peninsula

Muizenberg is a vibey, regentrifying spot, popular for learning to surf and grabbing a beer or ice cream on the beachfront, with Silvermine Nature Reserve nearby. Following False Bay south, pretty little Kalk Bay is popular for day-tripping Capetonians to wander the antiques shops and eat some fish and chips. Simon's Town, nautical HQ of the Dutch, British and now the South African Navy, is well preserved and atmospheric with a marina and two museums. Further south are the area's two major natural attractions, Boulders penguin colony (p108) and the Cape of Good Hope (p107), both part of Table Mountain National Park (p55).

MUIZENBERG, KALK BAY & AROUND

Muizenberg was established by the Dutch in 1743 as a staging post for horse-drawn traffic. Its heyday was the early 20th century, when it was a major seaside resort and the likes of Agatha Christie learnt to surf here.

Muizenberg & Kalk Bay

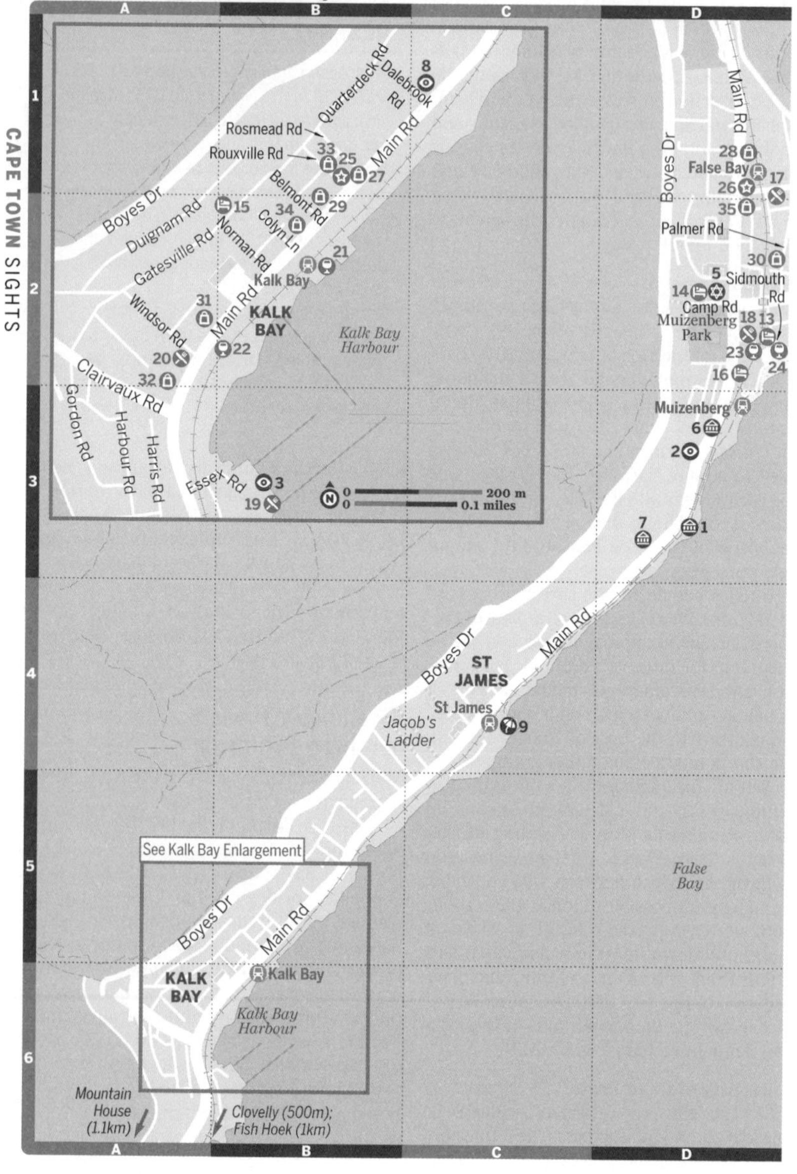

Kalk Bay is named after the lime ('kalk' in Afrikaans) that was produced by burning seashells in kilns and used for painting buildings in the 17th century. Under apartheid it was neglected by government and business as it was mainly a coloured area, with the upside being that it avoided the forced population removals that devastated Simon's Town.

Around False Bay, south of Kalk Bay, the communities of Fish Hoek and Clovelly have wide beaches that are safe for swimming.

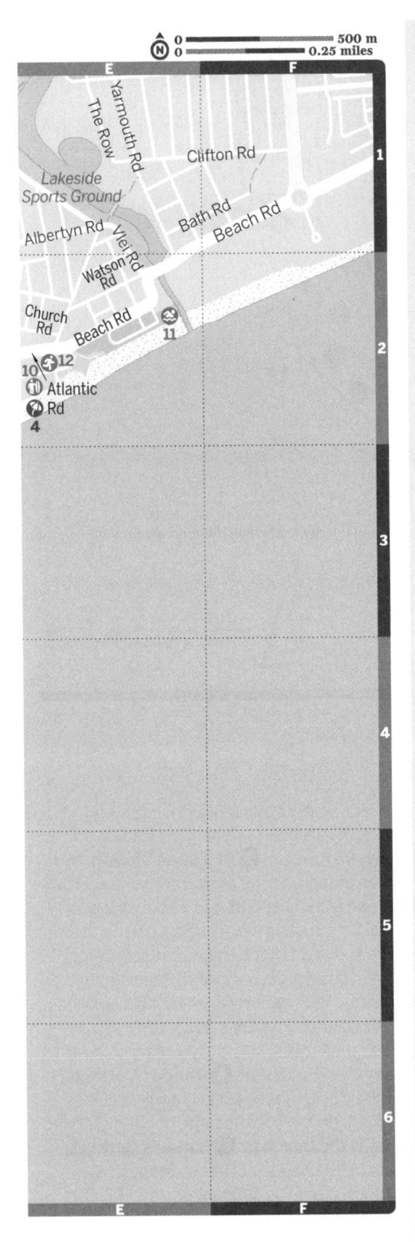

Muizenberg & Kalk Bay

Sights

1 Bailey's Cottage D3
2 Casa Labia Cultural Centre D3
3 Kalk Bay Harbour B3
4 Muizenberg Beach E2
5 Muizenberg Synagogue D2
6 Posthuys D3
7 Rhodes Cottage Museum D3
8 Save Our Seas Shark Education Centre C1
9 St James Beach C4

Activities, Courses & Tours

10 Gary's Surf School E2
11 Muizenberg Water Slides E2
Roxy Surf Club .... (see 10)
12 Surfstore Africa E2

Sleeping

13 African Soul Surfer D2
14 Bella Ev D2
15 Chartfield Guesthouse B2
16 Stoked Backpackers D2

Eating

17 Blue Bird Cafe D1
Bob's Bagel Cafe .... (see 33)
Cucina Labia .... (see 2)
18 Empire Cafe D2
19 Live Bait B3
20 Olympia Cafe & Deli A2
Salt .... (see 20)

Drinking & Nightlife

21 Brass Bell B2
22 Cape to Cuba B2
23 Striped Horse Bar & Grill D2
24 Tiger's Milk D2

Entertainment

25 Kalk Bay Theatre B1
26 Masque Theatre D1

Shopping

27 Artvark B1
Blue Bird Garage Food & Goods Market .... (see 17)
28 Blue Planet Fine Art D1
29 Catacombes B2
30 Gina's Studio D2
31 Kalk Bay Books A2
32 Kalk Bay Modern A2
33 Pottershop B1
34 Quagga Rare Books & Art B2
35 Sobeit Studio D2

Muizenberg Beach BEACH

(Map p104; Beach Rd, Muizenberg; P; Muizenberg) Popular with families, this surf beach is famous for its row of colourfully painted Victorian bathing chalets. Surfboards can be hired and lessons booked at several shops along Beach Rd. The beach shelves gently and the sea is generally safer here than elsewhere along the peninsula.

At the eastern end of the promenade is a fun **water park** (Map p104; 021-788 4759;

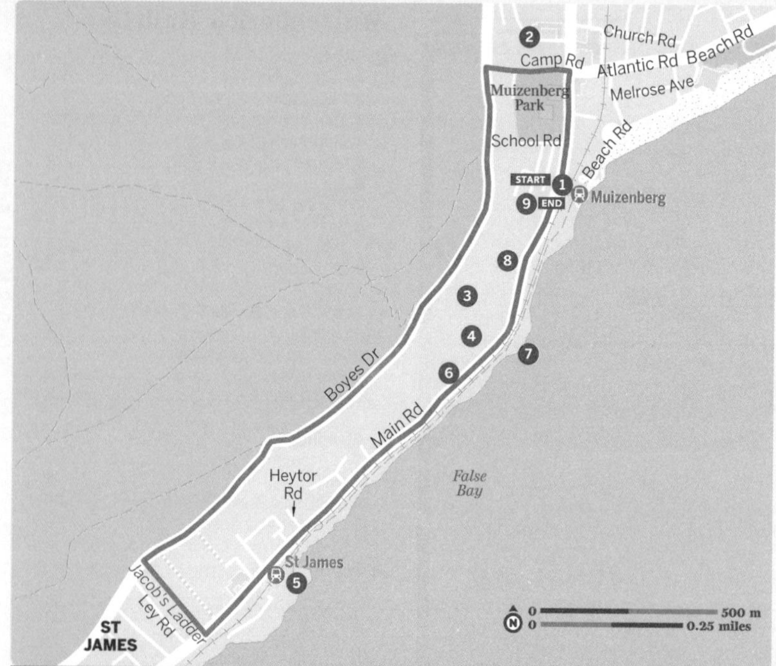

Neighbourhood Walk Muizenberg & St James

START MUIZENBERG STATION
END MUIZENBERG STATION
LENGTH 3KM; ONE HOUR

This invigorating coastal walk provides spectacular views of False Bay and gives you a sense of the history and once-grand nature of this seaside suburb.

From ❶ **Muizenberg Station**, head north past Muizenberg Park to Camp Rd, passing the red-and-white-painted ❷ **synagogue**, which dates from the 1920s, when Muizenberg had a large Jewish community. Concrete steps lead up to Boyes Dr, for a commanding view across Muizenberg and its broad, flat beach.

Head south on Boyes Dr, looking out for whales in season (roughly August to October). A wrought-iron gate on the left has steps leading down to the ❸ **grave of Sir Abe Bailey** (1864–1940): 'soldier, former sportsman, philanthropist, mining pioneer'. You should also be able to glimpse Bailey's house, ❹ **Rust-en-Vrede**, with its red tiles and high gables, on Main Rd below. The home was commissioned by the British imperialist Cecil Rhodes, but he never lived in it.

Keep walking along Boyes Dr until you reach the Jacob's Ladder steps leading down Capri Rd towards ❺ **St James Station**. Next to the station is a set of brightly painted Victorian-style bathing huts and a tidal rock pool – ideal for a cooling dip. A coastal path starts here and heads back towards Muizenberg.

As you approach a grand, Spanish-style mansion with green-glazed roof tiles (called 'Gracelands', after Elvis' pad), you'll see another underpass that lets you nip across to busy Main Rd to visit ❻ **Rhodes Cottage**, where Cecil Rhodes passed away in 1902.

Back on the coastal path, on the righthand side, is the thatched ❼ **Bailey's Cottage**, built in 1909 and another of Bailey's residences. Closer to Muizenberg, on Main Rd, is ❽ **Casa Labia** (p107), which belongs to the family of an Italian count who built the property in 1930.

Further along is the whitewashed ❾ **Posthuys**. Built in the 1670s, this one-time lookout post for ships entering False Bay is one of Cape Town's oldest European-style buildings. It's a minute's walk from here back to Muizenberg Station.

www.muizenbergslides.co.za; off Beach Rd, Muizenberg; 1hr/day passes R45/85; ⌚1.30-5.30pm Mon-Fri, from 9.30am Sat & Sun, plus 6-9pm Fri Nov-Feb; 👪; 🚆Muizenberg).

Casa Labia Cultural Centre ARTS CENTRE
(Map p104; ☎021-788 6068; www.casalabia.co.za; 192 Main Rd, Muizenberg; ⌚10am-4pm Tue-Sun; 🚆Muizenberg) FREE This magnificent seaside villa built in 1930 was once the palatial home of Italian ambassador Count Natale Labia and his South African wife. It now hosts a program of concerts, lectures and events, as well as exhibiting the Labia family's furniture, imported from Venice in the 1920s, and works from their art collection (including paintings by Irma Stern and Gerald Sekoto). The ornate building also houses Cucina Labia (p154) restaurant and the **South African Print Gallery**.

Capetonian architect Fred Glennie designed the grand palazzo in the style of 18th-century Venice, and a Venetian interior designer furnished it with antique fixtures and fittings. It served as the Italian, Canadian and finally Argentinian embassy for several decades, before entering its current incarnation in the 1980s. The rights to oversee the building were handed back to the Labias' son and granddaughter in 2008. It has since undergone a loving restoration.

Kalk Bay Harbour HARBOUR
(Map p104; Essex Rd, Kalk Bay; ⌚fish market 9am-5pm; P; 🚆Kalk Bay) This picturesque harbour is best visited in the morning, when the community's fishing boats pitch up with their daily catch and a lively quayside market ensues. This is an excellent place to buy fresh fish for a braai (barbecue), or to spot whales during the whale-watching season.

Nearby, next to Kalk Bay Station and the Brass Bell (p167) pub, are a couple of tidal swimming pools.

Save Our Seas Shark Education Centre SCIENCE CENTRE
(Map p104; ☎021-788 6694; www.saveourseas.com; 28 Main Rd, Kalk Bay; ⌚2-4pm Mon-Thu; 👪; 🚆Kalk Bay) 🍃 FREE This educational centre encourages awareness, protection, conservation and the sustainable fishing of sharks worldwide. The state-of-the-art exhibits, ranging from a touch pool to a microscope bench, appeal to adults and children alike. It's part of a not-for-profit foundation with similar centres in Florida and the Seychelles.

You can also find out about the pioneering **Shark Spotters** (http://sharkspotters.org.za) program, which monitors key beaches and raises the alarm if sharks are spotted swimming near them.

SIMON'S TOWN & REST OF SOUTHERN PENINSULA

On the False Bay side of the peninsula, Simon's Town is named after Simon van der Stel, 17th-century governor of the Cape. The winter anchorage for the Dutch East India Company (Vereenigde Oost-Indische Compagnie; VOC) from 1741, and a British naval base from 1814 to 1957, it's now a South African Navy HQ and you'll see many uniforms on the streets.

★**Cape of Good Hope** NATURE RESERVE
(Cape Point; Map p110; www.tmnp.co.za; adult/child R135/70; ⌚6am-6pm Oct-Mar, 7am-5pm Apr-Sep; P) This 77.5-sq-km section of Table Mountain National Park includes awesome scenery, fantastic walks, great birdwatching and often-deserted beaches. The reserve is commonly referred to as Cape Point, after it's most dramatic (but less famous) promontory. Bookings are required for the two-day **Cape of Good Hope Trail** (Map p110; R280, excl reserve entry fee), a spectacular 33.8km circular route

ℹ GETTING TO & AROUND THE SOUTHERN PENINSULA

Car Most useful for getting the best out of the region.

Taxi Try **HGTS Tours** (Map p108; ☎021-786 5243; www.hgtravel.co.za; Simon's Town Station, Main Rd, Simon's Town), **Noordhoek Taxis** (☎071 484 5721; www.noordhoektaxis.co.za) or Uber.

Tour A popular way to visit Cape Point, often including a stop at the Boulders penguin colony. Make sure your itinerary follows False Bay one way, and the Atlantic coast the other, so you see both sides of the peninsula.

Train Stops include Muizenberg, St James, Kalk Bay and Fish Hoek, before the terminus at Simon's Town. A single from Cape Town Station to Simon's Town costs R16.50.

Water taxi The **Mellow Yellow** (Map p108; ☎073 473 7684; www.watertaxi.co.za; single/return R100/150) runs between Kalk Bay and Simon's Town. We recommend taking the train to Simon's Town and the water taxi back to Kalk Bay, not the other way around.

Simon's Town

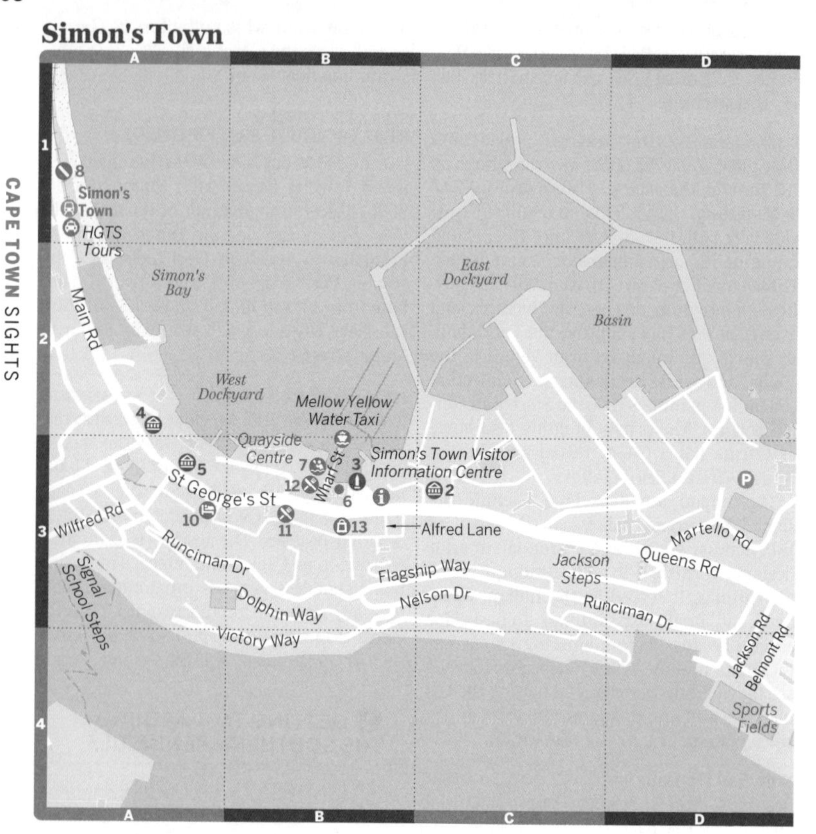

with one night spent in a basic hut. Contact the Buffelsfontein Visitor Centre (p57) for further details.

Some 250 species of birds have been spotted here, including cormorants and a family of ostriches that hang out near the Cape of Good Hope promontory, the southwestern-most point of the continent.

There are many bus tours to the reserve but, if you have the time, hiking or cycling through it is much more rewarding. Bear in mind, though, that there is minimal shade and that the weather can change quickly.

It's not a hard walk uphill, but if you're feeling lazy take the **Flying Dutchman Funicular** (www.capepoint.co.za; one way/return adult R50/65, child R20/25; 9am-5pm), which runs up from beside the restaurant to the souvenir kiosk next to the **old lighthouse** (which dates from 1859). A 1km trail runs from here to its successor. It takes less than 30 minutes to walk along a spectacular ridgeway path to look down on the new lighthouse and the sheer cliffs plunging into the pounding ocean.

★Boulders Penguin Colony BIRD SANCTUARY

(Map p108; 021-786 2329; www.tmnp.co.za; Simon's Town; adult/child R70/35; 7am-7.30pm Dec & Jan, 8am-6.30pm Feb, Mar, Oct & Nov, 8am-5pm Apr-Sep; P; Simon's Town) This picturesque area, with enormous boulders dividing small, sandy coves, is home to a colony of some 3000 delightful African penguins. A boardwalk runs from the Boulders Visitor Centre (p57) at the Foxy Beach end of the protected area – part of Table Mountain National Park (p55) – to Boulders Beach, where you can get down on the sand and mingle with the waddling penguins. Don't, however, be tempted to pet them: they have sharp beaks that can cause serious injuries.

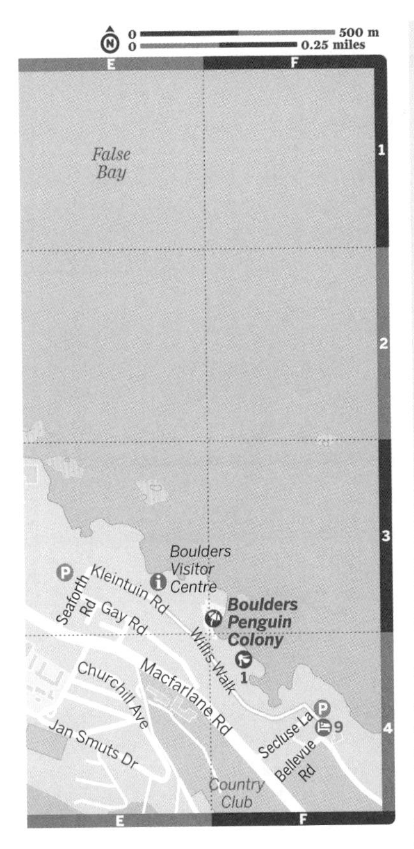

Simon's Town

Top Sights
1 Boulders Penguin Colony....................F4

Sights
2 Heritage Museum C3
3 Just Nuisance Statue B3
4 Simon's Town Museum.......................A2
5 South African Naval Museum............A3

Activities, Courses & Tours
6 Apex Shark Expeditions B3
7 Kayak Cape Town B3
8 Pisces Divers......................................A1
Simon's Town Boat Company .... (see 7)

Sleeping
9 Boulders Beach Lodge F4
10 Simon's Town Boutique Backpackers..................................A3

Eating
11 Lighthouse Cafe.................................B3
12 Salty Sea Dog.....................................B3

Shopping
13 Larij Works B3

The bulk of the colony, which has grown from just two breeding pairs in 1982, seems to prefer hanging out at Foxy Beach, where, like nonchalant, stunted supermodels, they blithely ignore the armies of camera-touting tourists snapping away on the viewing platforms. (The beach itself is off-limits to visitors.)

The aquatic birds, which are an endangered species, were formerly called jackass penguins on account of their donkey-like braying – you'll have a chance to hear it if you turn up during the main breeding season, which peaks from March to May. Parking is available at either end of the reservation, on Seaforth Rd and on Bellevue Rd, where you'll also find accommodation and places to eat. Boulders is around 3km southeast of Simon's Town.

Imhoff Farm FARM

(021-783 4545; www.imhofffarm.co.za; Kommetjie Rd, Kommetjie; 9am-5pm; P) FREE There's plenty to see and do at this attractive historic farmstead just outside Kommetjie. Among the attractions are craft shops and art studios; a cafe, sushi bar and the Blue Water Cafe (p154) restaurant; a snake and **reptile park** (adult/child R70/50); the **Higgeldy Piggeldy Farmyard** (R20), stocked with animals; **camel rides** (noon to 4pm Tuesday to Sunday; adult/child R70/50); and a **farm shop** selling tasty goat cheeses (made on-site by a French cheesemaker) and other provisions.

Noordhoek Beach BEACH

(Map p102; Beach Rd, Noordhoek) This magnificent 5km stretch of beach is favoured by surfers and horse riders. It tends to be windy, and dangerous for swimmers. The Hoek, as it is known to surfers, is an excellent right beach break at the northern end that can hold large waves (only attempt it at low tide); it's best with a southeasterly wind. The large beach is isolated in places and attacks have occurred here, so don't go alone and seek local advice beforehand.

In the middle of the beach, the rusted shell of the steamship *Kakapo* sticks out of the sand like a weird sculpture. It ran aground here in 1900, on its maiden voyage from Swansea, Wales, to Sydney, Australia.

Cape Point

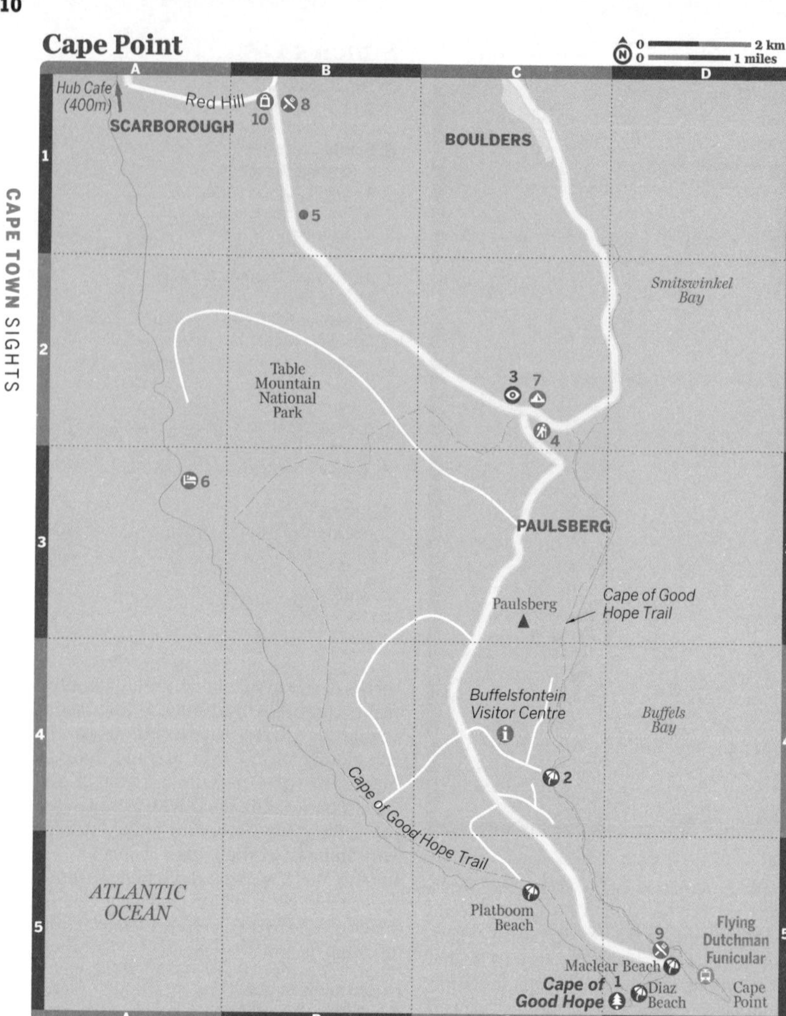

Cape Point

Top Sights
1 Cape of Good Hope D5

Sights
2 Buffels Bay C4
3 Cape Point Ostrich Farm C2

Activities, Courses & Tours
4 Cape of Good Hope Trail C2
5 Veld and Sea B1

Sleeping
6 Olifantsbos Guest House A3
7 Smitswinkel Tented Camp C2

Eating
8 Cape Farmhouse Restaurant B1
9 Two Oceans Restaurant D5

Shopping
Red Rock Tribal .... (see 8)
10 Redhill Pottery B1

★Cape Point Vineyards WINERY

(☎021-789 0900; www.cpv.co.za; Silvermine Rd, Noordhoek; tastings per wine R10; ⊙tastings 11am-6pm Fri-Wed, to 2pm Thu; P) This small vineyard known for its fine sauvignon blanc has a spectacular setting overlooking Noordhoek Beach. Enjoy the wines with a picnic (R395 for two, book at least a day ahead; 11am to 5pm Friday to Wednesday) on the grounds, or at the restaurant (noon to 3pm Friday to Wednesday, plus 6pm to 8.30pm Friday and Saturday).

The Thursday evening community market (4.30pm to 8.30pm), selling mainly food, is a weekly highlight for locals and great for kids, who can play on the lawns above the farm dam.

Buffels Bay BEACH

(Map p110; Cape of Good Hope, Table Mountain National Park; P) This sheltered bay within the Cape Point section of Table Mountain National Park (p55) offers sweeping views across False Bay and a sea pool for safe swimming.

Long Beach BEACH

(off Benning Dr, Kommetjie; P) For breezy beach walks, it doesn't get much better than this aptly named stretch of white sand. There are stunning views up the mountainous coastline as far as Hout Bay. To find the car park, follow Kirsten Ave from Kommetjie Rd and turn left.

South African Naval Museum MUSEUM

(Map p108; ☎021-787 4686; www.simonstown.com/navalmuseum/index.htm; off St George's St, Simon's Town; ⊙9.30am-3.30pm; Simon's Town) FREE Principally for naval enthusiasts, this museum nonetheless has plenty of interesting exhibits, including model ships and submarines, uniforms and a life-sized ship's bridge. The museum occupies the buildings of the original Dockyard Magazine (storehouse), built in the mid-18th century.

Ask about touring the **SAS Assegaai**, a Daphne-class, French-built submarine, which served the South African Navy from 1971 to 2003. It was open as a museum in Simon's Town Naval Dockyard, but has been closed for repairs.

Heritage Museum MUSEUM

(Map p108; ☎021-786 2302; King George Way, Simon's Town; R10; ⊙11am-4pm Tue-Thu & Sun; P; Simon's Town) Simon's Town had a 7000-strong community of people of colour before apartheid forcibly removed most of them, mainly to the suburb of Ocean's View, over on the Atlantic side of the peninsula. This small but interesting museum in Almay House (1858), with a lovely front garden, is dedicated to the evictees and their Islamic culture, which traces its roots to Simon's Town's 18th-century beginnings. The museum is curated by Zainab Davidson, whose family was evicted in 1975.

Simon's Town Museum MUSEUM

(Map p108; ☎021-786 3046; www.simonstown.com/museum/index.html; Court Rd, Simon's Town; adult/child R10/5; ⊙10am-4pm Mon-Fri, to 1pm Sat; P; Simon's Town) This rambling museum traces the history of Simon's Town, with displays ranging from maritime exhibits to a room dedicated to Just Nuisance, the local Great Dane adopted as a navy mascot in WWII. It's housed in the old governor's residence (1777).

Just Nuisance Statue STATUE

(Map p108; Jubilee Sq, Simon's Town; P; Simon's Town) Immortalised in bronze in 1985 by artist Jean Doyle, this famous local canine mascot lived from 1937 to 1944 and is fondly remembered for befriending naval sailors during WWII. Indeed, the Great Dane became the only dog to be enlisted in the Royal Navy. His statue overlooks the marina.

AVOID TRAFFIC & CROWDS

Main Rd is the coastal thoroughfare linking Muizenberg with Fish Hoek, although a prettier (and often less congested) alternative route between Muizenberg and Kalk Bay is the mountainside Boyes Dr, which provides fantastic views down the peninsula. You might spot whales from here between roughly August and October.

If you can spare only a day for the Southern Peninsula, one strategy for beating the crowds is to head down the Atlantic Coast via Chapman's Peak Dr, then follow Kommetjie/Main Rd (M65) to the entrance to the Cape of Good Hope nature reserve. Start early and you'll arrive at Cape Point well before the bulk of the tourist buses, which often stop at Boulders first (and you can hit this on the way back instead).

WORTH A TRIP

DURBANVILLE WINE ROUTE

About 25km (around a 30-minute drive) north of the City Bowl but still within Cape Town's metropolitan borders is the **Durbanville Wine Valley** (www.durbanvillewine.co.za). Vines have been grown here since 1698; the area's signature grape is sauvignon blanc, which benefits from the cooler winds off the coast that the hills receive. Among the dozen wineries on the wine route are the following:

De Grendel (021-558 6280; www.degrendel.co.za; Plattekloof Rd; tastings R60-80; tastings 9am-5pm Mon-Sat, 10am-4pm Sun; P; Potsdam) Established in 1720, the closest of the Durbanville wineries to Cape Town has a jaw-dropping view of Table Mountain from its tasting room. There's also a good **restaurant** (021-558 6280; www.degrendel.co.za; Plattekloof Rd, Durbanville; lunch mains R200, dinner 2/3 courses R350/385; noon-2.30pm & 7-9.30pm Tue-Sat, noon-2.30pm Sun; Potsdam) and conserved areas of indigenous *renosterveld* (grey shrubby 'rhinoceros field' vegetation), all located on a working farm on the slopes of Tygerberg.

Durbanville Hills (021-558 1300; www.durbanvillehills.co.za; M13; tastings R60-95; tastings noon-6pm Mon, from 10am Tue-Fri, 10am-4pm Sat, 11am-4pm Sun; P; Dunoon) Offering a change from the historic Cape Dutch wine estates, this winery, best known for its merlot and its sauvignon blanc, occupies an ultramodern building commanding a hilltop above the Durbanville vineyards. There's a good restaurant, splendid views of Table Bay and Table Mountain, and a *renosterveld* garden.

Hillcrest Estate (021-970 5800; www.hillcrestfarm.co.za; M13; tastings R30-50; tastings 10am-5pm Mon-Thu & Sat, to 6pm Fri, 11am-5pm Sun; P; Dunoon) There's lots going on here apart from excellent wine-making, such as growing olives and producing Havoc Brew craft beers, which you can enjoy with a pizza in the beer garden. The site's historic **quarry** (www.thequarry.co.za), with a fish-stocked dam, hosts open-air events such as concerts and film screenings. You can fish for bass, trout and more, as well as picnic and braai (barbecue) here.

Nitida (021-976 1467; www.nitida.co.za; M13; tastings R30-60; tastings 9.30am-5pm Mon-Fri, 11am-4pm Sat, 11am-3pm Sun; P; Dunoon) Excellent tastings of Nitida's award-winning wines are held in the wine cellar. Booking is recommended, as it's a small space. Also here are two restaurants: the excellent **Tables at Nitida** (021-975 9357; www.tablesatnitida.co.za; Nitida, M13, Durbanville; mains R105-165; 9am-4pm Mon-Sat, to 3pm Sun; Dunoon), where you can pre-book delicious gourmet picnics (R350 for two) or enjoy a luscious cake, and the more formal **Cassia**.

Meerendal (021-975 1655; www.meerendal.co.za; M48; tastings R30-75, mountain biking day pass R30; tastings 10am-6pm Mon-Sat, to 5pm Sun; P; Dunoon) Although it was established in 1702 and has some of South Africa's oldest pinotage and shiraz vineyards, as well as a handsome Cape Dutch homestead, Meerendal is no fuddy-duddy wine estate. The tasting room is very professionally run and combined with a contemporary art gallery and distillery, offering vodka, rum and gin tastings. There are two restaurants, **Carlucci's Deli** (021-612 0015; http://meerendal.co.za/carluccis-deli; M48; mains R100; 7.30am-5pm Mon-Wed & Sun, to 9pm Thu-Sat; Dunoon) and the more upmarket **Crown**, plus 18km of **mountain-biking trails**.

There are also craft stalls on Jubilee Sq, which hosts a market every second Saturday from 9.30am to 2.30pm.

Cape Point Ostrich Farm FARM
(Map p110; 021-780 9294; www.capepointostrichfarm.com; Sun Valley; guided tours adult/child R55/25; 9.30am-5.30pm; P) There's ostriches aplenty at this family-run farm, restaurant and tourist complex just 500m from Cape Point's main gate. Regular tours of the breeding facilities, which consist of 40 birds in 40 'camps', cover the ostrich's life cycle and offer glimpses of eggs incubating or even hatching. The well-stocked ostrich-leather and egg-shops are packed with items from handbags to carved eggshells.

Cape Flats & Northern Suburbs

The two main areas here are the townships of the Cape Flats, which flank the N2 highway as it heads out of town towards the airport and the Cape Winelands, and the wineries and beaches of the Northern Suburbs. The latter area is across town from the Cape Flats, and best visited on a separate trip. The two areas require no more than two days, one to get a sense of life in the townships and another to visit the Durbanville Wine Route and **Bloubergstrand** (P; Kleinbaai).

The beaches beside the pleasant coastal suburb of Bloubergstrand are where the British won their 1806 battle for the Cape. The panoramic view they provide of Table Mountain across Table Bay is fabulous, but these beaches are also popular with kite-surfers and windsurfers; watching them ride the waves on the weekends is an impressive sight. You can also see Robben Island clearly from here.

You can grab a bite to eat and buy a swimming costume at **Eden on the Bay Mall** (www.edenonthebaymall.co.za; Cormorant Ave, Bloubergstrand; Big Bay), which occupies a prime spot at the southern end of Big Bay Beach. Bloubergstrand is a good example of a poetic Cape name – it means 'blue mountain beach'.

TOWNSHIPS OF THE CAPE FLATS

A visit to the townships of the Cape Flats may end up providing your fondest memories of Cape Town, particularly if you choose to spend a night in one of the B&Bs that are found here or to have a meal in the growing range of restaurants and cafes.

If you don't feel confident driving yourself or taking public transport (it's always a good idea to have arranged for a local to meet you on arrival), there are plenty of tours and guides (p124) ready to show you around.

LANGA

Cape Town's oldest township is also one of the closest to the city centre, and the proximity of Langa's sights to the N2 highway makes this a straightforward option if you would like to visit a township independently.

Catch a taxi or drive to **Guga S'Thebe Arts & Cultural Centre** (Map p114; 021-695 3493; cnr King Langalibalele Ave & Church St, Langa; 8am-4.30pm Mon-Fri, to 2pm Sat & Sun; P; Langa) FREE, where there is a car guard.

> **OFF THE BEATEN TRACK**
>
> **INTAKA ISLAND**
>
> *Intaka* means 'bird' in Xhosa and you can see 120 feathered species, as well as 200-plus plant species, at this 1600-sq-metre **wetland reserve** (Map p114; 021-552 6889; www.intaka.co.za; Park Ln, Intaka Island, Century City; adult/child R20/12, incl ferry ride R60/50; 7.30am-7pm Sep-Apr, to 5.30pm May-Aug; P; Central Park). Learn about the wetlands and a host of green subjects in the Sustainability Area and Eco-Centre, from where you can take a 40-minute ferry ride through the canals that circle the island, or follow the 2km walking trail.

Decorated with polychromatic ceramic murals, this is one of the most impressive buildings in the townships – even more so now that it has a theatre, creatively constructed from recycled materials. You can watch pottery being made in one of several studio spaces here, and then buy samples from the centre's shop. Performances by local groups are often staged in the outdoor amphitheatre.

The huge mural painted on the building opposite the centre was done by Philip Kgosana, the man held aloft in the composition – it commemorates the 1960 defiance campaign against apartheid laws. Guga S'Thebe regularly hosts **Jazz in the Native Yards** (www.facebook.com/nativeyards) concerts.

From Guga S'Thebe take a short stroll along King Langalibalele Ave, past the **Langa Mosaic Plinths** (Map p114; King Langalibalele Ave, Langa; Langa). Each side of these colourful, mosaic-decorated plinths has a different theme related to township history. One is the only memorial to the *Mendi*, a troop ship that sank in the English Channel in 1917, drowning 607 members of the South African Native Labour Corps.

Drop into the **Langa Pass Museum** (Langa Heritage Museum; Map p114; 084 949 2153, 072 975 5442; cnr King Langalibalele & Lerotholi Aves, Langa; by donation; 9am-4pm Mon-Fri, to 1pm Sat; P; Langa). At this grim apartheid relic, black people had to present their identity cards. In the attached court they were tried for breaking the pass laws. There's a great collection of photographs and documentary evidence showing what life was like in Cape Town's oldest township during that era.

Pinelands, Langa & Milnerton

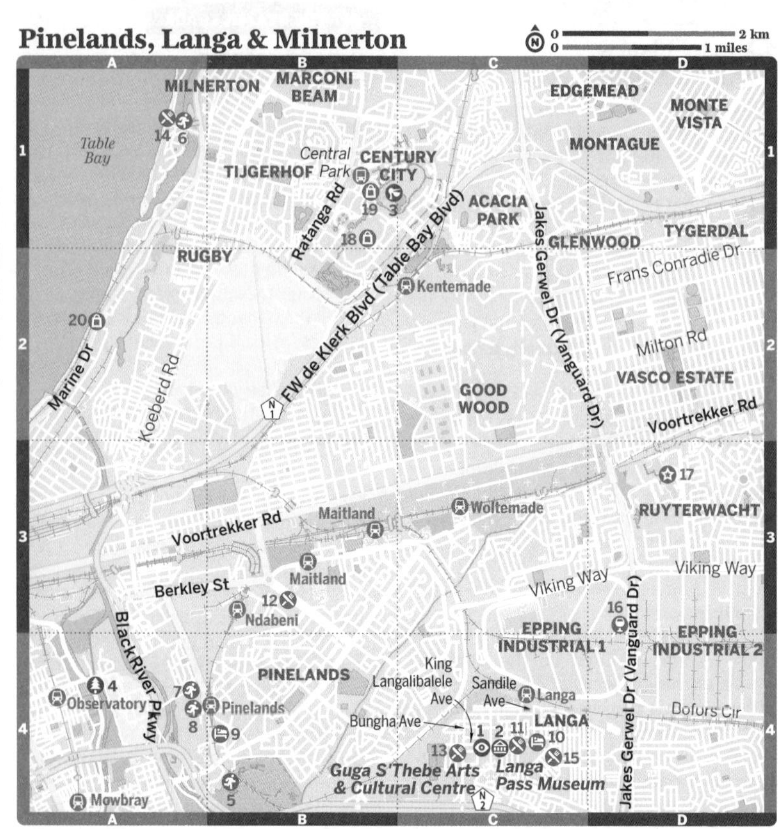

Pinelands, Langa & Milnerton

Top Sights

1 Guga S'Thebe Arts & Cultural Centre.. C4
2 Langa Pass Museum C4

Sights

3 Intaka Island B1
Langa Mosaic Plinths .... (see 1)
4 Two Rivers Urban Park A4

Activities, Courses & Tours

5 King David Mowbray Golf Club B4
6 Milnerton Golf Club............................. A1
7 Oude Molen Eco Village A4
8 Oude Molen Stables A4

Sleeping

9 Colette's.. B4
10 Nomase's Guesthouse.......................... C4

Eating

11 Eziko C4
12 Hog House Brewing Co........................ B3
13 Lelapa... C4
14 Maestro's on the Beach........................ A1
Millstone .... (see 8)
Mzansi... (see 13)
15 Nomzamo... C4

Drinking & Nightlife

16 Devil's Peak Brewing Company............ D3
Kaffa Hoist.. (see 1)

Entertainment

17 Grandwest Casino D3

Shopping

18 Canal Walk.. B1
19 Century City Natural Goods Market..... B1
20 Milnerton Flea Market......................... A2

GUGULETU

The granite **Gugulethu Seven Memorial** (cnr Steve Biko St (NY1) & Mananase Ndlebee St (NY121); Heideveld) commemorates seven young black activists from the townships who were murdered by the police here in 1986. Nearby is the **Amy Biehl Memorial** (Steve Biko St (NY1), Gugulethu; Heideveld) marking the spot where the young American anti-apartheid activist died, under tragic circumstances, in 1993.

KHAYELITSHA

The largest of Cape Town's townships, and the fastest growing in South Africa, Khayelitsha is a vast place. Climb the wooden staircase leading to the top of sandy **Lookout Hill** (021-361 7098; cnr Mew Way & Spine Rd; 8am-4.30pm Mon-Fri; P; Khayelitsha) FREE for a sweeping view. For access it's best to go into the cultural and tourism centre at its base, where you'll find the restaurant **Malibongwe** (021-361 6259; www.facebook.com/malibongwerestuarant; cnr Mew Way & Spine Rd, Khayelitsha; mains R60; 8am-5pm Mon-Sat; Makabeni) and a craft market. Ask there for a security guard to accompany you, as there have been incidents of muggings.

The **Isivivana Centre** (021-361 0181; https://isivivanacentre.org.za; 8 Mzala St, Khayelitsha; Khayelitsha), decorated with giant art murals by Breeze Yoko and Falko One, is a new cultural and community centre that is worthy of a look in its own right. However you'll also find here the **Bertha Movie House**, screening Africa-themed and family movies for free, and the pleasantly decorated **Isivivana Cafe** that acts as a canteen for the NGOs and charities based here.

Gangsterism is the blight of the Cape Flats, and the innovative new 18 Gangster Museum (p124) shows the treacherous path that too many in these communities follow into the gangs and, ultimately, prison. Hoping to persuade local youths to choose a more positive direction, the shipping-container museum's exhibits are curated by ex-offenders, who share their real-life experiences. There's text, images and a replica prison cell. Entrance is on a 45- to 60-minute guided tour; book ahead.

Activities

City Bowl, Foreshore, Bo-Kaap & De Waterkant

Long St Baths SWIMMING

(Map p70; 021-422 0100; www.capetown.gov.za; cnr Long & Buitensingel Sts, City Bowl; swimming adult/child R23/12, steam baths R64; Tue, Sat & Sun 10am-4pm, Fri from 1pm; Upper Loop, Upper Long) Dating from 1906, these nicely restored baths, featuring painted murals of city-centre life on the walls, are heated and very popular with the local community. The Turkish steam baths are a great way to sweat away some time, especially during the cooler months.

At the time of research, the baths were operating shorter hours because of the water restrictions – call before heading here to check on opening times. On Tuesdays the baths are open to ladies only.

DON'T MISS

HARBOUR CRUISES

For all the Waterfront's land-based attractions, the key way to experience this area is from a boat: nothing quite matches sailing across Table Bay with Table Mountain up ahead, a sight that has greeted mariners for generations.

There's a wide variety of boat rides available, from luxury yachts to the **Penny Ferry** (R5) row boat, which transports people between Pier Head and Clock Tower.

Waterfront Charters (Map p86; 021-418 3168; www.waterfrontcharters.co.za; Shop 5, Quay 5, V&A Waterfront; Breakwater) One-stop shop for cruises by a variety of operators, including highly recommended 1½-hour sunset cruises (adult/child R360/180) on the handsome wood-and-brass-fitted schooner *Esperance*. A 30-minute jet-boat ride is R440.

Yacoob Tourism (Map p86; 021-421 0909; www.ytourism.co.za; Shop 8, Quay 5, V&A Waterfront; ; Breakwater) Among the several trips that this company runs are those on the *Jolly Roger Pirate Boat* (adult/child from R170/85) and *Tommy the Tugboat* (adult/child R50/25), both perfect for families. Adults may prefer their *Adrenalin* speed-boat jaunts or a cruise on the catamarans *Ameera* and *Tigress*.

East City, District Six, Woodstock & Observatory

City Rock CLIMBING

(Map p79; 021-447 1326; http://cityrock.co.za; 21 Anson Rd, Observatory; day pass adult/child R150/125; 9am-9pm Mon & Wed, to 10pm Tue & Thu, to 6pm Fri-Sun; Observatory) This popular indoor-climbing gym offers climbing courses and hires out and sells climbing gear. They also have yoga classes.

Gardens & Surrounds

Table Mountain Aerial Cableway CABLE CAR

(Map p94; 021-424 8181; www.tablemountain.net; Tafelberg Rd, Table Mountain; one-way/return from adult R150/290, child R70/140; 8.30am-6pm mid-Jan–mid-Dec, 8am-9.30pm mid-Dec–mid-Jan; Lower Cable Car) If you want to reach the 1086m-high peak of Table Mountain without breaking much of a sweat, the cableway is the way to go; the views both from the revolving car and the summit are phenomenal. The cablecars run every 10 to 20 minutes; check online for first and last departures, as they vary throughout the year.

Note the cableway doesn't operate when it's very windy, which in Cape Town can be often; call or go online to see if it is running before setting out. The best visibility and conditions are likely to be first thing in the morning or in the evening. There's little point going up if you are simply going to be wrapped in the cloud known as the 'tablecloth'. Be sure to take something warm to wear – even when it's beach weather, it can be bitingly cold atop the mountain.

Abseil Africa ADVENTURE SPORTS

(Map p70; 021-424 4760; https://abseilafrica.co.za; 297 Long St; abseiling R995; Upper Long, Upper Loop) The 112m drop off the top of Table Mountain with this long-established outfit is a guaranteed adrenaline rush. Don't even think of tackling it unless you've got a head (and a stomach) for heights. You can tag on a guided hike up Platteklip Gorge (R1745) or just do the hike without the abseil (R800).

Abseil Africa also offers kloofing (canyoning) trips around Cape Town (R1395). The sport of clambering into and out of kloofs (cliffs or gorges) also entails abseiling, climbing, hiking, swimming and jumping.

Cape Town Tandem Paragliding PARAGLIDING

(076 892 2283; www.paraglide.co.za; flight R1150) Feel like James Bond as you paraglide off Lion's Head, land near the Glen Country Club, and then sink a cocktail at Camps Bay. Novices can arrange a tandem paraglide, where you're strapped to an experienced flyer who takes care of the technicalities. Make enquiries on your first day in Cape Town, as the weather conditions have to be right.

Enmasse MASSAGE

(Map p84; 021-461 5650; www.enmasse.co.za; 123 Hope St, Gardens; 1hr massage R425; 8am-10pm; Gardens) De-stress with Thai-style and Shiatsu massages (performed without oils) in a historic building that was once a hotel. Stay as long as you like afterwards, relaxing in their tea salon and enjoying any of the 15 different blends of mainly local teas and infusions (which you can also buy to take home). Enter via Gate 2, Schoonder Rd.

Green Point & Waterfront

Kaskazi Kayaks KAYAKING, TOUR

(Map p86; 074 810 2224, 083 346 1146; www.kayak.co.za; Shell service station, 179 Beach Rd, Three Anchor Bay; per person R400; Three Anchor Bay) Get up early to join the two-hour guided kayak trips (weather dependent) run by this professional operator from Three Anchor Bay to either Granger Bay or Clifton. There are astounding views of the mountains and coastline, as well as possible close encounters with dolphins, seals and penguins. Whale sightings in season are also on the cards.

Adrenalised Cape Town DIVING

(Map p86; 021-418 2870; www.adrenaliseddiving.co.za; Shop 8, Quay 5, V&A Waterfront; 9.30am-6pm Mon-Sat, from 10am Sun; Breakwater) Scuba diving is just one of the several water-based activities that this outfit offers, with PADI open-water courses at R5995 and a two-shore dive package at R1540. You can also learn or go freediving with them or sea snorkelling in Ouderkrall where you can hang out with a colony of Cape fur seals.

The 90-minute Ocean Safari in a Gemini 850 boat (R650 for a minimum of two people) also promises the chance to spot dolphins, seals, whales, penguins, sun fish and more.

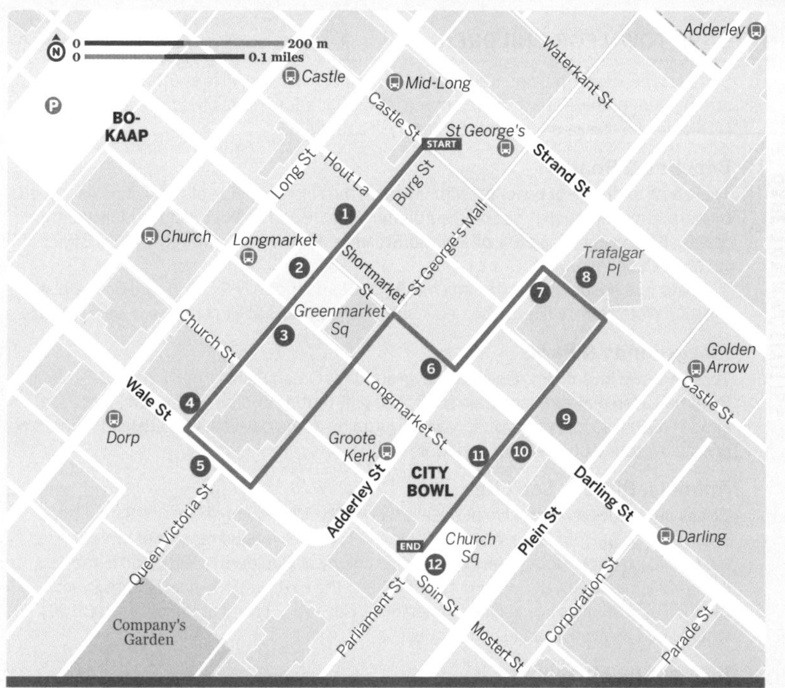

Neighbourhood Walk **Art & Architecture**

START CAPE TOWN TOURISM, CORNER CASTLE & BURG STS, CITY BOWL
END CHURCH SQ
LENGTH 1.5KM; ONE HOUR

A building boom in Cape Town during the 1930s resulted in the city centre having a remarkable number of grand art deco buildings. This walk takes you past some of the key buildings.

At 24 Burg St is ❶ **New Zealand House**, designed by WH Grant in a style known as Cape Mediterranean. Ahead is ❷ **Greenmarket Square** (p69), which hosts a daily crafts and souvenir market. Three quarters of the buildings surrounding the square hail from the 1930s, the main exception being the ❸ **Old Town House**, completed in 1761.

At the junction of Burg and Wale Sts, the ❹ **Waalburg Building** has a facade decorated with bronze and Table Mountain–stone panels depicting scenes of South African life. Opposite is the ❺ **Western Cape Legislature**, its grey bulk enlivened by stone-carved animal heads.

Turn into St George's Mall and continue to Shortmarket St, where a right turn will bring you to the junction with Adderley St. Here is the ❻ **First National Bank**, completed in 1913, and one of the final projects of Sir Herbert Baker: pop inside to see some of the bank's original fittings. Head up Adderley St, past the ❼ **Former Standard Bank**, a grand building topped by a statue of Britannia, and turn right into ❽ **Trafalgar Place** (p177), home to Cape Town's flower sellers since 1860.

At the end of Trafalgar Place is the ❾ **General Post Office**. The ground floor is clogged by market stalls, but look above them to view colourful painted panels of Cape Town scenes.

Emerge onto Darling St to face ❿ **Mutual Heights** (p73). At the crossing of Parliament and Longmarket Sts is ⓫ **Mullers Opticians**, one of the most beautifully preserved art deco shopfronts in the city. A few steps further along Parliament St will bring you to Church Square to see ⓬ **Groote Kerk** (p72), the mother church of the Dutch Reformed Church, facing the old National Building.

CAPE TOWN FOR CHILDREN

Soft sand beaches, the mountain and its myriad activities, wildlife spotting, the carnival atmosphere of the Waterfront and much more: Cape Town takes the prize as a *lekker* (Afrikaans for 'brilliant') location for family vacations.

Beaches & Boats

There's no shortage of beaches, with those on the False Bay side of the peninsula lapped by warmer waters than those on the Atlantic Coast. Good choices include Muizenberg (p105), **St James** (Map p104; off Main Rd, St James; St James), or lovely Buffels Bay (p111) at Cape Point.

Boat tours are abundant: *Tommy the Tugboat* and the *Jolly Roger Pirate Boat* are at the V&A Waterfront, while cruises leave from the harbours at Simon's Town and Hout Bay.

Playgrounds & Parks

There are two inventively designed playgrounds at Green Point Urban Park (p82). Mouille Point has a big play area, toy train (p88) and golf-putting course (p87). Sea Point Promenade (p96) also has playgrounds, and swimming at the pavilion. In Vredehoek, there's a good playground beside Deer Park Café (p146).

Animals, Birds & Sea Life

Check out the local marine life at the excellent Two Oceans Aquarium (p118); the birds and monkeys at Hout Bay's World of Birds (p93) or the wetland reserve of Intaka Island (p113); a happy-footed African penguin colony at Boulders (p108); wild ostriches, baboons and dassies at Cape Point (p107); and the birds at Rondevlei Nature Reserve (p125). Farm animals live at Oude Molen Eco Village (p123) and at Imhoff Farm (p109), where you can even arrange camel rides!

Interesting Museums

Science and technology is made fun at the Cape Town Science Centre (p76), where there's usually some special activity scheduled. The South African Museum (p79) offers giant whale skeletons, and star shows at the attached planetarium (p81). The Castle of Good Hope (p58), with its battlements, museums and horse-and-carriage rides, offers an entertaining visual history lesson.

Shopping & Eating

Toy and kids' clothing stores are found at all the major shopping malls. For a fine selection of secondhand items and a play area visit **Merry Pop Ins** (Map p70; 021-422 4911; www.merrypopins.co.za; 201 Bree St, City Bowl; 9.30am-5pm Mon-Thu, 9am-4pm Fri, 10am-2pm Sat; Upper Loop, Upper Long). The Book Lounge (p176) has a great kids' book section and story readings.

Weekly markets, including Neighbourgoods (p177), Bay Harbour Market (p177) and Blue Bird Garage (p177), have play areas, and kid-friendly food. For fish and chips, try the Waterfront, Hout Bay and Simon's Town.

Further Information

Cape Town Kids (www.capetownkids.co.za) Listings and features of local places and events that will appeal to kids.

Child Mag (www.childmag.co.za) South African parenting guide.

Two Oceans Aquarium DIVING
(Map p86; 021-418 3823; www.aquarium.co.za; Dock Rd, V&A Waterfront; dives R870, Discover Scuba course R750; Aquarium) A guaranteed way to swim with turtles and rays is to dive in the tanks at the Two Oceans Aquarium. With no sharks around to worry about, this makes for a delightful diving experience. The cost includes gear hire, and you need to be a certified diver, otherwise you also need to pay for the Discover Scuba course.

PADI diving courses are also available for around R5000.

Sports Helicopters SCENIC FLIGHTS
(☎021-419 5907; www.sport-helicopters.co.za; East Pier Rd, V&A Waterfront; flights from R1375; 🚌Waterfront) In this company's fleet is an ex-US Marine Corps Huey chopper from the Vietnam War era; it flies with open doors for that authentic *Apocalypse Now* experience (from R4400). Standard tours last 30 minutes and take you towards Hout Bay and back; the hour-long tour gets you from the Waterfront to Cape Point.

Cape Town Helicopters SCENIC FLIGHTS
(☎021-418 9462; www.helicopterscapetown.co.za; 220 East Pier, Breakwater Edge, V&A Waterfront; from R1650 per person; 🚌Waterfront) Unforgettable views of the Cape Peninsula are guaranteed with these scenic flights. A variety of packages are available, from a 30-minute journey out to Robben Island and back to the hour-long journey down to Cape Point (R4800 per person).

Ocean Sailing Academy BOATING
(Map p86; ☎021-425 7837; www.oceansailing.co.za; Marina Centre, West Quay Rd, V&A Waterfront; 🚌Marina) Contact the only Royal Yachting Association (RYA) school in South Africa to find out about its sailing courses, which are tailored to all skill levels.

Metropolitan Golf Club GOLF
(Map p86; ☎021-430 6011; www.metropolitangolfclub.co.za; Fritz Sonnenberg Rd, Mouille Point; green fees 9/18 holes R410/725, equipment hire 9/18 holes R250/350; 🚌Mouille Point) As part of the revamp of the sports facilities on Green Point Common, this course also got an upgrade, with four species of local grasses planted to give it a more natural look. The wind-sheltered position – between Cape Town Stadium and Green Point Park, with Signal Hill in the background – can't be beat.

Green fees are discounted between June and September.

Sea Point to Hout Bay

★**Animal Ocean** SNORKELLING, WILDLIFE, DIVING
(Map p92; ☎072 296 9132; www.animalocean.co.za; 8 Albert St, Hout Bay; snorkelling/diving per person R800/2150; 👪; 🚌Lower Victoria) Although it's weather-dependent (and not for those who suffer seasickness), don't miss the chance to go snorkelling or diving off Duiker Island. Chances are you'll be visited by some of the thousands of playful, curious Cape fur seals that live on the island and swim in the shark-free waters around it. All necessary gear, including thick neoprene wetsuits, is provided. Trips run from September to May.

★**Chapman's Peak Drive** DRIVING
(☎021-791 8220; www.chapmanspeakdrive.co.za; Chapman's Peak Dr; cars/motorcycles R45/29; 🚌Hout Bay) Take your time driving, cycling or walking along 'Chappies', a 5km toll road linking Hout Bay with Noordhoek – it's one of the most spectacular stretches of coastal highway in the world. There are picnic spots and viewpoints, and it's certainly worth taking the road at least one way en route to Cape Point.

The toll booth is at the Hout Bay end of the road; you're free to walk up here and along the road. Drivers can also obtain a free day pass (or 'picnic voucher') here, valid for the first 2.7km of the route, which allows you to stop at the picnic areas, viewing spots and mountain trails on this stretch before turning back. This option is offered between 6am and 8pm from October to March, and between 7am and 6.30pm from April to September.

On the approach from Hout Bay, look for a bronze **leopard statue** (Map p92; Chapman's Peak Dr, Hout Bay; 🚌Hout Bay). It has been sitting there since 1963 and is a reminder of the wildlife that once roamed the area's forests (which have also largely vanished).

Into the Blue DIVING
(Map p90; ☎021-434 3358; www.diveschoolcapetown.co.za; 88 Main Rd, Sea Point; open-water PADI courses R4995-5995, shore/boat dives R400/650, gear hire per day R650; 🚌Sea Point High) Conveniently located near Sea Point's accommodation, this operator runs diving courses and offers regular dives around the Cape, focusing on themes from shipwrecks to cow sharks, including shark-cage dives.

There has been much controversy regarding shark-cage diving, with detractors arguing that it is leading to increased shark attacks, while others (including some marine scientists and environmentalists) believe that it is a positive educational tool to encourage conservation.

Sea Point Pavilion SWIMMING
(Map p90; ☎021-434 3341; Beach Rd, Sea Point; adult/child R23/12; ⏰7am-7pm Dec-Apr, 9am-5pm May-Nov; 🚌Sea Point Pool) This huge outdoor pool complex, with its lovely art deco touches, is a Sea Point institution. It gets very busy on hot summer days – not surprisingly, since the four pools are always at least 10°C warmer than the always-frigid ocean.

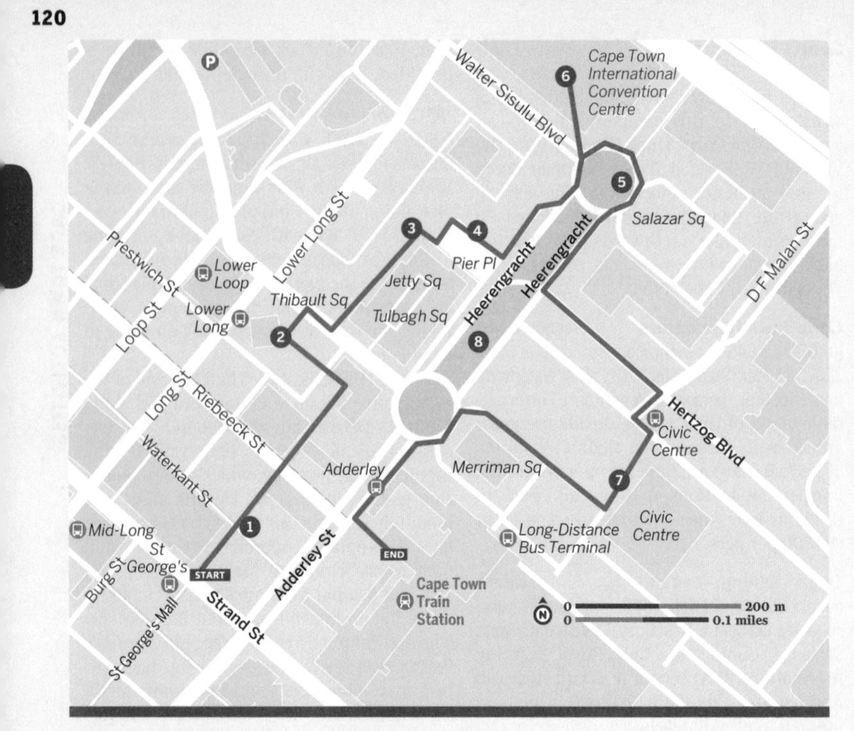

Neighbourhood Walks
Foreshore Public Art Walk

START **CORNER ST GEORGE'S MALL & STRAND ST, FORESHORE**
END **CAPE TOWN STATION**
LENGTH **1KM; ONE HOUR**

The Foreshore isn't big on sightseeing, but on this walk you can explore around the concrete towers and plazas and take in sculptures both old and new.

On pedestrianised St George's Mall, opposite Waterkant St, is Brett Murray's quirky statue 1 **Africa**. This African-curio bronze statue, sprouting bright-yellow Bart Simpson heads, is typical of Murray's satirical style and caused much public debate on its unveiling in 2000.

At the end of St George's Mall turn left into Thibault Sq, surrounded by some the Foreshore's oldest skyscrapers, including the ABSA Centre. In the square you can view 2 **Mythological Landscape**, a steel and bronze piece by John Skotnes that celebrates diversity.

Cross Mechau St and continue towards 3 **Jetty Square** where a school of steel sharks by Ralph Borland responds to passersby by swivelling on their poles. Around the corner 4 **Pier Place** is a pedestrianised square scattered with Egon Tania's statues of people going about their daily lives.

In the middle of the roundabout at the Foreshore end of Heerengracht is a small statue of the Portuguese sailor 5 **Bartholomeu Dias**, the first recorded European to have rounded the Cape of Good Hope, in 1488. Across the road is the 6 **Cape Town International Convention Centre** (p169); in the main entrance hall, *Baobabs, Stormclouds, Animals and People* is a giant relief sculpture, a collaboration between Brett Murray and the late San artist Tuoi Steffaans Samcuia of the !Xun and Khwe San Art and Cultural Project.

Return towards the city down Heerengracht, detouring left on Hertzog Blvd. Near the Civic Centre is Edoardo Villa's 7 **Knot**, which looks like a giant red paper clip bent out of shape. Back on Heerengracht, opposite Cape Town Train Station, are the twin statues of 8 **Jan van Riebeeck and Maria de la Queillerie**, the first Dutch boss of Cape Town and his wife. This is apparently the spot where they stepped ashore in 1652.

MORE PUBLIC ART

Apart from the sculptures you'll encounter on the Foreshore Walk (p120), there are several other public artworks in the City Bowl worth searching out.

Next to the Central Library, **We Are Still Here** (Map p70; cnr Longmarket & Parade Sts, City Bowl; Lower Buitenkant) is a powerful piece created by Lovell Friedman and Leora Lewis. A mosaic of ceramic tiles forms the image of a child and is surrounded by drawings and written contributions from street children. Look closely and you'll see each tile contains the print of an advert placed in the *Cape Government Gazette* between 1841 and 1921 calling for ownership of destitute children.

Open House (Map p70; cnr Dorp & Long Sts, City Bowl; Dorp, Leeuwen) by Jacques Coetzer is the winning entry from a World Design Capital competition in 2014 to create a piece of public art for the city. Rising up three stories to 10.5m, the bright-red house facade with stairs and balconies is envisioned as a place where people can go to speak, sing, cry or simply wave to passers by. Coetzer drew inspiration from corrugated metal structures, RDP homes (government-subsidised Reconstruction and Development Programme houses) and Long St itself.

On the pedestrianised portion of Church St, outside the **AVA Gallery** (p175), is the *Arm Wrestling Podium* by Johann van der Schijff. At the Burg St end, *The Purple Shall Govern* memorial is a piece of graphic art by Conrad Botes commemorating a 1989 anti-apartheid march.

Prestwich Memorial Garden (Map p74; cnr Somerset Rd & Buitengracht Sts, De Waterkant; Strand) is an attractive public space dotted with a collection of quirky sculptures and installations by Capetonian artists, including the rainbow arch *It's Beautiful Here* by Heath Nash, the *Full Cycle Tree* by KEAG and several Rock Girl benches (p69).

Duiker Island Cruises BOATING
(Map p92; cruises 8am-3.30pm; Fishmarket) From Hout Bay Harbour you can catch a boat to Duiker Island, also known as 'Seal Island' for its colony of Cape fur seals (not to be confused with the official Seal Island in False Bay). **Circe Launches** (Map p92; 082 552 2904; www.circelaunches.co.za; Hout Bay Harbour, Hout Bay; adult/child R75/45; Fishmarket), **Drumbeat Charters** (Map p92; 021-791 4441; www.drumbeatcharters.co.za; Hout Bay Harbour, Hout Bay; adult/child R90/50; Fishmarket) and **Nauticat Charters** (Map p92; 021-790 7278; www.nauticatcharters.co.za; Hout Bay Harbour, Hout Bay; adult/child R85/45; Fishmarket) run these 40- to 60-minute cruises daily, usually with guaranteed sailings in the mornings.

Some trips require a minimum of 15 to 20 passengers.

Simon's Town & Southern Peninsula

★**Kayak Cape Town** KAYAKING
(Map p108; 082 501 8930; www.kayakcapetown.co.za; Wharf St, Simon's Town; Simon's Town) Paddle out to the penguin colony (p108) at Boulders (R300, two hours) with this Simon's Town–based operation.

Gary's Surf School SURFING
(Map p104; 021-788 9839; www.garysurf.co.za; 34 Balmoral Bldg, Beach Rd, Muizenberg; 2hr lessons R500; 8am-5pm; Muizenberg) Genial surfing coach Gary Kleynhans and his team teach wave-riding novices aged four and upwards, using longboards and plenty of happy-go-lucky surf attitude. You can also hire boards and wetsuits (per hour/day R150/600) or join a sandboarding trip to the dunes at Fish Hoek (R350).

Veld and Sea FOOD
(Map p110; 060 509 4288; www.veldandsea.com; Good Hope Gardens Nursery, Plateau Rd, Scarborough; adult/child R550/250; 9am-4.30pm) Based at the Good Hope Gardens Nursery (www.goodhopegardensnursery.co.za) of indigenous plants, Veld and Sea runs fynbos and coastal foraging courses. Experienced guides will teach you sustainable techniques to harvest Mother Nature's edibles, including seaweed and mussels from nearby rock pools in Scarborough and the Cape of Good Hope (p107) nature reserve. Lunch is made from whatever you find.

If you want to harvest mussels, you need to get a mollusk permit, available from post offices.

Outer Kommetjie SURFING

(off Lighthouse Rd) A top surfing location, Kommetjie offers an assortment of reefs that hold a very big swell. Outer Kommetjie is a left point out from Slangkop Lighthouse, at the southern end of the village. Inner Kommetjie is a more protected, smaller left, with lots of kelp (only at high tide). They both work best with a southeasterly or southwesterly wind.

Surfstore Africa WATER SPORTS

(Map p104; 076 202 3703, 021-788 5055; www.surfstore.co.za; 48-50 Beach Rd, Muizenberg; kite-surfing lessons from R1600; Muizenberg) You can take lessons in kite-surfing and stand-up paddleboarding (SUP), as well as regular surfing, with these folks. Also here is a shop stocking a wide range of surf-related gear, and a cafe.

Pisces Divers DIVING

(Map p108; 021-786 3799; www.piscesdivers.co.za; Goods Shed, Main Rd, Simon's Town; guided dives from R1200, courses from R1300; Simon's Town) Just metres from the water's edge, this PADI dive centre offers a range of courses and scheduled dives.

Roxy Surf Club SURFING

(Map p104; 021-788 8687; www.surfemporium.co.za/roxy-surf-school; Empire Bldg, Beach Rd, Muizenberg; private lessons R360; 7.30am-5.30pm; Muizenberg) Started in 2003 as a women-only surf club to encourage more girls and women to get into this male-dominated sport, Roxy still runs female-only classes, but guys can get in on the action, too, as it's now part of the larger Surf Emporium shop.

Sleepy Hollow Horse Riding HORSE RIDING

(021-789 2341, 083 261 0104; www.sleepyhollowhorseriding.com; Sleepy Hollow Ln, Noordhoek; beach rides R530, bush trails R350; beach rides 9am, 1pm & 4pm, bush trails 11.30am & 3.30pm) This reliable operation offers two-hour rides along the wide, sandy beach at Noordhoek, as well as one-hour explorations of the mountainous hinterland. Advance booking is essential. Pony rides and lessons are also available.

CAPE CAMINO

Inspired by the Camino de Santiago, the famous long-distance pilgrimage hiking route in Spain, the 9-leg, 169km **Cape Camino** (083 997 7404, 084 844 7996; https://capecamino.co.za; passport R380) was launched by mother-and-daughter team Gabrielle Andrew and Peggy Coetzee-Andrew in 2015. Parts of the circular route around the Cape Peninsula follow trails through Table Mountain National Park, but at no point do you climb up to the top of the mountain.

Starting from the cableway up Table Mountain, the path runs across the mountain slopes, past Rhodes Memorial and Kirstenbosch National Botanical Garden to Constantia Nek. It then heads down to False Bay and Simon's Town before crossing to the west side of the Peninsula. Heading up from Scarborough to Green Point brings you back to where you started.

The route is broken up into chunks from 8km to 25km in length, depending on the walker's ability and the difficulty of the terrain. In line with the Cape Camino's core principles of promoting peace, unity and sustainability, the route follows roads into a diverse range of communities, connecting you also to a variety of sacred spaces including *kramats* (Islamic shrines), churches, synagogues and spiritual sites of the Khoe-San.

Local guides and small business, such as cafes and guesthouses, provide logistical services and the Camino's passport entitles you to discounts with them. Portering of your bags can be arranged between each of the legs (per day R250), as can accommodation and transfers. If you don't have time to do the entire circuit, it's possible to hike as many legs as you like or put together your own itinerary. At various times of the year, group hikes are also organised, such as a LGBT-friendly one around Mardi Gras time in February and ones to support various local charities. The Cape Camino Forum (www.facebook.com/groups/895423400589197) is the place to connect with others who have hiked or are planning to hike the route.

CYCLING, SKATEBOARDING & ROLLERBLADING

Every Monday at 6pm, up to 300 skateboarders, rollerbladers and cyclists gather at the parking lot beside Queen's Beach to take part in **Promenade Mondays** (Map p90; www.facebook.com/promenademondays; off Beach Rd, Sea Point). This super-social push-/roll-/skate-a-thon along Sea Point Promenade is organised by town planner and longboarder Marco Morgan, who is also a founding member of the National Skate Collective. The group has been lobbying the city for years to provide improved facilities for skaters.

The lifting of the ban on skateboarding and cycling along the promenade in recent years has also paved the way for **Up Cycles** (p185), which has a **rental bike station** next to Sea Point Pavilion and another **station** at the Bay Hotel in Camps Bay. So even as a visitor it's possible to join in the pedal- and push-powered event.

There are skateboard shops along Long St if you want to pick up your own set of wheels, and it's worth checking out the scene at the **Mill St Bridge Skate Park** (Map p84; Mill St, Gardens; 8am-9pm; Gardens) FREE in Gardens, where you may even catch South African champion skater (and Cape Town local) **Jean-marc Johannes** (www.facebook.com/jeanmarcskate) practising his moves.

Cape Flats & Northern Suburbs

Skydive Cape Town SKYDIVING
(082 800 6290; www.skydivecapetown.co.za; Delta 200 Airfield, Brakkefontein Rd, Melkbosstrand; R2850; 9am-4pm; Koeberg Power Station) Based about 40km north of the city centre in the Melkbosstrand area, this experienced outfit offers tandem skydives. Needless to say, the views – once you stop screaming – are spectacular. No Cape Town pickups offered, but the staff can recommend transport operators if you don't have your own vehicle.

Oude Molen Eco Village OUTDOORS
(Map p114; 021-448 9442; www.oudemolenecovillage.co.za; Alexandra Rd, Pinelands; pool adult/youth/child R30/20/10; 9am-5pm Tue-Sun; ; Pinelands) Many grass-roots-style operations occupy this once-abandoned section of the buildings and grounds of the Valkenberg psychiatric hospital.

The numerous activities include horse riding with **Oude Molen Stables** (Map p114; 073 199 7395; per hour R150; 9am-5pm; Pinelands) and swimming in the village's outdoor pool. Also here are the cafe and farm stall Millstone (p155).

Check the village's Facebook page (www.facebook.com/OudeMolenEcoVillage) for details of events such as the annual jazz festival, held over a weekend in late November.

Best Kiteboarding Africa WATER SPORTS
(021-556 2765; www.bestkiteboardingafrica.com; Portico Bldg, Athens Rd, Table View; half-/full-day lesson R1185/2350; 9.30am-5pm Mon-Fri, 10am-3pm Sat & Sun; Marine Circle) The long, broad, windswept beach at Table View is ideal for the sport of kite-surfing. This outfit, overlooking the beach, can teach you how to do it, or just rent you some gear if you already know how. It also teaches stand-up paddleboarding (SUP; two-hour lesson R1185).

Milnerton Golf Club GOLF
(Map p114; 021-552 1047; www.milnertongolf.co.za; Bridge Rd, Milnerton; 18 holes R650; 7am-5pm; Woodbridge) About 10km north of the city centre on Woodbridge Island, this 18-hole, par-72 course has a magnificent position overlooking Table Bay and great views of Table Mountain. (The wind can be challenging, though.)

King David Mowbray Golf Club GOLF
(Map p114; 021-685 3018; www.mowbraygolfclub.co.za; 1 Raapenberg Rd, Mowbray; 18 holes R580; 8am-6pm; Pinelands) Established in 1910, Mowbray is considered by some to be the best in-town course for its parkland setting and abundant birdlife. It certainly has a lovely view of Devil's Peak.

Tours

If you're short on time, have a specific interest, or want some expert help in seeing Cape Town, there's a small army of tour guides and companies waiting to assist you.

NOON GUN

Monday to Saturday you can set your watch by the **Noon Gun**, a cannon fired from the lower slopes of 350m-high Signal Hill, which separates Sea Point from the City Bowl. Traditionally, the blast allowed the burghers in the town below to check their watches. It's a stiff walk up here through the Bo-Kaap – take Longmarket St and keep going until it ends, just beneath the gun emplacement (which is off limits) – but the view is phenomenal. You can also drive or take a taxi up Signal Hill along Military Rd, accessed off Kloof Nek Rd.

The best will provide invaluable insight into Capetonian food and wine, flora and fauna, and history and culture.

City Walking & Biking Tours

VoiceMap (www.voicemap.me) This locally developed website and app provides high-quality self-guided walking tours that you can download to your smart phone or listen to on your computer. Narrated by local experts, they provide insight into corners of the city sometimes overlooked by regular guided tours.

Cape Town on Foot (Map p70; 021-462 2252; www.wanderlust.co.za; 66 Loop St, City Bowl; tours R250; 11am Mon, Wed & Fri; Church, Longmarket) These 2½-hour walking tours, leaving from Cape Town Tourism's office on Burg St, cover the central city sights and are led by a knowledgeable guide speaking either English or German.

Day Trippers (021-511 4766; www.daytrippers.co.za) Many of this long-established outfit's tours include the chance to go cycling. Their city cycle tour is R360.

Township & Cultural Tours

The best township tours provide a clear understanding of the Mother City's split nature and the challenges faced by the vast majority of Capetonians in their daily lives. They also reveal that these lives are not uniformly miserable and deprived, and that there are many inspiring things to see and do and people to meet.

Typically lasting half a day, township tours usually involve travel in a car or small coach, but there are also walking, cycling and even running tours, if you'd prefer.

Juma's Tours (073 400 4064; www.townshiparttours.co.za) Zimbabwean Juma is a talented street artist who lives and works in Khayelitsha where he leads excellent walking tours of the street art brightening up the area around Khayelitsha Station. He's also the go-to guide for insights into the rich stock of street art in Woodstock where he used to live and where he still leads walking tours.

Andulela (083 305 2599, 021-790 2592; http://andulela.com; cooking tours from R985) Offers a variety of cultural and culinary-themed tours, including an African cooking tour in Langa and a Cape Malay one in Bo-Kaap.

Siviwe Tours (076 483 5539; www.siviwetours.com; tours from R350) Personable guide Siviwe Mbinda is the founder of this company, offering two-hour walking tours around Langa. Itineraries often include a performance by the Happy Feet gumboot dance troupe that Siviwe established. Another of Siviwe's tour companies is **Vamos** (083 452 1112, 072 499 7866; www.vamos.co.za; cycling tours R320), which offers cycling tours of Langa.

Dinner@Mandela's (021-790 5817, 083 471 2523; www.dinneratmandelas.co.za; tours R400) A highly recommended alternative or addition to daytime township tours is this evening tour and dinner combination at Imizamo Yethu. It runs Mondays and Thursdays from 7pm (with pick-ups in the city centre). The meal, which includes African traditional dishes and is veggie-friendly, is held at Tamfanfa's Tavern and is preceded by lively African dancing and a choir singing.

Imizamo Yethu Tour (Map p92; 083 719 4870; www.suedafrika.net/imizamoyethu; R75; tours 10.30am, 1pm & 4pm; Imizamo Yethu) Local guide Afrika Moni offers a two-hour walking tour of Hout Bay's township, meeting local residents at the police station and then visiting the *spaza* (shop), *shebeen* (bar) and *sangoma* (traditional healer).

Transcending History Tours (084 883 2514; http://sites.google.com/site/capeslaveroutetours; 2½hr tours from R200) Lucy Campbell is the go-to academic for these tours, which offer a deeper insight into the rich and fascinating indigenous and slave history of the Cape.

18 Gangster Museum (021-821 7864, 073 707 3639; www.18gm.co.za; Dullah Omar St, Mandela Park, Khayelitsha; R60; 8.30am-6pm Mon-Fri, 10am-3pm Sat & Sun) One-hour walking tours, including this tiny museum (housed in a shipping container) that illustrates the

TOP TOURS

City Sightseeing Cape Town (☎086 173 3287; www.citysightseeing.co.za; adult/child 1 day R180/100, 2 days R280/200) These hop-on, hop-off buses, running two main routes, are perfect for a quick orientation, with commentary available in 16 languages. The open-top double-deckers also provide an elevated platform for photos. Buses run at roughly half-hourly intervals between 9am and 4.30pm, with extra services in peak season.

Coffeebeans Routes (Map p84; ☎021-813 9829; https://coffeebeansroutes.com; iKhaya Lodge Hotel, Dunkley Sq, Gardens; tours from US$90; Roodehek) The concept – hooking up visitors with interesting local personalities, including musicians, artists, brewers and designers – helps this long-running company stand out from the tour operator pack. Among innovative routes in Cape Town and surrounds are ones focusing on South Africa's recent revolutionary history, creative enterprises, and organic and natural wines.

Awol Tours (Map p86; ☎021-418 3803; www.awoltours.co.za; Information Centre, Dock Rd, V&A Waterfront; 9am-6pm; Nobel Sq) Discover Cape Town's cycle lanes on this superb city bike tour (daily, three hours, R600) from Awol's Waterfront base. Other pedalling itineraries include the Winelands, Cape Point and the township of Masiphumelele – a great alternative to traditional township tours. They also offer guided hikes on Table Mountain (from R1850).

Uthando (☎021-683 8523; www.uthandosa.org; R912) These township tours cost more because half of the money goes towards the social upliftment projects that the tours visit and are specifically designed to support. Usually three or so projects are visited: they could be anything from an organic farm to an old folks' centre.

Run Cape Town (Map p88; ☎072 920 7028; www.runcapetown.co.za; tours from R600) Sightsee while getting a workout on this innovative company's variety of running routes across the city, within Table Mountain National Park and further afield in Gugulethu and Darling.

treacherous path that too many in these communities follow into crime. They also offer a half-day walking, cycling and taxi tour, incorporating the museum alongside a visit to a reformed gangster's house, Khayelitsha Mall and Lookout Hill, as well as a braai lunch.

Maboneng Township Arts Experience (☎021-824 1773; www.maboneng.com) These walking tours of Langa, normally including Guga S'Thebe, the Langa Pass Museum, street art and a local artist's home gallery, are a fun way to experience the township's creative side. One-hour, half-day and full-day options are offered.

Nature Tours

Hiking and walking tours can be arranged in Table Mountain National Park (p55) and around the **Rondevlei Nature Reserve** (☎021-706 2404; rondevleinaturereserve@capetown.gov.za; cnr Perth Rd & Fishermans Walk, Zeekoevlei; 7.30am-5pm; P) FREE.

Boat trips to spot sharks, whales and pelagic birds can be arranged in **Simon's Town** (Map p108; ☎021-786 5717; www.apexpredators.com; Quayside Bldg, Simon's Town; shark-watching tours from R2400; Simon's Town).

Birdwatch Cape (☎021-592 7438, 072 211 9863; www.birdwatch.co.za; tours per person R4000) offers informative tours pointing out the many unique species of the Cape bird kingdom.

Festivals & Events

Sun Met SPORTS
(www.sunmet.co.za; Kenilworth Racecourse, Rosmead Ave, Kenilworth; Jan) South Africa's richest horse race, with a jackpot of R1.5 million, is a time for big bets and even bigger hats. Generally held on the last Saturday in January.

Design Indaba ART
(www.designindaba.com; Feb) This creative convention, bringing together the varied worlds of fashion, architecture, visual arts, crafts and media, is held at the end of February, usually at the Cape Town International Convention Centre.

Cape Town Minstrel Carnival CULTURAL
(www.facebook.com/capetownminstrelca; Jan & Feb) *Tweede Nuwe Jaar* (2 January) is when the satin- and sequin-clad minstrel troupes traditionally march through the city for the Kaapse Klopse (Cape Minstrel Festival) from Keizergracht St, along Adderley and Wale Sts to the Bo-Kaap. Throughout January into early February there are Saturday competitions between troupes at **Athlone Stadium** (☎021-637 6607; Cross Blvd, Athlone; Athlone).

Cape Town Carnival CULTURAL
(www.capetowncarnival.com; Walk of Remembrance, Green Point; ⌚mid-Mar) Held along the Walk of Remembrance (the former Fan Walk), this is a city-sponsored parade and street party that celebrates the many facets of South African identity.

Cape Town Cycle Tour SPORTS
(www.capetowncycletour.com; ⌚mid-Mar) Held on a Saturday, this is the world's largest timed cycling event, attracting more than 30,000 contestants. The route circles Table Mountain, heading down the Atlantic Coast and along Chapman's Peak Dr.

Infecting the City ART
(☎021-418 3336; http://infectingthecity.com; ⌚Mar) Cape Town's wonderful squares, fountains, museums and theatres are the venues for this innovative performing-arts festival, held every two years, featuring artists from across the continent. The next festival is in 2019.

Old Mutual Two Oceans Marathon SPORTS
(☎087 740 5260; www.twooceansmarathon.org.za; ⌚mid-Mar) This 56km marathon follows a route around Table Mountain. It generally attracts about 9000 competitors.

Cape Town International Jazz Festival MUSIC
(☎021-671 0506; www.capetownjazzfest.com; ⌚Mar or Apr) Cape Town's biggest jazz event, attracting big names from both South Africa and overseas, is usually held at the Cape Town International Convention Centre at the end of March. It includes a free concert in Greenmarket Sq.

Mercedes-Benz Fashion Week FASHION
(www.africanfashioninternational.com; ⌚Mar/Apr) Fashionistas line the catwalks at venues around the city to spot the hottest work from local designers and to pick up the latest trends.

Good Food & Wine Show FOOD & DRINK
(www.goodfoodandwineshow.co.za; ⌚May) Cape Town goes gourmet with this three-day event held at the Cape Town International Convention Centre.

Cape Town Nu World Festival MUSIC
(http://capetownnuworldfestival.com; ⌚mid-Jul) Held over Mandela Day weekend (around 18 July), this celebration of global beats and rhythms takes over old City Hall and parts of the Grand Parade.

Open Book Festival LITERATURE
(http://openbookfestival.co.za; ⌚Sep) The city's main literature festival has a packed schedule with talks, readings and discussions with local and international writers. It's organised by the Fugard Theatre, with events held there, the District Six Homecoming Centre and the Book Lounge.

Cape Town Fringe ART
(☎086 000 2004; www.capetownfringe.co.za; ⌚mid-Sep–early Oct) A jamboree of the performing arts, organised in conjunction with the respected Grahamstown Festival, that peppers the Mother City with interesting happenings for 11 days at the end of September and into October.

OUTsurance Kfm 94.5 Gun Run SPORTS
(http://thegunrun.co.za; ⌚early Oct) This popular half-marathon (21km) is the only time that the Noon Gun on Signal Hill gets fired on a Sunday – competitors try to finish the race before the gun goes off. There are also 10km and 5km races.

Mama City Improv Festival COMEDY
(www.mamacityimprovfest.com; ⌚Oct) Five laughter-packed days of shows at venues in Observatory – including Obviouzly Armchair (p170) – for this stand-up comedy and improvisation festival with workshops and performances by local and international talents.

Season of Sauvignon WINE
(www.durbanvillewine.co.za/festivals; ⌚late Oct) Durbanville celebrates its signature grape, sauvignon blanc, at this festival in late October, with the area's wineries hosting events from vertical tastings (tasting different vintages of one wine type) to live music.

Cape Town International Kite Festival AIR SHOW
(www.capementalhealth.co.za/kite; ⌚late Oct/early Nov) This colourful gathering of kite enthusiasts at Zandvlei, near Muizenberg, is held at the end of October or early November, in support of the Cape Mental Health Society.

Miss Gay Western Cape LGBT
(www.missgay.co.za; Joseph Stone Auditorium, Klipfontein Rd, Athlone; ⌚early Nov) Glam frocks are dusted off and created for this long-running transgender beauty pageant, usually held in early November.

Streetopia STREET CARNIVAL
(http://streetopia.co.za; ⌚Nov) The lively street festival is usually held on the last Saturday

in the November at various locations around central Observatory, including the Trill Rd, Station Rd and Lower Main Rd.

Wavescape Surf & Ocean Festival SURFING
(www.wavescapefestival.com; end Nov-early Dec) Events for this surfing-themed fest – which include art shows, movie screenings and masterclasses – are held at various places around the Cape, including Muizenburg and the Waterfront.

Adderley Street Christmas Lights MUSIC
(www.capetown.gov.za; Dec) Join the tens of thousands who turn out for the concert in front of Cape Town Railway Station that precedes the switching on of festive lights along Adderley St, and a parade. The same street is pedestrianised each night from around 17 to 30 December for a night market, with live music.

Cape Town Festival of Beer BEER
(www.capetownfestivalofbeer.co.za; Hamilton's Rugby Club, 1 Stephan Way, Green Point; early Dec) With the stadium as a backdrop, the continent's largest beer festival sees more than 200 beers available for tasting over three days.

Sleeping

From five-star pamper palaces and designer-chic guesthouses to creatively imagined backpackers, Cape Town's stock of sleeping options caters to all wallets. Choose your base carefully depending on your priorities – not everywhere is close to a beach or major sights.

Reserve well in advance, especially if visiting during school holidays (from mid-December to the end of January); most places slash their rates in the quiet winter season from May to October.

Rates usually include VAT of 14% and, often, the 1% tourism promotion levy. Check whether secure parking is included in your hotel rate, otherwise you could be charged anything up to R150 extra per day to park your car.

CHECK THE FACILITIES

As always, you get what you pay for, but you may be pleasantly surprised at the quality of what you get. Among the few things to watch out for are the following:

Internet access Wi-fi is common and often complimentary, but service may be slow, unsecure and with download limits; if you need a reliable connection, make detailed enquiries beforehand and check additional costs carefully.

Swimming pools Often more accurately described as plunge pools, particularly when found in guesthouses, though some top hotels have tiny pools, too.

Secure parking Not everywhere has it; some places that do, particularly in the City Bowl area, will slap on an extra daily charge of anything up to R150.

City Bowl, Foreshore, Bo-Kaap & De Waterkant

★**91 Loop** HOSTEL $
(Map p70; 021-286 1469; www.91loop.co.za; 91 Loop St, City Bowl; dm/r incl breakfast from R270/1000; ; Church, Longmarket) Jo'burg investors are behind this new and buzzing place offering a good range of rooms, including pods – essentially a dorm bed but instead of a bunk you sleep in a concrete, oblong pod with a tad more privacy. Rooms and dorms (all named after major world cities) offer big mattresses, and there are high housekeeping standards throughout.

The stylish **Honey Badger** restaurant and bar on the ground floor is a major social space, and there's a programme of daily activities – some free – to get guests mingling.

Happy Rhino Hotel HOTEL $
(Map p70; 021-424 5092; http://happyrhino.co.za; 179 Loop St, City Bowl; s/d from R800/950, parking R150 per night; ; Upper Loop, Upper Long) For such a central location this new but functional basic hotel offers a pretty good deal. The compact rooms feature exposed-brick walls and for R200 more you'll have a grand view of Table Mountain from the seventh floor. These also offer self-catering studios but they don't have a view.

Scalabrini Guest House GUESTHOUSE $
(Map p70; 021-465 6433; www.scalabrini.org.za; 47 Commercial St, City Bowl; dm/s/d R280/560/780; @; Roeland) The Italian monastic-order Scalabrini Fathers have provided welfare services to Cape Town's poor and to refugees since 1994. Housed in a former textile factory, they run several social programs, and a pleasant guesthouse with 11 immaculately clean en-suite rooms – plus a great kitchen for self-catering where you can also watch satellite TV.

SELF-CATERING & SERVICED APARTMENTS

For longer-term stays, a self-catering or serviced apartment or villa can be a good deal. Reliable agencies include the following:

African Elite Properties (Map p74; ☎021-421 1090; www.africaneliteproperties.com; Shop A21, Cape Quarter, Dixon St, De Waterkant; 1-bed apt from R3000; Alfred) Agency handling rental of luxury apartments atop the Cape Quarter.

Cape Stay (www.capestay.co.za) Accommodation across the Cape.

De Waterkant Cottages (Map p74; ☎021-421 2300; www.dewaterkantcottages.com; 40 Napier St, De Waterkant; apt/house from R1650/2200; Old Fire Station) Classy villas and apartments in De Waterkant, sleeping from two to eight people.

In Awe Stays (☎083 658 6975; www.inawestays.co.za; d from R1600) Stylish studios and cottages in Gardens and Fresnaye, with doubles from R1600.

Village & Life (Map p94; ☎021-437 9700; www.villageandlife.com; 69 Victoria Rd, Camps Bay; Old Fire Station) Focused mainly on properties in De Waterkant and Camps Bay.

Long Street Backpackers HOSTEL $
(Map p70; ☎021-423 0615; www.longstreetbackpackers.co.za; 209 Long St, City Bowl; dm/s/d R190/350/490; ; Dorp, Leeuwen) Little has changed at this backpackers since it opened in 1993 (making it the longest-running of the many that dot Long St). In a block of 14 small flats, with four to 10 beds and a bathroom in each, accommodation is arranged around a leafy courtyard decorated with funky mosaics, in which the resident cat pads around.

Rose Lodge B&B $
(Map p70; ☎021-424 3813; www.rosestreet28.com; 28 Rose St, Bo-Kaap; s/d inc breakfast from R890/990; ; Old Fire Station) Inside a grey-painted corner house is this cute B&B. The Canadian owner likes to play the grand piano and has two adorable dogs. There are just three cosy rooms (with private bathrooms), all decorated in contemporary style. They manage several more similar properties in the Bo-Kaap.

St Paul's B&B Guesthouse B&B $
(Map p70; ☎021-423 4420; www.stpaulsguesthouse.com; 182 Bree St, City Bowl; s/d incl breakfast R600/950, with shared bathroom R500/800; P; Upper Long, Upper Loop) This spotless, characterful B&B in a very handy location is a fine alternative to the backpacker lodges along Long St. The simply furnished and spacious rooms have high ceilings, and there's a vine-shaded courtyard where you can relax or eat breakfast.

★**Cape Heritage Hotel** BOUTIQUE HOTEL $$
(Map p70; ☎021-424 4646; www.capeheritage.co.za; Heritage Sq, 90 Bree St, City Bowl; d/ste/apt incl breakfast from R2850/4420/7000, parking per day R85; P@; Church, Longmarket) Each of the 19 rooms at this elegant boutique hotel, part of the Heritage Sq redevelopment of 18th-century buildings, has its own character. Some have four-poster beds and all have modern conveniences such as satellite TV and clothes presses. There's a roof terrace and a jacuzzi.

★**Rouge on Rose** BOUTIQUE HOTEL $$
(Map p70; ☎021-426 0298; www.rougeonrose.co.za; 25 Rose St, Bo-Kaap; s/d incl breakfast R1600/2300; ; Old Fire Station) This great Bo-Kaap option offers nine rustic-chic suites with kitchenettes, lounges and lots of workspace. The fun wall paintings are by a resident artist and all rooms have luxurious, open bath spaces with standalone tubs.

★**Grand Daddy Hotel** BOUTIQUE HOTEL $$
(Map p70; ☎021-424 7247; www.granddaddy.co.za; 38 Long St, City Bowl; r/trailer from R2895/3695; P@; Mid-Long, Church) The Grand Daddy's star attraction is its rooftop 'trailer park' of penthouse suites, made from seven vintage, artistically renovated Airstream trailers. The hotel's regular rooms are also stylish and incorporate playful references to South African culture.

Purple House B&B, APARTMENT $$
(Map p74; ☎021-418 2508; www.purplehouse.co.za; 23 Jarvis St, De Waterkant; s/d/apt from R1450/1650/1700; @; Alfred) Apart

from their stylish and cosy B&B, set in the eponymous purple-painted house, the personable Dutch owners Hank and Guido also offer a self-catering cottage on the same street and other apartments around town. It's all very LGBT friendly.

Dutch Manor HISTORIC HOTEL **$$**
(Map p70; ☎087 095 1375; www.dutchmanor.co.za; 158 Buitengracht St, Bo-Kaap; s/d incl breakfast R2050/2250, parking per day R100; P ❄ 📶; 🚌Dorp, Leeuwen) Four-poster beds, giant armoires and creaking floorboards lend terrific atmosphere to this six-room property crafted from a 1812 building. However, standards of service have slipped a bit and it overlooks busy Buitengracht, so you may get some traffic noise.

Cape Breaks APARTMENT **$$**
(Map p70; ☎083 383 4888; http://capebreaks.co.za; St Martini Gardens, 74 Queen Victoria St, City Bowl; studio from R1485; P 📶 🏊) Offers great studios and apartments in St Martini Gardens, a complex beside the Company's Garden, with Table Mountain and Lion's Head views. The complex also has a decent-sized pool and parking.

The Charles GUESTHOUSE **$$**
(Map p74; ☎021-409 2500; www.thecharles.co.za; 137 Waterkant St, De Waterkant; s/d incl breakfast from R1300/1550; ❄ @ 📶; 🚌Alfred) This appealing guesthouse and cafe has a central position in De Waterkant. The cafe's tables spill out onto a terrace with good views of the area. Rooms vary in size, the cheapest being small. Larger ones are open-plan and come with kitchens for self-catering.

La Rose B&B B&B **$$**
(Map p70; ☎021-422 5883; www.larosecapetown.com; 32 Rose St, Bo-Kaap; s/d incl breakfast from R1000/1200; P ❄ 📶; 🚌Old Fire Station) Adheena and Yoann are the very welcoming South African–French couple running this charming B&B, which has been so successful it has expanded into nearby properties. It's beautifully decorated and has a rooftop garden with the best views of the area. Yoann's speciality is making authentic crêpes for the guests.

Daddy Long Legs Hotel BOUTIQUE HOTEL **$$**
(Map p70; ☎021-422 3074; www.daddylonglegs.co.za; 134 Long St, City Bowl; r/apt from R950/1450; ❄ @ 📶; 🚌Dorp, Leeuwen) A stay at this boutique hotel-cum-art installation is anything but boring. Thirteen artists were given free rein to design the boudoirs of their dreams; the results range from a bohemian garret to a hospital ward! Our favourites include the karaoke room (with a mic in the shower) and the room decorated with cartoons of the South African pop group Freshlyground.

Breakfast is extra. They also offer super-stylish **apartments** (Map p70; 263 Long St, City Bowl; apt from R1450; ❄; 🚌Upper Long, Upper Loop) – an ideal choice if you crave hotel-suite luxury but want to self-cater.

The Grey BOUTIQUE HOTEL **$$**
(Map p74; ☎021-421 1106; www.thegreyhotel.co.za; 49 Napier St, De Waterkant; s/d from R1320/2750; ❄ @ 📶 🏊; 🚌Alfred) Rooms are smart (and, naturally, decorated in shades of grey), but most are very small, especially at the lower end of the price range when the bed practically fills the room. The rooftop plunge pool and bar is a prime spot for guests to check out the view – as well as each other.

Breakfast (R165 per person) is served in the Piano Bar (p168), which also serves as the hotel's reception.

De Waterkant House B&B **$$**
(Map p74; ☎021-409 2500; www.dewaterkant.com; 35 Loader St, De Waterkant; s/d incl breakfast from R1300/1550; @ 📶 🏊; 🚌Old Fire Station) This pleasant B&B, in a renovated Cape Georgian house, comes with a tiny plunge pool for hot summers and a lounge fireplace for chilly winters.

Townhouse HOTEL **$$**
(Map p70; ☎021-465 7050; www.townhouse.co.za; 60 Corporation St, City Bowl; s/d incl breakfast from R1685/2905, parking per day R95; P ❄ @ 📶 🏊; 🚌Groote Kerk) In the heart of the city, the Townhouse offers good service and high standards, making it justly popular. Rooms have been given a contemporary makeover, with wooden floors and chic black-and-white decor.

★ **Taj Cape Town** LUXURY HOTEL **$$$**
(Map p70; ☎021-819 2000; www.tajhotels.com; Wale St, City Bowl; r/ste incl breakfast R3000/5000; P ❄ @ 📶 🏊; 🚌Groote Kerk) India's luxury hotel group has breathed new life into the old Board of Executors building. There's plenty of heritage here but a new tower also houses the chic contemporary-styled rooms, many offering spectacular views of Table Mountain. Service and facilities, including the excellent restaurant Bombay Brasserie (p142), are top grade.

East City, District Six, Woodstock & Observatory

★ Wish U Were Here HOSTEL $
(Map p80; 021-447 0522; www.wishuwerehere capetown.com; 445 Albert Rd, Salt River; dm R280, d R845, s/d with shared bathroom R550/780; ; Kent) The designers clearly had a lot of fun with this place just a short stroll from the Old Biscuit Mill. One dorm is Barbie-doll pink; a romantic double has a swinging bed made from a suspended fishing boat; another is styled after an intensive care unit! The building's wrap-around balcony overlooks the Salt River roundabout (which is noisy during the day).

Bohemian Lofts Backpackers HOSTEL $
(Map p79; 021-447 6204; www.bohemian lofts.com; 41 Trill Rd, Observatory; dm R220, s/d R650/800, with shared bathroom R600/750; Observatory) With a wrap-around balcony overlooking the heart of Obs, this is one for backpackers who want to soak up all the comings and goings of Lower Main Rd. It's a pleasant place to crash, with decent rooms, pleasant shared spaces and a good kitchen for self caterers, although there are scores of places to eat just outside the door.

Observatory Backpackers HOSTEL $
(Map p79; 021-447 0861; http://observatory backpackers.com; 235 Lower Main Rd, Observatory; dm R240, d R800, with shared bathroom R700; ; Observatory) There's a funky African theme to this very appealing backpackers, just a short walk away from the heart of the Obs action further down Lower Main Rd. The spacious, shady backyard and lounges are a plus. Breakfast is not included, but there is a bakery cafe right next door.

33 South Backpackers HOSTEL $
(Map p79; 021-447 2423; http://33sout hbackpackers.com; 48 Trill Rd, Observatory; dm R190, s/d from R680/720, with shared bathroom R620/680; ; Observatory) This imaginative, cosy backpackers in a Victorian cottage has sought inspiration from different Cape Town suburbs as themes for its rooms. There's a delightful shared kitchen, a pretty courtyard and a convivial bar area. Staff conduct free tours of Observatory. Rates don't include breakfast.

Green Elephant HOSTEL $
(Map p79; 021-448 6359; www.green elephant.co.za; 57 Milton Rd, Observatory; dm R210, s/d R600/750, with shared bathroom R500/650, camping per tent R100; ; Observatory) This long-running backpackers, split between four houses, remains a popular alternative to the city-centre hostels. The en-suite rooms in the houses across the road from the main hostel are particularly pleasant, with wooden floors and rustic-chic furnishing. Rates include a basic breakfast.

Camping in their garden is also possible.

DoubleTree by Hilton Hotel Cape Town – Upper Eastside HOTEL $$
(Map p80; 021-404 0570; www.doubletree. hilton.com; 31 Brickfield Rd, Woodstock; r/ste from R1395/2595, parking per day R60; ; Upper Salt River) This snazzily designed property is tucked away in the revamped buildings of the old Bonwitt clothing factory. Rooms are large and pleasant, offering either mountain or city views. Most loft suites have kitchenettes. There's an indoor pool and a gym. Rates exclude breakfast.

Gardens & Surrounds

Backpack HOSTEL $
(Map p84; 021-423 4530; http://backpack ers.co.za; 74 New Church St, Tamboerskloof; dm R390, s/d from R1150/1440, with shared bathroom 910/1150; ; Upper Long, Upper Loop) This Fair Trade in Tourism–accredited operation offers affordable style, a buzzing vibe and fantastic staff. Its dorms may not be Cape Town's cheapest but they're among its best, while the private rooms and self-catering apartments are charmingly decorated. There's a lovely mosaic-decorated pool and relaxing gardens with Table Mountain views to chill out in. Rates include breakfast.

Once in Cape Town HOSTEL $
(Map p84; 021-424 6169; http://onceincape town.co.za; 73 Kloof St, Gardens; dm/d incl breakfast from R260/1260; ; Ludwig's Garden) Once has a great vibe and location, and every room has its own bathroom. While the rooms are pretty compact, they are all pleasantly decorated. There's a courtyard to chill in and a big kitchen for self-catering.

Ashanti Gardens HOSTEL $
(Map p84; 021-423 8721; https://ashanti.co.za; 11 Hof St, Gardens; dm R300, d R1100, s/d with shared bathroom R620/840, camping R180; ; Government Ave) This is one of Cape Town's slickest backpackers, with much of the action focused on the lively bar and deck that overlook Table Mountain. The beautiful old house, decorated with a tasteful collection

SLEEPING IN TABLE MOUNTAIN NATIONAL PARK

Private camping is banned here, but Table Mountain National Park does have places to stay.

Tented Camps

Partly constructed from materials gathered from the park – so as to blend with nature – these camps are made up of canvas, army-camp type tents, protected by wooden structures and housing comfortable beds. The bathroom facilities at all are excellent, as are the fully equipped communal kitchen and braai (barbecue) areas. You can drive to within relatively easy hiking reach of each. Bring your own bedding and towels.

Bookings can be made online (www.sanparks.org/parks/table_mountain) or by phone (021-428 9111).

Orange Kloof (Map p100; 012-428 9111; www.sanparks.org/parks/table_mountain; off Hout Bay Rd; tents for 2 people R580, additional adult/child R260/130) Perhaps the best, tucked away in a beautiful area near Constantia Nek and providing direct access to the last strand of Afromontane forest in the park.

Slangkop (Map p102; 012-428 9111; www.tmnp.co.za; off Lighthouse Rd, Kommetjie; tents R580; P) Near the lighthouse at Kommetjie, beneath a forest of rare, indigenous milkwood trees and decorated with the bones of a whale that washed up on the beach in 2006.

Smitswinkel (Map p110; 012-428 9111; www.tmnp.co.za; Cape Point; tents R715; P) The only camp to offer en suite bathrooms in its tents, this location is steps from the entrance to the Cape of Good Hope section of the park. Note that it does get windy here.

Cottages

The best of these are **Platteklip Wash House** (Map p88; 012-462 7861, 021-712 7471; www.sanparks.org/parks/table_mountain; Deer Park, Vredehoek; d R980, extra person R490; P; Herzlia) and **Olifantsbos Guest House** (Map p110; 021-780 9204; www.tmnp.co.za; Cape of Good Hope; up to 4 people R3885, extra adult/child R580/290; P). They are in lovely spots and you can drive right up to their doors. Linens are provided.

of contemporary art, holds the dorms and rooms with shared bathrooms; there's also a lawn where you can camp.

Excellent self-catering en-suite rooms are in two separate heritage-listed houses around the corner. There's also another branch in Green Point (p133).

Blencathra HOSTEL $

(Map p88; 073 389 0702, 021-424 9571; www.blencathra.co.za; cnr De Hoop & Cambridge Aves, Tamboerskloof; dm R200, s/d from R700/1000, with shared bathroom R350/500; P@; Cotswold) You're well on the way up Lion's Head at this delightful family home, which offers a range of attractive rooms, mostly frequented by long-stay guests. It's the ideal spot for those looking to escape the city and the more commercialised backpacker options. Rates are negotiable for longer stays.

★La Grenadine GUESTHOUSE $$

(Map p84; 021-424 1358; www.lagrenadine.co.za; 15 Park Rd, Gardens; r/2-bed cottage incl breakfast from R2590/3980; @; Ludwig's Garden) Expat couple Maxime and Mélodie ladle on the Gallic charm at this imaginatively renovated former stables, where the ancient stone walls are a feature of the rooms. The garden planted with fruit trees is a magical oasis, the lounge is stacked with books and vinyl LPs, and breakfast is served on actress Mélodie's prized collection of china.

★Cloud 9 BOUTIQUE HOTEL $$

(Map p84; 021-424 1133; www.hotelcloud9.com; 12 Kloof Nek Rd, Tamboerskloof; s/d incl breakfast from R1945/2590; @; Ludwig's Garden) This arty new boutique hotel and spa has been created from combining several formerly separate properties. Rooms differ depending on what part of the hotel you stay in, but could feature pressed-tin ceilings and tiled fireplace surrounds, kept as part of a contemporary makeover. Major pluses are the spacious rooftop bar and jacuzzi pool with Table Mountain views.

Trevoyan B&B $$

(Map p84; 021-424 4407; http://trevoyan.co.za; 12 Gilmour Hill Rd, Tamboerskloof; r incl breakfast from R2700; P@; Belle Ombre) This heritage building, with high-ceiling rooms, parquet floors and a faint art-deco style, has been transformed into a relaxed guesthouse that is smart but not too posh. A big plus is its lovely courtyard garden, partly shaded by a giant oak, with a pool big enough to swim in.

Cape Cadogan BOUTIQUE HOTEL **$$**

(Map p84; ☎021-480 8080; www.capecadogan.com; 5 Upper Union St, Gardens; s/d from R2190/2920; P ❄ @ ≋; 🚌 Belle Ombre) This *Gone with the Wind*–style, heritage-listed villa presents a very classy boutique operation, with some rooms opening onto the secluded courtyard. Treats abound, with a plate of macarons at reception, complimentary deserts in the lounge in the afternoon and an aperitif and canapés at sunset.

Abbey Manor B&B **$$**

(Map p88; ☎021-462 2935; www.abbey.co.za; 3 Montrose Ave, Oranjezicht; s/d incl breakfast from R2480/3260; P ❄ @ ≋; 🚌 Montrose) Occupying a grand Arts and Crafts–style home, built in 1905 for a shipping magnate, the interiors of this luxury guesthouse marry fine linen and antique furnishings with whimsical art nouveau flourishes. There are just nine rooms, a decent-sized pool and a rooftop terrace with spectacular views. Courteous staff enhance the experience.

Four Rosmead GUESTHOUSE **$$**

(Map p88; ☎021-480 3810; http://fourrosmead.com; 4 Rosmead Ave, Oranjezicht; d/ste incl breakfast from R3500/3900; P ❄ @ ≋; 🚌 Rayden) A heritage-listed building dating from 1903 has been remodelled into this luxury guesthouse. Rooms are a very chic with contemporary art and African crafts as decoration. Special touches include a saltwater swimming pool and a fragrant Mediterranean herb garden.

An African Villa B&B **$$**

(Map p84; ☎021-423 2162; www.capetowncity.co.za; 19 Carstens St, Tamboerskloof; r from R1450; ❄ @ ≋; 🚌 Belle Ombre) There's a sophisticated, colourful 'African modern' design theme at this appealing guesthouse, sheltering behind the facade of three 19th-century terrace houses. Relax in the evening in one of two comfy lounges while sipping the complimentary sherry or port.

★**Mannabay** BOUTIQUE HOTEL **$$$**

(Map p88; ☎021-461 1094; www.mannabay.com; 8 Bridle Rd, Oranjezicht; r/ste incl breakfast from R7000/8700; P ❄ @ ≋; 🚌 Upper Orange) Nothing seems too much bother for the staff at this knockout property, decorated with stunning pieces of contemporary art by local artists. The eight guest rooms are decorated in different themes. Its high hillside location on the edge of the national park provides amazing views. Rates include high tea, which is served in the library lounge.

★**Belmond Mount Nelson Hotel** HOTEL **$$$**

(Map p84; ☎021-483 1000; www.belmond.com; 76 Orange St, Gardens; r/ste incl breakfast from R10,050/12,635; P ❄ @ ≋; 🚌 Government Ave) A world apart from the rest of the city, sitting in three hectares of gardens, the sugar-pink-painted 'Nellie' is a colonial charmer with its chintz decor and doormen in pith helmets. Rooms sport elegant silver and moss-green decorations. Facilities include a large pool, tennis courts, a luxurious spa and several restaurants.

It's great for families since it pushes the boat out for the little ones, with kid-sized robes and bedtime cookies and milk. Even if you don't stay here, drop by for afternoon tea (p162) – it's a Cape Town institution.

15 on Orange HOTEL **$$$**

(Map p84; ☎021-469 8000; www.marriott.com/hotels/travel/cptoh-african-pride-15-on-orange-hotel; cnr Grey's Pass & Orange St, Gardens; r from R4400, parking per day R65; P ❄ @ ≋; 🚌 Michaelis) The lipstick-red marble walkway to the lobby gives an indication of the luxe nature of this hotel, which is built around a soaring atrium onto which some rooms face (perfect for exhibitionists). It's all very plush and design-savvy. Rates exclude breakfast.

Kensington Place BOUTIQUE HOTEL **$$$**

(Map p88; ☎021-424 4744; www.kensingtonplace.co.za; 38 Kensington Cres, Higgovale; r incl breakfast from R4800; P ❄ ≋; 🚌 Upper Kloof) High up the mountain, this exclusive, chic property offers eight spacious and tastefully decorated rooms, all with balconies and beautifully tiled bathrooms. Fresh fruit and flowers in the rooms are a nice touch.

To preserve the adult atmosphere, they don't allow guests with children under 12 to stay.

Green Point & Waterfront

★**B.I.G. Backpackers** HOSTEL **$**

(Map p86; ☎021-434 0688; www.bigbackpackers.co.za; 18 Thornhill Rd, Green Point; dm/s/d/tr R420/1050/1400/1900; P ❄ @ ≋; 🚌 Skye Way) Tucked away on the slopes of Green

Point, this backpackers has a fun, laid-back atmosphere with decently decorated rooms, chill areas and a big kitchen (with an honesty bar). Homemade bread is sometimes available for breakfast and there are three guitars and bicycles handy should you require either.

Ashanti Green Point HOSTEL $
(Map p86; 021-433 1619; www.ashanti.co.za; 23 Antrim Rd, Three Anchor Bay; dm/s/d with shared bathroom R320/640/900, d with private bathroom R1100; P @ ; St Bedes) This chilled backpacker lodge has a breezy hillside position with sea views and is nicely decorated with old Cape Town photos. Rates include a buffet breakfast.

★ **Villa Zest** BOUTIQUE HOTEL $$
(Map p86; 021-433 1246; www.villazest.co.za; 2 Braemar Rd, Green Point; s/d incl breakfast from R2070/2990; P @ ; Upper Portswood) This Bauhaus-style villa has been converted into a quirkily decorated boutique hotel. The seven guest rooms have bold, retro-design papered walls and furniture accented with furry pillows and shag rugs.

In the lobby, admire an impressive collection of '60s and '70s electronic goods, including radios, phones, Polaroid cameras and eight-track cassette players, displayed like artwork.

Radisson Red HOTEL $$
(Map p86; 087 086 1578; www.radissonred.com; Silo 6, Silo Sq, V&A Waterfront; r from R1750, parking R110; P ; Waterfront Silo) Radisson's youthful, fun hotel brand lands at the Waterfront's Silo district and it looks a little like a funky airport lounge. Superhero and Minnie Mouse dolls greet you at the lobby communal desk, there's a wall covered in Coca-Cola crates and a rather snazzy rooftop pool and bar. Rooms are functional and reasonably spacious with big beds.

La Splendida HOTEL $$
(Map p86; 021-439 5119; www.lasplendida.co.za; 121 Beach Rd, Mouille Point; s/d from R1170/1420, parking per day R25; P ; Lighthouse) You'll pay slightly extra for rooms with sea views at this hotel located on the Mouille Point Promenade, but the ones looking towards Signal Hill are just as nice and they're all quite spacious. There's a retro pop-art feel to the decor.

Breakfast (an extra R115 per person) is served in Sotano (p164), the buzzy cafe-bar on the ground floor.

Cape Standard BOUTIQUE HOTEL $$
(Map p86; 021-430 3060; www.capestandard.co.za; 3 Romney Rd, Green Point; s/d incl breakfast R1650/2100; P @ ; Ravenscraig) A chic property offering whitewashed beach-house rooms downstairs or contemporary rooms upstairs. The mosaic-tiled bathrooms have showers big enough to dance in. It recently extended into a neighbouring villa thus expanding its rooms, garden space and pool size (which is still not really big enough to swim much in).

Head South Lodge BOUTIQUE HOTEL $$
(Map p86; 021-434 8777; www.headsouth.co.za; 215 Main Rd, Three Anchor Bay; s/d incl breakfast from R1400/2100; P @ ; Ellerslie) A homage to the 1950s, with retro furnishings and a collection of Tretchikoff prints hung en masse in the bar. Its big rooms, decorated in cool white and grey, are decorated with equally striking modern art by Philip Briel.

★ **Cape Grace** LUXURY HOTEL $$$
(Map p86; 021-410 7100; www.capegrace.com; West Quay Rd, V&A Waterfront; r/ste incl breakfast from R9700/23,000; P @ ; Nobel Sq) One of the Waterfront's most appealing hotels, Cape Grace sports an arty combination of antiques and crafts decoration – including hand-painted bed covers and curtains – providing a unique sense of place and Cape Town's history.

★ **One&Only Cape Town** LUXURY HOTEL $$$
(Map p86; 021-431 5888; www.oneandonlycapetown.com; Dock Rd, V&A Waterfront; r/ste incl breakfast from R12,795/27,565; P @ ; Aquarium) Little expense seems to have been spared creating this luxury resort. Choose between enormous, plush rooms in the main building (with panoramic views of Table Mountain) or the even more exclusive island beside the pool and spa.

Silo Hotel BOUTIQUE HOTEL $$$
(Map p86; 021-670 0500; www.theroyalportfolio.com/the-silo; Silo Sq, V&A Waterfront; r/ste from R18,000/25,000; P ; Waterfront Silo) In counterpoint to its former industrial surroundings, and the clean lines of Thomas Heatherwick's redesign of the grain silo (p66), Silo Hotel opts for eye-popping maximalism in its interior decor. Be prepared for lush fabrics, floral prints, glitzy chandeliers and plenty of zingy colours everywhere.

Dock House BOUTIQUE HOTEL $$$
(Map p86; 021-421 9334; www.dockhouse.co.za; Portswood Close, Portswood Ridge, V&A Waterfront; d/ste incl breakfast R8000/10,000; ; Nobel Square) Butlers dressed in white kurta-style pyjamas greet you at this super-elegant six-bedroom property crafted out of the former harbour master's house. The luxurious bedrooms are decorated in dove-grey and olive and have spacious bathrooms. It's at the heart of the Waterfront but feels almost a world away.

The same company runs the appealing (and slightly cheaper) **Queen Victoria Hotel** (Map p86; 021-427 5900; www.queenvictoriahotel.co.za; Portswood Close, Portswood Ridge, V&A Waterfront; d/ste incl breakfast R6000/9000; ; Nobel Square) nearby.

Sea Point to Hout Bay

★ **Ocean View House** GUESTHOUSE $$
(Map p94; 021-438 1982; www.oceanview-house.com; 33 Victoria Rd, Bakoven; r incl breakfast from R2200; ; Bakoven) It's all about location at this family-run guesthouse, set in a fynbos (literally 'fine bush') garden between the Twelve Apostles range and the rocky shoreline, in Camps Bay's neighbouring suburb of Bakoven. Rooms are crisp, white and minimal, and each has a private balcony or terrace to enjoy the views.

★ **Glen Boutique Hotel** BOUTIQUE HOTEL $$
(Map p90; 021-439 0086; www.glenhotel.co.za; 3 The Glen, Sea Point; r incl breakfast from R2980; ; The Glen) This gorgeous, gay-friendly boutique hotel occupies an elegant old house and a newer block behind. Spacious rooms are decorated in natural tones of stone and wood. In the middle is a fabulous pool and spa, and outdoor dining for the hotel's restaurant.

★ **Winchester Mansions Hotel** HOTEL $$
(Map p90; 021-434 2351; www.winchester.co.za; 221 Beach Rd, Sea Point; s/d incl breakfast from R2785/3135; ; London) Offering a waterfront location (you'll pay extra for sea-view rooms), this elegant Sea Point institution dates to the 1920s, but adds contemporary appeal to its historic home with a spa and 50-sq-metre pool. There's a lovely courtyard with a central fountain – a romantic place to dine. Harvey's (p150) bar is a popular spot for a sundowner – and its legendary jazz brunch.

Cascades on the Promenade HOTEL $$
(Map p90; 021-434 2586; www.cascadescollection.com; 11 Arthurs Rd, Sea Point; s R2350-2550, d R2550-2750; ; Boat Bay) It's not technically on the promenade, but this trendily monochrome designer hotel is close enough that the (pricier) rooms with balconies have sea views. Rooms will delight with docking stations, Apple Macs and Nespresso coffee machines. The cafe on the veranda at the front is a lovely spot for breakfast or brunch/lunch, too. Rates include breakfast.

Thulani River Lodge GUESTHOUSE $$
(021-790 7662; www.thulani.eu; 14 Riverside Tce, Hout Bay; r incl breakfast from R1650; ; Imizamo Yethu) The word *thulani* is Zulu for 'peace and tranquillity' – the perfect description of this German-run guesthouse, an African-thatched mansion tucked away in a lush valley through which the Disa River flows towards Hout Bay. Lie in the four-poster bed in the honeymoon suite and you'll be treated to a sweeping panorama of the back of Table Mountain.

Amblewood Guesthouse B&B $$
(Map p92; 021-790 1570; www.amblewood.co.za; 43 Skaife St, Hout Bay; s/d incl breakfast from R1100/1490; ; Military) June and Trevor are the genial hosts of this convivial, upmarket B&B, which has six rooms decorated with period furniture or in breezy contemporary style. You can cool off in the small pool on the deck, which has a view over the beautiful sweep of Hout Bay.

Chapman's Peak Hotel HOTEL $$
(Map p92; 021-790 1036; www.chapmanspeakhotel.co.za; Chapman's Peak Dr, Hout Bay; s/d incl breakfast with mountain view from R1700/2550, sea view from R2300/3400; ; Hout Bay) Take your pick between chic, contemporary-designed rooms with balconies and to-die-for views across Hout Bay, and the smaller and more traditionally decorated mountain-facing options with indigenous forest outside the window. The historic main building houses a popular bar and seafood restaurant.

★ **Tintswalo Atlantic** LODGE $$$
(021-201 0025; www.tintswalo.com/atlantic; Chapman's Peak Dr, Hout Bay; s/d incl breakfast from R8085/10,780; ; Hout Bay) The only hotel in Table Mountain National Park (p55) has been rebuilt with its secluded seaside charm intact following a disastrous fire in March 2015. Luxurious Tintswalo hugs

the edge of Hout Bay beneath Chapman's Peak, with an unbroken view of the Sentinel towering over town, and whales passing in season.

★**Ellerman House** HISTORIC HOTEL $$$
(Map p90; 021-430 3200; www.ellerman.co.za; 180 Kloof Rd, Bantry Bay; r/ste/villas from R12,000/30,000/95,000; P; Bantry Bay) Imagine you've been invited to stay with an immensely rich, art-collecting Capetonian friend – that's what the vibe is like at the Ellerman House, an elegant mansion overlooking the Atlantic. The rooms are studies in tasteful design, with heated floors, studded headboards, ocean-facing bay windows and original artworks. Beautiful gardens and oodles of luxe services and conveniences are all on hand.

The mansion and its more contemporary-styled pair of private villas house an incredible contemporary art gallery. Two deluxe spa rooms have double sliding wooden doors opening to a pool deck.

★**Camps Bay Retreat** RESORT $$$
(Map p94; 021-437 8300; www.campsbayretreat.com; 7 Chilworth Rd, The Glen; r/ste incl breakfast from R6200/9200; P; Glen Beach) Based in the grand Earl's Dyke Manor (dating from 1929), this splendid place is set in a secluded nature reserve a short walk from the Camps Bay strip. Rooms range from those with dark wooden furniture, Turkish rugs and free-standing Victorian bath in the manor, to open-plan contemporary spaces with private decks nuzzling the treetops.

Twelve Apostles Hotel & Spa HOTEL $$$
(021-437 9000; www.12apostleshotel.com; Victoria Rd, Oudekraal; r incl breakfast from R8054; P; Ouderkraal) Silky wallpaper, piles of pillows and the owner's art collection bring a refined atmosphere to this seaside option, which, having happily survived a veld fire in 2017, perches in splendid isolation between its namesake mountain range and the Oudekraal rocks (p135). Other pluses include the Leopard Bar's (p165) afternoon tea, one of the city's best, and walking trails to secluded picnic spots.

Ritz Hotel HOTEL $$$
(Map p90; 021-439 6010; www.theritz.co.za; cnr Camberwell & Main Rds, Sea Point; s/d from R2550/2750; P) This 1960s landmark has received a massive overhaul after years of neglect and a long closure. Decked out in shades of grey, rooms are simple and stylish, all with ocean views. Request a corner room for the best vistas at no extra cost. The crowning glory is the 23rd-floor revolving restaurant (eight-course set menu R850).

OFF THE BEATEN TRACK

OUDEKRAAL

Maintained by Table Mountain National Park, **Oudekraal** (021-712 7471; www.tmnp.co.za; Victoria Rd/M6; adult/child R40/25; 8am-6pm Oct-May, Sat & Sun only Jun-Sep; P; Oudekraal) is a clump of granite boulders jutting into the Atlantic. The protected coves teem with marine life and are home to the oldest-known wreck in South Africa (dating from 1670) making this a prime diving location. It's also an attractive spot for a picnic or braai (barbecue).

Marly BOUTIQUE HOTEL $$$
(Map p94; 021-437 1287; www.themarly.co.za; 201 The Promenade, Camps Bay; ste incl breakfast with mountain/sea view from R4675/6375; P; Whale Rock) Exclusive and exquisite, the Marly's chic rooms decorated with black-and-white photography perch above the Camps Bay throng, close enough to hear the crash of waves (not to mention the Victoria Rd traffic). If a good night's sleep is needed, we recommend the quieter mountain-view suites.

POD BOUTIQUE HOTEL $$$
(Map p94; 021-438 8550; www.pod.co.za; 3 Argyle Rd, Camps Bay; r/ste incl breakfast from R5800/14,300; P; Camps Bay) Offering clean, contemporary design, POD is perfectly angled to catch the Camps Bay action from its bar and spacious pool and deck area. The cheapest rooms have mountain rather than sea views; luxury rooms have their own private plunge pools.

Hout Bay Manor BOUTIQUE HOTEL $$$
(Map p92; 021-790 0116; www.houtbaymanor.co.za; Baviaanskloof Rd, Hout Bay; r incl breakfast R4200-7600; P; Military) Your eyes will bulge at the flamboyant Afro-chic makeover to which the 1871 Hout Bay Manor has been treated. Contemporary art mixes with brightly coloured furnishings and handicrafts in African-themed rooms containing the expected electronic conveniences. Amenities also include a spa and the Pure restaurant.

Southern Suburbs

Off the Wall HOSTEL **$**

(Map p97; ☎076 322 4053, 021-671 6958; www.offthewallbackpackers.com; 117 Roscommon St, Claremont; dm R205-230, s/d R630/850, with shared bathroom R555/665; 📶; 🚉Claremont) In the thick of Claremont's shopping area, this is a handy and appealing hostel should you need to stay in the Southern Suburbs. It's colourfully painted inside and out, and has a great communal kitchen.

Andros Boutique Hotel BOUTIQUE HOTEL **$$**

(Map p100; ☎021-797 9777; www.andros.co.za; cnr Phyllis & Newlands Rds, Claremont; s/d incl breakfast from R2050/2550; P ❄ 📶 🏊; 🚉Kenilworth) Set in expansive gardens, this handsome Cape Dutch Revival homestead dating to 1908 was designed by Sir Herbert Baker. The rooms and suites are spacious and comfortable affairs, some with private terraces – perfect for people in town to work or socialise. There's a restaurant, bar, pool and spa, with an appealing mix of history and contemporary style throughout.

Summit Place GUESTHOUSE **$$**

(Map p100; ☎021-794 0895; http://summitplaceguesthouse.co.za; 15 Summit Way, Constantia; s/d from R1200/1800; P ❄ 📶 🏊) This attractive and well-appointed modern guesthouse offers light, contemporary rooms and self-catering cottages. Its balconies, lawn and pool are overlooked by the mountains.

Tucked away near Klein Constantia (p98) wine estate, it's a consistently good option for a low-key stay.

★ **Vineyard Hotel & Spa** LUXURY HOTEL **$$$**

(Map p97; ☎021-657 4500; www.vineyard.co.za; Colinton Rd, Newlands; r/ste incl breakfast from R3320/5420; P ❄ 📶 🏊; 🚉Claremont) This delightful hotel's rooms have a contemporary look and are decorated in soothing natural tones. Built around the 1799 home of Lady Anne Barnard, it's surrounded by lush gardens with Table Mountain views, where you can enjoy a guided walk and afternoon tea. The fabulous Angsana Spa, a great gym and pool, and a gourmet restaurant, Myoga, complete the picture.

Steenberg Hotel HISTORIC HOTEL **$$$**

(Map p100; ☎021-713 2222; www.steenberghotel.com; Steenberg Estate, Steenberg Rd, Constantia; r/ste incl breakfast from R4900/7750; P ❄ 📶 🏊) Fresh flowers in plush rooms decorated in soft tones – that's what you get at this elegant 24-room luxury hotel on the historic Steenberg wine estate, with its restaurants, golf course and spa. Guests receive complimentary wine tastings and there's a daily shuttle back and forth from the waterfront.

Alphen BOUTIQUE HOTEL **$$$**

(Map p100; ☎021-795 6300; www.alphen.co.za; Alphen Dr, Constantia; ste incl breakfast from R3570; P ❄ 📶 🏊; 🚉Wittebome) A glitzy makeover has transformed this historic estate into a bling-tastic property with 19 suites offering features such as 'his and her' bathrooms. There's a love-it-or-hate-it mix of antiques and bold, contemporary styling throughout. Either way, the property's La Belle (p152) bistro and bakery, and chic **Rose Bar**, overlooking the manicured gardens and pool, are worth a trip on their own.

To get here by car, take the Constantia exit from the M3 and follow the signs to Alphen.

Simon's Town & Southern Peninsula

Stoked Backpackers HOSTEL **$**

(Map p104; ☎021-709 0841; www.stokedbackpackers.com; 175 Main Rd, Muizenberg; dm R200-220, r R665-995; 📶; 🚉Muizenberg) Some of Stoked's four- to 12-bed dorms are nicer than others, so check out the options before deciding. Otherwise, you can't fault the location – next to the train station and offering beach views. With a cafe downstairs, activities available and the sand a short stroll away, it's consistently popular with travellers.

Eco Wave Lodge HOSTEL **$**

(☎073 927 5644; www.ecowave.co.za; 11 Gladioli Way, Kommetjie; d R700, dm/s/d with shared bathroom R200/550/600, apt R1200; P 📶) Just 100m from the beach – perfect for surfers – this spacious suburban house has a large dining room (complete with chandelier), lounge with pool table, and sun deck. Rooms range from a four-bed dorm, with exposed brickwork and wooden beams, to minimal doubles and twins with splashes of surf decor, most sharing bathrooms.

There's also a self-catering apartment with garage and braai (barbecue). Turn onto Somerset Way off Kommetjie Rd (M65); this leads into Gladioli Way.

African Soul Surfer HOSTEL **$**

(Map p104; ☎021-788 1771; www.africansoulsurfer.co.za; 13 York Rd, Muizenberg; dm R190, s/d R580/750; 📶; 🚉Muizenberg) Set in a heritage-listed building with splendid sea views, this backpackers is ideal for those who don't want to be more than 30 seconds from the sand. As well as nicely designed rooms with private or shared bathroom, there's a kitchen, comfy lounge, ping-pong and pool tables.

Simon's Town Boutique Backpackers HOSTEL $

(Map p108; ☎021-786 1964; www.capepax.co.za; 66 St George's St, Simon's Town; dm R240, s/d R700/820, with shared bathroom R550/690; P 📶; 🚉Simon's Town) The best-value place to stay in Simon's Town, with spacious, ship-shape rooms – several with harbour views. The staff can help you arrange activities in the area from whale watching to wine tours, and there's bike hire, a bar and a balcony overlooking the main drag.

★**Bella Ev** GUESTHOUSE $$

(Map p104; ☎021-788 1293; www.bellaevguesthouse.co.za; 8 Camp Rd, Muizenberg; s/d from R1000/1200; P 📶; 🚉Muizenberg) This charming guesthouse, with a delightful courtyard garden, could be the setting for an Agatha Christie mystery, one in which the home's owner has a penchant for all things Turkish – hence the Ottoman slippers for guests' use.

Mountain House COTTAGE $$

(☎083 455 5664; www.themountainhouse.co.za; 7 Mountain Rd, Clovelly; cottages R1450-1950; P 📶; 🚉Fish Hoek) This contemporary two-bedroom cottage in a local architect's mountainside garden is all windows and sea views. Accommodating up to four, it has a braai (barbecue) area and a terrace with sweeping views of Fish Hoek. It's located between Kalk Bay and Fish Hoek.

De Noordhoek Hotel HOTEL $$

(☎021-789 2760; www.denoordhoek.co.za; cnr Main Rd & Village Ln, Noordhoek; s/d incl breakfast R1500/2250; P ❄ @ 📶 🏊) Excellently located at the Noordhoek Farm Village (p182) complex, this hotel's rooms are spacious and comfortable and surround a pretty inner courtyard planted with fynbos (literally 'fine bush') and lemon trees. Some rooms are specially adapted for use by guests with disabilities. The complex resembles a latter-day Cape Dutch farmstead with restaurants, shops and a children's playground.

Monkey Valley Resort RESORT $$

(☎021-789 8000; www.monkeyvalleyresort.com; Mountain Rd, Noordhoek; s/d incl breakfast from R950/1480, cottages from R2360; P 📶 🏊) 🍃 Choose between sea- or garden-facing rooms and spacious self-catering cottages – all with thatched, open-rafter roofs – at this imaginatively designed, rustic 'beach nature resort' shaded by a milkwood forest. Nestled at the base of Chapman's Peak, it's moments away from a wide beach.

There's a restaurant and the resort is a winner with kids, offering a playground, three pools, a babysitting service and drumming workshops.

Boulders Beach Lodge B&B $$

(Map p108; ☎021-786 1758; www.bouldersbeach.co.za; 4 Boulders Pl, Simon's Town; s/d/f incl breakfast from R650/1300/2400; P 📶; 🚉Simon's Town) Penguins waddle right up to the doors of this smart guesthouse, with rooms decorated in wicker and wood, and two self-catering family units. Its excellent restaurant has an outdoor deck. Note: the penguins are not the quietest of creatures, so you may want to bring earplugs.

Chartfield Guesthouse GUESTHOUSE $$

(Map p104; ☎021-788 3793; www.chartfield.co.za; 30 Gatesville Rd, Kalk Bay; r R900-1200, f R2400; P 📶 🏊; 🚉Kalk Bay) This rambling, wooden-floored 1920s guesthouse is decorated with choice pieces of contemporary local arts and crafts. There's a variety of rooms, each with crisp linens and a bathroom with rain-style shower. You can eat breakfast on the lovely terrace and garden overlooking the harbour.

🛏 Cape Flats & Northern Suburbs

There are a number of family-run homestays and B&Bs on the Cape Flats, usually in or adjoining private homes. Staying with a Xhosa matriarch is an excellent and fun way to experience more of township life than you might on a day tour, including an African meal or two. You can book through Vamos (p124), **Ikhaya Le Langa** (☎076 530 5065; http://ikhayalelanga.co.za), **Khayelitsha Travel** (☎021-361 4505, 082 729 9715; www.facebook.com/Khayelitsha-Travel-618660584966170; Lookout Hill complex, cnr Mew Way & Spine Rd, Ilitha Park, Khayelitsha; 🚌Makabeni) and the usual home-sharing services.

In the Northern Suburbs you'll find accommodation on Durbanville wine estates such as Meerendal (p112), as well as in the Blourbergstrand and Century City areas.

★Liziwe Guest House B&B $
(☎021-633 7406; www.sa-venues.com/visit/liziwesguesthouse; 111 NY 112, Gugulethu; r R750-900; P; Heideveld) Liziwe has made her home into a palace, with seven delightful en-suite rooms all sporting TVs and African-themed decor. She was featured on a BBC cooking show, so you can be sure her food is delicious, all meals are available, and non-guests are welcome to book for lunch or dinner.

★Kopanong B&B $
(☎082 476 1278, 021-361 2084; www.kopanong-township.co.za; 329 Velani Cres, Section C, Khayelitsha; s/d incl breakfast R500/1000; P; Nonkqubela) Thope Lekau, also called 'Mama Africa', runs this excellent B&B with her equally ebullient daughter, Mpho. Her substantial brick home offers three stylishly decorated guest rooms, two with private bathroom. Dinner (per person R140, minimum two diners) is delicious and walking tours (one hour per person R150), guided by members of the local community, are available.

Nomase's Guesthouse GUESTHOUSE $
(Map p114; ☎083 482 8377, 021-694 3904; cnr King Langalibalele & Sandile Aves, Langa; r incl breakfast R480; P) Nomase's salmon-pink guesthouse offers four en-suite rooms in a useful location, a few minutes' walk east of the Langa Pass Museum (p113) and Guga S'Thebe Arts & Cultural Centre (p113). There's a self-catering kitchen.

Majoro's B&B B&B $
(☎021-794 1619; www.mycapetownstay.com/MajorosBB; 69 Helena Cres, Khayelitsha; s/d with shared bathroom incl breakfast R550/900; P; Khayelitsha) Friendly Maria Maile runs this B&B in her small brick bungalow in Graceland, an upmarket part of Khayelitsha. She can put up four people in her two homely rooms. Lunch and dinner are available, plus services ranging from transfers to gospel-themed tours, and there's safe parking should you drive here.

Malebo's B&B $
(☎083 475 1125, 021-361 2391; www.airbnb.com/rooms/2156844; 18 Mississippi Way, Khayelitsha; s/d R700/850; P; Khayelitsha) Lydia Masoleng has been opening up her spacious, modern home to guests since 1998. Her three comfy rooms have en-suite bathrooms. Tours and traditional Xhosa dinners (R120) are available, the latter including her self-brewed *umqombothi* (beer).

Colette's B&B $
(Map p114; ☎083 458 5344, 021-531 4830; www.colettesbb.co.za; 16 The Bend, Pinelands; s/d incl breakfast from R500/650; P; Pinelands) The lovely Colette runs this women-friendly B&B in her spacious and pretty Pinelands home, which she shares with pet ducks in the garden. The four en-suite rooms, including two loft doubles, are in a private wing.

★Hotel Verde HOTEL $$
(☎021-380 5500; www.hotelverde.com; 15 Michigan St, Airport Industria; s/d R2136/2380; P@; Airport) It's easy to see why the self-proclaimed 'greenest hotel' in Africa has won sustainability awards. Rooms are comfy, with creative design, and local arts and crafts abound throughout. Solar panels and wind generators cut down the hotel's power-grid use, and there's a beautiful garden in the preserved wetlands behind the hotel, as well as an ecofriendly pool.

There's a complimentary shuttle service to the nearby airport (p184) and the city.

Eating

It's a wonder that Capetonians look so svelte on the beach, because this is one damn delicious city to dine in – probably the best in the whole of Africa. There's a wonderful range of cuisines to sample, including local African and Cape Malay concoctions, superb seafood fresh from the boat and chefs working at the top of their game.

City Bowl, Foreshore, Bo-Kaap & De Waterkant

The City Bowl is packed with restaurants and cafes, but many are closed on Sundays. The Cape Quarter shopping centre is the focus of De Waterkant's dining scene but you'll also find plenty of places to eat outside of it. The Bo-Kaap offers a handful of dining options, too; locals swear by the takeaway grilled meats served up by the guy near the corner of Rose and Wale Sts.

Hail Pizza PIZZA $
(Map p70; www.hailpizza.com; 133 Bree St, City Bowl; pizza small/large R60/114; 7am-10.30pm Mon-Fri, from 8am Sat & Sun; Dorp, Leeuwen) The Capetonian equivalent of a pizza speakeasy, Hail hides in plain sight behind another popular eatery. Their delish thin-and-crispy pizzas cooked in a wood-fire oven, can be enjoyed with bottomless Bloody Marys or mimosas at weekend brunches

(R150 to R200). They also serve breakfast, including some interesting dishes such as kimchi fried organic rice, until 4pm.

Find them behind Clarke's Bar & Dining Room.

Hokey Poke HAWAIIAN $

(Map p70; 021-422 4382; www.hokeypoke.co.za; 1 Church St, City Bowl; mains R85-135; noon-9pm Mon-Sat;) Cape Town's first poke spot is a pleasing hole-in-the-wall with splashes of Asian-inspired kitsch livening up the white tiled walls. There are seven poke bowls to choose from, or you can build your own from scratch. Ingredients are fairly traditional, including raw tuna, salmon and prawns, shredded seaweed and fish roe. It's an upbeat place with friendly service.

Kleinsky's Delicatessen DELI $

(Map p70; 082 583 4162; www.kleinskys.co.za; 32 Parliament St, City Bowl; sandwiches R38-114; 7am-4pm Mon-Sat; Groote Kerk) Jewish soul food is the deal at this contemporary-styled deli fronting onto Church Sq, with bagels and 'shmers' (various flavoured cream cheeses), matzo-ball soup, chopped liver and hot pastrami on rye all present and correct.

Their main branch is in Sea Point (p149).

City Bowl Health Kitchen SOUTH AMERICAN $

(Map p84; 021-461 0334; www.facebook.com/citybowlhealthkitcken; Shop 6, Waalford Centre Bldg, 9 Commercial St, City Bowl; mains R55; 7am-4pm Mon-Fri; ;) A Columbian guy runs this pleasant, hidden-away cafe so you'll find a lot of South American–style items on the menu, including quesadillas, flour tortillas filled with meat, veggies and cheese, and traditional drinks such as *aromaticas,* a hot citrus and spice drink, and *canelazo,* a beverage made with sugar cane, cinnamon and lemon.

Marrow SOUP $

(Map p70; 082-963 3534; www.marrowbroth.co.za; 83 Loop St, City Bowl; cup/bowl of broth R30/65; 11am-4pm Mon-Tue, to 8pm Wed-Fri; Church, Longmarket) Here's a nifty idea. All halal beef, chicken or vegetable broths served either in a cup as a tasty savoury drink, or with a mix of other items such as roasted chicken or aubergine, steamed fish or slices of rare venison in a bowl. The food is beautifully presented in a narrow venue with room to seat just 12 people.

Bacon on Bree SANDWICHES $

(Map p70; 021-422 2798; http://bacononbree.com; 217 Bree St, City Bowl; sandwiches R55-90; 7.30am-5pm Mon-Thu, to 9pm Fri, 8.30am-9pm Sat, 8.30am-3pm Sun; Upper Loop, Upper Long) The 'number one baconporium in the Cape' serves superb sandwiches and decadent salads named for movies and TV shows, though the stars of this performance are the cured meats of owner Richard Bosman, a renowned local charcuterie master. The breakfasts are also excellent.

It's licensed, and on Friday and Saturday nights they stay open late for bacon, beer and bubbles dinners.

Plant VEGAN $

(Map p70; 021-422 2737; www.plantcafe.co.za; 8 Buiten St, City Bowl; mains R40-70; 8am-10pm Mon-Sat; ; Upper Loop, Upper Long) As their name suggests, Plant serves only vegan food, and it's so tasty that you may become converted to the cause. Mock cheese and egg substitutes are incorporated in sandwiches and salads, and giant portobello mushrooms or a mix of flaked potato and seaweed do service as alternative burgers. Their vegan cupcakes and brownies are delicious.

Clarke's Bar & Dining Room AMERICAN $

(Map p70; 021-424 7648; www.clarkesdining.co.za; 133 Bree St, City Bowl; mains R75-105; 7am-10.30pm Mon-Fri, 8am-3pm Sat & Sun; Dorp, Leeuwen) A focus of the Bree St hipster scene is this convivial spot with counter seating that pays homage to the US diner tradition. All-day breakfast dishes include grilled cheese sandwiches and huevos rancheros. There are Reubens and pork-belly sandwiches from lunchtime, as well as burgers and mac and cheese.

Olami MIDDLE EASTERN $

(Map p70; 231 Bree St, City Bowl; mains R75-100; 8am-4pm Mon-Fri; Upper Loop, Upper Long) All the flavours of the Mediterranean and Middle East are represented at this spotlessly white space serving delicious falafel sandwiches, salads, sweets and drinks. They can rustle up a takeaway box of goodies and sell you a copy of their cookbook as well as the cook's wonderful hand-crafted pottery dishes.

Jason Bakery BAKERY, CAFE $

(Map p70; 021-424 5644; www.jasonbakery.com; 185 Bree St, City Bowl; mains R50-85; 7am-3.30pm Mon-Fri, 8am-2pm Sat; Upper Loop, Upper Long) Move fast to secure a seat at this super-popular street-corner cafe that makes splendid breakfasts and sandwiches. It also serves decent coffee, a few craft beers and MCC bubbles by the glass and bottle. Good job it also has a takeaway counter.

You'll also find a new branch at Green Point.

Royale Eatery BURGERS $
(Map p70; 021-422 4536; www.royaleeatery.com; 279 Long St, City Bowl; mains R78-96; noon-11.30pm Mon-Sat; Upper Loop, Upper Long) They've been grilling gourmet burgers to perfection here for years; downstairs is casual and buzzy while upstairs is a restaurant where you can book a table. For something different, try the Sprinter ostrich burger. For non-red meat lovers, there are chicken, fish and veggie burgers, too.

Bread, Milk & Honey SANDWICHES $
(Map p70; 021-461 8872; www.breadmilkhoney.co.za; 10 Spin St, City Bowl; mains R45-65; 6.30am-3.45pm Mon-Fri; Groote Kerk) The spirited debate of politicos and bureaucrats from nearby parliament rings through this smart family-run cafe. The menu is delicious: the cakes and desserts are especially yummy and they have a pay-by-weight daily lunch, as well as plenty of stuff to go.

Lola's INTERNATIONAL $
(Map p70; www.lolas.co.za; 228 Long St, City Bowl; mains R60-80; 7.30am-4pm Mon-Sat, 8.30am-3pm Sun; ; Upper Loop, Upper Long) This old dame of the Long St scene has kept her looks and the vibe remains relaxed. The breakfasts, including sweetcorn fritters and eggs Benedict, are still good. Linger over a drink and watch Long St's passing parade.

★**Chef's Warehouse & Canteen** TAPAS $$
(Map p70; 021-422 0128; www.chefswarehouse.co.za; Heritage Sq, 92 Bree St, City Bowl; tapas for 2 people R700; noon-2.30pm & 4.30-8pm Mon-Fri, noon-2.30pm Sat; Church, Longmarket) Hurry here for a delicious and very generous spread of small plates from chef Liam Tomlin and his talented crew. Flavours zip around the world, from a squid with a tangy Vietnamese salad to comforting coq au vin. If you can't get a seat (there are no bookings), try their takeaway hatch **Street Food** in the space under the stoop.

Capetonian chefs come here to shop for ingredients and kitchen items, so browse the shop afterwards for a great selection of cookbooks and other culinary treats.

★**Hemelhuijs** INTERNATIONAL $$
(Map p74; 021-418 2042; www.hemelhuijs.co.za; 71 Waterkant St, Foreshore; mains R125-175; 9am-4pm Mon-Fri, to 3pm Sat; ; Strand) A quirky yet elegantly decorated space – think deer heads with broken crockery and contemporary art – showcases the art and culinary creations of Jacques Erasmus. The inventive food is delicious and includes local ingredients such as sandveld potato, lovely fresh juices and daily bakes.

Izakaya Matsuri JAPANESE $$
(Map p74; 021-421 4520; www.izakayamatsuri.com; Shop 6, The Rockwell, Schiebe St, De Waterkant; mains R50-125; 10.30am-3pm, 5-10pm Mon-Sat; Alfred) Genial Arata-san serves some of the best sushi and rolls to be found in Cape Town, along with other Japanese *izakaya* pub-grub including noodles and tempura. When the weather's warm, tables shift from the attractive interior hung with giant white and red paper lanterns out to the courtyard area.

Mulberry & Prince INTERNATIONAL $$
(Map p70; 021-422 3301; www.mulberryandprince.co.za; 12 Pepper St, City Bowl; mains R140-195; 7-10pm Wed-Sat, 10am-2pm Sun; Leeuwen/Dorp) Brass-topped tables, marble and contemporary art give this cosy restaurant and cocktail bar a sophisticated ambiance matched by the inventive food prepared by two chefs trained at the Culinary Institute of America. The tapas-style plates are not overly generous, so order several – not hard to do when there's tempting options such as twice-cooked pork belly on the menu.

Charango PERUVIAN $$
(Map p70; 021-422 0757; http://charango.co.za; 114 Bree St, City Bowl; mains R40-190; 5-10pm Mon, noon-10.30pm Tue-Sat; Church, Longmarket) Tuck into a variety of tasty small plates including fried calamari, Peruvian-style chicken and tacos as well as more substantial mains such as miso-cured fish. There's a lively vibe and plenty of outdoor seating for warm evenings when the bar can kick on for several hours after food orders have ceased.

Culture Club Cheese CHEESE $$
(☎021-422 3515; www.cultureclubcheese.co.za; 13 Boundary Rd, The Josphine Mill, Newlands; mains R65-85; ⏰9am-5pm Mon-Wed, to 10pm Thu-Sat, 9am-3pm Sun; Newlands) British-trained cheesemaker Luke and his partner Jessica set up this great little cafe and deli. Eighty percent of the 200-plus cheeses they stock here – and use in their dishes such as grilled cheese sandwiches and mac 'n cheese – are from South Africa, so it's a wonderful chance to taste something unusual.

They also make their own kefir and kombucha (two types of fermented drinks) and host monthly cheese-pairing gourmet events.

Cousins ITALIAN $$
(Map p84; ☎083 273 9604; www.thecousinsrestaurant.com; 3B Barrack St, City Bowl; mains R70-100; ⏰6-10pm;) If you have the urge for traditional Italian food, this friendly, busy place is the ideal spot for dinner. The menu includes perfect homemade pasta and all the theatricality of a giant wheel of parmesan wheeled to the table, likely by one of the three cousins from Romagna who set up the restaurant years ago.

Homage 1862 INTERNATIONAL $$
(Map p70; ☎021-422 0900; www.homage.co.za; 168 Loop St, City Bowl; mains R85-220; ⏰noon-3.30pm Tue-Sat; noon-3.30pm plus 6.30-9.30pm Wed-Sat; ; Leeuwen, Dorp) This building dates from 1862, which has been sensitively adapted into a pleasant restaurant and bar with a broad balcony, atrium and plenty of potted plants. The menu majors on vegetables – but there's meat too. The unifying factor is the use of a wood-burning grill to cook or finish the produce.

Check their Facebook page for events held at the bar upstairs, including live music performances.

La Tête INTERNATIONAL $$
(Map p74; ☎021-418 1299; www.latete.co.za; 17 Bree St, Foreshore; mains R130-180; ⏰noon-2.30pm Tue-Fri, 6-11pm; Lower Loop, Lower Long) Brothers Giles and James Edwards' nose-to-tail approach to cooking has found an enthusiastic audience with gourmet Capetonians, who are flocking here to sample dishes such as crispy pigs tails (they're actually quite rich and oily) or the superb baked pig cheek and quail eggs. Ox tongue, sweetbreads and devilled chicken hearts are also likely to make star appearances on the menu.

Lucy Ethiopian Restaurant ETHIOPIAN $$
(Map p84; ☎021-422 1797; www.lucyrestaurant.co.za; 281 Long St, City Bowl; mains R85-170; ⏰noon-11pm Mon-Sat; ; Upper Long, Upper Loop) Perch at one of the dozen traditional woven *mesob* tables in this bright dining room overlooking Long Street. Sample the authentic cuisine with a combo platter – six meaty or vegetarian dishes served on freshly made *injera* (a slightly sour, spongy flatbread). *Tej* (honey wine) is served and there's a traditional coffee ceremony on request.

Raw and Roxy VEGAN $$
(Map p70; ☎079 599 6277; www.facebook.com/rawandroxy; 38 Hout St, City Bowl; mains R110-135; ⏰10am-6pm Mon-Thu, to 9.30pm Fri, 10am-5pm Sat; ; Kent) Beatrice Holst seduces meat-loving Capetonians with her delicious raw and vegan repasts and drinks, including super vitamin-charged juices, a raw lasagne that has foodies reaching for superlatives, and a silky-smooth and super-rich avocado chocolate ganache cake.

Contact Beatrice about the vegan cooking classes (R600) she runs in the evenings.

Bocca ITALIAN $$
(Map p70; ☎021-422 0188; www.bocca.co.za; cnr Bree & Wale Sts, City Bowl; pizzas R75-136; ⏰noon-10pm; Dorp, Leeuwen) Superb Neopolitan-style softer-crust pizzas with creative toppings (kimchi, pork sausage and ginger on the Lady Zaza) fly out of the brick oven at this new and already very popular operation. Their menu covers other contemporary-style Italian dishes and sharing plates.

Bo-Kaap Kombuis CAPE MALAY $$
(Map p70; ☎021-422 5446; www.bokaapkombuisco.za; 7 August St, Bo-Kaap; mains R75-95; ⏰noon-4pm & 6-9.30pm Tue-Sat, noon-4pm Sun) You'll receive a hospitable welcome from Yusuf and Nazli and their staff at this spectacularly located restaurant, high up in the Bo-Kaap. The panoramic views of Table Mountain and Devil's Peak alone make it worth visiting. There are all the traditional Cape Malay dishes on the menu, plus vegetarian options such as sugar-bean curry.

They also have a few guesthouse and self-catering rooms for rent.

6 Spin St Restaurant INTERNATIONAL $$
(Map p70; 021-461 0666; www.6spinstreet.co.za; 6 Spin St, City Bowl; mains R75-180; 10am-10pm Mon-Fri, from 6pm Sat; Groote Kerk) Robert Mulders brings his personable restaurant skills and famous double-baked cheese soufflé to the elegant surrounds of this Sir Herbert Baker–designed building. You might also try Moroccan lamb with couscous or linefish roasted with a garlic crust. The space doubles as an **art gallery**, which you're welcome to look around whether dining or not.

Company's Garden Restaurant CAPE MALAY $$
(Map p70; 021-423 2919; www.thecompanysgarden.com; Company's Garden, Queen Victoria St, City Bowl; mains R75-130; 7am-6pm; ; Dorp, Leeuwen) The old Company's Garden cafe has been transformed into a chic contemporary space with charming outdoor features such as a giant chess set and wickerwork nests for kids (and young-at-heart adults) to play in. Menu items run from excellent breakfasts (try the French toast) to several Cape Malay dishes, some with a modern twist such as the spiced-mince spring rolls.

Addis in Cape ETHIOPIAN $$
(Map p70; 021-424 5722; www.addisincape.co.za; 41 Church St, City Bowl; mains R110-150; noon-10.30pm Mon-Sat; ; Church, Longmarket) Sit at a low basket-weave table and enjoy tasty Ethiopian cuisine served traditionally on plate-sized *injera* (sourdough pancakes), which you rip up and eat with in place of cutlery. They have a good selection of vegetarian and vegan dishes. Also try their home-made *tej* (honey wine) and authentic Ethiopian coffee.

Loading Bay BISTRO, CAFE $$
(Map p74; 021-425 6320; www.loadingbay.co.za; 30 Hudson St, De Waterkant; mains R80-100; 7.30am-5pm Mon-Fri, 8.30am-4pm Sat, 9am-2pm Sun; Old Fire Station) Hang with the De Waterkant style set at this spiffy cafe serving coffee with 'microtextured milk' (it's only heated to 70°C) and bistro-style dishes such as crispy bacon and avocado on toast.

There's an attached boutique offering menswear fashion lines from overseas labels and the Aesop skincare range.

Fork TAPAS $$
(Map p70; 021-424 6334; www.fork-restaurants.co.za; 84 Long St, City Bowl; tapas R60-85; noon-11pm Mon-Sat; Church, Longmarket) Whether you just want to graze on a few tapas-style dishes or cobble together a full meal, this super-relaxed venue is the business, serving inventive if not strictly Spanish nibbles alongside excellent wines, many by the glass.

Mink & Trout INTERNATIONAL $$
(Map p70; 021-426 2534; http://minkandtrout.com; 127 Bree St, City Bowl; mains R110-170; noon-3pm, 6-10pm Mon-Sat; ; Church, Longmarket) A grand old Dutch building is the setting for this casual bistro and wine bar with offering above-average meals and a large range of wines by the glass. The mussels steamed in a paper parcel with a delicious Malay curry sauce are sensational and come with slices of brioche to soak up the juices.

Anatoli TURKISH $$
(Map p74; 021-419 2501; www.anatoli.co.za; 24 Napier St, De Waterkant; meze R50-60, mains R120; 6.30-10.30pm Mon-Sat; Alfred) You can always rely on this atmospheric Turkish joint that's a little piece of Istanbul in Cape Town. Make a meal out of their delicious meze, both hot and cold, or try their kebabs.

★ **Shortmarket Club** INTERNATIONAL $$$
(Map p70; 021-447 2874; http://theshortmarketclub.co.za; 88 Shortmarket St, City Bowl; mains R150-290, 7-course tasting menu R790; 12.30-2pm, 7-10pm Mon-Sat; ; Church, Longmarket) Star chef Luke Dale-Roberts' latest venture hides in plain sight on the street it is named after. It's a gorgeous attic space with a wall of paper butterflies and clubby leather chairs and booths. Dishes include sustainable fish, grass-fed beef (displayed on wheeled trolleys), and plenty of locally grown vegetables. White-jacketed waiters provide a sleek European touch.

Unlike his other operations, the Test Kitchen (p145) and Pot Luck Club (p144), it's possible to walk in without a reservation here – at least for lunch during the week. Book well ahead for dinner, though.

★ **Bombay Brasserie** INDIAN $$$
(Map p70; 021-819 2000; www.tajhotels.com; Wale St, City Bowl; mains R110-200, tasting menus R625; 6-10.30pm; P; Groote Kerk) Far from your average curry house, the Taj Hotel's

main restaurant, hung with glittering chandeliers and mirrors, is darkly luxurious. Chef Harpreet Longani's cooking is creative and delicious, and the presentation spot on, as is the service. Go on a spice journey with the tasting menu, which comes in a vegetarian or non-vegetarian version.

Gold AFRICAN $$$
(Map p74; 021-421 4653; www.goldrestaurant.co.za; 15 Bennett St, De Waterkant; set menu R375, drumming R95; 6.30-10pm; Alfred) Occupying an enormous warehouse space, one part decorated with an organ salvaged from an old church, Gold offers an Africa-wide safari of tastes, from Xhosa corn pot breads and Cape Malay samosas to Tunisian spiced chicken wings and Zanzibar black bean and carrot stew, one of several vegetarian dishes that are part of the set menu.

Arrive at 6.30pm to take part in a 30-minute drumming session. The staff perform shows throughout the night, too.

95 Keerom ITALIAN $$$
(Map p70; 021-422 0765; http://95keerom.com; 95 Keerom St, City Bowl; mains R60-400; 6pm-10.30pm Mon-Sat; Upper Loop, Upper Long) Bookings are essential for this chic Italian restaurant, with an olive tree the centrepiece of the 1st floor. Chef-patron Giorgio Nava lays on the Italian charm with a trowel in his table-side presentations, but you can't fault his splendid pasta.

Meat lovers might want try Nava's premium steak restaurant **Carne SA** (Map p70; 021-424 3460; www.carne-sa.com; 70 Keerom St, City Bowl; mains R100-400; Upper Loop, Upper Long), which is just across the street; there's also a branch on Kloof St.

Africa Café AFRICAN $$$
(Map p70; 021-422 0221; www.africacafe.co.za; 108 Shortmarket St, City Bowl; set banquets R360; 6-11pm Mon-Sat; Church, Longmarket) Touristy, yes, but still one of the best places to sample African food. Come with a hearty appetite as the set feast comprises some 15 dishes from across the continent, of which you can eat as much as you like. The talented staff go on song-and-dance walkabout around the tables midmeal.

Savoy Cabbage MODERN SOUTH AFRICAN $$$
(Map p70; 021-424 2626; www.savoycabbage.co.za; 101 Hout Lane, City Bowl; mains R145-270; 6.30-10pm Mon-Sat; Church, Longmarket) The long-running Savoy Cabbage remains a great place for inventive cooking, and gives diners the chance to try local game meats such as eland and springbok. Also try their legendary tomato tart if it's on the menu.

East City, District Six, Woodstock & Observatory

The three main dining strips here are Woodstock's Roodebloem Rd, Salt River's Albert Rd and Lower Main Rd in Observatory. Also mark your calendar with a big red cross for Saturday's brunch fest at the Neighbourgoods Market (p177).

★ **Kitchen** DELI $
(Map p80; 021-462 2201; www.lovethekitchen.co.za; 111 Sir Lowry Rd, Woodstock; sandwiches & salads R60-75; 8am-3.30pm Mon-Fri; ; District Six) Of all the swanky restaurants in town, it was this little charmer that Michelle Obama chose for lunch, proving the ex-First Lady has excellent taste. Tuck into plates of divine salads, rustic sandwiches made with love, and sweet treats with tea served from china teapots.

Although it has recently expanded its space, Kitchen is still as popular as ever, so come before 11.30am or after 2pm if you don't want to wait for a table for lunch.

★ **Ocean Jewels** SEAFOOD $
(Map p80; 083 582 0829; www.oceanjewels.co.za; Woodstock Exchange, 66 Albert Rd, Woodstock; mains R50-95; shop 8.30am-4.30pm, restaurant 11am-3pm Mon-Fri; Woodstock) Fish straight from Kalk Bay Harbour is served at this seafood cafe and fishmonger that supports the South African Sustainable Seafood Initiative (SASSI). It does a mean tuna burger with wedge fries, and despite being in the industrial-chic Woodstock Exchange the vibe is as relaxed as the seaside, with white-washed wooden tables and food served on rustic enamel plates.

Lefty's AMERICAN $
(Map p80; 021-461 0407; 105 Harrington St, East City; mains R60-95; 4-10pm; Roeland) Appealing to students and lovers of grunge and shabby chic, this artfully crafted dive bar amps up it's hipster cred with sticky BBQ pork ribs and Kentucky chicken waffles, alongside brick-oven-baked pizza and beetroot and ginger falafel. There's plenty of craft beers to wash it all down, too.

Food orders finish at 10pm but the bar cranks on until midnight. Upstairs is the noodle bar Downtown Ramen.

Three Feathers Diner BURGERS $
(Map p80; ☎021-448 6606; 68 Bromwell Rd, Woodstock; burgers R90; ⏰11am-3pm Mon & Tue, to 9pm Wed-Fri, to 7pm Sat; 🚌Kent) Street art decorates this cavernous space that's a shrine to the owner's beloved American muscle cars, such as the bright-orange Pontiac Firebird parked inside next to the free pinball machine. Serves giant, juicy burgers (a veg option is available), shakes and craft beers.

Café Ganesh AFRICAN, INDIAN $
(Map p79; ☎021-448 3435; http://cafeganesh.co.za; 38 Trill Rd, Observatory; mains R50-80; ⏰11.30am-11.30pm Mon-Sat; 🚆Observatory) There are now two sides to this staple of the Obs dining scene. By day their colourful corner cafe serves up dishes such as veg curry and roti. By night sample pap (maize porridge) and veg, grilled springbok or lamb curry in the shack-chic, junk-filled space, squeezed into an alley between two buildings.

Superette CAFE $
(Map p80; www.superette.co.za; Woodstock Exchange, 66 Albert Rd, Woodstock; mains R70; ⏰9am-4pm Mon-Fri, to 2pm Sat; 🚆Woodstock) Feel-good food from farm to plate is on offer at this laid-back, tastefully turned out and oh-so-trendy neighbourhood cafe. Try their all-day breakfast sandwich or baked goods made with natural sugars.

Hello Sailor BISTRO $
(Map p79; ☎021-447 0707; www.hellosailorbistro.co.za; 86 Lower Main Rd, Observatory; mains R65-80; ⏰8am-10pm; 🚆Observatory) A tattooed mermaid in a round portrait on the wall looks down on the tattooed patrons of this slick bistro serving price-friendly comfort food – burgers, salads, pastas – all done well. The restaurant closes at 10pm, but the bar here can kick on until 2am on the weekend.

Charly's Bakery BAKERY, CAFE $
(Map p80; ☎021-461 5181; www.charlysbakery.co.za; 38 Canterbury St, East City; baked goods R25-35; ⏰8am-5pm Tue-Fri, 8.30am-2pm Sat; 🅿; 🚌Lower Buitenkant) Talk about the Great South African Bake-off. The fabulous female team here make – as they say – 'mucking afazing' cupcakes and other baked goods. Their heritage building is as colourfully decorated as their bakes.

★**Pot Luck Club** INTERNATIONAL $$
(Map p80; ☎021-447 0804; www.thepotluckclub.co.za; Silo top fl, Old Biscuit Mill, 373-375 Albert Rd, Woodstock; dishes R60-150; ⏰12.30-2.30pm & 6-10.30pm Mon-Sat, 11am-3pm Sun; 🚌Kent) The sister restaurant to Test Kitchen (p145) is a more affordable Luke Dale-Roberts option. Sitting at the top of an old silo, it offers panoramic views of the surrounding area, but the star attraction is the food. Dishes are designed to be shared; we defy you not to order a second plate of the beef with truffle-café-au-lait sauce.

Sunday brunch (without/with bottomless bubbly R450/650) is highly recommended. Book ahead.

★**Andalousse** MOROCCAN $$
(Map p80; ☎021-447 1708; http://andalousse-moroccan-cuisine.business.site; 148 Victoria Rd, Woodstock; mains R90-150; ⏰noon-9.30pm; 🚆Woodstock) Hiding in plain sight along a sketchy stretch of Victoria Rd is this little gem of a place. Started in 2016 by a group of friends from Morocco, this is the real deal, serving flavourful tagines, couscous, filo-pastry pastilla and a very moreish *harira* soup that, served with a crispy, cheese bread, is a meal in itself.

Do save space for mint tea, served hot and sweet in silver teapots with a plate of traditional biscuits.

★**Ferdinando's** PIZZA $$
(Map p79; ☎084 771 0485; www.ferdinandospizza.com; 205 Lower Main Rd, Observatory; pizza R80-110; ⏰Wed-Sat 6-11pm; 🚆Observatory) Bookings are required for this charming 'pizza parla' that's found its natural home in Obs. Diego is the pizza maestro and Kikki the bubbly host and creative artist, while their adorable mutt Ferdinando keeps them all in line. Toppings for their fantastic crispy thin-crust pizzas change with the season.

Downtown Ramen ASIAN $$
(Map p80; ☎021-461 0407; 103 Harrington St, East City; noodles R80; ⏰4-10pm Mon-Sat; 🚌Roeland) The menu here is pleasingly small – just four noodle dishes and a selection of *bao* (steamed buns filled with spiced pork, chicken or veggies). Ask for the chilli on the side if you don't like your noodles spicy. It's tiny, so book ahead on weekends.

Pesce Azzurro ITALIAN $$
(Map p80; ☎021-447 2009; www.pesceazzurro.co.za; 113 Roodebloem Rd, Woodstock; mains R105-165; ⏰noon-3pm & 6-10pm Mon-Sat; 🚌Balfour) Rustic Italian pasta and seafood dishes are the speciality of this casual joint, well patronised

by locals (despite less than stellar service). Round off the meal with grandma's tiramisu.

Raptor Room INTERNATIONAL $$
(Map p84; 087 625 0630; www.raptorroom.co.za; Shop 2, 79 Roeland St, East City; 10am-11pm Mon-Fri, to 5pm Sat, to 3pm Sun; Roeland) Who doesn't love dinosaurs, especially when they come as part of dusky-pink, leafy green decor? You can tell from the get-go that LGBT-friendly Raptor Room is quirky, but they also have an appealing menu of burgers, small plates (popcorn chicken, mushroom risotto balls) and brunch items, served alongside a full drinks menu including cocktails and wine.

★**Test Kitchen** INTERNATIONAL $$$
(Map p80; 021-447 2622; www.thetestkitchen.co.za; Shop 104a, Old Biscuit Mill, 375 Albert Rd, Woodstock; menu without/with wine R1650/2250; 6.30-9pm Tue-Sat; P; Kent) Luke Dale-Roberts creates inspired dishes with top-quality local ingredients at his flagship restaurant – generally agreed to be the best in Africa. However, the restaurant is so popular now that securing a reservation here is like winning the gourmet lottery – online bookings open three months ahead and you need to be quick off the mark.

★**Reverie Social Table** INTERNATIONAL $$$
(021-447 3219; www.reverie.capetown; 226a Lower Main Rd, Observatory; lunch R60-70, 5-course dinner with wine R700; noon-2.30pm Tue-Fri plus 7.30pm-late Wed-Sat; Salt River) With just one long wooden table seating up to 18, and the charming chef and host Julia Hattingh in charge, it's easy to see why this place is called Social. Book ahead for her five-course dinners where the dishes are matched with a particular region's wines, or sometimes with local gins.

Daytimes see regular visits from the artists and creatives in the area, who come to lunch on lovely dishes such as rare beef salad with peach achar or a cauliflower and gorgonzola soup.

Gardens & Surrounds

Kloof St is one of Cape Town's top eating strips, with a near-constant supply of new restaurants opening. You'll also find several places to eat clustered at the foot of Kloof Nek Rd.

Spirit Cafe VEGAN $
(Map p88; www.spiritcafe.co.za; 26 Dunkley Sq, Gardens; mains R50-98; 7.30am-5pm Mon-Fri, 9am-3pm Sat; ; Annandale) Not everything is vegan here but quite a lot is, including most of the salads and main dishes served in the daily buffet that sits, temptingly, on the kitchen counter. They also offer a variety of breakfast dishes, a Buddha bowl, wraps, and juices and smoothies made from fresh fruits and veggies.

Tamboers Winkel INTERNATIONAL $
(Map p84; 021-424 0521; www.facebook.com/Tamboerswinkel; 3 De Lorentz St, Tamboerskloof; mains R50-110; 7.45am-5pm Sun-Tue, to 10pm Wed-Sat; Welgemeend) A serious contender for the award for best breakfast or lunch spot around Kloof St, this rustic, country-kitchen-style cafe-shop is a charmer. The chicken pie, wrapped in flaky filo pastry, is indeed legendary. They also have free wine tastings for different vineyards on Wednesday from 6pm to 8pm.

Yard INTERNATIONAL $
(Map p84; www.facebook.com/YARDCT; 6 Roodehek St, Gardens; mains R85-99; 7am-10.30pm Mon-Fri, 9am-10.30pm Sat & Sun; Roodehek) Be prepared for very sticky fingers. The Dog's Bollocks' blockbuster burgers got this hip grunge spot going a few years ago; they've now expanded to all-day dining, with Mucky Mary's for breakfast fry-ups and sandwiches, and Bitch's Tits tacos. Deluxe coffee is also served.

Melissa's DELI $
(Map p84; 021-424 5540; www.melissas.co.za; 94 Kloof St, Gardens; mains R60-80; 7.30am-7pm Mon-Fri, from 8am Sat & Sun; Welgemeend) Pay by weight for the delicious breakfast and lunch buffets, then browse the grocery shelves for picnic fare or gourmet gifts.

Blue Cafe INTERNATIONAL $
(Map p84; 021-426 0250; www.thebluecafe.co.za; 13 Brownlow Rd, Tamboerskloof; mains R35-70; 7.30am-10pm; ; Belle Ombre) In business under various owners (and names) as a cafe and mini-deli since 1904, the Blue Cafe's latest incarnation is perhaps one of its best. It's a lovely, casual all-day dining spot that's particularly good for an early evening meal at its street tables – some of which afford beguiling views of the surrounding mountains as the sun sets.

Table Mountain Café CAFE $
(021-424 0015; www.tablemountain.net; Table Mountain; mains R35-95; 8.30am-30 min before last cableway down; Upper Cable Station) Hallelujah! Table Mountain finally gets the café it

so deserves. This self-serve place offers tasty deli items and meals, compostable plates and containers, and good coffee. They also sell wine and beer so there's no need to cart your bottle up the slopes to toast the view.

The kitchen closes at 4pm, but the cafe stays open for drinks until 30 minutes before the last cableway down the mountain.

Liquorice & Lime INTERNATIONAL **$**
(Map p88; ☎021-423 6921; 162 Kloof St, Gardens; sandwiches R50-80; ⊙7am-5pm Mon-Fri, to 4pm Sat & Sun; 🚌Upper Kloof) Pause at this convivial gourmet deli on your way from climbing up or down Table Mountain or Lion's Head. The French toast with grilled banana is yummy, and they have baked goods and sandwiches.

Deer Park Café INTERNATIONAL **$**
(Map p88; ☎021-462 6311; www.deerparkcafe.co.za; 2 Deer Park Dr West, Vredehoek; mains R55-90; ⊙8am-9pm; 📶🖉👪; 🚌Herzlia) Fronting a kid's playground in Rocklands Rd Park, this relaxed cafe has chunky wooden furniture that gives it the feel of a big nursery. The tasty food is anything but child's play, though. There are some great vegetarian options, as well as a kids' menu.

On the first Sunday of the month they usually host the **Deer Little Market** (9am to 2pm) in Rocklands Rd Park – check their Facebook page for details, including other events such as standup comedy shows on Wednesday nights.

Lazari INTERNATIONAL **$**
(Map p88; ☎021-461 9865; www.lazari.co.za; cnr Upper Maynard St & Vredehoek Ave, Vredehoek; mains R60-85; ⊙7.30am-4pm Mon-Fri, 8am-2.30pm Sat & Sun; 📶; 🚌Upper Buitenkant) Few proprietors work as hard as Chris Lazari to be friendly to their customers – who, understandably, are a loyal bunch. It's buzzy, gay-friendly and great for brunch or an indulgent moment over coffee and cake.

★**Chefs** INTERNATIONAL **$$**
(Map p84; ☎021-461 0368; www.chefscapetown.co.za; 81 St Johns Rd, Gardens; mains R150-190; ⊙noon-8.30pm Mon-Fri; 📶; 🚌Annandale) So called because you can see all the chefs at work in the open kitchen, this is a fab new addition to Cape Town's dining scene with an original concept of 'fast fine dining' that really works. The daily choice of three mains (always including a vegetarian option) look exactly as they do on the touchscreen menu and taste wonderful.

There's one dessert and a few good wines and other drinks on offer. Bookings are limited to set times so come early or risk being disappointed, as it's popular – especially for dinner.

★**The Stack** INTERNATIONAL **$$**
(Map p88; ☎021-286 0187; www.thestack.co.za; Leinster Hall, 7 Weltevreden St, Gardens; mains R125-190; ⊙8am-10pm; 🅿📶; 🚌Van Riebeek) Given a stylish makeover to become a brasserie and bar downstairs and a private members club upstairs, old Leinster Hall is a delightful place for a meal. The food is beautifully presented and includes dishes such as tuna Niçoise, springbok loin and a sinful smoked-chocolate mousse.

Other pluses: half-price cocktails from 3pm to 6pm and a gorgeous jasmine-scented garden to enjoy them in.

★**Kyoto Garden Sushi** JAPANESE **$$**
(Map p84; ☎021-422 2001; https://kyotogardensushict.com; 11 Lower Kloof Nek Rd, Tamboerskloof; mains R140-220; ⊙5.30-11pm Mon-Sat; 🚌Ludwig's Garden) Beechwood furnishings and subtle lighting lend a calm, Zen-like air to this superior Japanese restaurant with an expert chef turning out sushi and sashimi. Splurge on the sea urchin and try their peppy Asian Mary cocktail.

Thali INDIAN **$$**
(Map p84; ☎021-286 2110; www.thalitapas.co.za; 3 Park Rd, Gardens; tapas per person R325; ⊙5-9.30pm Mon, noon-2.30pm & 5-9.30pm Tue-Sat; 🚌Lower Kloof) Although the food here is described as Indian tapas, the portions in the four-course set meal are very generous so you'll end up having quite a feast. There's a sophisticated ambiance with brass platters adorning the brick and terracotta-painted walls. Presentation of the dishes is also good and the bar is a nice place for an boozy lassi if nothing else.

Cafe Paradiso ITALIAN **$$**
(Map p84; ☎021-422 0403; www.cafeparadiso.co.za; 101 Kloof St, Tamboerskloof; mains R90-205; ⊙9am-10pm Mon-Sat, 10am-4pm Sun; 👪; 🚌Welgemeend) Travellers with kids will love this place: it features a kitchen where little ones can make their own pizza, cookies, cupcakes or gingerbread figures (R55) while the adults dine in a pleasant garden setting.

Societi Bistro FRENCH **$$**
(Map p84; ☎021-424 2100; www.societi.co.za; 50 Orange St, Gardens; mains R100-180; ⊙noon-11pm Mon-Sat; 🚌Michaelis) Dine in

the courtyard garden for Table Mountain views (there are blankets provided if it gets chilly), or in the atmospheric, brick-walled and wine-rack-covered interior. The unfussy bistro dishes are well prepared and proficiently served.

Maria's GREEK $$
(Map p84; 021-461 3333; www.facebook.com/MariasGreekCafe; 31 Barnet St, Dunkley Sq, Gardens; mains R75-135; 8am-10.30pm Tue-Fri, from 9am Sat; P; Annandale) There are few places more romantic or relaxing for a meal than Maria's on a warm night, when you can tuck into classic Greek mezze and dishes such as moussaka on rustic tables beneath the trees in the square. There are tons of vegetarian and vegan options on the menu, too.

Manna Epicure BAKERY, CAFE $$
(Map p88; 021-426 2413; www.mannaepicure.com; 151 Kloof St, Gardens; mains R90-130; 8am-4pm Tue-Sat, to 3pm Sun; Welgemeend) Come for a deliciously simple breakfast or lunch, or for late-afternoon cocktails and tapas on the veranda of this white-box cafe. The freshly baked breads alone – coconut or pecan and raisin – are worth dragging yourself up the hill for.

★ **Chef's Table** INTERNATIONAL $$$
(Map p84; 021-483 1864; www.belmond.com/mountnelsonhotel; Belmond Mount Nelson Hotel, 76 Orange St, Gardens; lunch R545, dinner without/with wine R820/1395; noon-3pm Fri, 6.30-9pm Mon-Sat; P; Government Ave) There are several dining options at the Mount Nelson Hotel, but for a real treat book one of the four tables with a front-row view onto the drama and culinary magic unfolding inside the kitchen of this restaurant. The food is superb (vegetarians are catered for) and presented by the chefs who will take you on a behind-the-scenes tour.

★ **Aubergine** INTERNATIONAL $$$
(Map p84; 021-465 0000; www.aubergine.co.za; 39 Barnet St, Gardens; 3-course lunch R465, 3-/4-/5-course dinner R620/780/945; noon-2pm Wed-Fri plus 5-10pm Mon-Sat; ; Annandale) German-born Harald Bresselschmidt is one of Cape Town's most consistent chefs, producing creative, hearty dishes served with some of the Cape's best wines, several of which are made specially for the restaurant. Vegetarian menus are available, and the service and ambiance are impeccable.

Green Point & Waterfront

The Waterfront has a plethora of restaurants and cafes, many with outdoor decks with great ocean and mountain views. Less touristy alternatives are available a short walk away in Green Point and Mouille Point.

★ **Café Neo** CAFE $
(Map p86; 021-433 0849; 129 Beach Rd, Mouille Point; mains R85-100; 7am-7pm; P; Three Anchor Bay) This popular seaview cafe has a pleasingly contemporary design and atmosphere that sways from buzzy (at meal times) to laid-back – great for a late afternoon drink. Check out the big blackboard menu, featuring several Greek dishes, while sitting at the long communal table inside, or grab a seat on the deck overlooking the red-and-white lighthouse.

Nü VEGETARIAN $
(Map p86; 021-433 1429; www.nufood.co.za; Shop 4, Portside, Main Rd, Green Point; mains R60-80; 7am-7pm Mon-Fri, from 7.30am Sat, 7.30am-6pm Sun; ; Upper Portswood) A great place for a healthy veggie breakfast or lunch, with freshly squeezed juices, smoothies, nutritional salads and multigrain wraps on the menu. Order at the counter and enjoy in a bright, unfussy space. There's also a branch in **Sea Point** (Map p90; 021-439 7269; www.nufood.co.za; Piazza St John, Main Rd, Sea Point; mains R80; 7am-7pm Mon-Fri, 7.30am-6pm Sat & Sun; ; Arthur's).

Tashas INTERNATIONAL $
(Map p86; 021-421 4350; www.tashascafe.com; Shop 7117, Victoria Wharf, Breakwater Blvd, V&A Waterfront; mains R60-100; 7.30am-9pm Sun-Mon, to 10pm Tue-Sat; P; Waterfront) Muffins that could feed a small family and other delectable baked goods and desserts are the forte of this luxe-design cafe – a hit concept from Jo'burg imported to the Mother City. Also on the menu are plenty of salads, sandwiches and mains; many are served in half-portions for those times when you're not so hungry.

V&A Food Market FOOD HALL $
(Map p86; www.waterfrontfoodmarket.com; Pump House, Dock Rd, V&A Waterfront; mains from R75; 10am-8pm Sun-Thu, until 9pm Fri & Sat; P; Nobel Sq) There's no need to spend big to eat well (and healthily) at the Waterfront, thanks to this colourful, market-style food court in the old Pump House. Grab a coffee or freshly squeezed juice to go with a wrap or muffin, or opt for a larger meal such as Thai, Indian or Cape Malay curry.

Newport Market & Deli INTERNATIONAL, DELI **$**
(Map p86; ☎021-439 1538; www.newportdeli.co.za; Amalfi, 128 Beach Rd, Mouille Point; mains R55-100; ⏰7am-5pm; Ⓟ; 🚌Three Anchor Bay) This long-running deli and cafe occupies two floors. Grab a smoothie, power-blend or caffeinated beverage, plus sandwiches and deli goods to enjoy along Mouille Point Prom or in Green Point Park.

Giovanni's Deli World DELI **$**
(Map p86; ☎021-434 6893; 103 Main Rd, Green Point; mains R40-70; ⏰7.30am-8.30pm; 🚌Stadium) Its menu bursting with flavourful food, Giovanni's can make any sandwich you fancy, which is ideal for a picnic if you're on your way to the beach. The pavement cafe is a popular hangout.

★**The Yard** INDIAN **$$**
(Map p86; ☎021-879 1157; www.theyardatsilo.co.za/food; Silo 4, Silo District, V&A Waterfront; ⏰7.30am-10pm Mon-Fri, from 8am Sat, 8am-3pm Sun) Although the menu covers quite a bit of crowd-pleasing culinary ground, it's the Indian dishes that form the bulk and should not be missed – from crispy dosa (chickpea-flour pancakes) for breakfast to excellent tandoori chicken and daal for dinner. There's coffee from Rosetta Roastery, good cocktails and an attached deli and boutique with a carefully curated inventory.

Lily's INTERNATIONAL **$$**
(Map p86; ☎021-204 8545; www.lilysrestaurant.co.za; cnr Beach Rd & Surrey Pl, Mouille Point; mains R95-220; ⏰7.30am-10pm; 📶; 🚌Surrey) With brass-topped tables, a marble-clad bar and a photographic frieze of flowers in black and white, Lily's strikes a sophisticated note. Enjoy sea views as you tuck into competently made mains such as sesame tuna, crispy duck and lamb popsicles. For lunch the sandwich options include hot pastrami and the ultimate grilled cheese.

Cape Town Hotel School CONTEMPORARY **$$**
(Map p86; ☎021-440 5736; Beach Rd, Mouille Point; mains R70-200; ⏰11.30am-2.30pm & 6.30pm-9.30pm Tue-Fri, noon-2.30pm Sun; Ⓟ; 🚌Mouille Point) The dining room is elegantly decorated in shades of grey and silver, and the outdoor patio looks straight onto Granger Bay. Enthusiastic students train here as chefs and waiters, so things may not all go smoothly, but we've always found the experience pleasant and the food very tasty and nicely presented. The Sunday buffet or set menu is R280 per person.

El Burro MEXICAN **$$**
(Map p86; ☎021-433 2364; www.elburro.co.za; 81 Main Rd, Green Point; mains R100-140; ⏰noon-11.30pm Mon-Sat; Ⓟ🌶; 🚌Stadium) With a balcony providing views of Cape Town Stadium, the decor at this stylish restaurant is a bit more chic than your average Mexican joint and the food more inventive. Supplementing the usual tacos and enchiladas are traditional dishes such as chicken *mole poblano* and a whole vegan menu. Booking is advised as it's popular.

Downstairs is **Cabrito** (Map p86; ⏰4pm-2am Mon-Fri, from 2pm Sat), an ever-busy bar serving craft beer, wine and an impressive range of tequila.

Willoughby & Co SEAFOOD **$$**
(Map p86; ☎021-418 6115; www.willoughbyandco.co.za; Shop 6132, Victoria Wharf, Breakwater Blvd, V&A Waterfront; mains R70-180; ⏰noon-10.30pm; Ⓟ📶; 🚌Waterfront) Commonly acknowledged as one of the better places to eat at the Waterfront – and with long queues to prove it. Huge servings of sushi are the standout from a fish-based menu at this casual restaurant inside the mall.

★**Harbour House** SEAFOOD **$$$**
(Map p86; ☎021-418 4744; www.harbourhouse.co.za; Quay 4, V&A Waterfront; mains R100-435; ⏰noon-10pm; Ⓟ; 🚌Nobel Square) The Kalk Bay institution has set up shop at the Waterfront with a good white-tablecloth restaurant on the ground floor (ask for a table on the deck outside) at which to enjoy excellent seafood and other dishes.

The sushi and cocktail lounge bar on the upper deck is just the spot for a chilled glass of wine at sunset.

Nobu JAPANESE **$$$**
(Map p86; ☎021-431 4511; www.noburestaurants.com; One&Only Cape Town, Dock Rd, V&A Waterfront; mains R200-760, set meals from R900; ⏰6.30-11pm; Ⓟ; 🚌Aquarium) This branch of the upmarket global Japanese chain is a smooth-running operation. The chefs turn out expert renditions of Nobu Matsuhisa's signature ceviches and cod in miso sauce, along with the expected sushi and tempura. The soaring dining hall offers a New York–metro buzz.

The more intimate bar upstairs is a nice spot to work your way through the extensive sake menu.

Sea Point to Hout Bay

Sea Point is one of the city's most exciting neighbourhoods for food, with its cosmopolitan mix of sushi bars, burger joints, Korean restaurants, West African cafes and convenience stores serving fresh bagels. Running parallel with the prettier coastal Beach Rd, busy Main and Regent Rds yield the most interesting culinary discoveries, with numerous options, including the daily Mojo Market (p180), around the meeting of the two thoroughfares.

Camps Bay and Clifton have wonderful seafront cafes for an alfresco bite with beach views among Cape Town's beautiful people. Head to Hout Bay for fish and chips and the weekly Bay Harbour Market (p177).

★Jarryds Espresso Bar & Eatery CAFE **$**
(Map p90; 060 748 0145; www.jarryds.com; 90 Regent Rd, Sea Point; mains R95; 7am-4pm) When Jarryd and brother Ariel moved home from Sydney, they brought with them the concept of the come-as-you-are daytime eateries beloved of the Aussies. This has consequently become Sea Point's go-to for breakfasts, which range from coconut granola to eggs Benedict, and lunchtime sticky ribs or falafel bowls. Ingredients are sourced locally, including the coffee from Espresso Lab in Woodstock.

★Kleinsky's Delicatessen DELI **$**
(Map p90; 021-433 2871; www.kleinskys.co.za; 95 Regent Rd, Sea Point; sandwiches R50; 8am-4pm Mon-Fri, to 3pm Sat & Sun; ; Tramway) A hip homage to classic New York Jewish delis, Kleinsky's is a great casual daytime option, offering dishes such as toasted bagels with smoked salmon or free-range chicken-liver pâté, chicken soup with matzo balls, and latkes (potato pancakes). The deli serves good coffee, too. Its walls act as a gallery for local artists.

Hout Bay Coffee CAFE **$**
(Map p92; 083 263 9044; www.facebook.com/HoutbayCoffee; Main Rd, Hout Bay; mains R65; 9am-5pm Mon-Fri, to 3pm Sat & Sun; Military) Sip excellent coffee at this rustic cafe-roastery, occupying an 18th-century extension to the original 17th-century woodcutters' cottage at Hout Bay. The outdoor area is shaded by a 150-year-old Norfolk pine, with furniture made from old fishing boats. The cafe also bakes filo-pastry chicken pies, chocolate cakes and wheat-free quiches with free-range eggs. At the front of Mainstream Shopping Centre.

Hesheng CHINESE **$**
(Map p90; 021-433 0739; http://hesheng.co.za; cnr Main & Rocklands Rds, Sea Point; mains R70-98; 11am-10pm Mon & Wed-Sun, from 5pm Tue; Sea Point High) Sea Point is stacked with Chinese restaurants, but this inauspicious-looking hole-in-the-wall, classically located next to a pawnbroker, is the real deal. Frequented by Chinese expats, it's run by a friendly Chinese family, who pride themselves on serving authentic dishes (rather than gloppy sweet and sour pork) and make the dumplings and noodles by hand.

Fish on the Rocks SEAFOOD **$**
(Map p92; 021-790 0001; www.fishontherocks.com; Harbour Rd, Hout Bay; mains R50-92; 10am-8pm; Atlantic Skipper) This Hout Bay institution dishes up some of Cape Town's best fish and chips, in a breezy bayside location with outdoor tables. Watch out for the dive-bombing seagulls if you do eat on the rocks, though.

★Fuego MEXICAN **$$**
(Map p90; 021-200 4278; www.fuegotacos.co.za; 77 Regent Rd, Sea Point; tacos R60-75; 11am-10pm Tue-Sat, 9am-4pm Sun) Established by a New York chef, this taco joint specialises in Mexico's beloved corn snack, and cocktails. Enjoy fillings such as pulled pork and 'drunken' chicken (cooked in tequila), and tipples including the homemade rooibos-infused tequila. Tacos and drinks are both discounted during happy hour (4pm to 6.30pm).

★La Boheme Wine Bar & Bistro BISTRO **$$**
(Map p90; 021-434 8797; www.labohemebistro.co.za; 341 Main Rd, Sea Point; mains R100, 2-/3-course dinner menus R150/180; noon-11pm Mon-Sat; ; Firmount) Although you can fuel up on delicious tapas and espresso here during the day, La Boheme is best visited in the evening, when candles twinkle on the tables and you can take advantage of its superb-value two- or three-course menus. The dishes mix local ingredients with French and Spanish influences, resulting in a Capetonian take on European gastronomy.

★Massimo's ITALIAN **$$**
(021-790 5648; www.pizzaclub.co.za; Oakhurst Farm Park, Main Rd, Hout Bay; mains R70-135; noon-9.30pm; ; Imizamo Yethu) There's pasta and *spuntini* (tapas-style small plates) on offer, but the wood-fired thin-crust pizzas are Massimo's speciality – and very good they are, too. It's all served up with warmth and humour by the Italian Massimo

and his Liverpudlian wife Tracy. There are plenty of vegetarian and vegan options, plus one of the best kids' play areas in Cape Town.

Cheyne's ASIAN **$$**

(Map p92; 021-790 3462, 066 412 3289; www.facebook.com/cheyneshoutbay; 35 Main Rd, Hout Bay; small plates R65-95; 6-10pm Mon-Sat, noon-3pm Fri & Sat; ; Military) Cheyne Morrisby has gathered quite a following for his inventive Asian and Pacific Rim–inspired small plates, which combine adventurous flavours and textures. Not everything works, but when it does – such as with the tuna tacos, poke bowls and double-thick peanut-butter shakes – it can be sublime. The presentation, service and street-art decor are all great.

Mariner's Wharf SEAFOOD **$$**

(Map p92; 021-790 1100; www.marinerswharf.co.za; Harbour Rd, Hout Bay; mains R70-245; 10am-8.30pm; Northshore) A touristy complex of seafood restaurants, souvenir shops, and fish and chips stands beside sandy Hout Bay Beach. The **Wharfette Bistro & Takeaway** (mains R70 to R95) is a popular spot for hake and chips, while the **Wharfside Grill** (mains R125 to R245) offers more elaborate dishes such as Thai green curry linefish.

Harvey's INTERNATIONAL **$$**

(Map p90; 021-434 2351; www.winchester.co.za; Winchester Mansions Hotel, 221 Beach Rd, Sea Point; bar snacks R80, lunch mains R100-200; 7am-10pm Mon-Sat, from 11am Sun; London) Book for the Sunday jazz brunch (11am to 2pm; R320), where live music and a glass of bubbly will greet you in the century-old Winchester Mansions Hotel's (p134) flower-draped courtyard. The chic sea-facing bar-restaurant is good for lunch, drinks and nibbles, too. Book also for the Saturday high tea, featuring tiered stands of sweet and savoury delights (2.30pm to 5.30pm; R360 for two).

Duchess of Wisbeach INTERNATIONAL **$$**

(Map p90; 021-434 1525; www.duchessofwisbeach.co.za; 3 Wisbeach Rd, Sea Point; mains R105-175; 6.30-10.30pm Mon-Sat, 12.30-2.30pm Sun; Sea Point High) Under the stewardship of a celebrated Jo'burg chef, this Duchess is one romantic-looking lady who raises Sea Point's dining bar by several notches. The restaurant serves classic French bistro food with a modern South African spin. All of the ingredients are fresh, with the only thing frozen being the homemade ice creams and sorbets.

Kitima ASIAN **$$**

(Map p92; 021-790 8004; www.kitima.co.za; Kronendal, 140 Main Rd, Hout Bay; mains R130-225, Sun brunch R250; 5.30-10.30pm Tue-Sat, noon-3.30pm Sun; Imizamo Yethu) The Kronendal, a Cape Dutch farmhouse with parts dating back to 1713, has been sensitively restored to house this excellent pan-Asian restaurant specialising in Thai food and sushi. Smiling Thai chefs ensure that fusion dishes such as ostrich *phad chaa* (wok-fried with lemongrass) are delicious.

★ La Mouette FRENCH **$$$**

(Map p90; 021-433 0856; www.lamouette-restaurant.co.za; 78 Regent Rd, Sea Point; tapas R90, 3-/5-course menus R395/445, with wine pairings R720/820; 6-10.30pm, plus noon-3pm Sun; Kei Apple) New takes on the classics (such as herb gnocchi and smoked pork belly) and fresh inventions (including kudu loin with fermented cabbage, BBQ carrot puree and bolognese sauce) make this a standout culinary experience. Local art hangs in the maroon-walled interior and there's a lush outdoor courtyard with a bubbling fountain. Tapas are served for Sunday lunch.

Codfather SEAFOOD **$$$**

(Map p94; 021-438 0782; www.codfather.co.za; 37 The Drive, Camps Bay; meals R500; noon-11pm; Whale Rock) Book ahead to get a table at this Camps Bay institution, where an enjoyable meal awaits, whether you spend it at the sushi bar or dining with a view of Lion's Head. Order your wine and sides, then let your knowledgeable waiter talk you through the glistening choices on the counters, from angelfish and butterfish to hake and kingklip.

Depending on which fish you order, expect to spend around R500 per person for sushi starters, fish, sides and wine.

Roundhouse INTERNATIONAL **$$$**

(Map p94; 021-438 4347; www.theroundhouserestaurant.com; Round House Rd, Camps Bay; 5-course set menus R695, with wine pairings R995; 6-10pm Tue-Sat, plus noon-2.30pm Sat & Sun May-Sep; Kloof Nek) Overlooking Camps Bay, this heritage-listed 18th-century building, set in wooded grounds, houses an elegant restaurant. The menus mix South African recipes with European flair; dishes range from poached kingklip (a type of fish) to ostrich with red cabbage and mustard seeds.

From October to April, also consider a relaxed lunch on the lawns at Roundhouse's midrange **Rumbullion** restaurant, where you can snack on gourmet pizza and salads (mains R85 to R125). It's open noon to 5pm Tuesday to Thursday and 9am to 5pm Friday to Sunday.

La Perla ITALIAN **$$$**
(Map p90; 021-439 9538; www.laperla.co.za; cnr Church & Beach Rds, Sea Point; mains R95-285; 10am-11pm; Sea Point Pool) This eternally stylish restaurant, with its waiters in white jackets, has been a fixture of Sea Point's promenade since 1969. Enjoy something from the menu of pasta, fish and meat dishes on the terrace shaded by stout palms, or retreat to the atmospheric dining room.

Southern Suburbs

Constantia's wineries and hotels house some of the city's finest places to dine. Constantia Nek, the pass to Hout Bay, has a few upmarket restaurants among the trees, including a branch of La Parada (p159). There are good cafes and restaurants scattered through the rest of the Southern Suburbs – pleasant staging posts between the city centre and False Bay. On Wednesday and Saturday, there's also the **Earth Fair Food Market** (Map p100; 071 121 7367; www.earthfairmarket.co.za; South Palms Shopping Centre, 333 Main Road, Tokai; mains R60-100; 3-8.30pm Wed, 9am-2pm Sat; ; Steenberg) in Tokai.

★**Starlings Cafe** INTERNATIONAL **$**
(Map p97; 021-671 6875; www.starlings.co.za; 94 Belvedere Rd, Claremont; mains R60-120; 7am-5pm Mon-Fri, 8am-4pm Sat; ; Claremont) One of the Southern Suburbs' most charming dining spots. With its relaxed, arty cottage and shady garden environment, it's great for a lazy breakfast or lunch. Excellent coffee, too. For breakfast, choose the likes of French toast and poached eggs with parmesan and basil pesto; lunch dishes include aubergine bake and Asian yellow chicken curry.

It's well off the tourist route and a little tricky to find – hidden as it is behind a big hedge.

★**Gardener's Cottage** CAFE **$**
(Map p97; 021-689 3158; Montebello Design Centre, 31 Newlands Ave, Newlands; mains R80; 8am-4.30pm Tue-Fri, from 8.30am Sat & Sun; Newlands) After exploring the Montebello craft studios (p181), relax at this lovely cafe, which occupies the estate's original gatekeeper's cottage. Beyond the leafy garden and stoep (veranda), the interior has a contemporary-tearoom look with exposed floorboards and homemade cakes, jams and biscuits on display. The breakfasts range from eggs Benedict to sweetcorn flapjacks, and lunches from open sandwiches to the sushi stack.

The View CAFE **$**
(Map p100; 021-762 0067; www.theviewatchartfarm.com; Chart Farm, Klaasens Rd, Wynberg; mains R69-85; 9am-4.30pm Tue-Sun; ; Wynberg) Enjoy homemade cakes, breakfasts and lunch treats such as chicken pie at the resident coffee shop of Chart Farm, with its panoramic view across the farm to the mountains. Chestnuts, lemons and grapes are among the tasty things grown on the farm, where you can also pick your own roses and visit the farm stall. It's tucked away on the west side of the M3.

Rhodes Memorial Restaurant CAPE MALAY **$**
(Map p97; 021-687 0000; www.rhodesmemorial.co.za; Rhodes Memorial, off M3, Groote Schuur Estate; mains R80-105; 9am-5pm;) This pleasant restaurant and al-fresco tearoom is located in a 1920 thatched-roof cottage behind the Rhodes Memorial (p103). It's family-run and specialises in Cape Malay dishes, such as curries, ostrich and butternut *bobotie* (a delicately flavoured curry with a topping of beaten egg baked to a crust), *bredie* (slow-cooked lamb and tomato stew) and *potjie* (meat and vegetable pot stew).

Bookings are advised on the weekends – especially on Sunday, when there's live jazz from 1pm to 4pm. The restaurant has a children's play area.

O'ways Teacafe VEGETARIAN **$**
(Map p97; 021-671 2850; www.oways.co.za; 20 Dreyer St, Claremont; mains R70; 7.30am-5pm Mon-Fri, 9am-2pm Sat; ; Claremont) Pronounced 'always', this stylish, relaxing place is fully vegetarian, and offers tasty choices such as soya-chunk and chickpea curry, creamy gnocchi and a dim-sum platter. It's also one of the best places in Cape Town to come for tea, with 100-plus loose-leaf teas and infusions on offer, as well as locally roasted Origin coffee.

★**Rare Grill** STEAK **$$**
(Map p100; 076 460 0423; www.facebook.com/raregrillcpt; 166 2nd Ave, Kenilworth; mains R98-190; 6-10pm Mon-Sat; Kenilworth) In the unlikely setting of a scruffy car park next to Kenilworth train station, this small steakhouse is

one of the best in town, serving the finest wet-aged South African cuts overlooked by photos of cows. Book well ahead to experience this meltingly tender fillet and sirloin bursting with flavour; order the 500g T-bone if it's on the specials board.

★Bistro Sixteen82 BISTRO $$
(Map p100; 021-713 2211; www.steenbergfarm.com; Steenberg Estate, Steenberg Rd, Constantia; lunch mains R170; 9am-8pm) Perfectly complementing the slick and contemporary wine-tasting lounge at Steenberg Farm (p98), this appealing bistro serves everything from oysters for breakfast to braised lamb neck for lunch. Tapas (rather than dinner) are offered from 5pm and it's also justifiably popular as a restaurant to breakfast in style. Seating is both indoor and outdoor, with beguiling views of the gardens and mountain.

★Four & Twenty Cafe & Pantry DELI $$
(Map p100; 021-761 1000; www.fourandtwentycafe.co.za; 23 Wolfe St, Wynberg Village; mains R120; 8am-3.30pm Mon-Sat, from 9am Sun; ; Wynberg) A favourite among the Little Chelsea (Wynberg Village) crowd, this rustic but chic spot serves a small menu of delicious creations, from gourmet salads and sandwiches to inventive dishes such as 'man-sized' herbed fish cakes and sticky-beef-short-rib-filled steamed buns. The courtyard, draped with bougainvillea, is a lovely spot even just for tea and cake.

Tashas INTERNATIONAL $$
(Map p100; 021-794 5449; www.tashascafe.com; Shop 55, Constantia Village, Constantia Main Rd, Constantia; mains R110; 7am-9pm Mon-Sat, from 8am Sun;) Muffins that could feed a small family and other delectable baked goods and desserts are the forte of this luxe-design cafe offering 'beautiful food, stunning environments', inspired by country French cuisine. A hit Jo'burg concept imported to the Mother City (and the Middle East), it serves everything from quiches and burgers to waffles and scones.

La Belle BAKERY $$
(Map p100; 021-795 6336; www.alphen.co.za; Alphen Dr, Constantia; mains R95-250; 7am-11pm;) This bistro and bakery in front of the Alphen Hotel (p136) hotel is appealing both inside and out – for breakfast, lunch or a snack. Treat yourself to buttermilk pancakes and a speciality leaf tea for breakfast, or a lunch of griddled cheeseburger or smoked-salmon sandwich. There's also a branch in Camps Bay (p165).

Kirstenbosch Tea Room INTERNATIONAL $$
(Map p100; 021-797 4883; www.ktr.co.za; Gate 2, Kirstenbosch National Botanical Garden, Rhodes Dr, Newlands; mains R90-160; 8.30am-5pm; Kirstenbosch) Kirstenbosch's long-running tearoom serves a jolly English tea for two (R310), including sandwiches, mini-quiches and homemade scones with strawberry jam and clotted cream, to enjoy anywhere you please in the gardens (p95). Also offering gourmet picnics (R230 per person), light and not-so-light lunches, it's the gardens' best eating option.

A Tavola ITALIAN $$
(Map p100; 021-671 1763; www.atavola.co.za; Library Sq, Wilderness Rd, Claremont; mains R120; noon-3pm Mon-Fri & 6-11pm Mon-Sat; Claremont) This spacious, classy neighbourhood joint, its walls hung with photos of people tucking into food, starts proceedings with antipasti and salads, before moving to delicious pasta and other mains. No wonder the people in those photos are smiling.

Jonkershuis CAPE MALAY $$
(Map p100; 021-794 6255; www.jonkershuisconstantia.co.za; Groot Constantia Rd, Constantia; mains R90-198; 9am-9pm Mon-Sat, to 5pm Sun;) This casual brasserie-style restaurant on the grounds of Groot Constantia (p96) has a pleasant, vine-shaded courtyard and tables looking onto the manor house. Sample Cape Malay dishes (including a tasting plate for R198) or cured meats with a glass or two of the local wines, and satisfy your sweet tooth with traditional desserts such as milk tart and Malva pudding.

The Eatery GRILL $$
(Map p97; 021-003 4505; www.eaterywoodfiredgrill.co.za; Belvedere Sq, cnr Belvedere & Keurboom Rds, Claremont; mains R100-180; 9am-10pm; ; Claremont) This neighbourhood eatery in a small shopping plaza specialises in wood-fired steaks, burgers and milkshakes. It attracts everyone from students to families, and is a winner with kids because of the jungle gym adjoining its covered stoep.

★Greenhouse INTERNATIONAL $$$
(Map p100; 021-795 6226; www.greenhouserestaurant.co.za; The Cellars-Hohenort Hotel, 93 Brommersvlei Rd, Constantia; tasting menus R1200; 6-9.30pm Tue-Sat, plus noon-2pm Fri & Sat;) Chef Peter Tempelhoff's culinary imagination runs riot in this elegant restaurant that's one of the Cape's top dining destinations. The finest local produce and recipes, from Cape Malay curried octopus

to Outeniqua springbok, feature on the 12-course tasting menu. For serious foodies only; desserts are served on petrified Madagascan wood, to remind diners of the circle of life and death.

Greenhouse also offers a 'chef for the day' cooking experience, in which you do a shift in the kitchen followed by lunch or dinner.

★La Colombe FUSION $$$

(Map p100; 021-794 2390; www.lacolombe.co.za; Silvermist Estate, Constantia Nek; tasting menus R780-1280, with wine pairings R1530-2180; 12.30-2pm & 7-9.30pm) A veteran of Gordon Ramsay's kitchen, chef Scot Kirton rustles up skilful dishes combining French and Asian techniques and flavours, such as quail breast in coconut and miso, and Karoo lamb-loin bolognese. The coolly elegant setting and personable service couldn't be better.

Foxcroft FUSION $$$

(Map p100; 021-202 3304; www.foxcroft.co.za; High Constantia Centre, Groot Constantia Rd, Constantia; tasting menus R435; noon-2pm & 6-8.30pm) With a seasonal menu featuring dishes such as slow-cooked lamb with nettles and whisky mustard, Foxcroft is a delectable addition to the Southern Suburbs fine-dining scene. Tackle the four-course tasting menu in the minimalist dining room or on sunny days take tapas on the patio. It sits at the edge of the car park, but the mountain views are marvellous.

The attached bakery (open 8am to 4pm) serves some of Cape Town's finest pastries, freshly baked each morning.

Simon's Town & Southern Peninsula

The peninsula doesn't have the breadth of restaurants found elsewhere in Cape Town, but it does offer some scenic seaside spots for a light lunch. Kalk Bay is replete with vibey cafes and good restaurants, with plenty of options also in Muizenberg and Simon's Town. South of the latter, en route to Cape Point, roadside restaurants of varying quality cater to coach parties. Across the peninsula, Noordhoek Farm Village (p182) and Imhoff Farm (p109) are rustic, family-friendly complexes with cafes, delis and restaurants. Weekly food markets take place in the former, as well as at Blue Bird Garage (p177) and Cape Point Vineyards (p111).

Hub Cafe INTERNATIONAL $

(071 342 5210; www.facebook.com/pg/thehubcafescarborough; cnr Main Rd & Watsonia Ln, Scarborough; mains R95; noon-8.30pm Wed-Fri, from 9am Sat, 9am-3.30pm Sun) If you're looking for a bite in the deep south, Scarborough's favourite meeting point specialises in pizzas named after local surf breaks as well as breakfasts and dishes ranging from steak to beer-battered fish and chips.

Free Range Coffee Shop CAFE $

(021-783 4545; http://imhofffarm.co.za; Kommetjie Rd, Kommetjie; mains R70; 8am-4.30pm) Free Range sells quiches, pies, burgers, wraps and other wholesome lunches. Great cakes, too. It's located at the back of a farm shop, with tables overlooking Imhoff Farm's (p109) village green.

Blue Bird Cafe BURGERS $

(Map p104; 063 206 6911; www.bluebirdcafe.co.za; 39 Albertyn Rd, Muizenberg; mains R80; 4-9pm Sat-Thu; ; False Bay) Enjoy unpretentious dishes such as burgers, Asian ribs, pizza and crispy chicken wings while sitting beneath fairy lights at this bohemian eatery. There's a vegan menu, too. It's located in the same 1940s airplane hanger that hosts the Blue Bird Garage Food & Goods Market (p177) on Fridays.

Salty Sea Dog FISH & CHIPS $

(Map p108; 021-786 1918; saltydog@telkomsa.net; 2 Wharf St, Simon's Town; mains R70; 8.30am-9pm Mon-Sat, to 4.30pm Sun) The Sea Dog is always packed with Cape Point day-trippers feasting on fish and chips (the hake is excellent), with equally palatable milkshakes to follow. It's casual, licensed and has indoor and outdoor seating. Booking ahead recommended.

Bob's Bagel Cafe BAKERY $

(Map p104; 083 280 0012; 6 Rouxville Rd, Kalk Bay; bagels from R25; 7.45am-4pm Tue-Sun, to 2pm Mon; ; Kalk Bay) Bob's is the place for your bagel fix. They're all freshly baked here and you can have them au naturel, or as sandwiches, along with good coffee and other baked nibbles and organic ice creams. The streetside benches provide a good view of the small children's park opposite.

Empire Cafe CAFE $

(Map p104; 021-788 1250; www.empirecafe.co.za; 11 York Rd, Muizenberg; mains R80; 7am-4pm Mon-Thu & Sat, to 9pm Fri, 8am-4pm Sun; ; Muizenberg) The local surfers' favourite hang-out is a great place for a hearty breakfast of Mexican huevos rancheros or poached eggs on butternut rosti, accompanied by Tribe coffee, and lunches ranging from burgers to pastas. Local art enlivens the walls and a dramatic chandelier dangles from the ceiling.

★ Salt TAPAS $$

(Map p104; ☎021-788 3992; 136 Main Rd, Kalk Bay; mains R100; ⏰7am-9.30pm; 🚉Kalk Bay) Offering a gastronomic take on False Bay cool, Salt serves mains such as wild kudu goulash, but your best bet is to focus on the small plates (R45), which range from wasabi-dusted calamari to bratwurst with homemade kimchi. The seafood dishes use what's available from the harbour, normally yellowfish; order the angelfish ceviche when it's going.

The decor nicely complements the building's original black-and-white tiled floor with wrought ironwork, piping shelves, blackboard menus and big windows overlooking the harbour. Mellow tunes such as Kings of Convenience on the stereo and craft beers on draught add up to a memorable evening. Reservations are not taken so get here early.

★ Foodbarn INTERNATIONAL $$

(☎021-789 1390; www.thefoodbarn.co.za; cnr Main Rd & Village Ln; mains R180; ⏰noon-2.30pm daily, plus 7-9.30pm Tue-Sat; 📶) 🍃 Expect rustic, delicious bistro dishes with suggested wine pairings at master chef Franck Dangereux's restaurant in the relaxed surrounds of Noordhoek Farm Village (p182). The separate, book-lined deli-bakery-cafe (mains R35 to R145) and tapas bar (6pm to 9pm Tuesday to Saturday; small plates R50) is just as good, and stocks its freshly baked goodies and other locally sourced food and drinks.

The cafe is open 8am to 4.30pm daily; the deli 8am to 9pm Tuesday to Saturday, and until 5pm Sunday and Monday.

★ Blue Water Cafe INTERNATIONAL $$

(☎021-783 4545; www.imhofffarm.co.za; Kommetjie Rd, Kommetjie; mains R100; ⏰9am-9pm Wed-Sat, to 4pm Tue, to 6pm Sun; 👪) A lovely place to enjoy breakfast, simple-but-good lunch dishes including pizza, pasta, seafood and gourmet salads, or a craft beer with a sweeping view. The stoep of this historic property at the heart of Imhoff Farm (p109) looks out over Noordhoek Beach and Chapman's Peak. There's good service, a garden, jungle gym and the Higgeldy Piggeldy Farmyard next door.

★ Olympia Cafe & Deli BAKERY $$

(Map p104; ☎021-788 6396; http://olympiacafe.co.za; 134 Main Rd, Kalk Bay; mains R90-180; ⏰7am-9pm; 🚉Kalk Bay) Setting a high standard for relaxed rustic cafes by the sea, Olympia bakes its own breads and pastries. It's great for breakfast, and its Mediterranean-influenced lunch dishes are delicious, too – particularly the heaped bowls of mussels. There's live jazz on some Friday and Saturday nights.

★ Lighthouse Cafe INTERNATIONAL $$

(Map p108; ☎021-786 9000; www.thelighthousecafe.co.za; 90 St Georges St, Simon's Town; mains R70-140; ⏰8.30am-4pm Sun-Tue, to 10pm Wed-Sat; 🚉Simon's Town) Relaxed, beachcomber-chic cafe, with a menu big on seafood – from mussel-and-chorizo pasta to Jamie Oliver's beer-battered fish and chips. The Lighthouse Cafe also does burgers, pizzas and a meze platter.

Two Oceans Restaurant SEAFOOD $$

(Map p110; ☎021-780 9200; www.two-oceans.co.za; Cape of Good Hope; mains from R145; ⏰9-11am & noon-4.30pm) Two Oceans feeds tour-bus crowds en route between the Cape Point car park and the funicular to the old lighthouse, but it has some appeal if you don't mind a busy and bustling environment. Its False Bay views are superb and there's a good choice of breakfasts, sushi and seafood. Book ahead, natch.

Cucina Labia INTERNATIONAL $$

(Map p104; ☎021-788 6062; www.casalabia.co.za; 192 Main Rd, Muizenberg; mains R115-195; ⏰10am-4pm Tue-Fri, from 9am Sat & Sun, plus 6-10pm Fri; 🖉; 🚉Muizenberg) Enjoy brunch, Italian cuisine, afternoon tea and, on weekends, delicious breakfasts and lunchtime classical piano (1pm to 4pm) at this pleasant cafe in Muizenberg's gorgeous Italianate villa and cultural centre, Casa Labia (p107). Some of the meal ingredients come from the adjoining garden.

Live Bait SEAFOOD $$

(Map p104; ☎021-788 5755; www.livebait.co.za; Kalk Bay Harbour, Kalk Bay; mains R75-180; ⏰noon-11pm; 🚉Kalk Bay) This breezy, Aegean-style fish restaurant, set within arm's reach of the crashing waves and the bustle of Kalk Bay Harbour, is one of the best options around for a relaxed seafood meal. Dishes range from sushi to West Coast mussels, and there's another branch in Muizenberg.

The same company runs the upmarket **Harbour House** restaurant upstairs, and the neighbouring **Lucky Fish & Chips** takeaway.

Cape Farmhouse Restaurant INTERNATIONAL $$

(Map p110; 021-780 1246; www.capefarmhouse.com; cnr M65 & M66, Redhill; mains R100; 9am-5pm Thu-Sun;) This 250-year-old farmhouse with a rustic setting serves everything from breakfast to fillet steak, with as much of its produce as possible coming from the on-site organic garden.

It's set beside interesting craft stalls and a kids' playground. In summer the restaurant hosts music concerts on Saturdays from 2pm to 8pm (tickets R100); see its website for details.

Cape Flats & Northern Suburbs

You don't go to the Cape Flats for fine dining, but there are a few small restaurants where you can try traditional Xhosa cuisine or enjoy a braai (barbecue), often known as *shisa nyama* in the townships. It's best to call ahead to check that restaurants will be open, as they often don't stick to their advertised hours of business.

In the Northern Suburbs, the best restaurants are found on the estates of the Durbanville Wine Valley, but there are a few pleasant coastal spots with good views. Eden on the Bay Mall (p113) has cafes overlooking Bloubergstrand.

Cafe Blouberg CAFE $

(021-554 4462; http://cafe-blouberg.co.za; 20 Stadler Rd, Bloubergstrand; mains R65-105; 8am-5pm; ; Bokkombaai) At the southern end of Bloubergstrand is this delightful place in a whitewashed seaside cottage, its counter loaded with a tempting collection of cakes and baked goods. The menu focuses on all-day breakfasts ranging from poached eggs to tortillas, while lunch options include salads, sandwiches and quiches.

Spinach King BAKERY $

(073 892 5907; www.spinachking.co.za; Khayelitsha Mall, off Walter Sisulu Rd, Khayelitsha; snacks R20; 9am-6pm; ; Khayelitsha) Lufefe Nomjana is the young entrepreneur behind this very green business baking bread and muffins made with spinach. It's a welcome vegetarian respite from the fast-food outlets of Khayelitsha Mall and the grilled meats that are a feature of the townships.

Millstone CAFE $

(Map p114; 021-447 8226; www.facebook.com/MillstoneFarmstall; Oude Molen Eco Village, Alexandra Rd, Pinelands; mains R60; 8am-5pm Tue-Sat, to 3pm Sun & Mon; ; Pinelands) This rustic cafe and farm stall specialises in organic produce, hand-crafted breads, preserves and jams. Kids will love the tree house in its garden and the pony rides next door.

A market takes place here from 10am to 3pm on Sundays between November and January.

Eziko AFRICAN $

(Map p114; 021-694 0434; www.ezikorestaurant.co.za; cnr King Langalibalele Ave & Jungle Walk, Langa; mains R65; 9am-3.30pm Mon-Sat; Langa) Eziko offers good, simple food in a pleasant setting. Try the chef's special fried chicken and, if you're feeling adventurous, the 'delectable' tripe. Dishes are served with sides of samp (a mixture of maize and beans), pap (maize porridge), bread and vegetables. Phone ahead to check opening hours, or arrange to visit as part of a Maboneng (p125) tour. Eziko also offers cooking classes.

Clifford & Sandra's AFRICAN $

(off Ntlazane Rd, Khayelitsha; meals R30; 8am-6.30pm; Khayelitsha) At the market next to Khayelitsha Station, ask around to find this shack serving tasty and excellent traditional chow. Clifford will pour water over your hands before you start using them (no cutlery here) to tuck into beef stew, crispy fried chicken and pap.

Groova Park BRAAI $

(Ntutyana St, Khayelitsha; meals R50-100; 11am-10pm; Makabeni) It doesn't have a sign but you'll know this butchery and braai (barbecue) joint by the many cars parked outside on a weekend afternoon – and the happy patrons tucking into grilled meats.

Nomzamo BRAAI $

(Map p114; 021-695 4520; King Langalibalele Ave, Langa; meals R75-120; 9am-7pm; Langa) This spotlessly clean butchers generally has a relaxed, peaceful vibe since it doesn't sell alcohol. The cuts of meat – beef, lamb, pork, sausages and chicken wings – are top class. Call ahead if you want to add side dishes such as bread or salads to make a full meal.

★**Hog House Brewing Co.** BARBECUE $$

(Map p114; 021-810 4545; http://hhbc.co.za; Unit 4 Technosquare, 42 Morningside Rd, Ndabeni; meals R100-150; 5-9pm Mon-Sat;) It couldn't be in a more obscure spot – within a business park in an industrial part of town – but this barbecue restaurant is perpetually busy. The creations of chef PJ Vadas include smoked meats so tender you could cut them with a spoon. The veggie side dishes are just as impressive – you've never eaten cauliflower and aubergine this good. Wash it all down with beers produced in the attached microbrewery. Meat dishes are priced per 100g.

★**4Roomed eKasi Culture** AFRICAN $$
(☎076 157 3177; https://4roomedekasiculture.com; A605 Makabeni Rd, Khayelitsha; 3-course meals R165-230; ⊙noon-3.30pm & 6-8.30pm Fri-Sun; 📶) As gourmet as it gets in Khayelitsha with the lovely Abigail Mbalo, a self-taught cook and former contestant on SA's *MasterChef* TV show, in charge. Expect African food with a twist: delicious wedges of pap mixed with butternut squash and nutmeg, a rich lamb curry and a red velvet cake made with beetroot.

The whitewashed courtyard setting is delightful, with one wall lined with old bathtubs turned into planters for vegetables and herbs used in the cooking. Abigail also has a food truck out of which she can create a five-course feast if you have a group of at least 10 people. You can bring your own alcohol.

★**Maestro's on the Beach** INTERNATIONAL $$
(Map p114; ☎021-551 4992; www.maestros.co.za; Bridge Rd, Milnerton; mains R70-200; ⊙10am-11pm Mon-Fri, from 9am Sat & Sun; 🚌Woodbridge) This all-day dining operation has a grand beachside position with swoon-worthy views of Table Mountain. The broad menu includes plenty of seafood, steaks, pizzas and pasta dishes. It's located next to Milnerton Golf Club (p123), you enter through the club's car park.

★**Mzansi** AFRICAN $$
(Map p114; ☎073 754 8502; www.mzansi45.co.za; 45 Harlem Ave, Langa; buffet R190; ⊙noon-10pm; 🚆Langa) As much a cultural experience as a gastronomic one, Mzansi rates highly among travellers. Food is served buffet-style and features some traditional dishes, including plenty of pap (maize porridge). Host Mama Nomonde brings a personal touch with tales of her life in the Cape Flats, and there's live music in the form of a marimba band. Book ahead.

Moyo AFRICAN $$
(☎021-286 0662; www.moyo.co.za; Shop 50, Eden on the Bay Mall, Bloubergstrand; mains R95-190; ⊙noon-10pm Mon, from 11am Tue-Fri, from 8.30am Sat & Sun; 🚌Big Bay) Local meats such as ostrich and Karoo venison are on the menu at this fun African-themed restaurant, as are traditional South African dishes. Have your face painted and dangle your feet in a cooling paddle-pool beneath a table shaped like a surfboard, with spectacular beach and Table Mountain views outside.

Lelapa AFRICAN $$
(Map p114; ☎021-694 2681; www.lelapa.co.za; 49 Harlem Ave, Langa; buffet from R190; ⊙11am-3pm & 5-9pm; 🌱; 🚆Langa) Sheila Mahloane and her daughter Monica have been so successful with their delicious African buffets (which include plenty of vegetarian dishes) that they took over the neighbour's place, and now have a space big enough for large groups. As with all township eateries, phone ahead to avoid making the journey in vain.

🍷 Drinking & Nightlife

Cape Town didn't become known as the 'Tavern of the Seven Seas' for nothing. There are scores of bars – with stunning views of either beach or mountain – in which to sip cocktails, fine wines or craft beers. If strutting your stuff on the dance floor is more your thing, then there's bound to be a club to suit.

The busy nights are Wednesday, Friday or Saturday when you'll see how the locals like to party, or *jol*, as they say here. But it's not all about drinking and dancing. Cape Town's nightlife embraces cabaret and comedy venues, and live music gigs from jazz to rap as well as hybrid events such as First Thursdays (p172) and **Tuning the Vine** (☎083 357 4069; www.tuningthevine.co.za; ticket online/at venue R200/220; ⊙5.30-8.30pm, 2nd Wed of month).

🍷 City Bowl, Foreshore, Bo-Kaap & De Waterkant

★**Orphanage** COCKTAIL BAR
(Map p70; ☎021-424 2004; www.theorphanage.co.za; cnr Orphange & Bree Sts, City Bowl; ⊙4pm-2am Mon-Thu & Sat, to 3am Fri; 🚌Upper Loop, Upper Long) Named after the nearby lane, the mixologists here prepare some tempting artisan libations with curious names including Knicker-Dropper Glory, Dollymop and Daylight Daisy, using ingredients as varied as peanut butter, kumquat compote and 'goldfish'! It's dark, sophisticated and stylish, with outdoor seating beneath the trees on Bree. Even better, they donate a portion of their profits to an orphanage in Athlone – so you can knock back that extra cocktail with a clean conscience.

LGBT CAPE TOWN

Africa's pinkest city is a glam-to-the-max destination that any LGBT traveller should have on their bucket list. De Waterkant, the principal queer precinct, is welcoming to everyone, from Cape Town's finest drag queens to leathered-up muscle Marys.

The closure of the long-running Amsterdam Action Bar in De Waterkant in 2017 could be seen as something of a weather vane. The gay vibe of the district remains intact, but it's noticeably less busy than in previous years. Places to check out include **Beefcakes** (Map p74; 021-425 9019; www.beefcakes.co.za; 40 Somerset Rd, De Waterkant; burgers R55-85; 7pm-midnight; Gallow's Hill), a camp burger bar where you can play bitchy bingo on Tuesday and watch drag shows on other nights, starring characters such as Mary Scary and Princess Pop; the ever-popular **Crew Bar** (Map p74; 021-461 4920; www.facebook.com/CrewBarCapeTown; 30 Napier St, De Waterkant; cover after 10pm Fri & all Sat R50; 7pm-2am Sun-Thu, to 4am Fri & Sat; Alfred) which continues to draw a mixed crowd for its DJs and hunky bar dancers dressed only in skimpy shorts and glitter; **Beaulah** (Map p74; 021-418 5244; 28 Somerset Rd, De Waterkant; cover R50; 9pm-4am Fri & Sat; Alfred) a fun bar and dance venue, with a devoted crowd of young boys and girls who are always ready to bop to the DJ's poppy tunes; and **Bar Code** (Map p74; 076 469 1825; https://versatbar.wixsite.com/barcode; 18 Cobern St, De Waterkant; cover after 11pm Wed-Sat R70; 4pm-2am; Alfred) where, after 11pm Wednesday to Saturday, the doors are closed and blinds drawn across the windows as patrons either strip completely or down to their underwear.

Pink Panther 2 (Map p74; www.facebook.com/ThePinkPantherSocialClub; 120 Strand St, City Bowl; cover R50-150; 8pm-4am Fri & Sat) is a new LGBT-friendly dance venue on the far southern edge of De Waterkant, while further into the City Bowl there's **Alexander Bar & Cafe** (p168), which is a both a great bar and a performance venue; and the glam cabaret and theatre space **Gate69 Cape Town** (Map p70; 021-035 1627; http://gate69.co.za; 87 Bree St, City Bowl; dinner & show from R450; Strand), presided over by 7ft-tall (in high heels) platinum-blonde drag queen Cathy Specific. Your tickets here gets you a tapas-style meal and a show.

In the old District Six/East City area, you'll find another new dance venue, **Babylon** (Map p80; 44 Constitution St, East City; cover R50; 8-4pm Fri & Sat; Lower Buitenkant). The vibe here is laid-back and friendly, with plush grey-velvet-upholstered booths, topless twinks and cubs behind the bars and a DJ playing crowd-pleasing music. It also has a broad balcony that provides panoramic views towards Table Mountain.

Camp and Afrikaans cultures collide at the **Pienk Piesang** (081 249 5604; www.facebook.com/HeSheLangarm; R50) events. Meaning 'Pink Banana', at these gatherings local gays and lesbians twirl around *langarm*-style (a local type of ballroom dance) to country-and-western-style tunes. The events take place irregularly at different venues around the Northern Suburbs; check the Facebook page for details.

Cape Town's lesbian community continues to party on with the MISS (Make It Sexy Sisters; www.facebook.com/MISSmakeitsexysisters) events and the Unofficial Pink Parties (www.facebook.com/pinkpartyza). These are lesbian-run but welcoming to everyone.

If you fancy going hiking with gays and gay-friendly folk while in the Mother City, check out the Cape Town Gay Hiking Club (www.facebook.com/groups/6068816435).

For the latest openings and events check out GayCapeTown4u.com (www.gaycapetown4u.com) and *Pink Tongue*, the free monthly newspaper covering local LGBT news and events. **Triangle Project** (081 257 6693; https://triangle.org.za; 2nd fl, Leadership House, cnr Burg & Shortmarket Sts, City Bowl; Mowbray) is the leading local gay-support organisation, offering legal advice and a range of education programs.

Also mark your calendar for the city's two main LGBT events: **Cape Town Pride** (www.capetownpride.org; Feb-Mar) and the huge dance and fancy-dress party **MCQP** (Mother City Queer Project; 021-461 4920; https://mcqp.co.za; Dec).

★ **Lady Bonin's Tea Bar** TEAHOUSE

(Map p70; 021-422 0536; http://ladybonins tea.com; 213 Long St, City Bowl; 9am-5pm Mon-Fri, 9.30am-2.30pm Sat; Upper Loop, Upper Long) A charmingly decorated, relaxing place in which to sample organic and sustainable artisan teas, fruity and herbal brews, and vegan baked treats. At front is the shop selling all their blends, while the tea room is a through the vine-covered courtyard to the rear.

★ **Openwine** WINE BAR

(Map p70; 021-422 0800; http://openwineza.co.za; 72 Wale St, City Bowl; noon-10pm Mon-Fri, from 5pm Sat; Church, Longmarket) The motto here is 'wine first, food second', so while there is a short menu, it's the range of 200-plus different wines from across the Western Cape that are the focus. Check out what they have by the glass on their 'drinkable blackboard' and then settle down either inside or outside to enjoy a drop or two.

Beerhouse BAR

(Map p70; 021-424 3370; www.beerhouse.co.za; 223 Long St, City Bowl; 11am-2am; Upper Loop, Upper Long) With 99 brands of bottled beer, both local and international, and several more brews on tap, this brightly designed and spacious joint in the heart of Long St will have beer lovers thinking they've died and gone to heaven. The balcony is a great spot from which to watch the world go by.

Honest Chocolate Cafe BAR

(Map p70; 076 765 8306; http://honest chocolate.co.za; 64a Wale St, City Bowl; 9am-6pm Mon-Fri, to 9pm Sat, to 4pm Sun; Dorp, Leeuwen) Following a successful crowdfunding campaign, Honest Chocolate launched this homage to fine dark chocolate in liquid, solid, ice-cream and cake form. It's a chocoholic's dream come true, with vegan and gluten-free options.

If you want to see where they make their artisan sweet treats, head to the Woodstock Exchange (p176).

Upstairs on Bree BAR

(Map p70; 021-422 4147, 083 417 3624; http://upstairsonbree.co.za; 103 Bree St, City Bowl; Church, Longmarket) You'll most likely find this New York–inspired loft-like bar and events space open for First Thursday (p172), when it hosts a techno-music after party. There's also a pretty regular series of one-off parties, product launches and music nights too, with a full list on their Facebook page.

Between 11am and 5pm Monday to Friday, you'll also find the place open as a cafe serving fresh veggie Buddha bowls and poke bowls (R70 to R80) – eat in or take away in biodegradable containers.

Outrage of Modesty COCKTAIL BAR

(Map p70; https://anoutrage.com; 88 Shortmarket St, City Bowl; 6pm-1am Tues-Sat; Church, Longmarket) An inventive twist at this speakeasy-style, unmarked cocktail bar is the menu of hessian pouches you'll be presented with: sniff each pouch to decide which smell you like and that will clue you into the cocktail to order. Every season the menu changes, as does the compact bar's interior art.

The bar shares an address with the Shortmarket Club (p142) but has a separate entrance; if you're dining at the restaurant, there's a connecting door.

Ka Pa Tée TEAHOUSE

(Map p70; 072 329 4443; www.facebook.com/Kapateecpt; 7 Church St, City Bowl; 7am-4.30pm Mon-Fri, 9am-2pm Sat; Groote Kerk) As well as being a rather stylish place to revive over their various house blends of organic teas, served alongside nice cakes and other sweets, you can also take home packaged bags of loose leaves and browse a small, colour-coordinated selection of arts and crafts.

House of H ROOFTOP BAR

(Map p70; 076 699 6146; www.houseofh.co.za; 112 Loop St, City Bowl; 4pm-4am Wed-Sat) There's a cafe and restaurant on the ground floor, but the big attraction lies on the roof where they've created one of the city's less pretentious rooftop bars. Street art decorates the wall and big cushions on wooden pallets provide a comfy place to sit on the broad decks at both the back and front end of the building.

The Vue LOUNGE

(Map p74; 021-418 3065; www.the-vue.com; 15th fl, 40 Chiappini St, De Waterkant; 6.45am-midnight; Old Fire Station) Knockout views of the city, mountains and harbour envelope this rooftop bar, restaurant and lounge. Exhibitionists should bring their swimming cossies, as they also have a small plunge pool in which to relax and splash about in. Food ranges from breakfast buffets (R195) to tapas (R50 to R90).

Harvest CAFE

(Map p70; 079 448 1618; www.facebook.com/harvestcafect; 102 Wale St, Bo-Kaap; 7.30am-4.30pm

Mon-Sat, to 1pm Sun) This contemporary-styled cafe and deli in the heart of the Bo-Kaap offers a rooftop area where you can enjoy stunning views towards Table Mountain and Lion's Head as you sip coffee or one of their freshly pressed juices. They also run early-morning yoga classes.

14 Stories COCKTAIL BAR

(Map p74; 021-492 9999; www.tsogosun.com; 23 Buitengracht St, City Bowl; 4-11pm; ; Strand) Perched on the 14th floor of the **SunSquare Cape Town City Bowl hotel** (Map p74; 021-492 9999; www.tsogosun.com; 23 Buitengracht St, City Bowl; r from R2130; ; Strand), this rooftop bar is one of several in the area that provides great views of Table Mountain, Signal Hill and the Foreshore while you enjoy a sundowner.

Nitro Brew CAFE

(Map p70; 078 455 7955; http://nitrobrewbev.co; 130 Bree St, City Bowl; 6.30am-4.30pm Mon-Fri, 8.30am-2pm Sat; ; Dorp, Leeuwen) This small cafe, stylish in its simplicity, serves nitro coffee – iced coffee poured from a draught tap. The nitrogen lends the appearance of a pint of Guinness and adds a smooth, velvety texture. Also on tap are various flavours of kombucha, all brewed on site. There are salads, sandwiches and a couple of heartier meals on the menu.

Localli CAFE

(Map p70; 021-422 2647; 136 St George's Mall, City Bowl; 7am-6pm Mon-Fri; Groote Kerk) The speciality at this diminutive pavement cafe is mille-crêpe cakes (R45), made from 20 wafer-thin pancakes held together with flavoured pastry cream. Try the rooibos masala version for some local flavour. Everything served is sourced in South Africa, including loose leaf tea and excellent coffee, cultivated in KwaZulu-Natal.

Gin Bar COCKTAIL BAR

(Map p70; www.theginbar.co.za; 64a Wale St, City Bowl; 5pm-2am Mon-Thu, 3pm-2am Fri & Sat; Dorp, Leeuwen) Tucked away in the courtyard of what used to be a mortuary (but set to move to the same building's upper floor), this secret little bar is the perfect place to get a taste for Cape Town's burgeoning craft gin scene. Grab one of the four expertly made house cocktails to sip on the interior patio.

Find the bar by heading through Honest Chocolate Cafe (p158).

I Love My Laundry CAFE

(Map p70; 074 992 1481; http://ilovemylaundry.co.za; 59 Buitengracht St, City Bowl; 7am-7pm; ; Church, Longmarket) Primarily this is a laundry, which is hidden behind a shopfront festooned with colourful, arty whatnots and wine, as the place triples up as a cafe-bar, gift shop and wine cellar. Come for a glass of wine or a coffee along with a plate of steamed Korean dumplings, their main food offering.

Hard Pressed Cafe CAFE

(Map p74; www.hardpressed.co.za; 4 Bree St, Foreshore; 7.30am-5.30pm Mon-Fri, 9.30am-2.30pm Sat; Lower Loop, Lower Long) At the base of the Portside Building, Cape Town's tallest building, this groovy cafe gives others a run for their money with their expertly made coffees and delicious coconut-and-date cake. They also sell (and play) old LPs.

La Parada BAR

(Map p70; 021-426 0330; http://laparada.co.za; 107 Bree St, City Bowl; noon-10pm Mon-Sat, to 9pm Sun; Church, Longmarket) Cerveza-quaffing and tapas-munching crowds spill out from this spacious and authentically Spanish-looking bar all days of the week.

They also have branches at Camps Bay and Constantia Nek.

Orchard on Long JUICE BAR

(Map p70; 021-424 3781; www.orchardonlong.co.za; 211 Long St, City Bowl; 9am-5pm Mon-Fri, 9.30am-2pm Sat; ; Dorp, Leeuwen) Eye-popping displays of fresh fruits and vegetables lure in the Long St passing parade for the super-healthy and tasty juice mixes and smoothies here. Try their Dr Ozzy's Lemonade, which has a peppery kick, or Fine Lady, which promises an improved complexion. Their wraps, sandwiches and salads are all vegetarian, too.

House of Machines BAR

(Map p70; 021-426 1400; www.thehouseofmachines.com; 84 Shortmarket St, City Bowl; 7am-1am Mon-Fri, 9am-2am Sat; Church, Mid-Long) Combining a motorbike workshop with barbers, a boutique and a live music/DJ space, this is a homage to Americana, with tasty, inventive bourbon cocktails, imported craft beers and Evil Twin Coffee from NYC.

Twankey Bar COCKTAIL BAR

(Map p70; 021-819 2000; www.tajhotels.com; Taj Hotel, cnr Adderley & Wale Sts, City Bowl; 7am-11pm Mon-Fri, 2pm-midnight Sat; Groote Kerk)

For those not familiar with the conventions of British theatre, this elegant bar is named after pantomime dame Widow Twankey – which also happens to be the nickname for the shepherdess statue on the building's corner facade. The cocktails are good, and they serve fresh oysters and other tasty bar snacks.

Tjing Tjing BAR
(Map p70; 021-422 4920; www.tjingtjing.co.za; 165 Longmarket St, City Bowl; 4pm-2am Tue-Fri, 6.30pm-2am Sat; ; Church, Longmarket) This slick rooftop bar is a stylish hangout for cocktails and wine. The barnlike interior has exposed beams, a photo mural of Tokyo and a scarlet lacquered bar. Down one floor is the restaurant **Tjing Tjing Tori**, serving Japanese-influenced tapas with a contemporary twist (not always successful!).

Bean There COFFEE
(Map p70; 087 943 2228; www.beanthere.co.za; 58 Wale St, City Bowl; 7.30am-4pm Mon-Fri, 9am-2pm Sat; Dorp, Leeuwen) Not much other than Fair Trade coffees from across Africa and a few sweet snacks are served in this chic cafe, which has space to spread out and a relaxed vibe despite all the caffeine.

Origin COFFEE
(Map p74; 021-421 1000; http://originroasting.co.za/v3; 28 Hudson St, De Waterkant; 7am-5pm Mon-Fri, 8am-3pm Sat, 8am-2pm Sun; ; Alfred) Apart from great coffee, the traditional bagels are pretty awesome too. They train baristas here and you can book online for their courses – a three-hour home barista class is R600.

Waiting Room BAR
(Map p70; 021-422 4536; www.facebook.com/WaitingRoomCT; 273 Long St, City Bowl; cover Fri & Sat R50-70; 7pm-2am Mon-Sat; Upper Loop, Upper Long) Climb the narrow stairway beside the Royale Eatery to find this hip bar decorated in retro furniture with DJs spinning funky tunes. Climb even further and you'll eventually reach the roof deck, the perfect spot from which to admire the city's glittering night lights.

Fireman's Arms PUB
(Map p74; 021-419 1513; http://firemansarms.co.za; cnr Buitengracht & Mechau Sts, De Waterkant; 11am-2am Mon-Sat; Alfred) Here since 1906, the Fireman's is a Capetonian institution. Inside, the Rhodesian and old South African flags remain pinned up alongside a collection of firemen's helmets and old ties. Come to watch rugby on the big-screen TV, grab some seriously tasty pizza or down a lazy pint or two. Thursday is quiz night.

31 CLUB
(Map p70; 021-421 0581; http://thirtyonecpt.co.za; 31st fl, ABSA Bldg, 2 Riebeeck St, Foreshore; cover R50; 10pm-4am Fri & Sat; Adderley) Taking its name from the lofty storey it occupies, this glitzy club with white leather sofas to lounge on provides stunning views of the city should you need a breather from the dance floor.

Yours Truly CAFE
(Map p70; 021-422 3788; http://yourstrulycafe.co.za; 175 Long St, City Bowl; 6am-4pm Mon-Fri; Dorp, Leeuwen) Inspirational sayings in bold, graphic, white-on-black lettering cover the wall at this cute cafe that is the original in what is now a small chain. You don't need to hang around, as there's a street-side serving hatch – although you might as well since their sandwiches and baked goods are good.

East City, District Six, Woodstock & Observatory

★Truth COFFEE
(Map p80; 021-200 0440; www.truthcoffee.com; 36 Buitenkant St, East City; 7am-6pm Mon-Thu, 8am-midnight Fri & Sat, 8am-2pm Sun; ; Lower Buitenkant) This self-described 'steampunk roastery and coffee bar', with pressed-tin ceilings, naked hanging bulbs and mad-inventor-style metalwork, is an awe-inspiring space in which to mingle with city slickers. Apart from coffee, craft beers, quality baked goods (including fresh croissants) and various sandwiches are on the menu.

★Espressolab Microroasters COFFEE
(Map p80; 021-447 0845; www.espressolabmicroroasters.com; Old Biscuit Mill, 375 Albert Rd, Woodstock; 8am-4pm Mon-Fri, to 2pm Sat; Kent) Geek out about coffee at this lab staffed with passionate roasters and baristas. Their beans, which come from single farms, estates and co-ops from around the world, are packaged with tasting notes such as those for fine wines.

Inventive coffee drinks include a vitamin C shot of espresso mixed with freshly pressed ginger, honey and lemon, and a refreshing soda made with cascara, a sugar made from coffee-bean skins.

★Brewers Co-op CRAFT BEER
(Map p80; 061 533 6699; www.facebook.com/BrewersCoopCPT; 135 Albert Rd, Woodstock; 1-10pm

Mon-Fri) Some 16 craft beer brewers get to showcase their efforts at this co-op bar. You could have a very entertaining time working your way through their various IPAs, and golden and summer ales (lager and pilsner fans note there are few of those types of beer on offer). Happy hour is 4.30pm to 6pm.

Check their Facebook page for details on meet-a-brewer events. Also in the same colourfully painted building is a Mexican restaurant and a pizza parlour.

Woodstock Gin Company DISTILLERY

(Map p80; 021-821 8208; www.woodstockgin co.co.za; 399 Albert Rd, Woodstock; 9am-6pm Mon-Fri, to 4pm Sat; Kent) Sample the small-batch premium gins of this company here. Buchu (a local type of fynbos), citrus and lavender flavours feature in the 'wine-base' gin; the 'beer-base' one has a more malty profile, and the High Tea gin offers a rooibos and honeybush after taste. They also make their own tonic as a mixer.

Touch of Madness PUB

(Map p79; 021-447 4650; http://atouchof madness.webflow.io; 12 Nuttall Rd, Observatory; mains R55-70; noon-10pm Tue-Sat, to 6pm Sun; ; Observatory) This long-running bar and restaurant has new management but still offers an eclectic art-house atmosphere and a varied menu of global favourites. There's a good range of craft beer on tap and a variety of events from DJ nights to poetry slams and the monthly LGBT Unofficial Pink Party (www.facebook.com/pg/pinkpartyza).

From the food menu, choose between spring rolls, mezze, tacos, burgers and bunny chow (bread rolls filled with curry – a Durban favourite).

Hope on Hopkins DISTILLERY

(Map p80; 021-447 1950; www.hopeon hopkins.co.za; 7 Hopkins St, Salt River; noon-5pm Sat; Upper Salt River) As the boutique gin wave washes over South Africa, Hope on Hopkins remains one of the country's most progressive micro-distilleries. Occupying a disused warehouse in a yet-to-be-gentrified part of town, it's a real locals' haunt. The convivial tasting space overlooks the distillery and offers a relaxed way to sample the gins – ask about the latest special releases.

As well as the Saturday tasting sessions, they're open for an in-depth tour and tasting on the first Wednesday of the month. Bookings are essential for all visits.

Saint James COFFEE

(Map p79; 079 761 8627; www.facebook.com/SaintJamesCafeOBZ; 43 Station Rd, Observatory; 7.30am-5pm Mon-Fri, 8am-3.30pm Sat & Sun; ; Observatory) A strong contender for the hippest cafe in Obs, Saint James serves its own blend of java in all the various permutations in a cool design space that's dripping with foliage and also acts as a gallery for local photographers.

Woodstock Brewery BREWERY

(Map p80; 021-447 0953; www.woodstock brewery.co.za; 252 Albert Rd, Woodstock; taproom noon-7pm Tue-Thu, to 8pm Fri, 10am-3pm Sat; restaurant 10am-10pm Mon-Sat; Kent) In the ground-floor taproom you can do a tasting (R30) of the eight seasonal beers produced here. If you'd prefer to pair the beers with food, there's a large restaurant upstairs serving the usual suspects of burgers, steaks and the like. It's all very slick and professional.

Hidden Leaf BAR

(Map p80; 021-447 4868; www.hiddenleaf.co.za; 77 Roodebloem Rd, Woodstock; 11.30am-11pm Tue-Sat; Balfour) It's hard to beat the views of Table Mountain and Devil's Peak from the wrap-around plant-potted balcony of this appealing and very Woodstock restaurant and bar. They do some interesting cocktails and have craft beer and wine as well as a tasty, low-alcohol homemade pineapple beer.

The chef and waiters will also run through the blackboard menu with you; we found some items a bit overly ambitious with muddled flavours, though.

Drawing Room Cafe CAFE

(Map p114; 082 672 0515; http://thedrawing roomcafe.co.za; 87 Station Rd, Observatory; 8am-4pm Mon-Fri, 9am-3pm Sat; ; Observatory) As well as being a rather cool cafe serving Deluxe roasted coffee and various snacks (including vegan all-day breakfast dishes), this space serves as a gallery and a place for artists to meet. Check their Facebook page for details of evening events such as jazz and folk music sessions.

They're one of the businesses that are part of Art Thursday (p172).

Taproom MICROBREWERY

(Map p80; 021-200 5818; www.devilspeak brewing.co.za; 95 Durham Ave, Salt River; mains R50-90; 11am-10pm Mon-Sat, noon-5pm Sun; Upper Salt River) Devil's Peak Brewing Company make some of South Africa's best craft beers. Their taproom and restaurant provide a panoramic view up to Devil's Peak itself. The food is hearty fare (think burgers and fried chicken), designed to balance their stellar selection of on-tap beers. There are also barrel-aged brews and one-off experiments available on tap.

Ukhamba Beerworx MICROBREWERY

(Map p80; ☎072 757 6427; www.ukhambabeerworx.co.za; The Palms, 145 Sir Lowry Rd, Woodstock; ⏰4pm-midnight Fri, 10am-7pm Sat, 11am-9pm Sun; 🚌District Six) At one of Woodstock's many new boutique breweries, Lethu Tshabangu is the brewer creating ales with witty names such as the IPA State Capture and the black IPA Pursuit of Hoppiness. Also sample his sorghum saison, Utgwala.

Flat Mountain COFFEE

(Map p80; ☎074 115 8441; www.flatmountainroasters.co.za; 101 Sir Lowry Rd, Woodstock; ⏰6am-3pm Mon-Fri, 9am-1pm Sat; 🚌District Six) These artisan coffee guys specialise in blends, including an organic one and a full-flavour decaf. It's handy if you're browsing the galleries in the area and need a caffeine kick.

Haas CAFE

(Map p80; ☎021-461 1812; http://haascollective.com; 19 Buitenkant St, East City; ⏰7am-5pm Mon-Fri, 8am-3pm Sat & Sun; 📶; 🚌Lower Buitenkant) Come more for the arty design boutique – where you can sip artisan coffee, lounge, and work on your laptop – than for the food, which is OK, but not outstanding.

Field Office CAFE

(Map p80; ☎021-447 2771; www.fieldoffice.co.za; Woodstock Exchange, 66 Albert St, Woodstock; ⏰7.30am-4.30pm Mon-Fri, 9am-2pm Sat; 🚆Woodstock) Take a moment to gather your thoughts and enjoy a well-made coffee at this cool cafe and showroom for furniture- and lighting-designers Pedersen & Lennard (www.pedersenlennard.co.za).

Rosetta Roastery CAFE

(Map p80; ☎021-447 4099; www.rosettaroastery.com; Woodstock Exchange, 66 Albert Rd, Woodstock; ⏰8am-4pm Mon-Fri, 9am-1pm Sat; 🚆Woodstock) Tucked away in the courtyard of the Woodstock Exchange, these guys have a singularly appreciative hipster audience on tap to enjoy their single-origin and estate coffees from around the world, each roasted differently to bring out the best flavours. No wonder they've been named one of the 25 coffee shops to visit before you die.

SurfaRosa BAR

(Map p80; ☎076 070 4474; https://thefirmct.co.za/surfarosa; 61 Harrington St, East City; ⏰3pm-2am Tue-Sat; 🚌Lower Buitenkant) 'Too drunk to punk' is the apt motto for this styled-to-the-max surfers' dive bar where the music is loud and the vibe edgy.

Downstairs in the same building you'll also find the upmarket, plush cocktail bar and live jazz venue Harringtons (p170) and the dance club **District**.

Tribe Woodstock CAFE

(Map p80; ☎021-448 3362; www.tribecoffee.co.za; Woodstock Foundry, 160 Albert Rd, Woodstock; ⏰7am-4pm Mon-Sat, 9am-2pm Sun; 🚆Woodstock) Woodstock's creative hub developments wouldn't be complete without an on-site artisan coffee roaster and cafe, and the Woodstock Foundary is no exception. Here Tribe does the duties with a pleasant cafe fronting onto a quiet courtyard.

Stardust BAR

(Map p80; ☎021-462 7777; www.stardustcapetown.com; 118 Sir Lowry Rd, Woodstock; ⏰5pm-2am Tue-Sat; 🚌District Six) This cheesy but hugely popular 'theatrical diner' gets packed with groups who come to enjoy their tagines (R160-180) and other dishes while listening to their waiters – all professional singers – hop up on stage periodically to belt out tunes. There's a spacious bar so you don't need to eat if you just want to watch the show, which starts around 8pm.

Gardens & Surrounds

★Mount Nelson Lounge LOUNGE

(Map p88; ☎021-483 1948; www.belmond.com; Belmond Mount Nelson Hotel, 76 Orange St, Gardens; afternoon tea R365; ⏰1pm or 3.30pm; 📶; 🚌Government Ave) Afternoon tea in the lounge or (in good weather) the gardens of the 'Nellie' is pure pleasure. There are two sessions daily, where a piano player provides the background music for a classy selection of cakes, pastries and savouries washed down with the hotel's signature blend of tea, flavoured with rose petals from the garden.

★Chalk & Cork WINE BAR

(Map p84; ☎021-422 5822; www.chalkandcork.co.za; 51 Kloof St, Gardens; tapas R25-90, pizza R95-110; ⏰11am-10.30pm Mon-Sat, to 6pm Sun; 🚌Lower Kloof) This wine bar and restaurant has a pleasant courtyard fronting Kloof St. The menu runs the gamut from breakfast dishes to tapas and sharing platters, but you're welcome to drop in just for the wines, plenty of which are served by the glass and sourced from some of the region's best estates.

★ Yours Truly Cafe & Bar BAR

(Map p84; ☎021-426 2587; http://yourstruly cafe.co.za; 73 Kloof St, Gardens; ⌚6am-11pm; 🚌Ludwig's Garden) This place is hopping from early morning to late at night. Travellers mingle with hipster locals, who come for the excellent coffee, craft beer, gourmet sandwiches, thin-crust pizzas and the occasional DJ event.

Publik WINE BAR

(Map p70; www.publik.co.za; 11D Kloof Nek Rd, Gardens; ⌚4-11pm Mon-Fri, 12-6pm Sat; 🚌Church, Longmarket) This relaxed, unpretentious bar does a brilliant job at digging out hidden gems of the Cape's wine and gin scenes. Taste drops from sustainably farmed vineyards, interesting and unusual varietals, and rare vintages.

Tiger's Milk BAR

(Map p84; ☎021-286 2209; http://tigers milk.co.za/kloof-street; 55 Kloof St, Gardens; ⌚noon-midnight; 🚌Lower Kloof) With entrances on both Kloof St and Rheede St, and a large courtyard in between, this branch of the Tiger's Milk chain is proving to be one of its most popular. They have a wall mural based on Picasso's *Guernica* – a tongue-in-cheek metaphor for the alcoholic carnage that can happen here as the night wears on.

The Sorrows BAR

(Map p84; ☎021-422 3655; https://the sorrows.co.za; 16 Kloof Nek Rd, Tamboerskloof; ⌚7am-4pm Mon, to 11pm Tue-Sat, to 11am Sun) On one side of this cafe-bar they serve 'libations' – hipster-speak for anything from an espresso to a glass of wine – and on the other 'victuals': grub such as Karoo lamb chops and salted-peanut-butter cheesecake. It's an interesting, old-fashioned space and a good addition to the Kloof Nek drinking/dining scene.

Cause Effect COCKTAIL BAR

(Map p84; ☎071 096 2995; www.facebook.com/CauseEffectBar/; 2a Park Rd, Gardens; ⌚4pm-2am Tue-Sat; 🚌Lower Kloof) A stylish new addition to Cape Town's growing cocktail-bar scene, Cause Effect trains its alcoholic focus on brandy – some 70 different types, all South African. The tipple turns up in classics, such as a sazarac and a sidecar with a twist, as well as other inventive concoctions, some including their homemade vermouth.

Deluxe Coffeeworks COFFEE

(Map p84; ☎072 569 9579; www.deluxecoffee works.co.za; 171a Buitenkant St, Gardens; ⌚7am-5pm Mon-Fri, 9am-2pm Sat & Sun; 🚌Gardens) This is both the roasting operation for Deluxe and a sleek, simple cafe where you can sample their highly-regarded coffee – as served by suitably tattooed and bearded baristas. They also have a small outlet on Church St in the City Bowl.

Power & the Glory/Black Ram BAR

(Map p84; ☎021-422 2108; www.facebook.com/The-Power-and-the-Glory-129092450488495; 13b Kloof Nek Rd, Tamboerskloof; ⌚8am-midnight Mon-Sat; 🚌Ludwig's Garden) The coffee and food (pretzel hot dogs, crusty pies and other artisan munchies) are good, but it's the smoky, cosy bar that packs the trendsters in, particularly on Thursday to Saturday nights.

Perseverance Tavern PUB

(Map p84; ☎021-461 2440; http://perseverance tavern.co.za; 83 Buitenkant St, Gardens; ⌚noon-10pm; 🚌Roeland) This convivial, heritage-listed pub, which is affectionately known as 'Persies' and has been around since 1808, was once Cecil Rhodes' local. There are beers on tap and the pub grub is decent.

Van Hunks BAR

(Map p84; ☎021-422 5422; http://vanhunks.co.za; cnr Kloof & Upper Union St, Gardens; ⌚10am-1am Mon-Fri, from 11.30am Sat & Sun; 🚌Belle Ombre) Ponder the legend of Van Hunks, who challenged the devil to a smoking match atop the peak that can be seen from this bar and restaurant's deck. It's a good spot to watch the comings and goings along Kloof St.

The Vic BAR

(Map p84; ☎072 192 2518; www.facebook.com/theviconkloof; 84 Kloof St, Gardens; ⌚noon-1am Mon-Sat, to 9pm Sun; 🚌Welgemeend) There's craft beer on tap, wood-fired pizzas and live music every Wednesday from around 8pm and sometimes on the weekends (check their Facebook page) at this spacious bar in an old house on Kloof St. They also have some outside seats.

Asoka BAR

(Map p84; ☎021-422 0909; www.asoka.za.com; 68 Kloof St, Gardens; 🚌Ludwig's Garden) Pronounced 'ashoka', a Zen-mellow vibe pervades this groovy Asian restaurant-bar with a tree growing in the middle of it. Live jazz is a regular feature of Tuesday nights (performances from 8pm), while on other nights DJs play suitably chilled sounds.

Green Point & Waterfront

★Bascule BAR

(Map p86; ☎021-410 7082; www.basculebar.com; Cape Grace Hotel, West Quay Rd, V&A Waterfront; ⏲9am-1am; 🚌Nobel Sq) Over 480 varieties of whisky are served at the Grace's sophisticated, nautical-themed bar, with a few slugs of the 50-year-old Glenfiddich still available (at just R18,000 a tot). Outdoor tables facing the marina are a superb spot for drinks and tasty tapas.

Make a booking for a whisky tasting (from R395), during which you can sample various drams paired with food.

★Shift COFFEE

(Map p86; ☎021-433 2450; 47 Main Rd, Green Point; ⏲6.30am-6pm Mon-Sat, 7am-3pm Sun; 📶; 🚌Upper Portswood) Sporting an industrial-chic look with a cosy library corner inside and sheltered, spacious front courtyard outside, this is one of the area's most inviting cafes. Owner Luigi Vigliotti works hard to please customers, and he's come up with a few intriguing signature brews, including Hashtag, which blends espresso with vanilla gelato and Oreo cookies.

Life Grand Cafe CAFE

(Map p86; ☎021-205 1902; www.life.za.com/home/lifegrandcafe; Old Pierhead, V&A Waterfront; ⏲7.30am-11pm; 🚌Nobel Square) The food is so-so, but the drinks are fine at this classy all-day cafe serving everything from breakfast coffee and croissants to nightcaps. It's a lovely spot to rest your feet and have some refreshments with a grandstand view onto the buzz of the Waterfront.

Tobago's Bar & Terrace COCKTAIL BAR

(Map p86; ☎021-441 3414; www.radissonblu.com/en/hotel-capetown/bars; Radisson Blu Hotel Waterfront, Beach Rd, Granger Bay; ⏲6.30am-10.30pm; 🚌Granger Bay) Walk through the hotel to the spacious deck bar and restaurant with a prime Table Bay position. It's a great place to enjoy a sunset cocktail; you can take a stroll along the breakwater afterwards.

Sotano BAR

(Map p86; ☎021-433 1757; www.sotano.co.za; 121 Beach Rd, Mouille Point; ⏲7am-11pm; 🚌Three Anchor Bay) With a relaxed vibe and a spacious deck open to Mouille Point Promenade, this is an ideal spot for sundowners or a coffee and light bite with an ocean view. There's live music on Friday from 7pm to 9pm and Sunday from 4pm to 7pm.

Shimmy Beach Club CLUB

(☎021-200 7778; www.shimmybeachclub.com; 12 South Arm Rd, V&A Waterfront; cover charge for events R250; ⏲11am-4am Mon-Sat, until 2am Sun; 🚌Waterfront Silo) Drive past the smelly fish-processing factories to discover this glitzy mega-club and restaurant, arranged around a small, fake beach with a glass-sided pool. Pool parties with scantily clad dancers shimmying to grooves by top DJs, including the electro-jazz group Goldfish, who has a summer residency here (bookings advised).

Vista Bar & Lounge COCKTAIL BAR

(Map p86; ☎021-421 5888; www.oneandonlyresorts.com; One&Only Cape Town, Dock Rd, V&A Waterfront; ⏲6.30am-3am; 🚌Aquarium) The bar at the luxury hotel One&Only offers plush surrounds and a perfectly framed view of Table Mountain. Alcohol is served from 11am and it's a classy spot for afternoon tea (R295; from 2.30pm to 5.30pm) or a creative cocktail, including classics with a local twist.

Grand Africa Café & Beach BAR

(Map p86; ☎021-425 0551; www.grandafrica.com; Haul Rd, V&A Waterfront; ⏲noon-11pm; 🚌Somerset Hospital) Sand was dumped here to created the private beach for this oh-so-chic bar and restaurant operating out of a former warehouse. Locals love to gather on weekends here to enjoy the laid-back vibe, rather than the so-so food. DJs kick in later at night.

Belthazar WINE BAR

(Map p86; ☎021-421 3753; www.belthazar.co.za; Shop 153, Victoria Wharf, V&A Waterfront; ⏲noon-11pm; 🚌Breakwater) Claiming to be the world's largest wine bar, Belthazar offers 600 different South African wines, around 250 of which you can get by the glass. The attached restaurant specialises in top-class Karan beef, and it does plenty of seafood dishes, too.

Mitchell's Scottish Ale House PUB

(Map p86; ☎021-418 5074; www.mitchells-ale-house.com; cnr East Pier & Dock Rd, V&A Waterfront; ⏲10am-2am; 🚌Nobel Square) Check all airs and graces at the door of South Africa's oldest microbrewery (established in 1983 in Knysna), which serves a variety of freshly brewed ales and good-value meals. The 7% proof Old Wobbly packs an alcoholic punch.

Sea Point to Hout Bay

★ Leopard Bar COCKTAIL BAR

(021-437 9000; www.12apostleshotel.com; Twelve Apostles Hotel & Spa, Victoria Rd, Oudekraal; 7am-2am; ; Oudekraal) With a dress-circle view over the Atlantic, the Twelve Apostles Hotel's (p135) bar is an ideal spot to escape the hoi polloi of nearby Camps Bay for a classy cocktail or – better yet – a deliciously decadent afternoon tea (R295; served from 10am to 4pm).

★ Dunes BAR

(Map p92; 021-790 1876; www.dunesrestaurant.co.za; 1 Beach Rd, Hout Bay; 9am-11pm; ; Hout Bay) You can hardly get closer to the beach than this – in fact, the front courtyard *is* the beach. Up on the terrace or from inside the restaurant-bar, you'll get a great view of Hout Bay, along with some decent sushi, nibbles and pub grub ranging from pizza to seafood. There's also a safe play area for kids.

★ Bungalow BAR

(Map p94; 021-438 2018; www.thebungalow.co.za; Glen Country Club, 3 Victoria Rd, Clifton; noon-2am; Maiden's Cove) This Euro-chic restaurant and lounge bar is a great place for a long lunch, languorous-afternoon craft beers or sunset mojitos and martinis, overlooked by the Twelve Apostles range. Crash on a daybed under a billowing white awning, or dangle your feet in the tiny bar-side splash pool. DJs create a more clubby atmosphere by night. Bookings are advised.

La Belle CAFE

(Map p94; 021-437 1278; www.labellecampsbay.co.za; 201 The Promenade, Camps Bay; 8am-11pm; Whale Rock) This bistro and bakery is one of the loveliest belles on Camps Bay's seafront strip, and a whole lot more relaxed and less pretentious than some of its neighbours. Choose between coffees, speciality teas, smoothies, shakes and cocktails – ranging from gin smash to whisky sours – plus some extremely tempting baked goods, cakes and other light eats.

Ta Da! CAFE

(Map p92; 021-790 8132; its.ta.da.4@gmail.com; 37 Victoria Rd, Hout Bay; 8am-5pm; ; Lower Victoria) This coffee bar and crêperie has shaded outdoor seating and a pleasant interior, which are also the venues for regular live music and movie nights, respectively. A popular local hang-out for its coffee, breakfasts, burgers and sweet or savoury pancakes.

Dizzy's Restaurant & Pub PUB

(Map p94; 021-438 2686; www.dizzys.co.za; 41 The Drive, Camps Bay; noon-2am; Whale Rock) There's regular entertainment at this convivial British-style watering hole with a good selection of craft beers and pub grub. Come for karaoke on Tuesday, live music on Friday and Saturday (sometimes attracting a cover charge of around R40), and a beer-pong battle on Sunday (also R40).

Set back from the seafront, it's a laid-back place for coffee or a beer and to hang out with locals.

Mynt Cafe BAR

(Map p94; 31 Victoria Rd, Camps Bay; 8am-11pm; Camps Bay) At the northern end of the Camps Bay dining strip, this place offers coffee, cocktails and light meals (R100) with a beach view. It's more casual and relaxed than the strip's self-consciously fashionable cafes with their booming DJ music.

Southern Suburbs

★ Banana Jam CRAFT BEER

(Map p100; 021-674 0186; www.bananajamcafe.co.za; 157 2nd Ave, Harfield Village, Kenilworth; 11am-11pm Tue-Sat, to 10pm Sun; ; Kenilworth) Real beer lovers rejoice – this convivial Caribbean restaurant and bar is like manna from heaven, with over 30 beers on draught (including Banana Jam's own brews) and bottled ales from all the top local microbrewers, including Jack Black, Devil's Peak and CBC. Cocktail happy hour is 5pm to 6pm daily.

★ Martini Bar COCKTAIL BAR

(Map p100; 021-794 2137; www.thecellars-hohenorthotel.com; 93 Brommerslvei Rd, Constantia; 11am-11.30pm;) The magnificent pink, lemon, burgundy and teal lounge at the Cellars-Hohenort Hotel specialises in martinis such as the sweet and spicy white-chocolate-and-chilli flavour, with many other cocktails on offer, as well as single-origin coffees and Constantia wines. You can take high tea here (R225 per person) or retire to another part of the grounds wandered by peacocks.

★ Forester's Arms PUB

(Map p97; 021-689 5949; www.forries.co.za; 52 Newlands Ave, Newlands; 11am-11pm Mon-Sat, 9am-10pm Sun; ; Newlands) 'Forries' has been around for well over 150 years. The English-style pub offers a convivial atmosphere in which to enjoy a dozen draught beers (mostly large-brewery, with a few craft), good pub meals (including wood-fired pizzas), and a very pleasant beer garden with a play area for the kids.

Salt Yard BAR

(Map p114; 021-685 0307; www.facebook.com/pg/thesaltyardSA; 74 Klipfontein Rd, Mowbray; 9am-11pm Mon-Thu, to 1am Fri-Sun; ; Mowbray) With surfboards and recycled decor on the walls, this bar in the university area has a beach-house aesthetic despite being firmly inland of Table Mountain. There's cocktails, steaks, seafood, periodic live music and a mixed clientele of students and locals.

Jack Black's Brewery BREWERY

(Map p100; 021-286 1220; www.jackblackbeer.com; 10 Brigid Rd, Diep River; 10am-10pm Wed-Fri, to 4pm Sat; ; Diep River) One of the pioneers of South Africa's craft-beer culture, Jack Black's is a cavernous space with beer-hall-style seating. The brewery takes pride of place and tours can be arranged. Otherwise, grab a tasting tray of its pilsner, pale ale, IPA and flagship lager to sip at leisure. The menu features charcuterie boards, tempting salads and excellent fries.

There are regular special events, including Food Truck Fridays, open mike nights and a pub quiz.

Twigs with Beans CAFE

(Map p100; 021-674 1193; www.twigswithbeans.co.za; 48 2nd Ave, Harfield Village; 7am-5pm Mon-Fri, 8am-2.30pm Sat & Sun; ; Kenilworth) This neighbourhood cafe nestled in the heart of historic Harfield Village attracts the area's young professionals, freelancers, joggers, dog walkers and so on. With local art on the walls and a sunny front stoep overlooking 2nd Ave, it serves Truth coffee, freshly squeezed juices, muffins, breakfasts and light lunches (R50 to R70). Good chocolate brownies, too.

LOCAL KNOWLEDGE

PARTIES & EVENTS

➡ Look out for the **Secret Sunrise beach parties** (www.facebook.com/secretsunrisecapetown) and the **Silent Disco sunset beach parties** (www.facebook.com/silenteventssa), held at various spots around the Cape including St James' Beach and Clifton 3rd Beach.

➡ Attend a book launch or author talk at the **Book Lounge** (p176).

➡ Catch local musicians or dancers close up at **Studio 7 Sessions** (p171), **Youngblood Africa** (p69) or **Alma Café** (p171).

Zhivago CLUB

(Map p97; 083 784 1644; www.zhivago.co.za; 103 Main Rd, Claremont; 9pm-4am Thu & Sat; Claremont) If you're looking for a late-night party and dance spot in the Southern Suburbs, with a young, up-for-it crowd, Zhivago (the old Tiger Tiger) is the place to head to. Bop to upbeat '90s and noughties pop and house and learn about South Africans' love of Jägermeister shooters. Admission varies and is usually under R100.

No women under 18 or men under 19. Dress code is smart casual; no shorts, tracksuits, flip flops, vests, hoodies or caps.

Barristers PUB

(Map p97; 021-671 7907; www.barristersgrill.co.za; cnr Kildare Rd & Main St, Newlands; 11am-11pm; ; Newlands) A locals' favourite watering hole, with a series of cosy rooms hung with an eye-catching assortment of items in ye-olde-country-pub style. It's also an excellent spot for warming pub grub on a chilly night. There are R65 pub lunches daily and live music from time to time.

Caffé Verdi BAR

(Map p100; 021-762 0849; www.caffe-verdi.co.za; 21 Wolfe St, Wynberg Village; 9am-midnight Mon-Sat, 11am-7pm Sun; Wynberg) This local watering hole, set in a century-old house with a pretty courtyard, is a pleasant place for a drink after exploring Chelsea Village (as Wynberg Village is nicknamed). There are big screens for watching sports matches.

Simon's Town & Southern Peninsula

★**Tiger's Milk** BAR

(Map p104; 021-788 1860; www.tigersmilk.co.za; cnr Beach & Sidmouth Rds, Muizenberg; 11am-2am; ; Muizenberg) There's a panoramic view of Muizenberg Beach through the floor-to-ceiling window of this hangar-like bar and restaurant. It's open all day for food (good pizza and steaks; mains R110), but is more of a sundowner venue and nightspot with its long bar, stools and exposed-brick walls hung with quirky decor including a motorbike.

Striped Horse Bar & Grill BAR
(Map p104; ☎021-788 2979; www.facebook.com/TheStripedHorse; 12-14 York Rd, Muizenberg; ⏰noon-1am Mon-Sat, to 9pm Sun; 🚆Muizenberg) With its mishmash of eclectic decor, this local hang-out does Paarl-brewed Striped Horse beers on draught and burgers on boards. Regular live music adds to the fun.

Cape to Cuba BAR
(Map p104; ☎021-788 1566; www.capetocuba.com; 165 Main Rd, Kalk Bay; ⏰9am-midnight; 🚆Kalk Bay) Every city has a little corner of Havana, and this is one of the bars touting cocktails and revolution in the Cape Town area. This comrade has been around forever: the latest incarnation features a faux beach bar with sandy floors and swing seats, while the restaurant is packed with antiques and Latino trimmings. Popular on Friday and Saturday nights.

There's live music every summer Sunday (4pm to 7pm; R20).

Brass Bell BAR
(Map p104; ☎021-788 5455; www.brassbell.co.za; Kalk Bay Station, Main Rd, Kalk Bay; ⏰11.30am-10pm; 🚆Kalk Bay) On a sunny day there are few better places to drink and eat (mains R100) by the sea than this local institution, which is lapped by the waves of False Bay. You can also take a dip in the adjacent tidal pools before or after. Follow the tunnel beneath the train tracks to get here.

Beach Road Bar BAR
(☎021-789 1783; cnr Beach Rd & Pine St, Noordhoek; ⏰noon-11pm Tue-Sun, from 4.30pm Mon) If you're down this way – say, after a drive along Chapman's Peak Dr (p119) – the bar above the Red Herring restaurant is a pleasant place for a craft beer and a pizza. The sunset deck has excellent beach views, there's occasional live music and the bar serves beers made on-site by **Aegir Project Brewery** (www.aegirprojectbrewery.com).

Cape Flats & Northern Suburbs

★Blue Peter BAR
(☎021-554 1956; www.bluepeter.co.za; Popham St, Bloubergstrand; ⏰noon-11pm; 🚌De Mist) At this perennial favourite, the deal is to grab a beer (13 types on draught), order a pizza (R100) and settle in at a wooden table outside to enjoy the classic views of Table Mountain and Robben Island. There's live music on Friday, Saturday and Sunday afternoons.

It's also a hotel.

Devil's Peak Brewing Company BREWERY
(Map p114; ☎021-001 4290; www.devilspeakbrewing.co.za; 166 Gunners Circle, Epping 1; ⏰8am-7pm Mon-Wed, to 2am Thu & Fri; 📶) One of South Africa's most innovative breweries has moved to colossal premises outside the city. It's a somewhat unlikely location, on a large industrial estate, but once you're inside the diner-inspired taproom, you quickly forget the surrounds. There are experimental brews on draught alongside the core range, and a small menu featuring truffle mac 'n' cheese and a legendary cheeseburger.

Free guided tours (11.30am and 4pm Monday to Friday) take you through the brewery and offer a peek into Afrofunk – the barrel-ageing room, where brewers are experimenting with sour styles and wooded ales.

Siki's Kofee Kafe COFFEE
(☎082 369 8229; 7 Ntaba St, Village 1 South, Khayelitsha; ⏰7am-5pm Mon-Fri, 8.30am-3pm Sat; 📶; 🚌Khayelitsha) Siki Dibela, an ex-employee of the Vida e Caffè chain, is the business brains and barista behind the township's coolest cafe. He sells his own blend of coffee, muffins and cookies out of a converted garage.

Plans are in the works for a lounge, internet cafe and adjacent restaurant with Siki's mum, an experienced cook, in the kitchen.

Rands Cape Town CLUB
(☎071 742 4322; www.facebook.com/RandsCPT; Makabeni Rd, Village 1 North, Khayelitsha; ⏰10am-9pm Mon-Fri, to midnight Sat, to 11pm Sun) Although it's a barbecued-meat restaurant in true township style (line up to order a platter of chicken wings, sausages or steak with various sides), Rands is really about cracking open a beer, sinking a glass of wine and grooving down with locals as the DJs do their thing. It can be quite a scene here on a sunny day.

Devil's Peak De Oude CRAFT BEER
(www.devilspeakbrewing.co.za/de-oude; 1 Pandoer St, Bellville; ⏰8am-11pm Tue-Sat, to 6pm Sun; 🚆Oosterzee) The Devil's Peak brewery has split De Oude Welgemoed, a 350-year-old Cape Dutch property, into three sections: the **Alpha Beer Hall**, the **Manor** and the **Bistro**. Alpha is the best bet for a casual beer under the oak tree and some quality pub grub, with 10 craft beers on draught and a menu of boards and burgers (mains R100).

The Manor places more emphasis on eating, with a longer menu of similar cuisine and six craft beers on draught, while the Bistro is a pizzeria.

Kaffa Hoist CAFE

(Map p114; ☎071 120 6345; www.facebook.com/kaffahoist; Guga S'thebe Arts & Cultural Centre, cnr King Langalibalele Ave & Church St, Langa; ⏲7am-7pm) Cheery owner Chris Bangira serves homemade ginger beer, herbal teas and a range of caffeinated options at this open-air cafe tucked behind the cultural centre (p113). Light meals are also served and a roastery is on the cards. Opening hours are slightly shorter from June to November.

Kefu's BAR

(☎082 353 9742; www.facebook.com/pg/kefusjp; 39-41 Mthawelanga St, Ilitha Park, Khayelitsha; ⏲10am-midnight Mon-Thu, to 2am Fri & Sat; 🚆Khayelitsha) Ms Kefuoe Sedia has come a long way since opening a six-seater pub in her front lounge in 1990. This spiffy, two-level, 140-seat place, with mellow jazz playing in the background, also serves food. Check the Facebook page for upcoming nights (sometimes with a cover charge of around R50), and call ahead from Monday to Thursday to check it's open.

Department of Coffee CAFE

(☎078 086 0093; www.facebook.com/Department-of-Coffee-455306021156615; 158 Ntlazani St, Khayelitsha; ⏲6am-6pm Mon-Fri, 8am-3pm Sat; 🚆Khayelitsha) Artisan coffee comes to Khayelitsha – even though it's served from a kiosk with uninviting barred windows, and the hours can be erratic. There are some outdoor tables and chairs nearby for you to sit and sip your coffee and nibble on the cafe's muffins.

Galaxy CLUB

(☎021-637 9027, 082 650 2756; College Rd, Rylands Estate; ⏲9pm-4am Fri & Sat) This legendary 40-year-old Cape Flats dance venue is where you can get down to R&B, hip hop and live bands with a black and coloured crowd. Cover charges range up to R100, and are generally cheaper before 11pm, while women often get in for free.

The plush live-music venue **West End** is in the same building.

☆ Entertainment

Rappers and comedians performing in a mix of Afrikaans and English; a cappella township choirs and buskers at the Waterfront; theatre on the streets and in old churches; intimate performances in suburban living rooms – the Mother City dazzles with a diverse and creative range of entertainment, with live music a particular highlight.

☆ City Bowl, Foreshore, Bo-Kaap & De Waterkant

★ **Alexander Bar & Café** THEATRE

(Map p70; ☎021-300 1088; www.alexanderbar.co.za; 76 Strand St, City Bowl; ⏲bar 11am-1am Mon-Sat; 🚌Strand) Playwright Nicholas Spagnoletti and software engineer Edward van Kuik are the driving duo behind this fun, eccentric space in a gorgeous heritage building. Downstairs is a very popular LGBT-friendly bar while upstairs is a studio theatre with a packed programme of plays, musical performances and other speaking events.

In the bar, use antique telephones on the tables to chat with fellow patrons and to place your order. Their regular Wednesday night quizzes are a hoot and a great way to meet locals.

★ **Café Roux** LIVE MUSIC

(Map p70; ☎061 339 4438; www.caferouxsessions.co.za; 74 Shortmarket St, City Bowl; tickets R100-150; ⏲6pm-midnight; 🚌Church, Longmarket) The City Bowl has been crying out for a quality live-music venue for a while and it's taken Café Roux (who already run a successful operation in Noordhoek) to provide it. Most nights a different singer or band plays here, and with tiered seating (and all seats bookable online) you're guaranteed to get a good view.

Come early if you also wish to eat here before the start of the show – usually around 8.30pm.

Cape Philharmonic Orchestra CLASSICAL MUSIC

(CPO; Map p70; ☎021-410 9809; www.cpo.org.za; Old City Hall, Darling St, City Bowl; tickets R160-230; 🚌Darling) The grand auditorium to the rear of the old City Hall has very good acoustics that are taken advantage of by this orchestra and accompanying local choirs. Entrance is on Corporation St. Concerts happen throughout the year: check online for the schedule.

Piano Bar LIVE MUSIC

(Map p74; http://thepianobar.co.za; 47 Napier St, De Waterkant; cover Fri & Sat R50; ⏲12.30pm-midnight Mon-Sat, to 11pm Sun; 🚌Alfred) Proving a hit with one-and-all in the heart of De Waterkant is this slick music revue bar and restaurant with a nightly line-up of different performers who

LOCAL KNOWLEDGE

SPORTS IN CAPE TOWN

Capetonians are avid sports fans – attending a soccer, rugby or cricket game here is highly recommended.

Soccer

The biggest game on the Cape is soccer (football, known locally as *diski*). Cape Town has two teams in the national Premier Soccer League (www.psl.co.za): Cape Town City (http://capetowncityfc.co.za) and Ajax Cape Town (www.ajaxct.com). If either of these teams is playing the nation's top soccer teams, the Kaizer Chiefs and the Orlando Pirates (both based in Jo'burg), you'll have to fight for tickets, which start at R60. The season runs from August to May, with matches played at either Cape Town Stadium (p83) or **Athlone Stadium** (021-637 6607; Cross Blvd, Athlone; Athlone).

Cricket

Capetonians have a soft spot for cricket, and **Newlands Cricket Ground** (Map p97; 021-657 2003; www.newlandscricket.com; 146 Campground Rd, Newlands; Newlands) is where all top national and international games are played. The game was the first of the 'whites-only' sports to wholeheartedly adopt a nonracial attitude, and development programs in the townships have paid dividends: hailing from Langa is Thami Tsolekile, who played three Test matches for South Africa as wicket-keeper; unfortunately he and three other teammates were handed bans in 2016 by Cricket South Africa for breaching the board's Anti-Corruption Code. The local team is the Cape Cobras (www.wpca.org.za).

Rugby

Rugby (union, not league) is the traditional Afrikaner sport. Games are held at the **Newlands Rugby Stadium** (Map p97; 021-659 4600; www.wprugby.com; Boundary Rd, Newlands; Newlands), with the most popular matches being those in the Super 14 tournament – teams from South Africa, Australia and New Zealand compete from late February until the end of May.

hit the piano keys around 8pm. Expect top-class pianists, jazz singers and players.

OnPointe Dance Studios DANCE

(Map p70; 061 198 6355, 021-422 3368; www.onpointedancestudio.wordpress.com; 5th fl, 112 Loop St, City Bowl; tickets R100, classes from R150; ; Dorp, Leeuwen) Theo Ndindwa and Tanya Arshamian use dance to change the lives of kids in the townships. On the first Thursday of the month this studio, where classes are held, hosts **Art in the City with iKapa Dance**, a wonderful chance to meet up with a host of local dance companies and watch them perform in a very relaxed environment.

Crypt Jazz Restaurant JAZZ

(Map p70; 079 683 4658; www.thecryptjazz.com; 1 Wale St, City Bowl; cover R100; 7pm-midnight Tue-Sat; Groote Kerk) Occupying part of the St George's Cathedral's vaulted stone crypt, this restaurant, which serves a continent-hopping menu of dishes, is best visited for its live jazz. Concerts start at around 8pm and last most of the evening. Some very accomplished performers take to the stage here; for some concerts booking ahead is advisable.

Cape Town International Convention Centre CONCERT VENUE

(CTICC; Map p74; 021-410 5000; www.cticc.co.za; 1 Lower Long St, Foreshore; Convention Centre) Since opening in 2003, the CTICC has barely paused for breath, packing in a busy annual programme of musical performances, exhibitions, conferences and other events, such as the Cape Town International Jazz Festival (p126) and Design Indaba (p125).

Artscape THEATRE

(Map p74; 021-410 9800; www.artscape.co.za; 1-10 DF Malan St, Foreshore; Civic Centre) Consisting of three different-sized auditoriums, this behemoth is the city's main arts complex. Theatre, classical music, ballet, opera and cabaret shows – Artscape offers it all. The desolate nature of the area means it's not recommended to walk around here at night; there's plenty of secure parking.

LOCAL KNOWLEDGE

LIVE MUSIC GUIDE

Indoor Venues

Studio 7 Sessions (p171), House of Machines (p159), **Mercury Live** (www.facebook.com/MercuryLive) and both branches of Café Roux (p172) can always be relied on for cool, up-and-coming and edgy bands. If you like jazz, check out **Kloof St House** (Map p84; ☎021-423 4413; www.kloofstreethouse.co.za; 30 Kloof St, Gardens; mains R95-175; ⏰5-11pm Mon, noon-11pm Tue-Sun; 🚌Lower Kloof) for their Sunday lunch session; the same owners run Asoka (p163), which also has sessions on Tuesday night. If it's Monday, head to **HQ** (www.hqrestaurant.co.za) at Heritage Square (although it's not always a jazz band), and on Thursday you can't go wrong with **Harringtons** (www.facebook.com/harringtonsct), which plays a mix of live jazz followed by the best local funk, soul and house DJs. Also don't rule out the bigger venues such as Artscape (p169), City Hall (p72), Grandwest Casino (p172) and the Baxter Theatre (p171), as they often have larger musical productions from across various genres.

Outdoor Venues

In summer you can't miss the concerts in **Kirstenbosch National Botanical Garden** (p95). Although it's a 45-minute drive out of town, the **Paul Cluver Forest Amphitheatre** (p215) in Elgin is really beautiful – a very different environment in which to catch a gig. Also look for outdoor shows at other wine estates, which often produce their own picnic concerts across the Constantia, Stellenbosch and Durbanville areas. Durbanville's **Hillcrest** (p112) quarry is a great spot to catch some live music during summer. If you head out to Noordhoek, Kalk Bay and Scarborough, there are a host of restaurants with great outdoor sections that regularly stage some excellent local artists – well worth the trip out of town.

Artists to Watch

Look out for folk singer Paige Mac; electro-jazz combo GoodLuck; the internationally known Black Coffee, Goldfish and Jeremy Loops; Matthew Mole from Johannesburg; Majozi from Durban; the indie-pop trio Beatenberg; jazz cats Lee Thomson and Jason Reolon; if he's in town, blues king Dan Patlansky; rock rebels The Sweet Resistance; and trip-hop band Astrafunk and the Space Cats.

☆ East City, District Six, Woodstock & Observatory

Fugard Theatre THEATRE

(Map p80; ☎021-461 4554; www.thefugard.com; Caledon St, District Six; 🚌Lower Buitenkant) Named in honour of Athol Fugard, South Africa's best-known living playwright, this very impressive arts centre was created from the former Congregational Church Hall. There are two stages, the largest theatre also doubling up as a 'bioscope' – a fancy word for a digital cinema where top international dance and opera performances are screened.

Harringtons JAZZ

(Map p80; ☎021-461 2276; www.facebook.com/harringtonsct; 61b Harrington St, District Six; cover R100; ⏰5pm-2am Wed & Thu, to 4pm Fri & Sat; 🚌Lower Buitenkant) On Thursday nights you can catch live jazz sets in this plush cocktail lounge. On other nights DJs play for an up-for-it crowd of party seekers.

Obviouzly Armchair LIVE PERFORMANCE

(Map p79; ☎021-460 0458; http://obviouzlyarmchair.com; 135 Lower Main Rd, Observatory; ⏰5pm-2am Mon-Wed, noon-2am Thu-Sun; 🚆Observatory) Live acoustic rock is a firm feature of Friday nights at this pub, and there's often live music and other events such as comedy slots, open mic and cinema on other nights. The atmosphere is Obs in spades, so dress down and come to chill.

☆ Gardens & Surrounds

Labia CINEMA

(Map p84; ☎021-424 5927; www.thelabia.co.za; 68 Orange St, Gardens; tickets R50; 🚌Michaelis) A Capetonian treasure and lifeline to the independent movie fan, the four-screen Labia is named after the old Italian ambassador and local philanthropist Count Labia. Their African Screen program is one of the rare opportunities you'll have to see locally made films; check the website for session times.

☆ Green Point & Waterfront

Galileo Open Air Cinema CINEMA
(Map p86; www.thegalileo.co.za/waterfront.html; Croquet Lawn, off Portswood Rd, V&A Waterfront; tickets R100, blanket/chair hire R10/20; ⏱Nov-Apr; 🚌Nobel Square) From November to April, this open-air cinema sets up shop on Thursday nights to screen classic and crowd-pleasing movies on the croquet lawn next to the Dock House Hotel (p134). Sadly, you're not allowed to bring your own blanket or chair, but they're available to rent from the venue.

Galileo also screens movies at other venues, including Kirstenbosch and several wine estates – check online for the current program.

Market Square Amphitheatre LIVE MUSIC
(Map p86; www.waterfront.co.za/events/overview; off Dock Rd, V&A Waterfront; 🚌Nobel Square) The Waterfront's Market Square Amphitheatre is the focus for much free entertainment, including buskers and various musical and dance acts. Apart from the giant electronic screen showing videos, the Amphitheatre acts as a platform for up-and-coming artists, and there are always live shows from 5pm to 6pm on Saturdays and Sundays.

Cape Town Comedy Club COMEDY
(Map p86; ☎021-418 8880; www.capetowncomedy.com; Pump House, Dock Rd, V&A Waterfront; tickets from R60; ⏱6-10pm, shows 8.30pm; 🚌Nobel Sq) This long-running comedy club, which hosts the cream of South Africa's comedy talent, has found a permanent home at the back of the old Pump House next to Robinson Dry Dock. You don't need to understand Afrikaans slang to get the jokes of host Kurt Schoonraad and the other performers.

☆ Sea Point to Hout Bay

★**Theatre on the Bay** THEATRE
(Map p94; ☎021-438 3301; www.theatreonthebay.co.za; 1 Link St, Camps Bay; 🚌Lower Camps Bay) A great venue for an evening of lighthearted theatrical entertainment, offering everything from comic plays to classic musicals.

Should you want to eat before curtain, there's the chic **Sidedish Theatre Bistro** (http://dishfood.co.za/side-dish) on-site.

Studio 7 Sessions LIVE MUSIC
(Map p90; www.studio7sessions.com; 213 High Level Rd, Sea Point; 🚌Rhine) These bimonthly live gigs, going since 2010, are hosted in unique, unusual venues throughout the city and surrounds. They mix new, up-and-coming artists with inspiring keynote speakers from various fields to appeal to both mind and soul. Venues include the relaxed and intimate surroundings of founder Patrick Craig's Sea Point living room, as well as libraries, rooftops, gardens and beaches.

Usually no more than 40 to 350 tickets are sold (online) – check the website for details, as it's a fantastic experience for music lovers and fans of inspiring talks.

☆ Southern Suburbs

★**Baxter Theatre Centre** THEATRE
(Map p97; ☎021-685 7880; www.baxter.co.za; Main Rd, Rondebosch; tickets R100-380; 🚆Rosebank) Since the 1970s the Baxter has been the focus of Capetonian theatre. There are three main venues at the centre – a 674-seat theatre, a concert hall and a studio – and between them they cover everything from comedy and kids' shows to classical music and African dance spectaculars.

Alma Cafe LIVE MUSIC
(Map p97; ☎021-685 7377; www.almacafe.co.za; 20 Alma Rd, Rosebank; ⏱6-10pm Wed, 11am-4pm Thu, 6-11pm Fri & Sat, 5-10pm Sun; 🚆Rosebank) This cosy venue, which also serves food and drinks, usually has live music on Wednesday (free) and weekends (cover charge R170 to R190; bookings necessary). Check the cafe's Facebook page for details of upcoming events.

Maynardville Open-Air Theatre THEATRE
(Map p100; ☎083 915 8000; www.facebook.com/maynardvilleopenairtheatre; cnr Church & Wolfe Sts, Wynberg; 🚆Wynberg) It wouldn't be

ℹ ONLINE ENTERTAINMENT GUIDES

Cape Town Magazine (www.capetownmagazine.co.za)

Inside Guide (https://insideguide.co.za)

IOL (www.iol.co.za/entertainment/whats-on/cape-town)

More Than Food (www.morethanfood.co.za)

The Next 48 Hours (http://48hours.co.za)

DON'T MISS

THURSDAY ART EVENTS

First Thursdays (www.first-thursdays.co.za; ⏲5-9pm, 1st Thu of month Feb-Dec) is a popular monthly event centred on the galleries and design shops clustered around Church and Bree Sts – it's a chance to dip into the local art scene, as well as a roving street party.

Observatory holds its own smaller-scale **Art Thursday** (www.facebook.com/ARTthursdaysInObz; Observatory) event on the second Thursday of the month. Pick up a leaflet showing participants from AHEM! Art Collective (p78).

summer in Cape Town without a visit to Maynardville Park's open-air theatre to see some Shakespeare. Bring a blanket, pillow and umbrella, though, as the weather can be dodgy and the seats are none too comfy. The annual Shakespeare in the Park season runs from late January to late February; ticket prices range from R108 to R180.

At other times of the year, dance, jazz and theatre performances take place here.

☆ Simon's Town & Southern Peninsula

Kalk Bay Theatre THEATRE

(Map p104; ☎021-788 7257; www.kalkbaytheatre.co.za; 52 Main Rd, Kalk Bay; 🚂Kalk Bay) One of the city's intimate dinner-and-a-show venues, this theatre is housed in an atmospheric converted church. You don't need to eat here to see the productions, which are fun showcases of local talent and often reasonably short, and after a performance you can join the cast at the upstairs bar.

Masque Theatre THEATRE

(Map p104; ☎021-788 1898; www.masquetheatre.co.za; 37 Main Rd, Muizenberg; 🚂False Bay) The program at this small theatre (seating 171) changes on a pretty regular basis, veering from stand-up comedy and live music to musical revues and more serious plays.

Cafe Roux LIVE MUSIC

(☎021-789 2538; www.caferouxsessions.co.za; Noordhoek Farm Village, cnr Main Rd & Village Ln, Noordhoek; ⏲8.30am-5pm daily, plus 6-11pm Wed-Sat) One of the best places on the peninsula for live music and comedy, and a great cafe to boot. Tickets typically cost around R100; check www.caferouxsessions.co.za for the lineup. There's another branch in the city at 74 Shortmarket St.

☆ Cape Flats & Northern Suburbs

Grandwest Casino CASINO

(Map p114; ☎021-505 7777; www.suninternational.com/grandwest; 1 Jakes Gerwel Dr, Goodwood; ⏲24hr; 👪; 🚂Goodwood) Even if gambling isn't your thing, there's plenty to keep you entertained at Grandwest, including a six-screen cinema, many restaurants, a food court, an Olympic-sized ice rink, kids' play areas, a bowling alley and regular concerts by major international singers and bands. It's 15km east of the city centre.

Shopping

Bring an empty suitcase, because chances are you'll be leaving Cape Town laden with booty. There's an almost irresistible range of products on offer, including traditional African crafts, ceramics, fashion, fine wines and contemporary art. You'll also find antiques and curios from all over Africa, but shop carefully as there are many fakes among the originals.

City Bowl, Foreshore, Bo-Kaap & De Waterkant

★ **Africa Nova** ARTS & CRAFTS

(Map p74; ☎021-425 5123; www.africanova.co.za; Cape Quarter, 72 Waterkant St, De Waterkant; ⏲10am-5.30pm; 🚌Alfred) One of the most stylish and desirable collections of tribal and contemporary African textiles, arts and crafts. You'll find potato-print fabrics made by women in Hout Bay, Ronel Jordaan's handmade felt rock cushions (which look like giant pebbles) and a wonderful range of high-end ceramics and jewellery.

There's a smaller branch at the Watershed (p179) at the V&A Waterfront.

★ **Stable** DESIGN

(Map p70; ☎021-426 5922; www.stable.org.za; 65 Loop St, City Bowl; ⏲9am-5pm Mon-Fri, 10am-1pm Sat; 🚌Strand) A one-stop shop for a variety of South African designers' products, including very portable items such as clothes hooks, fridge magnets, skinny leather ties and jewellery. If you've a house to decorate, there are bigger pieces of furniture, too, such as chairs and sofas, as well as wall art.

★ **Chandler House** ARTS & CRAFTS

(Map p70; ☎021-424 4810; www.chandlerhouse.co.za; 53 Church St, City Bowl; ⏰10am-5pm Tue-Fri, to 2pm Sat; 🚌Church, Longmarket) Michael Chandler showcases his quirky ceramic homewares and decorative pieces in this well-edited collection of imaginative local arts and crafts, which includes cushions, prints and playful design pieces. He also has an expert eye for art as showcased on the walls and in a small gallery section.

★ **Monkeybiz** ARTS & CRAFTS

(Map p70; ☎021-426 0145; www.monkeybiz.co.za; 61 Wale St, Bo-Kaap; ⏰9am-5pm Mon-Thu, to 4pm Fri, 9.30am-1pm Sat; 🚌Church, Longmarket) Colourful beadwork crafts, made by local township women, are Monkeybiz's super-successful stock in trade – you'll find their products around the world, but the largest selection – in a myriad of colour combinations – is here. Profits are reinvested back into community services such as soup kitchens and a burial fund for artists and their families.

★ **Rialheim** ARTS & CRAFTS

(Map p70; ☎021-422 2928; www.rialheim.co.za; 117 Long St, City Bowl; ⏰9am-5pm Mon-Fri, to 3pm Sat; 🚌Church, Longmarket) Locally sourced clay is used in the Robertson-based factory to make these stylish, mainly monochrome ceramics which range from plates and mugs to decorative items such as dogs and rams heads. Upstairs check out the Walter Battiss Gallery (https://walterbattiss.co.za) – they have the rights to reproduce images of this important South African artist.

Mami Wata SPORTS & OUTDOORS

(Map p70; www.mamiwata.surf; 81 Rose St, Bo-Kaap; ⏰9am-5pm Mon-Fri, 9am-1pm Sat; 🚌Church, Longmarket) A large yellow banana sticking out of the shop front greets you at this surfboard and fashion store. All the colourful products are locally designed and produced, and there is a great map of 133 surf spots around Africa you can contemplate while sipping on their African coffee and listening to some LPs for local label Rostin' Records.

Eclectica Contemporary ART

(Map p70; ☎021-422 4145; www.eclecticacontemporary.co.za; 69 Burg St, City Bowl; 🚌Longmarket, Church) This commercial gallery lives up to its name, being both contemporary and eclectic in its choices of art. The curators have a good eye when it comes to local talent and there's plenty of affordable printed works as well as eye-catching paintings.

Mali South Clothing FASHION & ACCESSORIES

(Map p70; ☎021-426 1519; www.malisouthclothing.com; 96 Long St, City Bowl; ⏰7am-8pm Mon-Sat, 9am-6pm Sun) There are several tailoring shops dotted along Long St where you can buy ready-to-wear items or have custom-designed clothing made from vibrantly colourful African prints. Mali South offers a dazzling range of patterns that come in suits, shirts, dresses, skirts and more – plus they're open on Sunday.

Mungo HOMEWARES

(Map p70; ☎021-201 2374; www.mungo.co.za; 78 Hout St, City Bowl; ⏰9am-5pm Mon-Fri, to 2pm Sat; 🚌Strand) The Cape Town retail outpost for this fabric-weaving business from Plettenberg Bay. They design, weave and make a wide range of attractive homeware items, such as towels and bed linen in subtle, earthy colours and patterns. In the basement is a small exhibition on their weaving process.

Bo-op FASHION & ACCESSORIES

(Map p70; www.facebook.com/BoOpCollective; 102 Wale St, Bo-Kaap; ⏰9am-5pm Mon-Fri, to 3pm Sat; 🚌Church, Longmarket) Some 14 Capetonian designers, including Ballo sunglasses, Sealand bags made from recycled materials, and Grandt Mason shoes, are stocked in this Mondrian-painted shop that pops with colour on a prime corner in Bo-Kaap.

Real + Simple FASHION & ACCESSORIES

(Map p70; www.realandsimpledenim.com; 69 Shortmarket St, City Bowl; ⏰10am-7pm Mon-Fri, to 1pm Sat) Having started out at the Neighbourgoods Market (and still selling there on Saturdays), the makers of this locally tailored brand of denim jeans and shirts have set up a concept shop in the centre of town. They share space here with shirt-and-jacket brand Proper, which has a complementary utility look in their choice of fabrics.

Wild Olive COSMETICS

(Map p70; ☎021-422 2777; www.wildolive.eu; 29 Pepper St, City Bowl; ⏰10am-6pm Mon-Fri; 🚌Dorp, Leeuwen) Olive oil and other locally sourced organic ingredients are used for the high-quality bath, body and perfumery products, including scented candles, displayed in this chic artisan apothecary.

Unknown Union FASHION & ACCESSORIES

(Map p70; ☎021-422 2166; www.facebook.com/Unknownunion; 44 Bloem St, City Bowl; ⏰9am-7pm

Mon-Sat; Upper Loop, Upper Long) The showroom for this unisex Capetonian streetwear brand is a friendly, colourful and appealing place to shop for fashion statements as well as more casual clothing. They use South African *shweshwe* textiles and wools from the Basotho mills in their collections.

Espadril SHOES

(Map p70; www.espadril.co.za; 100 Bree St, City Bowl; 9am-5pm Mon-Fri; Church, Longmarket) Two Spanish girls are the creative team behind this women's espadrille-making operation. They have some styles already made up, but you can also create your own design by choosing from the fabrics and suedes they have in their atelier.

On Saturdays you'll find them on a stall at the Neighbourgoods Market (p177).

Cape Gallery ART

(Map p70; 021-423 5309; www.capegallery.co.za; 60 Church St, City Bowl; 9.30am-5pm Mon-Fri, 10am-2pm Sat; Church, Longmarket) Packed with a wide selection of local artworks at a range of price points. Look for the humorous, colourful pieces by David Kuijers, as well as the puppets and ceramics.

Alexandra Höjer Atelier FASHION & ACCESSORIES

(Map p70; 021-424 1674; www.alexandrahojer.com; 156 Bree St, City Bowl; 10am-5pm Mon-Fri, to 2pm Sat; Upper Loop, Upper Long) Swedish immigrant Alexandra Höjer has her workshop here, fronted by a boutique that stocks her chic men's and women's fashions in tailored linen, denim, cotton and leather. The distressed T-shirts are neatly packaged in boxes decorated with snaps of her rock-and-roll dad, who collaborates with her on the Metro brand of menswear.

Missibaba & Kirsten Goss ACCESSORIES, JEWELLERY

(Map p70; www.missibaba.com; 229 Bree St, City Bowl; 10am-6pm Mon-Fri, to 2pm Sat; Upper Loop, Upper Long) Two fashion businesses share premises here: Missibaba, the brand of Capetonian designer Chloe Townsend, who hand-makes colourful bags, belts and other accessories, some with craft input from the townships; and jeweller Kirsten Goss (www.kirstengoss.com), who takes inspiration from South Africa for her gold-plated sterling-silver pieces.

Ma Se Kinners CHILDREN, TOYS

(Map p70; 083 982 1748; www.masekinners.co.za; 1b-c Church St, City Bowl; 8am-7pm Mon-Fri, to 4pm Sat; Groote Kerk) Meaning 'Mother's Children' but also slang for 'How's it going?', this attractive place stocks high-quality, locally made kids and women's clothing and soft toys, as well as ceramics, art and other things for grown ups, such as their own range of body creams and cleansers.

Olive Green Cat JEWELLERY

(Map p70; 021-424 1101; www.olivegreencat.com; 76 Church St, City Bowl; 9.30am-5pm Mon-Fri; Church, Longmarket) At the studio of Philippa Green and Ida-Elsje, you'll find the work of two talented jewellery designers, both of whom have caught international attention. Green's signature pieces are her chunky Perspex cuffs, hand-stitched with patterns and graphic text, while Elsje specialises in delicate earrings and necklaces. They also collaborate on the striking Nunc range of diamond jewellery.

What If The World ART

(Map p70; 021-447 2376; www.whatiftheworld.com; 16 Buiten St, City Bowl; 9.30am-5pm Tue-Fri, to 2pm Sat) This gallery can be credited with kicking Capetonian creativity up the backside. Drop by to witness the unruly forces of young South African art.

Skinny La Minx ARTS & CRAFTS

(Map p70; 021-424 6290; www.skinnylaminx.com; 201 Bree St, City Bowl; 10am-5pm Mon-Fri, to 2pm Sat; Upper Loop, Upper Long) The full range of Heather Moore's designs, printed on cotton and cotton-linen mix, are on view here, made up into cushions, table runners, lamp shades, bags and the like. You can also purchase cloth by the metre.

Klûk & CGDT FASHION & ACCESSORIES

(Map p74; 083 377 7780; http://klukcgdt.com; 43-45 Bree St, City Bowl; 9am-5pm Mon-Fri, to 2pm Sat; Lower Loop, Lower Long) The showroom and atelier of Malcolm Klûk (once an apprentice to John Galliano) and Christiaan Gabriel Du Toit are combined here. Expect haute couture, with similarly haute prices, and some more affordable prêt-à-porter pieces.

Lucky Fish CLOTHING, CRAFTS

(Map p70; 084 380 0090; 43 Long St, City Bowl; 8am-6.30pm Mon-Thu, 8am-7pm Fri, 9am-7pm Sat; Church, Mid-Long) A very groovy little shop stocking a great range of locally produced souvenirs, including their own brand of design T-shirts and some African music CDs.

Merchants on Long FASHION, GIFTS

(Map p70; ☎021-422 2828; www.merchantsonlong.com; 34 Long St, City Bowl; ⏲10am-6pm Mon-Fri, to 2pm Sat; 🚌Church, Mid-Long) This 'African salon store', in one of Long St's more beautiful buildings and boasting a terracotta art nouveau facade, is a gallery of top contemporary design – from fashion to stationery and the scents of Karen Frazer (frazerparfum.com) – sourced from across the continent.

Avoova ARTS & CRAFTS

(Map p70; ☎021-422 1620; http://avoova.com/za; 97 Bree St, City Bowl; ⏲9am-5pm Mon-Fri, to 1pm Sat; 🚌Church, Longmarket) Stocks the beautiful ostrich-eggshell-decorated accessories made by Avoova – each one is a unique piece. You'll also find Masai beadwork from Kenya, and a few other carefully selected crafts.

Cape Quarter SHOPPING CENTRE

(Map p74; ☎021-421 1111; www.capequarter.co.za; 27 Somerset Rd, Green Point; ⏲9am-6pm Mon-Fri, 9am-4pm Sat, 10am-4pm Sun; 🚌Alfred) With the Cape Quarter's original 20-year-old location undergoing a major renovation, the shopping mall action has moved over to the newer, larger block anchored by a snazzy branch of the supermarket **Spar** (Map p74; ☎021-418 0360; http://sparcapequarter.co.za; Cape Quarter, 27 Somerset Rd, Green Point; ⏲7am-9pm Mon-Sat, 8am-9pm Sun), handy if you're self-catering in the area – or indeed staying in one of the complex's luxury penthouse apartments.

Baraka GIFTS & SOUVENIRS

(Map p74; ☎021-425 8883; www.barakashop.co.za; Shop 35, Cape Quarter, Dixon St, De Waterkant; ⏲9am-6pm Mon-Sat, 10am-2pm; 🚌Alfred) Baraka means 'blessing' in Arabic. Co-owner Gavin Terblanche has an eclectic eye for what works as a gift or quirky piece of home decor. Products include handmade leather journals and photo albums by Terblanche's own company Worlds of Wonder (www.worldsofwonder.co.za).

Carole Nevin HOMEWARES

(Map p70; ☎021-422 1615; www.carolenevin.com; 52 Burg St, City Bowl; ⏲8am-5pm Mon-Fri, 8.30am-2pm Sat; 🚌Church, Longmarket) Carole's colourful hand-printed and hand-painted fabrics can be bought by the metre or sewn into table linens, cushion covers, tea towels and the like. There are several other locally made handicrafts sold here, too.

There's also a branch in Victoria Wharf (p180).

Tribal Trends ARTS & CRAFTS

(Map p70; ☎021-423 8007; http://tribal-trends.business.site; Winchester House, 72-74 Long St, City Bowl; ⏲9am-5pm Mon-Fri, to 2pm Sat; 🚌Church, Longmarket) Colour-coordinated items pack this emporium of all things African, tribal and crafty. They support local artists, who sell some of their beadwork and jewellery here.

AVA Gallery ART

(Map p70; ☎021-424 7436; www.ava.co.za; 35 Church St, City Bowl; ⏲10am-5pm Mon-Fri, to 1pm Sat; 🚌Church, Longmarket) Exhibition space for the nonprofit Association for Visual Arts (AVA), which shows some very interesting work by local artists. Pick up signed prints of works by the famous local cartoonist Zapiro.

Clarke's Bookshop BOOKS

(Map p70; ☎021-423 5739; www.clarkesbooks.co.za; 199 Long St, City Bowl; ⏲9am-5pm Mon-Fri, 9.30am-1pm Sat; 🚌Dorp, Leeuwen) Take your time leafing through the best range of books on South Africa and the continent, with a great second-hand section upstairs. If you can't find what you're looking for here, it's unlikely to be in any of the other bookshops around town (although there's no harm in browsing).

Mememe FASHION & ACCESSORIES

(Map p70; ☎021-424 0001; www.mememe.co.za; 117a Long St, City Bowl; ⏲9.30am-5.30pm Mon-Fri, 9am-3pm Sat; 🚌Church, Longmarket) A forerunner of the funky boutiques blooming along Long St, Mememe was started by award-winning sculptor and fashion designer Doreen Southwood in 2001. It's a showcase for young Capetonian designers and labels such as Adam & Eve, Morphe Odonata and the bespoke leather shoes of Diomonde.

Pan African Market ARTS & CRAFTS

(Map p70; 76 Long St, City Bowl; ⏲8.30am-5.30pm Mon-Sat; 🚌Church, Longmarket) A microcosm of the continent, packed into three floors, with a bewildering range of arts and crafts (which you should certainly bargain over). On the top floor you'll find an art gallery and Chimurenga (www.chimurenga.co.za), publishers of the pan-African newspaper *Chronic* and other publications.

Prins & Prins JEWELLERY

(Map p70; ☎021-422 0148; www.prinsandprins.com; 66 Loop St, City Bowl; ⏲9am-5pm Mon-Fri, to 1pm Sat; 🚌Church, Mid-Long) An old Huguenot house makes a suitably salubrious venue for investing in some of South Africa's mineral wealth, in wearable form.

East City, District Six, Woodstock & Observatory

★Streetwires ARTS & CRAFTS
(Map p80; www.streetwires.co.za; Maxton Centre, 354 Albert Rd, Woodstock; 8am-5pm Mon-Fri, 9am-2pm Sat; Salt River) Their motto is 'anything you can dream up in wire we will build'. And if you visit this social project, designed to create sustainable employment, and see the wire sculptors at work, you'll see what that means! They stock an amazing range, including working radios and chandeliers, life-sized animals and artier products such as the Nguni Cow range.

★Woodstock Exchange SHOPPING CENTRE
(Map p80; 021-486 5999; www.woodstockexchange.co.za; 66 Albert Rd, Woodstock; 8am-5pm Mon-Fri, to 2pm Sat; Woodstock) As well as good places to eat and drink, there's a fair amount of original retail at the Exchange, including the boutique Kingdom, which mixes fashion and accessories with interior design, and Ballo, which makes trendy eyewear from a combo of recycled paper and off-cut timber.

Also here are the atelier and showroom of **Grandt Mason Originals** (Map p80; 072 258 0002; https://grandtmason.com; Shop 13, Woodstock Exchange, 66 Albert Rd, Woodstock; Woodstock), which uses luxurious fabrics from ends of rolls and swatch books to make one-off footwear; **Chapel** (Map p80; 061 426 4270; https://chapelgoods.co.za; Woodstock Exchange, 66 Albert Rd, Woodstock; Woodstock) leather goods; and the factory shop for Honest Chocolate (p158).

★Old Biscuit Mill SHOPPING CENTRE
(Map p80; 021-447 8194; www.theoldbiscuitmill.co.za; 373-375 Albert Rd, Woodstock; 10am-4pm Mon-Fri, 9am-2pm Sat; Kent) This former biscuit factory houses an ace collection of arts, craft, fashion and design shops, as well as places to eat and drink.

Favourites include **Clementina Ceramics** (Map p80; 021-447 1398; http://clementina.co.za; Old Biscuit Mill, 373-375 Albert Rd, Woodstock; 9am-5pm Mon-Fri, to 3pm Sat; Kent) and **Imiso Ceramics** (Map p80; 021-447 2627; www.imisoceramics.co.za; Old Biscuit Mill, 373-375 Albert Rd, Woodstock; Kent); the organic bean-to-shop chocolate factory **Cocofair** (Map p80; 021-447 7355; www.cocoafair.com; Old Biscuit Mill, 373-375 Albert Rd, Woodstock; 8.30am-5pm Mon-Fri, to 3pm Sat, 10am-3pm Sun; Kent); and **Mü & Me** (Map p80; 021-447 1413; Old Biscuit Mill, 373-375 Albert Rd, Woodstock; 9am-4pm Mon-Fri, to 2pm Sat; Kent) for supercute graphic art for cards, wrapping paper, stationery and kids' T-shirts. This is also the location of the massively successful Neighbourgoods Market.

★Book Lounge BOOKS
(Map p80; 021-462 2425; www.booklounge.co.za; 71 Roeland St, East City; 9.30am-7.30pm Mon-Fri, 8.30am-6pm Sat, 10am-4pm Sun; Roeland) The hub of Cape Town's literary scene, thanks to its great selection of titles, comfy chairs, simple cafe and busy program of events. There are up to three talks or book launches a week, generally with free drinks and nibbles, and readings for kids on the weekend.

One of a Kind FASHION & ACCESSORIES
(Map p80; 078 818 2327; www.navaapparel.com; 137 Sir Lowry Rd, Woodstock; 9am-5pm Mon-Fri; District Six) You can chat to Alwyn about his handmade shoes in leather and fancy fabrics at this boutique that showcases several fashion and accessory designers' products, as well as local art and deli goods. A small cafe and juice bar is also part of the mix.

Welkin Supply Store FASHION & ACCESSORIES
(Map p80; www.facebook.com/WelkinSupplyStore; 133 Sir Lowry Rd, Woodstock; 9.30am-3.30pm Mon-Fri; District Six) Frontier Provisions are the local menswear label stocked on one side of this boutique, with Gray Dawn womenswear on the other. The look is vintage with a contemporary twist, with a lot of earthy colours, canvas and utility styles.

Threads Project FASHION & ACCESSORIES
(Map p80; 021-447 0722; http://threadsproject.co.za; 349 Albert Rd, Woodstock; 9am-5pm Mon-Sat; Kent) Like a mini fashion department store, a variety of mens- and womens-wear brands are showcased here – it's a good spot to browse for colourful, locally designed T-shirts, shirts, swimwear and dresses as well as accessories.

Black Chillie Style CLOTHING
(Map p79; 021-447 3020; 98 Lower Main Rd, Observatory; 9am-6pm Mon-Fri, to noon Sat; Observatory) Stocking high-quality, Dutch-manufactured waxed-cotton prints in dazzling West African designs, this fabric shop and tailor can turn out all kinds of attire – from suits and shirts to shoes and bags. Trousers are R600, shirts R700 and a jacket R2500. The cloth itself goes for R100 per metre.

DON'T MISS

CAPE TOWN'S MARKETS

Joining the long-established **Trafalgar Place** (Map p70; off Adderley St, City Bowl; ⏲7am-6pm; Groote Kerk) flower market and the bric-a-brac vendors at Milnerton Flea Market (p183) is a trendy breed of artisan-food and designer-goods-and-crafts markets. As well as the following, a market at Cape Point Vineyards (p111) on Thursday evening also draws crowds.

Neighbourgoods Market (Map p80; www.neighbourgoodsmarket.co.za; Old Biscuit Mill, 373-375 Albert Rd, Woodstock; ⏲9am-3pm Sat; Kent) This is the artisan goods markets that kickstarted the craze for similar markets across the Cape – and it's still one of the best. Food and drinks are gathered in the main area where you can pick up groceries and gourmet goodies or just graze, while the separate Designergoods area hosts a must-buy selection of local fashions and accessories. Come early, unless you enjoy jostling with crowds.

OZCF Market Day (Map p86; www.ozcf.co.za/market-day; Granger Bay Rd, Granger Bay, V&A Waterfront; ⏲9am-2pm Sat; Upper Orange) Produce grown on the Oranjezicht City Farm (p83) and other local farms is sold every Saturday here alongside many other edible and souvenir products. It's a great event – one of the best of its kind in Cape Town – with plenty of food and drink stalls for brunching, a DJ and a community-coming-together atmosphere.

Bay Harbour Market (Map p92; www.bayharbour.co.za; 31 Harbour Rd, Hout Bay; ⏲5-9pm Fri, 9.30am-4pm Sat & Sun; Atlantic Skipper) This imaginatively designed indoor market at the far end of Hout Bay Harbour is one of Cape Town's best. There's a good range of stalls selling items from clothes to craftwork, as well as very tempting food and drink. Live music gives the former fish factory a relaxed, party-like atmosphere.

Blue Bird Garage Food & Goods Market (Map p104; ☎082 920 4285; www.bluebirdgarage.co.za; 39 Albertyn Rd, Muizenberg; ⏲4-10pm Fri; False Bay) This hip, artisan food-and-goods market is located in a 1940s hangar, once the base for the southern hemisphere's first airmail delivery service, and then a garage in the 1950s. It's a fun place to shop and graze, accompanied by live music.

City Bowl Market (Map p84; ☎083 676 6104; www.citybowlmarket.co.za; 14 Hope St, Gardens; ⏲4.30pm-8.30pm Thu; Roodehek) Based in a lovely old building with a lofty hall and outside courtyard areas, this weekly market sells mainly food and drink, including freshly made salads, roast-pork sandwiches, craft beers, wines and fruit juices. There's also some fashion on sale.

EarthFair Food Market (Map p70; www.earthfairmarket.co.za; St Georges Mall, City Bowl; ⏲11am-3pm Thu) This weekly takeaway food market is very popular with city office workers. It's held at the southern end of St Georges Mall and also includes a few craft stalls and a secondhand book seller.

Woodstock Cycleworks SPORTS & OUTDOORS
(Map p80; ☎021-461 5634; www.woodstockcycleworks.com; 14 Searle St, Woodstock; ⏲9am-6pm Mon-Fri, 9.30am-1pm Sat; District Six) Swing by this converted warehouse complex even if you're not in the market for a custom-built bike. They also sell fashionable, locally made biking tops, arty T-shirts and prints, and have the Le Jeune cafe (named after a South African brand of bike).

In the courtyard, check out the naturally tanned leather products made by **Stockton Goods** (Map p80; ☎021-461 0107; www.stocktongoods.com; 14 Searle St, Woodstock; ⏲9am-5pm Mon-Fri; District Six). The side of the building is painted with a bicycle-themed mural by Freddy Sam.

SMAC ART
(Map p80; ☎021-461 1029; https://smacgallery.com; the Palms, 145 Sir Lowry Rd, Woodstock; ⏲9am-5pm Mon-Fri, to 3pm Sat; District Six) SMAC specialises in artworks from 1960 to the 1980s and occupies a series of roomy spaces in the Palms, where you'll find a few other, smaller art and interior-design dealers and galleries.

Woodstock Co-op SHOPPING CENTRE
(Map p80; http://woodstockcoop.co.za; 357-363 Albert Rd, Woodstock; 9am-5pm Mon-Sat; Kent) At this co-op you'll find a rough-and-ready collection of start-ups, try outs and established traders, hawking a range of appealing items including accessories, and old and new interior design. The main anchor is the **Attic**, which specialises in retro collectables and other household junk.

Also check out **Ashley Heather** (http://ashleyheather.co.za), who makes jewellery out of precious metals reclaimed from circuit boards.

Vamp HOMEWARES
(Map p80; www.vampfurniture.co.za; 368c Albert Rd, Woodstock; 9.30am-4.30pm Mon-Fri, 8.30am-3pm Sat; Kent) Capetonian interior-design adventures can be had at this place, set back from Albert Rd, where you may be able to pick up original framed Trechtikoff prints alongside retro suitcases, globes, and contemporary arts and crafts.

Salt Circle Arcade SHOPPING CENTRE
(Map p80; 374 Albert Rd, Salt River; Kent) Among the retail options to hunt out here are the second-hand bookshop Blank Books, the owner of which writes the local blog www.ilovewoodstock.co.za and Isobel Sippel Studio, where the designer's choice of art prints and dyework on cotton and linen are turned into cushion covers, napkins and wall-hangings. Food trucks gather in the central courtyard.

Recreate HOMEWARES
(Map p80; 021-447 0007; https://recreatesa.com; 6 Stowe St, Salt River; 9am-4pm Mon-Thu, to 3pm Fri & Sat; Kent) Extraordinary repurposed furniture and lighting by Katie Thompson – think suitcases turned into chairs, crockery as lamp stands, and fridge magnets made from computer keyboard letters.

Woodhead's FASHION & ACCESSORIES
(Map p80; 021-261 7185; www.woodheads.co.za; 29 Caledon St, East City; 8am-5pm Mon-Fri, 8.30am-1pm Sat; Lower Buitenkant) If you're after a full hide – cow, buffalo, antelope, zebra etc – head over to these savvy guys who've been catering to Cape Town's leather trade since 1867. They also stock locally made hide boots, bags and belts. Small springbok hides go from around R450, while for a zebra skin you're looking at around R20,000 including VAT. Zebra skins (and meat) are byproducts of compulsory culls used to maintain healthy populations of the species.

Note: zebra skins (and meat) are byproducts of compulsory culls used to maintain healthy populations of the species.

Mnandi Textiles & Design CLOTHING
(Map p79; 021-447 6814; 90 Station Rd, Observatory; 9am-5.30pm Mon-Fri, to 2pm Sat; Observatory) Mnandi sells cloth from all over Africa, including the local *shweshwe* cotton printed with everything from animals to traditional African patterns. You can also have clothes tailor-made and find lots of cute gifts, including the adorable Zuka cloth dolls of Xhosa women and Desmond Tutu.

Gardens & Surrounds

★ **Handmade by Me** HOMEWARES
(Map p88; www.handmadebyme.co.za; 21 De Lorentz St, Tamboerskloof; 11am-5pm Tue-Fri, 9.30am-1pm Sat; Welgemeend) Sera Holland is the artist responsible for the colourful, floral and abstract designs on the fabric items – cushion covers, napkins, table runners etc – and other products at this cute shop that also sells plants.

★ **Stefania Morland** FASHION & ACCESSORIES
(Map p88; 021-422 2609; www.stefaniamorland.com; 153A Kloof St, Gardens; 9am-5pm Mon-Fri, to 2pm Sat; Welgemeend) Gorgeous gowns and more casual wear made from silks, linens, lace and other natural fibres seduce fashionistas in this chic showroom and atelier.

★ **Ashanti** HOMEWARES
(Map p84; 021-461 0367; www.ashantidesign.com; 77 Kloof St, Gardens; 8am-5pm Mon-Fri, 10am-3pm Sat; District Six) Baskets, mats, lampshades, pillows, bags and cushions are among the many rainbow-coloured products on sale at this great artisan design shop that creates its own fabric from T-shirt offcuts that would otherwise go to landfill. No two pieces are alike and you can also buy their fabrics by the metre.

LIM HOMEWARES
(Map p84; 021-423 1200; www.lim.co.za; 86a Kloof St, Gardens; 9am-5pm Mon-Fri, 9.15am-1.15pm Sat; Welgemeend) Although the shop's name is an acronym for 'Less is More', this interior design shop has been so successful that they've had to add more room by expanding into the neighbouring house. Wander through the rooms admiring the stylish, pared-back selection of homewares, including fashion accessories made from buckskin.

Bluecollarwhitecollar FASHION & ACCESSORIES
(Map p84; ☎021-422 1593; www.bluecollarwhitecollar.co.za; Lifestyles on Kloof, 50 Kloof St, Gardens; ⏲9am-5pm Mon-Fri, 9am-4pm Sat; 🚌Lower Kloof) There's an eye-catching selection of tailored men's and women's shirts from this locally based fashion brand – formal (white collar) and informal (blue collar), as well as T-shirts and shorts.

Roastin' Records MUSIC
(Map p88; ☎073 129 6799; http://roastinrecords.com; 28 Wandel St, Gardens; ⏲8am-6pm Mon-Fri, to 2pm Sat) Vinyl junkies can score their fix at this small emporium run by a local record publisher – they have CDs and even a few lo-fi cassettes too. While you browse the racks and listen to the tunes you can also order a coffee.

Erf 81 Market MARKET
(Map p84; www.facebook.com/tyisanabanye; cnr Leeuwenvoet & Military Rd, Tamboerskloof; ⏲10am-2pm Sun; 🚌Lower Kloof) This small market is one of the projects of a worthy, non-profit urban agriculture project that exists without a lease on prime city land. Food security activists Tyisa Nabanye (Xhosa for 'feed the others') moved from the townships into this former military site, cleaned up a shed and planted a market garden with a spectacular view of Table Mountain. Follow the road uphill to find the market and garden.

AKJP Collective FASHION & ACCESSORIES
(Map p84; ☎021-424 5502; www.adriaankuiters.com; 73 Kloof St, Gardens; ⏲10am-6pm Mon-Fr, to 4pm Sat; 🚌Ludwig's Garden) The brainchild of designer Keith Henning and Jody Paulsen, this stylish boutique stocks clothes such as shirts, shorts and trousers under the Adriaan Kuiters mens brand, as well as accessories like canvas and leather bags and belts. You'll also find pieces by other fashion brands including Take Care, Drotsky and the fragrance line House of Gozdawa.

Mr & Mrs FASHION, HOMEWARES
(Map p84; ☎021-424 4387; www.mrandmrs.co.za; 98 Kloof St, Gardens; ⏲9am-6pm Mon-Fri, to 4pm Sat; 🚌Welgemeend) A tasteful selection of fashion, gifts and homewares from South African and international designers. The choices of products reflect the owners' travels through Indonesia, Argentina and India.

Lifestyles on Kloof MALL
(Map p84; www.lifestyleonkloof.co.za; 50 Kloof St, Gardens; ⏲9am-7pm Mon-Fri, to 5pm Sat, 10am-3pm Sun; 🚌Lower Kloof) At this handy, small shopping centre are several places to eat, fashion boutiques, the supermarket Woolworths and, upstairs, the health-food store and chemists **Wellness Warehouse**.

Also here are branches of the wine merchant **Wine Concepts** (Map p84; ☎021-426 4401; http://wineconcepts.co.za; Lifestyles on Kloof, 50 Kloof St, Gardens; ⏲9am-7pm Mon-Fri, to 5pm Sat; 🚌Lower Kloof) and the fashion brand Bluecollarwhitecollar.

Gardens Centre MALL
(Map p84; ☎021-465 1842; www.gardensshoppingcentre.co.za; cnr Mill & Buitenkant Sts, Gardens; ⏲9am-7pm Mon-Fri, to 5pm Sat, to 2pm Sun; 🚌Gardens) A handy, well-stocked mall covering all the bases, with good cafes, bookshops, Pick n Pay and Woolworths supermarkets, a travel agency and a Cape Union Mart for camping and outdoor-adventure gear.

Mabu Vinyl BOOKS, MUSIC
(Map p84; ☎021-423 7635; www.mabuvinyl.co.za; 2 Rheede St, Gardens; ⏲9am-8pm Mon-Sat, 11am-3pm Sun; 🚌Lower Kloof) New and secondhand LPs, CDs, DVDs, books and comics are bought, sold and traded at this reputable shop that features in the award-winning documentary *Searching For Sugarman*. Ask here about independently released CDs by local artists.

Green Point & Waterfront

★**Guild** ARTS & CRAFTS
(Map p86; ☎021-461 2856; www.southernguild.co.za; Shop 5b, Silo 5, South Arm Rd, V&A Waterfront; ⏲9am-6pm Mon-Fri, 10am-2pm Sat; 🚌Watefront Silo) Trevyn and Julian McGowan have made a business out of cherry-picking the cream of the South African design community and promoting it to the world in annual collections. Opened in 2017, this is their permanent showcase, so the go-to location for spotting emerging talents and to buy incredible, distinctive pieces.

For something more affordable – not to mention portable – check out the boutique gift section co-curated by Guild and Wallpaper. The company has teamed up with local designers such as Wola Nani to create its own range of products.

★**Watershed** SHOPPING CENTRE
(Map p86; www.waterfront.co.za/shop/watershed; Dock Rd, V&A Waterfront; ⏲10am-6pm; 🚌Nobel Sq) One of the best places to shop for souvenirs in Cape Town, this inventively

designed retail market gathers together over 150 tenants representing the cream of Capetonian and South African producers of fashion, arts, crafts and design – there's something here for every pocket. On the upper level is an exhibition space, and a wellness centre offering holistic products and massages.

Many boutiques and craft stores you'll find elsewhere in the city have outlets here, but there are also unique stalls such as **Township Guitars** (www.townshipguitars.com), which makes and sells all-electric guitars made from oil cans, wood and fishing wire.

★Out of this World ARTS & CRAFTS

(Map p86; 021-434 3540; www.outofthisworld.co.za; 1 Braemar Rd, Green Point; 8.30am-4.30pm Mon-Fri) Buddha statues meet Nigerian tribal crowns at this interior design emporium piled high with treasures from across Africa and Asia. Here also, in a courtyard garden, is the pleasant **Stranger's Club** cafe, which is good for a quiet coffee and snack.

There are branches in Victoria Wharf and in the Promenade complex at Camps Bay.

Donald Greig Gallery & Foundry ART

(Map p86; 021-418 0003; www.donaldgreig.co.za; 1 Coode Cr, Port of Cape Town; 9.30am-5.30pm Mon-Fri, to 1pm Sat; Watefront Silo) The striking, life-sized bronze animal sculptures of Donald Greig grace many public and private spaces around the Western Cape. At his foundry, set in a 19th-century former customs warehouse, you can watch the crafting and casting process and buy pieces small enough to fit easily in your luggage.

Victoria Wharf SHOPPING CENTRE

(Map p86; 021-408 7500; www.waterfront.co.za; Breakwater Blvd, V&A Waterfront; 9am-9pm; Breakwater) All the big names of South African retail (including Woolworths, CNA, Pick n Pay, Exclusive Books and Musica), as well as international luxury brands, are represented at this appealing mall – one of Cape Town's best.

Everard Read ART

(Map p86; 021-418 4527; www.everard-read-capetown.co.za; 3 Portswood Rd, V&A Waterfront; 9am-6pm Mon-Fri, to 4pm Sat; Nobel Square) Browse or buy works by some of South Africa's leading contemporary artists at this classy gallery. Works on display include paintings by John Meyer and Lionel Smit, mixed media projects from Velaphi Mzimba, and sculptures by Brett Murray and Angus Taylor.

Cape Union Mart Adventure Centre SPORTS & OUTDOORS

(Map p86; 021-425 4559; www.capeunionmart.co.za; Quay 4, V&A Waterfront; 9am-9pm; Nobel Square) This emporium is packed with backpacks, boots, clothing and practically everything else you might need for outdoor adventures, from a hike up Table Mountain to a Cape-to-Cairo safari.

There's a smaller branch in Victoria Wharf, as well as in the Gardens Centre (p179) and Cavendish Square malls.

Shimansky JEWELLERY

(Map p86; 021-421 2788; www.shimansky.co.za; 1st fl, Clock Tower Centre, V&A Waterfront; 9am-9pm; Nobel Square) Diamonds are synonymous with South Africa – here you'll find plenty of them, set in a range of jewellery designs.

Shimansky also has a small museum (p85) and a workshop where you can take a peek at how all that bling is made.

Sea Point to Hout Bay

★Ethno Bongo JEWELLERY

(Map p92; 021-791 0757; www.andbanana.com; Harvest Centre, Harbour Rd, Hout Bay; 10am-5.30pm Mon-Fri, to 4pm Sat & Sun; Military) A court order may have stopped this shop from using the name Dolce & Banana for its bead jewellery, but otherwise it hasn't put a dent in this long-running business that sells fun fashion items made by local craftspeople. The products include home decor made from materials such as reclaimed wood and driftwood.

★Hout Bay Lions Craft Market MARKET

(Map p92; Baviaanskloof Rd, Hout Bay; 10am-3pm Sun; Military) Browsing the stalls at this little village-green market, a fundraiser for the Lions Club of Hout Bay social-upliftment organisation, is a lovely way to while away an hour or so on a Sunday. You'll find crafts made by locals, including impressive beadwork, colourfully printed cloths and cute guinea-fowls crafted from pine cones.

Mojo Market MARKET

(Map p90; www.mojomarket.co.za; 30 Regent Rd, Sea Point; shops 10am-6pm, food stalls 7am-10pm) Pick up items ranging from contemporary African craftwork to fashion at this buzzing indoor market, where 45 shops mix with 25 food stands and a fresh produce section. Between shopping, enjoy goodies such as masala dosas and poke bowls.

The live music (at 7pm during the week, 12.30pm, 4pm and 7.30pm Saturday and 12.30pm Sunday) draws the locals for a beer on Friday night in particular. At other times, such as Sunday morning, some traders can be disorganised and you are better off going elsewhere.

T-Bag Designs ARTS & CRAFTS
(Map p92; 021-790 0887; www.tbagdesigns.co.za; Klein Kronendal, 144 Main Rd, Hout Bay; 9am-4.30pm Mon-Fri; Imizamo Yethu) Recycled tea bags are used to produce an attractive range of greetings cards, stationery, and other quality paper products; it's a worthwhile project that employs people from the neighbouring township of Imizamo Yethu. T-Bag also has a stall in the Watershed (p179) at the V&A Waterfront.

Shipwreck Shop ANTIQUES
(Map p92; 021-790 1100; www.marinerswharf.com; Mariner's Wharf, Harbour Rd, Hout Bay; 9am-5.30pm; Northshore) For anything to do with the Cape's maritime heritage and seafaring in general – from scrimshaw (old carved ivory) and skippers' caps to charts and models – point your prow at this treasure trove, containing more than 20,000 pieces of nautical memorabilia.

Iziko Lo Lwazi ARTS & CRAFTS
(Map p92; 021-790 2273; www.izikoll.co.za; Hout Bay Community Centre, 1 Baviaanskloof Rd, Hout Bay; 8.30am-4pm; Military) What began as an adult literacy programme has morphed into a craft collective, producing creative beadwork, recycled-paper products and stationery, the latter incorporating (among other things) seaweed, reeds, maize, rooibos tea and even horse dung.

Southern Suburbs

★ Montebello Design Centre ARTS & CRAFTS
(Map p97; 021-685 6445; www.montebello.co.za; 31 Newlands Ave, Newlands; 9am-4pm Mon-Sat, to 3pm Sun; ; Newlands) This development project has helped several great craftspeople and designers along the way. In the leafy compound, artists' studios are scattered around the central craft shop, where you can buy a range of gifts, from Irma Stern cushions to tyre handbags.

There's also a plant nursery, the excellent Gardener's Cottage cafe (p151) and a farm shop.

Balu Legacy Boutique FASHION & ACCESSORIES
(Map p97; www.balu.co.za; 9 Cavendish Pl, off Cavendish St, Claremont; 9am-5pm Mon-Fri, to 2pm Sat; Claremont) Balu Nivison's designs using original print fabrics are temptingly displayed in this chic boutique in one of the heritage cottages behind Cavendish Square mall. There's a cafe and juice bar here, too, as well as jewellery, essential oils and more – including a few pieces for men by Balu's son Benjamin.

Cavendish Square MALL
(Map p97; 021-657 5600; www.cavendish.co.za; Dreyer St, Claremont; 9am-7pm Mon-Sat, 10am-5pm Sun; Claremont) The focal point of Claremont's shopping scene, this top-class mall has outlets of many local and international fashion designers, as well as supermarkets, department stores, restaurants and a Ster-Kinekor **multiplex cinema** (www.sterkinekor.com).

Constantia Village SHOPPING CENTRE
(Map p100; 021-794 5065; www.constantiavillage.co.za; cnr Constantia Main & Spaanschemat River Rds, Constantia; 9am-6pm Mon-Fri, to 5pm Sat, to 2pm Sun) Constantia's main shopping hub covers all the basics and more, with a couple of major supermarkets and many other stores, including an Exclusive Books bookshop and numerous fashion retailers.

Kirstenbosch Craft Market ARTS & CRAFTS
(Map p100; 074 333 2170; cnr Kirstenbosch Dr & Rhodes Av, Newlands; 9am-3pm last Sun of month; ; Kirstenbosch) There's lots to choose from at this large monthly craft market spread across the commons outside Kirstenbosch (p95). It's possible to use a credit card to pay for most purchases: payments are made in one of the stone cottages on the site. Proceeds from the market go to the development fund for the botanical gardens.

YDE FASHION & ACCESSORIES
(Map p97; 081 171 0811; www.yde.co.za; F66, Cavendish Square, Dreyer St, Claremont; 9am-7pm Mon-Sat, 10am-5pm Sun; Claremont) Standing for 'Young Designers Emporium', this place is all a bit of a jumble, but you'll most likely find something reasonably inexpensive to suit among the clothes and accessories, created for both sexes by South African streetwear designers.

Simon's Town & Southern Peninsula

★Kalk Bay Modern ARTS & CRAFTS
(Map p104; 021-788 6571; www.kalkbaymodern.co.za; 136 Main Rd, Kalk Bay; 9.30am-5pm; Kalk Bay) This wonderful gallery is stocked with an eclectic and appealing range of arts and crafts, and there are often exhibitions here by local artists. Check out the Art-I-San collection of printed cloth, based on designs by San artists in Namibia and Angola.

Francoise V PHOTOGRAPHY
(021-783 0153; www.francoisev.co.za; Imhoff Farm, Kommetjie Rd, Kommetjie; 9am-5pm) This gallery sells gorgeous wildlife and savannah landscape photos in black-and-white, sepia and faded blues and greens, with images of elephants and baobabs overlooking the cool brick floor. Offering smaller prints around the R700 mark, it's worth considering for a stylish African souvenir.

Noordhoek Farm Village SHOPPING CENTRE
(021-789 2654; www.thefarmvillage.co.za; cnr Main Rd & Village Ln, Noordhoek; 9am-5pm;) This leafy complex, which has the pastoral charm of a Cape Dutch farmstead, is a pleasant place to buy gifts and souvenirs from African craft to local fashion. There are restaurants, a children's playground and a weekly **food market** (4pm to 8pm) on Wednesday.

Blue Planet Fine Art ART
(Map p104; 021-788 3154; www.facebook.com/BluePlanetFineArt; 25 Main Rd, Muizenberg; 10am-5pm Mon-Sat; False Bay) Offering the buzzy feel of an art studio rather than a sterile gallery, Blue Planet is the seaside portfolio of artists Koos de Wet and Anastasia Sarantinou, but offers a window on the broader Muizenberg art scene. There's an interesting and appealing selection of works, from abstract to pop, by local artists who you're unlikely to find represented elsewhere.

Studio Art Gallery ART
(083 310 3220; www.studioartgallery.co.za; Kommetjie Rd, Kommetjie; 9am-5pm) One of several galleries at Imhoff Farm (p109), Cape Town artists Marc Alexander and Donna McKellar's space exhibits their oil paintings and prints in a former blacksmith's workshop dating to 1743. McKellar focuses on South African landscapes and Alexander on wildlife, while other local artists are also represented.

Sobeit Studio ARTS & CRAFTS
(Map p104; 021-788 9007; www.sobeitstudio.com; 51 Main Rd, Muizenberg; 8am-5pm Mon-Sat; False Bay) Occupying the top floor of a pink-and-turquoise art deco building, this modern curiosity shop of crazy creatives includes wax artists, graphic and furniture designers and jewellery makers. Pick up a distinctive souvenir, such as a skull candle or a ceramic Chairman Mao bust.

Pottershop CERAMICS
(Map p104; 021-788 7030; 6 Rouxville Rd, Kalk Bay; 9.30am-4.30pm; Kalk Bay) Pick up works by local ceramicists, including rejects of hand-painted plates and cups by the Potter's Workshop (www.pottersworkshop.co.za), which often have so little wrong with them that you'd hardly notice.

It's on the same premises as Bob's Bagel Cafe (p153).

Redhill Pottery CERAMICS
(Map p110; 021-780 9297; www.redhillpotterycape.co.za; Kilfinan Farm, Scarborough; 8am-5pm Tue-Fri, from 10am Sat & Sun) In a forested valley between Simon's Town and Scarborough, Redhill specialises in pottery that mimics old enamelware in its glaze and incorporates bright African colours in the designs. It's also possible to decorate your own pot and pick it up later (or have it shipped home).

Catacombes FASHION & ACCESSORIES
(Map p104; 021-788 8889; www.facebook.com/pages/Catacombes-Kalkbay/127570887056; 71 Main Rd, Kalk Bay; 9am-5pm; Kalk Bay) Get the floaty boho look at this boutique, which stocks a beautiful range of dresses, separates and accessories. They're locally made and designed with original prints, some inspired by the Mexican Day of the Dead or flowers. The shop also carries some art and crafts.

LarIJ Works ARTS & CRAFTS
(Map p108; 083 977 9182; www.larijworks.com; 112 St George's St, Simon's Town; 10am-4pm; Simon's Town) Reflecting the maritime heritage of Simon's Town, this gallery sells contemporary, nautical-themed artwork and decor, alongside clothing from cotton sleepwear to crocheted naval caps for babies. The woven rope mats are particularly appealing.

Gina's Studio ARTS & CRAFTS
(Map p104; 084 558 5268; www.journeyinstitches.co.za; 38 Palmer Rd, Muizenberg; 10am-4pm Wed-Fri, to 2pm Sat; Muizenberg) Austrian-born Gina Niederhumer is the crafter be-

hind this small boutique packed with appealing items, from crocheted jewellery and organic gingerbread to patchwork bags and patterned quilts.

Kalk Bay Books BOOKS

(Map p104; 021-788 2266; www.kalkbaybooks.co.za; 124 Main Rd, Kalk Bay; 9am-5pm; Kalk Bay) The Southern Peninsula's book lovers gather at this shop that's been dealing literature since 2006. Check the website for details of upcoming book launches, readings, discussions and workshops.

Artvark ARTS & CRAFTS

(Map p104; 021-788 5584; www.artvark.org; 48 Main Rd, Kalk Bay; 9am-5pm; Kalk Bay) This contemporary folk-art gallery is a great place to find attractive souvenirs. It stocks a range of interesting arts and crafts by local artists, including paintings, ceramics, wirework, woodcarvings and jewellery.

Quagga Rare Books & Art BOOKS

(Map p104; 021-788 2752; www.quaggabooks.co.za; 86 Main Rd, Kalk Bay; 9am-5pm Mon-Sat, from 10am Sun; Kalk Bay) It's hard to pass by this appealing bookshop if you're looking for old editions and antiquarian books. The shop also has local art, as well prints and maps, for sale.

Red Rock Tribal ARTS & CRAFTS

(Map p110; 082 269 1020; www.redrocktribal.co.za; Cape Farm House, cnr M65 & M66, Redhill; 10am-5pm Thu-Sun) Hidden away in the peninsula hinterland, this quirky trove of crafts and African tribal artefacts, from tin-can planes made in KwaZulu Natal to old Ethiopian silver and Coptic crosses, has been amassed by owners Steven and Juliette on their travels. Opposite is a giant metal zebra made for an advertisement.

Cape Flats & Northern Suburbs

Century City Natural Goods Market MARKET

(Map p114; 021-552 6889; http://events.centurycity.co.za; Central Park, Century City; 9am-2pm last Sun of month; ; Central Park) Held on the last Sunday of the month, this well-established market – with plenty of eating options and kids' entertainment – sets up in the park opposite Intaka Island (p113). Go onto the island to see local artists in the Eco-Centre.

Milnerton Flea Market MARKET

(Map p114; www.milnertonfleamarket.co.za; Marine Dr (R27), Paarden Eiland; 8am-2pm Sat, to 3pm Sun; Zoarvlei) Hunt for vintage pieces and collectables among the junk and cheap goods at this car-boot sale that fills up a car park on the edge of Table Bay. The views of Table Mountain are matched by the interesting characters you'll encounter here. Established in Milnerton, the market now takes place in neighbouring Paarden Eiland.

Canal Walk SHOPPING CENTRE

(Map p114; 021-529 9699; www.canalwalk.co.za; Century Blvd, Century City; 9am-9pm; ; Canal Walk North) With more than 400 shops, 50-odd restaurants, 18 cinema screens and 8000 parking bays, this faux palazzo is one of Africa's largest malls. Entertainment for kids includes the Canal Walk Express train.

Information

CONSULATES

Most foreign embassies are based in Johannesburg or Pretoria, but a few countries also maintain a consulate in Cape Town. Most are open from 9am to 4pm Monday to Friday.

Angolan Consulate (021-425 8700; www.angolanembassy.org/consular.html; 15th fl, Metlife Centre, 7 Walter Sisulu Ave, Foreshore; Convention Centre)

Dutch Consulate (021-421 5660; http://southafrica.nlembassy.org; 100 Strand St, City Bowl; Strand)

French Consulate (021-423 1575; https://lecap.consulfrance.org; 78 Queen Victoria St, Gardens; 9am-1pm & 2-5pm Mon-Thu, 9am-1pm Fri; Upper Long, Upper Loop)

German Consulate (021-405 3000; www.southafrica.diplo.de; Roeland Park, e-tv Bldg, 4 Stirling St, District Six; Lower Long, Lower Loop)

Italian Consulate (021-487 3900; www.conscapetown.esteri.it/Consolato_Capetown; 2 Grey's Pass, Queen Victoria St, City Bowl; 9am-11.30am Mon, Tue & Fri, 9am-noon & 2-4pm Wed; Upper Long, Upper Loop)

Mozambican Consulate (021-418 2131; www.embamoc.co.za/contact-us; 3rd flr, 1 Thibault Sq, Long St, City Bowl)

UK Consulate (021-405 2400; www.gov.uk/world/organisations/british-consulate-general-cape-town; 15th fl, Norton Rose House, 8 Riebeeck St, Foreshore; Adderley)

US Consulate (021-702 7300; https://za.usembassy.gov; 2 Reddam Ave, Westlake)

DISCOUNT CARDS

iVenture Card (www.iventurecard.com/sg/cape-town) Savings of up to 50% on attractions around Cape Town including tours, cruises and the cableway.

Go Cards Cape Town City Pass (www.gocards.co.za) Available as either as Day Passes (valid for 1, 2, 3 or 7 days) or as Explorer Passes covering 4, 6 or 8 attractions and lasting 90 days from first use. You'll need to be a busy tourist to take full advantage of the discounts they offer on entry to various places.

EMERGENCY & IMPORTANT NUMBERS

Country code	☎27
International access code	☎00
Emergency (landline/mobile)	☎107/112
Table Mountain National Park	☎086 110 6417
Sea Rescue	☎021-449 3500

INTERNET ACCESS

Wi-fi access is available at hotels and hostels, as well as most cafes, some restaurants and tourist hot spots throughout the city. It is usually free (just ask for the password), but don't expect it to be fast or that reliable. Some establishments will also have download limits.

POST

There are post office branches across Cape Town; see www.postoffice.co.za to find the nearest.

TOURIST INFORMATION

Cape Town Tourism (Map p70; ☎086 132 2223, 021-487 6800; www.capetown.travel; Pinnacle Bldg, cnr Castle & Burg Sts, City Bowl; ⏱7am-6pm Mon-Fri, 8.30am-2pm Sat, 9am-1pm Sun; 🚌Church, Mid-Long) Head office books accommodation, tours and car hire, and provides information on national parks and reserves. There are several other branches around town.

Simon's Town Visitor Information Centre (Map p108; ☎021-786 8440; Jubilee Sq, Simon's Town; ⏱8am-5pm Mon-Fri, 9am-1pm Sat & Sun; 🚆Simon's Town)

V&A Waterfront Visitor Information Centre (Map p86; ☎021-408 7600; 280 Dock Rd, V&A Waterfront; ⏱9am-6pm; 🚌Nobel Sq)

Kirstenbosch Visitor Information Centre (Map p100; ☎021-762 0687; www.capetown.travel; Gate 1, Kirstenbosch National Botanical Garden, Rhodes Dr, Newlands; ⏱8am-5pm)

Getting There & Away

AIR

Cape Town International Airport (CPT; Map p50; ☎021-937 1200; www.airports.co.za), 22km east of the city centre, has a tourist information office located in the arrivals hall.

There are many direct international flights into Cape Town. Generally it's cheaper to book and pay for domestic flights within South Africa on the internet (rather than via a local travel agent).

BUS

Interstate buses arrive at the bus terminus at **Cape Town Railway Station**, where you'll find the booking offices for the bus companies, all open from 6am to 6.30pm daily.

Greyhound (☎021-418 4326, reservations 083 915 9000; www.greyhound.co.za; Cape Town Railway Station; ⏱6am-6.30pm)

Intercape (☎021-380 4400; www.intercape.co.za)

Translux (☎021-449 6209, 086 158 9282; www.translux.co.za; Cape Town Railway Station; ⏱6am-6.30pm)

Baz Bus (☎021-422 5202, SMS bookings 076 427 3003; www.bazbus.com) Offers hop-on, hop-off fares and door-to-door service between Cape Town and Jo'burg/Pretoria via Northern Drakensberg, Durban and the Garden Route.

CAR & MOTORCYCLE

The three main arterial routes leading into Cape Town are:

N1 from Johannesburg via the Karoo and the Cape Winelands

N2 from the Garden Route and Overberg via Somerset West and Cape Town International Airport

N7 from the West Coast and Namibia.

TRAIN

Long distance trains arrive at **Cape Town Railway Station** on Heerengracht in the City Bowl. There are services Wednesday, Friday and Sunday to and from Jo'burg via Kimberley on the **Shosholoza Meyl** (☎0860 008 888, 011-774 4555; www.shosholozameyl.co.za): these sleeper trains offer comfortable accommodation and dining cars. Other services include the luxurious **Blue Train** (☎012-334 8459; www.bluetrain.co.za) and **Rovos Rail** (☎012-315 8242; www.rovos.co.za).

Getting Around

GETTING TO/FROM THE AIRPORT

MyCiTi buses (p185) Run every 30 minutes between 4.45am and 10.15pm to the city centre and the Waterfront. A single trip is R100; if you use a 'myconnect' card (which costs a non-refundable R35), the fare varies between R90.40 and R98.80 depending on whether you travel in off-peak or peak times.

Backpacker Bus (082 809 9185; www.backpackerbus.co.za) Book in advance for airport transfers (from R220 per person) and pick-ups from hostels and hotels.

Major car-hire companies have desks at the airport. Driving along the N2 into the city centre from the airport usually takes 15 to 20 minutes, although during rush hour (7am to 9am and 4.30pm to 6.30pm) this can extend up to an hour.

Expect to pay around R250 for a nonshared taxi.

BICYCLE

If you're prepared for the many hills and long distances between sights, the Cape Peninsula is a terrific place to explore by bicycle. Dedicated cycle lanes are a legacy of the World Cup: there's a good one north out of the city towards Table View, and another runs alongside the Walk of Remembrance from Cape Town Train Station to Green Point. Bear in mind it's nearly 70km from the centre to Cape Point. Unfortunately, bicycles are banned from suburban trains.

Pick up a free copy of the *Cape Town Green Map Cycle Map* at one of the tourist offices or download it from www.capetowngreenmap.co.za/cyclemap.

Check out **Critical Mass Cape Town** (www.facebook.com/CriticalMassCapeTown) for news about the monthly full moon rides from Green Point along Granger Bay Boulevard through Mouille Point and Three Anchor Bay, culminating in Long Street.

Hire

There are numerous places in Cape Town that offer bicycle hire.

&Bikes (021-823 8790; www.andbikes.co.za; 32 Loop St, Foreshore; half-/full day from R150/250; 7.30am-5pm Mon-Fri, 8am-1pm Sat)

Awol Tours (p125) Bikes for rent (per half/full day R200/300).

Bike & Saddle (021-813 6433; www.bikeandsaddle.com; half-/full day R950/1380)

Cape Town Cycle Hire (084 400 1604, 021-434 1270; www.capetowncyclehire.co.za; per day from R300) Delivers and collects bikes free of charge to/ from the City Bowl, and down the Atlantic seaboard to Llandudno.

Downhill Adventures (Map p84; 021-422 0388; www.downhilladventures.com; cnr Orange & Kloof Sts, Gardens; 8am-5pm Mon-Fri, to 1pm Sat; Upper Loop, Upper Long)

Up Cycles (076 135 2223; www.upcycles.co.za; 1hr/half-day/full day R70/200/250) Has pick-up and drop-off points in the **City Bowl** (074 100 9161; www.upcycles.co.za; Breakaway Cafe, 50 Waterkant St, Foreshore; bike rental per hr/day from R70/250; 6am-5pm Mon-Fri; Strand), **Silo District** (www.upcycles.co.za; Silo 5, Silo Sq, V&A Waterfront; one hour/day R70/250; 8.30am-7pm; Nobel Square) at the Waterfront, **Sea Point Pavilion** (p123) and **Camps Bay.** (p123)

BUS

The **MyCiTi** (0800 656 463; www.myciti.org.za) network of commuter buses runs daily between 5am and 10pm, with the most frequent services between 8am and 5pm. Routes cover the city centre up to Gardens and out to the Waterfront; along the Atlantic seaboard to Camps Bay and Hout Bay; up to Tamboerskloof along Kloof Nek Rd, with a shuttle service to the cableway; to Woodstock and Salt River; to Blouberg and Table View; to Khayelitsha; and to the airport.

Fares have to be paid with a stored-value 'myconnect' card (a non-refundable R35), which can be purchased from MyCiTi station kiosks and participating retailers. It's also possible to buy single-trip tickets (R30 or R100 to or from the airport). A bank fee of 2.5% of the loaded value (with a minimum of R1.50) will be charged, eg if you load the card with R200 you will have R195 in credit. The card, issued by ABSA (a national bank), can also be used to pay for low-value transactions at shops and businesses displaying the MasterCard sign.

Fares depend on the time of day (peak-hour fares are charged from 6.45am to 8am and 4.15pm to 5.30pm, Monday to Friday) and whether you have pre-loaded the card with the MyCiTi Mover package (costing between R50 and R1000), which can cut the standard fares by 30%.

For journeys of under 5km (ie from Civic Centre to Gardens or the Waterfront), standard fares are peak/off-peak R13.90/9.10; city centre to Table View is peak/off-peak R17.50/11.70; city centre to airport peak/off-peak R98.80/90.40; city centre to Hout Bay peak/off-peak R17.50/11.70.

The rather old **Golden Arrow** (0800 656 463; www.gabs.co.za) buses run from the Golden Acre Bus Terminal, with most services stopping early in the evening. You might find them handy for journeys into the Cape Flats, Northern Suburbs and south to Wynberg through the Southern Suburbs. The fare to Wynberg is R16.

CAR

Cape Town has an excellent road system. Rush hour is from around 7am to 9pm and 4.30pm to 6.30pm.

Car-hire companies include:

Around About Cars (021-422 4022; www.aroundaboutcars.com; 20 Bloem St, City Bowl; 7.30am-7pm Mon-Fri, to 4pm Sat, 8am-1pm Sun; Upper Long, Upper Loop) Friendly local operation offering one of the best independent deals in town, with rates starting at R140 per day.

Avis (021-424 1177; www.avis.co.za; 123 Strand St, City Bowl; 7am-7pm Mon-Fri, 8am-3pm Sat & Sun; Strand)

Hertz (021-410 6800; www.hertz.co.za; 40 Loop St, City Bowl; 7am-6pm Mon-Fri, 8am-4pm Sat & Sun; Strand)

Status Luxury Vehicles (086 110 0108; www.slv.co.za) Contact them if you wish to cruise around town in a Bentley or a sporty Porsche Boxster S Cab convertible (per day R6550).

Rates range from R140 per day for a Hyundai i10 to around R5000 for a Porsche convertible. Standard rates generally include 100km to 200km per day. If you're sticking to the Cape Peninsula, you will probably get by, but if you plan a few jaunts to the Winelands, Overberg or West Coast, it might be better to opt for unlimited kilometres.

When you're getting quotes, make sure that they include VAT, as that 14% slug makes a big difference.

Parking

Monday to Saturday during business hours there will often be a one-hour limit on parking within the city centre in a particular spot – check with a parking marshal (identified by their luminous yellow vests), who will ask you to pay for the first half-hour up front (around R5).

If there's no official parking marshal, you'll almost always find someone on the street to tip a small amount (say, R5) in exchange for looking after your car. Charges for off-street parking vary, but you can usually find it for R10 per hour.

MOTORCYCLES & SCOOTERS

The following places hire out two-wheeled motors:

Cape Sidecar Adventures (Map p90; 021-434 9855; www.sidecars.co.za; 1 Dickens Rd, Salt River; 2-/4-hr rides R2100/3850) Hire a motorbike chauffeur to drive you around in one of this company's vintage CJ750 sidecars, manufactured between the 1950s and 1970s for the Chinese army to WWII BMW specifications.

Harley Davidson Cape Town (021-401 4260; www.harley-davidson-capetown.com; Harbour Edge Bldg, 2 Hospital St, De Waterkant; 8am-5.30pm Mon-Fri, 8.30am-1pm Sat; Alfred)

Scoot Dr (021-418 5995; www.scootdr.com; Castle Mews, 16 Newmarket St, Foreshore; 8am-5pm Mon-Fri, to 1pm Sat; Strand) Rents out Vespa and Yamaha scooters.

TAXI

Consider taking a nonshared taxi at night or if you're in a group. Rates are about R10 per kilometre. Uber is very popular and works well.

Excite Taxis (021-448 4444; www.excitetaxis.co.za)

Marine Taxi (0861 434 0434, 021-447 0384; www.marinetaxis.co.za)

Rikkis (021-447 3559, 086 174 5547; www.rikkis.co.za)

Telecab (021-788 2717, 082 222 0282) For transfers from Simon's Town to Boulders and Cape Point.

Shared Taxi

The main rank is on the upper deck of Cape Town Train Station, accessible from a walkway in the Golden Acre Centre or from stairways on Strand St. It's well organised and finding the right rank is easy. Anywhere else, you just hail shared taxis from the side of the road and ask the driver where they're going.

TRAIN

Cape Metro Rail (0800 656 463; http://capetowntrains.freeblog.site) trains are a cheap and – potentially – handy way to get around. However, there are few (or no) trains after 6pm on weekdays and after noon on Saturday. The service is also very unreliable, prone to breakdowns and, on certain services, sometimes unsafe. Over 100 carriages have been lost to arson and vandalism since October 2015, all having an impact on punctuality and reliability.

The difference between MetroPlus (first class) and Metro (economy class) carriages in price and comfort is negligible. The most important line for visitors is the Simon's Town line, which runs through Observatory and around the back of Table Mountain, through upper-income suburbs such as Newlands, and on to Muizenberg and the False Bay coast. These trains run at least every hour from 6am to 9pm and, in theory, as often as every 15 minutes during peak times (6am to 9am and 3pm to 6pm).

For all routes security is best at peak times when the carriages are busy – but then they can also be dangerously overcrowded.

Around Cape Town

Includes ➡

Stellenbosch 194
Franschhoek 202
Paarl 207
Tulbagh 211
Robertson 213
The Elgin Valley...........215
Hermanus 216
Gansbaai 220
Stanford 221
Darling........................ 223
Langebaan 224
Paternoster................ 225

Best Places to Eat

- ➡ La Petite Colombe (p206)
- ➡ Die Strandloper (p225)
- ➡ Karoux (p215)
- ➡ Boschendal at Oude Bank (p200)

Best Places to Stay

- ➡ Grootbos Private Nature Reserve (p221)
- ➡ Oudebosch Eco Cabins (p216)
- ➡ Pat Busch Mountain Reserve (p214)
- ➡ Banghoek Place (p199)

Why Go?

There's an abundance of day and overnight trips you can make from Cape Town. Northeast the magnificent mountain ranges around Stellenbosch, Franschhoek and Paarl provide ideal microclimates for growing vines: this is South Africa's premier wine region with a history of over 300 years.

All roads leading to the Overberg are great ones to follow. The N2 up Sir Lowry's Pass takes you to the Elgin Valley, while Rte 44 is a breathtaking coastal drive en route to the whale-watching hot spot of Hermanus. Alternatively, head for less crowded whale-watching spots in Gansbaai, Arniston and the magical De Hoop Nature Reserve. Or, you can't go wrong with a drive along Rte 62 inland towards the Garden Route.

Heading north, the windswept West Coast offers peaceful, whitewashed fishing villages, arty country towns, unspoilt beaches, a lagoon and wetlands teeming with birds.

When to Go

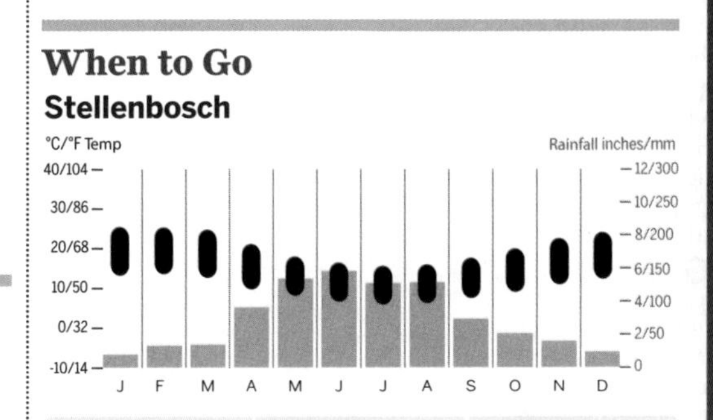

Around Cape Town Highlights

❶ **Stellenbosch** (p194) Exploring an elegant town with colonial architecture, good museums and scores of wineries.

❷ **Franschhoek** (p202) Deciding which of the many excellent restaurants to eat at in this gourmet paradise.

❸ **Paarl** (p207) Admiring old Cape Dutch architecture and vineyards in the Winelands' largest town.

❹ **Robertson** (p213) Heading further afield to the Breede River Valley and dipping into a blissfully uncrowded wine route.

❺ **Hermanus** (p216) Walking the cliff path or taking to the seas in a kayak to watch for whales.

❻ **Stanford** (p221) Having fabulous off-the-beaten-track foodie experiences in this picture-perfect village on the banks of the Klein River.

❼ **Darling** (p223) Attending the village's inimitable drag show, sipping its wine and hanging out with its arty community.

❽ **Langebaan** (p224) Enjoying the seafood restaurants, phenomenal sunsets and kite-surfing lessons on the lagoon.

❾ **Route 62** (p190) Driving from Robertson to Oudtshoorn, stopping off to taste wines, climb rock faces and relax in hot springs.

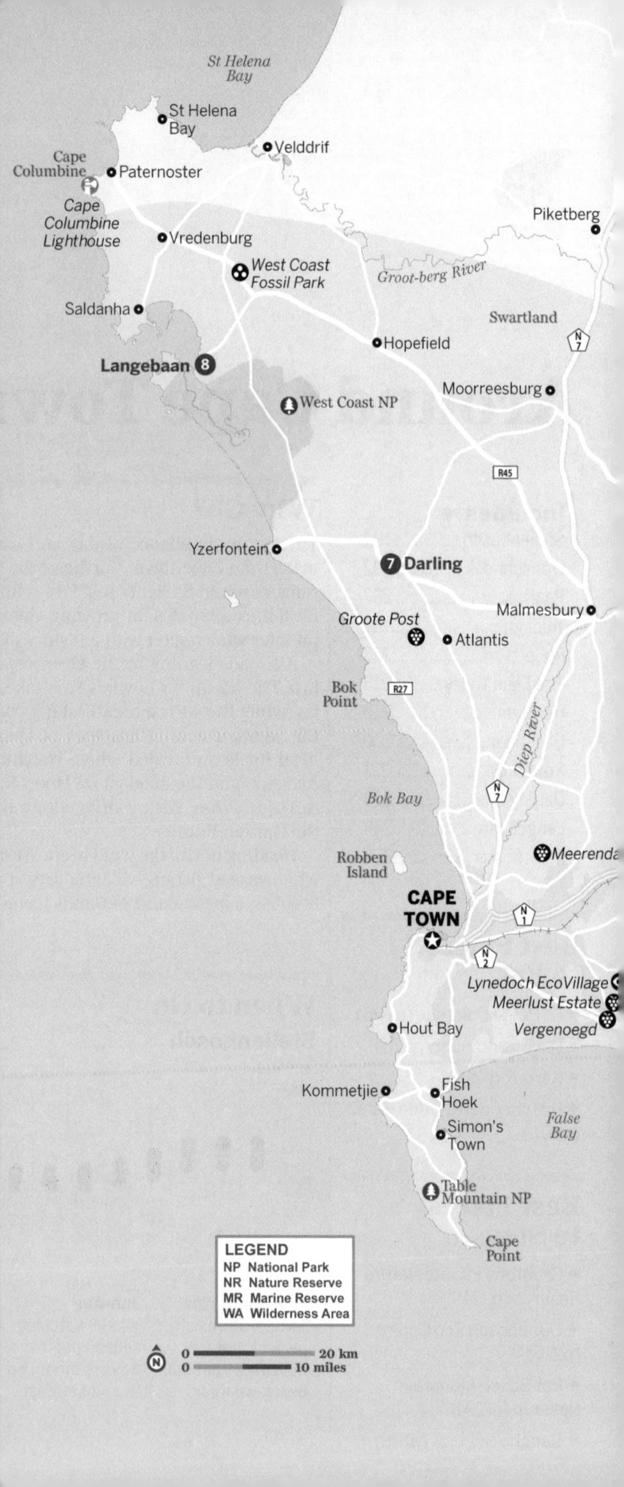

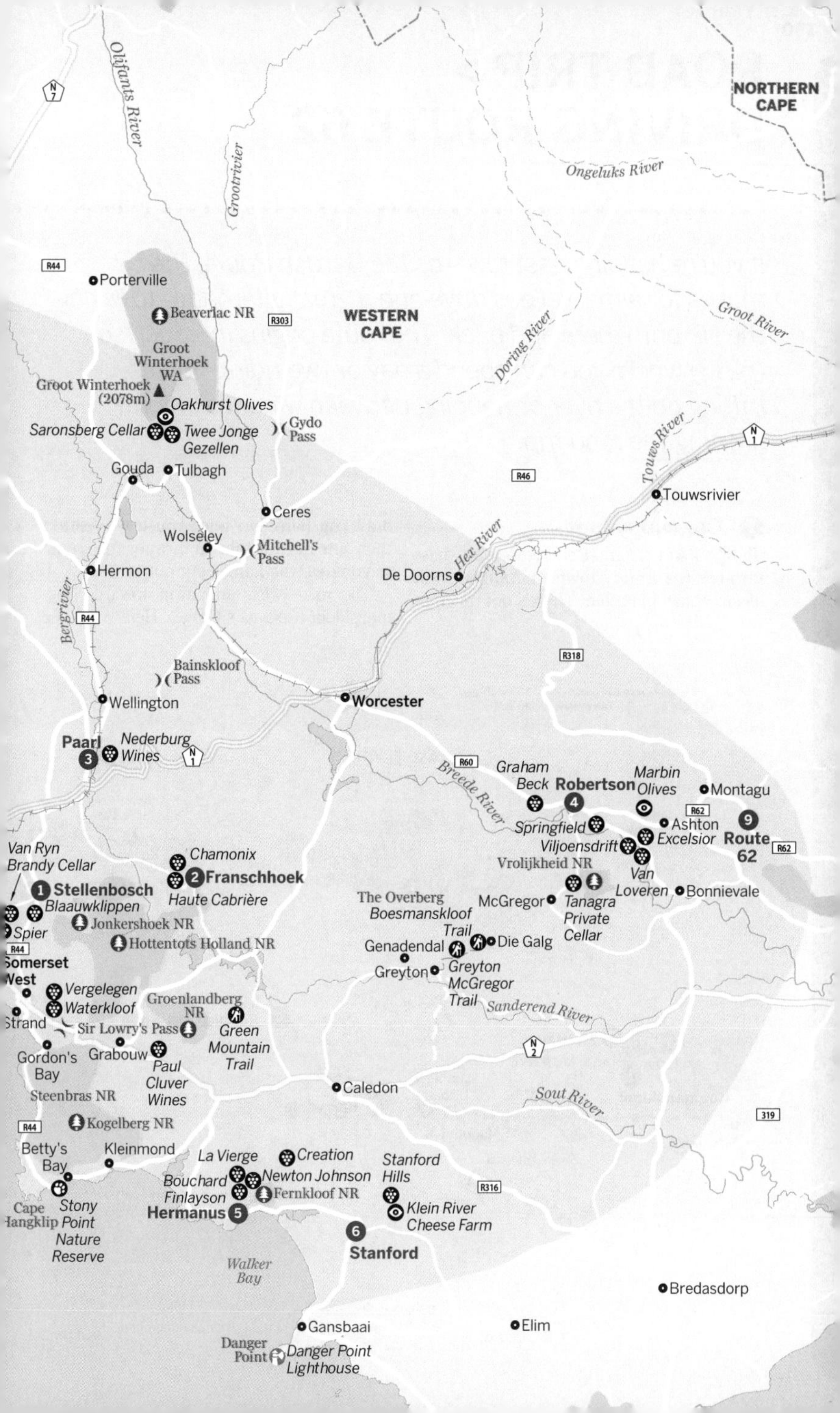

NORTHERN CAPE
WESTERN CAPE
Olifants River
Grootrivier
Ongeluks River
Groot River
Doring River
Touws River
Hex River
Breede River
Bergrivier
Sanderend River
Sout River
Porterville
Beaverlac NR
Groot Winterhoek WA
Groot Winterhoek (2078m)
Oakhurst Olives
Saronsberg Cellar
Twee Jonge Gezellen
Gydo Pass
Gouda
Tulbagh
Ceres
Touwsrivier
Wolseley
Mitchell's Pass
Hermon
De Doorns
Bainskloof Pass
Wellington
Worcester
Paarl
Nederburg Wines
Graham Beck
Robertson
Marbin Olives
Montagu
Ashton
Springfield
Excelsior
Viljoensdrift
Van Loveren
Route 62
Van Ryn Brandy Cellar
Stellenbosch
Chamonix
Franschhoek
Haute Cabrière
Blaauwklippen
Spier
Jonkershoek NR
Hottentots Holland NR
Vrolijkheid NR
The Overberg
Boesmanskloof Trail
McGregor
Tanagra Private Cellar
Bonnievale
Genadendal
Die Galg
Greyton
Greyton McGregor Trail
Somerset West
Vergelegen
Waterkloof
Strand
Groenlandberg NR
Green Mountain Trail
Sir Lowry's Pass
Gordon's Bay
Grabouw
Paul Cluver Wines
Caledon
Steenbras NR
Kogelberg NR
Betty's Bay
Kleinmond
La Vierge
Creation
Newton Johnson
Bouchard Finlayson
Fernkloof NR
Stanford Hills
Klein River Cheese Farm
Hermanus
Stanford
Cape Hangklip
Stony Point Nature Reserve
Walker Bay
Bredasdorp
Gansbaai
Elim
Danger Point
Danger Point Lighthouse
N7
N1
N2
R44
R303
R46
R318
R60
R62
R316
319

ROAD TRIP > DRIVING ROUTE 62

If you're heading east towards the Garden Route, Rte 62 makes for a marvellous drive and a great alternative to taking the N2 both there and back. The route begins in Robertson (p213) where you can spend a day or two riding horses, rafting on the river or hopping between wineries before starting the road trip.

1 Cogmanskloof

About 15km from Robertson you pass through the untidy town of **Ashton** with its sizeable wine cellar. There's not much to hold you here, but once you leave Ashton the route quickly takes a turn for the scenic as you near the Langeberg range.

The road twists and turns towards Cogmanskloof (Cogmans Gorge). Here you'll see

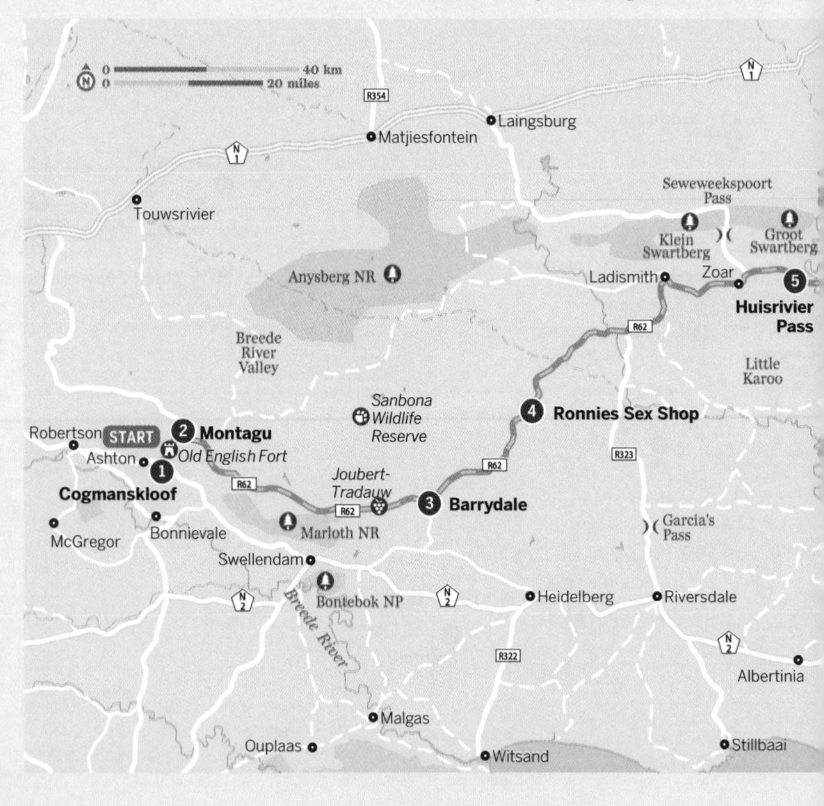

3 to 4 days 260km/161 miles

Great for... Food & Drink

September–November Enjoy Springtime greenery

a sign denoting the **Old English Fort**. Built in 1899 in anticipation of the Anglo-Boer War, the fort sits above the road – keep an eye out for it as you pass through an archway in the mountains which heralds your arrival in Montague.

2 Montagu

Pretty Montagu's wide streets are bordered by 24 restored national monuments, including some fine art deco architecture. There's plenty to do here for visitors, including taking a dip in the hot springs at **Avalon Springs** (023-614 1150; www.avalonsprings.co.za; Uitvlucht St; Mon-Fri R55, Sat & Sun R100; 8am-8pm;) and a number of walks and superlative **rock climbing** (082 696 4067; www.montaguclimbing.com; 45 Mount St; 2hr climbing/abseiling trip R750/400).

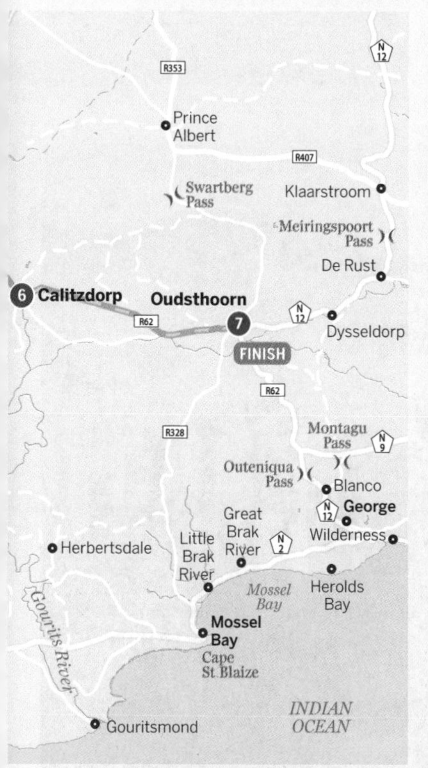

Excellent accommodation includes the upmarket guesthouses **7 Church Street** (023-614 1186; www.7churchstreet.co.za; 7 Church St; d incl breakfast from R1500;) and pleasantly located **Montagu Caravan Park** (082 920 7863; www.montagucaravanpark.co.za; 4 Middel St; camping R100, 4-person chalet from R800;). At **Barn on 62** (082 824 2995; 60 Long St; mains R50-80; 8.30am-4pm Tue-Sun;) enjoy lunch or a slice of cake with Montagu's best cup of coffee in a shady garden with a kids' play area.

Leaving Montagu, the road straightens out and passes by orchards. This is perhaps the least interesting stretch of the trip, but do keep an eye out for **Joubert-Tradauw** (028-125 0086; www.joubert-tradauw.co.za; tastings R30; 9am-5pm Mon-Fri, 10am-2pm Sat;) after about 50km. The winery makes for a lovely lunch stop and offers tastings – grab a bottle of its R62 red blend as a memento of your drive. From here it's only 12km to Barrydale.

3 Barrydale

Barrydale is one of Rte 62's most underrated treats. Venture off the main road and you'll find stylish accommodation, small galleries and quirky restaurants with a bohemian feel. Hiking, birdwatching and the Big Five are on offer in **Sanbona Wildlife Reserve** (021-010 0028; www.sanbona.com; d incl meals & wildlife drives from R11,900;), 18km west of the town.

Although **Barrydale Cellar** (028-572 1012; www.barrydalewines.co.za; 1 Van Riebeeck St; tastings R30; tasting room 9am-5pm Mon-Fri, to 3pm Sat, pizzeria 11.30am-5pm Tue-Sun;) looks characterless and industrial from the roadside, its tasting room and restaurant on the river bank are actually quite charming. The cellar is best known for brandy but you can also taste wine or beer brewed at the on-site microbrewery. There's a kids' play area inside and wood-fired pizzas on the menu (mains R75 to R90).

4 Ronnies Sex Shop

Some 27km east of Barrydale, you can't miss the tatty whitewashed building on the right, with fluttering flags and untidy lettering proclaiming that you have reached 'Ronnies Sex Shop'. **Ronnies** (☎028-572 1153; www.ronniessexshop.co.za; ⊙8.30am-9pm) has become one of the most famous spots on Rte 62. It began life as a simple shop and the owner, struggling to get customers in, painted 'Ronnies Shop' on the facade. Some prankster pals added the word 'sex' and suggested he start a bar rather than sticking with the road stall idea. Today Ronnies is a dingy biker bar and most don't stick around longer than it takes to snap a few photos of the bar, endowed with row upon row of bras and knickers. Nearby there is a spa with warm water pumped from underground springs.

5 Huisrivier Pass

The scenery remains the same – undulating semidesert scrubland typical of the Little Karoo – until you pass Ladismith, a pleasant town with a couple of decent farm stalls, and Zoar, a small farming settlement. Suddenly the mountains begin to rise and you reach the highly scenic Huisrivier Pass, which counts two river crossings along its 13km of dips and hills. This is the prettiest part of the drive, so take time to stop at one of the lay-bys set up for view-hunters.

Ostriches, Oudtshoorn

MERTEN SNIJDERS/GETTY IMAGES ©

Ronnies Sex Shop (p191)

6 Calitzdorp

On the other side of the pass is Calitzdorp, best known for its port-style wines. The main road isn't the most relaxing place to pause, but turn right onto Van Riebeek St and you'll find a higgledy-piggledy maze of roads lined with handsome old buildings. There are wineries within walking distance of the town, including **Boplaas** (044-213 3326; www.boplaas.co.za; Saayman St; tastings R30; 9am-5pm Mon-Fri, to 3pm Sat, 10am-2pm Sun; P) and **De Krans** (044-213 3314; www.dekrans.co.za; Station Rd; tastings R30; 9am-4.30pm, bistro closed Tue; P). Sample the various dessert wines or pop into **Porto Deli** (044-213 3007; Calitz St, cnr Voortrekker St; mains R85-180; 11am-3.30pm & 6-9pm) for a lunch inspired by Portuguese and Mozambican cuisine.

Should you decide to stay over, **Port-Wine Guest House** (044-213 3131; www.portwine.net; 7 Queen St; d incl breakfast R900;) is a beautifully appointed, thatched Cape cottage with four-poster beds.

7 Oudtshoorn

Oudtshoorn likes to call itself the 'ostrich capital of the world', with its industry that dates back to Victorian times. The town lies 55km east of Calitzdorp and is home to a number of ostrich farms where you can learn about the industry and meet the birds. This is also the home of the impressive **Cango Caves** (044-272 7410; www.cango-caves.co.za; adult/child R110/65; 9am-4pm; P); the interesting **CP Nel Museum** (044-272 7306; www.cpnelmuseum.co.za; 3 Baron van Rheede St; adult/child R25/5; 8am-5pm Mon-Fri, 9am-1pm Sat) with its extensive displays about ostriches and Karoo history; and the much-loved **Meerkat Adventures** (084 772 9678; www.meerkatadventures.co.za; per person R600), a dawn wildlife encounter with the curious meerkats as they emerge from their burrows to warm up in the morning sun.

Recommended places to stay include the hostel **Karoo Soul Travel Lodge** (044-272 0330; www.karoosoul.com; 1 Adderley St; dm R160, d with shared bathroom R480; P) and the stylish guesthouse **La Pension** (044-279 2445; www.lapension.co.za; 169 Church St; s/d incl breakfast from R800/1200; P) while a meal at **Jemima's** (044-272 0808; www.jemimas.com; 94 Baron van Rheede St; mains R75-200; 11am-11pm) is a great way to celebrate the near end of your road trip. Make for the N12, which connects Oudtshoorn with the Garden Route.

WINELANDS

Immediately inland and upwards from Cape Town you'll find the Boland, meaning 'upland'. It's a superb wine-producing area, and indeed the best known in South Africa.

There's been colonial settlement here since the latter half of the 17th century, when the Dutch first founded Stellenbosch and the French Huguenots settled in Franschhoek. Both towns pride themselves on their innovative young chefs, many based at wine estates, and the region has become the mainspring of South African cuisine. Along with Paarl, these towns make up the core of the Winelands, but there are many more wine-producing places to explore. Pretty Tulbagh, with its many historical buildings, is known for MCC (Méthode Cap Classique – the local version of Champagne), and Robertson's scattered wineries offer unpretentious, family friendly places to taste.

Stellenbosch

☎021 / POP 155,000

If there's one thing that Stellenbosch is renowned for, it is wine. There are hundreds of estates scattered around the outskirts of the town, many of which produce world-class wines. A tour of the wineries with their many tasting options and superlative restaurants will likely form the backbone of your visit, but there is a lot more to see.

An elegant, historical town with stately Cape Dutch, Georgian and Victorian architecture along its oak-lined streets, Stellenbosch is full of interesting museums, quality hotels and a selection of bars, clubs and restaurants. A university town, it is constantly abuzz with locals, students, Capetonians and tourists.

OFF THE BEATEN TRACK

LYNEDOCH ECOVILLAGE

An initiative of the Sustainability Institute, **Lynedoch EcoVillage** (☎021-881 3196; www.sustainabilityinstitute.net) is an ecologically designed and socially mixed, self-sustaining community. You can visit and learn more about the community projects or join one of the short courses covering topics such as sustainable development and food security. There is a cafe that uses produce grown in the community garden and simple accommodation is also available (double from R500).

Established by the governor of the Cape (Simon van der Stel) in 1679 on the banks of the Eerste River, Stellenbosch was – and still is – famed for its rich soil, just what was needed to produce vegetables and wine for ships stopping off at the Cape.

Sights

The Town

Stellenbosch University Botanical Garden PARK
(Map p196; ☎021-808 3054; www.sun.ac.za/botanicalgarden; cnr Neethling & Van Riebeeck Sts; R10; ⊙8am-5pm) This glorious inner-city garden is an unsung Stellenbosch sight and well worth a wander. Themed gardens include a bonsai area and tropical glasshouse, and there's a host of indigenous plants. For those not mad about botany, it's a peaceful place to walk and there's a pleasant tea garden for coffee, cake or a light lunch (mains R55 to R130).

Village Museum MUSEUM
(Map p196; ☎021-887 2937; www.stelmus.co.za; 18 Ryneveld St; adult/child R35/15; ⊙9am-5pm Mon-Sat year-round, 10am-1pm Sun Apr-Aug, to 4pm Sun Sep-Mar) A group of exquisitely restored and period-furnished houses dating from 1709 to 1850 make up this museum, which is a must-see. At each house you'll find a staff member in relevant period costume ready to tell tales about the house's history. Also included are charming gardens and a small exhibition at the main entrance.

University Museum MUSEUM
(Map p196; 52 Ryneveld St; by donation; ⊙10am-4.30pm Mon, 9am-4.30pm Tue-Sat) This fabulous Flemish Renaissance-style building houses an interesting and varied collection of local art, an array of African anthropological treasures and exhibits on South African culture and history.

Jonkershoek Nature Reserve NATURE RESERVE
(☎021-866 1560; www.capenature.co.za; Jonkershoek Rd; adult/child R40/20; ⊙7.30am-4pm) This small nature reserve is 8km southeast of town and set within a timber plantation. There is a 10km scenic drive, plus hiking trails ranging from 5km to 18km. A hiking map is available at the entrance.

Braak PARK
(Map p196; Town Sq) At the north end of the Braak, an open stretch of grass, you'll find the neo-Gothic **St Mary's on the Braak Church**

WORTH A TRIP

HELDERBERG

There are around 30 wineries in the Helderberg region, an offshoot of the Stellenbosch wine route. Sitting on the lower slopes of the Helderberg mountains near Somerset West, this region has some of the country's oldest estates.

If you have time, also consider visiting **Helderberg Nature Reserve** (☎021-851 4060; www.helderbergnaturereserve.co.za; Verster Ave, Somerset West; adult/child R20/10, per vehicle R15; ⏲7.30am-7pm Nov-Mar, to 5.30pm Apr-Oct; P). There are several short day trails and you're likely to see tortoises, bonteboks and plenty of fynbos (literally 'fine bush' – indigenous vegetation featuring ericas and proteas).

Simon van der Stel's son Willem first planted vines at **Vergelegen** (☎021-847 2100; www.vergelegen.co.za; Lourensford Rd, Somerset West; adult/child R10/5, tastings from R30, tours R50; ⏲9am-5pm, garden tour 10am, cellar tour 11am & 3pm; P ♿) in 1700. The buildings and elegant grounds have ravishing mountain views and a 'stately home' feel to them. You can take a tour of the gardens, a cellar tour or just enjoy a tasting of four of the estate's wines. Tasting the flagship Vergelegen Red costs an extra R10. There are also two restaurants.

The bistro-style **Stables** (mains R80 to R165, 9am to 5pm) overlooks the Rose Garden and has a super cool kids' playground. For a more upmarket meal, try **Camphors** (three courses R395, noon to 3pm Wednesday to Sunday, 6.30pm to 9pm Friday and Saturday). Picnic hampers (R255 per person, November to April only) are also available – bookings are essential for these and Camphors.

The stunning contemporary architecture at **Waterkloof** (☎021-858 1292; www.waterkloofwines.co.za; Sir Lowry's Pass Village Rd, Somerset West; tastings from R40; ⏲10am-5pm Mon-Sat, 11am-5pm Sun; P) is a fine contrast to the familiar Cape Dutch buildings at older estates. The estate specialises in biodynamic wines and ecofriendly farming methods – take a two-hour guided walk (10am and 4.30pm, R710 with two-course lunch/dinner) around the estate to learn more. Horse riding (R750 with lunch) is also offered, and if you're feeling particularly flush you could fly in from Cape Town by helicopter (R11,250 per person with six-course meal). The restaurant is one of the Winelands' best and advance bookings are recommended.

(Map p196; ☎021-887 6912; Braak; ⏲by appointment 9am-4pm Mon-Fri) FREE, completed in 1852. West of the church is the **VOC Kruithuis** (Powder House; Map p196; Market St; adult/child R5/2; ⏲9am-2pm Mon-Fri Sep-May), built in 1777 to store the town's weapons and gunpowder – it now houses a small military museum. On the northwest corner of the square is **Fick House**, a fine example of Cape Dutch architecture from the late 18th century.

Toy & Miniature Museum MUSEUM
(Map p196; ☎021-882 8861; Rhenish Parsonage, 42 Market St; adult/child R15/5; ⏲9am-4.30pm Mon-Fri, to 2pm Sat; ♿) This delightful museum features a remarkable collection of detailed toys ranging from railway sets to dollhouses. The highlight for kids is probably the model railway, which operates on R5 coins.

Wineries Around Stellenbosch

There is an abundance of good wineries in the Stellenbosch area. Get the free booklet *Stellenbosch and Its Wine Routes* from Stellenbosch Tourism (p201) for the complete picture.

★ **Spier** WINERY
(☎021-809 1100; www.spier.co.za; Rte 310; tastings from R40; ⏲9am-5pm Mon-Wed, to 6pm Thu-Sat, 11am-6pm Sun; P ♿) Spier has some excellent shiraz, cabernet and red blends, though a visit to this vast winery is less about wine and more about the other activities available. There are superb birds-of-prey displays (adult/child R75/65), Segway tours through the vines, three restaurants, and picnics to enjoy in the grounds. Look out for special events in the summer months, including open-air cinema evenings and live entertainment.

★ **Warwick Estate** WINERY
(Map p198; ☎021-884 4410; www.warwickwine.com; tastings R50, wine safari R80; ⏲9am-5pm; P ♿) Warwick's red wines are legendary, particularly its Bordeaux blends. The winery offers an informative Big Five wine safari (referring to grape varieties, not large mammals) through the vineyards and picnics (R550 for two people) to enjoy on the lawns. Advance bookings are required for picnics, but simple cheeseboards are available if you just rock up.

Stellenbosch

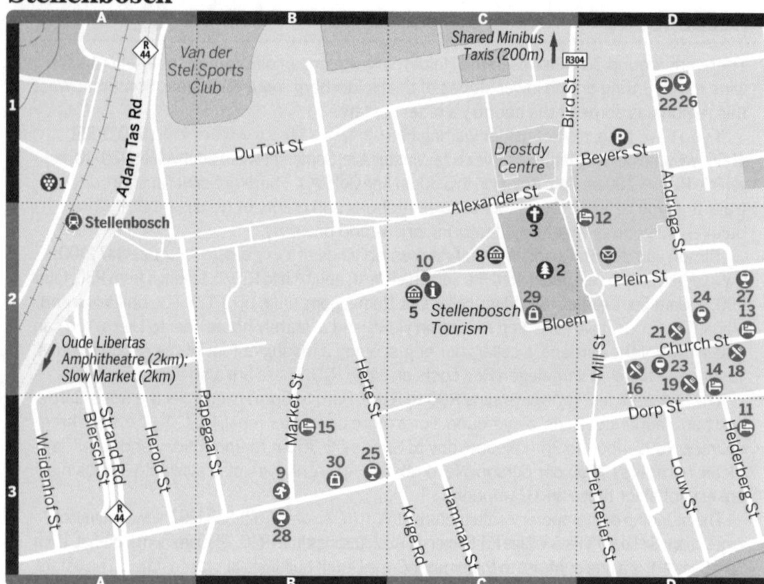

Stellenbosch

Sights

1 Bergkelder A1
2 Braak C2
3 St Mary's on the Braak Church C2
4 Stellenbosch University Botanical Garden E2
5 Toy & Miniature Museum C2
6 University Museum E1
7 Village Museum E2
8 VOC Kruithuis C2

Activities, Courses & Tours

9 Adventure Shop B3
Easy Rider Wine Tours .... (see 15)
10 Guided Walk C2
Vine Hopper .... (see 9)

Sleeping

11 Bertha's Guest Flats D3
12 Ikhaya Backpackers D2
13 Oude Werf Hotel D2
14 Stellenbosch Hotel D2
15 Slumble Inn B3

Eating

16 Boschendal at Oude Bank D2
17 Decameron E2
18 Helena's D2
19 Jardine D2
20 Katjiepiering Restaurant F1
21 Wijnhuis D2

Drinking & Nightlife

22 Bohemia D1
23 Brampton Wine Studio D2
24 Craft Wheat & Hops D2
25 De Akker B3
26 Mystic Boer D1
27 Nu Bar D2
28 Trumpet Tree B3

Shopping

29 Craft Market C2
30 Oom Samie se Winkel B3

Villiera WINERY
(Map p198; 021-865 2002; www.villiera.com; tastings R30; 9am-5pm Mon-Fri, to 3pm Sat; P) Villiera produces several excellent Méthode Cap Classique wines and a highly rated and well-priced shiraz. Excellent two-hour wildlife drives (adult/child R220/110) with knowledgable guides take in antelope, zebras, giraffes and various bird species on the farm and are followed by a tasting. Bookings are essential for the game drives.

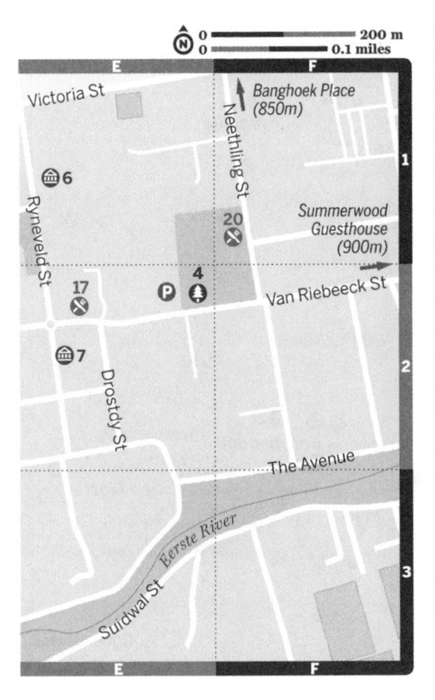

Bergkelder WINERY

(Map p196; ☎021-809 8025; www.fleurducap.co.za/die-bergkelder; George Blake St; tastings R65; ⏲9am-5pm Mon-Fri, to 2pm Sat; P) For wine lovers without wheels, this cellar a short walk from the town centre is ideal. Hour-long tours (R60) are followed by an atmospheric candlelit tasting in the cellar. The tours run at 10am, 11am, 2pm and 3pm Monday to Friday, and at 10am, 11am and noon Saturday. A wine and salt pairing (R110) is also on offer. Bookings are required for all activities.

Delaire Graff Estate WINERY

(Map p198; ☎021-885 8160; www.delaire.co.za; Helshoogte Pass; tastings from R65; ⏲tastings 10am-5pm; P) The views are magnificent from this 'vineyard in the sky', which has a gorgeous hotel and spa and two gourmet restaurants including **Indochine** (mains R225 to R410), which specialises in pan-Asian cuisine. Their wines get top marks from critics.

Art buffs will be thrilled to know that the original painting of the *Chinese Girl* by Vladimir Tretchikoff is on display in the estate's diamond boutique.

Tokara WINERY

(Map p198; ☎021-808 5900; www.tokara.co.za; Rte 310; tastings R75-100; ⏲10am-5.30pm; P) Tokara is renowned for its excellent wines – particularly chardonnay and sauvignon blanc – and for its upmarket restaurant (mains R210 to R260; bookings advised), fine art collection and sleek design. In summer enjoy intricate dishes and mountain views. In winter, snuggle up by the fire with a taster of the noble late harvest (dessert wine) or pot still brandy (R25). There's a fantastic deli/sculpture gallery for less fancy lunches (mains R110 to R150), and you can taste the estate's olive oil.

Hartenberg Estate WINERY

(Map p198; ☎021-865 2541; www.hartenbergestate.com; Bottelary Rd; tastings R40; ⏲9am-5pm Mon-Fri, 9am-4pm Sat, 10am-4pm Sun Oct-Apr, closed Sun May-Sep; P) Thanks to a favourable microclimate, Hartenberg produces super red wines, particularly cabernet, merlot and shiraz. Light lunches in the courtyard are available (mains R70 to R130), and from October to April gourmet picnics (adult/child R230/90) can be enjoyed under trees on the lawns (bookings essential). Kids are well catered for with a trampoline and jungle gym.

Vergenoegd WINERY

(☎021-843 3248; www.vergenoegd.co.za; Baden Powell Dr; tastings R50; ⏲8am-5pm Mon-Sat, 10am-4pm Sun) Other than tastings, there's lots of kid-friendly fun, including a chance to meet the workforce of ducks that help keep the vineyards pest- and pesticide-free. There's also plenty for adults including the opportunity to blend your own tea, coffee, wine and olive oil (R250 per experience). Picnics (adult/child R450/125) can be nibbled on the lawns or in the old barn, and there's a popular market on Sundays, featuring food, crafts and an awesome kids' area.

Van Ryn Brandy Cellar WINERY

(☎021-881 3875; www.vanryn.co.za; off Rte 310; tastings R55-90, tour & tasting R75-115; ⏲9am-5.30pm Mon-Fri, 9am-3.30pm Sat, 11am-3.30pm Sun Oct-Apr, closed Sun May-Sep) This brandy distillery runs superb tours (10am, 11.30am and 3pm), which include a barrel-making display and end with your choice of tasting. Options include pairing brandy with chocolate or sampling brandy cocktails.

Marianne Wines WINERY

(Map p198; ☎021-875 5040; www.mariannewines.com; Rte 44; tastings R60; ⏲11am-6pm) Perched at the end of a rutted road, Marianne has a light-filled tasting room and a scenic balcony on which to sip. You can try pairing wine with biltong (R95) or a selection of sweets (R65). Wine buffs should book ahead for the vertical

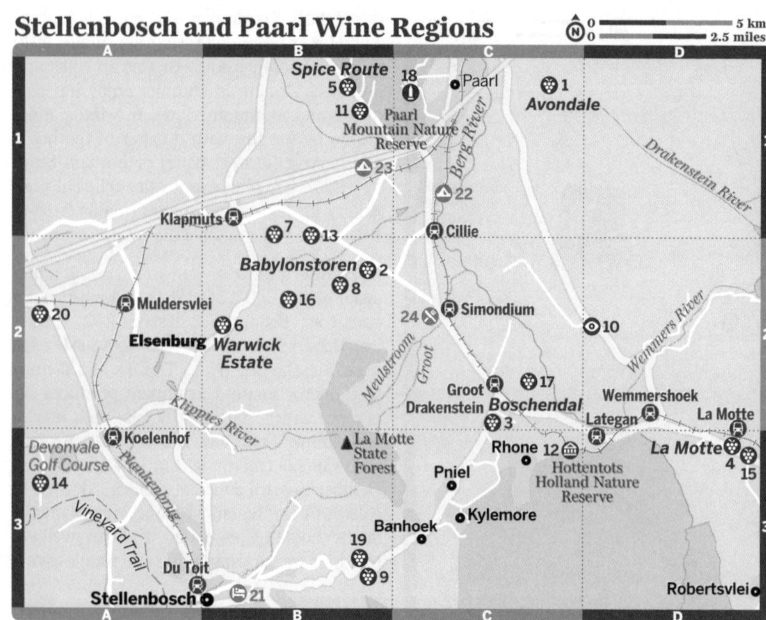

Stellenbosch and Paarl Wine Regions

Top Sights

1	Avondale	C1
2	Babylonstoren	B2
3	Boschendal	C2
4	La Motte	D3
5	Spice Route	B1
6	Warwick Estate	B2

Sights

7	Anura	B1
8	Backsberg	B2
9	Delaire Graff Estate	B3
10	Drakenstein Correctional Centre	D2
11	Fairview	B1
12	Franschhoek Motor Museum	C3
13	Glen Carlou	B1
14	Hartenberg Estate	A3
15	Leopard's Leap	D3
16	Marianne Wines	B2
17	Solms-Delta	C2
18	Taal Monument	C1
19	Tokara	B3
20	Villiera	A2

Sleeping

21	Banghoek Place	B3
22	Berg River Resort	C1
23	Ingonyama Tented Camp	B1

Eating

	Fyndraai Restaurant	(see 17)
	Glen Carlou	(see 13)
24	Lust Bistro & Bakery	C2
	Pierneef à la Motte	(see 4)

tasting (R200) – four vintages of the flagship Floreal, a red blend. There's a restaurant and accommodation on the premises if you can't tear yourself away.

Meerlust Estate WINERY

(☎021-843 3587; www.meerlust.com; Rte 310; tastings R30; ⏰9am-5pm Mon-Fri, 10am-2pm Sat) Hannes Myburgh is the eighth generation of his family to have run this historic wine estate since 1756. Most famous for its Rubicon claret, it's a much quieter alternative to many wineries, with no restaurant or pairing options.

Its tasting room, decorated with the owner's collection of posters and a fine history of the winery, is worth a look.

Blaauwklippen WINERY

(☎021-880 0133; www.blaauwklippen.com; Rte 44; tastings R79; ⏰10am-5pm, cellar tours 11am & 2pm; P 👪) This rustic, 300-year-old estate with several fine Cape Dutch buildings is known for its excellent red wines, particularly its cabernet sauvignon and zinfandel. There's a wine and chocolate pairing option (R135) and lunch is available (mains R75 to

R135). On Sundays there's a popular market with food, crafts and horse-and-carriage rides around the estate.

Activities & Tours

★ **Bikes 'n Wines** TOURS
(021-823 8790; www.bikesnwines.com; tours from R795) This carbon-negative company comes highly recommended. Cycling routes range from 9km to 21km and take in three or four Stellenbosch wineries. There are also Cape Town city tours and trips to lesser-visited wine regions such as Elgin, Wellington and Hermanus.

Adventure Shop CYCLING
(Map p196; 021-882 8112; www.adventureshop.co.za; cnr Dorp & Market Sts; per hr/day R80/250) A good option for bicycle rental if you're not interested in a tour, though it does offer guided bike rides and a huge range of other trips and activities as well.

Vine Hopper TOURS
(Map p196; 021-882 8112; www.vinehopper.co.za; cnr Dorp & Market Sts; 1-/2-day pass R300/540) A hop-on, hop-off bus with three routes each covering five or six estates. There are seven departures per day, departing from Stellenbosch Tourism (p201), where you can buy tickets. You can also buy tickets at Vine Hopper's office on the corner of Dorp and Market Sts.

Guided Walk WALKING
(Map p196; 021-883 3584; 36 Market St; R140; 11am & 3pm Mon-Fri, 9.30am Sat & Sun) If you've had all the wine you can take, Stellenbosch's many historical buildings are worth a visit. Guided 90-minute walks around town leave from Stellenbosch Tourism. Evening ghost walks are also available if you book ahead.

Easy Rider Wine Tours TOURS
(Map p196; 021-886 4651; www.winetour.co.za; 12 Market St) This long-established company operates from the Stumble Inn and offers good value for a full-day trip at R650 including lunch and all tastings.

Festivals & Events

Stellenbosch Wine Festival WINE
(www.stellenboschwinefestival.co.za; Feb) This event in late February offers visitors the chance to sample wines from more than 60 vineyards all in one spot as well as attend talks and tutorials on wine. There's also live music and kids' entertainment.

Sleeping

★ **Banghoek Place** HOSTEL $
(Map p198; 021-887 0048; www.banghoek.co.za; 193 Banghoek Rd; dm/r incl breakfast R200/700; P) This stylish suburban hostel provides a quiet budget alternative, away from the town centre. The recreation area has satellite TV and a pool table and there's a nice swimming pool in the garden.

Bertha's Guest Flats APARTMENT $
(Map p196; 021-887 4113; www.berthasguestflats.com; 16 Helderberg St; apt from R720; P) Some of the furnishings are a bit chintzy, but you can't beat this spot for good-value in a central location. Each apartment sleeps up to four people and comes with a well-equipped kitchen and satellite TV plus there's a shared garden. Minimum stay of three nights.

Ikhaya Backpackers HOSTEL $
(Map p196; 021-883 8550; www.stellenboschbackpackers.co.za; 56 Bird St; dm R165, d with shared bathroom R460;) The central location means you're within easy stumbling distance of some of the more popular bars. Rooms are in converted apartments, so each dorm comes with its own kitchen and bathroom, shared with the adjoining double rooms.

Stumble Inn HOSTEL $
(Map p196; 021-887 4049; www.stumbleinnbackpackers.co.za; 12 Market St; camping per site R120, dm R180, d with shared bathroom R500; P) Although it's grown up in recent years, this is still Stellenbosch's party hostel. It's split over two old houses – the second building is the quieter option, away from the bar. The wine tours are recommended.

Summerwood Guesthouse GUESTHOUSE $$
(021-887 4112; www.summerwood.co.za; 28 Jonkershoek Rd; s/d incl breakfast from R1750/2400; P) In a suburban neighbourhood bordering a small nature reserve east of the town centre is this elegant guesthouse. The immaculate rooms are bright and spacious, with excellent amenities. Rates drop considerably between April and September.

Stellenbosch Hotel HISTORIC HOTEL $$
(Map p196; 021-887 3644; www.stellenboschhotel.co.za; 162 Dorp St, cnr Andringa St; s/d incl breakfast from R1290/1490; P) A comfortable country-style hotel with a variety of rooms, including some with self-catering facilities and others with four-poster beds. A section dating from 1743 houses the Stellenbosch Kitchen (mains R110 to R190), a good spot for a drink and some people-watching.

Oude Werf Hotel HISTORIC HOTEL $$
(Map p196; 021-887 4608; www.oudewerfhotel.co.za; 30 Church St; r incl breakfast from R2400;) This appealing, old-style hotel dates back to 1802, though it has had a dramatic facelift. Deluxe rooms are furnished with antiques and brass beds, while the superior and luxury rooms are bright and modern.

Lanzerac Hotel & Spa LUXURY HOTEL $$$
(021-887 1132; www.lanzerac.co.za; Lanzerac Rd, Jonkershoek Valley; P) This opulent place consists of a 300-year-old manor house and winery set in grassy grounds with awesome mountain views. One suite even has a private pool. The hotel was severely damaged by a fire in mid-2017 and is closed for renovations until October 2018.

Eating

The town centre has a few excellent restaurants and plenty of casual cafes. Many of the best restaurants though are found on wine estates. These often offer a fine-dining experience and should be booked ahead.

★ **Boschendal at Oude Bank** BAKERY $
(Map p196; 021-870 4287; www.decompanje.co.za; cnr Church & Bird Sts; mains R75-120; 7am-5pm Mon-Fri, 8am-5pm Sat & Sun;) A vibrant bakery and bistro priding itself on locally sourced ingredients. The menu features salads, sandwiches and mezze-style platters, as well as fresh cakes and pastries and local craft beer. There are tables on the pavement, while inside has a market-hall feel, with plenty of seating and some shops to browse.

Root 44 Market MARKET $
(021-881 3052; www.root44.co.za; Audacia Winery, Rte 44; dishes R40-90; 10am-4pm Sat & Sun; P) A large indoor-outdoor market with fresh produce, plenty of crafts and clothing as well as wine by the glass, draught craft beer and a host of food stalls serving everything from pad Thai to burgers to slabs of cake.

Slow Market MARKET $
(021-886 8514; www.slowmarket.co.za; Oude Libertas Rd, Oude Libertas; 9am-2pm Sat; P) Stellenbosch's original farmers market features lots of artisanal produce as well as crafts.

Katjiepiering Restaurant CAFE $
(Map p196; Van Riebeeck St; mains R50-120; 9am-5pm) Tucked away in the corner of the botanical garden (p194) and surrounded by exotic plants, this is a lovely spot for coffee, cake or a light lunch. Some traditional meals are served.

96 Winery Road INTERNATIONAL $$
(021-842 2020; www.96wineryroad.co.za; Zandberg Farm, Winery Rd; mains R135-225; noon-10pm Mon-Sat, to 3.30pm Sun; P) Off Rte 44 between Stellenbosch and Somerset West, this is a long-established restaurant, best known for its dry aged beef. There's plenty of other meat on the menu, plus two token vegetarian dishes.

Wijnhuis ITALIAN $$
(Map p196; 021-887 5844; www.wijnhuis.co.za; cnr Andringa & Church Sts; mains R120-220; 9am-11pm) There's an interesting menu and an extensive wine list with more than 500 choices. Around 20 wines are available by the glass and tastings are available (R50).

Decameron ITALIAN $$
(Map p196; 021-883 3331; 50 Plein St; mains R85-165; noon-9.30pm Mon-Sat) This Italian-food stalwart of Stellenbosch's dining scene has a shady patio next to the botanical garden.

★ **Rust en Vrede** FUSION $$$
(021-881 3757; www.rustenvrede.com; Annandale Rd; 4-course menu R720, 6-course menu with/without wines R1450/850; 6.30-11pm Tue-Sat) Expect innovative dishes like rabbit-leg wontons or beetroot chocolate fondant at this stylish winery restaurant. Book ahead.

Jardine FUSION $$$
(Map p196; 021-886-5020; www.restaurantjardine.co.za; 1 Andringa St; lunch R160-220, 3-/6-course dinner R380/580; noon-2pm & 6.30-8pm Wed-Sat) Celebrated chef George Jardine of the long-established Jordan restaurant opened this small and very special spot in 2016. The emphasis is on local produce showcased in simple but extraordinarily good dishes. Book ahead.

Jordan BISTRO, BAKERY $$$
(021-881 3612; www.jordanwines.com; Stellenbosch Kloof Rd; bakery R90-135, 3-course menu R425; bakery 8am-4pm, restaurant noon-2pm & 6.30-10.30pm Thu-Sat, noon-2pm Sun-Wed; P) It's a little off the beaten Stellenbosch path, but it's worth the drive to get to this well-respected restaurant in a winery. The delectable menu is filled with high-end, inventive dishes, and, for those looking for something more casual, the bakery serves salads and cheese platters with freshly baked bread.

Overture Restaurant FUSION $$$
(021-880 2721; https://bertusbasson.com; Hidden Valley Wine Estate, off Annandale Rd; 3-/6-course menu R510/735; noon-3pm daily, 7-11pm Thu-Sat)

A modern wine estate and restaurant where celebrated TV chef Bertus Basson focuses on local, seasonal produce prepared to perfection and paired with Hidden Valley wines.

Helena's SOUTH AFRICAN $$$
(Map p196; 021-883 3132; www.helenasrestaurant.co.za; Coopmanhuijs Boutique Hotel, 33 Church St; mains R135-295; 12.30-3pm & 6-9.30pm) A cosy, charming restaurant within a boutique hotel. The menu is small but features some traditional dishes and lots of locally sourced goodies – the mushroom risotto is superb. Bookings essential.

Drinking & Nightlife

Stellenbosch's nightlife scene is geared largely towards the interests of the university students, but there are classier options. It's safe to walk around the centre at night, so a pub crawl could certainly be on the cards (if you're staying at the Stumble Inn (p199), one will probably be organised for you).

★ **Craft Wheat & Hops** CRAFT BEER
(Map p196; 021-882 8069; www.craftstellenbosch.co.za; Andringa St; 11am-10pm) This place has a dozen local craft beers on tap and plenty more in bottles. There's also a decent wine list and a great selection of spirits. If you can't decide, ask to do the beer tasting (R65) or a gin sampler (R60). Open sandwiches and burgers (R60 to R110) are available to soak it all up.

Brampton Wine Studio WINE BAR
(Map p196; 021-883 9097; www.brampton.co.za; 11 Church St; 10am-9pm) Scribble on chalkboard tables while sipping shiraz at this trendy pavement cafe that also serves as Brampton winery's tasting room. Sandwiches, wraps and cheeseboards (R60 to R130) are served throughout the day.

Mystic Boer BAR
(Map p196; 021-886 8870; www.diemysticboer.co.za; 3 Victoria St; 11am-2am Mon-Sat, to midnight Sun) This funky bar is a Stellenbosch institution. There's regular live music and decent bar food.

Trumpet Tree PUB
(Map p196; 021-883 8379; www.thetrumpettree.com; Dorp St; 11am-11pm) Popular with both locals and students, Trumpet Tree has a shady beer garden where you can nibble pizzas and sip on craft beer during the lengthy happy hour (2pm to 5pm Monday to Friday).

De Akker PUB
(Map p196; 063 797 3257; 90 Dorp St; 11am-2am Mon-Sat, to 11pm Sun) Stellenbosch's second-oldest pub attracts a slightly older crowd than many places in town, with its well-priced pub grub, large array of craft beer, live music and tables on the pavement.

Bohemia BAR
(Map p196; 021-882 8375; cnr Victoria & Andringa Sts; 11am-2am Mon-Sat, to midnight Sun) A chilled, student-filled place that also serves lunch – opt for the pizza. There's often live music as well as regular drinks specials.

Nu Bar CLUB
(Map p196; 021-886 8998; www.nubar.co.za; 51 Plein St; 9pm-2am Mon-Sat) This club has a small dance floor beyond the long bar where DJs pump out dance and house music.

Entertainment

Oude Libertas Amphitheatre PERFORMING ARTS
(www.oudelibertas.co.za; Oude Libertas Rd) Open-air performances of theatre, music and dance are held here from November to March.

Shopping

Oom Samie se Winkel GIFTS & SOUVENIRS
(Uncle Sammy's Shop; Map p196; 021-887 0797; 84 Dorp St; 8.30am-6pm Mon-Fri, 9am-5pm Sat & Sun) This place was on the Stellenbosch map before Stellenbosch was on the map. It's an unashamedly touristy general dealer but still worth visiting for its curious range of goods – everything from joke-shop tat to African crafts and local foodstuffs.

Craft Market MARKET
(Map p196; Braak; 9am-5pm Mon-Sat) This open-air market is a great spot to haggle for African carvings, paintings and costume jewellery.

Information

Internet cafes are a dying breed, but virtually all cafes and bars in Stellenbosch have free wi-fi. Plans to roll out a town-wide network of wi-fi hot spots have hit a few snags, but you do find patches with free wi-fi.

Post Office (Map p196; 021-883 2233; cnr Bird & Plein Sts)

Stellenbosch Tourism (Map p196; 021-883 3584; www.stellenbosch.travel; 36 Market St; 8am-5pm Mon-Fri, 9am-2pm Sat, 9am-1pm Sun;) The staff are extremely helpful. Pick up the excellent brochure *Historical Stellenbosch on Foot* (R10), with a walking-tour map and information on many of the historic buildings (also available in French and German).

Getting There & Away

Long-distance bus services charge high prices for the short sector to Cape Town and do not take bookings.

Shared minibus taxis (cnr Bird & Merriman Sts) to Paarl (about R50, 45 minutes) leave from the stand on Bird St.

Metro trains run the 46km between Cape Town and Stellenbosch (1st/economy class R19.50/13, about one hour). To be safe, travel in the middle of the day.

Getting Around

Stellenbosch is navigable on foot and, being largely flat, is good cycling territory. Bikes can be hired from the **Adventure Shop** (p199). **Tuk Tuk Stellies** (☎076 011 3016; www.tuktukstellies.co.za) offers short trips around town on a tuk tuk (wine tours are also available).

Franschhoek

☎021 / POP 17,500

French Huguenots settled in this spectacular valley over 300 years ago, bringing their vines with them. Ever since, this Winelands town has clung to its French roots, and July visitors will find that Bastille Day is celebrated here. Franschhoek bills itself as the country's gastronomic capital, and you'll certainly have a tough time deciding where to eat. Plus, with a clutch of art galleries, wine farms and stylish guesthouses thrown in, it really is one of the loveliest towns in the Cape.

Sights

There are some wineries within walking distance of the town centre, but you'll need your own wheels or to join a tour to really experience Franschhoek's wines.

★La Motte WINERY
(Map p198; ☎021-876 8000; www.la-motte.com; Main Rd; tastings R50; ⌚9am-5pm Mon-Sat) There's enough to keep you occupied for a full day at this vast estate just west of Franschhoek. As well as tastings on offer of the superb shiraz range, wine-pairing lunches and dinners are served at the Pierneef à la Motte (p206) restaurant. The restaurant is named for South African artist Jacob Hendrik Pierneef and a collection of his work is on show at the on-site museum.

This is also the starting point for historical walks (R50) through the estate, taking in four national monuments and a milling demonstration and ending with a bread tasting (Wednesday 10am, bookings essential). If you've overindulged, walk off a few calories on the 5km circular hike that starts at the farm.

★Boschendal WINERY
(Map p198; ☎021-870 4210; www.boschendal.com; Groot Drakenstein, Rte 310; tastings from R45, cellar tours R50, vineyard tours R80; ⌚9am-5.30pm) This is a quintessential Winelands estate, with lovely architecture, food and wine. Tasting options include bubbly, brandy or wine and chocolate pairing. There are excellent vineyard and cellar tours; booking is essential.

When it comes to eating, there are various options, from sandwiches or cake at the Farmshop & Deli to bistro lunches featuring produce grown on the farm at the Werf. On Sundays you can partake in a huge buffet lunch (adult/child R325/160) in the 1795 homestead, while picnics (basket for two R480, bookings essential) can be ordered to enjoy under parasols on the lawn from September to May. Mountain-biking trails start from the farm, for those who feel like working up an appetite.

Grande Provence WINERY
(☎021-876 8600; www.grandeprovence.co.za; Main Rd; tastings from R40, cellar tours R40; ⌚10am-7pm, cellar tours 11am & 3pm Mon-Fri) A beautifully revamped, 18th-century manor house that is home to a stylish restaurant and a splendid gallery showcasing contemporary South African art. There is a range of tasting options, including a canapé pairing (R120), nougat pairing (R70) and grape-juice tasting for the kids (R20) plus the chance to blend your own wine (R350). It's within walking distance of the town centre.

Franschhoek Motor Museum MUSEUM
(Map p198; ☎021-874 9002; www.fmm.co.za; L'Ormarins, Rte 45; adult/child R80/40; ⌚10am-5pm Mon-Fri, to 4pm Sat & Sun) If you're all wined out, check out the amazing collection of classic cars here. There are 80 mint-condition automobiles on show, from a 1903 Ford Model A right through to a McLaren F1 car from 1998. The museum is part of the Anthonij Rupert wine estate, which has two tasting rooms plus spectacular grounds to wander. Visits to the museum must be prebooked, even if that just means calling from the bottom of the drive.

Leopard's Leap WINERY
(Map p198; ☎021-876 8002; www.leopardsleap.co.za; Rte 45; tastings from R25; ⌚9am-5pm Tue-Sat, 11am-5pm Sun; P 🚸) The bright, modern, barn-like tasting room has com-

Franschhoek

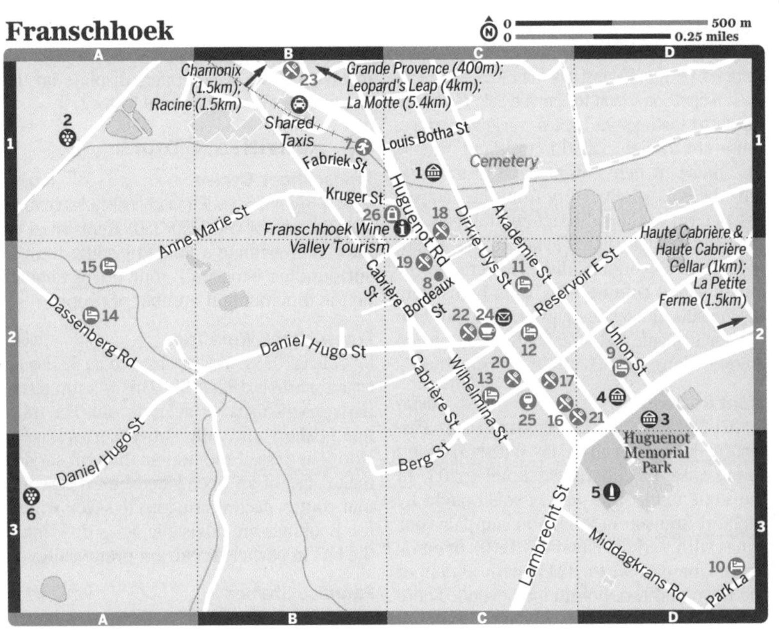

Franschhoek

Sights
1 Ceramics Gallery C1
2 Grande Provence A1
3 Huguenot Memorial Museum D2
4 Huguenot Memorial Museum Annexe D2
5 Huguenot Monument D3
6 Mont Rochelle A3

Activities, Courses & Tours
7 Franschhoek Cycles B1
8 Franschhoek Wine Tram C2

Sleeping
9 Akademie Street D2
10 La Cabrière Country House D3
11 La Fontaine C2
12 Le Ballon Rouge C2
13 Le Quartier Français C2
Mont Rochelle Hotel .... (see 6)
14 Otter's Bend Lodge A2
15 Reeden Lodge A2

Eating
16 De Villiers Chocolate Cafe C2
17 Foliage C2
18 Franschhoek Market C1
19 French Connection C2
20 La Petite Colombe C2
21 Marigold D2
22 Reuben's C2
23 Ryan's Kitchen B1

Drinking & Nightlife
24 Hoek C2
25 Tuk Tuk Microbrewery C2

Shopping
26 Huguenot Fine Chocolates C1

fy couches strewn around – you can either take your tasters to enjoy at leisure or sit at the bar for a slightly more formal affair. The large lawns have a jungle gym for kids, while the rotisserie restaurant (11.30am to 3pm Wednesday to Sunday) is very popular with families. You pay by weight, but you can budget for around R150 per person. Cooking classes are available once a month – booking ahead is essential.

Haute Cabrière WINERY

(☎021-876 8500; www.cabriere.co.za; Franschhoek Pass Rd; tastings from R55, cellar tours R85; ⏰10am-6pm Mon-Sat, to 4pm Sun, cellar tours 11am Mon-Sat; Ⓟ) Best known for Méthode Cap Classique (MCC; wine made in the Champagne method), there is also an excellent range of white and red wines, plus a brandy. The recommended cellar tours come with a demonstration of *sabrage:* slicing open a bottle of bubbly with a sword.

Solms-Delta WINERY
(Map p198; 021-874 3937; www.solms-delta.com; Delta Rd, off Rte 45; tastings from R25, tours R50; 9am-5pm Sun & Mon, to 6pm Tue-Sat; P) In addition to tastings and sales, various heritage tours are available at this excellent winery. The museum here covers Cape history and tells the Solms-Delta story from the perspective of farm workers throughout the years. On the culinary side, there's Fyndraai Restaurant (p205), serving original dishes inspired by the Cape's varied cultures and using herbs from the on-site indigenous garden. You can also opt for a picnic (adult/child R235/75), to be enjoyed along an enchanting riverside trail.

Mont Rochelle WINERY
(021-876 2770; www.montrochelle.co.za; Dassenberg Rd; tastings from R45; 10am-7pm; P) Along with the uberplush hotel (p205) of the same name, this winery was bought by Richard Branson in 2014. You can pair your wines with a trio of canapés (R140), or enjoy lunch (mains R95 to R245) with a view of the town and the mountains beyond. There are free cellar tours on weekdays at 11am.

Ceramics Gallery GALLERY
(021-876 4304; www.davidwalters.co.za; 24 Dirkie Uys St; 10am-5pm) Franschhoek boasts many fine galleries, mostly along Huguenot Rd. At the Ceramics Gallery you can watch David Walters, one of South Africa's most distinguished potters, at work in the beautifully restored home of Franschhoek's first teacher. There are also exhibits of work by other artists.

Chamonix WINERY
(021-876 8426; www.chamonix.co.za; Uitkyk St; tastings from R60, game drives R700; 9.30am-4pm) The tasting room at this small winery is in a converted blacksmith's; there's also a range of grappa to sample. Game drives to see wildebeest, zebras and a variety of antelope are available and include a wine tasting in the vineyards. Bookings are essential for the drives. The restaurant, Racine (p206), has a lovely deck overhanging a stream. It's walkable from the town if you don't mind the uphill slog.

Huguenot Memorial Museum MUSEUM
(021-876 2532; www.museum.co.za; Lambrecht St; adult/child R20/5; 9am-5pm Mon-Sat, 2-5pm Sun) This museum celebrates South Africa's Huguenots and houses the genealogical records of their descendants. Behind the main complex is a pleasant cafe, in front is the **Huguenot Monument** (9am-5pm) FREE, opened in 1948, and across the road is the **annexe** (9am-5pm Mon-Sat, 2-5pm Sun; admission included), which offers displays on the Anglo-Boer War and natural history.

Activities & Tours

Franschhoek Cycles CYCLING
(021-876 4956; www.franschhoekcycles.co.za; 2 Main Rd; half/full day R250/350) Rent bikes or have staff arrange a guided cycling tour of surrounding wineries – tour prices depend on the itinerary and number of people.

Franschhoek Wine Tram TOURS
(021-300 0338; www.winetram.co.za; 32 Huguenot Rd; adult/child R220/90) This is a fun alternative to the usual Winelands tour. The tram line is short and only two wineries have a stop. The rest of the hop-on, hop-off service makes use of an open-sided bus. There are four routes, each visiting up to seven wineries. Bookings are advisable, as is dressing – the bus in particular can get pretty chilly.

Paradise Stables HORSE RIDING
(021-876 2160; www.paradisestables.co.za; per hr R300; rides 7.30am, 8.45am, 1.15pm & 5.45pm Mon-Sat) As well as hour-long rides through Franschhoek's surrounds, there are four-hour trips taking in two vineyards (R950 including tastings).

Sleeping

Otter's Bend Lodge HOSTEL $
(021-876 3200; www.ottersbendlodge.co.za; Dassenberg Rd; camping per site R220, dm/d R220/600; P) A delightful budget option in a town not known for affordable accommodation. Basic double rooms lead to a shared deck shaded by poplar trees, and there's space for a couple of tents on the lawn. There are also two four-sleeper cabins (R880) with kitchenette, one of which is wheelchair-friendly. A 15-minute walk from town and close to a winery.

★ **Reeden Lodge** CHALET $$
(021-876 3174; www.reedenlodge.co.za; Anne Marie St; cottage from R1000; P) A good-value, terrific option for families, with well-equipped, self-catering cottages sleeping from two to 10 people, situated on a farm about 10 minutes' walk from town. Parents will love the peace and quiet and their kids will love the sheep, tree house and open space.

Chamonix Guest Cottages CHALET $$
(021-876 8406; www.chamonix.co.za; Uitkyk St; d from R2100) There are various lodges and self-catering cottages at this wine farm-

cum-game reserve. You can walk to town (though it's a long slog uphill to get back).

La Cabrière Country House GUESTHOUSE $$
(☎021-876 4780; www.lacabriere.co.za; Park Lane; s/d incl breakfast from R2100/2850; P❄📶≋) The sumptuously decorated rooms at this boutique guesthouse have underfloor heating and sweeping views to the mountains. You can stroll into town.

La Fontaine GUESTHOUSE $$
(☎087 095 2017; www.lafontainefranschhoek.co.za; 21 Dirkie Uys St; s/d from R1375/1950; ❄📶≋) A stylishly appointed, very comfortable family home featuring 14 spacious rooms with wooden floors and mountain views.

Le Ballon Rouge GUESTHOUSE $$
(☎021-876 2651; www.ballonrouge.co.za; 7 Reservoir East St; s/d incl breakfast from R1000/1200; ❄📶≋) A small, friendly guesthouse with good-quality rooms and stylish suites with stunning bathrooms.

Akademie Street BOUTIQUE HOTEL $$$
(☎082 517 0405; www.aka.co.za; 5 Akademie St; r incl breakfast R5500; P📶≋) If there's anywhere in South Africa that you're going to blow the budget, Franschhoek might as well be it. The opulent rooms at this quiet hotel are a fine place to splurge. Part of the guesthouse dates back to 1860 and rooms honour the building's history with heavy four-poster beds and occasional antiques, though there is a distinctly modern flair.

Le Quartier Français BOUTIQUE HOTEL $$$
(☎021-876 2151; www.lqf.co.za; cnr Wilhelmina & Berg Sts; r incl breakfast from R7500; P❄📶≋) Set around a leafy courtyard and pool, the large rooms at this opulent hotel have fireplaces, huge beds and stylish decor. If you're feeling flush, try one of the suites (from R12,500), which come with private pools.

Mont Rochelle Hotel BOUTIQUE HOTEL $$$
(☎central reservations 011-325 4405; www.montrochelle.co.za; Dassenberg Rd; s/d incl breakfast from R4950/6600; ❄📶≋) Along with the winery of the same name, this boutique hotel and restaurant were bought by Richard Branson in 2014. It offers gilt-edged luxury as well as magnificent views across the valley.

Eating

Franschhoek's compactness means it's possible to stroll around and let your nose tell you where to eat. Many places are well established, though, and advance booking is best.

De Villiers Chocolate Cafe DESSERTS $
(☎021-874 1060; www.dvchocolate.com; Heritage Sq, 9 Huguenot Rd; pastries from R30; ⏲9am-5.30pm) The excellent single-origin chocolate here is made at a boutique chocolatier in Paarl and used in all the cakes, pastries and ice cream on offer. There's also excellent coffee. If you just can't decide, try the ice cream or coffee tasting (R55).

Franschhoek Market MARKET $
(☎082 786 7927; 29 Huguenot Rd; mains R40-70; ⏲9am-2pm Sat; 👪) Based in the grounds of the church, this market has a real country fete vibe. Shop for crafts and lunch on a range of light dishes, or buy a bag of goodies to take on a picnic.

Marigold INDIAN $$
(☎021-876 8970; www.marigoldfranschhoek.com; Heritage Sq, 9 Huguenot Rd; mains R80-150; ⏲noon-2.30pm & 6-9pm; 🌶) If you fancy a change from all the French-inspired fine dining, Marigold serves elegant North Indian cuisine in its contemporary dining room.

Reuben's FUSION $$
(☎021-876 3772; www.reubens.co.za; 2 Daniel Hugo St; mains R175-235; ⏲noon-3pm & 6-9pm Wed-Mon) Franschhoek's favourite son, celebrity chef Reuben Riffel, is behind this Asian fusion restaurant in a fabulous, light-filled space off the main road. In summer, grab a poké bowl to enjoy on the large patio. There's a carefully curated wine list plus beers from a nearby microbrewery.

Lust Bistro & Bakery BISTRO $$
(Map p198; ☎021-874 1456; www.lustbistro.com; cnr Simondium Rd & Rte 45; mains R85-160; ⏲7.30am-5pm Mon-Sat, 8am-4pm Sun) Based at Vrede en Lust winery, this is a refreshingly unfussy place to eat in a region known for haute cuisine. You'll find salads, sandwiches and a build-your-own pizza option. Daily blackboard specials include some Asian-inspired eats and on Sunday there's a buffet lunch (adult/child R195/99) where you can eat away the day – bookings essential.

Fyndraai Restaurant SOUTH AFRICAN $$
(Map p198; ☎021-874 3937; www.solms-delta.com; Delta Rd, off Rte45; mains R140-185; ⏲10am-5pm; 🌶) Serves original dishes inspired by the Cape's varied cultures and using herbs from the on-site indigenous garden. A handy glossary on the menu helps you to learn some traditional foodstuffs.

French Connection INTERNATIONAL $$
(☎021-876 4056; www.frenchconnection.co.za; 48 Huguenot Rd; mains R165-220; ⏰noon-3pm & 6.30-9pm) No-nonsense bistro-style food using only fresh ingredients is dished up at this long-standing and deservedly popular place.

Racine BISTRO $$
(☎021-876 8426; www.chamonix.co.za; Uitkyk St; mains R100-185; ⏰noon-3pm daily, 7-9.30pm Fri & Sat) One of the restaurants of celebrity chef Reuben Riffel, Racine has a small menu of fairly rich food to be enjoyed on a pretty deck overhanging a river.

★ **La Petite Colombe** FUSION $$$
(☎021-202 3395; www.lapetitecolombe.com; Le Quarter Français, Huguenot Rd; 7-course menu with/without wine R750/395) The award-winning Cape Town restaurant has opened a breezy sister branch here. The French-inspired menu comes in seven- or 12-course versions and you can opt to pair each course with a different wine.

Foliage FUSION $$$
(☎021-876 2328; http://foliage.co.za; 11 Huguenot Rd; mains R175-265; ⏰noon-2pm & 7-9pm Mon-Sat) Chef and owner Chris Erasmus has brought the foraging culture to the Cape at this hugely popular restaurant. Forest-floor ingredients such as river cress, dandelion and mushrooms complement decadent dishes like roasted swordfish and braised kudu shank. The restaurant is decked out with creations from Chris' artist wife, Alisha. Book ahead.

Pierneef à la Motte SOUTH AFRICAN $$$
(Map p198; ☎021-876 8800; www.la-motte.com; Main Rd; mains R185-240; ⏰11.30am-3pm Tue-Sun, 7-10pm Thu-Sat) Named for South African artist Jacob Hendrik Pierneef, whose work is on show at the on-site museum, this elegant restaurant serves modern takes on traditional cuisine. Local ingredients like sorghum, springbok rooibos and *waterblommetjies* (Cape pondweed) feature in many dishes.

Ryan's Kitchen FUSION $$$
(☎021-876 4598; www.ryanskitchen.co.za; Place Vendome, Huguenot Rd; mains R170-260, 4-course menu with/without wine R740/540; ⏰12.30-2.30pm & 6.30-9.30pm Mon-Sat) Loved by locals and recommended by travellers, this long-running restaurant marries South African ingredients with fine-dining techniques. Watch chefs prepare intricate dishes such as Madagascan sea bass with seaweed-soya broth in the open kitchen. The menu changes every two weeks.

Haute Cabrière Cellar FUSION $$$
(☎021-876 3688; www.cabriere.co.za; Franschhoek Pass Rd; 3-course menu R370; ⏰noon-2.30pm daily, 6-9pm Mon-Sat) If you want to go all-out on the French-inspired cuisine here, try the five-course menu with wine pairings (R595). Tastings (from R55) are available and there are cellar tours at 11am, which include a demonstration of *sabrage* – slicing open a bottle of bubbly with a sword .

La Petite Ferme SOUTH AFRICAN $$$
(☎021-876 3016; www.lapetiteferme.co.za; Franschhoek Pass Rd; mains R155-280; ⏰noon-3.30pm daily, 6.30-9pm Fri & Sat; 📶) In a stupendous setting overlooking Franschhoek Valley, this contemporary restaurant makes a big deal of local ingredients. Try the biltong-dusted ostrich steak or harissa-coated Karoo lamb. There are some luxurious rooms if you can't bear to leave.

🍷 Drinking & Nightlife

Tuk Tuk Microbrewery MICROBREWERY
(☎021-4922207; www.tuktukbrew.com; 14 Huguenot Rd; ⏰11am-10pm) There are three permanent beers on tap, plus ever-changing experimental brews so be sure to ask what's new. It also serves beers from Cape Brewing Company in Paarl. The menu is a breath of fresh air if you're looking for a light lunch in Franschhoek – tamales, buffalo wings and tacos.

Hoek COFFEE
(☎079 451 3019; Daniel Hugo St; ⏰7am-3pm Mon-Sat, from 8am Sun) Franschhoek's strip gets swamped with tourists in summer, so locals retreat to side-street haunts like this diminutive coffee shop. There are a few pastries and cookies, but it's really all about the coffee – grab a cup of house blend to sip on the patio.

🛍 Shopping

Huguenot Fine Chocolates CHOCOLATE
(☎021-876 4096; www.huguenotchocolates.com; 62 Huguenot Rd; ⏰8am-5.30pm Mon-Fri, from 9am Sat & Sun) An empowerment program gave the two local guys who run this chocolatier a leg up and now people are raving about their confections. There are daily chocolate-making demonstrations including a tasting (R40) at 11am and 3pm – booking is recommended.

ℹ Information

Franschhoek Wine Valley Tourism (☎021-876 2861; www.franschhoek.org.za; 62 Huguenot Rd; ⏰8am-5pm Mon-Fri, 9am-5pm Sat, 9am-4pm Sun) Staff can provide you with a map of the area's scenic walks (R40) and issue permits

(R40) for hikes in the Mont Rochelle Nature Reserve, as well as book accommodation.

Post Office (☎021-876 2342; 21 Huguenot Rd)

Getting There & Away

Franschhoek is 32km east of Stellenbosch and 32km south of Paarl. The best way to reach Franschhoek is in your own vehicle. Some visitors choose to cycle from Stellenbosch, but roads are winding and can be treacherous. Alternatively, take a **shared taxi** (Huguenot Rd) from Stellenbosch (R25) or Paarl station (R28). If you're looking for a private taxi, try **Call a Cab** (☎082 256 6784).

Paarl

☎021 / POP 112,000

Surrounded by mountains and vineyards, and set on the banks of the Berg River, Paarl is the Winelands' largest town. It's often overlooked by people heading for Stellenbosch and Franschhoek, but it does have its own charm, including interesting Cape Dutch architecture and gracious homesteads, a good range of places to stay and some decent restaurants.

The main road is over 11km long, so not exactly walkable, but there are a couple of wineries within an easy stroll of the train station.

Sights

The Town

Drakenstein Correctional Centre HISTORIC SITE

(Map p198) On 11 February 1990, when Nelson Mandela walked free from incarceration for the first time in over 27 years, the jail he left was not on Robben Island, but here. Then called the Victor Verster, this was where Mandela spent his last two years of captivity in the warders' cottage, negotiating the end of apartheid. It's still a working prison, so there are no tours, but there's a superb statue of Mandela, fist raised in *viva* position.

Afrikaans Language Museum MUSEUM

(Map p208; ☎021-872 3441; www.taalmuseum.co.za; 11 Pastorie Ave; adult/child R20/5; ⏲9am-4pm Mon-Fri) Paarl is considered the wellspring of the Afrikaans language, a fact covered by this interesting museum. It also shows, thanks to a multimedia exhibition, how three continents contributed to the formation of the language. There's a discount if you buy a combo ticket for the Taal Monument as well.

Taal Monument MONUMENT

(Map p198; ☎021-863 0543; www.taalmuseum.co.za; adult/child R30/10; ⏲8am-5pm Apr-Nov, to 8pm Dec-Mar) The somewhat phallic Taal Monument is in the Paarl Mountain Nature Reserve. The giant, needle-like edifice commemorates the language (*taal* is Afrikaans for 'language'). On a clear day there are stunning views as far as Cape Town. There's also an adjoining restaurant and curio shop. If you're here when it's a full moon, join locals for a night-time picnic. It's 3km from the main road. Follow signs from Flambeau St.

Paarl Mountain Nature Reserve NATURE RESERVE

(per vehicle R52, per person R17; ⏲7am-7pm) The three giant granite domes that dominate this reserve glisten like pearls when washed by rain – hence the name 'Paarl'. The reserve has mountain fynbos (literally 'fine bush'; primarily proteas, heaths and ericas), a cultivated wildflower garden that's a delightful picnic spot, and numerous walks with excellent views over Drakenstein Valley. Hiking maps are sold at the main gate. On a clear day there are stunning views as far as Cape Town.

Access is via Jan Phillips Mountain Dr, from where it's about 6km on a winding gravel road to the main picnic area, Meulwater.

Paarl Museum MUSEUM

(Map p208; ☎021-872 2651; 303 Main St; R10; ⏲9am-4pm Mon-Fri, to 1pm Sat) Housed in the Oude Pastorie (Old Parsonage), built in 1714, this museum has an interesting collection of Cape Dutch antiques and relics of Huguenot and early Afrikaner culture, plus information on the history of Paarl.

Wineries Around Paarl

★**Avondale** WINERY

(Map p198; ☎021-863 1976; www.avondalewine.co.za; Lustigan Rd, Klein Drakenstein; tastings R70, ecotour R300; ⏲10am-4pm; P) This quiet spot in a gracious old homestead serves delectable, organically made wines. The formal tasting takes around an hour, or you can join a two-hour eco-safari through the vineyards on the back of a tractor, which culminates in a tasting. The restaurant, **Faber** (mains R160 to R220), is one of the Winelands' best, with dishes like roasted springbok loin, truffled leeks and sourdough bread-and-butter pudding.

If you'd like a less formal way to taste the cuisine, the **Garden Bar** is open on Friday evenings. You can enjoy wines and sharing plates from the Faber kitchen.

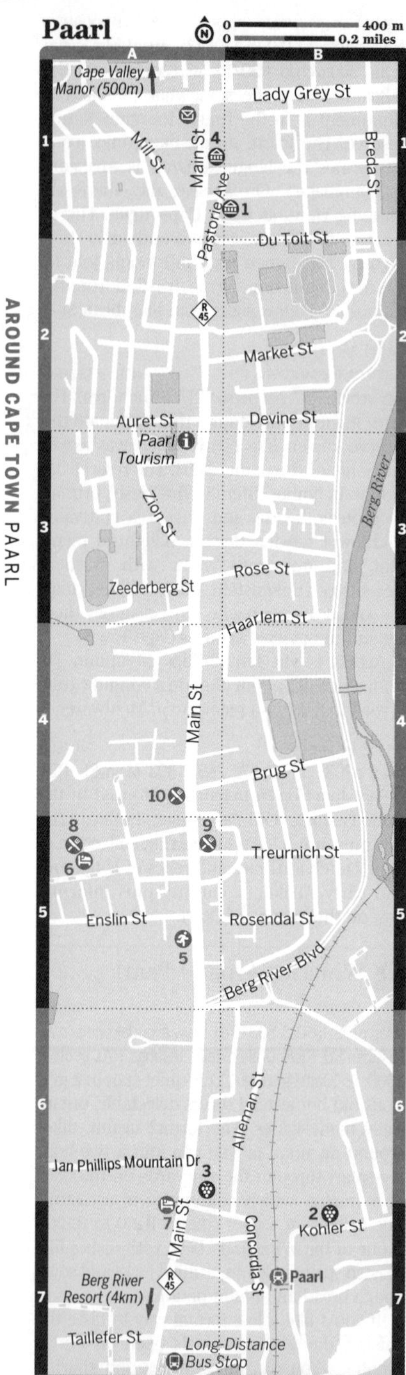

Paarl

Sights

1 Afrikaans Language Museum B1
2 KWV Emporium B7
3 KWV Sensorium A6
4 Paarl Museum A1

Activities, Courses & Tours

5 Wineland Ballooning A5

Sleeping

6 Grande Roche Hotel A5
7 Oak Tree Lodge A7

Eating

8 Bosman's Restaurant A5
9 Noop A5
10 Terra Mare A4

★Spice Route WINERY

(Map p198; 021-863 5200; www.spiceroute.co.za; Suid-Agter-Paarl Rd; tastings from R40; 9am-5pm; P) Spice Route is known for its complex red wines, particularly the Flagship syrah. Aside from wine there is a lot going on, including glass-blowing demonstrations, wine and charcuterie pairings (R85), a chocolatier (tutored tasting R35), grappa distillery and a superlative microbrewery (tastings R35). As well as the upmarket restaurant headed by celebrity chef Bertus Basson (mains R140 to R215), there is a pizzeria (mains R70 to R150).

Fairview WINERY

(Map p198; 021-863 2450; www.fairview.co.za; Suid-Agter-Paarl Rd; wine & cheese tastings R40; 9am-5pm; P) This hugely popular estate off Rte 101, 6km south of Paarl, is a wonderful winery, but not the place to come for a tranquil tasting. It's great value, since tastings include six wines *and* a wide range of cheeses (you can just do cheese for R20). The well-respected restaurant (mains R90 to R180) is open for breakfast and lunch.

Fairview is famous for its goats and you can even partake in goat yoga on weekends – just watch out for poop when you put down your mat!

KWV Emporium WINERY

(Map p208; 021-863 3803; www.kwvwine emporium.co.za; Kohler St; tastings R40-65, cellar tours R55; 9am-4.30pm Mon-Sat, 10am-5pm Sun, cellar tours 10am, 10.30am & 2.15pm; P) Operating since 1918, this wine-making cooperative is particularly well known for its award-winning fortified wines and brandies. Cellar tours are available and there is a range of tasting options, including chocolate and brandy, biltong and wine, bubbly and cheesecake and a tea and chocolate pairing. It's a short walk from the train station.

KWV Sensorium WINERY
(Map p208; 021-807 3094; www.kwv.co.za; 57 Main St; art & wine pairing R55; 9am-4.30pm Mon-Fri, to 1pm Sat) Just when you thought you'd seen every possible pairing option, KWV chooses to couple its wines with local art inspired by the region. It's a fun way to taste or you can visit the gallery for free. There's also a chocolate and brandy pairing and a pinotage journey, although most of the tasting fun happens at the KWV Emporium on the other side of the train tracks.

Anura WINERY
(Map p198; 021-875 5360; www.anura.co.za; off Simondium Rd, Klapmuts; wine & cheese tastings R60; 9am-5pm; P) Foodies could hang out here for a while, tasting cheese made on the premises, grabbing a platter or picnic featuring cured meats from the deli, or swapping grape for grain and sipping a beer from the microbrewery beside the pond. Wine-wise, Anura is best known for syrah and malbec.

Backsberg WINERY
(Map p198; 021-875 5141; www.backsberg.co.za; tastings from R30; 8.30am-5pm Mon-Fri, 9.30am-4.30pm Sat, 10.30am-4.30pm Sun;) Backsberg is a hugely popular estate thanks to its reliable label and lavish outdoor lunches – book ahead for the Sunday lamb spit braai (barbecue; R295) or a picnic to enjoy in the grounds (R180). Tasting options include wine and chocolate, wine and cheese, and a chance to create your own blend.

Glen Carlou WINERY
(Map p198; 021-875 5528; www.glencarlou.co.za; Simondium Rd, Klapmuts; tastings R25-35; 9am-5pm Mon-Fri, 10am-4pm Sat & Sun; P) Sitting south of the N1, the tasting room has a panoramic view of Tortoise Hill. Enjoy a glass of the sumptuous chardonnay or renowned bordeaux blend, Grand Classique, over lunch (three-course meal R295). There's an art gallery too, with rotating exhibits.

Nederburg Wines WINERY
(021-862 3104; www.nederburg.co.za; tastings from R60, cellar tours incl tasting R60; 9am-5pm Mon-Fri, 10am-4pm Sat & Sun, tours 10.30am & 3pm Mon-Fri, 11am Sat & Sun; P) This is one of South Africa's best-known labels, a big but professional and welcoming operation featuring a vast range of wines. As well as various wine-tasting options, there is a kids' grape juice and snack pairing experience. There's a small museum detailing Nederburg's history and an elegant restaurant open for lunch.

Activities

Wineland Ballooning BALLOONING
(Map p208; 021-863 3192; www.kapinfo.com; 64 Main St; per person R3900) You'll need to get up very early in the morning, but a hot-air balloon trip over the Winelands will be unforgettable. Trips run between November and April when the weather conditions are right.

Sleeping

Since Paarl tends to be overshadowed by Stellenbosch and Franschhoek, there are comparative bargains to be found here. You'll find guesthouses on suburban streets leading off Main St, and some plush high-end options further afield.

Oak Tree Lodge GUESTHOUSE $
(Map p208; 021-863 2631; www.oaktreelodge.co.za; 32 Main St; s/d incl breakfast from R720/980; P) This old house has comfortable, well-appointed rooms, some with balconies. The larger garden rooms are quieter, being off the main road. It's very conveniently located – you can walk to restaurants, wineries and the train station from here.

Berg River Resort CAMPGROUND $
(Map p198; 021-007 1852; www.bergriverresort.co.za; Rte 45; camping per site from R330, chalets from R940; P) An attractive camping ground with simple chalets (sleeping two) beside the Berg River, 5km from Paarl on Rte 45 towards Franschhoek. Facilities include canoes, trampolines and a cafe. It gets very crowded during school holidays and prices rise dramatically.

★**Cascade Country Manor** BOUTIQUE HOTEL $$
(021-868 0227; www.cascademanor.co.za; Waterval Rd; r incl breakfast from R2190; P) Tucked away along a dirt road 10km east of the centre, this place will make you feel like you're far from anywhere, although it's an easy drive back to town. Rooms are just what you'd expect but it's the grounds that wow, with vast lawns, a large pool, olive groves and a short walk to a pretty waterfall. Olive tastings and excellent dinners are on offer.

Cape Valley Manor GUESTHOUSE $$
(021-872 4545; www.capevalleymanor.co.za; Plein St; s/d incl breakfast from R900/1200; P) In a peaceful side street not far

DON'T MISS

BABYLONSTOREN

This 2.5-sq-km **wine and fruit farm** (Map p198; 021-863 3852; www.babylonstoren.com; Simondium Rd, Klapmuts; entrance R10, tastings R30; 9am-5pm; P) is on the north slope of the Simonsberg mountain between Klapmuts and Paarl. Its highlight is an 800-sq-metre, formally designed garden; inspired by Cape Town's Company's Garden, it is an incredible undertaking, featuring edible and medicinal plants, lotus ponds and espaliered quince trees, chicken coops and a maze of prickly-pear cacti. Reserve a place on one of the garden tours (10am).

Better yet, check into one of the super-chic guest rooms (single/double from R4200/5700), crafted from the old workers' cottages, so that once the day visitors have left you can enjoy the gardens – not to mention the spa and pool in one of the farm's old reservoir tanks.

There's no need to reserve if you'd like lunch at the **Greenhouse** (mains R75 to R100), hidden deep in the garden. However, bookings are essential for the **Babel** (mains R100 to R280), which serves delicious meals made with produce from the garden and quaffable wines that the farm has recently resumed making. The new wine cellar is a model of contemporary design with interesting exhibits related to the wine-making process. There are cellar tours on the hour (R35, including tasting). You can also buy freshly baked bread and charcuterie cured on-site if you feel like picnicking.

from Main St, Cape Valley has four individually decorated rooms and a delightful garden – a great spot to open that bottle of wine you bought while touring the vineyards.

Under Oaks GUESTHOUSE $$
(021-869 8535; http://underoaks.co.za; Noord-Agter-Paarl Rd, Northern Paarl; s/d R1150/1440; P @) On a peaceful wine farm just 3km north of central Paarl, Under Oaks has spacious rooms decked out in muted shades. There's wine tasting on the premises as well as a rustic pizzeria and some magnificent mountain vistas.

Ingonyama Tented Camp TENTED CAMP $$
(Map p198; 021-863 3290; www.lionrescue.org.za; Drakenstein Lion Park, Rte 101; d tent R1500; P) The tents here are fairly basic – two single beds and a private bathroom – but it's really about the location. The camp is at Drakenstein Lion Park, a sanctuary for mistreated lions and chimps born in captivity. A traditional braai (barbecue) dinner is available in the evenings and you can wake up and stroll past the lions in the morning.

Grande Roche Hotel LUXURY HOTEL $$$
(Map p208; 021-863 5100; www.granderoche.com; Plantasie St; ste incl breakfast from R3270; P) A superluxurious hotel set in a Cape Dutch manor house, offering wonderful mountain views, a heated swimming pool and the excellent Bosman's Restaurant (p211). It's a short walk to Paarl's main road.

Eating

Many wineries have excellent restaurants or offer picnic lunches and there are also some good eateries in town.

★ **Tea Under the Trees** BISTRO $
(072 871 9103; www.teaunderthetrees.co.za; Main St, Northern Paarl; mains R40-55; 9am-4pm Mon-Fri Oct-Apr; P) The only downside to this fabulous tea garden is that it's only open for half the year. Based on an organic fruit farm, it's a wonderful place to sit under century-old oak trees and enjoy an alfresco cuppa, a light lunch or a large slice of home-baked cake. There's no indoor seating. Saturdays tend to get booked well in advance. It's 4km north of the town centre.

★ **Glen Carlou** INTERNATIONAL $$
(Map p198; 021-875 5528; www.glencarlou.co.za; mains R150-190; 11am-3pm) The food at this stylish winery is on a par with the views: magnificent. Dishes, such as pan-roasted sea bass, Parmesan mousse and lamb shoulder with sweetbreads, come with a recommended wine pairing. There's also a three-course set menu (R295). Book ahead on weekends.

Blacksmith's Kitchen BISTRO $$
(021-870 1867; www.pearlmountain.co.za; Pearl Mountain Winery, Bo Lang St; mains R65-195; 11.30am-9.30pm Tue-Sat, to 4pm Sun; P) Grab a table under the trees and enjoy an unfussy lunch of wood-fired pizza or roast pork belly with views of the vineyards, town and mountains beyond.

Terra Mare FUSION $$
(Map p208; ☎021-863 4805; 90a Main St; mains R130-200; ⊙noon-10pm Mon-Sat; P) The menu is fairly small but superb, offering a mix of Asian, Italian and South African dishes. Tables inside can be a little noisy due to the proximity to busy Main St, but there's a delightful garden at the back with views of Paarl Mountain Nature Reserve (p207).

Noop FUSION $$
(Map p208; ☎021-863 3925; www.noop.co.za; 127 Main St; mains R135-225; ⊙11am-11pm Mon-Sat) Recommended by locals all over the Winelands, this restaurant and wine bar has a comprehensive menu of upmarket dishes like slow-roasted lamb neck, roast duck and wild-mushroom risotto. Check out the South African dessert platter, featuring Malva pudding (a traditional sticky sponge pudding with citrus fruit) and milk-tart millefeuille. Bookings recommended for dinner.

Bosman's Restaurant INTERNATIONAL $$$
(Map p208; ☎021-863 5100; www.granderoche.com; Plantasie St; 3 courses R525; ⊙noon-2pm & 7-11pm) This elegant spot within the Grande Roche Hotel is one of Paarl's top restaurants, serving multicourse gourmet dinners and more casual bistro-style lunches (mains R175 to R240). Bookings highly recommended.

Information

Paarl Tourism (Map p208; ☎021-872 4842; www.paarlonline.com; 216 Main St; ⊙8.30am-5pm Mon-Fri, 10am-1pm Sat & Sun) This office has an excellent supply of information on the whole region.

Post Office (Map p208; ☎021-872 5791; Lady Grey St)

Getting There & Away

BUS

All the major long-distance bus companies offer services going through Paarl, making it easy to build the town into your itinerary. The bus segment between Paarl and Cape Town is disproportionately expensive, so consider taking the cheaper train to Paarl and then linking with the buses.

The **long-distance bus stop** (Map p208) is opposite the Shell petrol station on Main St as you enter town from the N1.

TRAIN

Metro trains run roughly every hour between Cape Town and Paarl (1st/economy class R19.50/13, 1¼ hours). Services are less frequent on weekends. Take care to travel on trains during the busy part of the day, for safety reasons.

You can travel by train from Paarl to Stellenbosch; take a Cape Town–bound train and change at Muldersvlei.

Getting Around

If you don't have your own transport, your only option for getting around Paarl, apart from walking and cycling, is to call a taxi; try **Paarl Taxis** (☎021-872 5671; www.paarltaxisandtours.co.za).

Tulbagh

☎023 / POP 9000

Beneath the dramatic backdrop of the Witzenberg range, Tulbagh (established in 1699) is a pretty town with historic buildings and delightful places to stay and eat. Church St, lined with trees and flowering shrubs, is a near-perfect example of an 18th- and 19th-century Cape Dutch village street. It was badly damaged in an earthquake in 1969, but the painstaking restoration has paid off.

Sights & Activities

Church Street is one of the Western Cape's most beautiful roads and wandering from house to house is a pleasant way to spend a morning. Many of the buildings are national monuments and have information plaques outside detailing the history of the building. The **community garden** at the northern end of town is also worth a wander. The region is known for its wines, particularly bubbly.

Oakhurst Olives FARM
(☎023-230 0842; www.oakhurstolives.co.za; Lemoendrif Farm, Waveren Rd; tastings R20; ⊙9am-4pm Mon-Fri, to 2pm Sat; P) The magnificent, airy tasting room tucked beneath the Winterhoek Mountains is a fine place to hang out for an hour. Tutored tasting sessions start with some background on the olive industry and production process, before moving on to the best bit – sampling the various olives, oils and tapenades. The last tour begins 30 minutes before it closes.

Twee Jonge Gezellen WINERY
(☎023-230 0680; www.tweejongegezellen.co.za; Waveren Rd; tastings free; ⊙10am-4pm Mon-Sat, cellar tours 11am; P) This long-established winery has had a revamp and is once again a marvellous place to sip bubbly all afternoon. Unpretentious tastings take place in the stylish tasting room, on the deck or in the garden. There are tours explaining the Méthode Cap Classique–making process.

OFF THE BEATEN TRACK

WELLINGTON

This sedate and reasonably pretty town is 15km north of Paarl. Like surrounding towns, the main draw is the wineries, which often offer a less touristy experience than those in Paarl. Ask at the **tourism bureau** (021-864 1378; www.wellington.co.za; 104 Main Rd; 9am-5pm Mon-Fri, 10am-1pm Sat & Sun) for a list of local wineries and information on the **Wellington Wine Walk**. If you're looking for something stronger than wine, visit **Jorgensen's Distillery** (021-864 1777; www.jd7.co.za; Regent St; by appointment), which produces handmade gin, brandy and absinthe.

While in the area, don't miss the chance to drive the spectacular **Bainskloof Pass**, one of South Africa's finest. It was built between 1848 and 1852 by legendary pass builder Thomas Bain, and other than having its surface tarred, the road has not been altered since.

There are several walks from the pass, including the 8km **Bobbejaans River Walk** to a waterfall. This walk starts at Eerste Tol and you need to buy a permit (adult/child R40/20), available from the tourism bureau.

Saronsberg Cellar WINERY
(www.saronsberg.com; Waveren Rd; tastings R80; 8.30am-5pm Mon-Fri, 10am-2pm Sat, 10am-1pm Sun) Sip superlative reds while admiring the contemporary art that lines the walls of this smart cellar 6km north of town.

Oude Kerk Volksmuseum MUSEUM
(Old Church Folk Museum; 4 Church St; adult/child R15/5; 9am-5pm Mon-Fri, 9am-3pm Sat, 11am-3pm Sun) This museum made up of four buildings is worth a pause. Start at No 4, which has a photographic history of Church St, covering the earthquake and reconstruction; visit the beautiful Oude Kerk itself (1743); move to No 14, featuring Victorian furnishings; and end at No 22, a reconstructed town dwelling from the 18th century.

Maker's Mark GALLERY
(023-230 0048; http://makersmark.co.za; 42 Church St; 10am-4pm Wed-Sun) Opened in late 2017, this gallery has rotating exhibitions from local and international artists. A brasserie, wine-and-oyster bar, and gin-and-cigar lounge are all due to open in 2018.

Detour Bike Shop CYCLING
(084 052 4102; www.detourcycles.co.za; bike hire half/full day R150/250; 8am-5.30pm Mon-Fri, to 1pm Sat) As well as renting bikes, Detour Bike Shop offers guided cycling tours to nearby wineries (R750 per person).

Sleeping

★**Vindoux Guest Farm** CABIN $$
(023-230 0635; www.vindoux.com; Waveren Rd; d incl breakfast R1950; P) These luxury tree houses each have a spa bath and views of a small wildlife area with zebras, wildebeest and springbok. Hire bikes for a self-guided vineyard cycle then revive with a fynbos aromatherapy massage at the day spa (R480). There are also simpler cottages (R850 for two people).

Cape Dutch Quarter GUESTHOUSE $$
(079 051 2059; www.cdq.co.za; 33 Van der Stel St; r from R1100;) There is a variety of accommodation on offer here, from simple apartments (two people R650) to more luxurious self-catering houses (four people R1600) and smart doubles with four-poster beds. The owner is a mine of information on the area and can arrange hiking and mountain-biking permits and maps. Most of the accommodation is on Church St, but you'll find reception on Van der Stel St.

De Oude Herberg HISTORIC HOTEL $$
(023-230 0260; www.deoudeherberg.co.za; 6 Church St; s/d incl breakfast R865/1130;) A guesthouse since 1885, this is a friendly place with traditional country furniture and a lovely patio. There are just four rooms so advance bookings are highly recommended.

Rijk's Country House BOUTIQUE HOTEL $$
(023-230 1006; www.rijkscountryhouse.co.za; Van der Stel St; r incl breakfast R1550; P) Rijk's provides pleasant accommodation in thatched cottages on a beautiful wine estate with manicured lawns. There are tours and tastings at the winery and a good restaurant (mains R95 to R170) in the main building. The hotel is 2km north of the town centre.

Eating

★**Olive Terrace** INTERNATIONAL $$
(www.tulbaghhotel.co.za; 22 Van der Stel St; mains R75-150; 7am-10pm) Based in the Tulbagh Hotel, this restaurant serves a range of dishes

including a few vegetarian options. The shady terrace is a delight in the Tulbagh summer heat.

Readers Restaurant SOUTH AFRICAN $$
(023-230 0087; 12 Church St; mains R105-155; 9am-10pm Wed-Mon) The menu changes regularly, but always features a few traditional South African dishes and plenty of local ingredients. The attached gift shop is aimed at feline lovers, with an array of catty collectables.

Things I Love CAFE $$
(023-230 1742; 61 Van de Stel St; mains R70-140; 9am-7pm Mon-Sat, to 5pm Sun;) A friendly spot serving decent coffee and a little bit of everything, food-wise. There are tables on the front *stoep*, but the shady terrace at the back is much quieter There's also a shop selling crafts, clothing and foodstuffs.

Information

Tulbagh Tourism (023-230 1348; www.tulbaghtourism.co.za; 4 Church St; 9am-5pm Mon-Fri, 9am-3pm Sat, 10am-3pm Sun) Helpful staff provide information and maps about the area, including the Tulbagh Wine Route.

Getting There & Away

There is no public transport to Tulbagh. The town is 121km northeast of Cape Town via N1 to Paarl and then the Rte 44 via Wellington – about a three-hour drive in total.

Robertson

023 / POP 22,000

In a valley located between the Langeberg and Riviersonderendberge, Robertson is the prosperous centre of one of the largest wine-growing areas in the country. It offers an excellent wine route encompassing the neighbouring villages of Ashton, Bonnievale and McGregor, as well as a wider range of outdoor activities than other towns on Rte 62. There's hiking in the mountains, rafting on the river and horse riding – the town is famous for its horse studs.

Sights & Activities

★ **Viljoensdrift** WINERY
(023-615 1017; www.viljoensdrift.co.za; tastings free; 10am-5pm Mon-Fri, to 4pm Sat;) One of Robertson's most popular places to sip, especially on weekends. Put together a picnic from the deli, buy a bottle from the cellar door and taste on an hour-long boat trip along the Breede River (adult/child R70/20). Boats leave on the hour from noon. Bookings essential.

Excelsior WINERY
(023-615 1980; www.excelsior.co.za; off Rte 317; tastings free; 10am-4pm Mon-Fri, to 3pm Sat;) Tastings take place on a wooden deck overlooking a reservoir – it's a delightful spot. The real draw, though, is the 'blend your own' experience, where you can mix three wine varieties to your liking and take home a bottle of your own creation, complete with your own label (R70). The restaurant serves *roosterbrood* (traditional bread cooked over coals) sandwiches.

Marbin Olives FARM
(073 840 8228; www.marbin.co.za; off Klaasvoogds East Rd; tastings R50; 9am-4pm Mon-Sat) Travellers rave about the tutored tastings of olives, balsamic vinegar and olive oil offered at this family-run farm with jaw-dropping views of the Langeberg. Bookings are recommended.

Graham Beck WINERY
(023-626 1214; www.grahambeckwines.com; tastings from R75; 9am-5pm Mon-Fri, 10am-4pm Sat & Sun;) Taste the world-class bubblies in a striking modern building with huge plate-glass windows. The winery comes as a breath of fresh air after all those Cape Dutch estates.

Springfield WINERY
(023-626 3661; www.springfieldestate.com; Rte 317; tastings free; 8am-5pm Mon-Fri, 9am-3pm Sat) Some of the wines here are unfiltered – try the uncrushed Whole Berry for something different. Bring your own picnic to enjoy in the peaceful grounds, overlooking a lake. Cellar tours are available on request.

Van Loveren WINERY
(023-615 1505; www.vanloveren.co.za; tastings R55; 8.30am-5pm Mon-Fri, 9.30am-3.30pm Sat, 11am-3pm Sun, bistro closed Tue;) Specialising in affordable wines, Van Loveren offers a range of tasting options including pairings with cheese, chocolate and charcuterie as well as a grape juice tasting for kids (R35). Each of the trees in the tropical garden tells a story – grab a pamphlet from reception or join a guided tour (R45). Cellar tours are also available. The low-key bistro (mains R65 to R130) serves excellent burgers and pizzas.

Nerina Guest Farm HORSE RIDING
(082 744 2580; www.nerinaguestfarm.com; Goree Rd; hour-long rides R200) This long-running outfit offers hour-long horse trails along the Breede River or through the vineyards with an option to swim with the horses afterwards (R50). Longer rides can be arranged.

Festivals & Events

There are a number of wine-related events, including the Hands on Harvest in February, the Wacky Wine Weekend (023-626 3167; www.wackywineweekend.com) in late May/early June and the Wine on the River Festival (023-626 3167; www.wineonriver.com) in late October. Accommodation in the town is scarce at these times, so book well in advance.

Sleeping

★ Pat Busch Mountain Reserve COTTAGE $
(023-626 2033; www.patbusch.co.za; Bergendal Rd, Klaasvoogds West; 4-person cottage from R680;) These well-equipped cottages are based on the edge of a nature reserve 15km northeast of Robertson off Rte 60. Hiking, mountain biking, fishing and birdwatching are available. If you fancy some glamping, there are also luxury tents (double R1490) operated by Africamps. The tents have two bedrooms, a bathroom, well-equipped kitchen and stellar views of the Langeberg.

Robertson Backpackers HOSTEL $
(023-626 1280; www.robertsonbackpackers.co.za; 4 Dordrecht Ave; campsites R100, dm/s/d with shared bathroom R160/350/420, d R520;) A suburban backpackers with spacious dorms and pleasant en-suite doubles in the garden. There's a big grassy backyard, a shisha lounge, and wine and activity tours can be arranged, including a gentle half-day rafting trip on the Breede River (R550).

Gubas De Hoek GUESTHOUSE $$
(023-626 6218; www.gubas-dehoek.com; 45 Reitz St; s/d from R720/1160;) Highly recommended by readers is this friendly home with well-appointed rooms and family-friendly self-catering units (from R1200). Owner-chef Gunther Huerttlen will cook you dinner (three courses R360) and there's a shared self-catering kitchen for preparing light meals. The owners are working to produce all of their own electricity.

Ballinderry GUESTHOUSE $$
(023-626 5365; www.ballinderryguesthouse.com; 8 Le Roux St; s/d incl breakfast from R1100/1500;) This colourful boutique guesthouse is impeccable, thanks to hosts Luc and Hilde. A champagne breakfast is served, as are superb dinners on request, and Dutch, French and German are spoken. Try to get one of the rooms that opens onto the garden.

Eating

There are restaurants at many of the wine estates, though Robertson lags a little behind the likes of Stellenbosch and Franschhoek when it comes to culinary pursuits.

★ Strictly Coffee CAFE $
(023-626 6691; www.strictlycoffee.co.za; 5 Voortrekker St; mains R70-90; 7am-5.30pm Mon-Fri, 9am-2pm Sat;) As well as excellent coffee roasted on-site, you'll find a selection of cakes, plus tasty salads and sandwiches made with the freshest ingredients. Locals rave about the eggs Benedict for breakfast.

@ Four Cousins INTERNATIONAL $$
(023-615 1505; www.fourcousins.co.za; 3 Kromhout St; mains R80-160; 8.30am-9.30pm Mon-Sat, to 5pm Sun;) There's something to keep everyone entertained here – wine tasting, a microbrewery, sweetie pairings for the kids and an excellent jungle gym. The menu runs the gamut from salads and wraps to pizzas, burgers and steaks.

Bourbon Street INTERNATIONAL $$
(023-626 5934; www.bourbonst.co.za; 22 Voortrekker St; mains R70-170; 11am-10pm Mon-Sat, to 5pm Sun;) A firm favourite with locals, this long-running restaurant offers everything from jambalaya and Southern-style ribs to Thai green curry or a hearty game meat platter. It's also a good place for drinks, with a wide selection of craft beer and a decent cocktail menu.

Information

Robertson Tourism Bureau (023-626 4437; www.robertsontourism.co.za; 9 Voortrekker St; 8am-5pm Mon-Fri, 9am-2pm Sat, 10am-2pm Sun) A friendly office with information about the wine region and Rte 62.

Getting There & Away

Translux (086 158 9282; www.translux.co.za) buses stop opposite the police station on Voortrekker St. Routes include Knysna (R250, five hours), Cape Town (R240, two hours, daily) and Port Elizabeth (R390, nine hours, daily).

Shared taxis (Voortrekker St) to and from Bellville in the northern suburbs of Cape Town (R95, 1½ hours) also stop opposite the police station.

THE OVERBERG

Literally meaning 'over the mountain', Overberg refers to the region east of the Hottentots Holland range, where rolling wheat fields

OFF THE BEATEN TRACK

MCGREGOR

Just 20km south of Robertson at the end of a road going nowhere (you need your own wheels to visit) sits the pretty town of McGregor. The main reason to visit, other than a dose of peace and quiet, is to tackle the spectacular **Boesmanskloof Trail** (Greyton McGregor Trail; www.capenature.co.za; day permit adult/child R40/20), a 14km hike through the Riviersonderend mountains to Greyton. There's also a shorter hike to a waterfall if you don't feel like a full day of walking.

The town has a superb restaurant, **Karoux** (023-625 1421; www.karoux.co.za; 42 Voortrekker St; mains R90-160; 6-10pm Wed-Sat, noon-3pm Sun), and a couple of wineries scattered around the outskirts. Try **Tanagra Private Cellar** (023-625 1780; www.tanagra-wines.co.za; tastings free; by appointment) for its range of reds and good grappa.

McGregor Backpackers (023-004 0018; www.mcgregorbackpackers.co.za; 34 Bree St; dm/s/d R200/300/550; P) is more a budget guesthouse than a backpackers. Set around a lovely, rambling garden it offers brightly decorated rooms all with their own bathrooms and there's a communal kitchen, lounge and braai area. If McGregor isn't quiet enough for you, head to the luxury **Lord's Guest Lodge** (023-625 1881; www.lordsguestlodge.co.za; s/d cottage incl breakfast R1000/1450; P) 13km north of town. The thatched, stone cottages sit atop a hill and have wow vistas across the region.

are bordered by the Breede River, the coast and the peaks of three mountain ranges.

There are no unattractive routes leading to the Overberg; the N2 snakes up Sir Lowry's Pass, which has magnificent views from the top, and leads to the lovely Elgin Valley with its wine farms and the magnificent Hottentots Holland Nature Reserve.

Rte 44 stays at sea level and winds its way round Cape Hangklip, skirting the Kogelberg Nature Reserve on its way to Hermanus. It's a breathtaking coastal drive, on a par with Chapman's Peak Dr in Cape Town, but without the toll.

The Elgin Valley

Best known for its apple orchards, this verdant and sparsely populated region is little known to travellers. This makes its wineries (known for sauvignon blanc, chardonnay and pinot noir), hiking trails and other outdoor activities refreshingly uncrowded, except for the very popular Canopy Tour, which must be booked in advance. The main town in the region is **Grabouw**. It's easy to visit on a day trip from Cape Town.

Sights & Activities

Hottentots Holland Nature Reserve NATURE RESERVE
(028-841 4301; www.capenature.co.za; adult/child R40/20; 7am-5pm) This mountainous and forested reserve stretches from Jonkershoek in the west to Villiersdorp in the east, skirting the Theewaterskloof Dam. There are day walks and overnight hikes, mountain-bike routes and *kloofing* (canyoning) trails, but the main attraction is the **Canopy Tour** (021-300 0501; www.canopytour.co.za; per person R895), a zip-lining adventure that sees you soaring above the treetops.

Paul Cluver Wines WINERY
(021-844 0605; www.cluver.com; N2, Grabouw; tastings R40; 9am-5pm Mon-Fri, 10am-2pm Sat & Sun) A worthy stop on the Elgin wine route, offering fine wine, a country-style restaurant and mountain-bike trails (permits R80).

Green Mountain Trail HIKING
(028-284 9827; www.greenmountaintrail.co.za; s/d with full board R13,520/19,350) A four-day, 57km, 'slackpacking' hike through the mountains, where your bags are transported as you hike in relative luxury – think white-table-clothed picnics with fine wines and, at the end of the day, a handsome country manor to stay in.

Eating & Drinking

★ **Hickory Shack** BARBECUE $$
(021-300 1396; www.hickoryshack.co.za; N2; mains R70-165; 9am-5pm Tue-Fri & Sun, to 9pm Sat; P) This smokehouse has quickly gained a huge following for its slow-cooked and perfectly seasoned meats and Texan-inspired sides like corn salad, baked beans and slaw. There's craft beer on tap and a selection of ciders from around the Elgin Valley.

WORTH A TRIP

ROUTE 44 TO HERMANUS

If you have an extra half an hour to spare, taking the ocean road to Hermanus is a spectacular way to arrive and only adds 30 minutes to your trip (plus the time it takes to stop for photos and admire the view). As you reach Strand, veer off the N2 onto Rte 44, a road that hugs the coast once you reach Gordon's Bay. Known as Clarence Dr, this coastal route is a very worthy, toll-free alternative to Cape Town's Chapman's Peak Dr. Allow time to stop at the many lookout points for photos, and between June and December keep an eye on False Bay for frolicking whales.

There are a few worthy stops en route, starting with the **Kogelberg Nature Reserve** (☎087 288 0499; www.capenature.co.za; Rte 44; adult/child R40/20; ⏰7.30am-7pm) which has incredibly complex biodiversity, including more than 1880 plant species. Day walks are available as well as mountain-biking routes, but all activities must be prebooked. If you decide to have an overnight stay here, **Oudebosch Eco Cabins** (☎central reservations 021-483 0190; www.capenature.co.za; d cabin from R1170; P) offers delightful, well-equipped accommodation that is highly sought after, so be sure to reserve in advance.

Do take the time to stop at the **Stony Point Nature Reserve** (☎028-272 9829; www.capenature.co.za; off Wallers Rd; adult/child R20/10; ⏰8am-4.30pm; P). It's a much quieter place to watch the diminutive penguins than at the infinitely more famous Boulders Beach, on the other side of False Bay.

After driving through Betty's Bay, you'll find the **Harold Porter National Botanical Gardens** (☎028-272 9311; www.sanbi.org; adult/child R25/10; ⏰8am-4.30pm Mon-Fri, to 5pm Sat & Sun; P), worth a quick visit. There are paths exploring the indigenous plant life in the area and, at the entrance, a tearoom and plenty of places to picnic.

Close to a wild and beautiful beach, **Kleinmond** is a great place to spend an afternoon, eat some fresh seafood and browse the shops. It's much less commercialised than Hermanus and has excellent opportunities for whale watching, consistent waves for surfers and good walking.

Peregrine Farm Stall FOOD & DRINKS
(☎021-848 9011; www.peregrinefarmstall.co.za; N2; ⏰7.30am-6pm) Locals love to stop here for a freshly baked pie and some just-pressed apple juice before heading off on a road trip. As well as the farm stall, there's a cafe (mains R60 to R120) serving excellent lemon meringue pie and a range of shops and attractions, including the tasting room of Everson's Cider (tastings R42).

Getting There & Away

The valley begins after you reach the top of Sir Lowry's Pass in the Hottentots Holland Mountains east of Somerset West.

DMJ Transport (☎021-419 4368; www.dmjtransport.com) buses stop in Grabouw on their route from Cape Town (R150, 1½ hours, daily) to the Eastern Cape via the Garden Route.

Hermanus

☎028 / POP 10,500

Hermanus is generally considered the best land-based whale-watching destination in the world. From June to December, the bay becomes the swimming grounds for a large number of southern right whales. So what might have otherwise just been a small fishing village is today a large, bustling town with an excellent range of accommodation, restaurants and shops.

The town stretches over a long main road but the centre is easily navigable on foot. There's a superb cliff-path walk and plenty of other hikes in the hills around the town, as well as good wine tasting, and the **Hermanus Whale Festival** (www.whalefestival.co.za) in September. The town gets very crowded at this time and during the December and January school holidays. Only 122km from Cape Town, Hermanus is also perfect for a day trip.

Sights

Fernkloof Nature Reserve NATURE RESERVE
(☎028-313 0819; www.fernkloof.com; Fir Ave; ⏰7am-7pm) FREE This 15-sq-km reserve is wonderful if you're interested in fynbos (literally 'fine bush' – shrubby plants with thin leaves). There's a 60km network of hiking trails for all fitness levels, and views over the sea are spectacular. A hiking map is available from the tourist information office. Guided tours are available – book ahead.

Old Harbour HISTORIC SITE

The harbour clings to the cliffs in front of the town centre and is the hub of Hermanus. You'll find three museums here: the **Old Harbour Museum** (028-312 1475; www.old-harbour-museum.co.za; Marine Dr; adult/child R20/5; 9am-4.30pm Mon-Sat, noon-4pm Sun), **Whale House Museum** (Market Sq; adult/child R20/5; 9am-4.30pm Mon-Sat, noon-4pm Sun) and **Photographic Museum** (Market Sq; adult/child R20/5; 9am-4.30pm Mon-Sat, noon-4pm Sun). There's a permanent craft market in the square as well.

Activities

While Hermanus is renowned for its land-based whale watching, boat trips are also available. Approaching whales in the water is highly regulated and the boats must stay a minimum of 50m from the whales.

★ **Cliff Path Walking Trail** HIKING

FREE This scenic path meanders for 10km from New Harbour, 2km west of town, along the sea to the mouth of the Klein River; you can join it anywhere along the cliffs. It's simply the finest thing to do in Hermanus, whales or not.

Along the way you pass Grotto Beach, the most popular beach; Kwaaiwater, a good whale-watching lookout; as well as Langbaai and Voelklip Beaches. The tourism office has a pamphlet with more details on the trail.

Walker Bay Adventures WATER SPORTS

(082 739 0159; www.walkerbayadventures.co.za; Old Harbour; kayaking R400, boat-based whale watching adult/child R800/380) Watching whales from a sea kayak is a gobsmacking, if at times rather nerve-wracking, experience. Other activities on offer include sandboarding, horse riding and boat trips.

Southern Right Charters BOATING

(082 353 0550; www.southernrightcharters.co.za; 2hr trip adult/child R800/380) A licensed boat operator that runs whale-watching trips from New Harbour.

Sleeping

Hermanus Backpackers HOSTEL $

(028-312 4293; www.hermanusbackpackers.co.za; 26 Flower St; dm R170, d R490, with shared bathroom R440; P) This is a great place with upbeat decor, good facilities and clued-up staff who can help with activities. The simple, help-yourself breakfast is free, and evening meals are available. It's a pretty chilled spot and the annexe around the corner is even quieter.

Zoete Inval Travellers Lodge HOSTEL $

(028-312 1242; www.zoeteinval.co.za; 23 Main Rd; dm from R200, d R650, with shared bathroom R550; P) A budget option in suburbia, this is a quiet place with good amenities (including a spa bath) and neatly furnished rooms.

★ **Potting Shed** GUESTHOUSE $$

(028-3121712; www.thepottingshedaccommodation.co.za; 28 Albertyn St; d incl breakfast from R1100; P) This friendly guesthouse offers delightful personal touches, including homemade biscuits on arrival. The neat rooms are comfortable and have bright, imaginative decor. There's a spacious loft studio and the owners also operate self catering apartments (four people R1450) closer to the sea.

Baleia de Hermanus GUESTHOUSE $$

(028-312 2513; www.baleia.co.za; 57 Main Rd; s/d incl breakfast R630/1100; P) The smart, comfortable rooms are set around a swimming pool. Owner-run, it's a friendly and welcoming spot.

Hermanus Esplanade APARTMENT $$

(028-312 3610; www.hermanusesplanade.com; 63 Marine Dr; sea-facing apt from R800) When we last visited, these ocean-facing apartments had just been taken over by the Windsor Hotel and were about to receive a much-needed facelift.

Marine LUXURY HOTEL $$$

(028-313 1000; www.themarinehotel.co.za; Marine Dr; r incl breakfast from R4700; P) The town's poshest option is right on the sea with immaculate grounds and amenities, including two sea-facing restaurants. Pavilion (p219) is only open for breakfast, while Origins (p219) boasts gourmet fare with a focus on seafood.

Auberge Burgundy GUESTHOUSE $$$

(028-313 1201; www.auberge.co.za; 16 Harbour Rd; s/d incl breakfast from R1080/1440; P) This wonderful place, built in the style of a Provençal villa, is right in the centre of town. Many rooms have ocean views. Rates do not rise during peak season.

Harbour House Hotel HOTEL $$$

(028-312 1799; www.harbourhousehotel.co.za; 22 Harbour Rd; s/d incl breakfast from R1100/1380; P) Some of the bright, modern rooms have kitchenettes and all have a balcony or

Hermanus

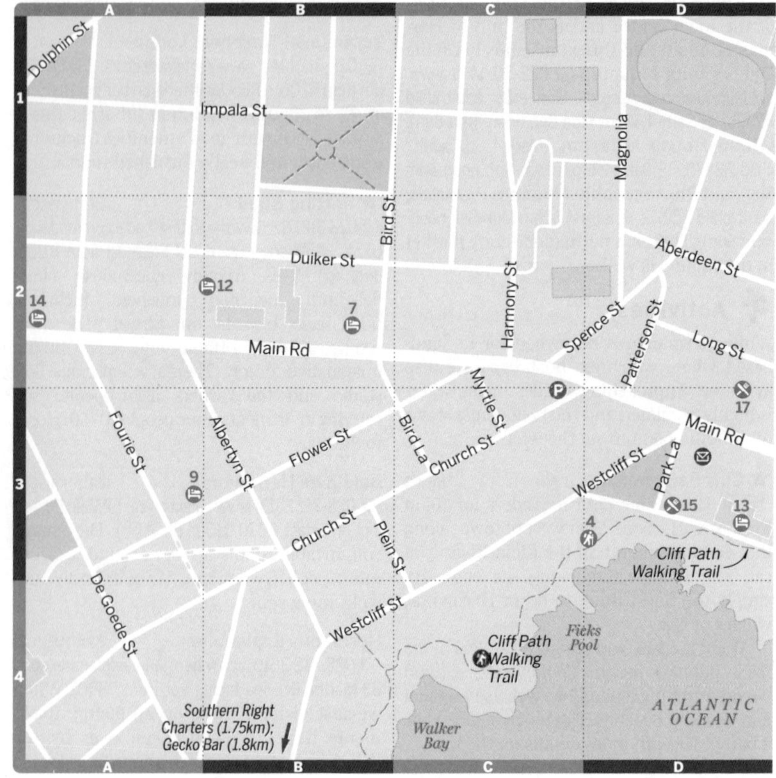

terrace. It's a delightful seaside hotel and the ocean views from the infinity pool are phenomenal.

Windsor Hotel HOTEL $$$
(☎028-312 3727; www.windsorhotel.co.za; 49 Marine Dr; s/d incl breakfast R950/1150, with sea views R1450/1650; P) A sea-facing room at this stalwart overlooking the ocean means you'll be able to whale-watch from your bed in season. Rooms have had a bit of a revamp but are still true to the hotel's Victorian roots. There are also large, sea-facing apartments (four people R2100).

Eating

Eatery CAFE $
(☎028-313 2970; Long St Arcade, Long St; mains R55-95; 7am-4pm Mon-Fri, to 1pm Sat;) Tucked away in a side street, this is a local hang-out lauded for its excellent coffee, fresh salads and sandwiches plus a range of tasty cakes baked on-site.

Bistro at Just Pure CAFE $$
(☎028-313 0060; www.justpurebistro.co.za; cnr Marine Dr & Park Lane; mains R65-115; 8.30am-4.30pm Mon-Fri, to 3pm Sat & Sun;) Adjoining a shop selling natural cosmetics, this seafront bistro is all about fresh, local, organic ingredients. Try the 'famous' cheesecake and watch whales from the patio as you eat. Dinners are served from October to February.

Burgundy Restaurant SEAFOOD $$
(☎028-312 2800; www.burgundyrestaurant.co.za; Marine Dr; mains R95-240; 8am-9pm) This long-standing restaurant is still going strong, popular with both locals and tourists as much for its superb sea view as for its menu. Seafood is the star, though vegetarians and carnivores are also well served.

Fisherman's Cottage SEAFOOD $$
(☎028-312 3642; www.fishermanscottage.co.za; Lemm's Corner; mains R105-270; noon-3pm Fri-Sun, 6-9.30pm Mon-Sat) The emphasis is on seafood at this 1860s thatched cottage

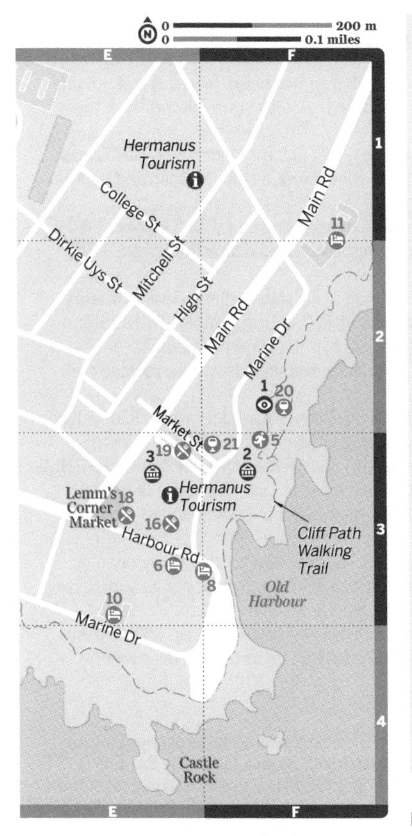

Hermanus

Sights

1 Old Harbour F2
2 Old Harbour Museum F3
Photographic Museum .... (see 3)
3 Whale House Museum E3

Activities, Courses & Tours

4 Cliff Path Walking Trail D3
5 Walker Bay Adventures F3

Sleeping

6 Auberge Burgundy E3
7 Baleia de Hermanus B2
8 Harbour House Hotel F3
9 Hermanus Backpackers A3
10 Hermanus Esplanade E3
11 Marine F1
12 Potting Shed B2
13 Windsor Hotel D3
14 Zoete Inval Travellers Lodge A2

Eating

15 Bistro at Just Pure D3
16 Burgundy Restaurant E3
17 Eatery D3
18 Fisherman's Cottage E3
Origins .... (see 11)
Pavilion .... (see 11)
19 Pear Tree E3

Drinking & Nightlife

20 Bientang's Cave F2
21 Mock Turtle F3

draped with fishing nets, though it also serves steaks and traditional meals.

★ **Pear Tree** FUSION $$$
(☎028-313 1224; http://peartree-hermanus.co.za; 2 Godfrey Cottages, Village Sq; mains R110-180; ⊙11am-11pm) One of the town's top restaurants is an intimate venue decorated in bodega style – all bare brick and wine bottles. The small menu features delights like pulled lamb tagliatelle with truffle oil, braised pork belly and naartjie Malva pudding (a traditional sticky sponge pudding with citrus fruit) with pink peppercorns. Book ahead.

Origins SEAFOOD $$$
(☎028-313 1000; www.themarine.co.za; Marine Dr; mains R135-250; ⊙noon-2.30pm & 7-9.30pm; P) Based within the plush Marine (p217) hotel, the focus here is perfectly prepared seafood dishes, plus a few meaty options and some enticing desserts.

Pavilion BREAKFAST $$$
(☎028-313 1000; www.themarinehotel.co.za; Marine Dr; breakfast R180; ⊙7-10.30am) Found within the Marine (p217) hotel, this is the place for a special breakfast with ocean views – try the croissant French toast with maple syrup and bacon, then attack the buffet.

Drinking & Nightlife

Bientang's Cave BAR
(☎028-312 3454; www.bientangscave.com; Marine Dr; ⊙11.30am-8pm) This cave, occupied by the last Strandlopers (coastal indigenous people) at the turn of the 19th century, has a truly remarkable setting and is definitely worth a stop for a drink. Access is only via a steep flight of cliff-side stairs.

Gecko Bar BAR
(☎028-312 4665; New Harbour; ⊙11am-2am) The decor is a bit shabby but the ocean views more than make up for it. There's sushi and pizza on the menu (mains R55 to R115), local beer on tap, sport on the big screen and live music on weekends.

LOCAL KNOWLEDGE

WINE TASTING AROUND HERMANUS

The area is best known for whales but there are also some superb wineries just outside Hermanus. The **Hemel-en-Aarde** (Heaven and Earth) valley starts 5km west of the town and follows a winding route north for 15km.

If you don't have a nondrinker in your party, the highly recommended **Tuk-Tuk Transporter** (p220) provides transport between three wine farms, a stop for lunch and return to your accommodation for R275 per person.

For an alternative way to see the wineries, join a quad-biking tour with **SA Forest Adventures** (in Cape Town 021-795 0225; www.saforestadventures.co.za; activities from R350) (per person R650).

As with other wineries in the region, the pinot noir really shines at **Newton Johnson** (021-200 2148; www.newtonjohnson.com; tastings from R50; 9am-4pm Mon-Fri, 10am-2pm Sat, restaurant noon-3pm Wed-Sun). The real star, though, is the superb restaurant (mains R150 to R200), which serves fairly simple but perfectly executed dishes like roasted pork loin with broad beans.

Creation (028-212 1107; www.creationwines.com; Hemel en Aarde Rd; tastings R50; 10am-5pm; P) is best known for its various wine-pairing options, which include a superb brunch pairing (R495) as well as tea pairings (R435) and even a juice pairing for kids (R115). The restaurant menu lists the local butchers, bakers, cheese makers and the like who supply the ingredients. It's 20km from Hermanus on the Hemel-en-Aarde road. Bookings essential for pairing experiences.

The picturesque **Bouchard Finlayson** (028-312 3515; www.bouchardfinlayson.co.za; Rte 320; tastings R40; 9am-5pm Mon-Fri, 10am-1pm Sat; P) is best known for its superlative pinot noir. There are gentle walks through fynbos vegetation on the estate.

La Vierge (028-313 0130; www.lavierge.co.za; Hemel-en-Aarde Rd; tastings R50; 10am-5pm Tue-Sun) offers tastings and lunch (mains R120 to R185) in its ubermodern winery decked out in hot pink and glass.

Mock Turtle BAR

(083 639 1222; Village Sq, Marine Dr; noon-9pm Mon-Thu, to 2am Fri & Sat) A chilled-out bar with good cocktails and DJs most nights. In the early evening it's a great place to enjoy sunset with a beer.

Information

Internet City (Waterkant Bldg, Main Rd; per hr R40; 8am-5pm Mon-Fri, 8.30am-3pm Sat)

Post Office (028-312 1500; 93 Main Rd)

Although **Hermanus Tourism** (028-313 1602; www.hermanustourism.info; Market Sq; 9am-5pm Mon-Fri, to 4pm Sat, 10am-2pm Sun) is not the main tourism office, it's in a much more convenient location. Staff are exceptionally helpful.

The larger **tourism office** (028-312 2629; www.hermanustourism.info; Old Station Bldg, Mitchell St; 8am-5pm Mon-Fri, 9am-4pm Sat, 10am-2pm Sun) is just north of the town and can help with accommodation bookings.

Getting There & Away

Bernardus Tours (028-316 1093; www.bernardustransfershermanus.co.za) offers shuttles to Gansbaai (R450, 30 minutes) and Cape Town (R1000, 1½ hours). Prices are per vehicle (up to three passengers).

The hostels run a shuttle service (one way from R100, 30 minutes) to the **Baz Bus** (p184) drop-off point in Botrivier, 50km west of town. There are shared taxis from Bellville (R90, two hours) in Cape Town's northern suburbs.

Getting Around

Hermanus town centre is compact but if you're staying in the suburbs you will find the handy **Tuk-Tuk Transporter** (084 688 5885; www.hermanustaxi.com) a cheap way to get around. A standard fare is R40 for two people.

Gansbaai

028 / POP 11,600

Gansbaai's unspoilt coastline is perfect for those wishing to explore more out-of-the-way Overberg nature spots. The town's star has risen in recent years thanks to shark-cage diving, though most people just visit on a day trip from Cape Town.

The nearby village of **De Kelders** (on the road to Gansbaai from Hermanus) is a great spot for secluded whale watching. Shark boats leave from the harbour at Kleinbaai.

Sights

★Walker Bay Nature Reserve NATURE RESERVE
(☎028-314 0062; www.capenature.co.za; adult/child R40/20; ⏱7am-7pm) This coastal reserve has excellent hikes and is a prime birdwatching spot. The main attractions though, other than the ocean vistas, are the impressive **Klipgat Caves**, site of an archaeological discovery of Khoe-San artefacts. There are informative panels within the caves. The reserve is in two sections, though most people stick to the area just north of De Kelders. You can also access the park from Stanford and from Uilenkraalsmond, south of Gansbaai.

Danger Point Lighthouse LIGHTHOUSE
(☎028-384 0530; Lighthouse.Tourism@transnet.net; adult/child R16/8; ⏱10am-3pm Mon-Fri; P) Dating from 1895, the lighthouse is set in pretty grounds and has some information on the 1852 HMS *Birkenhead* shipwreck. Call in advance, as opening hours aren't always observed. There's also a simple self-catering cottage in the grounds (four people from R900).

Sleeping

Gansbaai Backpackers HOSTEL $
(☎083 626 4150; www.gansbaybackpackers.com; 6 Strand St; dm R180, d R500, d with shared bathroom R450; P 📶) This efficient and friendly place close to the harbour offers homely budget accommodation, including small garden studios with TV and basic kitchen facilities (double R500). Staff can assist with booking adventure activities in the area.

Aire del Mar GUESTHOUSE $$
(☎028-384 2848; www.airedelmar.co.za; 77 Van Dyk St, Kleinbaai; s/d incl breakfast R765/1275; P 📶) A friendly place offering a good range of prices, including basic self-catering units (for two people R950). Rooms have panoramic sea views out to Dyer Island.

★Grootbos Private Nature Reserve LODGE $$$
(☎028-384 8008; www.grootbos.com; Rte 43; s/d full board R9600/12,800; P ❄ 📶 🏊) 🍃 This superb luxury choice set on 25 sq km includes horse riding, hiking, local excursions and great food in the price. Each of the free-standing cottages has an outdoor shower on the deck. The Grootbos Foundation runs a number of environmental and community projects – ask about the Progressive Tourism Package.

Eating

★Coffee on the Rocks CAFE $$
(☎028-384 2017; http://coffee-on-the-rocks.com; 81 Cliff St, De Kelders; mains R50-110; ⏱10am-5pm Wed-Sun; 📶) All breads are baked daily onsite and everything else is homemade too. The ocean-facing deck is a great place for a sandwich, a salad or just a coffee while you look out for whales in season.

Blue Goose SOUTH AFRICAN $$
(☎079 310 1770; 12 Franken St; mains R90-155; ⏱10am-3pm Tue-Sun, 5.30-10pm daily) Based in an old fishing cottage, this local favourite has a menu that showcases local, seasonal ingredients. It's best known for seafood, though the lamb shank is also very good.

Great White House SEAFOOD $$
(☎028-384 3273; www.thegreatwhitehouse.co.za; 5 Geelbek St, Kleinbaai; mains R60-180; ⏱8am-10pm Wed-Mon, to 5pm Tue) A multifarious place that dishes up fresh seafood (including hard-to-find abalone), clothing and curios, helps with tourist information and offers accommodation in pleasant thatched cottages (single/double including breakfast R570/1000).

Information

Gansbaai Tourism (☎028-384 1439; www.gansbaaiinfo.com; Main Rd, Great White Junction; ⏱9am-5pm Mon-Fri, 9am-4pm Sat, 10am-2pm Sun) Staff can help with activities and accommodation.

Getting There & Away

Public transport to Gansbaai is sporadic and unreliable. Your best bet is **Bernardus Tours** (p220), which runs shuttles to Hermanus (R450, 30 minutes) and Cape Town (R1400, two hours).

Stanford

☎028 / POP 4800

This picture-perfect village on the banks of the Klein River is a popular spot with Capetonians on weekends, and for good reason. The surrounding area boasts a handful of uncrowded wineries while in Stanford itself you'll find trips on the river, kayaks for hire, a couple of good restaurants and a brewery.

Sights

★Stanford Hills WINERY
(☎028-341 0841; www.stanfordhills.co.za; off Rte 43; tastings R40; ⏱8.30am-5pm; P 👪) Taste the Jacksons pinotage here – a fine example

of South Africa's home-grown grape variety. There's also charming self-catering accommodation available (cottage from R1100), a glamping option (single/double luxury tent R1290/1490) and a family-friendly restaurant (mains R95 to R120) offering a chalkboard menu of rustic fare. The views are marvellous.

Robert Stanford Estate WINERY
(☎028-341 0647; www.robertstanfordestate.co.za; Rte 43; tastings free; ⏰9am-4pm Thu-Mon) The white wines here are good, particularly the sauvignon blanc. There's also a small distillery producing grappa and *mampoer* (moonshine) and a country restaurant for lunch.

Klein River Cheese Farm FARM
(☎028-341 0693; www.kleinrivercheese.co.za; Rte 326; ⏰9am-4pm Mon-Sat; P 👪) The cheese from this farm has become wildly popular – the aged gruyère is particularly good. Taste and buy a selection of cheese and put together your own picnic to eat in the grounds. Children will love the petting farm and playground.

Birkenhead Brewery BREWERY
(☎028-341 0013; www.walkerbayestate.com; Rte 326; tour & tasting R80; ⏰10am-5pm, tours 10am & 3pm Wed-Fri; P 👪) Birkenhead is one of the country's oldest microbreweries and one of its most scenic, with a lovely view of the Klein River Mountains. Sip your way through a tasting tray on the lawns in summer or grab a pint of English bitter next to the log fire in winter. It's just out of town on Rte *326* towards Bredasdorp.

Activities

River Rat BOATING
(☎083 310 0952; www.riverratstanford.wordpress.com; per person R150; ⏰by appointment) Book a three-hour trip along the Klein River and bring along your own meat to braai on board. There are also kayaks available to hire (per day R100).

African Queen BOATING
(☎082 732 1284; www.africanqueenstanford.co.za; Du Toit St; per person R160; ⏰9am, noon, 3pm & 6pm Sep-May) Three-hour boat trips along the Klein River, docking part way to allow passengers to swim in the river and braai on the deck. Bring your own booze and food. Bookings essential.

Eating

Marianna's BISTRO $$
(☎028-341 0272; 12 Du Toit St; mains R120-145; ⏰noon-2pm Sat & Sun; ✎) This award-winning, eclectic place serves a mixture of traditional and contemporary fare, much of it made with produce from the owner's garden. Advance booking is essential. If all the private tables are taken, you might end up sharing with other guests. No children under 10.

Havercroft's BISTRO $$$
(☎028-341 0603; Rte 43; mains R140-165; ⏰noon-2.30pm Thu-Sun; P) The food from husband-and-wife team Brydon and Innes gets excellent reviews. The small menu is inventive and refined, utilising plenty of local produce. Sunday lunch is highly recommended. Bookings

SHARK-CAGE DIVING

A number of shark-cage diving operators are clustered around Kleinbaai's harbour, including **Marine Dynamics** (☎079 930 9694; www.sharkwatchsa.com; 5 Geelbek St, Kleinbaai; adult/child R1900/1100) and **White Shark Projects** (☎076 245 5880; www.whitesharkprojects.co.za; 16 Geelbek St, Kleinbaai; dives R1800), which both have Fairtrade accreditation.

There is ongoing controversy regarding shark-cage diving. Detractors believe that 'chumming' – throwing blood and guts from other fish into the water to attract the sharks – teaches the animals that boats and humans are associated with food. Attacks on swimmers and surfers are said to have increased as a direct result. But the activity has many supporters, including marine scientists and even some environmentalists. Their argument is that shark-cage diving is a positive education tool that helps to remove fear and alleviate the bad rep these fish have had since the *Jaws* movie back in 1975.

Once the sharks come close, participants clad in wetsuits and snorkel masks take a deep breath and submerge themselves in the water for a close encounter with the great whites. No scuba experience is necessary and underwater visibility is best from May to September.

If you want to experience this close encounter with a wild animal, make sure you use a licensed operator who is fully insured. If you prefer to avoid shark-cage diving, get in touch with an operator such as **Simon's Town Boat Company** (Map p108; ☎083 257 7760; www.boatcompany.co.za; Town Pier, 🚉Simon's Town), which offers boat trips to Seal Island, where sharks go to feast on penguins and seals.

essential and no under 12s allowed. It's based in a farmhouse on Rte 43 as you enter Stanford from Hermanus.

Information

Tourist Office (022-341 0340; www.stanfordinfo.co.za; 18 Queen Victoria St; 8.30am-4.30pm Mon-Fri, 9am-4pm Sat, 9am-1pm Sun)

Getting There & Away

It's a scenic 25km drive from Hermanus to Stanford along Rte 43. There are infrequent shared taxis to and from Hermanus (R20, 30 minutes).

WEST COAST

Darling

022 / POP 1100

A quiet country town, Darling has long been known as the home of actor and satirist Pieter-Dirk Uys – or more so his alter ego, Evita Bezuidenhout. But in recent years, reasons to visit have multiplied and Darling has become a foodie town of note.

The long-established wineries offer a more relaxed tasting experience than many of their busier counterparts in the Winelands and the region is well known for its olives. On the edge of town is a highly popular brewery that has played an integral part in Darling's culinary awakening.

Sights

Darling Brewery BREWERY
(079 182 9001; www.darlingbrew.co.za; 48 Caledon St; tastings from R10; 9am-5pm Tue-Thu, 10am-9pm Fri & Sat, 10am-4pm Sun; P) Darling is one of the country's best-known breweries, pouring a wide range of beers including Africa's first carbon-neutral brew. You can taste any or all of the beers in the cheery tasting room overlooking the brewery itself. The restaurant (mains R60 to R160) serves upscale bar food showcasing produce from Darling's various artisanal producers.

Groote Post WINERY
(022-492 2825; www.grootepost.com; tastings free, 2hr wildlife drive adult/child R170/75; 10am-4pm; P) Of all the Darling wineries, Groote Post has the most to offer the visitor, with wildlife drives, self-guided nature walks, a superb restaurant and free tastings of its excellent chardonnays and sauvignon blancs. It's 7km along a dirt road, off Rte 307. Book ahead for the restaurant and wildlife drives.

Sleeping & Eating

Darling Lodge GUESTHOUSE $$
(022-492 3062; www.darlinglodge.co.za; 22 Pastorie St; s/d incl breakfast R850/980;) An elegant and imaginatively decorated place. Rooms are named after local artists, whose work is displayed on the walls, and there's a lovely garden to relax in.

Chicory Cheese CAFE $$
(076 975 6197; www.chicorycheese.co.za; 5 Long St; mains R80-105; 8.30am-4pm Mon-Fri, to 2pm Sat;) Grab a seat in the garden and slurp down a freshly squeezed juice at this chilled cafe. The menu features wraps, sandwiches, pancakes and some calorie-laden salads. There's also a decent deli, if you're looking to stock up for picnics.

Hilda's Kitchen BISTRO $$
(022-492 2825; www.grootepost.com; Groote Post Winery; mains R110-150; noon-2pm Wed-Sun) Perhaps Darling's most upmarket place to dine, with a constantly changing menu that is designed to pair with Groote Post's wines.

Marmalade Cat CAFE $$
(022-492 2515; www.marmaladecat.co.za; 19 Main Rd; mains R60-115; 7am-4.30pm daily, 6-9pm Fri;) For an afternoon coffee or all-day breakfast, this is the place to go. It also serves sandwiches, delicious cheeses and homemade sweet treats. Friday night is pizza night – bookings essential.

Entertainment

★**Evita se Perron** CABARET
(022-492 2851; www.evita.co.za; Old Darling Station, 8 Arcadia St; tickets R165, buffet meal R135; 2pm & 7pm Sat, 2pm Sun) This uniquely South African cabaret, featuring Pieter-Dirk Uys as his alter ego Evita Bezuidenhout, touches on everything from South African politics to history to ecology. Nothing is off limits – including the country's racially charged past. Although the shows include a smattering of Afrikaans, they're largely in English and always hilarious and thought-provoking. Buffet meals are available for those attending a show.

Even if you're not seeing a show, a visit to the complex is well worth it. There's a politically themed sculpture garden and some fascinating apartheid memorabilia on show. The splendidly kitsch restaurant (mains R45-65; 10am-4pm Tue-Sun) serves traditional Afrikaner food. Uys also set up the Darling Trust (www.thedarlingtrust.org) to assist Swartland communities to empower themselves through participation in education and health programs. The **A en C Shop** at the complex stocks beading, clothes, wire-art and paintings.

Shopping

Darling Sweet FOOD
(☎083 235 4002; www.darlingsweet.co.za; 7a Long St; ⏰8am-5pm Mon-Sat, 10am-2pm Sun) Specialising in handmade toffees, Darling Sweet is a popular addition to the town's foodie scene. You can watch the toffee being made then indulge in a free tasting before stocking up on your favourites. There's an emphasis on locally sourced ingredients, including red wine and chocolate, sour fig and bird's eye chilli.

Information

Tourist Information (☎022-492 3361; www.darlingtourism.co.za; cnr Hill & Pastorie Sts; ⏰9am-1pm & 2-4pm Mon-Thu, to 3.30pm Fri, 10am-3pm Sat & Sun) In the museum.

Getting There & Away

Darling is 90km north of Cape Town along the scenic Rte 27. **Golden Arrow** (p185) offers a service that leaves Cape Town at 5pm with return buses leaving Darling at 5am. At other times you can catch a **MyCiTi** (p185) bus (R36, 1½ hours) from the Civic Centre in Cape Town to Atlantis from where you can take a shared taxi (R20, 30 minutes) to Darling. Just keep your wits about you at the taxi rank in Atlantis.

Langebaan

☎022 / POP 8300

Its beautiful location overlooking the Langebaan Lagoon has made this seaside resort a favourite holiday destination with South Africans. But, while it is popular, it's fairly spread out so you can still easily find solitude. The town is known for its water sports, particularly kite-surfing and windsurfing on the lagoon. There are phenomenal sunset views and a few good beaches, the best of which is **Langebaan Beach** – in town and popular with swimmers. The town is also a good base for exploring the West Coast National Park (p226).

OFF THE BEATEN TRACK

DE HOOP NATURE RESERVE

Covering 340 sq km and extending 5km out to sea, **De Hoop Nature Reserve** (☎028-542 1114; www.capenature.co.za; adult/child R40/20; ⏰7am-6pm) has a magnificent coastline, with long stretches of pristine beach and huge dunes. It's an important breeding and calving area for the southern right whale. You'll find exceptional coastal fynbos (fine bush) and animals such as endangered Cape mountain zebras and bontebok. There is also prolific birdlife, including a breeding colony of the rare Cape vultures. The accommodation ranges from camping to basic huts to luxury rooms.

Sights & Activities

★**West Coast Fossil Park** ARCHAEOLOGICAL SITE
(☎022-766 1606; www.fossilpark.org.za; guided tour adult/child R80/50, entry only adult/child R35/25; ⏰8am-4pm Mon-Fri, 10am-1pm Sat & Sun; P) The first bear discovered south of the Sahara, lion-size sabre-toothed cats, three-toed horses and short-necked giraffes are all on display at this excellent fossil park on Rte 45 about 16km outside Langebaan. Fascinating tours depart hourly from 10am to 3pm (until 1pm on weekends) and take you to the excavation sites – among the richest fossil sites in the world. There are also mountain-biking and walking trails, and a coffee shop. A new exhibition centre funded by the national lottery was about to open when we last visited.

Cape Sports Center WATER SPORTS
(☎022-772 1114; www.capesport.co.za; 98 Main Rd) Langebaan is a water-sports mecca, particularly for windsurfing and kite-surfing. This cheery office offers kite-surfing courses (three-day course from R3950), windsurfing lessons (two hours R900) and rents out surfboards, SUPs and kayaks (R320/395/395 per day).

Sleeping & Eating

★**Friday Island** B&B $$
(☎022-772 2506; www.fridayisland.co.za; Main Rd; s/d R600/880; 📶) There are bright rooms and cheery staff at this popular beachfront B&B. You're going to want one of the two-level sea-facing rooms (single/double R900/1380), each with its own deck. The popular restaurant (mains R75 to R180) serves seafood, burgers, steak and budget-friendly breakfast.

Farmhouse Hotel HOTEL $$
(☎022-772 2062; www.thefarmhousehotel.com; 5 Egret St; r incl breakfast from R1100; P❄📶🏊) Langebaan's oldest hotel sits on a hill overlooking the bay with lovely views. Rooms are large, with country decor and fireplaces. The restaurant is reasonably priced (mains R95 to R190) and has a varied menu. The hotel also has some self-catering cottages (www.kitequarters.co.za) aimed at kite-surfers.

OFF THE BEATEN TRACK

!KHWA TTU

!Khwa ttu (022-492 2998; www.khwattu.org; Rte 27; tours R195; 9am-5pm, tours 10am & 2pm; P) is the only San-owned and -operated culture centre in the Western Cape. It's based on an 8.5-sq-km nature reserve within the ancestral lands of the San. Tours involve a nature walk on which you learn about San culture, and a wildlife drive – you'll likely see various antelope, zebras and ostriches. There are hiking and biking trails on the reserve and a quality gift shop stocking work from San artists. A museum was in progress when we last visited.

There is a restaurant open for breakfast and lunch and a range of accommodation including a basic bush camp (R325 per person) and a guesthouse (double R1760). It's off Rte 27, 70km north of Cape Town.

Club Mykonos INTERNATIONAL $$
(080 022 6770; www.clubmykonos.co.za; Mykonos Access Rd; mains R60-190; P) This Greek-themed, pseudo-Mediterranean resort might not appeal as a place to stay over, but it is a fun spot to spend an evening. There are eight restaurants to choose from plus numerous bars and a casino, all open to nonguests. Four of the restaurants have fabulous ocean views.

★ **Die Strandloper** SEAFOOD $$$
(022-772 2490; www.strandloper.com; buffet R310; noon-4pm & 6-10pm Dec & Jan, noon-4pm Fri-Sun, 6-10pm Fri Feb-Nov) The West Coast life exemplified – a *10*-course fish and seafood braai right on the beach. There's also freshly made bread, bottomless *moerkoffie* (freshly ground coffee) and a local crooner who wanders the tables strumming his guitar. You can BYO (corkage free) or get drinks from the rustic bar, from where the view is sensational. Bookings highly recommended.

Drinking & Nightlife

Black Eagle MICROBREWERY
(022-772 0594; http://bebc.co.za; Suffren St; 11am-6pm Fri & Sat) If you happen to be in town on a weekend, join the locals for a couple of pints at this tiny brewery. Tasters (R10) are available or just grab a pint of the Weskus Brekfis witbier or Moedersmelk stout and nibble on a cheese and charcuterie platter (R180).

Ginja Beanz COFFEE
(022-772 2221; www.ginjabeanz.co.za; Waterfront Sq, Bree St; 8am-4pm Mon-Fri, 9am-3pm Sat) As well as superb coffee from Langebaan's one and only roastery, Wings, this busy place serves Black Insomnia – the world's strongest cup of joe.

Information

Tourist Information Centre (022-772 1515; www.visitwestcoast.co.za; 120 Oostewal Rd; 9am-5pm Mon-Fri, to 2pm Sat & Sun)

Getting There & Away

Langebaan is about 90 minutes' drive north of Cape Town. **Shared taxis** (Oostewal Rd) run from the OK Mart car park to Cape Town (R110, two hours). **Elwierda** (021-557 9002; www.elwierda.co.za) operates regular buses to Cape Town (R130, two to three hours); booking a day in advance is essential.

Paternoster

022 / POP 2000

Not so many years ago, Paternoster was the West Coast's last traditional fishing village, little more than a clutch of simple whitewashed homes set against the blue sea. Today it's a second home to wealthy Capetonians and foreigners captivated by its calm waters, an expansive and often empty beach.

It's best to steer clear of the many roadside vendors selling crayfish *(kreef)*, considered an endangered species here.

Sights & Activities

Cape Columbine Lighthouse LIGHTHOUSE
(021-449 2400; www.transnetnationalportsauthority.net; Cape Columbine Nature Reserve; adult/child R16/8; 10am-3pm Mon-Fri; P) Built in 1936, the diminutive lighthouse is worth a brief pause. You can also stay over here in a simple cottage (double from R650).

Cape Columbine Nature Reserve NATURE RESERVE
(022-752 2718; adult/child R21/14; 7am-7pm) Three kilometres south of Paternoster, along a rutted gravel road, lies this windswept but beautiful reserve. It has campsites with basic facilities at Tieties Bay (R167 per site). The lighthouse tower is worth a climb and you can also stay here in renovated keepers' cottages (double from R650).

DON'T MISS

WEST COAST NATIONAL PARK

The focal point at this 310-sq-km **park** (022-772 2144; www.sanparks.org; adult/child R80/40, Aug & Sep R170/85; 7am-7pm), 120km north of Cape Town and 7km south of Langebaan, is the Langebaan Lagoon, whose clear blue waters are perfect for sailing and swimming. The park also attracts birding enthusiasts, its wetlands providing important seabird breeding colonies. Wading birds flock here in summer, with the curlew sandpiper seen in the greatest numbers. The park is also famous for its **wildflower display**, usually between August and September when the entry fee doubles and it can get fairly crowded.

Aside from the white-sand beaches and turquoise waters of the ocean and lagoon, the park's greatest allure is that it is undervisited. If you visit midweek (and outside school holidays) you might find that you're sharing the roads only with zebras, ostriches and the occasional leopard tortoise ambling across your path.

Should you wish to stay over there are five park-owned cottages (from R1380 per cottage), the nicest of which is **Jo Anne's Beach Cottage** (www.sanparks.org; cottage from R1380; P). Other recommended options are **Duinepos** (022-707 9900; www.duinepos.co.za; s/d chalet from R700/1025; P), bight, modern and well-equipped chalets in the heart of the park; and **Kraal Luxury Houseboats** (076 017 4788; www.kraalbaailuxury houseboats.com; Kraalbaai; 6-person boat R2530), which offers a six-sleeper and a 24-sleeper boat permanently anchored in pretty Kraalbaai. Both have kitchen and braai facilities.

The only restaurant in the park is **Geelbek** (072 698 6343; mains R95-165; 9am-5pm; P), otherwise, bring along your own picnic to enjoy in pristine surrounds. Go shopping in Langebaan before you arrive – there is no shop within the park.

Geco Adventures KAYAKING
(082 584 1907; www.gecoadventures.co.za; per person R200) Hour-long kayaking trips take you out onto the calm but cold waters to see penguins and other seabirds.

Sleeping & Eating

Paternoster Lodge GUESTHOUSE $$
(022-752 2023; www.paternosterlodge.co.za; s/d incl breakfast R950/1340; P) This is a bright, well-priced place offering seven minimalist rooms, all with a sea view, and a breezy restaurant (mains R95 to R190) that's open all day. From the sun deck you can watch the fisherfolk bringing in their catch.

Sea Shack CABIN $$
(079 820 6824; www.seashack.co.za; Cape Columbine Nature Reserve; cabin R750; P) The bright cabins here are just large enough for a double bed. Ablutions are shared and there is a cheery bar-restaurant. It's right on the water in the Cape Columbine Nature Reserve; entrance to the reserve is included in the rates.

Abalone House GUESTHOUSE $$$
(022-752 2044; www.abalonehouse.co.za; 3 Kriedoring St; d from R6000;) A five-star guesthouse with artsy rooms, a rooftop hot tub and plunge pool and a health spa. The restaurant (mains R145 to R210), also open to nonguests, is part of a small chain of swanky eateries started by local celebrity chef Reuben Riffel.

Voorstrandt Restaurant SEAFOOD $$
(022-752 2038; www.voorstrandt.com; Strandloperweg; mains R75-185; 11am-9pm; P) A better location you couldn't wish for – you can hop from your table right onto the sand. Specialising in seafood, this is also an excellent spot to watch the sunset over a beer.

Information

The **tourist information office** (022-752 2323; www.visitwestcoast.co.za; Fish Market, Seeduiker St; 9am-5pm Mon-Thu, to 2pm Fri-Sun) is found at the fish market.

Getting There & Away

Shared minibus taxis to Vredenburg (R25) leave from the corner of St Augustine Rd and Mosselbank St. From Vredenburg there are buses to Cape Town.

Garden Route

Includes ➡

Mossel Bay 232
George 235
Wilderness 237
Buffalo Bay 238
Knysna 239
Plettenberg Bay 246
Nature's Valley 250

Best Places to Eat

- Ile de Pain (p244)
- 101 Meade (p236)
- Serendipity (p238)
- Nguni (p250)

Best Places to Stay

- Views Boutique Hotel (p238)
- Point Village Hotel (p234)
- French Lodge International (p236)
- Turbine Hotel & Spa (p244)
- Hog Hollow (p249)

Why Go?

You can't help but be seduced by the glorious natural beauty of the Garden Route. The distance from Mossel Bay in the west to Storms River in the east is just over 200km, yet the range of topography, vegetation, wildlife and outdoor activities is remarkable.

The coast is dotted with excellent beaches and world-class surfing breaks. Inland you'll find picturesque lagoons and lakes, rolling hills and eventually the mountains of the Outeniqua and Tsitsikamma ranges that divide the verdant Garden Route from the arid Little Karoo.

Overlooking a beautiful lagoon, Knysna is the Garden Route's tourism hub, but also make time for lovely Plettenberg Bay. The Tsitsikamma section of Garden Route National Park is deservedly well known for nature and multiday hiking, including the Otter Trail, which ends in Nature's Valley. Outdoorsy types will be in seventh heaven with plenty of activities to keep them busy.

When to Go

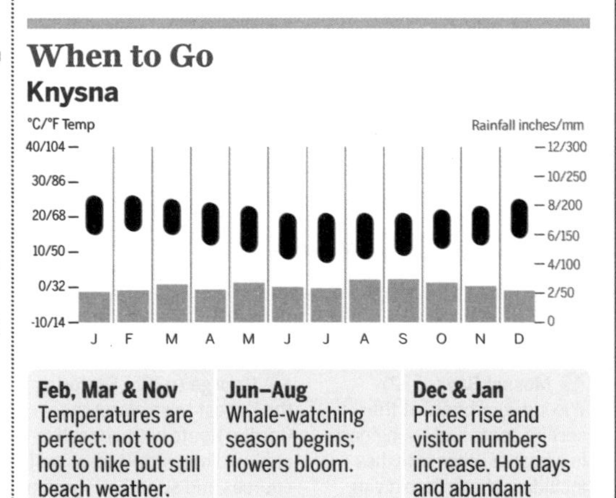

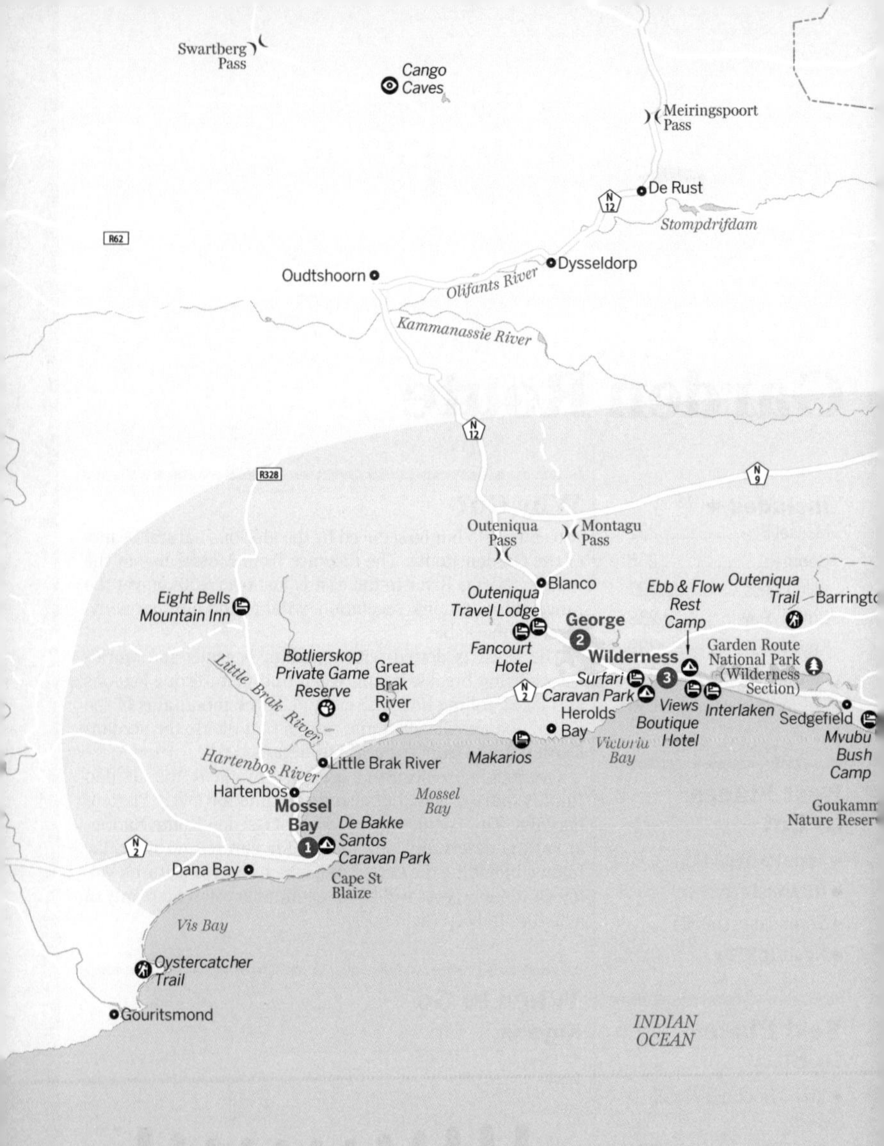

Garden Route Highlights

1. **Mossel Bay** (p232) Waxing your board at the surfing spots and taking part in a host of other activities including shark-cage diving and coastal hikes.

2. **George** (p235) Exploring the largest town along the Garden Route with attractive old buildings, world-class golf courses and superb mountain drives.

3. **Wilderness** (p237) Strolling along the windswept beach and kayaking the lagoons.

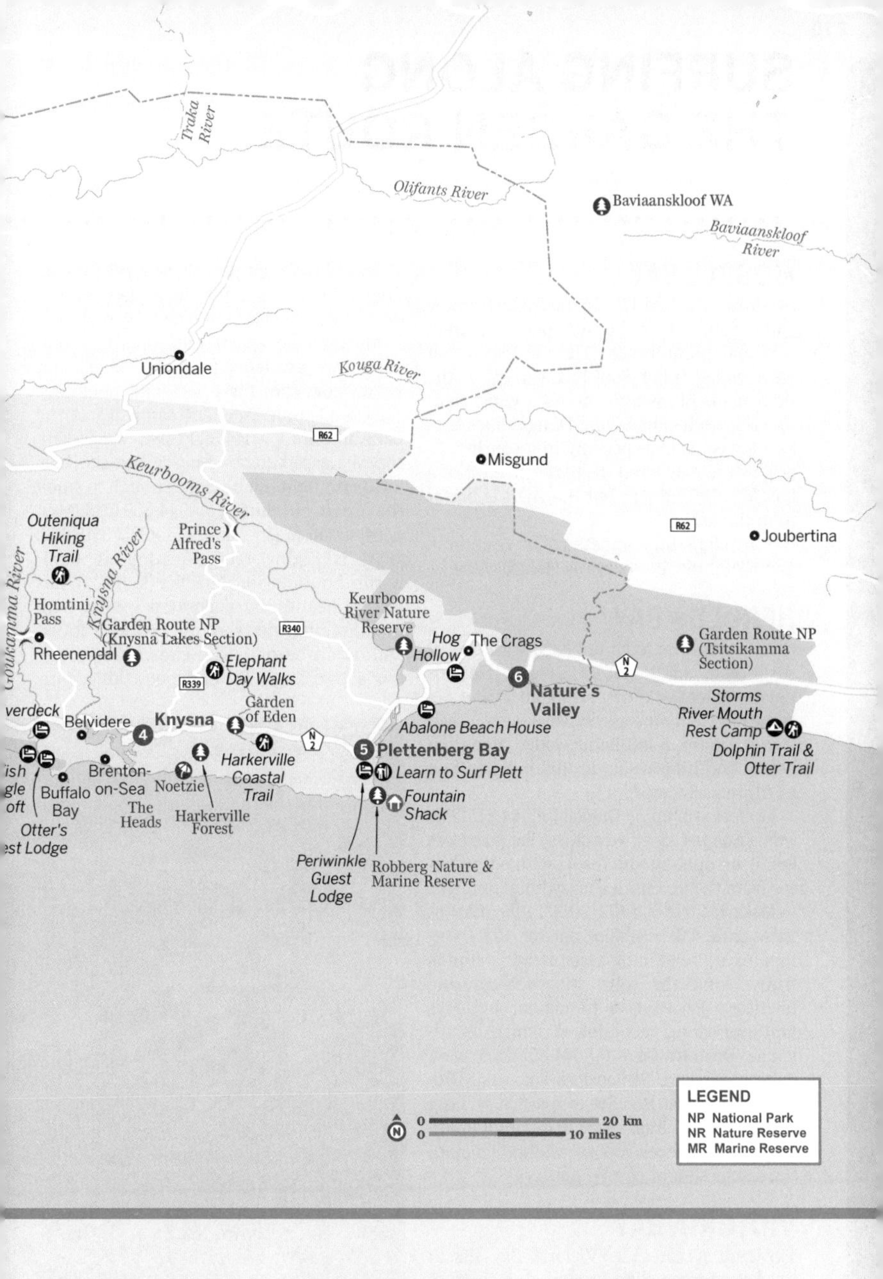

❹ **Knysna** (p239) Hiking and biking through the forests or exploring the lagoon by boat.

❺ **Plettenberg Bay** (p246) Swooning at the verdant mountains, white sand and crystal-blue waters around one of the country's top tourist spots.

❻ **Nature's Valley** (p250) Hiking in the Tsitsikamma section of the Garden Route National Park.

SURFING ALONG THE GARDEN ROUTE

MOSSEL BAY

In Mossel Bay (p232), the main surf spot is Outer Pool (left of the tidal pool) – a great reef and point break. There's also a soft wave called Inner Pool to the right of the tidal pool. Elsewhere there's a good right in a big swell called Ding Dangs that's best at a lowish tide, especially in a southwesterly or easterly wind. It might be a bit of a hassle paddling out, but the right is better than the left.

You might find something at Grootbrak and Kleinbrak, but better is Herold's Bay.

HEROLDS BAY

On a beautiful stretch of beach with decent surf, 16km southwest of George, Herolds Bay is generally quiet, although it can become crowded on summer weekends. When it's on, there's a left-hand wedge along the beach, and it's unusual in that it works in a northwesterly wind.

Golfers will enjoy **Oubaai** (☎044-851 1234; www.oubaaigolf.co.za; Herolds Bay Rd; green fees R800), an opulent golf resort with ocean vistas from the greens, a snazzy hotel and spa. **Makarios** (☎044-872 9019; www.makariosonsea.co.za; 4 Gericke's Cnr; apt from R1260) offers luxury sea-facing apartments a stone's throw from the sand with self-catering facilities. Prices rise in school holidays and everything gets booked months in advance. **Dutton's Cove** (☎044-851 0155; www.duttonscove.co.za; 21 Rooidraai Rd; mains R70-180; ⏰10am-9pm Mon-Sat, to 4pm Sun; Ⓟ) is a popular local lunch spot sitting high above the beach. There's lots of seafood, including a selection of combo platters.

VICTORIA BAY

Tiny and picturesque, Victoria Bay sits at the foot of steep cliffs, around 8km south of George. One of the Western Cape's top surf spots, it has the most consistent breaks along this coast. It's perfect when the swell is about 1m to 2m and you get a great right-hander. There's also a tidal pool that's good for children. All this means the village gets overrun during school holidays and on long weekends.

Most of the apartments on the promenade are available to rent – check out www.vicbay.com for prices and bookings. There's also an excellent campsite at the **Caravan Park** (☎044-889 0081; www.victoriabaycaravanpark.co.za; camping per site from R330). It might not be close enough to smell the ocean, but **Surfari** (☎044-889 0113; www.vicbaysurfari.co.za; dm/s/d R220/350/800; Ⓟ📶) is highly recommended. A family-run boutique backpacker lodge, it has bright, beautifully decorated rooms with breathtaking views of the coastal forest and ocean beyond. The enormous lounge has a bar, large TV and pool table, plus

Bottlenose dolphins, Herolds Bay

Beyond Cape Agulhas, the warmer waters of the Indian Ocean enable happy surfing in board shorts or a short wetsuit during summer. You'll need a full wetsuit in winter, though.

DEYAN DENCHEV/SHUTTERSTOCK ©

Surfer at Victoria Bay

the owners rent out surfboards (R300 per day)..There's only one restaurant - a fish and chips joint on the seafront that also serves burgers and pizzas.

There is no public transport to either Herolds Bay or Victoria Bay. If you don't have your own wheels, take a taxi from George.

BUFFALO BAY

A little further along is Buffalo Bay (Buffel's Bay; p238) where there's another right-hand point. Buffalo Bay is at one end of Brenton Beach; at the northern end, you'll find some good peaks, but watch out for sharks.

PLETTENBERG BAY

On to Plettenberg Bay (p246): avoid Robberg Peninsula as that's home to a seal colony. But the swimming area at Robberg Beach (where lifeguards are stationed) can have good waves if the swell isn't too big. Central Beach has one of the best known waves, the Wedge, which is perfect for goofy-footers. Lookout Beach can have some sandbanks and the Point can be good, but there's a lot of erosion here and the beach is slowly disappearing. Watch out for rip currents, especially when there are no lifeguards on duty.

Mossel Bay

044 / POP 30,000

With gnarly surf spots, some fine beaches, a menu of outdoor activities that covers everything from coastal hikes to leaping out of a plane, and a solid range of places to stay for every budget, Mossel Bay is an excellent destination for the independent traveller.

At first glance, the town is the ugly sister of the Garden Route. It was a hugely popular destination until the 1980s, when the building of the world's largest gas-to-oil refinery and concomitant industrial sprawl uglified it, and it fell into a slump. But if you can see beyond the unimpressive approach road, you'll find a cheery town with plenty of sunny-day pursuits.

Much of the holiday action happens around the Point, a promontory with an old-school seaside vibe. There are ice-cream kiosks, a caravan park and mini golf, and it's also a prime spot to surf.

Sights

★Dias Museum Complex MUSEUM

(044-691 1067; www.diasmuseum.co.za; Market St; adult/child R20/5; 9am-4.45pm Mon-Fri, to 3.45pm Sat & Sun; P) This excellent museum offers insight into Mossel Bay's role as an early stomping ground for European sailors. Named for 15th-century Portuguese explorer Bartholomeu Dias, the museum contains the 'post office tree' (p234) where sailors left messages for one another, the 1786 Dutch East India Company (Vereenigde Oost-Indische Compagnie; VOC) granary, a small aquarium and a local history museum. The highlight is the replica of the caravel that Dias used on his 1488 voyage of discovery.

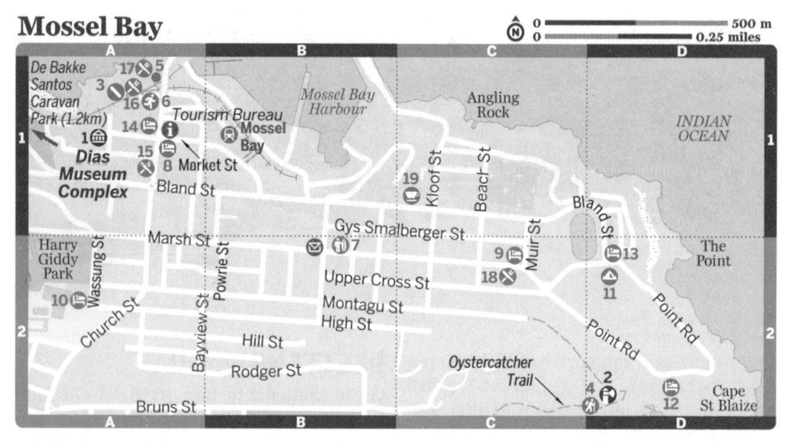

Mossel Bay

Top Sights
1 Dias Museum Complex ... A1

Sights
2 Cape St Blaize Lighthouse ... D2

Activities, Courses & Tours
3 Electrodive ... A1
4 Oystercatcher Trail ... D2
5 Romonza ... A1
6 Seven Seas ... A1
7 Waves School of Surfing ... B2
White Shark Africa ... (see 8)

Sleeping
8 Mile Crunchers ... A1
9 Mossel Bay Backpackers ... C2
10 Park House Lodge & Travel Centre ... A2
11 Point Caravan Park ... D2
12 Point Hotel ... D2
13 Point Village Hotel ... D2
14 Protea Hotel Mossel Bay ... A1

Eating
Café Gannet ... (see 14)
15 Carola Ann's ... A1
16 Kaai 4 ... A1
17 Mossel Bay Oyster Bar ... A1
18 Route 57 ... C2

Drinking & Nightlife
19 Blue Shed Coffee Roastery ... C1

Its small size brings home the extraordinary skill and courage of the early explorers. The replica was built in Portugal and sailed to Mossel Bay in 1988 to commemorate the 500th anniversary of Dias' trip. There's an extra fee to board the boat (adult/child R20/5).

Botlierskop Private Game Reserve WILDLIFE RESERVE
(044-696 6055; www.botlierskop.co.za; Little Brak River; P) This reserve contains a vast range of wildlife, including lions, elephants, rhinos, buffaloes and giraffes. Day visitors are welcome for a variety of activities including three-hour wildlife drives (adult/child R450/225) and horseback safaris (per hour R310). The reserve is about 20km northeast of Mossel Bay along the N2 (take the Little Brak River turn-off and follow the signs towards Sorgfontein). Bookings essential.

Cape St Blaize Lighthouse LIGHTHOUSE
(044-690 3015; lighthouse.tourism@transnet.net; The Point; adult/child R20/10; 10am-3pm Mon-Fri) There are wonderful views from the lighthouse, but call ahead to ensure it's open as the hours aren't always observed. There are plans to open a coffee shop at the base of the lighthouse.

Activities

It's easy to see where Mossel Bay's tourism slogan comes from. 'Do stuff', the authorities tell you, and the town is chock-full of stuff to do, including surfing, skydiving, hiking and boat trips.

Oystercatcher Trail HIKING
(044-699 1204; www.oystercatchertrail.co.za; per person self-catering/full board R6200/7450) Hikers can tackle this fabulous coastal trail over five days. It follows 48km of coastline from Mossel Bay to Gourits River via Cape St Blaize, where you're likely to see the endangered black oystercatcher. You can self-cater or choose the fully catered option. All rates include accommodation and guides.

Waves School of Surfing SURFING
(078 297 3999; www.wavesschoolofsurfing.com; 47 Marsh St; 1½hr lesson R300) Mossel Bay is one of the Garden Route's top surfing spots; beginners can get started here. Board rental is also available (R150 per day).

Skydive Mossel Bay ADVENTURE SPORTS
(082 824 8599; www.skydivemosselbay.com; Mossel Bay Airfield, 69 Rooikat St, Aalwyndal; from R2800) Tandem skydives start from 3000m and when the weather and tides cooperate you get to land on Diaz Beach.

Electrodive DIVING
(082 561 1259; www.electrodive.co.za; Mossel Bay Harbour; PADI open-water course R4980, boat-based dives incl equipment R610) While diving in Mossel Bay offers the opportunity to see quite a lot of coral, fish and other sea creatures, these aren't tropical waters and you're not going to have perfect visibility.

White Shark Africa DIVING
(044-691 3796; www.whitesharkafrica.com; 7 Church St; adult/child R1750/1050) Half-day cage-diving trips to view great white sharks, including breakfast, lunch, drinks and snacks.

Seven Seas BOATING
(079 251 1326; www.se7enseas.co.za; Mossel Bay Harbour; adult/child R150/80) There are hour-long trips to see Seal Island's 3000-strong colony of seals as well as short turns on a speed boat (from R200).

Tours

Point of Human Origins CULTURAL
(079 640 0004; www.humanorigin.co.za; tours R450) Led by an archaeology professor, this fascinating four-hour tour includes a hike to the Pinnacle Point Caves, where discoveries have shed light on human life from 162,000 years ago. You can also visit the caves on a 90-minute scramble with a local guide (R350).

Romonza BOATING
(082 701 9031; www.romonzaboattrips.co.za; Mossel Bay Harbour; 1hr boat trips R170) Regular boat trips head out to Seal Island to see the seals, birds and dolphins that frequent these waters. From July to October there are also whale-watching trips (adult/child R730/430, 2½ hours).

Sleeping

De Bakke Santos Caravan Park CAMPGROUND, CHALET $
(076 058 7153; www.debakkesantos.co.za; Santos Beach; camping per site from R190, chalet from R550; P) As well as more than 300 campsites – many of which have ocean views – there are well-equipped thatched chalets here (the chalets were about to be

LOCAL KNOWLEDGE

THE MILKWOOD TREE POST

The Portuguese explorers Bartholomeu Dias and Vasco da Gama were the first Europeans to visit the bay, late in the 15th century. It became a useful place for ships to stop because there was fresh water available and deals could be struck with the local Khoekhoen people. A large milkwood tree beside the spring was used as a postal collection point – expeditions heading east would leave mail to be picked up by ships returning home. The spring and the tree still exist, and are now part of the **Dias Museum Complex** (p232). You can post letters (they receive a special postmark) from a letterbox within the museum.

renovated when we last visited). Rates rise slightly on weekends and during school holidays.

Mossel Bay Backpackers HOSTEL $
(☎044-691 3182; www.mosselbaybackpackers.co.za; 1 Marsh St; dm R180, d R580, d with shared bathroom R380;) This well-run and long-established backpackers has two sections – a backpacker wing where rooms share a bathroom and a more upmarket wing with en-suite rooms and dorms. There's even a honeymoon suite, complete with spa bath (R890). Staff can arrange surfing, boat trips and other water sports.

Park House Lodge & Travel Centre HOSTEL $
(☎044-691 1937; www.park-house.co.za; 121 High St; camping R110, dm R170, s/d R385/640, with shared bathroom R290/480;) This place, in a gracious old sandstone house next to the park, is friendly, smartly decorated and has beautiful gardens. Breakfast is R55, and staff can organise activities.

Mile Crunchers HOSTEL $
(☎044-690 4462; 7 Church St; dm R160, d with shared bathroom R400;) This friendly place has a great location a short walk from the harbour, the museum and plenty of restaurants. It's fairly rudimentary but the dorms and doubles are clean and comfortable and there's a pool table in the lounge. Rates include a DIY breakfast.

Point Caravan Park CAMPGROUND $
(☎044-690 3501; Point Rd; camping per site from R160) This caravan park and campground has an excellent location within walking distance of the Point's restaurants, bars and surf. There is a small supplement for seafront sites, but it's worth paying the extra. Note that rates triple in December and January.

★**Point Village Hotel** HOTEL $$
(☎044-690 3156; www.pointvillagehotel.co.za; 5 Point Rd; s/d R600/1100; P) The quirky, fake lighthouse on this exceptionally well-priced hotel's exterior speaks to what you'll find inside: a range of fun, funky, bright rooms and cheery service. Rooms have a kitchenette and some have balconies. There are also two- and three-bedroom apartments with good sea views (from R1800).

Protea Hotel Mossel Bay HOTEL $$$
(☎044-691 3738; www.oldposttree.co.za; cnr Market & Church Sts; s/d from R1235/1530; P) Part of the Protea chain, this is a classy hotel set in the old post office building. Its restaurant, Café Gannet (p235), has a large seafood, meat and pizza menu.

Eight Bells Mountain Inn LODGE $$$
(☎044-631 0000; www.eightbells.co.za; Rte 328; s/d from R1010/1610; P) This country inn oozes old-world charm and boasts a lovely mountain setting at the foot of the Robinson Pass. Its large grounds feature tennis and squash courts, horse trails, kids' play areas and hiking routes. You'll find a variety of rooms; the rondavels (round huts with conical roofs) are delightful. Prices rise sharply during school holidays. It's 35km north of Mossel Bay on Rte 328 to Oudtshoorn (50km).

Point Hotel HOTEL $$$
(☎044-691 3512; www.pointhotel.co.za; Point Rd; s/d with half board R2200/2500; P) This modern hotel boasts a spectacular location, right above the wave-pounded rocks at the Point. There's a decent restaurant (mains R60 to R120) and the spacious rooms have balconies with ocean views – request a south-facing room for the best vistas. There's no pool, but there are tidal rock pools nearby.

Eating

Mossel Bay Oyster Bar SEAFOOD $
(044-333 0202; www.mosselbayoysterbar.co.za; Mossel Bay Harbour; sushi R40-50; 9.30am-9pm) On the water's edge, this is one of the best places in town for a sundowner. Sushi and oysters are on the menu alongside a selection of cocktails (R40 to R60).

Carola Ann's CAFE $
(044-690 3477; www.carolaann.com; 12 Church St; mains R60-95; 8am-5pm Mon-Fri, to 2pm Sat) Close to the museum (p232), Carola Ann's serves inventive breakfasts, delicious, healthy lunches and not-so-healthy slabs of cake. Grab a packet of the chocolate-chip cookies for the road. Delicious.

★**Kaai 4** BRAAI $$
(044-691 0056; www.kaai4.co.za; Mossel Bay Harbour; mains R60-100; 10am-10pm) Boasting one of Mossel Bay's best locations, this low-key restaurant has picnic tables on the sand overlooking the ocean. Most of the dishes – including stews, burgers, boerewors (farmer's sausage) and some seafood – are cooked on massive fire pits and there's local beer on tap.

Route 57 SOUTH AFRICAN $$
(044-691 0057; www.route57.co.za; 12 Marsh St; mains R90-190; 11am-10pm Tue-Sun) This elegant place in a century-old house is one of Mossel Bay's swankiest dining options. Try the seafood *potjie* (stew) or the fillet steak topped with marrow bone. Dinner bookings recommended.

Café Gannet INTERNATIONAL $$
(044-691 3738; www.cafegannet.co.za; Market St; mains R115-225; 7am-10pm; P) Part of the Protea Hotel (p234), this bright bistro has an extensive menu featuring seafood, steaks, sushi and pizza.

Drinking & Nightlife

★**Blue Shed Coffee Roastery** CAFE
(044-691 0037; www.blueshedroasters.co.za; 33 Bland St; 6.30am-8pm;) Enjoy great coffee and homemade cakes at this funky cafe with eclectic decor and ocean views from the deck. It's an awesome spot to spend a couple of hours chilling or playing vinyl on the old-school jukebox.

Information

Post Office (044-691 1308; 55 Marsh St)

Tourism Bureau (044-691 2202; www.visitmosselbay.co.za; Market St; 8am-6pm Mon-Fri, 9am-4pm Sat & Sun) Staff are very friendly and can help with accommodation bookings. Pick up a brochure detailing a self-guided walking tour of historic Mossel Bay.

Getting There & Away

Mossel Bay is off the highway, so the long-distance buses don't come into town; they drop passengers at the Voorbaai Shell petrol station, 8km away. The hostels can usually collect you if you give notice, but private taxis (R80) are often waiting for bus passengers who need onward travel. Try **Smith Taxis** (072 924 5977), or during the day take a shared taxi (R12). The **Baz Bus** (p184) will drop you in town.

All major bus companies stop here on their Cape Town–Port Elizabeth runs. Intercape fares from Mossel Bay include Knysna (R230, 1½ hours), Plettenberg Bay (R260, 2½ hours) and Cape Town (R410, six hours).

George

044 / POP 114,000

George, founded in 1811, is the largest town on the Garden Route yet remains little more than a commercial centre and transport hub. It has some attractive old buildings, including the tiny St Mark's Cathedral and the more imposing Dutch Reformed Mother Church, but it's 8km from the coast and for most visitors its chief draw is the range of championship golf courses.

Sights & Activities

Outeniqua Transport Museum MUSEUM
(044-801 8289; www.outeniquachootjoe.co.za/museum.htm; 2 Mission St; adult/child R20/10; 8am-5pm Mon-Fri, to 2pm Sat; P) The starting point and terminus for journeys on the Outeniqua Power Van (p236), this museum is worth a visit if you're even remotely interested in trains. A dozen locomotives and 15 carriages, as well as many detailed models, have found a retirement home here, including a carriage used by the British royal family in the 1940s. There's also an impressive collection of classic cars.

WORTH A TRIP

MONTAGU & OUTENIQUA PASSES

Montagu Pass is a quiet dirt road that winds its way through the mountains north of George; it was opened in 1847 and is now a national monument. Head back on the Outeniqua Pass, a tarred road where views are even better.

Alternatively, you could opt for the **Outeniqua Power Van** (p236), a motorised trolley van that will take you from the Outeniqua Transport Museum on a 2½-hour trip into the Outeniqua mountains. You can even take a bike and cycle back down the Montagu Pass.

George Museum MUSEUM
(044-873 5343; Courtenay St; by donation; 9am-4.30pm Mon-Fri, to 12.30pm Sat) George was the hub of the indigenous timber industry and, thus, this museum contains a wealth of related artefacts.

Links at Fancourt GOLF
(044-804 0844; www.fancourt.co.za; 18 holes from R950) Designed by Gary Player, this is one of the most elite and famous golf courses in South Africa. Green fees double from September to March.

Tours

★**Outeniqua Power Van** TOURS
(082 490 5627; Outeniqua Transport Museum, 2 Mission St; adult/child R150/130; Mon-Sat) A trip on this motorised trolley van is one of the best things to do in George. It takes you from the Outeniqua Transport Museum on a 2½-hour trip into the Outeniqua mountains with a brief picnic stop. Departure times vary and all bookings are done via SMS.

Sleeping

Outeniqua Travel Lodge HOSTEL **$**
(082 316 7720; www.outeniqualodge.co.za; 19 Montagu St; s/d R430/580; P) It's about 6km from the centre, but this is a decent budget option with en-suite rooms in a quiet, residential area. Staff can arrange activities.

★**French Lodge International** GUESTHOUSE **$$**
(044-874 0345; www.frenchlodge.co.za; 29 York St; s/d incl breakfast from R750/900; P@) Rooms at this town-centre guesthouse are in luxurious thatched-roof rondavels (round huts with a conical roof) set around the pool, with satellite TV and bathrooms with spa baths.

Fancourt Hotel LUXURY HOTEL **$$$**
(044-804 0000; www.fancourt.co.za; Montagu St, Blanco; s/d incl breakfast from R2580/3440; P) This is the area's most luxurious option, with three 18-hole golf courses designed by Gary Player, a health spa and four restaurants. It's about 6km from the town centre.

Eating & Drinking

★**101 Meade** FUSION **$$**
(044-874 0343; www.101meade.co.za; 101 Meade St; mains R80-210; 7am-9.30pm Mon-Sat, 9am-9pm Sun;) Whether you're after freshly baked bread and good coffee to start the day, inventive tapas plates to share at lunchtime or heavier evening fare like braised springbok shank or Durban lamb curry, the excellent cuisine and minimalist decor at 101 Meade make it George's top eating option.

Old Townhouse STEAK **$$**
(044-874 3663; Market St; mains R75-200; 11.30am-5pm & 6-10pm Mon-Fri, 6-10pm Sat) In the one-time town administration building dating back to 1848, this long-standing restaurant is known for its excellent steaks and ever-changing game-meat options. The homemade ice cream is a great way to finish off a meal.

Robertson Brewery BREWERY
(www.robertsonbrewery.com; 1 Memoriam St; tastings R35, light meals R75-100; 10am-10pm Mon-Sat) There's not a lot to keep you occupied in George, so this family-run microbrewery is a welcome addition. Sip a taster tray of the eight staple beers brewed on-site and munch on basic pub grub while listening to classic rock.

Information

CapeNature (044-802 5300; www.capenature.org.za; York St)

George Tourism (044-801 9299; www.georgetourism.org.za; 124 York St; 7.45am-4.30pm Mon-Fri, 9am-1pm Sat) Dishes out information for George and the surrounding area.

Getting There & Away

Kulula (086 158 5852; www.kulula.com), **Airlink** (086 160 6606; www.flyairlink.com) and **SA Express** (086 172 9227; www.flyexpress.aero) fly to George Airport, which is 9km southwest of town.

Greyhound (customer care 24hr 011-611 8000, reservations 087 352 0352; www.greyhound.co.za) bus services stop at the Caltex petrol station on York St, while **Translux** (p214) and **Intercape** (p184) stop at the main station at the end of Hibernia St. Intercape fares include Knysna (R310, 1½ hours, twice daily), Plettenberg Bay (R330, two hours) and Cape Town (R440, seven hours, twice daily).

The **Baz Bus** (p184) drops off passengers in town.

Wilderness

044 / POP 6200

The name says it all: dense old-growth forests and steep hills run down to a beautiful stretch of coastline of rolling breakers, kilometres of white sand, bird-rich estuaries and sheltered lagoons. All this has made Wilderness very popular, but thankfully it doesn't show – the myriad holiday homes blend into the verdant green hills, and the town centre is compact and unobtrusive. Beach bums beware: the beach here is beautiful, but a strong rip tide means swimming is not advised. The only other drawback is that everything is quite widely scattered, making life difficult if you don't have a vehicle.

Sights

Garden Route National Park (Wilderness Section) NATIONAL PARK
(044-877 1197; www.sanparks.org; adult/child R130/65; 7am-6pm) Formerly the Wilderness National Park, this section has now been incorporated into the vast and scattered Garden Route National Park along with the Knysna Forests and Tsitsikamma. The park covers a unique system of lakes, rivers, wetlands and estuaries that are vital for the survival of many species. There are several nature trails in the national park for all levels of fitness, taking in the lakes, the beach and the indigenous forest.

The **Kingfisher Trail** is a day walk that traverses the region and includes a boardwalk across the intertidal zone of the Touws River. The lakes offer anglers, canoeists, windsurfers and sailors an ideal venue. Canoes (R250 per day) can be hired from **Eden Adventures** (044-877 0179; www.eden.co.za; Fairy Knowe Hotel, 1 Dumbleton Rd), which also offers abseiling (R600), kloofing (canyoning; R600) and tours of the area.

There is just one camp in this section of the park, the expansive **Ebb & Flow Rest Camp** (camping per site from R200, d rondavel from R480, with shared bathroom R425). Alongside the river, it has campsites and a variety of self-catering cabins, chalets and rondavels (round huts with conical roofs).

Sleeping

Wilderness Beach House Backpackers HOSTEL $
(044-877 0549; www.wildernessbeachhouse.com; Wilderness Beach; d from R550, dm/d with shared bathroom R180/450; P) Southwest of town, this breezy hostel provides awesome ocean views, simple rooms, and a *lapa* (circular area with a fire pit) bar and cafe serving breakfast and dinner. If you're after a dorm bed, request the upstairs dorm with its ocean-facing balcony.

Fairy Knowe Backpackers HOSTEL $
(044-877 1285; www.wildernessbackpackers.com; Dumbleton Rd; camping R120, s/d R400/600, dm/s/d with shared bathroom R160/250/400; P) Set in leafy grounds overlooking the Touws River, this long-running hostel is based in a 19th-century farmhouse. The bar is in another building some distance away, so boozers won't keep you awake. There's an activity centre offering kayaking, abseiling, horse riding and paragliding. To get here, drive through town and follow the road for 2km to the Fairy Knowe turn-off.

Interlaken GUESTHOUSE $$
(044-877 1374; www.interlaken.co.za; 713 North St; s/d incl breakfast from R1100/1200; P) It gets rave reviews from readers, and we can't argue: this is a well-run and very friendly guesthouse offering magnificent lagoon views. Delicious dinners are available on request.

★**Views Boutique Hotel** BOUTIQUE HOTEL $$$
(044-877 8000; www.viewshotel.co.za; South St; sea-facing s/d incl breakfast R3715/4800;) With bright, modern, glass-fronted rooms looking on to the glorious beach, this hotel makes the most of its awesome location. It's worth paying the premium for an ocean-facing room if you can, though the mountain-view rooms are also delightful (and are half the price). The hotel has a rooftop pool, spa and steps leading straight to the sand.

Eating & Drinking

Beejuice CAFE $
(044-877 0608; www.beejuicecafe.co.za; Sands Rd; light meals R50-120; 8.30am-9pm Mon-Sat, to 4pm Sun;) Although no trains ply the tracks any more, this cafe filling the old station building is still a nice spot for salads and sandwiches. In the evenings, traditional South African fare is served.

Zucchini EUROPEAN $$
(044-882 1240; www.zucchini.co.za; Timberlake Organic Village, N2; mains R90-195; 9am-5pm Sun-Wed, to 9pm Thu-Sat;) Stylish decor combines with home-grown organic produce, free-range meats and lots of vegetarian options at this delightful place. There's a coffee roastery on-site and the complex also has shops and a kids' play area.

★**Serendipity** SOUTH AFRICAN $$$
(044-877 0433; www.serendipitywilderness.com; Freesia Ave; 5-course menu R495; 6.30-9.30pm Mon-Sat;) Readers and locals all recommend this elegant restaurant with a deck overlooking the lagoon. The South African–inspired menu changes monthly but always features original takes on old classics, such as cardamom milk tart brûlée. It's the town's fine-dining option; bookings essential.

Girl's Restaurant INTERNATIONAL $$$
(044-877 1648; www.thegirls.co.za; 1 George Rd; mains R110-285; 7-9.30pm Tue-Sun;) It doesn't look much from afar – a restaurant tucked down the side of a petrol station – but Girl's gets rave reviews. Try the venison fillet or the fresh prawns in a range of increasingly spicy sauces.

Blind Pig CRAFT BEER
(083 640 5403; Palms Garden Sq, Owen Grant St; 1-8pm Tue-Thu, noon-midnight Fri & Sat, 11am-7pm Sun;) This tiny bar serves a wide range of craft beer from around the country and there's even an equally tiny brewery on-site. Grab a pint and a bar snack to enjoy on the shady patio.

Shopping

Timberlake Organic Village ARTS & CRAFTS
(www.timberlakeorganic.co.za; N2; 9am-5pm;) This complex off the N2 between Wilderness and Sedgefield has the pleasant Zucchini (p238) and some small shops selling fresh produce, boutique foodstuffs and crafts. You can also partake in quad biking and zip-line tours here.

Information

Wilderness Tourism Bureau (044-877 0045; George Rd; 7.45am-4.30pm Mon-Fri, 9am-1pm Sat) Just past the cluster of restaurants on the right as you enter the village.

Getting There & Away

Long-distance buses stop at the Caltex petrol station en route to Cape Town (R300, 7½ hours) and Plettenberg Bay (R180, 1¼ hours).

Buffalo Bay

044 / POP 71

Buffalo Bay is a blissful place with an almost deserted surf beach, the Goukamma Nature Reserve and only a tiny enclave of holiday homes. That's about it, and it's all you need. It's 17km west of Knysna; signposts also read Buffel's Bay or Buffelsbaai.

Sights

Goukamma Nature Reserve NATURE RESERVE
(044-383 0042; www.capenature.co.za; adult/child R40/20; 8am-6pm) This reserve is accessible from the Buffalo Bay road, and protects 14km of rocky coastline, sandstone cliffs, dunes covered with coastal fynbos (fine bush) and forest, and **Groenvlei**, a large freshwater lake. The nature reserve also extends 1.8km out to sea and you can often see dolphins (and whales, in season) along the coast. Goukamma was badly affected by wildfires in 2017 and remains closed until mid-2018.

There are day trails ranging from a two-hour forest walk to a 15km hike that takes you through the sand dunes. Permits can be obtained on arrival from the reserve's reception. Canoeing and fishing are great, and canoes can be hired (R30 per day).

Sleeping & Eating

There are only a couple of options – the **Buffelsbaai Waterfront** (044-383 0038; Walker Dr; mains R80-130; 9am-5pm; P) in town and Riverdeck, which serves pizzas alongside the river.

CapeNature (021-483 0190; www.capenature.co.za) rents numerous cabins, cottages and chalets throughout In town. Buffelsbaai Waterfront offers apartments and houses. Accommodation in the reserve was badly damaged during wildfires in 2017, but was being rebuilt when we last visited.

Riverdeck CABIN $
(078 134 5873; www.riverdeckaccommodation.co.za; Buffalo Bay Rd; camping R80, d R600, with shared bathroom R300; P) Just off the N2, on the Goukamma River's banks, this backpacker resort offers safari tents and simple cabins as well as en-suite rooms and four-sleeper cottages (from R1400). There's a simple spa and an outdoor restaurant (open 8am to 7pm) serving wood-fired pizzas and traditional meals. You can rent out canoes or water bikes, and horse riding can be arranged.

Fish Eagle Loft APARTMENT $$
(www.capenature.co.za; d from R820) A stylishly decorated loft apartment with awesome views of the ocean. The loft is closed until mid-2018 due to fire damage in the Goukamma Nature Reserve.

Mvubu Bush Camp COTTAGE $$
(www.capenature.co.za; 4-person cottage from R950) Mvubu is a large, wooden chalet set amid milkwood trees and with views of Groenvlei lake. Sleeping four in two bedrooms, it also has an expansive deck and free use of a canoe.

Buffelsbaai Waterfront APARTMENT $$
(044-383 0038; www.buffelsbaai.co.za; Walker Dr; apt from R850) A one-stop shop for accommodation, meals and information on the area. Accommodation is in apartments and houses dotted about the town. It's best to book in advance rather than just rocking up. It's a vast building behind the beach – you can't miss it.

Otter's Rest Lodge COTTAGE $$
(www.capenature.co.za; cottage from R1000) A self-contained house with two double bedrooms. There's modern decor throughout and the open-plan kitchen opens onto a deck with braai (barbecue) facilities.

LOCAL KNOWLEDGE

SEDGEFIELD FARMERS MARKET

A Garden Route institution, **Wild Oats Community Farmers Market** (082 376 5020; www.wildoatsmarket.co.za; N2, Sedgefield; 7.30am-noon Sat;) has been operating for over a decade. Arrive early to get your pick of the pies, biltong, cheese, cakes, bread, beer, fudge – all from small, local producers. The market is just off the N2, 1.5km east of Sedgefield's town centre.

Getting There & Away

It is 8km from the N2 to Buffalo Bay. You will need your own vehicle as there is no public transport.

Knysna

044 / POP 51,000

Embracing an exquisitely beautiful lagoon and surrounded by ancient forests, Knysna (pronounced ny-znah) is probably the most famous town on the Garden Route. Formerly the centre of the timber industry, supplying yellowwood and stinkwood for railway lines, shipping and house-building, it still has several shops specialising in woodwork and traditional furniture. The lagoon is popular with sailing enthusiasts, and there are plenty of boat trips on offer.

With its serene setting, arty and gay-friendly vibe, excellent places to stay, eat and drink, and wide range of activities, Knysna has plenty going for it. But if you're after something quiet and undeveloped, you might like to look elsewhere – particularly in high season.

In June 2017, a massive wildfire ravaged the area, destroying more than 1000 homes and devastating the landscape. It will take decades for the forests to recover, though the town was welcoming tourists back within a couple of weeks.

Sights

Knysna Lagoon PARK
(Map p240) FREE The Knysna Lagoon opens between two sandstone cliffs known as the Heads – once proclaimed by the British Royal Navy to be the most dangerous harbour entrance in the world. There are good views from the eastern head, and from the

Knysna

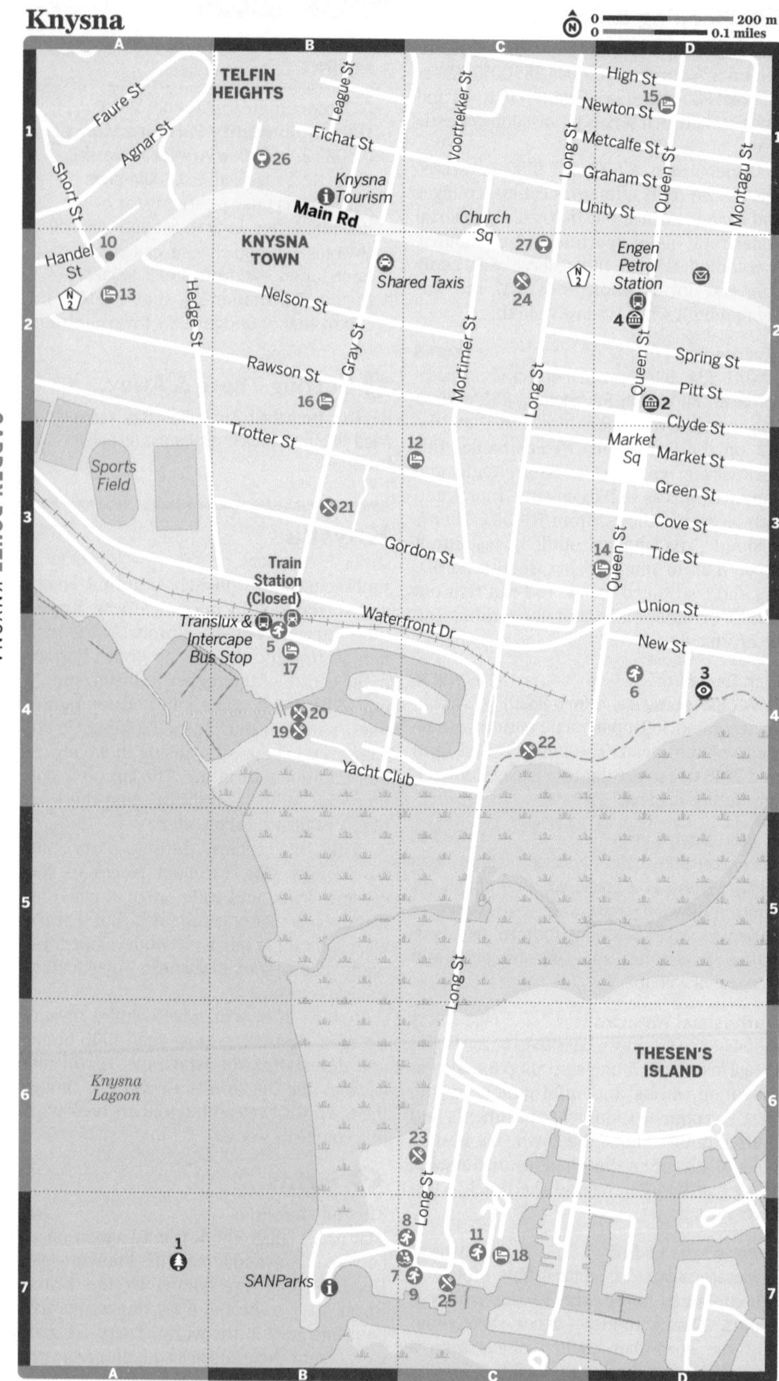

TELFIN HEIGHTS
Faure St
Agnar St
Short St
League St
Fichat St
Voortrekker St
High St
Newton St
Metcalfe St
Graham St
Unity St
Queen St
Montagu St
Long St
Knysna Tourism
Main Rd
Church Sq
Handel St
KNYSNA TOWN
Shared Taxis
Engen Petrol Station
Hedge St
Nelson St
Gray St
Mortimer St
Spring St
Rawson St
Pitt St
Clyde St
Trotter St
Market Sq
Market St
Sports Field
Green St
Cove St
Gordon St
Tide St
Train Station (Closed)
Union St
Translux & Intercape Bus Stop
Waterfront Dr
New St
Yacht Club
Knysna Lagoon
THESEN'S ISLAND
SANParks
200 m
0.1 miles

Knysna

Sights
1 Knysna Lagoon ... A7
2 Millwood House ... D2
3 Mitchell's Brewery ... D4
4 Old Gaol Museum ... D2

Activities, Courses & Tours
5 Featherbed Company ... B4
6 Knysna Cycle Works ... D4
7 Knysna Kayak Hire ... C7
8 Ocean Odyssey ... C7
9 Oyster Tour ... C7
10 Peggy's Tours ... A2
Scootours ... (see 7)
11 Turbine Water Club ... C7

Sleeping
12 Inyathi Guest Lodge ... C3
13 Island Vibe ... A2
14 Jembjo's Knysna Lodge ... D3
15 Knysna Backpackers ... D1
16 Knysna Log Inn ... B2
17 Protea Hotel Knysna Quays ... B4
18 Turbine Hotel & Spa ... C7

Eating
19 34 South ... B4
20 Caffé Mario ... B4
21 Chatters Bistro ... B3
22 Freshline Fisheries ... C4
23 Ile de Pain ... C6
24 Olive Tree ... C2
25 Sirocco ... C7

Drinking & Nightlife
26 King's ... B1
27 Vinyl ... C2

Featherbed Nature Reserve (Map p245; www.knysnafeatherbed.com) on the western head.

The best way to appreciate the lagoon is by boat; the Featherbed Company (p242) operates various vessels.

Although regulated by SANParks (p246), Knysna Lagoon is not a national park or wilderness area. Much of it is still privately owned, and the lagoon is used by industry and for recreation. The protected area starts just to the east of Buffalo Bay and follows the coastline to the mouth of the Noetzie River.

Belvidere VILLAGE
(Map p245) Belvidere, 10km from Knysna, is so immaculate it's positively creepy. But it's worth a quick look for the beautiful Norman-style **Belvidere church** (Map p245) that was built in the 1850s by homesick English expats. Further on is the Featherbed Nature Reserve (p241) and, on the seaward side, Brenton-on-Sea.

Garden of Eden FOREST
(adult/child R40/20; 8am-6pm) There are lovely forest picnic spots, short walks through the forest and an 800m-long wheelchair-friendly path.

Mitchell's Brewery BREWERY
(Map p240; 044-382 4685; www.mitchellsbrewing.com; 10 New St; tastings R75, tour & tasting R150; 11am-5pm Tue & Wed, to 10pm Thu-Sat, tours 12.30pm & 2.30pm Mon-Sat; P) South Africa's oldest microbrewery occupies bright, new premises on the edge of the lagoon. You can join a tour or just taste its range of English-style brews in the beer garden. Pub meals (R65 to R110) are also served. Bookings essential for tours.

Millwood House MUSEUM
(Map p240; Queen St; by donation; 9.30am-4.30pm Mon-Fri, to 12.30pm Sat) Millwood House is a mini complex of museums detailing Knysna's history. It's a quaint set of buildings dating back to the town's booming timber era. This is the main focus of the museum, though it also houses information on Knysna's involvement in the Anglo-Boer War and details on the town's founder George Rex.

Noetzie BEACH
Reached by a turn-off along the N2 10km east of Knysna, Noetzie is a quirky little place with holiday homes in mock-castle style. There's a lovely surf beach (spacious but dangerous) and a sheltered lagoon running through a forested gorge. The trail between the car park and beach is steep.

Old Gaol Museum MUSEUM
(Map p240; 044-302 6320; cnr Main & Queen Sts; 9am-4pm Mon-Fri, to noon Sat) FREE Since this region has plenty of wet weather, a rainy-day option is welcome. The main museum is a pleasant complex in a mid-19th century building that was once the jail. There's a gallery showcasing local art, a display on the Knysna elephants and a community art project.

OFF THE BEATEN TRACK

KNYSNA'S RASTAFARIANS

Knysna is home to South Africa's largest Rastafarian community, **Judah Square**. You can take an impassioned walking tour of the community, which is within the township, with **Brother Zeb** (☎076 649 1034; www.judahsquare.co.za; tours from R100), an\ unforgettable local character.

Activities

Elephant Day Walks HIKING
(adult/child R68/34) A series of forest walks in the Diepwalle area. Keep an eye out for signs of the legendary Knysna elephants living in the forest. There are still thought to be a couple of elephants here, with a rare sighting caught on camera in early 2016.

Outeniqua Trail HIKING
(☎044-302 5606; adult/child per day R134/67) This 108km-long trail takes a week to walk, although you can also do two- or three-day sections. The trail fee includes overnight accommodation in basic huts. You will need your own bedding.

Ocean Odyssey WATER SPORTS
(Map p240; ☎044-382 0321; www.oceanodyssey.co.za; Thesen's Island; boat trip adult/child R710/510) As well as 1½-hour boat trips on the lagoon (p239), Ocean Odyssey rents out stand-up paddle boards (per hour R180) and offers sunset yachting trips (from R900). From June to November there are whale-watching trips as well (adult/child R900/700).

Oyster Tour BOATING
(Map p240; ☎082 892 0469; www.knysnacharters.com; jetty at Quay 4, Thesen's Island; adult/child R570/160; ⏲3pm) In South Africa, Knysna is synonymous with oysters. Learn about cultivation on this 90-minute lagoon cruise, which includes tasting of wild and farmed oysters and some wine to wash them down with.

Turbine Water Club OUTDOORS
(Map p240; ☎044-302 5751; Sawtooth Lane, Thesen's Island) The menu of activities here includes bicycle hire (half day R180), fishing trips (R650), kayak hire (R180) and hour-long boat cruises (R250).

Scootours ADVENTURE SPORTS
(Map p240; ☎079 148 3751; http://scootours.co.za; tours R450) Explore the Knysna Forest on a monster scooter – that is, a nonmotorised scooter with chunky tyres capable of navigating the terrain. The guided tours last two hours and include transfers to the forest from Thesen's Island.

Knysna Kayak Hire KAYAKING
(Map p240; ☎082 892 0469; www.knysnacharters.com; per hr R100) A peaceful way to explore the lagoon (p239) – just steer clear of the Heads! Book online and collect the kayaks from Whet Restaurant on Thesen's Island.

Trip Out WATER SPORTS
(☎083 306 3587; www.tripout.co.za; 2hr surfing class R400) Offers surfing classes for beginners in nearby Buffalo Bay, snorkelling around the Heads (R350) and boat cruises, as well as a half-day kloofing (canyoning) trip (R650).

Knysna Cycle Works CYCLING
(Map p240; ☎044-382 5153; www.knysnacycles.co.za; Waterfront Park, Queen St; per day R250; ⏲8.30am-5pm Mon-Fri, 9am-1pm Sat) Long-running agency that rents out mountain bikes and supplies maps of the region's trails.

Go Vertical ADVENTURE SPORTS
(☎082 731 4696; www.govertical.co.za) Offers guided kayaking, canoeing and hiking around the Garden Route.

Featherbed Company BOATING
(Map p240; ☎044-382 1693; www.knysnafeatherbed.com; Remembrance Ave, off Waterfront Dr; boat trips adult/child from R140/75; ⏲8am-5pm) Operates various boat trips, ranging from a short ferry trip into the Heads to a sunset catamaran cruise (adult/child R730/375). The most popular trip is a 90-minute cruise on the *John Benn*, leaving at 12.30pm and 5pm (adult/child R190/90).

Trips to the Featherbed Nature Reserve (p241) itself came to a halt in June 2017 when the reserve was ravaged by wildfire. There are plans to start the trips again but call in advance for the latest update.

Harkerville Coastal Trail HIKING
(per person R256) This challenging 20km, two-day hike follows a circular route through the Harkerville forest and along tricky sections

of coast. Accommodation in a simple hut is included in the price, but conservation fees are extra (R32 per day). Book through SANParks (p246).

Tours

The tourism office has an up-to-date list of the numerous operators offering tours to Knysna's hilltop townships. If you want to stay overnight in the townships, contact Knysna Tourism (p246) and ask for its brochure, *Living Local.*

★ Emzini Tours CULTURAL
(044-382 1087; www.emzinitours.co.za; adult/child R400/150; 10am & 2pm Mon-Sat) Led by township resident Ella, this three-hour trip visits some of this tour company's community projects. Tours can be tailored to suit your interests, but generally end at Ella's home for tea, drumming and a group giggle as you try to wrap your tongue around the clicks of the Xhosa language.

Other options include a music and drumming experience and a hands-on lunch where you help prepare the food (lunch is R120 extra). A meeting point (or hotel pick-up) is arranged at booking.

Peggy's Tours CULTURAL
(Map p240; 044-382 1283; www.peggysart.co.za; 66 Main St; tours R400) Local artist Peggy Dlephu operates tours of the township, where she has launched various art-based projects with schoolchildren. Tours leave from Peggy's gallery in the town centre.

Festivals & Events

Pink Loerie Festival LGBT
(www.pinkloerie.co.za; late May) Knysna celebrates its gay-friendliness with a flamboyant Mardi Gras around the end of May.

Oyster Festival FOOD & DRINK
(www.oysterfestival.co.za; late Jun/early Jul) This is an homage to the oyster with oyster-based specials at restaurants around town, live concerts and sporting events including the Knysna Marathon.

Sleeping

Jembjo's Knysna Lodge HOSTEL $
(Map p240; 044-382 2658; www.jembjosknysnalodge.co.za; 4 Queen St; dm R170, s/d R550/600, s/d with shared bathroom R450/500; P) A small, friendly hostel run by two former overland truck drivers. There's lots of info on activities in the area, mountain bikes to rent (R20 per hour) and a free DIY breakfast.

Inyathi Guest Lodge CHALET $
(Map p240; 044-382 7768; www.inyathiguestlodge.co.za; 38 Trotter St; chalet from R600;) This lodge has changed address and had a complete overhaul, but the cheery owners and tasteful African decor remain. Accommodation is self-catering chalets each with its own private garden. It's an excellent budget option for those who don't fancy a backpackers.

HIKING & MOUNTAIN BIKING

Perfect for hikers of all levels, the Knysna Forests fall under the Knysna Lakes section of the Garden Route National Park. At the easy end of the hiking scale is the Garden of Eden (p241), where there are lovely forest picnic spots and a wheelchair-friendly path. The **Millwood Gold Mine Walk** is also a gentle hike, while the Elephant trails (p242) at Diepwalle offer varying degrees of difficulty.

More challenging is the Harkerville Coastal Trail (p242), a two-day hike that leads to the popular Outeniqua Trail. The Harkerville Coastal Trail sustained serious damage in the 2017 wildfires and was closed when we last visited, but park authorities were working to rehabilitate the paths.

The Outeniqua Trail (p242) is 108km long and takes a week to walk, although you can do two- or three-day sections. The daily fee (adult/child R134/67) includes accommodation in basic huts along the trail; bring your own bedding. For permits, maps and further information, contact SANParks (p246). There are also plenty of mountain-biking trails – contact Knysna Cycle Works (p242) for rentals and maps.

Island Vibe HOSTEL $
(Map p240; 044-382 1728; www.islandvibe.co.za; 67 Main St; dm R170, d R600, with shared bathroom R550;) A funky backpackers with excellent communal areas, cheery staff and nicely decorated rooms. There's a lively bar and a small pool on the deck.

Woodbourne Resort CAMPGROUND $
(Map p245; 044-384 0316; www.woodbourneknysna.com; George Rex Dr; campsites R250, chalet R650;) Here you'll find spacious, shaded camping and simple chalets with TVs. It's a quiet place a little way out of town; follow the signs to the Heads. Prices more than double from mid-December to mid-January.

Knysna Backpackers HOSTEL $
(Map p240; 044-382 2554; www.knysnabackpackers.co.za; 42 Queen St; dm R200, d R695, with shared bathroom R495;) You'll find mainly double rooms at this large Victorian house a few blocks up from Main St. It's a fairly quiet, family-run hostel.

Brenton Cottages CHALET $$
(Map p245; 044-381 0082; www.brentononsea.net; 242 CR Swart Dr, Brenton-on-Sea; 2-person cabins R990, 6-person chalets R1680;) On the seaward side of the lagoon (p239), the hills drop to Brenton-on-Sea, overlooking a magnificent 8km beach. The chalets have a full kitchen while cabins have a kitchenette; many have ocean views. There are plenty of braai (barbecue) areas dotted around the manicured lawns. Prices rise steeply in December and January.

★ **Turbine Hotel & Spa** BOUTIQUE HOTEL $$$
(Map p240; 044-302 5746; www.turbinehotel.co.za; Sawtooth Lane, Thesen's Island; s/d incl breakfast from R1900/2840;) The clever design of this power station-turned-boutique hotel makes it one of Knysna's coolest places to stay. Elements of the original building have been cleverly incorporated into the rooms and public areas. It's a great location a short walk from cafes and restaurants and some rooms have magnificent views of the lagoon.

★ **Under Milkwood** CHALET $$$
(Map p245; 044-384 0745; www.milkwood.co.za; George Rex Dr; s/d cabin from R950/1460;) Perched on the shores of Knysna Lagoon (p239) are these highly impressive self-catering log cabins, each with its own deck and braai area. There's no pool but there is a small beach. The water-facing chalets are more expensive and prices skyrocket in December.

Belvidere Manor HOTEL $$$
(Map p245; 044-387 1055; www.belvidere.co.za; Duthie Dr; s/d incl breakfast R1330/2220;) A tremendously peaceful place to stay, with luxury cottages around an immaculate lawn, some with lagoon views. There is a restaurant (mains R85 to R170) in the historical main house serving regional and international dishes, and an atmospheric pub, open to nonguests.

Protea Hotel Knysna Quays HOTEL $$$
(Map p240; 044-382 5005; www.protea.marriott.com; Waterfront Dr; s/d R1520/1920;) Rooms are tastefully decorated at this stylish hotel. It has an inviting, heated pool and is moments away from shopping and eating options at the Waterfront. You'll want a lagoon-facing room.

Knysna Log Inn HOTEL $$$
(Map p240; 044-382 5835; www.log-inn.co.za; 16 Gray St; s/d incl breakfast R1540/2160;) This inn is said to be the largest log structure in the southern hemisphere. The rooms are comfortable, many with balconies, and there's a lovely pool in the garden.

Eating

★ **Ile de Pain** CAFE, BAKERY $$
(Map p240; 044-302 5705; www.iledepain.co.za; Thesen's Island; mains R55-115; 8am-3pm Tue-Sat;) Ile de Pain is a wildly popular bakery and cafe that's as much a hit with locals as it is with tourists. There's an excellent breakfast menu, lots of fresh salads, some inventive lunch specials and quite a bit for vegetarians. Expect to queue for a table at weekends or in peak season – reservations are not accepted.

Freshline Fisheries SEAFOOD $$
(Map p240; 044-382 3131; www.freshlinefisheries.co.za; Long St, Railway Siding Dockyard; mains R70-170; 11.30am-8pm Mon-Sat;) It can work out to be quite pricey since sides are ordered separately, but the seafood here really is worth it. It's a simple spot with tables on a sandy terrace. It has so much character you quickly forget you're basical-

Around Knysna

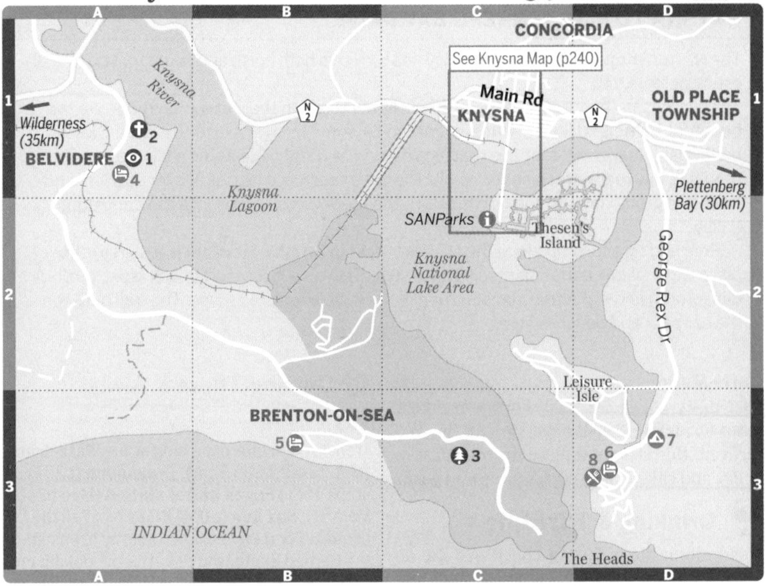

See Knysna Map (p240)

ly lunching at the side of a car park. Bring your own booze – there's no corkage fee.

Chatters Bistro PIZZA $$
(Map p240; ☎044-382 0203; www.chattersbistro.co.za; 9a Gray St; mains R60-130; ⏰noon-10pm Tue-Sat) Restaurants seem to come and go in Knysna, but this pizza joint has been around a while. You'll also find burgers, pasta and some salads, plus a pleasant garden to enjoy them in.

Olive Tree BISTRO $$
(Map p240; ☎044-382 5867; 21 Main St; mains R100-170; ⏰6-9pm Mon-Sat) One of Knysna's more upmarket restaurants is a romantic spot with a blackboard menu that changes regularly. Bookings advisable.

Sirocco INTERNATIONAL $$
(Map p240; ☎044-382 4874; www.sirocco.co.za; Main Rd, Thesen's Island; mains R60-150; ⏰11am-10pm) Inside, it's a stylish place to dine on sushi, steak and seafood; outside, it's a laid-back bar with wood-fired pizzas and a range of Mitchell's beers. The cocktail menu is also worth a look.

East Head Café INTERNATIONAL $$
(Map p245; ☎044-384 0933; www.eastheadcafe.co.za; 25 George Rex Dr, Eastern Head; mains R75-145; ⏰8am-3pm; P ✎ ♿) There's an outdoor deck overlooking the lagoon and ocean, lots of fish and seafood, plus a few vegetarian dishes. It's a very popular spot so expect to wait for a table in high season. Reservations not accepted.

34 South INTERNATIONAL $$
(Map p240; ☎044-382 7331; www.34south.biz; Knysna Waterfront; mains R70-170; ⏰8.30am-10pm) With outdoor tables overlooking the water, decent sushi, deli produce and lavish seafood platters, this is a nice spot for lunch. The wine selection is one of the best in town.

Around Knysna

Sights
1 Belvidere A1
2 Belvidere Church A1
3 Featherbed Nature Reserve C3

Sleeping
4 Belvidere Manor A1
5 Brenton Cottages B3
6 Under Milkwood D3
7 Woodbourne Resort D3

Eating
8 East Head Café D3

OFF THE BEATEN TRACK

KNYSNA TO PLETTENBERG BAY DRIVE

The N2 from Knysna to Plettenberg Bay has turn-offs both north and south that offer interesting detours.

The Knysna–Avontour road, Rte 339, climbs through the Outeniqua range via the beautiful **Prince Alfred's Pass**, regarded by some as even better than the Swartberg Pass. Be warned that the road is a bit on the rough side and it's slow going. The road has few really steep sections but the pass reaches a height of over 1000m, and there are great views to the north before the road winds its way into the Langkloof Valley.

Reached by a turn-off along the N2 10km east of Knysna, **Noetzie** is a quirky little place with holiday homes in mock-castle style. There's a lovely surf beach (spacious but dangerous) and a sheltered lagoon running through a forested gorge. The trail between the car park and beach is steep.

Caffé Mario ITALIAN $$
(Map p240; ☎044-382 7250; Knysna Waterfront; mains R65-195; ⏰8am-9.30pm; 📶) At the Waterfront, this is a good place for breakfast or coffee and cake. It also serves pizza and pasta.

Drinking & Nightlife

Head along Main St and check out the local bars, many of which are seasonal. The town's microbrewery, Mitchell's (p241), is South Africa's oldest.

King's PUB
(Map p240; ☎044-382 6641; Pledge Sq, Main St; ⏰11am-2am Mon-Sat, to 11pm Sun) A slightly grungy but popular pub with draught beer and pool tables.

Vinyl CLUB
(Map p240; ☎044-382 0386; Main St; ⏰7pm-2am) Knysna's top spot for late-night dancing offers a relaxed vibe and a balcony area for lounging. DJs play when there are no live bands.

Information

You'll find a couple of internet cafes on Main St. Access is around R50 per hour, or most cafes provide free, if not altogether reliable, wi-fi.

Knysna Tourism (Map p240; ☎044-382 5510; www.visitknysna.co.za; 40 Main St; ⏰8am-5pm Mon-Fri, 8.30am-1pm Sat year-round, plus 9am-1pm Sun Dec, Jan & Jul) An excellent office, with very knowledgable staff.

SANParks (Map p240; ☎044-302 5600; www.sanparks.org; Long St, Thesen's Island; ⏰7.30am-4pm Mon-Fri)

Post Office (Map p240; ☎044-382 1211; 6 Main St)

Getting There & Away

BUS

Translux and Intercape stop at the **Waterfront** (Map p240; Waterfront); **Greyhound** (p237) stops at the **Engen petrol station** (Map p240; Main St); **Baz Bus** (p184) drops off at all the hostels. For travel between nearby towns on the Garden Route, you're better off looking for a shared taxi than travelling with the major bus lines, which are very expensive for short sectors.

Intercape destinations include George (R240, 45 minutes), Mossel Bay (R240, 1½ hours) and Cape Town (R370, eight hours).

TAXI

Routes from the main **shared taxi stop** (Map p240; cnr Main & Gray Sts) is at the corner of Main and Gray Sts. Routes include Plettenberg Bay (R20, 30 minutes, daily) and Cape Town (R270, 7½ hours, daily). If you want a private taxi, try **Eagle Cabs** (☎076 797 3110).

Plettenberg Bay

☎044 / POP 6500

Plettenberg Bay, or 'Plett' as it's more commonly known, is a resort town through and through, with mountains, white sand and crystal-blue water making it one of the country's top local tourist spots. As a result, things can get very busy, but the town retains a relaxed, friendly atmosphere and does have excellent hostels. The scenery to the east in particular is superb, with some of the best coast and indigenous forest in South Africa.

Plettenberg Bay

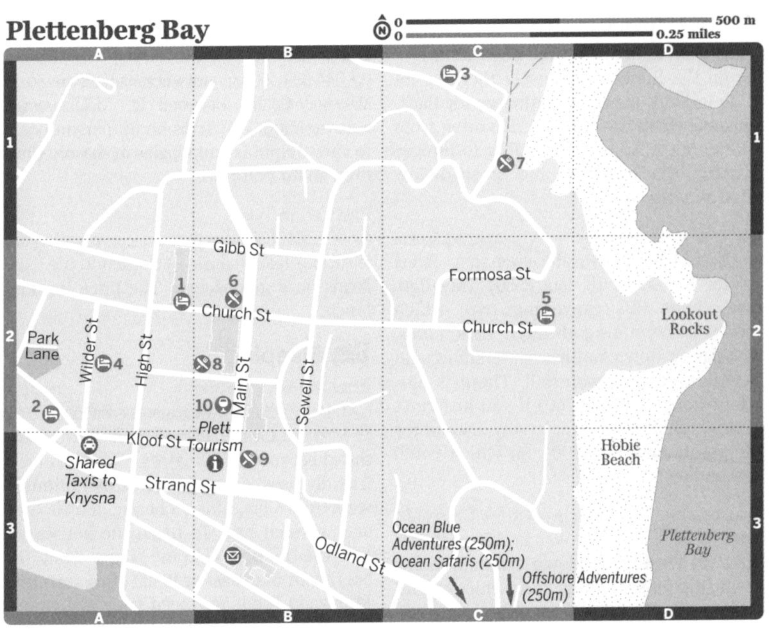

Plettenberg Bay

Sleeping

1 Albergo for Backpackers.....A2
2 Amakaya Backpackers.....A2
3 Milkwood Manor.....C1
4 Nothando Backpackers Hostel.....A2
5 Plettenberg.....C2

Eating

6 Le Fournil de Plett.....B2
7 Lookout Deck.....C1
8 Nguni.....B2
9 Table.....B3

Drinking & Nightlife

10 Flashbacks.....B2

Sights

Monkeyland WILDLIFE RESERVE

(044-534 8906; www.monkeyland.co.za; The Crags; 1hr tour adult/child R210/105; 8am-5pm) This very popular attraction helps rehabilitate wild monkeys that have been in zoos or private homes. The walking safari through a dense forest and across a 128m-long rope bridge is superb. A combo ticket with Birds of Eden costs R320/160 per adult/child.

Bramon WINERY

(044-534 8007; www.bramonwines.co.za; N2; tastings per wine R10; 11am-5pm) Operating since 2000, this was the first wine estate in the region. It's best known for its bubbly. Tucked away in the vines is the mezze-style restaurant (dishes R35 to R90), where bread is baked to order and the whole wine range is available by the glass.

Keurbooms River Nature Reserve NATURE RESERVE

(044-533 2125; www.capenature.co.za; adult/child R40/20; 8am-6pm) This riverine reserve is a glorious place to swim, angle, picnic or paddle. There are canoes to rent (R135 per day) or you can take a ferry trip (p248) down the river.

Birds of Eden BIRD SANCTUARY

(044-534 8906; www.birdsofeden.co.za; The Crags; adult/child R210/105; 8am-5pm) This is one of the world's largest free-flight aviaries with a 200-sq-metre dome over the forest and over 280 species of bird to spot. A combo ticket with Monkeyland costs R320/160 per adult/child.

Activities

Apart from lounging on the beaches or hiking on the Robberg Peninsula there's a lot to do in Plett; check with Albergo for Backpackers, which can organise anything from hiking, horse riding and surfing to bungee jumping, blackwater tubing or skydiving, often at a discount.

Africanyon ADVENTURE SPORTS
(☎044-534 8055; www.africanyon.com; Forest Hall Rd, The Crags; 2hr tour R550) Travellers rave about this canyoning trip, which sees you swimming through rock pools, whooshing down natural waterslides and abseiling down a waterfall. There is also a four-hour option (R750) if you just can't get enough. If you prefer to stay dry, opt for the abseiling trip (R400), on which you'll descend a 50m rock face.

Keurbooms River Ferries BOATING
(☎083 254 3551; www.ferry.co.za; N2; adult/child R180/90) Placid trips down the Keurbooms River stop for swimming and picnics at a little river beach. Ferries depart from the Keurbooms River Nature Reserve (p247), so the reserve entrance fee is also payable.

Learn to Surf Plett SURFING
(☎082 436 6410; www.learntosurfplett.co.za; 2hr group lesson incl equipment R400) A long-running surfing outfit that also offers stand-up paddle boarding lessons (R100 per hour) and rents out equipment.

Ocean Safaris BOATING
(☎082 784 5729; www.oceansafaris.co.za; Milkwood Centre, Hopwood St; whale watching adult/child R750/450) Two-hour boat trips to view southern right and humpback whales operate at 9.30am, noon and 2.30pm from July to December. Dolphin-viewing trips (adult/child R500/250) operate throughout the year.

Sky Dive Plettenberg Bay ADVENTURE SPORTS
(☎082 905 7440; www.skydiveplett.com; Plettenberg Airport; tandem jump from R2600) Although all skydives offer pretty impressive views, you can't beat soaring over the Garden Route coast. This recommended operator has over a decade of skydiving experience.

Tours

Ocean Blue Adventures BOATING
(☎044-533 5083; www.oceanadventures.co.za; Milkwood Centre, Hopwood St; dolphin/whale watching R500/750) Trips on 30-person boats to view dolphins and whales in season. Children go for half price.

Plett Wine Tours WINE
(☎081 270 0658; www.plettwinetours.com; half-day tour R750) Take in a trio of Garden Route wine farms on a guided tour. The price includes lunch.

Sleeping

Abalone Beach House HOSTEL $
(☎044-535 9602; www.abalonebeachhouse.co.za; 13 Milkwood Glen, Keurboomstrand; d R700, with shared bathroom R600; P 📶) This extremely friendly backpackers hostel is two minutes' walk from a magnificent beach; body boards are provided free. To reach the house, follow the Keurboomstrand signs from the N2 (about 6km east of Plett), then turn into Milkwood Glen. You need your own transport to get here.

Nothando Backpackers Hostel HOSTEL $
(☎044 533 0220; www.nothando.com; 5 Wilder St; dm R180, d R550, with shared bathroom R480; P 📶) This excellent budget option is owner-run and it shows. There's a great bar area with satellite TV, yet you can still find peace and quiet in the large grounds. Rooms are worthy of a budget guesthouse.

Albergo for Backpackers HOSTEL $
(☎044-533 4434; www.albergo.co.za; 8 Church St; camping R90, dm R160, d with shared bathroom R450; P 📶) Well-run and friendly, Albergo can organise just about any activity in the area and there are free body boards to use. The upstairs dorm has huge windows and a spacious balcony.

Amakaya Backpackers HOSTEL $
(☎044-533 4010; www.amakaya.co.za; 15 Park Lane; dm R160, d R600, with shared bathroom R450; P 📶) The focal point is the bar and deck with views of the Tsitsikamma Mountains. There are two 'private dorms' – basically a twin room with bunks – offering a cheaper alternative for two people travelling together (but at the same price as regular dorm beds).

OFF THE BEATEN TRACK

ROBBERG NATURE & MARINE RESERVE

This **reserve** (044-533 2125; www.capenature.co.za; adult/child R40/20; 8am-6pm May-Sep, 7am-8pm Oct-Apr), 8km southeast of Plettenberg Bay, protects a 4km-long peninsula with a rugged coastline of cliffs and rocks. There are three circular day walks of increasing difficulty, but it's very rocky and not for the unfit or anyone with knee problems! Basic accommodation is available at the spectacularly located **Fountain Shack** (044-802 5300; www.capenature.org.za; 4 people R920), which is reachable only by a two-hour hike.

You can also take a boat trip to view the peninsula – and its colony of Cape fur seals – from the water and even take a dip to see if the seals come for a closer look. Contact **Offshore Adventures** (082 829 0809; www.offshoreadventures.co.za; Hopwood St; boat trip R400, swimming with seals R700) to book.

To get to the reserve head along Robberg Rd, off Piesang Valley Rd, until you see the signs. There is no public transport. A private taxi from Plettenberg Bay's town centre costs around R100 each way.

★ **Hog Hollow** LODGE $$$
(044-534 8879; www.hog-hollow.com; Askop Rd, The Crags; s/d incl breakfast R2700/3975; P) Hog Hollow, 18km east of Plett along the N2, provides delightful accommodation in African-art-decorated units overlooking the forest. Each luxurious unit comes with a private wooden deck and hammock. You can walk to Monkeyland (p247) from here; staff will collect you if you don't fancy the walk back.

Plettenberg LUXURY HOTEL $$$
(044-533 2030; www.theplettenberghotel.com; 40 Church St; r incl breakfast from R4300; P) Built on a rocky headland with breathtaking vistas, this five-star place is pure decadence, with fantastic rooms, a spa and a top-class restaurant (mains R150 to R250).

Milkwood Manor HOTEL $$$
(044-533 0420; www.milkwoodmanor.co.za; Salmack Rd, Lookout Beach; r incl breakfast from R1400; P) A remarkable location, right on the beach and overlooking the lagoon. Rooms have a bright, beachy feel. There's an on-site restaurant (mains R110 to R200) and kayaks are free for guests.

Periwinkle Guest Lodge GUESTHOUSE $$$
(044-533 1345; www.periwinkle.co.za; 75 Beachy Head Dr; s/d incl breakfast from R2145/2860; P) This bright beachfront guesthouse offers airy rooms, all with great views – you might even be able to spot whales and dolphins.

Eating & Drinking

Le Fournil de Plett CAFE $
(044-533 1390; Lookout Centre, Church St; mains R60-115; 8am-5pm Mon-Fri, to 4pm Sat, to 1pm Sun;) Enjoy a good cup of coffee and a freshly baked pastry in the courtyard or on the balcony overlooking Plett's main road. There's also a small lunch menu, largely focusing on salads and sandwiches.

Ristorante Enrico SEAFOOD $$
(044-535 9818; www.enricorestaurant.co.za; Main Beach, Keurboomstrand; mains R90-170; noon-10pm Tue-Sun; P) Highly recommended by readers and right on the beach, this is *the* place for seafood in Plett (well, just outside Plett). Enrico has his own boat that, weather permitting, heads out each morning. If you book ahead you can join the fishing trip and have your catch cooked at the restaurant.

Table ITALIAN $$
(044-533 3024; www.thetable.co.za; 9 Main St; mains R60-115; noon-11pm Mon-Sat, to 6pm Sun;) A funky, minimalist venue with pizzas, seafood and a very tasty lamb shank. There's an indoor kids' area and live music on Fridays.

Lookout Deck SEAFOOD $$
(044-533 1379; www.lookout.co.za; Hill St, Lookout Beach; mains R90-185; 9am-9pm) With a deck overlooking the beach, this is a great place for a simple meal and perhaps views of dolphins surfing the waves.

★ **Nguni** STEAK $$$
(044-533 6710; www.nguni-restaurant.co.za; 6 Crescent St; mains R135-225; 11am-10pm Mon-Fri, from 6pm Sat) Tucked away in a quiet courtyard, this is one of Plett's most upscale eateries. The speciality is dry-aged beef, though you'll also find some South African favourites including ostrich, springbok and the odd traditional dish such as a vegetarian version of *bobotie* (curry topped with beaten egg baked to a crust). Reservations recommended.

Flashbacks BAR
(044-533 4714; Marine Bldg, Main St; noon-2am Mon-Sat, from 5pm Sun) A long-established bar in the centre of town with sports on the big screen in the early evening and DJs playing pop and dance tunes later on.

Shopping

Old Nick Village ARTS & CRAFTS
(044-533 1395; www.oldnickvillage.co.za; N2; 9am-5pm) For a bit of retail therapy, head for this complex 3km east of town, with resident artists, a weaving museum, antiques and a restaurant.

Information

There is an **internet cafe** (Melville's Corner Shopping Centre, Main St; per hr R60; 8am-5pm Mon-Fri, 9am-1pm Sat) in Melville's Corner Shopping Centre on Main St. Most cafes offer free wi-fi.

Plett Tourism (044-533 4065; www.plett-tourism.co.za; Melville's Corner Shopping Centre, Main St; 9am-5pm Mon-Fri, to 1pm Sat) Plenty of useful information on accommodation plus walks in the surrounding hills and reserves.

Post Office (044-533 1215; 30 Main St)

Getting There & Away

All the major buses stop at the Shell Ultra City petrol station on the N2; the **Baz Bus** (p184) comes into town. **Intercape** (p184) destinations from Plett include George (R230, one hour) and Cape Town (R470, eight hours).

If you're heading to Knysna you're better off taking a **shared taxi** (Kloof St, near cnr High St; R20) (30 minutes). Long-distance shared taxis stop at the Shell Ultra City.

Nature's Valley

Nature's Valley is nestled in yellowwood forest next to a magnificent beach and lagoon in the Tsitsikamma section of the **Garden Route National Park** (042-281 1607; www.sanparks.org; adult/child R216/108; gate 6am-9pm), which encompasses 650 sq km between Plettenberg Bay and Humansdorp, as well as a Marine Protected Area covering 80km of coastline. A 77m-long suspension bridge spans the Storms River Mouth near the rest camp of the same name (not to be confused with the village of Storms River in the Eastern Cape), where several walking trails pass thickets of ferns, lilies, orchids, coastal and mountain fynbos, and yellowwood and milkwood trees. Millennia-old sandstone and quartz rock formations line the gorges and rocky shoreline, and southern right whales and dolphins are visible out in the ocean.

Elusive Cape clawless otters, after which the 46km Otter Trail (a multiday hike) is named, inhabit this park; there are also baboons, monkeys, small antelope and furry little dassies. Birdlife is plentiful, including endangered African black oystercatchers. Nature's Valley is where the Otter Trail ends and the 60km Tsitsikamma Mountain Trail begins. There are also plenty of shorter hikes in this part of the park.

Activities

Otter Trail HIKING
(in Pretoria 012-426 5111; www.sanparks.org; per person R1200) The 45km Otter Trail is one of South Africa's most acclaimed hikes, hugging the coastline from Storms River Mouth to Nature's Valley. The five-day, four-night walk involves fording a number of rivers and gives access to some superb stretches of coast. A good level of fitness is required, as it goes up- and downhill quite steeply in many places.

Accommodation is in six-bed rest huts with mattresses (without bedding), rainwater tanks, braais (barbecues) and firewood. Camping is not allowed.

Book at least nine months ahead (six months if you are flexible about dates). There are often cancellations, however, so it's always worth trying, especially if you are in a group of only two or three people. Single hikers are permitted; you'll be tagged onto a group so you do not walk by yourself.

Tsitsikamma Mountain Trail HIKING
(042-281 1712; www.mtoecotourism.co.za; per night R155) This 62km trail begins at

Nature's Valley and ends at Storms River, taking you inland through the forests and mountains. The full trail takes six days, but you can also opt for two, three, four or five days, because each overnight hut has its own access route. Porterage is also available, as are day hikes (R50) and mountain-bike trails.

Bloukrans Bridge Bungee BUNGEE JUMPING
(042-281 1458; www.faceadrenalin.com; bungee jumps R990; 8.30am-4.45pm) At 216m, this is one of the highest (and most spectacular) bungee jumps in the world. If you're not sure whether you have the guts to take the plunge, walk out to the jumping-off point under the bridge for R150. Jumps take place 21km west of Storms River directly under the N2.

Unexpectedly scary is the post-jump upside-down hang while you wait to be reeled back up. Photos and video of your glorious lapse of judgment are available. If jumping is not for you, you can instead take in the spectacle of people leaping off the bridge from the safety of the cliff-top terrace or the aptly named Cliffhanger bar-restaurant.

Dolphin Trail HIKING
(042-280 3588; www.dolphintrail.co.za; s/d R7080/11,800) Ideal for well-heeled slackpackers who don't want to hoist a rucksack or sleep in huts, this two-day, 17km hike runs from **Storms River Mouth Rest Camp** (042-281 1607; www.sanparks.org; camping per site from R370, hut/cottage/chalet from R600/1100/1200; P) to **Misty Mountain** (042-280 3699; www.mistymountainreserve.co.za; s/d/f from R1395/1860/2200; P), and then onto the **Fernery Lodge & Chalets** (042-280 3588; www.forestferns.co.za/Fernery; s/d incl breakfast from R1800/2600; P) for the last night. Book through the trail's website at least a year in advance (yes, really!).

Luggage is transported by vehicle between the overnight stops, and the price also includes three nights of accommodation, all meals, guides and a 4WD trip back to Storms River Mouth.

Untouched Adventures ADVENTURE SPORTS
(073 130 0689; www.untouchedadventures.com; kayak & lilo trip R450, scuba diving R600, guided snorkelling trip R400; 8.30am-6pm) This renowned venture offers a popular three-hour kayak and lilo trip up Storms River, plus scuba diving and guided snorkelling trips in the national park Marine Protected Area (trips are weather dependent). Located near the beach at Storms River Mouth Rest Camp.

Sleeping

A range of accommodation options are above the village, signposted from Rte 102 as it runs 9km down to Nature's Valley from the N2 near Kurland Village. You'll also find a few B&Bs and self-catering facilities in the village, but no hotel. Nature's Valley Properties (www.naturesvalleyproperties.co.za/accommodation) lists self-catering accommodation on its website.

Nature's Valley Guesthouse & Hikers Haven GUESTHOUSE $
(044-531 6805; www.hikershaven.co.za; 411 St Patrick's Ave; s/d incl breakfast R490/960, d with shared bathroom R380; closed Dec; P) This thatched brick building has a big lawn, a self-catering kitchen, a lounge, and small, tidy rooms with outdated bathrooms. Transport to the start of the Otter Trail is offered (R480 for up to four people).

Nature's Valley Rest Camp CAMPGROUND $
(044-531 6700; www.sanparks.org; camping per site R205, chalet R1120, cabin with shared bathroom R550) The national park campsite is a lovely spot at the edge of the river east of town, and it's a 2km walk from the beach. There are clean bathrooms and shared kitchens and laundry. Keep food well stored: there are pesky primates everywhere. In addition to accommodation charges, guests must pay the park's daily conservation fee (adult/child R96/48).

Rocky Road HOSTEL $
(044-534 8148; www.rockyroadbackpackers.com; Loredo South; dm R190, safari tent s/d R240/480, cabin s/d R270/540; P) Rocky Road is like an enchanted clearing in the wood. Swing chairs, a donkey-boiler jacuzzi and offbeat bathrooms are scattered on the fringes of indigenous forest. Accommodation options include two dorms, comfortable safari tents and cabins with adjoining bathrooms. Breakfast and dinner are available on request. It is signposted from Rte 102 about 1km from the N2.

Tranquility B&B B&B $$
(044-531 6663; www.tranquilitylodge.co.za; 130 St Michael's Ave; s incl breakfast R650-750, d incl breakfast R1300-1500;) Soundtracked by a trickling fountain and the roaring waves, Tranquility has seven clean rooms decked out with beach-house furniture, African art and surf trimmings. Guests get free kayaks for the lagoon and discounts on bungee jumping at Bloukrans Bridge.

Eating

Nature's Valley Trading Store PUB FOOD $$
(044-531 6835; 135 St Michael's Ave; mains R60-125; 9am-7.30pm;) A spade's throw from the beach (but without sea views), the only eatery in the village serves burgers, salads, steaks and seafood, and the adjoining shop sells basic groceries. Also offers local information and brochures.

Nature's Way Farm Stall CAFE $
(044-534 8849; Rte 102; snacks R35-40; 9am-5pm;) This charming roadside store on a dairy farm sells light breakfasts and lunches, tapas, cake, coffee and a smorgasbord of local produce, including cheese, jam and fruits. It also rents a few fully equipped cottages.

Information

Nature's Valley Trust (044-531 6820; www.naturesvalleytrust.co.za; 388 Lagoon Dr; 8am-4pm Mon-Fri) Located at the entrance to the village.

Getting There & Away

Mzansi Experience (021-001 0651; www.mzansi.travel) stops in the Crags (near Nature's Valley) en route between Cape Town and Hogsback. **Baz Bus** (p184) also stops in the Crags en route between Cape Town and Port Elizabeth. The other bus companies stop in Plettenberg Bay, from where accommodation in Nature's Valley will pick you up, if given advance notice.

Understand Cape Town

CAPE TOWN TODAY 254

Tap water running out due to drought is only one of many crises the Mother City is having to deal with.

HISTORY 256

From the Khoekhoen and San peoples to Zille and de Lille, Cape Town's history is rich in characters and events.

PEOPLE & CULTURE 266

One city, many cultures – Cape Town is a melting pot of different people and lifestyles.

ARCHITECTURE 271

A stone castle, graceful Cape Dutch, florid Victoriana and art deco towers are all part of the architectural mix.

THE ARTS 273

Cape Town's vibrant mix of communities and cultures inspire the arts, from literature and cinema to painting and music.

THE NATURAL ENVIRONMENT 277

Shaped over millions of years, the Cape's dramatic features are carpeted by the richest floral kingdom in the world.

Cape Town Today

Of late, the Mother City has been fighting fires on multiple fronts – and we're not only talking about those that regularly scorch their way through the national park or decimate township communities. The city is in the midst of a catastrophic drought, its commuter train system is at breaking point, crime is on the rise and students have been rioting on university campuses.

Best in Print

What Will People Say? (Rehana Rossouw, 2015) A funny and emotionally moving debut novel set in the crime-plagued coloured community of Hanover Park in the Cape Flats in 1986.

Sunset Claws (Brent Meersman, 2017) Cape Town is a key setting for this epic trilogy about South Africa's move from apartheid to democracy as seen through a cast of vividly drawn characters.

Gang Town (Don Pinnock, 2016) Award-winning book by an investigative journalist that shines a light on gangsterism in Cape Town.

Best on Film

Black Butterflies (2011) Biopic about Afrikaaner poet Ingrid Jonkers (a powerful performance by Carice van Houten) set in Cape Town in the 1950s and '60s.

Sea Point Days (2008; www.seapointdays.co.za) Documentary by François Verster focusing on the suburb and its promenade as a multicultural crossroads.

Love the One You Love (2014) A phone-sex operator, a dog handler and an IT technician are the main characters in Jenna Bass' debut feature, set in Cape Town.

Running Out of Water

The drought has forced the city to recommend a per person limit of 50L or less of water per day. Fines are issued to heavy users, municipal swimming pools have been shuttered, a ban put on car washes, and citizens encouraged to adopt water-saving measures such as two-minute showers and flushing their toilets with grey water and only when necessary.

At the time of research Day Zero – when the city's reservoirs hit 13% capacity, taps are turned off and people will have to queue at water collection points – was set for July 2018. Temporary desalination plants are up and running and there are plans in the works for a more permanent facility in the harbour that will be able to process 50 million litres per day. For more on the situation and what you as a visitor can do to help, see www.capetown.gov.za/thinkwater.

Trouble with the Trains

Anything up to 700,000 people use Metrorail to get to work in the Cape Town area. However, the system suffers from dilapidated rolling stock, severe delays are common and security is practically nonexistent. Since January 2017, at least 28 coaches have been set alight by angry commuters. Metrorail only has 58 train sets, but to meet its current timetable it requires 84. It's easy to do the maths and see why commuters are finding themselves crammed on overcrowded and long-delayed trains.

At the end of October 2017 a plan was approved by the city council to take over management of Metrorail from the national Passenger Rail Agency of South Africa (Prasa). However, this is going to take quite a bit of time and negotiation. For the plan to succeed, the city will have to prise prime assets off Prasa *and* make a major investment in the network, the funds for which currently just don't exist.

Most Dangerous Place in South Africa

The 2017 State of Urban Safety Report in South Africa confirmed what many residents have long suspected: the Mother City has the highest rates of robbery, murder and property-related crime in the country. Along with Nelson Mandela Bay in the Eastern Cape, Cape Town is top of the league when it comes to murders, a direct result of the high level of violent gang activity across the Cape Flats.

However, the situation is complex. Suburbs such as Camps Bay and Claremont are among the safest places to live – not just in South Africa, but the world. Many years no murders occur in these suburbs at all. In comparison, Khayelitsha clocked up 161 murders in 2016, while Nyanga had 279 murders, 351 sexual offences and 1053 assaults – making it the nation's most dangerous place to live.

Drill down further into the stats and you'll find that the killings generally don't involve unfortunate tourists, but are between family members or drug gangs.

Rhodes (and Fees) Must Fall

The protest movement dubbed 'Rhodes Must Fall' began at the University of Cape Town (UCT) and has since rippled out across South Africa and even to the hallowed halls of Oxford in the UK. UCT stands on land bequeathed to Cape Town by Cecil Rhodes and a bronze statue of the man had stood on campus since 1934. Calls for its removal, which had been steady over the decades, reached a crescendo in March 2015 when students rioted in front of the statue. A month later it was gone.

The protests have continued, however, with the true targets becoming institutional racism and increasing university fees that hamper equality of access to education. The occupation of UCT's administration building in October 2015 led to riot police being called in and 25 students were arrested. The protest spread to the Cape Peninsula University of Technology where the campus was locked down. Students then marched to Parliament and the riot police were again called. The national government eventually agreed to a Commission of Inquiry into Higher Education and Training to look at the feasibility of providing free tertiary education. It concluded it wasn't feasible.

Her tweets in March 2017 on the positive aspects of colonialism also caused problems for Western Cape Premier Helen Zille. Accused of racism and fundamentally misunderstanding African history, Zille later apologised and stepped down from the Democratic Alliance's leadership structures, but the drama is yet another example of how raw domestic sensitivities over such matters remain.

POPULATION: **3.74 MILLION**

AREA: **2445 SQ KM**

POPULATION GROWTH RATE: **2.57%**

UNEMPLOYMENT RATE: **23.9%**

FEMALE HEADED HOUSEHOLDS: **38.2%**

belief systems

(% of population)

if Cape Town were 100 people

History

Humans lived on the Cape for millennia before the first Europeans visited in the 15th century. Dutch rule lasted nearly 200 years before the British took over in 1814, prompting many Afrikaners (Boers) to trek inland – only to come back to power with a vengeance during the apartheid years. In 1990 Nelson Mandela became a free man 75km from Cape Town, hailing the start of a democratic South Africa.

The Khoekhoen & San People

Academics don't know whether the earliest recorded inhabitants of South Africa – the San people – are direct descendants or if they returned to the area after æons of travel, between 40,000 and 25,000 years ago. For centuries, perhaps even millennia, the San and the Khoekhoen, another early Southern African people, intermarried and coexisted. The distinction is by no means clear, hence the combined term Khoe-San.

Culturally and physically, the Khoe-San developed differently from the Negroid peoples of Africa, but it's possible they came into contact with pastoralist Bantu-speaking tribes as – in addition to hunting and gathering food – they too became pastoralists, raising cattle and sheep. There's evidence that the Khoe-San lived on the Cape of Good Hope about 2000 years ago.

South Africa lays strong claim to being the cradle of mankind. At Langebaan Lagoon (north of Cape Town), the discovery of 117,000-year-old fossilised footprints prompted one researcher to speculate that 'Eve' (the very first human or common ancestor of us all) lived here.

First European Visitors

The first Europeans to record a sighting of the Cape were the Portuguese, who passed by on their search for a sea route to India and spices. The land here offered the Portuguese little more than fresh water, since their attempts to trade with the Khoe-San often ended in violence. But by the end of the 16th century, English and Dutch traders were beginning to challenge the Portuguese, and the Cape became a regular stopover for ships. In 1647 the Dutch vessel the *Haarlem* was wrecked in Table Bay; its crew built a fort and stayed for a year before they were rescued. This crystallised the value of a permanent settlement in the minds of the directors of the Vereenigde Oost-Indische Compagnie (VOC; Dutch East India Company). They had no intention of colonising the country, but simply wanted to establish a secure base where ships could shelter and stock up on fresh food supplies.

TIMELINE

AD 1488

Bartolomeu Dias, the first European to sail around the Cape, dubs it Cabo da Boa Esperança (Cape of Good Hope). Others prefer Cabo das Tormentas (Cape of Storms).

1510

The Khoe-San fight back when Portuguese soldiers try to kidnap two of their number; Captain de Almeida and 50 of his troops are killed.

1652

Jan van Riebeeck, instructed by the Vereenigde Oost-Indische Compagnie (VOC; Dutch East India Company) to establish a supply station en route to India, arrives on 6 April.

The Dutch Arrive

The task of establishing the VOC station fell to Jan van Riebeeck (1619–77), Commander of the Cape from 1652 to 1662. The Dutch were not greeted with open arms by the Khoe-San and intermittent hostilities broke out. But the locals – who are thought to have numbered between 4000 and 8000 people – hardly stood a chance against the Europeans' guns and diseases.

With the Khoe-San uncooperative, the Cape settlement was soon suffering a chronic labour shortage. From 1657 Van Riebeeck started releasing VOC employees, allowing them to farm land independently, thus beginning the colonisation of Southern Africa and giving birth to the Boers. The following year he began to import slaves from West Africa, Madagascar, India, Ceylon, Malaya and Indonesia. By the time the slave trade ended in 1807, some 60,000 slaves had been brought to the Cape, laying the foundation for its unique mix of cultures and races.

The San were nomadic hunters and gatherers, and the Khoekhoen (also known as Khoikhoi, possibly meaning 'Men of Men') were seminomadic hunters and pastoralists. European settlers later called the Khoekhoen 'Hottentots', and the San 'Bushmen'.

The Settlement Grows

The process of colonisation kicked off a series of wars between the Dutch and the Khoe-San further inland, who were no match for the well-armed Europeans. The Dutch also allowed some 200 Huguenots (French Calvinists fleeing religious persecution) to settle on the Cape in 1688. There was a shortage of women in the colony, so female slaves and Khoe-San women were exploited for both labour and sex. In time, the slaves intermixed with the Khoe-San, too. The children of these unions were the ancestors of some of today's coloured population.

Under the VOC's almost complete control, Kaapstad (the Dutch name for Cape Town) provided a comfortable European lifestyle for a growing number of artisans and entrepreneurs servicing ships and crews. By the middle of the 18th century there were around 3000 people living in the riotous port, known as the 'Tavern of the Seas' by every sailor travelling between Europe and the East.

Bartolomeu Dias rounded the Cape in 1488, but didn't linger, as his sights were fixed on the trade riches of the east coast of Africa and the Indies.

The British Take Over

As the 18th century progressed, the global power of the Dutch was waning and under challenge by the British. Between 1795 and 1806 the Cape was passed like a parcel between the two colonial powers, with the French also briefly drawn into the power play. Even before the colony was formally ceded to the British Crown on 13 August 1814, the British had abolished the slave trade. The remaining Khoe-San were given the explicit protection of the law in 1828. These moves contributed to Afrikaners' dissatisfaction and their mass migration inland from the Cape Colony, which came to be known as the Great Trek.

Despite outlawing slavery, the British introduced new laws that laid the basis for an exploitative labour system little different from it. Thousands of

1660

Van Riebeeck plants a wild almond hedge to protect his European settlement from the Khoe-San – a section of it remains in the Kirstenbosch National Botanical Garden.

1679

Simon van der Stel, the son of a VOC official and a freed Indian slave, arrives in the Cape as its commander. Two years later he is promoted to governor.

1699

After retiring to develop his estate of Constantia, the birthplace of the Cape's wine industry, Van der Stel is succeeded by his son Willem Adriaan.

1795

The British take control of the Cape after winning the Battle of Muizenberg. Eight years later the Treaty of Amiens puts the Dutch back in power.

dispossessed blacks sought work in the colony, but it was made a crime to be in the colony without a pass – and without work. It was also a crime to leave a job.

Cape Economy Booms

Under a policy of free trade Cape Town's economy flourished. In 1854 a representative parliament was formed in Cape Town, but much to the dismay of Dutch and English farmers to the north and east, the British government and Cape liberals insisted on a multiracial constituency (albeit with financial requirements that excluded the vast majority of blacks and coloureds).

The opening of the Suez Canal in 1869 dramatically decreased the amount of shipping that sailed via the Cape, but the discovery of diamonds and gold in the centre of South Africa in the 1870s and '80s helped Cape Town maintain its position as the country's premier port. Immigrants flooded into the city and the population trebled, from 33,000 in 1875 to over 100,000 people at the turn of the 20th century.

During the first half of the 19th century, before the Suez Canal opened, British officers serving in India would holiday at the Cape.

Boer War

After the Great Trek, the Boers established several independent republics, the largest being the Orange Free State (today's Free State Province) and the Transvaal (today's Northern Province, Gauteng and Mpumalanga). When the world's richest gold reef was found in the Transvaal (a village called Johannesburg sprang up beside it), the British were miffed that the Boers should control such wealth – which precipitated war in 1899. The Boers were outnumbered, but their tenacity and local knowledge meant the war dragged on until 1902, when the British triumphed. Cape Town was not directly involved in any of the fighting, but did play a key role in landing and supplying the half-million imperial and colonial troops who fought for Britain.

WHO ARE THE BOERS?

South Africa's Afrikaner population has its roots in the Dutch and early European settlers of the Cape. The more independent of these settlers soon began drifting away from the strict regime of the VOC and into the countryside. These were the first of the Trekboers (literally 'trekking farmers'), later known as Boers.

Fiercely independent and with livelihoods based on rearing cattle, the Boers were not so different from the Khoe-San with whom they came into conflict with as they colonised the interior. Many Boers were illiterate and most had no source of information other than the Bible. Isolated from other Europeans, they developed their own separate culture and eventually their own language, Afrikaans, derived from the argot of their slaves.

1806

As part of the Napoleonic Wars, the British return. With their decisive victory at the Battle of Blouberg, they secure the cape for the British Crown.

1808

The new government proclaims free trade and abolishes the local slave trade. Still, slaves in the Malmesbury and Tygerberg area revolt and march on Cape Town.

1814

The Cape Colony is formally ceded to Britain, making it the empire's second possession in Africa after Sierra Leone. English replaces Afrikaans as the official language.

1834

Following emancipation, Cape Town's free slaves establish their own neighbourhood, the Bo-Kaap. In the same year, the Cape Town Legislative Council is also founded.

Act of Union

After the war, the British made some efforts towards reconciliation, and instituted moves towards the union of the separate South African provinces. In 1910 the Act of Union was signed, bringing the republics of Cape Colony, Natal, Transvaal and Orange Free State together as the Union of South Africa. Under the provisions of the act, the Union was still a British territory, with home-rule for Afrikaners. In the Cape, blacks and coloureds retained a limited franchise (although only whites could become members of the national parliament, and eligible blacks and coloureds constituted only around 7%), but did not have the vote in other provinces.

The first government of the new Union was headed by General Louis Botha, with General Jan Smuts as his deputy: statues of both these figures are found in the City Bowl. Their South African National Party (later known as the South African Party, or SAP) followed a generally pro-British, white-unity line.

The Dutch Reformed Church justified apartheid on religious grounds, claiming the separateness of the races was divinely ordained – that the *volk* (literally, the 'people'), meaning Afrikaners, had a holy mission to preserve the purity of the white race in its promised land.

Apartheid Rules

Afrikaners were economically and socially disadvantaged when compared with the English-speaking minority, which controlled most of the capital and industry in the new country. This, plus lingering bitterness over the war and Afrikaners' distaste at having to compete with blacks and coloureds for low-paying jobs, led to strident Afrikaner nationalism and the formation of the National Party (NP) in 1914. The NP championed Afrikaner interests, advocating separate development for the two white groups and independence from Britain.

In 1948 the NP came to power on a platform of apartheid (literally, 'the state of being apart'). Nonwhites were denied the vote, mixed marriages were prohibited, interracial sex was made illegal and every person was classified by race. The Group Areas Act defined where people of each 'race' could live and the Separate Amenities Act created separate public facilities: separate beaches, separate buses, separate toilets, separate schools and separate park benches. Blacks were compelled to carry passes at all times and were prohibited from living in or even visiting towns without specific permission.

Within months of opening in 1899, the Mount Nelson Hotel became the headquarters for the British Army, led by Lords Roberts and Kitchener, during the Boer War. Winston Churchill recuperated at the hotel and filed newspaper dispatches from here after escaping a Boer prison camp.

Fictional Homelands

A system of homelands was set up in 1951, whereby the proportion of land available for black ownership in South Africa increased very slightly to 13%. Blacks then made up about 75% of the population. The homelands idea was that each black group had a traditional area where it belonged – and must now stay. The area around Cape Town was declared a 'coloured preference area', which meant no black person could be employed unless it could be proved that there was no coloured person suitable for the job. The plan

1835

Afrikaner dissatisfaction with British rule prompts the start of the Great Trek; some 10,000 families go in search of their own state, opening up the country's interior.

1849

Governor Sir Harry Smith, anxious that the Cape not become a penal colony, bars 282 British prisoners from leaving the ship *Neptune*, forcing it to continue to Tasmania.

1869

The discovery of the world's largest diamond deposit in Kimberley and later gold in the Transvaal boosts Cape Town's economy as the port becomes the gateway for mineral wealth.

1890

Two decades after first arriving in Cape Town, self-made mining magnate Cecil Rhodes, founder of De Beers, becomes the colony's prime minister at the age of 37.

ignored the huge numbers of blacks who had never lived in their 'Homeland'. Millions of people who had lived in other areas for generations were forcibly removed into bleak, unproductive areas with no infrastructure.

The homelands were regarded as self-governing states, and it was planned that they would become independent countries. Four of the 10 Homelands were nominally independent by the time apartheid was demolished (though they were not recognised as independent countries by the UN), and their leaders held power with the help of the military.

Meanwhile, white South Africa depended on cheap black labour to keep the economy booming, so many black 'guest workers' were admitted back to the country. But unless a black person had a job and a pass, they were

NELSON MANDELA

Nelson Mandela, son of a Xhosa chief, was born on 18 July 1918 in the Eastern Cape village of Mveso, on the Mbashe River. After attending the University of Fort Hare, Mandela headed to Johannesburg, where he soon became immersed in politics. He finished his law degree and, together with Oliver Tambo, opened South Africa's first black law firm. Meanwhile in 1944, along with Tambo and Walter Sisulu, Mandela formed the Youth League of the African National Congress (ANC). During the 1950s, Mandela was at the forefront of the ANC's civil disobedience campaigns, for which he was arrested in 1952, and tried and acquitted. After the ANC was banned in the wake of the Sharpeville massacre, Mandela led the establishment of its underground military wing, Umkhonto we Sizwe. In 1964 Mandela was brought to trial for sabotage and fomenting revolution in the widely publicised Rivonia Trial. After brilliantly arguing his own defence, he was sentenced to life imprisonment, and spent the next 18 years in the infamous Robben Island prison before being moved to the mainland.

Throughout his incarceration, Mandela repeatedly refused to compromise his political beliefs in exchange for freedom, saying that only free men can negotiate. In February 1990 Mandela was finally released, and in 1991 he was elected president of the ANC. In 1993 Mandela shared the Nobel Peace Prize with FW de Klerk and, in the country's first free elections the following year, was elected president of South Africa. In his much-quoted speech 'Free at Last!', made after winning the 1994 elections, he focused the nation's attention firmly on the future, declaring, 'This is the time to heal the old wounds and build a new South Africa'.

In 1997 Mandela – or Madiba, his traditional Xhosa name – stepped down as ANC president, although he continued to be revered as an elder statesman. On 5 December 2013 Nelson Mandela, aged 95 years, died from an ongoing respiratory infection. South Africans grieved openly for the man who had given so much of himself to his country. Then South African president Jacob Zuma said, 'Our nation has lost its greatest son. Nothing can diminish our sense of a profound and enduring loss'. The world also grieved for the man who had inspired so many with his moral authority. One of the largest gatherings of world leaders came together for the memorial service.

1899

Lord Kitchener dubs the British campaign to gain control of the Boer republics as 'a teatime war', but the Anglo-Boer War is fiercely fought for three years.

1902

Bubonic plague arrives on a ship from Argentina, giving the government an excuse to introduce racial segregation – 6000 blacks are forcibly sent to live on the Cape Flats.

March 1902

Following Rhodes' death, his vast estate is bequeathed to the city, providing the grounds for both the University of Cape Town and Kirstenbosch National Botanical Garden.

1910

The British colonies and the old Boer republics are joined in the Union of South Africa. Cape Town is made the seat of the legislature.

liable to be jailed and sent back to their homeland. This caused massive disruption to black communities and families. Unsurprisingly, people without jobs gravitated to cities such as Cape Town to be near their spouses and parents. But no new black housing was built; as a result, illegal squatter camps mushroomed on the sandy plains to the east of Cape Town. In response, government bulldozers flattened the shanties, and their occupants were forced into the homelands. Within weeks, the shanties would rise again.

Mandela Jailed

In 1960 the African National Congress (ANC) and the Pan Africanist Congress (PAC) organised marches against the hated Pass laws, which required blacks and coloureds to carry passbooks authorising them to be in a particular area. At Langa and Nyanga on the Cape Flats, police killed five protesters. The Sharpeville massacres in Gauteng were concurrent and resulted in the banning of the ANC and PAC. In response to the crisis, a warrant for the arrest of Nelson Mandela and other ANC leaders was issued. In mid-1963 Mandela was captured; at trial he was sentenced to life imprisonment on Robben Island.

The government tried for decades to eradicate squatter towns, such as Crossroads, which were focal points for black resistance to the apartheid regime. Violent removals and killings failed and the government, forced to accept the inevitable, began to upgrade conditions. Since then, vast townships have sprung up across the Cape Flats. No one knows exactly how many people call them home, but it's thought to be in excess of 1.5 million.

The Coloured Experience

Apartheid's divide-and-rule tactics – favouring coloureds above blacks – stoked the animosity that still lingers between those Cape communities today. Even so, coloureds did suffer under apartheid, such as the residents of the poor inner-city area of District Six, which in 1966 was classified as a white area. Its 50,000 people, some of whose families had been there for five generations, were gradually evicted and removed to bleak and soulless Cape Flats suburbs like Athlone, Mitchell's Plain and Atlantis. Friends, neighbours and relatives were separated. Bulldozers moved in and the multiracial heart was ripped out of the city, while in the townships, depressed and dispirited youths increasingly joined gangs and turned to crime.

The coloured Muslim community of the Bo-Kaap, on the northeastern edge of Signal Hill, was more fortunate. Home to Cape Town's first mosque (the Owal Mosque on Dorp St dates back to 1798), the district was once known as the Malay Quarter, because it was where many of the imported slaves from the start of the Cape Colony lived with their masters. In 1952 the entire Bo-Kaap region was declared to be a coloured area under the terms of the Group Areas Act. There were forced removals, but the residents of

Mandela Reads

Long Walk to Freedom (Nelson Mandela)

Mandela: The Authorised Biography (Anthony Sampson)

The Long Walk of Nelson Mandela (www.pbs.org/wgbh/pages/frontline/shows/mandela)

Nelson Mandela Foundation (www.nelsonmandela.org)

1914

Lingering bitterness over the Anglo-Boer war and Afrikaners' distaste at competing with blacks and coloureds for low-paying jobs leads to formation of the National Party.

1923

The Black Urban Areas Act restricts the entry of blacks into the city centre. Three years later the prison-like settlement of Langa becomes the first planned township for blacks.

1939

The peninsula's rugged tip is protected within the Cape of Good Hope Nature Reserve. It's 60 years before a single Cape Peninsula national park is created.

1940

Cape Town's pier, built in 1925, is demolished as an ambitious reclamation project extends the city centre 2km from the Strand into Table Bay, creating the Foreshore district.

the community banded together in order to successfully fight for and retain ownership of their homes. Many were declared National Monuments in the 1960s, which saved them from the bulldozers.

Path to Democracy

In 1982 Mandela and other ANC leaders were moved from Robben Island to Pollsmoor Prison in Cape Town. (In 1986 senior politicians began secretly talking with them.) Concurrently, the state's military crackdowns in the townships became even more pointed. In early 1990 President FW de Klerk began to repeal discriminatory laws, and the ANC, PAC and Communist Party were legalised. On 11 February the world watched as a living legend emerged from Victor Vester Prison near Paarl. Later that day Nelson Mandela delivered his first public speech since being incarcerated 27 years earlier, to a massive crowd overspilling from Cape Town's Grand Parade.

The Sunday Times Heritage Project (http://sthp.saha.org.za) is an online collaboration between the newspaper and the South African History Archive. It includes a map detailing the stories of many prominent activists and events in South Africa's 20th-century history.

From this time onwards virtually all the old apartheid regulations were repealed; in late 1991, the Convention for a Democratic South Africa (Codesa) began negotiating the formation of a multiracial transitional government, and a new constitution extending political rights to all groups. Two years later a compromise was reached and an election date set. In the frustration of waiting, political violence exploded across the country during this time, some of it sparked by the police and the army.

Despite this, the 1994 election was amazingly peaceful, with the ANC winning 62.7% of the vote. In Western Cape, the majority coloured population voted in the NP as the provincial government, seemingly happier to live with the devil they knew than with the ANC.

Truth & Reconciliation Commission

One of the first acts of the new ANC government was to set up the Truth & Reconciliation Commission (TRC) to expose the crimes of the apartheid era. This institution carried out Archbishop Desmond Tutu's dictum: 'Without forgiveness there is no future, but without confession there can be no forgiveness.' Many stories of horrific brutality and injustice were heard during the commission's three-year life, offering some catharsis to individuals and communities shattered by their past.

The TRC operated by allowing victims to tell their stories and perpetrators to confess their guilt, with amnesty offered to those who came forward. Those who chose not to appear before the commission face criminal prosecution if their guilt can be proven. Although some soldiers, police and 'ordinary' citizens have confessed their crimes, it seems unlikely that those who gave the orders and dictated the policies will ever come forward (former president PW Botha was one famous no-show), and gathering evidence against them has proven difficult.

1948

The National Party wins government. The right of coloureds to vote in the Cape is removed (blacks had been denied the vote since 1910) as apartheid is rolled out.

1964

Following the Rivonia Trial, Nelson Mandela, Walter Sisulu and others escape the death penalty, but are sentenced to life imprisonment on Robben Island in Table Bay.

1976

Students in Langa, Nyanga and Gugulethu march against the imposition of Afrikaans as the language of instruction in schools; 128 people are killed and 400 injured.

1982

Mandela and other senior African National Congress (ANC) leaders are moved from Robben Island to Pollsmoor Prison in Tokai, facilitating the beginning of discreet contact between them and the National Party.

Rise, Fall & Rise Again of Pagad

The governmental vacuum that existed between Mandela's release from jail and the election of a democratic government left Cape Town in a shaky social position. The early 1990s saw drugs and crime become such a problem that communities began to take matters into their own hands. People against Gangsterism and Drugs (Pagad) was formed in 1995 as an offshoot of the Islamic organisation Qibla. The group saw itself as defending the coloured community from the crooked cops and drug lords who allowed gangs to control the coloured townships.

At first the police tolerated Pagad, but their vigilante tactics turned sour in 1996 with the horrific (and televised) death of gangster Rashaad Staggie. A lynch mob burned then repeatedly shot the dying gangster. Other gang leaders were killed, but Capetonians really began to worry when bombs, some believed to have been planted by the more radical of Pagad's members, began to go off around the city. The worst attack was in 1998, when an explosion at the Waterfront killed one woman and injured 27 other people. In September 2000 a magistrate presiding in a case involving Pagad members was murdered in a drive-by shooting.

Pagad leader Abdus Salaam Ebrahim was imprisoned in 2002 for seven years for public violence, but no one has ever been charged, let alone convicted, for the Cape Town bombings. For a time, Pagad was designated a terrorist organisation by the government. However, in 2009 it began a comeback campaign, rebranding itself the 'new Pagad', yet still operating like the organisation of old by marching on the homes of suspected drug dealers and demanding they cease their activities. In 2013, murder charges

For more about the TRC read the award-winning account *Country of My Skull*, by journalist and poet Antjie Krog.

DESMOND TUTU

Few figures in South Africa's anti-apartheid struggle are as recognisable as Desmond Mpilo Tutu, the retired Anglican Archbishop of Cape Town. Tutu, born in 1931 in Klerksdorp, Transvaal (now in North West Province), rose from humble beginnings to become an internationally recognised activist. During the apartheid era, Tutu was a vigorous proponent of economic boycotts and international sanctions against South Africa. Following the fall of the apartheid government, he headed South Africa's Truth & Reconciliation Commission, an experience that he chronicles in his book *No Future Without Forgiveness*.

Today Tutu continues to be a tireless moral advocate. He has been a particularly outspoken critic of the ANC government, lashing out against corruption, AIDS and poverty, and taking the government to task for failing to adequately tackle poverty. Tutu has been awarded the Nobel Peace Prize, the Gandhi Peace Prize and numerous other distinctions. It is Tutu who is generally credited with coining the phrase 'rainbow nation' as a description for post-apartheid South Africa.

1986

An estimated 70,000 people are driven from their homes and hundreds killed as the government tries to eradicate the squatter towns of Nyanga and Crossroads in the Cape Flats.

1989

President PW Botha suffers a stroke and is replaced by FW de Klerk, who continues the secret negotiations that lead to the ANC, Pan Africanist Congress (PAC) and Communist Party becoming legalised.

1990

Mandela walks a free man from Victor Verster Prison in Paarl, and delivers his first public speech in 27 years from the balcony of Cape Town City Hall.

1994

Following democratic elections, Mandela succeeds FW de Klerk as president, saying 'This is the time to heal the old wounds and build a new South Africa'.

were dropped against Ebrahim, who had been arrested following the slaying of three Tanzanians (alleged to be drug dealers) in Cape Town.

Shifting Alliances

In 1999, two years after Mandela had stepped down as ANC president and was succeeded by his deputy, Thabo Mbeki, South Africa held its second free elections. Nationally, the ANC increased its vote, coming within one seat of the two-thirds majority that would allow it to alter the constitution, but in the Western Cape a pact between the old NP (restyled as the New National Party, or NNP) and the Democratic Party (DP) created the Democratic Alliance (DA), bringing them victory not only in the provincial elections but also in the metropolitan elections.

In 2002 the political landscape shifted radically when the NNP completed a merger with the ANC, which gave the ANC control of Cape Town and brought the city its first black female mayor, Nomaindia Mfeketo. In national and provincial elections two years later the ANC were equally triumphant, and Ebrahim Rasool – a practising Muslim whose family had been moved out of District Six when he was 10 – was appointed premier of the Western Cape.

Conscious of their core vote in the Cape Flats, the ANC-led city council vowed to improve the lot of township folk by upgrading the infrastructure in the informal settlements and boosting investment in low-cost housing, such as the N2 Gateway Project. Urban renewal projects were also announced for Mitchells Plain, one of the deprived coloured areas of the city blighted, like so many Cape Flats suburbs, by the murderous drug trade. Particularly deadly has been the rise in addiction to methamphetamine, known locally as 'tik'.

South Africa's constitution is one of the most enlightened in the world. Apart from forbidding discrimination on practically any grounds, among other things it guarantees freedom of speech and religion, and access to adequate housing and health care and basic adult education.

History Reads

- *Dinosaurs, Diamonds & Democracy: A Short, Short History of South Africa (Francis Wilson)*
- *Diamonds, Gold and War (Martin Meredith)*
- *Cape Lives of the Eighteenth Century (Karel Schoeman)*

Xenophobia & Soccer

Battling charges of corruption and blamed for disruptive rolling power cuts caused by the Western Cape's overstretched nuclear power station at Koeberg, the ANC narrowly lost out to the Democratic Alliance (DA) in the municipal elections of March 2006. The DA's Helen Zille became Cape Town's mayor. In July 2008, Rasool – mired in controversy over the sale of the V&A Waterfront and nearby Somerset Hospital site – was replaced as Western Cape premier by Lynne Brown.

For the poorest Capetonians, however, the political circus counted for little against lives blighted by dire economic, social and health problems. In May 2008 frustrations in the townships, fuelled by spikes in food and fuel prices, boiled over in a series of horrific xenophobic attacks on the most vulnerable members of society – immigrants and refugees from wars and political violence. As some 30,000 people fled in panic, the vast majority of Capetonians rallied to provide assistance.

1998

After two years of emotionally painful testimonies the Truth & Reconciliation Commission in Cape Town delivers its verdict, condemning both sides in the liberation struggle.

2002

Cape Town elects its first black female mayor, Nomaindia Mfeketo, as the New National Party (NNP) ditches the Democratic Party (DP) to join forces with the ANC.

2004

Ebrahiem Murat, 87, and Dan Mdzabela, 82, are handed keys to new homes in District Six, the first returnees among thousands who hope to rebuild their lives in the demolished suburb.

2008

African immigrants are targeted in the xenophobic violence that engulfs Cape townships. Over 40 people are killed and 30,000 driven from their homes in nearly two weeks of attacks.

ZILLE & DE LILLE

Helen Zille (pronounced Ziller, hence her nickname 'Godzille') and Patricia de Lille have both been at the forefront of Capetonian politics for over a decade. Zille was Cape Town's mayor for three years from 2006, and in the May 2009 elections she became premier of the Western Cape. She was also formerly the leader of the Democratic Alliance (DA), the official national opposition party, but this position passed to charismatic Mmusi Maimane in 2015.

Jo'burg-born Zille began her career as a journalist in 1974, during which time she exposed the circumstances of the freedom fighter Steve Biko's death while in police custody. As mayor and the state's premier, she has impressed (and sometimes infuriated) locals with her no-nonsense, practical style of government, fearlessly wading into issues as thorny as drugs and gangsterism, teenage pregnancies and prevention of HIV/AIDS transmission. In 2017, however, her reputation took a severe dent following an ill-advised tweet about colonialism, an issue that has distanced her from the DA's leadership.

De Lille has been no less fiery and controversial in her political career. Starting as a union rep in her hometown of Beaufort West, De Lille progressed to become leader of the Independent Democrats (ID) and as a campaigner is famous for shedding light on a shady arms deal that still dogs the upper echelons of the ANC. The ID merged with the DA in 2010, and in 2011 De Lille was chosen as the mayoral candidate, a post she was elected to that year. It had been thought that De Lille would follow Zille as the Western Cape premier at the next election in 2019 (when Zille's second and final term of office finishes) but it's now more likely that current Western Cape DA leader Bonginkosi Madikizela will be the party's candidate.

Despite controversies over the location and spiralling costs of the new Cape Town Stadium, the city's various factions united to support the hosting of soccer's World Cup in 2010. The event was judged a huge success but, facing global recession and social problems, many locals wonder if the money could not have been better spent.

The 2014 & 2016 Elections

Prior to the 2014 national and provincial elections, disenchantment with corruption, crime and slow progress on providing critical services to poor communities fed a growing desire for change; one beneficiary was firebrand politico Julius Malema's Economic Freedom Fighters (EFF) party. Nationally the ANC won comfortably with 62.1% of the vote (down from 65.9% in 2009), with the the DA lagging way behind on 22.2%. However, in the Western Cape, the DA held onto power with 59.4% of the vote, and the ANC at 32.9%.

In the 2016 municipal elections, the DA made major gains in ANC strongholds, particularly in major metros such as Tshwane (Pretoria), Johannesburg and Nelson Mandela Bay (Port Elizabeth), as well as holding onto their majorities in Cape Town and the Western Cape.

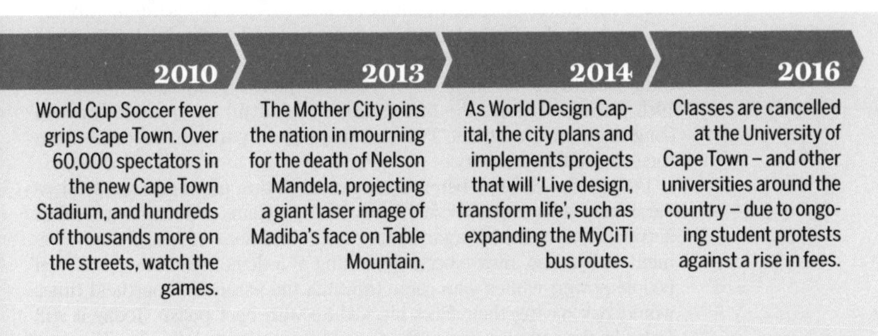

People & Culture

Cape Town's racial mix is different from the rest of South Africa. Of its metropolitan population of 3.7 million, more than half are coloured; blacks account for about a third of the total, while whites and others comprise the balance. However, this is the just the starting point for the rich mix of cultures that coexists here.

Racial Groups

Although there are many people who find the old apartheid racial terms 'white', 'black', 'coloured' and 'Indian' distasteful and want to break away from the stereotypes they imply, it's a fact that in South Africa these words are used by everyone, quite often without any rancour or ill feeling.

The ethnic composition of Afrikaners is difficult to quantify but it has been estimated at 40% Dutch, 40% German, 7.5% French, 7.5% British and 5% other. Some historians have argued that the '5% other' figure includes a significant proportion of blacks and coloureds.

Coloureds

Coloureds, sometimes known as Cape coloureds or Cape Malays, are South Africans of long standing. Although many of their ancestors were brought to the early Cape Colony as slaves, others were political prisoners and exiles from the Dutch East Indies. Slaves also came from India and other parts of Africa, but their lingua franca was Malay (at the time an important trading language), hence the term Cape Malays.

Many coloureds practise Islam, and Cape Muslim culture has survived intact over the centuries, resisting some of the worst abuses of apartheid. The slaves who moved out with the Dutch to the hinterland, many losing their religion and cultural roots in the process, had a much worse time of it. And yet practically all of the coloured population of the Western Cape and Northern Cape Provinces today are bound by Afrikaans, the unique language that began to develop from the interaction between the slaves and the Dutch over three centuries ago.

Cape Town Minstrel Carnival

The most public secular expression of coloured culture today is the riotous Cape Town Minstrel Carnival. This parade, also known in Afrikaans as the Kaapse Klopse, is a noisy, joyous and disorganised affair, with practically every colour of satin, sequin and glitter used in the costumes of the marching troupes, which can number over a thousand members.

Although the festival dates back to the early colonial times when slaves enjoyed a day of freedom on the day after New Year, the look of today's carnival was inspired by visiting American minstrels in the late 19th century – hence the face make-up, colourful costumes and ribald song-and-dance routines. The vast majority of participants come from the coloured community.

Despite the carnival being a permanent fixture on Cape Town's calendar, it has had a controversial history with problems over funding, clashes between rival carnival organisations and allegations of gangster involvement. It has also always been something of a demonstration of coloured people power: whites who came to watch the parade in apartheid times would risk having their faces blacked-up with boot polish. Today it still feels like the communities of the Cape Flats coming to take over the city.

Blacks

Although most blacks in Cape Town are Xhosa, hailing from Eastern Cape Province, they are not the only group in the city. Cape Town's economy has attracted people from all over Southern Africa, including many immigrants from the rest of the continent – a lot of the car-parking marshals, traders at the city's various craft markets and waiters in restaurants are from Zimbabwe, Nigeria, Mozambique and the like.

Xhosa culture is diverse, with many clan systems and subgroups. Within the black community there are also economic divisions and subgroups based on culture, such as the Rastafarian community in Knysna.

Many South Africans proudly identify themselves as black, white or coloured – for example, you'll meet black South Africans who happily refer to themselves as black rather than South African or African (which is the African National Congress' preferred collective expression for all people of African, Indian and mixed-race origin).

Whites

There are distinct cultural differences in the white community here, depending on whether people are descendants of the Boers or the British and other later European immigrants to South Africa. The Boers' history of geographical isolation and often deliberate cultural seclusion has created a unique people who are often called 'the white tribe of Africa'.

Afrikaans, the only Germanic language to have evolved outside Europe, is central to the Afrikaner identity, but it has also served to reinforce their isolation from the outside world. You'll find Afrikaans to be a much stronger presence in the northern suburbs of Cape Town and in the country towns of the Cape, especially around Stellenbosch, which has a prominent Afrikaans university.

Most other white Capetonians are of British extraction. Cape Town, as the seat of British power for so long, is somewhat less Afrikaner in outlook than other parts of the country. White liberal Capetonians were regarded with suspicion by more conservative whites during the apartheid years.

INITIATION RITES

Male initiation ceremonies, which take place from around the ages of 16 to the early 20s, are a consistent part of traditional black African life (and coloured Muslim life, where teenage boys are also circumcised, albeit with much less ritual). Initiations typically take place near the end of the year and in June to coincide with school and public holidays.

In the Eastern Cape, young Xhosa men would once go into a remote area in the mountains to attend the Ukwaluka – the initiation school where they would be circumcised, live in tents and learn what it is to be a man in tribal society. Some still do return to the Eastern Cape for the ceremony, but others cannot afford to go, or choose not to do so, so similar initiation sites are created in makeshift tents erected amid the wastelands around the townships.

Initiations used to take several months, but these days they're likely to last a month or less. Initiates shave off all their hair, shed their clothes and wear just a blanket, and daub their faces in white clay before being circumcised. They receive a stick that symbolises the traditional hunting stick; they use it instead of their hands for shaking hands during the initiation period. For about a week immediately after the circumcision, while the wound heals, initiates eat very little and drink nothing. No women are allowed to go near the initiation ground.

Initiations are expensive – around R8000, mainly for the cost of the animals (typically sheep or goats) that have to be slaughtered for the various feasts that are part of the ceremony. At the end of the initiation all the items used, including the initiate's old clothes, are burned together with the hut in which he stayed, and the boy emerges as a man. You can spot recent initiates in the townships and Cape Town's city centre by the smart clothes they are wearing, often a sports jacket and a cap.

DEALING WITH RACISM

Cultural apartheid still exists in South Africa. To an extent, discrimination based on wealth is replacing that based on race; most visitors will automatically gain high status. There are, however, still plenty of people who think that a particular skin colour means a particular mindset. A few believe it means inferiority.

The constant awareness of race, even if it doesn't lead to problems, is an annoying feature of travel in South Africa, whatever your skin colour. Racial discrimination is illegal, but it's unlikely that the overworked and under-resourced police force will be interested in most complaints. Tourism authorities are likely to be more sensitive. If you encounter racism in any of the places mentioned by us, please let us know.

African

If you are of African descent, you may well encounter racism from some white and coloured people. Do not assume a special bond with black South Africans either. The various indigenous peoples of South Africa form distinct and sometimes antagonistic cultural groups.

Indian

Although Indians were discriminated against by whites during apartheid, blacks saw them as collaborating with the whites. If you are of Indian descent this could mean some low-level antagonism from both blacks and whites.

Asian

East Asians were a problem for apartheid – Japanese were granted 'honorary white' status, but Chinese were considered coloured. Grossly inaccurate stereotyping and cultural ignorance will probably be the main annoyances you will face.

Religion

Islam

The progressive **Open Mosque** (Map p100; www.theopenmosque.co.za) preaches enlightened, egalitarian and erudite Islam. It also organises interfaith events, which bring together Muslims, Christians and Jews.

Islam first came to the Cape with the slaves brought by the Dutch from the Indian subcontinent and Indonesia. Although the religion could not be practised openly in the colony until 1804, the presence of influential and charismatic political and religious figures among the slaves helped a cohesive Cape Muslim community to develop. One such political dissident was Imam Abdullah Ibn Qadi Abdus Salaam, commonly known as Tuan Guru, from Tidore (now in Indonesia), who was exiled to Robben Island in 1780 and released 13 years later in Cape Town. Four years later he helped establish the city's first mosque, the Owal Mosque, in the Bo-Kaap, thus making this area the heart of the Islamic community in Cape Town – as it still is today.

Tuan Guru's grave is one of the 20 or so *kramats* (tombs of Muslim saints) encircling Cape Town and visited by the faithful on mini pilgrimages. Other *kramats* are found on Robben Island (that of Sayed Abdurahman Matura); on Signal Hill, which has two (for Sheikh Mohammed Hassen Ghaibie Shah and Tuan Kaape-ti-low); at the gate to the Klein Constantia wine estate (for Sheik Abdurahman Matebe Shah); and at Ouderkraal, where there are another two (that of Sheikh Noorul Mubeen and possibly his wife or one of his followers). For a full list see www.capemazaarsociety.com.

Cape Town has managed to avoid becoming embroiled in violent Islamic fundamentalism. You'll encounter many friendly faces while wandering around the Bo-Kaap, where you can drop by the local museum to find out more about the community. A sizeable Muslim community also lived in Simon's Town before the Group Areas Act evictions of the late 1960s; its history can be traced at Simon's Town's Heritage Museum.

Christianity

The Afrikaners are a religious people and the group's brand of Christian fundamentalism, based on 17th-century Calvinism, is still a powerful influence. Urbanised middle-class Afrikaners tend to be considerably more moderate. Whites of British descent tend to be Anglican and this faith, along with other forms of Christianity, is also very popular among sections of the black and coloured communities.

Spirit Worship

Elements of traditional African spiritual culture persist, lending a distinctively African air to the townships. At important junctions in life, such as birth, coming of age and marriage, various old rites and customs are followed as well.

Herbal medicine shops are regularly used, and *sangomas* (traditional medicine practitioners, usually women) are consulted for all kinds of illnesses. Certain *sangomas* can also help people get in touch with their ancestors, who play a crucial role in the lives of many black Capetonians. Ancestors are believed to watch over their kin and act as intermediaries between this world and that of the spirits. People turn to their ancestors if they have problems or requests – an animal may be slaughtered in their honour and roasted on an open fire, as it's believed the ancestors eat the smoke.

Ubuntu, best translated as 'humanity to others', is one of the core principles of traditional South African life and is often witnessed in the townships despite, or perhaps because of, people having so little and needing to support each other.

Judaism

South Africa's oldest Jewish community is in Cape Town. Even though the rules of the Vereenigde Oost-Indische Compagnie (VOC; Dutch East India Company) allowed only for Protestant settlers at the Cape, there are records of Jews converting to Christianity in Cape Town as early as 1669. Jewish immigration picked up speed after the British took charge, with settlers coming mainly from England and Germany. The first congregation was established in 1841, while the first synagogue (now part of the South African Jewish Museum) opened in 1863.

Jewish immigration boomed between 1880 and 1930, when an estimated 15,000 families arrived in South Africa, mainly from Lithuania, Latvia, Poland and Belarus. During this period Jews began to make a large contribution to the city's civic and cultural life. Max Michaelis donated his art collection to the city and Hyman Liberman became the first Jewish mayor of Cape Town in 1905, the same year the Great Synagogue was consecrated.

Cape Town's Jewish population has dropped from 25,000 (second in number only to the community in Jo'burg) in 1969 to around 16,000 today. Sea Point is the most visibly Jewish area of the city.

Spanish director Pablo Pinedo Bóveda's documentary film *Noma* (2016) shadows shack dweller Nomaliphathwe Gwele as she struggles to build a life in Philippi.

Township Life

The vast majority of Capetonians – of which there are an estimated 2.4 million in Khayelitsha alone – live in what are termed townships. These areas, mostly on the windswept, sandy Cape Flats, were demarcated during apartheid as locations for black and coloured South Africans to live. To a large extent they remain so. While poverty and all its associated ills are ingrained in the townships, it is very far from a universally bleak situation.

The Shaping of Townships

South Africa's oldest planned township is Langa, founded in 1927. Today it's home to 250,000 people – the same number who live in the city centre, but squashed into an area some 48 times smaller.

When it was first set up Langa, like other early townships such as Nyanga, was mainly made up of hostels (basic units, each accommodating 16 men, who shared one shower, one toilet and one small kitchen) and 30-sq-metre terrace housing accommodation. Built originally for

SHACK LIFE

Formally called 'informal settlements', shacks are the type of homes most widely associated with the townships. It's estimated that around 20% of township residents live in shacks. Cobbled together from a variety of materials, such as old packing crates, and decorated with (among other things) magazine pages and old food-tin labels, the design and structure of a shack depends on the financial situation of the owner and how long they have lived there. Driving around the townships, you'll see ready-made shacks for sale. This is a sound business prospect as people are constantly moving to the townships from the countryside – and because of the need to replace housing after the frequent fires that burn many shacks to the ground.

migrant labourers before WWII, these homes were very basic, poorly constructed and crowded.

After the Pass laws (which stated that those without a job outside the homelands were not allowed to leave) were abolished, most men brought their families to live with them. The population of the original townships boomed, eventually leading to the creation of Gugulethu, Crossroads, Philippi and Khayelitsha. Elsewhere on the Cape you'll also find smaller black townships such as Imizamo Yethu in Hout Bay and Masiphumelele in the south between Noordhoek and Kommetjie.

Khayelitsha: uMlungu in a Township (Steve Otter, 2007) is a vivid account by a white South African of his time living in Khayelitsha.

Coloured Townships

It wasn't just black South Africans who were dumped out in the Cape Flats before and during apartheid. Cape Town's coloured population also suffered forced removals, the most notorious being those from the city centre's District Six. Many of the city's most crime- and poverty-stricken suburbs, such as Mitchell's Plain and Hanover Park, are a consequence of those removals.

A generation on from the end of apartheid, the racial divisions that defined these different township areas remains largely intact – blacks live in Langa while neighbouring Bonteheuwel is predominantly coloured. The tragedy is that all the township communities are united in facing the same ingrained problems of crime, poor infrastructure and lack of social services when compared to the wealthier suburbs of the city.

During his 13 years on Robben Island, Tuan Guru is said to have transcribed three copies of the Quran from memory. He's buried in Bo-Kaap's Tana Baru Cemetery.

Townships Today

Since 1994, the South African government has striven to build proper houses in the townships, first through the Reconstruction and Development Programme (RDP) and currently through the Breaking New Ground (BNG) scheme, both of which provide a very basic, free house to former shack residents. Averaging around 28 sq metres in size, these 'matchbox' houses are little more than four concrete-block walls topped with a corrugated iron roof. There's no insulation, ceiling or hot water provided.

So called 'gap' housing is also being built in the townships for low-income families who earn between R3500 and R15,000 a month. Residents are expected to contribute towards buying these subsidised homes, which are typically of a better quality than BNG housing.

Not everyone in the townships lives in poverty, though. There are areas of Gugulethu, Langa and Khayelitsha that are very middle-class, and where you'll find spacious, bungalow-style houses and villas of a high standard. Improving local incomes and investment by government are reflected in such places as Gugulethu Square, a glittering mall that would not be out of place in Camps Bay; and spiffy public complexes such as Khayelitsha District Hospital, the Isivivana Centre and Langa's Guga S'Thebe Arts & Cultural Centre.

Architecture

From the 17th-century Castle of Good Hope to the 21st-century towers rising on the Foreshore, Cape Town's range of architecture is one of its most attractive features. Much that might have been destroyed in other places has been preserved here, and can be viewed on walking or cycling tours of the city and surroundings.

Dutch Colonial

When the Dutch colonists arrived in 1652, they brought their European ideas of architecture with them, but had to adapt to local conditions and available materials. Stone from Table Mountain was used to build the Castle of Good Hope between 1666 and 1679. The first Capetonian houses were utilitarian structures, such as the thatched and whitewashed Posthuys in Muizenberg, dating from 1673.

Governor Simon van der Stel's quintessential manor house, Groot Constantia, went up in 1692, setting a precedent for other glorious estates to follow further inland in the Winelands. On Strand St, the fancy facade of the late-18th-century Koopmans–de Wet House is attributed to Louis Thibault, who, as lieutenant of engineers for the Vereenigde Oost-Indische Compagnie (Dutch East India Company; VOC), was responsible for the design of most of Cape Town's public buildings in this period. Thibault also had a hand in the handsome Rust en Vreugd: completed in 1778, the house is notable for its delicately carved rococo fanlight above the main door, as well as its double balconies and portico.

Of course, not everyone lived in such a grand manner. In the city centre, the best place to get an idea of how Cape Town looked to ordinary folk during the 18th century is the Bo-Kaap. You'll notice flat roofs instead of gables and a lack of shutters on the windows, all the result of VOC building regulations.

Best Books

Hidden Cape Town (Paul Duncan and Alain Proust)

Cape Town: Architecture & Design (Pascale Lauber)

Cape Dutch Houses & Other Old Favourites (Phillida Brooke Simons)

British Colonial

When the British took over from the Dutch in the early 19th century, they had their own ways of doing things, and this extended to the architectural look of the city. British governor Lord Charles Somerset made the biggest impact during his tenure (1814–26). It was he who ordered the restyling of Tuynhuis – first built as a guesthouse and later a summer residence for the Dutch governors of the Cape – to bring it into line with Regency tastes for verandas and front gardens, and renamed it Government House.

As the British Empire reached its zenith in the late 19th century, Cape Town boomed and a slew of monumental buildings were erected. These include the Standard Bank building, with its pediment, dome and soaring columns; the Houses of Parliament; and the Byzantine-influenced Old Synagogue, dating from 1863. The neighbouring and neo-Egyptian-styled Great Synagogue, with its twin towers, is from 1905. Long St is where you can see Victorian Cape Town at its most appealing, with the wrought-iron balconies and varying facades of shops and buildings.

Another building boom in the 1920s and '30s led to the construction of many fine art deco buildings in the city centre. Prime examples include the blocks around Greenmarket Sq and the handsome 1939 Mutual Heights

At the Foreshore end of Bree St, the 42-storey, 142m-high Portside Tower (2014) is currently Cape Town's tallest building. Designed by DHK and Louis Karol Architects, the building was South Africa's first Green Star–rated skyscraper.

SIR HERBERT BAKER

Like his patron Cecil Rhodes, Herbert Baker (1862–1946) was an ambitious young Englishman who seized the chance to make his mark in South Africa. Baker arrived in Cape Town in 1892 and a year later, through family connections, had gained himself an audience with Rhodes and been commissioned to remodel Groote Schuur, the prime minister's mansion on the slopes of Table Mountain. This kicked off a style known as Cape Dutch Revival.

Many more commissions followed, and Cape Town is littered with buildings of Baker's design, including several cottages in Muizenberg (where Baker lived for a while), St George's Cathedral and the First National Bank on Adderley St. In 1900, Rhodes sent Baker to Italy, Greece and Egypt to study their classical architecture to inspire him to design the sort of grand buildings Rhodes wished to see constructed in South Africa. Two years later, though, Rhodes was dead – and Baker was designing his memorial.

building – the continent's first skyscraper – decorated with friezes and frescoes, all with South African themes.

Apartheid Era

Apartheid laws labelled Cape Town a mainly coloured city – this meant that the national government was unwilling to support big construction projects (hampering the development of the Foreshore for decades), while the local authorities went about applying the Group Areas Act, demolishing areas such as District Six and rezoning Green Point (including De Waterkant) as a whites-only area.

Examples of rationalist architecture from this era include the brutalist Artscape arts centre and the adjoining Civic Centre on the Foreshore, which demonstrate the obsession with concrete that was typical of international modernism. Far more attractive is the Baxter Theatre designed by Jack Barnett and completed in 1977; its flat roof is famously dimpled with orange fibreglass downlights that glow fabulously at night.

During apartheid, official architectural planning ignored the townships. Still, it is worth mentioning the tremendous ingenuity and resilience that residents have shown in creating liveable homes from scrap. A visit to the townships today reveals colourfully painted shacks and murals, homes and churches made from shipping crates, and more recent imaginative structures, such as the Guga S'Thebe Arts & Cultural Centre in Langa.

Best Modern Buildings

Guga S'Thebe Arts & Cultural Centre (2000)

Cape Town Stadium (2010)

Zeitz MOCAA Museum (2017)

Contemporary Architecture

The death knell of apartheid coincided with the redevelopment of the Victoria & Alfred Waterfront in the early 1990s. More recent architectural additions to the Waterfront include the Nelson Mandela Gateway and Clock Tower Precinct, built in 2001 as the new departure point for Robben Island, the ritzy millionaire's playground of the V&A Marina, with some 600 apartments and 200 boat moorings, and most recently the Silo District surrounding the Zeitz MOCAA Museum designed by Heatherwick Studio.

The recent Cape Town property boom has created an environment for some interesting new residential buildings and conversions of old office blocks into apartments, such as the Mutual Heights building, the three old buildings that are part of Mandela Rhodes Place, and the adjacent Taj Cape Town hotel, all of which sensitively combine the original structures with new towers.

Opening in 2003, the Cape Town International Convention Centre (CTICC), with its ship-like prow and sleek glass-and-steel hotel, drew favourable nods and has helped push the City Bowl down towards the waterfront, from which it had been cut off for decades. An extension to the CTICC has recently been completed and more towers are rising or planned for the Foreshore district and City Bowl.

The Arts

Cape Town's mash-up of cultures and the sharply contrasting lives of its citizens make it a fertile location for the arts. Music is a pulsing constant in the Mother City, with jazz a particular forte. There's a surprisingly good range of performing arts, and a host of imaginative authors shed light on more obscure corners of the urban experience.

Visual Arts

At the South African National Gallery (p78), you may find paintings by Gerard Sekoto, a black artist whose works capture the vibrancy of District Six, and Peter Clarke, a distinctive printer, poet and painter hailing from Simon's Town. Irma Stern's German-expressionism-inspired works can be found in the Irma Stern Museum (p96) and at Casa Labia Cultural Centre (p107) in Muizenberg.

Notable among contemporary local artists is Conrad Botes, who first made his mark with his weird cult comic *Bitterkomix,* founded with Anton Kannemeyer. Botes' colourful graphic images, both beautiful and horrific, have been shown in exhibitions in New York, the UK and Italy, as well as at the Havana Biennale in 2006.

Also look out for works by the painter Ndikhumbule Ngqinambi; Willie Bester, whose mixed-media creations of township life are very powerful; and the more conventional John Kramer (www.johnkramer.net), who captures the ordinary, serene quality of the South African landscape. A rising star is Zanele Muholi, an out-and-proud lesbian artist who uses photography, video and installations to striking effect – see her work at Stevenson (p78), (which represents her) and the Zeitz MOCAA Museum (p66).

The Cape's history of visual art stretches back to the original San inhabitants, who left their mark on the landscape in the form of rock paintings and subtle rock engravings.

THE PEOPLE'S PAINTER

Across Cape Town you'll see the striking multiracial faces that inspired the portraits of Vladimir Tretchikoff (1913–2006). The most famous of these is the iconic *Chinese Girl* – a mesmerising image of a blue-faced, red-lipped Asian beauty as instantly recognisable as the *Mona Lisa*.

Born in Petropavlovsk in present-day Kazakhstan, the twists of fate that transported Tretchikoff – via Harbin, Shanghai, Singapore and Indonesia – to Cape Town just after WWII are the stuff of high adventure. Against all odds, and with little assistance from Cape Town's established art circles, Tretchikoff made a fortune marketing his art as prints around the world; the 252 exhibitions organised by the skilled businessman and self-promoter were attended by over two million people.

However, it wasn't until 2011 that a major retrospective of his work, which included many of the original oils, was held at the South African National Art Gallery in Cape Town. The accompanying book, *Tretchikoff: The People's Painter,* is a fine introduction to the artist's work.

Natasha Mercorio, Tretchikoff's granddaugher, has also launched the Tretchikoff Foundation (www.vladimirtretchikoff.com) with the aim of helping creative youths realise their dreams. A percentage of sales of new prints from Tretchikoff's collection help fund the project; you'll find stalls at various shops and markets selling official Tretchikoff merchandise (including Mojo Market (p180) in Sea Point).

Music

Jazz

Cape Town has produced some major jazz talents, including the singer-songwriter Jonathan Butler and the saxophonists Robbie Jansen and Winston 'Mankunku' Ngozi. So important has the city been to the development of jazz that there is a subgenre of the music called Cape Jazz, which is improvisational in character and features instruments that can be used in street parades, such as the drums and trumpets favoured in the **Cape Town Minstrel Carnival** (www.facebook.com/capetownminstrelca; ⌚Jan & Feb).

The elder statesman of the scene is pianist Abdullah Ibrahim. Born Adolph Johannes Brand in District Six in 1934, he began performing at 15 under the name Dollar Brand, and formed the Jazz Epistles with the legendary Hugh Masekela. In 1962, after moving to Zurich, he was spotted by Duke Ellington, who arranged recording sessions for him at Reprise Records and sponsored his appearance at the Newport Jazz Festival in 1965. Brand converted to Islam in 1968 and took the name Abdullah Ibrahim. In 1974 he recorded the seminal album *Manenberg* with saxophonist Basil Coetzee. He occasionally plays in Cape Town.

Goema-style jazz takes its rhythmic cues from the *goema* drum and has been popularised by musicians such as Mac McKenzie and Hilton Schilder. Other respected local artists to watch out for include guitarists Jimmy Dludlu and Reza Khota, pianist Paul Hanmer and singer Judith Sephuma.

Online Art Resources

Artthrob *(www.artthrob.co.za) Showcases the best in South African contemporary art (and has plenty of up-to-the-minute news).*

ArtSouthAfrica *(www.artsouthafrica.com) – Magazine on local art scene.*

Art Meets *(www.artmeetsapp.com) Web-based app with news on art exhibitions, events and artist studios around Cape Town.*

Dance, Rock & Pop

Few Afro-fusion groups have been as big recently as the multiracial seven-piece band Freshlyground (www.freshlyground.com), who draw huge crowds whenever performing in their hometown. Their song 'Waka Waka', with Colombian artist Shakira, was the official 2010 FIFA World Cup anthem; on their 2013 album *Take Me to the Dance* they collaborated with Steve Berlin of Los Lobos.

Bridging the divide between jazz and electronic dance music are Goldfish (www.goldfishlive.com), aka the duo David Poole and Dominic Peters, who combine samplers, a groove box, keyboards, vocoder, upright bass, flute and saxophone in their live performances. Dominic's brother Ben Peters is a member of Goodluck (www.goodlucklive.com), who are also gaining a strong following for their similar sound.

Techno, trance, hip hop, jungle and rap are wildly popular. Afrikaans rapper Jack Parow (www.jackparow.com) is the Capetonian answer to the national rap sensation Die Antwoord (www.dieantwoord.com) – both acts embody the subculture of 'zef', a 'white trash'-style fashion with lots of exaggerated bling, tattoos and the like. Also tune in to *kwaito,* a mix of *mbaqanga* (a Zulu style of music), jive, hip hop, house and ragga. The music of local singing superstar Brenda Fassie (1964–2004) has a strong *kwaito* flavour – listen to her hits such as 'Weekend Special' and 'Too Late for Mamma'. Fassie, who was born in Langa, struggled with drug problems throughout her brief life.

Among the many indie rock bands and singers to catch at gigs around town are Arno Carstens (https://arnocarstensmusic.wordpress.com), the one-time lead singer of the legendary Springbok Nude Girls; the incredible one-man-band Jeremy Loops (http://jeremyloops.com); 13-member ska/reggae/hip-hop/dance/you-name-it band The Rudimentals (www.therudimentals.co.za); folk singer Paige Mac (www.paigemac.com); and the internationally renowned DJ and record producer Black Coffee.

Controversial Artists

When Michael Elion's sculpture of a giant pair of Ray-Bans, *Perceiving Freedom,* was vandalised on Sea Point promenade in November, 2014 the artist expressed a fear for his life. In creating a controversial piece of art, Elion joined a long list of fellow Capetonian artists who have upset the establishment and/or the public.

Censorship of the arts was standard under apartheid. In recent years, such government-sanctioned censorship has again reared its ugly head. Capetonian cartoonist Zapiro (www.zapiro.com) was twice sued by Jacob Zuma when he was president for defamation (both cases were eventually dropped). Zuma and the African National Congress (ANC) also took umbrage against *The Spear,* by Brett Murray (www.brettmurray.co.za), when it was displayed at the Goodman Gallery in Johannesburg in 2012; this provocative painting of Zuma was later defaced by two members of the public. Murray's sculpture *Africa,* standing in St George's Mall, was also a controversial winner of a Cape Town public sculpture competition in 1998.

Literature

Cape Town has nurtured several authors of international repute, including Nobel Prize–winner JM Coetzee (the first part of his Man Booker award–winning novel *Disgrace* is set in Cape Town); André Brink (1935–2015) who wrote in both English and Afrikaans; and the Man Booker–prize nominated Damon Galgut.

Out of the coloured experience in District Six came two notable writers, Alex La Guma (1925–85) and Richard Rive (1931–89). La Guma's books include *And a Threefold Cord,* which examines the poverty, misery and loneliness of slum life, and *A Walk in the Night,* a collection of short stories set in District Six. Rive's *'Buckingham Palace', District Six* is a thought-provoking and sensitive set of stories.

Charting a more contemporary coloured experience on the Cape Flats is Rehana Rossouw's debut novel *What Will People Say?* (2015) which garnered praises and award nominations. She followed this up in 2017 with *New Times,* also set in Cape Town during Mandela's second term as president. Also look out for *The Yearning* by promising young writer Mohale Mashigo.

Sindiwe Magona grew up in Gugulethu in the 1940s and '50s. The feisty writer's early life experiences inform her autobiographical works *To My Children's Children* (1990) and *Forced to Grow* (1992). *Beauty's Gift* (2008) deals unflinchingly with AIDS in the black community and, in particular, its impact on five women who consider themselves to be in faithful relationships.

The Cape's incredible true crime stories have also provided easy inspiration for a slew of thriller writers, including Mike Nicol, Deon Meyer, Margie Orford, Sarah Lotz and Andrew Brown.

Public Artworks

- *Africa by Brett Murray*
- *The Knot by Edoardo Villa*
- *Nobel Square by Claudette Schreuders*
- *Open House by Jacques Coetzer*

Cinema

Cape Town is a major centre for South African movie-making and, increasingly, for international productions. The city acts as a magnet for many talented people in the industry and you'll frequently see production crews shooting on location around town. On the city's outskirts are the Cape Town Film Studios (www.capetownfilmstudios.co.za), where several major Hollywood productions have been shot, including *Safe House,* the Cape Town–set thriller with Denzel Washington and Ryan Reynolds.

Oliver Hermanus followed up his 2009 debut feature *Shirley Adams,* a bleak Ken Loach–style drama set in Mitchell's Plains on the Cape Flats, with *Skoonheid* (Beauty); it was the first ever Afrikaans movie to play at the Cannes Film Festival (in 2011) and won the Queer Palm award. His third feature *Endless River* premiered at the Venice Film Festival in 2015. Among other recent local movies to feature Cape Town are *Long Street,* directed by Revel Fox and starring his daughter Sannie and wife Roberta, and the charming *Visa/Vie* directed by Elan Gamaker.

Search online for the American documentary *Long Night's Journey into Day,* nominated for Best Documentary at the 2001 Oscars. This very moving Sundance Film Festival winner follows four cases from the Truth & Reconciliation Commission hearings, including that of Amy Biehl, the white American murdered in the Cape Flats in 1993. *U-Carmen eKhayelitsha,* winner of the Golden Bear at the 2005 Berlin International Film Festival, is based on Bizet's opera *Carmen* and was shot entirely on location in Khayelitsha.

The Labia's African Screen and the Isivivana Centre's Bertha Movie House regularly screen African movies. At the multiplexes you might also catch the odd South African–made feature. Otherwise, your best chance of watching home-grown products is at the city's several film festivals.

Theatre & Performing Arts

Cape Town's lively and diverse performing arts scene mounts large-scale musicals, one-person shows, edgy dramas reflecting modern South Africa and intimate poetry-reading soirees. The city has produced some notable actors, including the Sea Point–born Sir Anthony Sher, who returns occasionally to the city to perform.

Among local theatre companies that have gone international are Handspring Puppet Company (www.handspringpuppet.co.za), whose amazingly lifelike creations formed the heart of the hit UK National Theatre production *War Horse;* and director Brett Bailey's Third World Bunfight (http://thirdworldbunfight.co.za), which specialises in using black actors to tell uniquely African stories – his thought-provoking show *Exhibit B* sparked controversy across Europe in 2014.

Songwriter and director David Kramer and musician Taliep Petersen (1950–2006) teamed up to work on two musicals, *District Six* and *Poison,* before hitting the big time with their jazz homage *Kat and the Kings,* which swept up awards in London in 1999 and received standing ovations on Broadway. Their collaboration *Goema* celebrates the tradition of Afrikaans folk songs while tracing the contribution made by the slaves and their descendants to the development of Cape Town. Kramer's 2015 musical *Orpheus in Africa* is about American impresario Orpheus McAdoo and his African American troupe of Jubilee Singers, who visited South Africa in the 1890s.

The Natural Environment

Cape Town is defined by its magnificent natural environment, part of the Unesco World Heritage–status Cape Floristic Region (CFR) – the richest and smallest of the world's six floral kingdoms and home to around 9600 plant species, more than three times as many per square kilometre as in the whole of South America.

The Land

Table Mountain's flat-top shape as we see it today probably first came about 60 million years ago, although the mountain as a whole started forming about 250 million years ago, making it the elder statesman of world mountains. (For comparison, the Alps are only 32 million years old and the Himalayas 40 million years old.) Over time the mountain was weathered to create the distinctive hollows and oddly shaped rocks found on the summit today.

Three major types of rock make up the Cape Peninsula. Malmesbury shale is the oldest, dating back 540 million years. It forms the base of most of the City Bowl and can be seen along the Sea Point shoreline, on Signal Hill and on the lower slopes of Devil's Peak. Cape granite is the second oldest. It's tough, forms the foundation for Table Mountain and can also be seen on Lion's Head and the boulders at Clifton and Boulders Beaches. The third type is Table Mountain Sandstone, a combination of sandstone and quartzite.

Table Mountain and the peninsula alone contain 2285 plant species – more than in all of Britain – and it's also home to over 100 invertebrates and two vertebrates not found anywhere else on earth.

Flora

Fynbos (fine-bos; from the Dutch, meaning 'fine bush') thrives in the Cape's nitrogen-poor soil – it's thought that the plants' fine, leathery leaves improve their odds of survival by discouraging predators. The three main types of *fynbos* are: proteas (including the king protea, South Africa's national emblem), ericas (heaths and mosses) and restios (reeds). Examples of *fynbos* flowers that have been exported to other parts of the world include gladiolus, freesias and daisies.

On Signal Hill and the lower slopes of Devil's Peak you'll find *renosterbos* (literally, 'rhinoceros bush'), composed predominantly of a grey ericoid shrub and peppered with grasses and geophytes (plants that grow from underground bulbs). In the cool, well-watered ravines on the eastern slopes of Table Mountain you'll also find small pockets of Afro-montane forest, such as at Orange Kloof, where entry is by permit only (one issued daily for up to 12 people).

More than 1730 *fynbos* plants are endangered or vulnerable to extinction; some have minute natural ranges. Most *fynbos* needs fire to germinate and flower, but unseasonal and accidental fires can cause great harm. The fires can also burn far longer and more fiercely because of the presence of invasive alien plants, such as the various pines and wattles that also pose a threat because of the vast amounts of water they suck up.

Reading Up

- *Wild About Cape Town (Duncan Butchart)*
- *The Rocks and Mountains of Cape Town (John Compton)*
- *How the Cape Got Its Shape (fold-out map and chart by Map Studio)*

CREATING TABLE MOUNTAIN NATIONAL PARK

Future prime minister General Jan Smuts – a keen hiker – started a public appeal in the 1920s to secure formal protection for Table Mountain; today there's a track on the mountain named after him.

The Cape of Good Hope Nature Reserve was secured in 1939. This was the first formal conservation on the Cape, although mining magnate and South African politician Cecil Rhodes had used a small part of his vast fortune to buy up much of the eastern slopes of Table Mountain; he gifted this land, which includes Kirstenbosch and the Cecilia Estate stretching to Constantia Nek, to the public in his will.

In the 1950s the Van Zyl Commission baulked at creating a single controlling authority for the park, but in 1958 all land on Table Mountain above the 152m-contour line was declared a National Monument. The city created the Table Mountain Nature Reserve in 1963 and the Silvermine Nature Reserve in 1965.

It wasn't until 1998 that a single Cape Peninsula National Park became a reality. In 2004 the park was renamed Table Mountain National Park.

For several years the national park has been carrying out an alien-plant-clearing program to rehabilitate fire-damaged areas and to educate vulnerable communities, such as the townships, about fires. Around 85% of the park's management area has so far been cleared of alien plants.

The first farms were granted at Cape Point in the 1780s, but the area really didn't become fully accessible until 1915, when the coastal road from Simon's Town was completed.

Fauna

The animal most closely associated with Table Mountain is the dassie, also known as the rock hyrax. Despite the resemblance to a plump hamster, these small furry animals are – incredibly – distantly related to the elephant. You'll most likely see dassies sunning themselves on rocks around the upper cableway station.

Among the feral population of introduced fallow deer that roam the lower slopes of Table Mountain (around the Rhodes Memorial) is an animal once regarded as extinct: the quagga. This partially striped zebra was formerly thought to be a distinct species, but DNA obtained from a stuffed quagga in Cape Town's South African Museum showed it to be a subspecies of the widespread Burchell's zebra. A breeding program started in 1987 has proved successful in 'resurrecting' the quagga. Mammals found at the Cape of Good Hope include eight antelope species, Cape mountain zebras and a troupe of chacma baboons.

The Cape's most famous birds are the African penguins (formerly called jackass penguins for their donkey-like squawk). You'll find some 2100 of the friendly penguins at Boulders Beach, and a smaller colony on Robben Island.

Cape Point itself isn't exactly where the warm waters of the Indian Ocean meet the cold seas of the Atlantic. The actual meeting point fluctuates along the southwestern coast between Cape Point and Cape Agulhas.

Marine Life

The seas surrounding the Cape Peninsula host many types of marine life. Southern right and humpback whales, dolphins, Cape fur seals and loggerhead and leatherback turtles are among the species you might be able to spot. One you would hope to not see – unless you're in the safety of a diving cage or a boat – is the great white shark.

In order to protect and conserve threatened marine species (such as abalone and west coast rock lobster) that had until recent times flourished in the waters around the Cape, Table Mountain National Park created a Marine Protected Area (MPA) in 2004. Covering around 1000 sq km of waters from Moullie Point to Muizenberg, the MPA includes six 'no-take' zones, where no fishing or extractive activities are allowed.

Survival Guide

DIRECTORY A–Z . . . 280
Accessible Travel 280
Accommodation. 280
Children 280
Customs Regulations . . . 280
Discount Cards. 280
Electricity 281
Health. 281
Insurance. 281
Internet Access. 281
LGBT Travellers. 281
Money. 281
Opening Hours 282
Photography 282
Post. 282
Public Holidays. 282
Safe Travel. 282
Taxes & Refunds. 282
Telephone 283
Time 283
Toilets. 283
Tourist Information 283
Visas. 283
Volunteering 284
Women Travellers. 284

TRANSPORT 285
GETTING THERE & AWAY 285
Entering the Country/Region 285
Air 285
Land 285
Sea 286
GETTING AROUND 286
Air 286
Bicycle 286
Bus 286
Car & Motorcycle. 286
Hitching 288
Local Transport. 288
Train 288

LANGUAGE 289

Directory A–Z

Accessible Travel

➡ South Africa is one of the best destinations on the continent for travellers with disabilities, with an ever-expanding network of facilities catering to those who are mobility or visually impaired.

➡ We've noted establishments and destinations with facilities and access for travellers with disabilities.

➡ Several gardens and nature reserves have Braille trails for the visually impaired.

➡ Boardwalks for wheelchair access are found at many parks and attractions, and some can organise activities for travellers with disabilities.

➡ Hand-controlled vehicles can be hired at major car-rental agencies.

➡ Download Lonely Planet's free Accessible Travel guides from http://lptravel.to/AccessibleTravel.

Accommodation

You can often get away with booking a few days in advance, or not at all, but if you're travelling at Christmas or Easter, plan several months ahead. Always book national-park accommodation in advance.

Lodges Can be uber-luxe or fairly rustic, but tend to boast some of the best locations.

Guesthouses Often owner-run, with comfortable rooms, hearty breakfasts and priceless local information.

Self-catering cottages Usually spacious and excellent value for money.

Backpacker hostels Often have a bar, swimming pool and campsites; ideal for budget or solo travellers.

Hotels Everything from stylish boutique hotels to vast and luxurious chains.

Booking Services

SA-Venues.com (www.sa-venues.com) Directory of accommodation in Cape Town and the Western Cape.

Cape Town Tourism (www.capetown.travel) Accommodation bookings through member hotels.

Portfolio Collection (www.portfoliocollection.com) Curated listings of top hotels, guesthouses and boutique rental properties.

Lonely Planet (www.lonelyplanet.com/south-africa/cape-town/hotels) Hotel and hostel bookings.

BOOK YOUR STAY ONLINE

For more accommodation reviews by Lonely Planet authors, check out http://lonelyplanet.com/hotels/. You'll find independent reviews, as well as recommendations on the best places to stay. Best of all, you can book online.

Children

Cape Town and the surrounding Western Cape have great infrastructure for family-friendly holidays. Garden Route spots such as Mossel Bay and Nature's Valley are particularly well set up for family holidays, with beaches and activities galore.

Customs Regulations

➡ You're permitted to bring 2L of wine, 1L of spirits and other alcoholic beverages, 200 cigarettes and up to R5000 worth of goods into South Africa without paying duties.

➡ Imported and exported protected-animal products such as ivory must be declared.

➡ For more information, visit www.brandsouthafrica.com and search for its customs guide.

Discount Cards

Various types of **Wild Cards** (www.wildcard.co.za) provide unlimited access to South Africa's national parks for a year. International visitors must purchase the All Parks Cluster card (single/couple/family

R2430/3800/4545). South African citizens and Cape Town residents can buy either a SANParks Cluster card (single/couple/family R540/880/1055) covering just the national parks, or an All Parks Cluster card (R565/930/1140), which also covers Cape Nature reserves. Cards can be bought at the park's information centres.

Electricity

Power cuts are quite common although the situation has improved in Cape Town.

Type M
230V/50Hz

Health

With the exception of HIV/AIDS, there's little need to worry about health issues in Cape Town. Having said that, hundreds do die daily from HIV/AIDS, so make sure you use protection.

Insurance

➡ Travel insurance covering theft, loss and medical problems is highly recommended.

➡ Before choosing a policy, shop around; policies designed for short European package tours may not be suitable for the South African veld.

➡ Read the fine print – some policies specifically exclude 'dangerous activities', which can mean scuba diving, motorcycling, bungee jumping and more.

➡ Some policies ask you to call (reverse charges) a centre in your home country, where an immediate assessment of your problem is made.

➡ Worldwide travel insurance is available at www.lonelyplanet.com/travel-insurance. You can buy, extend and claim online any time – even if you're already on the road.

Internet Access

Wi-fi access is available at hotels and hostels, as well as most cafes, some restaurants and tourist hot spots throughout the city. It is usually free (just ask for the password), but don't expect it to be fast or that reliable. Some establishments will also have download limits.

LGBT Travellers

South Africa's constitution is one of the few in the world that explicitly prohibits discrimination on the grounds of sexual orientation. Gay sexual relationships are legal and same-sex marriages are recognised. There are active gay and lesbian communities and scenes in Cape Town and Jo'burg, and to a lesser degree in Pretoria and Durban. Cape Town is the focal point, and is the most openly gay city on the continent.

But despite the liberality of the new constitution, it will be a while before attitudes in the more conservative sections of society begin to change towards acceptance. Particularly in black communities, homosexuality remains frowned upon, if not taboo – homosexuals are attacked in the townships. Outside larger city centres, exercise discretion.

Money

➡ South Africa's currency is the rand (R), which is divided into 100 cents. The notes are R10, R20, R50, R100 and R200; the coins are R1, R2 and R5, and five, 10, 20 and 50 cents. Transactions are often rounded up or down by a few cents.

➡ The rand is weak against Western currencies, making travelling in South Africa less expensive than in Europe and North America.

➡ The best foreign currencies to bring in cash are US dollars, euros or British pounds, but a debit or credit card will be more useful, as most businesses only accept rand.

➡ Cash is readily exchanged at banks and foreign-exchange bureaus in the cities.

➡ Keep at least some of your exchange receipts, as you'll need them to reconvert leftover rand when you leave.

➡ ATMs are common and cards are widely accepted. Inform your bank of your travel plans to avoid declined credit-card transactions.

Tipping

Wages are low here, and tipping is expected.

Restaurants & cafes 10% to 15% of the total in restaurants; 10% in cafes.

TAP WATER

High-quality water is widely available in South Africa and drinking from taps is fine, except in rural and drought-struck areas.

SLEEPING PRICE RANGES

Rates quoted are for high season (November to March), with a private bathroom. Exceptions are noted in listings.

$ less than R700

$$ R700–R1400

$$$ more than R1400

In Cape Town and the Winelands, prices are higher:

$ less than R1000

$$ R1000–R4000

$$$ more than R4000

Hotels A standard tip of R10 to R20 is welcomed.

Car guards Offer R5 or more for longer periods.

Petrol stations Anything from R5 – more if the attendant washes the windscreen and checks the tyres.

Taxis Tips not expected but rounding up the fare will be appreciated.

Opening Hours

The following are general hours. Individual reviews list more specific variations.

Banks 9am to 3.30pm Monday to Friday, 9am to 11am Saturday

Post offices 8.30am to 4.30pm Monday to Friday, 8am to noon Saturday

Shops 8.30am to 5pm Monday to Friday, 8.30am to 1pm Saturday. Major shopping centres are open 9am to 9pm daily.

Cafes 7.30am to 5pm Monday to Saturday. Cafes in the City Bowl are open 8am to 3pm on Saturday and closed on Sunday.

Restaurants Noon to 3pm and 6pm to 10pm Monday to Saturday.

Photography

➡ In South Africa cameras, memory cards, film and accessories are readily available in large towns.

➡ Don't photograph or film soldiers, police, airports, defence installations, border posts and government buildings.

➡ You should always ask permission before taking a photo of anyone, but particularly if you're in a tribal village.

➡ In Cape Town a recommended camera and equipment shop is **Orms** (www.ormsdirect.co.za).

➡ Pick up *Lonely Planet's Guide to Travel Photography* for inspiration and advice.

Post

➡ Domestic and international deliveries are generally reliable but can be slow.

➡ Periodic postal strikes cause further delays.

➡ Delivery times are considerably quicker for items leaving South Africa than for items entering the country.

➡ For mailing anything valuable or important, use a private mail service such as **PostNet** (www.postnet.co.za).

➡ **Post Office** (www.postoffice.co.za) branches are widespread.

➡ Do not have anything of value sent to you from overseas, as parcels are often impounded by customs.

Public Holidays

On public holidays government departments, banks, offices, post offices and some museums are closed. Public holidays in South Africa include the following:

New Year's Day 1 January

Human Rights Day 21 March

Easter (Good Friday/Easter Monday) March/April

Family Day 13 April

Constitution Day (Freedom Day) 27 April

Worker's Day 1 May

Youth Day 16 June

Women's Day 9 August

Heritage Day 24 September

Day of Reconciliation 16 December

Christmas Day 25 December

Boxing Day (Day of Goodwill) 26 December

Safe Travel

Keep things in perspective and don't be overly paranoid, but do remember that South Africa has a high crime rate and you need to be much more cautious than in most Western countries.

➡ Look out for ATM and credit-card scams.

➡ If you're using public transport and venturing outside tourist environments, preferably travel with a friend or in a group.

➡ Female travellers, remember that violence against women is widespread throughout South Africa; exercise caution when interacting with men.

➡ Ask locals about areas to avoid and don't walk around after dark, when the risk of mugging is high.

Taxes & Refunds

South Africa has a value-added tax (VAT) of 14%, but departing foreign visitors can reclaim most of it on goods being taken out of the country. To make a claim, the goods must have been bought at a VAT-registered vendor, their total value must exceed R250 and you need a tax invoice for each item. Visit www.taxrefunds.co.za for comprehensive information.

Claiming Tax Refunds

➡ Your receipt usually covers the requirements for a tax invoice. It must include the following: the words 'VAT invoice', the seller's name, address and 10-digit VAT registration number (starting with a 4); a description of the goods purchased; the cost of the goods in rand; the amount of VAT charged, or a statement that VAT is included in the total cost; an invoice number; the date of the transaction; the quantity or volume of the goods; and for purchases more than R3000, the buyer's name and physical address.

➡ All invoices must be originals – no photocopies.

➡ A commission of 1.3% of the reclaimed sum is charged for the service (minimum R10, maximum R250).

➡ At your point of departure, you'll need to fill in a form or two and show the goods to a customs inspector.

➡ At airports, if your purchases are too large for hand luggage, make sure you have them checked by the inspector before you check in your bags.

➡ After going through immigration, make the claim and pick up your refund, normally issued as a MasterCard or Visa card, which will be loaded with your home (or another foreign) currency, and can be used to make purchases or withdraw money within three days.

➡ If your claim comes to more than R3000, the refund will not be given on the spot; it will be loaded onto the card you are given up to three months later.

➡ You can claim at Jo'burg, Cape Town and Durban's major international airports, and in the smaller airports at Lanseria (Jo'burg), Bloemfontein, Polokwane (Pietersburg), Nelspruit, Pilansberg, Port Elizabeth and Upington.

➡ It's also possible to claim at major harbours and some train stations.

➡ You can claim the refund by post within three months of leaving South Africa, but it is much easier to do it in person.

Telephone

South Africa's country code is 27 and Cape Town's area code is 021, as it also is for Stellenbosch, Paarl and Franschhoek; the area code must be included even when dialling locally. Sometimes you'll come across phone numbers beginning with 0800 for free calls or 0860 for calls shared 50/50 between the caller and receiver. Note that it's cheaper to make a call between 7pm and 7am.

Forget about public telephones, which rarely work (if you can even find them).

Mobile Phones

The main operators are:

Cell C (www.cellc.co.za)

MTN (https://brightside.mtn.co.za)

Virgin Mobile (www.virginmobile.co.za)

Vodacom (www.vodacom.co.za)

Both Vodacom and MTN have desks at Cape Town International Airport, where you can sort out a local prepaid or pay-as-you-go SIM card to use in your phone during your visit. Otherwise you'll find branches of each company across the city, as well as many places where you can buy vouchers to recharge the credit on your phone account. Call charges average about R2.50 per minute.

Time

South African Standard Time is two hours ahead of Greenwich Mean Time (GMT; at noon in London, it's 2pm in Cape Town), seven hours ahead of USA Eastern Standard Time (at noon in New York, it's 7pm in Cape Town) and eight hours behind Australian Eastern Standard Time (at noon in Sydney, it's 4am in Cape Town). There is no daylight saving time.

Toilets

➡ Finding a clean, sit-down toilet in Cape Town is usually not a problem.

➡ There are few public toilets, but malls generally have them.

➡ Restaurants, cafes and bars are normally happy to let you use their facilities.

Tourist Information

Almost every town in the country has a tourist office. These are often private entities, which will only recommend member organisations and may add commissions to bookings they make on your behalf. They are worth visiting, but you may have to push to find out about all the possible options.

In state-run offices, staff are often badly informed and lethargic; asking for assistance at your accommodation may prove more useful.

South African Tourism (www.southafrica.net) has a helpful website, with practical information and inspirational features.

Visas

Visitors on holiday from most Commonwealth countries (including Australia and the UK), most Western European countries, Japan and the USA don't require visas. Instead, you'll be issued with a free entry permit on arrival, which is valid for a stay of up to 90 days. But if the date of your flight out is sooner than this,

PRACTICALITIES

Newspapers & Magazines

Cape Times (www.iol.co.za/capetimes) Local morning newspaper, Monday to Friday.

Cape Argus (www.iol.co.za/capeargus) Local afternoon newspaper, Monday to Saturday.

Mail & Guardian (https://mg.co.za) National weekly, published Friday; includes excellent investigative and opinion pieces and arts-review supplement.

Cape Etc (www.capetownetc.com) Listings and features magazine published three times a year.

Big Issue (www.bigissue.org.za) Monthly magazine that helps provide an income for the homeless; sold at many of Cape Town's busiest traffic intersections.

TV & Radio

South African Broadcasting Corporation (SABC; www.sabc.co.za) National radio and TV channels.

Cape Talk (www.capetalk.co.za) 567 MW; talkback radio.

Fine Music Radio (www.fmr.co.za) 101.3FM; jazz and classical.

KFM (www.kfm.co.za) 94.5FM; pop music.

Good Hope FM (www.goodhopefm.co.za) Between 94FM and 97FM; pop music.

Heart (www.1049.fm) 104.9FM; pop music, soul, R&B.

the immigration officer may use that as the date of your expiry, unless you request otherwise.

All children aged under 18 must show an unabridged birth certificate, with additional paperwork needed in some cases. Where only one parent's particulars appear on the UBC or equivalent document, no parental consent affidavit is required when that parent travels with the child. For further information and updates, check www.brandsouthafrica.com, www.home-affairs.gov.za, or with your government's travel advisory or your airline.

If you aren't entitled to an entry permit, you'll need to get a visa (also free) before you arrive. These aren't issued at the borders, and must be obtained from a South African embassy or consulate in your own country. Allow several weeks for processing.

For any entry – whether you require a visa or not – you need to have at least two completely blank pages in your passport, excluding the last two pages.

Apply for a visa extension or a re-entry visa at Cape Town's **Department of Home Affairs** (Map p84; ☎021-468 4500; www.home-affairs.gov.za; 56 Barrack St, City Bowl; ⏰7.30am-4.30pm Mon-Fri, 8.30am-12.30pm Sat; 🚌Lower Buitenkant).

Volunteering

Useful starting points for information are Greater Good SA (www.greatergoodsa.co.za) and For Good (www.forgood.co.za), with details on many local charities and development projects.

Greenpop (www.greenpop.org) is an award-winning social enterprise that has planted over 80,000 indigenous and fruit trees at schools, other urban sites, community farms and forests across South Africa and further afield. You can volunteer and take part in various programs it runs.

Uthando (☎021-683 8523; www.uthandosa.org; R912) is a tour company that supports a vast range of charitable projects; they can let you know which ones might need volunteers.

Volunteer Centre (www.volcent.co.za) is a Cape Town–based nonprofit that can also help place people in various communities and projects.

Women Travellers

Old-fashioned attitudes to women are still common among South African men, regardless of colour. However, this doesn't mean you should tolerate sexist behaviour.

There's a high level of sexual assault and other violence against women in South Africa, the majority of which occurs in townships and poor rural areas. Given the HIV/AIDS epidemic, the problem is compounded by the transfer of infection. Some rape victims have escaped infection by persuading the attacker to wear a condom.

For most female visitors, patriarchal attitudes and mildly sleazy behaviour are the main issues. However, there have been incidents of travellers being raped, and women should not walk alone at night or in deserted areas. Use a legitimate taxi company and join a tour if travelling to remote areas where you might be the only person at a particular site or accommodation option.

Transport

GETTING THERE & AWAY

Entering the Country

South Africa is straightforward and hassle-free to enter, although airport customs officers often check bags for expensive gifts and items purchased overseas.

Immigration officials rarely ask to see it, but travellers should be able to show an onward ticket – preferably an air ticket, although an overland ticket is also acceptable. The same applies to proof that you have sufficient funds for your stay; it pays to be neat, clean and polite.

➡ Immigration rules have been changing with regards to travelling with children, which involve unabridged birth certificates (UBC) etc, so check the latest details well before departure. Where only one parent's particulars appear on the UBC or equivalent document, no parental consent affidavit is required when that parent travels with the child.

➡ If you have travelled in a yellow-fever area or have even transited in such an area for more than 12 hours en route, you need to show a vaccination certificate to enter South Africa.

➡ For more information, see www.brandsouthafrica.com.

Air

South African Airways (SAA; ☎0861 606 606; www.flysaa.com) is South Africa's national airline, with an excellent route network and safety record. In addition to its long-haul flights, it operates regional and domestic routes together with its partners **Airlink** (☎086 160 6606; www.flyairlink.com) and **SA Express** (☎086 172 9227; www.flyexpress.aero).

Cape Town International Airport (CPT; Map p50; ☎021-937 1200; www.airports.co.za) is the region's main airport.

Land

Long distance trains arrive at **Cape Town Railway Station**, where you'll also find the bus terminus and booking offices for the major interstate bus companies.

The three main arterial routes leading into Cape Town are:

N1 from Johannesburg via the Karoo and the Cape Winelands

N2 from the Garden Route and Overberg via Somerset West and Cape Town International Airport

N7 from the West Coast and Namibia.

CLIMATE CHANGE & TRAVEL

Every form of transport that relies on carbon-based fuel generates CO_2, the main cause of human-induced climate change. Modern travel is dependent on aeroplanes, which might use less fuel per kilometre per person than most cars but travel much greater distances. The altitude at which aircraft emit gases (including CO_2) and particles also contributes to their climate change impact. Many websites offer 'carbon calculators' that allow people to estimate the carbon emissions generated by their journey and, for those who wish to do so, to offset the impact of the greenhouse gases emitted with contributions to portfolios of climate-friendly initiatives throughout the world. Lonely Planet offsets the carbon footprint of all staff and author travel.

DEPARTURE TAX

Departure tax is included in the price of a ticket.

Sea

Many cruise ships stop at Cape Town. Useful contacts:

Cruise Compete (www.cruisecompete.com) Site with an up-to-date list of all cruises visiting Cape Town.

MSC Starlight Cruises (☎087 075 0850; www.msccruises.co.za) South African–based operator.

GETTING AROUND

Air

For air connections further afield, budget airlines serve all the major South African cities, and it rarely works out cheaper to fly with South African Airways (SAA).

Keep costs down by booking online months before travelling, either directly, or through the likes of **Computicket Travel** (☎0861 915 4000; www.computickettravel.com) or **Travelstart** (www.travelstart.co.za).

Bicycle

Public transport Trains can carry bicycles (although bicycles are banned from Cape Town's suburban trains), but most bus lines don't want bikes in their luggage holds, and shared taxis don't carry luggage on the roof.

Purchase Cape Town has a good selection of mountain and touring bikes for sale. To resell your bicycle at the end of your trip, try hostel noticeboards, bike shops and clubs, and www.gumtree.co.za.

Rental For day rides, some hostels offers short-term mountain-bike rental. Rentals can also sometimes be arranged through bike shops in the cities, though you'll usually be required to leave a credit-card deposit.

Safety Many roads don't have a hard shoulder; on those that do, motorists use the shoulder as an unofficial slow lane. It's illegal to cycle on highways, and roads near urban areas are busy and hazardous. Before heading off anywhere, contact other cyclists through local cycling clubs or bicycle shops to get recent information on the routes you're considering. Bring a good lock to counter the ever-present risk of theft; store the bike inside your accommodation (preferably inside your room) and chain it to something solid.

Spare parts Mountain bikes and parts are widely available in the cities. It's often difficult to find specialised parts for touring bikes, especially outside Cape Town. Establish a relationship with a good bike shop in a city before you head off into the veld, in case you need something couriered to you.

Weather Be prepared for rain and sometimes violent thunderstorms. When it isn't raining, summer days can be unpleasantly hot.

Bus

Classes There are no class tiers on the bus lines, although major companies generally offer a 'luxury' service, with features such as air-con, a toilet and films.

Discounts The major bus lines offer student, frequent-traveller and senior-citizen discounts, as well as specials – check their websites for details.

Fares Roughly calculated by distance, though short runs are disproportionately expensive. Your fare may also be based on the bus's whole journey. Prices rise during school holidays.

Safety Lines are generally safe. Note, however, that many long-distance services run through the night. On overnight journeys, travellers should take care of their valuables and women might feel more comfortable sitting near the front of the bus.

Ticket purchase For the main lines, purchase tickets at least 24 hours in advance, and as far in advance as possible for travel during peak periods. Tickets can be bought through bus offices, **Computicket Travel** (☎0861 915 4000; www.computickettravel.com) and Shoprite/Checkers supermarkets.

Bus Lines

City to City (☎0861 589 282; www.citytocity.co.za) In partnership with Translux, this no-frills service is less expensive than other lines, and serves many off-the-beaten-track places.

Greyhound (☎customer care 24hr 011-611 8000, reservations 087 352 0352; www.greyhound.co.za) An extensive nationwide network of comfortable buses. Also operates other lines, including the cheaper Citiliner buses.

Intercape (☎021-380 4400; www.intercape.co.za) An extensive network stretching from Cape Town to Limpopo and beyond.

Translux (☎086 158 9282; www.translux.co.za) The main long-distance operator, serving destinations including Cape Town and the Garden Route.

Baz Bus (☎021-422 5202, SMS bookings 076 427 3003; www.bazbus.com) Caters almost exclusively to backpackers and travellers. Offers hop-on, hop-off fares and door-to-door services between Cape Town and Jo'burg via the Garden Route and other popular South African destinations.

Mzansi Experience (☎021-001 0651; www.mzansi.travel) Offers a similar service to Baz Bus but at lower prices.

Car & Motorcycle

Driving Licence

➡ You can use your driving licence from your home country, provided it is in

English (or you have a certified translation).

➡ For use in South Africa, your licence should also carry your photo. Otherwise you'll need an international driving permit.

➡ Police generally ask to see foreign drivers' passports, so keep a photocopy in your car.

➡ You can be fined for not being able to show your licence, passport or other ID.

Fuel & Spare Parts

➡ Unleaded petrol costs about R12 per litre.

➡ An attendant will fill your tank and clean your windows – tip R2 to R5; if they check your oil, water or tyres, tip R5 to R10.

➡ Along main roads, there are plenty of petrol stations. Many stay open 24 hours.

➡ There are petrol stations in most South African towns.

➡ In rural areas, fill up whenever you can.

Campervans, 4WD & Motorcycles

➡ Some campervan/motorhome rentals include camping gear.

➡ One-way rental is not always possible.

➡ 'Bakkie' campers, sleeping two in the back of a canopied pick-up, are cheaper.

➡ Mopeds and scooters are available for hire in Cape Town and other tourist areas.

➡ Besides standard rental-car companies, check **Britz** (☎011-230 5200; www.britz.co.za) for 4WDs; **Drive South Africa** (www.drivesouthafrica.co.za) for 4WDs and campervans; and **Maui** (www.maui.co.za) for motorhomes.

Insurance

Insurance for third-party damage and damage to or loss of your vehicle is highly recommended, though it's not legally required for private-vehicle owners. Generally it is only available on an annual basis.

If you're renting a vehicle, insurance with an excess should be included, with an excess waiver or reduction available at an extra cost.

Check that hire-car insurance or the rental agreement covers hail damage, a costly possibility during summer in the highveld and lowveld regions.

Insurance providers include the following:

Automobile Association of South Africa (AASA; ☎011-799 1000, 086 100 0234; www.aa.co.za)

Old Mutual iWyze (www.oldmutual.co.za)

Outsurance (www.outsurance.co.za)

Sansure (www.sansure.co.za)

Road Conditions

➡ A good network of highways covers the country.

➡ Major roads are generally in good condition.

➡ Outside large towns and cities, you may encounter gravel (dirt) roads, most of which are graded and reasonably smooth.

➡ Check locally on tertiary and gravel roads' conditions, which can deteriorate when it rains.

➡ In rural areas beware of hazards such as dangerous potholes, washed-out roads, unannounced hairpin bends, and livestock, children and dogs on the road.

Road Hazards

➡ South Africa's roads can be treacherous, with a horrific accident rate and well over 10,000 deaths annually.

➡ The main hazards are your fellow drivers. Motorists from all sections of society drive sloppily and often aggressively. Be particularly wary of shared-taxi drivers, who operate under pressure on little sleep in sometimes shoddy vehicles.

➡ Overtaking blind and with insufficient passing room is common.

➡ On major roads, drivers coming up behind you will flash their lights at you and expect you to move into the hard shoulder to let them pass, even if you are approaching a corner and regardless of what is happening in the hard shoulder. Motorists often remain hard on your tail until you move over.

➡ Drivers on little-used rural roads often speed and assume there is no other traffic.

➡ Watch out for oncoming cars at blind corners on secondary roads.

➡ Despite roadblocks and alcohol breath-testing in South Africa, particularly in urban areas, drink-driving is widespread.

➡ Do not be seduced by the relaxed local attitude to drink-driving; you can end up in a cell, so nominate a designated driver.

➡ Farm animals, wildlife (particularly baboons) and pedestrians stray onto the roads, especially in rural areas. If you hit an animal in an area where you're uncertain of your safety, continue to the nearest police station and report it there.

➡ In roads through townships (such as the N2 from Cape Town International Airport to the city), foreign objects are occasionally placed on the road, and motorists are robbed when they pull over after driving over the object. If you encounter this, do not stop but continue to a garage to inspect your car and to a police station to report the incident.

Road Rules

➡ Driving is on the left-hand side of the road.

➡ Seatbelts are mandatory for the driver and all passengers.

➡ The main local idiosyncrasy is the 'four-way stop' (crossroad), found even on major roads. All vehicles are required to stop, with those arriving first being the first to go (even if they're on a minor cross street).

Speed Limits

Stick to speed limits, as speed traps (cameras and guns) are increasingly common in South Africa, although limits remain widely ignored by locals.

➡ 120km/h on most major highways

➡ 100km/h on open roads

➡ 60km/h in built-up areas

➡ 40km/h in most wildlife parks and reserves

Parking & Car Guards

Parking is readily available at sights, eateries and accommodation throughout South Africa.

If you are parking in the street, or even a car park in larger South African towns and cities, you will often be approached by a 'car guard'. They will keep an eye on your vehicle in exchange for a tip: R2 for a short period, R5 to R10 for long stays. They may also offer to wash your car for an extra R20. Do not pay them until you are leaving, or if they did not approach you when you arrived. Ensure you give the money to the right person; in Cape Town, for example, approved car guards often wear high-visibility vests.

Hitching

Hitchhiking and picking up hitchers is inadvisable.

If you're strapped for cash, you can look into drive-shares. Hostel noticeboards often have details of free or shared-cost lifts. Also check out **FindALift** (https://findalift.co.za) and **Jumpin Rides** (www.jumpinrides.co.za).

Local Transport

Bus

➡ Urban areas, including Cape Town, have city bus networks.

➡ Fares are cheap.

➡ Routes, which are often signboarded, are extensive.

➡ Services often stop running early in the evening, and there aren't many on weekends.

➡ In terms of safety and convenience, Cape Town's MyCiTi buses are recommended.

Shared Taxi

Shared minibus taxis run almost everywhere – around cities, and to the suburbs, townships and neighbouring towns. Riding them offers an insight into local life, but be aware that there are safety issues.

➡ They leave when full – though 'full' in South Africa isn't as packed as in many African countries.

➡ Most accommodate 14 to 16 people. Slightly larger 'sprinters' accommodate about 20.

➡ Away from train and bus routes, shared taxis may be the only choice of public transport.

➡ At weekends they generally have reduced services or no departures.

➡ Visit **TaxiMap** (http://taximap.co.za) for a useful database of minibus-taxi routes, fares and other information.

Car taxis are sometimes shared.

➡ In some towns, and on some longer routes, a shared car taxi may be the only transport option.

➡ Shared car taxis are more expensive than minibus taxis, and similar in terms of safety.

SHARED TAXI ETIQUETTE

➡ Passengers with luggage should sit in the first row behind the driver.

➡ Move along the seat to the window to give others easy access.

➡ Pass the money forward (your fare and those of the people around you) to the driver's assistant.

➡ If you sit on the folding seat by the sliding door, it's your job to open and close the door when passengers get out. You'll have to get out of the taxi each time.

➡ Some shared taxis, for example in Cape Town, have a conductor who calls out to potential passengers and handles the minibus door.

➡ Say: 'Thank you, driver!', when you want to get out, rather than just: 'Stop!'

Private Taxi

➡ Cape Town has private taxi services and there are taxi stands in popular areas.

➡ Phoning for a cab is often safer; you will have to wait for the taxi to arrive, but the vehicle will likely be better quality than those at the stands.

➡ Rates vary between cities; in Cape Town, they average R10 per kilometre, often with a minimum charge of R30 or more.

➡ Uber is popular in larger cities and operates in Cape Town.

Train

Cape Metro Rail (☎0800 656 463; http://capetowntrains.freeblog.site) trains run out to Strand on the eastern side of False Bay, and into the Winelands to Stellenbosch and Paarl. They are the cheapest and easiest means of transport to these areas. For all routes, security is best at peak times when the carriages are busy – but then they can also be dangerously overcrowded.

Language

South Africa has 11 official languages: English, Afrikaans, Ndebele, North Sotho, South Sotho, Swati, Tsonga, Tswana, Venda, Xhosa and Zulu. In the Cape Town area only three languages are prominent: Afrikaans, English and Xhosa.

AFRIKAANS

Afrikaans developed from the dialect spoken by the Dutch settlers in South Africa from the 17th century. Until the late 19th century it was considered a Dutch dialect (known as 'Cape Dutch'), and in 1925 it became one of the official languages of South Africa. Today, it's the first language of around six million people. Most Afrikaans speakers also speak English, but this is not always the case in small towns and among older people.

If you read our coloured pronunciation guides as if they were English, you'll be understood. The stressed syllables are in italics. Note that aw is pronounced as in 'law', eu as the 'u' in 'nurse', ew as the 'ee' in 'see' with rounded lips, oh as the 'o' in 'cold', uh as the 'a' in 'ago', kh as the 'ch' in the the Scottish *loch*, r is trilled, and zh is pronounced as the 's' in 'pleasure'.

Basics

Hello.	*Hallo.*	ha·*loh*
Goodbye.	*Totsiens.*	tot·*seens*
Yes./No.	*Ja./Nee.*	yaa/ney
Please.	*Asseblief.*	a·si·*bleef*
Thank you.	*Dankie.*	*dang*·kee
Sorry.	*Jammer.*	*ya*·min

How are you?
Hoe gaan dit? — hu khaan dit

Fine, and you?
Goed dankie, en jy? — khut *dang*·kee en yay

What's your name?
Wat's jou naam? — vats yoh naam

My name is ...
My naam is ... — may naam is ...

Do you speak English?
Praat jy Engels? — praat yay *eng*·ils

I don't understand.
Ek verstaan nie. — ek vir·*staan* nee

WANT MORE?

For in-depth language information and handy phrases, check out Lonely Planet's *Africa Phrasebook*. You'll find it at **shop.lonelyplanet.com**, or you can buy Lonely Planet's iPhone phrasebooks at the Apple App Store.

Accommodation

Where's a ...?	*Waar's 'n ...?*	vaars i ...
campsite	*kampeerplek*	kam·*peyr*·plek
guesthouse	*gastehuis*	*khas*·ti·hays
hotel	*hotel*	hu·*tel*

Do you have a single/double room?
Het jy 'n enkel/ dubbel kamer? — het yay i *eng*·kil/ *di*·bil *kaa*·mir

How much is it per night/person?
Hoeveel kos dit per nag/ persoon? — *hu*·fil kos dit pir nakh/ pir·*soon*

Eating & Drinking

Can you recommend a ...?	*Kan jy 'n ... aanbeveel?*	kan yay i ... *aan*·bi·feyl
bar	*kroeg*	krukh
dish	*gereg*	khi·*rekh*
place to eat	*eetplek*	*eyt*·plek

NUMBERS – AFRIKAANS

1	*een*	eyn
2	*twee*	twey
3	*drie*	dree
4	*vier*	feer
5	*vyf*	fayf
6	*ses*	ses
7	*sewe*	*see*·vi
8	*agt*	akht
9	*nege*	*ney*·khi
10	*tien*	teen

I'd like ..., please.	*Ek wil asseblief ... hê.*	ek vil a·si·*bleef* ... he
a table for two	*'n tafel vir twee*	i *taa*·fil fir twey
that dish	*daardie gereg*	*daar*·dee khi·*rekh*
the bill	*die rekening*	dee *rey*·ki·ning
the menu	*die spyskaart*	dee *spays*·kaart

Emergencies

Help!	*Help!*	help
Call a doctor!	*Kry 'n dokter!*	kray i *dok*·tir
Call the police!	*Kry die polisie!*	kray dee pu·*lee*·see

I'm lost.
Ek is verdwaal. ek is fir·*dwaal*

Where are the toilets?
Waar is die toilette? vaar is dee toy·*le*·ti

I need a doctor.
Ek het 'n dokter nodig. ek het i *dok*·tir *noo*·dikh

Shopping & Services

I'm looking for ...
Ek soek na ... ek suk naa ...

How much is it?
Hoeveel kos dit? *hu*·fil kos dit

What's your lowest price?
Wat is jou laagste prys? vat is yoh *laakh*·sti prays

I want to buy a phonecard.
Ek wil asseblief 'n foonkaart koop. ek vil a·si·*bleef* i *foon*·kaart koop

I'd like to change money.
Ek wil asseblief geld ruil. ek vil a·si·*bleef* khelt rayl

I want to use the internet.
Ek wil asseblief die Internet gebruik. ek vil a·si·*bleef* dee *in*·tir·net khi·*brayk*

Transport & Directions

A ... ticket, please.	*Een ... kaartjie, asseblief.*	eyn ... *kaar*·kee a·si·*bleef*
one-way	*eenrigting*	*eyn*·rikh·ting
return	*retoer*	ri·*tur*

How much is it to ...?
Hoeveel kos dit na ...? *hu*·fil kos dit naa ...

Please take me to (this address).
Neem my asseblief na (hierdie adres). neym may a·si·*bleef* naa (*heer*·dee a·*dres*)

Where's the (nearest) ...?
Waar's die (naaste) ...? vaars dee (*naas*·ti) ...

Can you show me (on the map)?
Kan jy my (op die kaart) wys? kan yay may (op dee kaart) vays

What's the address?
Wat is die adres? vat is dee a·*dres*

XHOSA

Xhosa belongs to Bantu language family, along with Zulu, Swati and Ndebele. It is the most widely distributed indigenous language in South Africa, and is also spoken in the Cape Town area. About six and a half million people speak Xhosa.

In our pronunciation guides, the symbols b', ch', k', p', t' and ts' represent sounds that are 'spat out' (only in case of b' the air is sucked in), a bit like combining them with the sound in the middle of 'uh-oh'. Note also that hl is pronounced as in the Welsh *llewellyn* and dl is like hl but with the vocal cords vibrating. Xhosa has a series of 'click' sounds as well; they are not distinguished in this chapter.

Basics

Hello.	*Molo.*	*maw*·law
Goodbye.	*Usale ngoxolo.*	u·*saa*·le ngaw·*kaw*·law
Yes./No.	*Ewe./Hayi.*	e·*we*/haa·*yee*
Please.	*Cela.*	*ke*·laa
Thank you.	*Enkosi.*	e·*nk'aw*·see
Sorry.	*Uxolo.*	u·*aw*·law
How are you?	*Kunjani?*	k'u·*njaa*·nee

Fine, and you?
Ndiyaphila, unjani wena? ndee·yaa·*pee*·laa u·*njaa*·nee *we*·naa

What's your name?
Ngubani igama lakho? ngu·*b'aa*·nee ee·*gaa*·maa laa·*kaw*

My name is ...
Igama lam ngu ... ee·*gaa*·maa laam ngu ...

Do you speak English?
Uyasithetha isingesi? u·yaa·see·te·taa ee·see·nge·see

I don't understand.
Andiqondi. aa·ndee·kaw·ndee

Accommodation

Where's a ...?	*Iphi i ...?*	ee·pee ee ...
campsite	*ibala loku-khempisha*	ee·b'aa·laa law·k'u·ke·mp'ee·shaa
guesthouse	*indlu yama-ndwendwe*	ee·ndlu yaa·maa·ndwe·ndwe
hotel	*ihotele*	ee·haw·t'e·le

Do you have a single/double room?
Unalo igumbi kanye/kabini? u·naa·law ee·gu·mb'ee k'aa·nye/k'aa·b'ee·nee

How much is it per night/person?
Yimalini ubusuku/umntu? yee·maa·lee·nee u·b'u·su·k'u/um·nt'u

Eating & Drinking

Can you recommend a ...?	*Ugakwazi ukukhuthaza ...?*	u·ngaa·k'waa·zee u·k'u·ku·taa·zaa ...
bar	*ibhari*	ee·baa·ree
dish	*isitya*	ee·see·ty'aa
place to eat	*indawo yokutya*	ee·ndaa·waw yaw·k'u·ty'aa

I'd like ..., please.	*Ndiyafuna ...*	ndee·yaa·fu·naa ...
a table for two	*itafile yababini*	ee·t'aa·fee·le yaa·b'aa·b'ee·nee
that dish	*esasitya*	e·saa·see·ty'aa
the bill	*inkcukacha ngama-xabiso*	ee·nku·k'aa·haa ngaa·maa·kaa·b'ee·saw
the menu	*isazisi*	e·saa·zee·see

Emergencies

Help!	*Uncedo!*	u·ne·daw
I'm lost.	*Ndilahlekile.*	ndee·laa·hle·k'ee·le
Call a doctor!	*Biza ugqirha!*	b'ee·zaa u·gee·khaa

Call the police!
Biza amapolisa! b'ee·zaa aa·maa·paw·lee·saa

Where are the toilets?
Ziphi itoylethi? zee·pee ee·taw·yee·le·tee

I need a doctor.
Ndifuna ugqirha. ndee·fu·naa u·giee·khaa

Shopping & Services

I'm looking for ...
Ndifuna ... ndee·fu·naa ...

How much is it?
Yimalini? yee·maa·li·nee

What's your lowest price?
Lithini ixabiso elingezantsi? lee·tee·nee ee·kaa·b'ee·saw e·lee·nge·zaa·nts'ee

I want to buy a phonecard.
Ndifuna uku thenga ikhadi lokufowuna. ndee·fu·naa u·k'u te·ngaa ee·kaa·dee law·k'u·faw·wu·naa

I'd like to change money.
Ndingathanda tshintsha imali. ndee·ngaa·taa·ndaa ch'ee·nch'aa ee·maa·lee

I want to use the internet.
Ndifuna uku sebenzisa i intanethi. ndee·fu·naa u·k'u se·b'e·nzee·saa ee ee·nt'aa·ne·tee

Transport & Directions

A ... ticket, please.	*Linye ... itikiti nceda.*	lee·nye ... ee·t'ee·k'ee·t'ee ne·daa
one-way	*ndlelanye*	ndle·laa·nye
return	*buyela*	b'u·ye·laa

How much is it to ...?
Kuxabisa njani u ...? ku·kaa·b'ee·saa njaa·nee u ...

Please take me to (this address).
Ndicela undise (kule dilesi). ndee·ke·laa u·ndee·se (k'u·le dee·le·see)

Where's the (nearest) ...?
Iphi e(kufutshane) ...? ee·pee e·(k'u·fu·ch'aa·ne) ...

Can you show me (on the map)?
Ungandibonisa (kwimaphu)? u·ngaa·ndee·b'aw·nee·saa (k'wee·maa·pu)

What's the address?
Ithini idilesi? ee·tee·nee ee·dee·le·see

NUMBERS – XHOSA

English numbers are commonly used.

1	*wani*	waa·nee
2	*thu*	tu
3	*thri*	tree
4	*fo*	faw
5	*fayifu*	faa·yee·fu
6	*siksi*	seek'·see
7	*seveni*	se·ve·nee
8	*eyithi*	e·yee·tee
9	*nayini*	naa·yee·nee
10	*teni*	t'e·nee

GLOSSARY

ANC – African National Congress

apartheid – literally 'the state of being apart'; the old South African political system in which people were segregated according to race

bobotie – traditional Cape Malay dish of delicate curried mince with a topping of savoury egg custard, usually served on turmeric-flavoured rice

braai – barbecue featuring lots of grilled meat and beer; a South African institution, particularly in poorer areas, where having a communal braai is cheaper than using electricity

bredie – traditional Cape Malay pot stew of vegetables and meat or fish

cafe – in some cases, a pleasant place for a coffee, in others, a small shop selling odds and ends, plus unappetising fried food; also kaffie

coloureds – South Africans of mixed race

DA – Democratic Alliance

farm stall – small roadside shop or shelter that sells farm produce

fynbos – literally 'fine bush'; the vegetation of the area around Cape Town, composed of proteas, heaths and reeds

karamat – tomb of a Muslim saint

kloof – ravine

line fish – catch of the day

mealie – an ear of maize; also see mealie meal and mealie pap

mealie meal – finely ground maize

mealie pap – mealie porridge; the staple diet of rural blacks, often served with stew

Mother City – another name for Cape Town; probably so called because it was South Africa's first colony

NP – old apartheid-era and now defunct National Party

PAC – Pan-African Congress

Pagad – People against Gangsterism and Drugs

rondavel – round hut with a conical roof; frequently seen in holiday resorts

SABC – South African Broadcasting Corporation

sangoma – traditional African healer

shared taxi – relatively cheap form of shared transport, usually a minibus; also known as a black taxi, minibus taxi or long-distance taxi

shebeen – drinking establishment in a township; once illegal, now merely unlicensed

strand – beach

township – black residential district, often on the outskirts of an otherwise middle-class (or mainly white) suburb

venison – if you see this on a menu it's bound to be some form of antelope, usually springbok

VOC – Vereenigde Oost-Indische Compagnie (Dutch East India Company)

Voortrekkers – original Afrikaner settlers of the Orange Free State and Transvaal who migrated from the Cape Colony in the 1830s

Behind the Scenes

SEND US YOUR FEEDBACK

We love to hear from travellers – your comments keep us on our toes and help make our books better. Our well-travelled team reads every word on what you loved or loathed about this book. Although we cannot reply individually to your submissions, we always guarantee that your feedback goes straight to the appropriate authors, in time for the next edition. Each person who sends us information is thanked in the next edition – the most useful submissions are rewarded with a selection of digital PDF chapters.

Visit **lonelyplanet.com/contact** to submit your updates and suggestions or to ask for help. Our award-winning website also features inspirational travel stories, news and discussions.

Note: We may edit, reproduce and incorporate your comments in Lonely Planet products such as guidebooks, websites and digital products, so let us know if you don't want your comments reproduced or your name acknowledged. For a copy of our privacy policy visit lonelyplanet.com/privacy.

OUR READERS

Many thanks to the travellers who used the last edition and wrote to us with helpful hints, useful advice and interesting anecdotes:

Caren Bender, Dominique Barnett, Elizabeth Heddes, Emily Apple, Jonathan Jones, Lauren Smith, Matt Roughley, Mike Saunders, Samantha Carter, Tessa Söbbeke

WRITER THANKS

Simon Richmond

Many thanks for the help, friendship and advice from the following: fellow authors James and Lucy, Heather Mason, Bheki Dube, Gerald Garner, Mike Luptak, Sheryl Ozinsky, Nicole Biondi, Iain Harris, Lee Harris, Brent Meersman and Amber April.

James Bainbridge

Thanks in 11 languages to my fellow writers Simon, Lucy, Shawn and Ashley for beers and banter in the Southern Suburbs during this update; to the rest of the author team for your contributions; to everyone who helped me on the road in Mpumalanga and Cape Town; and to Leigh-Robin, Oliver and Thomas for putting up with my long hours typing in the garden shed.

Jean-Bernard Carillet

A huge thanks to everyone who helped out and made this trip an enlightenment, especially Doné, Renée, Esti, Leigh and all the people I met on the road. At Lonely Planet, I'm grateful to Matt for his trust, and to the hard-working editors. At home, a *gros bisou* to Eva and lots of love to Morgane, whose support was essential.

Lucy Corne

Huge thanks to the team in Kimberley – Dianna, Romano, Kim, Joy and Tebogo – and to Fayroush, Christa, Brian and Nadia at SAN Parks. *Baie dankie* to Ailsa Tudhope for making me fall in love with Prince Albert all over again and to Johan, Debbie, Martiens and Cathy for making my life easier on the road. Big love to Shawn, who didn't help because he was busy with his own chapter, and a huge high five to Kai, who makes a pretty awesome travel buddy and helps me to see everything through the eyes of a four-year-old.

ACKNOWLEDGEMENTS

Climate map data adapted from Peel MC, Finlayson BL & McMahon TA (2007) 'Updated World Map of the Köppen-Geiger Climate Classification', Hydrology and Earth System Sciences, 11, 163344.

Cover photograph: Greater double-collared sunbird on pincushion protea plant, Kirstenbosch National Botanical Garden, Danita Delimont Stock, AWL ©

THIS BOOK

This 9th edition of Lonely Planet's *Cape Town & the Garden Route* guidebook was curated by Simon Richmond, and was researched and written by Simon Richmond, James Bainbridge, Jean-Bernard Carillet and Lucy Corne. The previous two editions were also written by Simon Richmond and Lucy Corne. This guidebook was produced by the following:

Destination Editor Matt Phillips

Senior Product Editor Elizabeth Jones

Product Editor Jessica Ryan, Kate Mathews

Senior Cartographer Diana Von Holdt

Book Designer Lauren Egan

Assisting Editors Michelle Bennett, Jacqueline Danam, Samantha Forge, Jennifer Hattam, Alexander Knights, Anne Mulvaney, Gabrielle Stefanos

Cartographer James Leversha

Cover Researcher Naomi Parker

Thanks to Heather Champion, Gwen Cotter, Corey Hutchison, Sandie Kestell, Chris Lee Ack, Angela Tinson, Sam Wheeler

Index

!Khwa ttu 225

A

abseiling 116
accessible travel 280
accommodation 280, 282, *see also individual locations*
activities 21, 42-4, *see also individual activities, individual locations*
Afrikaans 267, 289-90
Afrikaners 266, 267
air travel 31, 285, 286
animals 278
apartheid 259
aquariums 82
archaeological sites 224
archaeological tours 233
architecture 271-2
area codes 17, 283
arts 273-6
Atlas Trading Company 65, **65**

B

Babylonstoren 210
Bainskloof Pass 212
Baker, Sir Herbert 272
ballooning 209
Banting 33
Barrydale 191
bathrooms 283
beaches 19
  Bloubergstrand 113
  Buffels Bay 111
  Camps Bay Beach 93
  Clifton 3rd Beach 93
  Clifton 4th Beach 93
  Glen Beach 93
  Llandudno Beach 94
  Long Beach 111
  Muizenberg Beach 105-7
  Noetzie 241
  Noordhoek Beach 109
  Sandy Bay 94
beer 24, 35, *see also* breweries
Belvidere 241
bicycle travel, *see* cycling
biltong 35, **34**
bird sanctuaries
  Birds of Eden 247
  Boulders Penguin Colony 108-9
  World of Birds 93
birdwatching 42, 125
boat tours
  Cape Town 115, 121
  Hermanus 217
  Mossel Bay 233
  Plettenberg Bay 248
Boer War 258
boerewors 35
Boers 258, 267
Bo-Kaap 10, 65, **10**, **65**, *see also* City Bowl, Foreshore, Bo-Kaap & De Waterkant
books 254, 261, 263, 264, 270, 275, 277
brandy 40
breweries
  Birkenhead Brewery 222
  Darling Brewery 223
  Mitchell's Brewery 241
  Newlands Brewery 102
  Tuk Tuk Microbrewery 206
Buffalo Bay 231, 238-9
bungee jumping
  Nature's Valley 251
  Plettenberg Bay 248
bus travel 31, 184, 185, 286, 288
business hours 17, 281

C

cabaret 223-4
cable cars 116
Calitzdorp 193
campervans 287
Camps Bay 93, **94**, **5**
canoeing, *see* kayaking & canoeing
canyoning, *see* kloofing
Cape Camino 122
Cape Columbine Lighthouse 225
Cape Flats & Northern Suburbs 51
  accommodation 137-8
  drinking & nightlife 167-8
  entertainment 172
  food 155-6
  shopping 183
  sights 113-115
Cape Flats townships 113-15
Cape of Good Hope 11, 107-8, **11**
Cape Point **110**
Cape St Blaize Lighthouse 233
Cape Town 45, 49-186, **28-9**, **50**, **52-3**
  accommodation 49, 27-38
  activities 115-23
  children, travel with 118, 280
  climate 49
  drinking & nightlife 156-68
  entertainment 168-72
  festivals & events 125-7
  food 49, 138-56
  gay travellers 157
  highlights 52-3
  internet access 184
  internet resources 171
  itineraries 26, **26**
  lesbian travellers 157
  markets 177
  shopping 172-83
  sights 58-115
  tourist information 184
  tours 123-5
  travel seasons 49
  travel to/from 184
  travel within 184-6
Cape Town City Hall 72
Cape Town International Airport 184, 285
Cape Town Minstrel Carnival 22, 125, 266, 274
Cape Town Stadium 83
Cape Wheel 83, 85
car travel 30-1, 184, 286-7
  car guards 288
  car hire 30, 185-6
  driving licences 286-7
  fuel 287
  insurance 287
  parking 127, 186, 288
  road conditions 287
  road rules 31, 287-8
  safety 287
  speed limits 288
casinos 172
Castle of Good Hope 58-9, **58**
cathedrals, *see* churches & cathedrals
caves
  Cango Caves 193
  Elephant's Eye 102
  Klipgat Caves 221
  Pinnacle Point Caves 233
cell phones 16, 283
Chapman's Peak Drive 119, **30**
children, travel with 37, 118, 280
Christianity 269
churches & cathedrals
  Evangelical Lutheran Church 75
  Groote Kerk 72
  St George's Cathedral 88
cinema 170-1, 254, 275-6

Map Pages **000**
Photo Pages **000**

City Bowl, Foreshore, Bo-Kaap & De Waterkant 50 **70-1**, **74-5**
accommodation 127-9
drinking & nightlife 156, 158-60
entertainment 168-9
food 138-43
shopping 172-5
sights 58-61, 65, 68-76
walks 117, 120, **117**, **120**
Clifton **94**
climate 16, 22-4, *see also individual regions*
Clock Tower 88
Cogmanskloof 190-1
comedy 171
Company's Garden 60-1, **60**
Constantia **100**
consulates 183
courses
brewing 35
cooking 35
drink 35
food 35
foraging 35, 121
wine 36
cricket 169
crime 255
cultural tours 124-5, 233, 243
culture 266-70
culture centres 225
currency 16, 281
customs regulations 280
cycling 31, 123, 185, 199, 286
cycling tours
Cape Town 22, 124
Franschhoek 204
Knysna 242
Tulbagh 212

D

dance 169
Danger Point Lighthouse 221
Darling 223-4
De Lille, Patricia 265
De Waterkant, *see* City Bowl, Foreshore, Bo-Kaap & De Waterkant
disabilities, travellers with 283-4
discount cards 184, 280
distilleries 212
District Six, *see* East City, District Six, Woodstock & Observatory
District Six Museum 11, 62-3, **11**, **62**
diving & snorkelling 43, 116, 118, 119, 122, 233, 242
dolphins 250
Drakenstein Correctional Centre 207
drinking, *see individual locations*, wineries
courses 35
driving, *see* car travel
drought 254
Durbanville 112

E

East City, District Six, Woodstock & Observatory 50-1, **79**, **80-1**
accommodation 130
drinking & nightlife 160-2
entertainment 170
food 143-5
shopping 176-8
sights 62-3, 76-7
ecotourism
Lynedoch EcoVillage 194
Oudebosch Eco Cabins 216
electricity 280, 281
elephants 242
Elgin Valley 215-16
embassies 183
emergencies 17
entertainment 21, *see also individual locations*
environment 277-8
etiquette 17
Evita se Perron 223-4
exchange rates 17

F

farms
Babylonstoren 210
Cape Point Ostrich Farm 112
Imhoff Farm 109
Klein River Cheese Farm 222
Marbin Olives 213
Oakhurst Olives 211
Oranjezicht City Farm 83
Ferris wheels 83, 85
festivals & events 22-4, 125-7
56 Good Food & Wine Show 23
Adderley St Christmas Lights 24, 127
Cape Town Carnival 22, 126
Cape Town Cycle Tour 22, 126
Cape Town Festival of Beer 24, 127
Cape Town Fringe 23, 126
Cape Town International Jazz Festival 22-3, 126
Cape Town International Kite Festival 23, 126
Cape Town Minstrel Carnival 22, 125, 266, 274
Cape Town Nu World Festival 23, 126
Cape Town Pride 22
Design Indaba 22, 125
First Thursdays 172
Franschhoek Literary Festival 23
Freedom Swim 23
Galileo Outdoor Cinema 24
Good Food & Wine Show 126
Hands on Harvest 214
Hermanus Whale Festival 216
Infecting the City 23, 126
Kirstenbosch Summer Sunset Concerts 24
Mama City Improv Festival 24, 126
MCQP 24
Mercedes-Benz Fashion Week 23, 126
Miss Gay Western Cape 24, 126
Old Mutual Two Oceans Marathon 23, 126
Open Book Festival 23, 126
OUTsurance Kfm 94.5 Gun Run 24, 126
Oyster Festival 243
Pink Loerie Festival 23, 243
Season of Sauvignon 24, 126
Stellenbosch Wine Festival 199
Streetopia 24, 126-7
Sun Met 22, 125
Wacky Wine Weekend 214
Wavescape Surf & Ocean Festival 24, 127
Wine on the River Festival 214
films 254, 269, 275-6
fishing 43
food 32-5, *see also individual locations*
African cuisine 35
Afrikaner cuisine 35
Banting 34
biltong 35, **34**
Cape Malay cuisine 33, 35
courses 35
foraging 34
internet resources 32
opening hours 32
sustainability 33
vegetarian 35, 36
Foreshore, *see* City Bowl, Foreshore, Bo-Kaap & De Waterkant
forests
Garden of Eden 241
Tokai Forest 102
fossils 224
Franschhoek 12, 202-7, **203**, **12**
accommodation 204-5
activities 204
drinking & nightlife 206
food 205-6
sights 202-4
shopping 206
tours 204
wineries 202
free attractions 19
fynbos 63, 277

G

galleries, *see* museums & galleries
Gansbaai 220-1
Garden Route 46, 227-52, **228-9**, **13**
accommodation 227
climate 227
food 227
highlights 13, 228-9
itineraries 25, 28-9, **25**, **28-9**
surfing 13, 230-1
travel seasons 227
Garden Route National Park 237, 250
gardens, *see* parks & gardens
Gardens & Surrounds **84**
accommodation 130-2
drinking & nightlife 162-3

Map Pages **000**
Photo Pages **000**

entertainment 170-1
food 145-7
shopping 178-9
sights 77-81
gay travellers 22, 157, 281
geography 277
geology 277
George 235-7
golf
King David Mowbray Golf Club 123
Links at Fancourt 236
Metropolitan Golf Club 119
Milnerton Golf Club 123
Oubaai 230
Green Point & Waterfront 51, **86**
accommodation 132-4
drinking & nightlife 164
entertainment 171
food 147-8
shopping 179-80
sights 66-7, 81-9
Green Point Lighthouse 87-8
Groote Schuur 98
Guguletu 115

H

health 281
Helderberg 195
Hermanus 15, 216-20, **218-19**, **2-3**, **15**
Herolds Bay 230, **230**
Higgovale **88-9**
hiking 43, 56, *see also* walks
Boesmanskloof Trail 215
Cape of Good Hope Trail 56
Cape Camino 122
Cliff Path Walking Trail 217
Contour Path: Constantia Nek to Rhodes Memorial 56
Dolphin Trail 251
Elephant Day Walks 242
Elgin Valley 215
Green Mountain Trail 215
Harkerville Coastal Trail 242-3
India Venster Trail 56
Kasteelspoort 57
Kingfisher Trail 237
Knysna 243
Lion's Head Trail 55
Otter Trail 250
Outeniqua Trail 242
Oystercatcher Trail 233
Pipe Track 56
Platteklip Gorge 54-5
Robberg Nature & Marine Reserve 249
Smuts Track 55
Stellenbosch 199
Table Mountain National Park 54-7
Tsitsikamma Mountain Trail 250-1
history 20, 256-65
Act of Union 259
apartheid 259
Boer War 258
books 261, 264
British takeover 257-8
democracy 262
Dutch arrival 257
Europan arrival 256-7
homelands 259-60
Mandela, Nelson 64, 260, 261
Pagad 263
Truth & Reconciliation Commission 262
websites 261
wineries 38
hitch-hiking 288
holidays 282
homelands 259-60
horse riding 122, 123, 213, 248
Houses of Parliament 69
Hout Bay, *see* Sea Point to Hout Bay
Hout Bay Harbour 92
Huisrivier Pass 192
human rights 38

I

immigration 285
initiation rites 267
insurance 281, 287
Intaka Island 113
internet access 127, 281
internet resources 43
Islam 268
itineraries 25-9, **25**, **26**, **27**, **28-9**, *see also* scenic drives, walks

J

Judaism 269

K

Kalk Bay 12, 103-7, **104-5**, **12**, **35**
Kalk Bay Harbour 107
kayaking & canoeing 43
Anchor Bay 116
Hermanus 217
Knysna 242
Nature's Valley 251
Simon's Town 121
West Coast 226
Wilderness 237
Khayelitsha 115
Khoekhoen people 256
Kirstenbosch **100-1**
Kirstenbosch National Botanical Garden 13, 95-6, **2**, **13**
kite-surfing 123, 224
Kleinmond 216
kloofing 43-4, 215, 248
Knysna 13, 239-46, **240**, **245**, **13**
accommodation 243-4
activities 242-3
festivals & events 243
food 244-6
sights 239-41
tours 243

L

Langa 113, **114**
Langebaan 224-5
languages
Afrikaans 267, 289-90
Xhosa 290-1
lesbian travellers 22, 157, 280-1
Lion's Head 55
literature 254, 275
live music 21, 168, 169, 170, 171, 172
Long St Baths 115
Long Street 69
luxury travel 21
Lynedoch EcoVillage 194

M

magazines 284
Mandela, Nelson 64, 260, 261
Marine Protected Areas 278
markets 21, 177, 201, 239, **20**
massage 116
McGregor 215
microlighting 44
Milkwood Tree Post 234
Milnerton **114**
mobile phones 16, 283
money 16, 17, 281-2
Montagu 191
Montagu Pass 236
monuments, sculptures & statues
Arch for Arch 59
Just Nuisance Statue 111
Prestwich Memorial 74
Rhodes Memorial 103
Taal Monument 207
mosques 67
Mossel Bay 230, 232-5, **232**
motorcycle travel 184, 286-7
mountain biking 44, 243, *see also* cycling
Muizenberg 103-7, **104-5**,
museums & galleries 19-20
A4 Arts Foundation 76
Afrikaans Language Museum 207
AHEM! Art Collective 78
Bo-Kaap Museum 65
Cape Town Holocaust Centre 77
Cape Town Science Centre 76-7
Casa Labia Cultural Centre 107
Castle Military Museum 61
Ceramics Gallery 204
Chavonnes Battery Museum 83
CP Nel Museum 193
Diamond Museum 85, 87
Dias Museum Complex 232-3
District Six Museum 11, 62-3, **11**, **62**
Franschhoek Motor Museum 202
George Museum 236
Goodman Gallery Cape 78
Greatmore Studios 78
Groot Constantia 96
Guga S'Thebe Arts & Cultural Centre 113
Heart of Cape Town Museum 77
Heritage Museum 111
Huguenot Memorial Museum 204
Irma Stern Museum 96
Iziko Slave Lodge 68
Jetty 1 89
John H Marsh Maritime Research Centre 88
Koopmans-de Wet House 75

museums & galleries *continued*
Langa Pass Museum 113
Maker's Mark 212
museums & galleries *continued*
Maritime Centre 88
Millwood House 241
Old Gaol Museum 241
Old Harbour Museum 217
Oude Kerk Volksmuseum 212
Outeniqua Transport Museum 235
Paarl Museum 207
Photographic Museum 217
Rust en Vreugd 80
Simon's Town Museum 111
South African Jewish Museum 77-8
South African Museum 79-80
South African National Gallery 61, 78, **60**
South African Naval Museum 111
South African Print Gallery 78
Springbok Experience 83
Stevenson 78
Toy & Miniature Museum 195
University Museum 194
Village Museum 194
Whale House Museum 217
William Fehr Collection 61
Youngblood Africa 69
Zeitz MOCAA 66-7, **20**, **66**
music 274-5, *see also* live music
Mutual Heights 73, 74

N

National Library of South Africa 63
national parks & reserves
Botlierskop Private Game Reserve 233
Cape Columbine Nature Reserve 225
Cape of Good Hope 11, 107-8, **11**
De Hoop Nature Reserve 224
Fernkloof Nature Reserve 216
Garden Route National Park 237, 250
Goukamma Nature Reserve 238
Helderberg Nature Reserve 195
Hottentots Holland Nature Reserve 215
Intaka Island 113
Jonkershoek Nature Reserve 194
Keurbooms River Nature Reserve 247
Knysna Lagoon 239, 241
Kogelberg Nature Reserve 216
Paarl Mountain Nature Reserve 207
Robberg Nature & Marine Reserve 249
Sanbona Wildlife Reserve 191
Silvermine Nature Reserve 103
Stony Point Nature Reserve 216
Table Mountain National Park 54-7
Tokai Forest 102
Walker Bay Nature Reserve 221
West Coast National Park 15, 226
Nature's Valley 250-2
Newlands Cricket Ground 169
Newlands Rugby Stadium 169
newspapers 284
Noetzie 246
Noon Gun 124
Northern Suburbs, *see* Cape Flats & Northern Suburbs

O

Observatory, *see* East City, District Six, Woodstock & Observatory
opening hours 17, 281
Oranjezicht 83, **88-9**
ostriches 193, **192**
otters 250
Oudekraal 135
Oudtshoorn 193, **192**
Outeniqua Pass 236
Overberg, the 214-23

P

Paarl 207-11, **198**, **208**
accommodation 209-10
activities 209
food 210-11
sights 207
wineries 207-9
Pagad 263-4
paragliding 44, 116
parking 127, 186
parks & gardens 19
Arderne Gardens 103
Braak 194-5
Green Point Urban Park 82-3
Harold Porter National Botanical Gardens 216
Kirstenbosch National Botanical Garden 13, 95-6, **2**, **13**
Maiden's Cove 93
Rust en Vreugd 80
Stellenbosch University Botanical Garden 194
Two Rivers Urban Park 76
passports 285
Paternoster 225-6
people 266-70
performing arts 276
photography 282
Pinelands **114**
planetariums 81
planning, *see also individual regions*
budgeting 17
Cape Town basics 16-17
Cape Town & the Garden Route's regions 45-6
internet resources 17
itineraries 25-9, **25**, **26**, **27**, **28-9**
repeat visitors 18
travel seasons 16, 22-4
plants 277-8
Plettenberg Bay 231, 246-50, **247**
politics 254-5
population 255
postal services 282
public art 77, 96, 121, 275
public holidays 282

R

racial groups 266-7
racism 268
radio 284
rafting 43
Rastafarians 242
religion 255, 268-9
restrooms 283
Rhodes Must Fall 255
riots 255
Robben Island 10, 64, **10**, **64**
Robberg Nature & Marine Reserve 249
Robertson 213-15
Robinson Dry Dock 85
rock climbing 43-4, 116, 191, **44**
Rock Girl Benches 69
rollerblading 123
Ronnies Sex Shop 191-2, **192-3**
Route 62 190-3, **190**, **192-3**
rugby 83, 169

S

safety 255, 282
Table Mountain National Park 57
taxis 31
sailing 119, 242
San people 256
Save Our Seas Shark Education Centre 107
scenic drives
Bainskloof Pass 212
Chapman's Peak Drive 119, **30**
Knysna to Plettenberg Bay 246
Montagu Pass 236
Outeniqua Pass 236
Route 44 to Hermanus 216
Route 62 190-3, **190**, **192-3**
scenic flights 119
scooter travel 186
sea life 278
Sea Point to Hout Bay **90-1**, **92**
accommodation 134-5
drinking & nightlife 165
entertainment 171
food 149-51
shopping 180-1
sights 89-94
seals 249
self-catering 128
serviced appartments 128
shacks 270
shared taxis 31, 288
shark-cage diving 222, **43**
shopping 21, *see also individual locations*

Map Pages **000**
Photo Pages **000**

Signal Hill 78
Simon's Town & Southern Peninsula 51, **108-9**
accommodation 136-7
drinking & nightlife 166-7
entertainment 172
food 153-5
shopping 182-3
sights 103-12
travel to/from 107
skateboarding 123
skydiving 123, 233, 248
snoek 35
snorkelling, *see* diving & snorkelling
soccer 169, 264-5
South African Planetarium 81
Southern African Sustainable Seafood Initiative 33
Southern Suburbs 51, **97**
accommodation 136
drinking & nightlife 165-6
entertainment 171-2
food 151-3
shopping 181
sights 94-103
walk 99, **99**
spirit worship 269
sports 21, 169, *see also individual sports*
squares
Church Square 58
Grand Parade 73
Greenmarket Square 69
Heritage Square 76
Nobel Square 85
stand-up paddle boarding 242
Stanford 221-3
stargazing 81
Stellenbosch 14, 194-202, **196-7**, **198**, **14**
accommodation 199-200
activities 199
drinking & nightlife 201
entertainment 201
festivals & events 199
food 200-1
shopping 201
sights 194-9
tourist information 201
tours 199
travel to/from 202
travel within 202
wineries 195-9
student riots 255
surfing 44
Buffalo Bay 231
Garden Route 13, 230-1, **13**, **231**
Knysna 242
Mossel Bay 230, 233
Muizenberg 105, 121, 122
Plettenberg Bay 231, 248
Victoria Bay 230-1
swimming 115, 119
synagogues 77

T

Table Mountain 9, 54-7, **8-9**, **48**
Table Mountain Frames 80
Table Mountain National Park 54-7, **54**, **102**, **48**
accommodation 131
books 57
guided walks 57
history 278
information 57
maps 57
safety 57
trails 54-57
Tamboerskloof **84**, **88-9**
tap water 281
taxes 282-3
taxis 31, 186, 288
telephone services 16, 283
theatre 168, 169, 170, 171, 172, 276
time 16, 283
tipping 281-2
toilets 283
tourist information 184, 283
tours, *see also individual locations*
cultural tours 124-5, 233, 243
cycling tours 124, 204, 242, 212
nature tours 125
Outeniqua Power Van 236
townships 124-5, 243
walking tours 124
wineries 40, 199, 212
townships 113-15, 269-70
tours 124-5, 243
traffic 111
train crisis 254
train travel 31, 184, 186, 288
transport 17, 30-1, 285-8
Tretchikoff, Vladimir 273
Truth & Reconciliation Commission 262
tubing 248
Tulbagh 211-13
Tutu, Archbishop Desmond 263
TV 284
Twelve Apostles 92

U

Ubuntu 269
University of Cape Town 103

V

V&A Waterfront 9, 81-2, **9**
vegan travellers 35
vegetarian travellers 35
Victoria Bay 230-1, **231**
viewpoints 19, 78
visas 16, 283-4
visual arts 273
volunteering 284

W

walking tours 124
walks, *see also* hiking
Bobbejaans River Walk 212
City Bowl 117, **117**
Foreshore Public Art Walk 120, **120**
Muizenberg & St James 106, **106**
Southern Suburbs 99, **99**
Wellington Wine Walk 212
water, drinking 281
water shortages 254
water sports 122, *see also individual sports*
Waterfront, *see* Green Point & Waterfront
weather 16, 22-4
Wellington 212
West Coast Fossil Park 224
West Coast National Park 15, 226
whale watching 216, 217, 220, 242, 248
wi-fi 127, 281
Wild Cards 280
Wilderness 14, 237-8, **15**
wildlife 278
windsurfing 224
wine 36-41, **39** *see also* wineries
courses 36
glossary 41
history 38
trends 41
varieties 40
workers' wines 40
Winelands 37-41, 194-214
ballooning 209
itineraries 27, **27**
wineries 37-42, **198**, **39**
Anura 209
Avondale 207
Backsberg 209
Beau Constantia 102
Bergkelder 197
Blaauwklippen 198-9
Boschendal 202
Bouchard Finlayson 220
Bramon 247
Buitenverwachting 98, **39**
Cape Point Vineyards 111
Chamonix 204
Constantia Glen 98
Constantia Uitsig 102
Creation 220
De Grendel 112
Delaire Graff Estate 197
Durbanville Hills 112
Durbanville Wine Route 112
Eagle's Nest 102
Excelsior 213
Fairview 208
Glen Carlou 209
Graham Beck 213
Grande Provence 202
Groot Constantia 96
Groote Post 223
Hartenberg Estate 197
Haute Cabrière 203
Hillcrest Estate 112
history 38
human rights 38
internet resources 36
itineraries 27, 38, 40, **27**
Klein Constantia 98
KWV Emporium 208-9
KWV Sensorium 209
La Motte 202
La Vierge 220
Leopard's Leap 202-3
Marianne Wines 197-8
Meerendal 112
Meerlust Estate 198
Mont Rochelle 204
Nederburg Wines 209
Newton Johnson 220
Nitida 112
Paul Cluver Wines 215
Robert Stanford Estate 222

wineries *continued*
Saronsberg Cellar 212
Solms-Delta 204
Spice Route 208
wineries *continued*
Spier 195
Springfield 213
Stanford Hills 221-2
Steenberg Farm 98
Tanagra Private Cellar 215
Tokara 197
tours 38, 199, 204, 212, 220, 248
Twee Jonge Gezellen 211
Van Loveren 213
Van Ryn Brandy Cellar 197
Vergelegen 195, **39**
Vergenoegd 197
Viljoensdrift 213
Villiera 196
Warwick Estate 195
Waterkloof 195
women travellers 284
Woodstock, *see* East City, District Six, Woodstock & Observatory
World Cup 2010 265
Wynberg 95, **100**

X

Xhosa 267
Xhosa language 290-1

Y

yachting, *see* sailing

Z

Zeitz MOCAA Museum 66-7, **66**
Zille, Helen 265
zip-lining 215
zoos & wildlife reserves
Meerkat Adventures 193
Monkeyland 247

SORINA CHIRITA

Map Legend

Sights
- Beach
- Bird Sanctuary
- Buddhist
- Castle/Palace
- Christian
- Confucian
- Hindu
- Islamic
- Jain
- Jewish
- Monument
- Museum/Gallery/Historic Building
- Ruin
- Shinto
- Sikh
- Taoist
- Winery/Vineyard
- Zoo/Wildlife Sanctuary
- Other Sight

Activities, Courses & Tours
- Bodysurfing
- Diving
- Canoeing/Kayaking
- Course/Tour
- Sento Hot Baths/Onsen
- Skiing
- Snorkelling
- Surfing
- Swimming/Pool
- Walking
- Windsurfing
- Other Activity

Sleeping
- Sleeping
- Camping
- Hut/Shelter

Eating
- Eating

Drinking & Nightlife
- Drinking & Nightlife
- Cafe

Entertainment
- Entertainment

Shopping
- Shopping

Information
- Bank
- Embassy/Consulate
- Hospital/Medical
- Internet
- Police
- Post Office
- Telephone
- Toilet
- Tourist Information
- Other Information

Geographic
- Beach
- Gate
- Hut/Shelter
- Lighthouse
- Lookout
- Mountain/Volcano
- Oasis
- Park
- Pass
- Picnic Area
- Waterfall

Population
- Capital (National)
- Capital (State/Province)
- City/Large Town
- Town/Village

Transport
- Airport
- Border crossing
- Bus
- Cable car/Funicular
- Cycling
- Ferry
- Metro station
- Monorail
- Parking
- Petrol station
- Subway station
- Taxi
- Train station/Railway
- Tram
- Underground station
- Other Transport

Routes
- Tollway
- Freeway
- Primary
- Secondary
- Tertiary
- Lane
- Unsealed road
- Road under construction
- Plaza/Mall
- Steps
- Tunnel
- Pedestrian overpass
- Walking Tour
- Walking Tour detour
- Path/Walking Trail

Boundaries
- International
- State/Province
- Disputed
- Regional/Suburb
- Marine Park
- Cliff
- Wall

Hydrography
- River, Creek
- Intermittent River
- Canal
- Water
- Dry/Salt/Intermittent Lake
- Reef

Areas
- Airport/Runway
- Beach/Desert
- Cemetery (Christian)
- Cemetery (Other)
- Glacier
- Mudflat
- Park/Forest
- Sight (Building)
- Sportsground
- Swamp/Mangrove

Note: Not all symbols displayed above appear on the maps in this book

OUR STORY

A beat-up old car, a few dollars in the pocket and a sense of adventure. In 1972 that's all Tony and Maureen Wheeler needed for the trip of a lifetime – across Europe and Asia overland to Australia. It took several months, and at the end – broke but inspired – they sat at their kitchen table writing and stapling together their first travel guide, *Across Asia on the Cheap*. Within a week they'd sold 1500 copies. Lonely Planet was born.

Today, Lonely Planet has offices in Franklin, London, Melbourne, Oakland, Dublin, Beijing and Delhi, with more than 600 staff and writers. We share Tony's belief that 'a great guidebook should do three things: inform, educate and amuse'.

OUR WRITERS

Simon Richmond

Cape Town (City Bowl, Foreshore, Bo-Kaap & De Waterkant; East City, District Six, Woodstock & Observatory; Gardens & Surrounds; Green Point & Waterfront) Journalist and photographer Simon has specialised as a travel writer since the early 1990s, and first worked for Lonely Planet in 1999 on their *Central Asia* guide. He's long since stopped counting the number of guidebooks he's researched and written for the company, but countries covered include Australia, China, India, Iran, Japan, Korea, Malaysia, Mongolia, Myanmar (Burma), Russia, Singapore, South Africa and Turkey. For Lonely Planet's website, he's penned features on topics from the world's best swimming pools to the joys of Urban Sketching. Simon also wrote the Plan Your Trip, Understand and Survival Guide chapters.

James Bainbridge

Cape Town (Cape Flats & Northern Suburbs, Sea Point to Hout Bay, Simon's Town & Southern Peninsula, Southern Suburbs) James is a British travel writer and journalist based in Cape Town, South Africa, from where he roams the globe and contributes to publications worldwide. He has been working on Lonely Planet projects for over a decade, updating dozens of guidebooks and TV hosting everywhere from the African bush to the Great Lakes. The coordinating author of several editions of Lonely Planet's *South Africa, Lesotho & Swaziland*, *Turkey* and *Morocco* guides, his articles on travel, culture and investment appear in the likes of BBC Travel, the UK *Guardian* and *Independent*, *Condé Nast Traveller* and *Lonely Planet Traveller*.

Jean-Bernard Carillet

Garden Route (Nature's Valley) Jean-Bernard is a Paris-based freelance writer and photographer who specialises in Africa, France, Turkey, the Indian Ocean, the Caribbean and the Pacific. He loves adventure, remote places, islands, outdoors, archaeological sites and food. His insatiable wanderlust has taken him to 114 countries across six continents, and it shows no sign of waning. It has inspired lots of articles and photos for travel magazines and some 70 Lonely Planet guidebooks, both in English and in French.

Lucy Corne

Around Cape Town, Garden Route Lucy left university with a degree in journalism and a pair of perpetually itchy feet. She taught EFL for eight years in Spain, South Korea, Canada, China and India, while writing freelance features for a range of magazines, newspapers and websites. She joined the Lonely Planet team in 2008, and has since worked on a range of titles including *Africa*, *The Canary Islands*, *South Africa, Lesotho & Swaziland* and several foodie titles. Lucy lives in Cape Town with her husband and young son, where she writes on travel, food and beer. Her popular blog, www.brewmistress.co.za, documents the South African beer scene.

Published by Lonely Planet Global Limited
CRN 554153
9th edition – Oct 2018
ISBN 978 1 78657 167 0

10 9 8 7 6 5 4 3 2 1
Printed in Singapore